Communication for Management and Business

Second Edition

Communication for Management and Business

Second Edition

Norman B. Sigband
University of Southern California

Scott, Foresman and Company • **Glenview, Illinois**
Dallas, Tex. • Oakland, N.J. • Palo Alto, Cal. • Tucker, Ga.

To My Mother and Father

Photos on pages 49 and 487 courtesy of Design Photographers International, Inc.

Sigband, Norman B.
  Communication for management and business.

  Published in 1969 under title: Communication for
management.
  Includes bibliographical references and index.
  1. Communication in management. I. Title.
HF5718.S53 1976   658.4'5   75-34093
ISBN 0-673-07884-1

6 7 8 9 10 - MUR - 82 81 80 79

Preface

Communication and the World Today

Today we live in a world where words are easily conveyed to millions of people in minutes or seconds.

Words are like a vital fluid that ebbs and flows through the formal and informal structures of society. We can all contribute something toward harmony by using communication consciously and sensibly as a tool. We can study this tool and its uses in our personal lives, in our careers, and in the larger world of politics and international affairs.

That's what this book is all about: *The more efficient use of communication.* The emphasis is on the business environment. However, the principles discussed and the examples given are easily translatable into politics, social situations, and family relationships.

Changes in This Edition

This second edition has been revised dramatically on the basis of responses received from a great many instructors who have used the initial edition. The organization of chapters has been changed to conform more closely to course outlines. Specific sections have been strengthened: career search and résumé preparation; research techniques; and oral reports and speaking. The segments on business reports and business letters have been brought up to date, and the Readings section revised thoroughly. Articles not used frequently have been dropped; papers with interesting concepts have been added; and several essays which are somewhat controversial have been included.

How This Book Can Be Used

The book is so arranged that it can be used for a one-semester course in business communications, business letters, and business reports; a combination letters/reports course; or a two-semester course stressing communication theory, research, and principles in the first segment, and letters and reports in the second. (See the Instructor's Manual for various course syllabi.) In any format, the instructor will find the readings valuable. They will serve to:

- Broaden the students' horizons
- Provide a basis for class discussions and presentations
- Eliminate the cost of a "readings text"
- Prevent the crisis that occurs when 100 students descend on the library to read "the assigned article for tomorrow's class"

The book can be used effectively as a college text and also in various types of organizational training programs in industry and government. In addition, it can serve as a valuable reference guide for managers engaged in various forms of communication on an interpersonal and organizational basis.

Organization and Content

The structure of the book is logical and easy to follow. The first segment examines the process of communication: how it functions, why it breaks down, and ways to improve it. Certainly every manager (in business, in a public job, in the home) should be aware of these principles. From that point, the text makes recommendations on how to exercise various communication techniques: listening, interviewing, conference leadership, speaking, job hunting, business-letter writing, report presentation, research, preparation of employee communications, and a dozen other aspects of organizational and interpersonal communications.

Most of these areas are reinforced by comments from experts in the form of articles and essays contained in the Readings. And finally, the individual who has a question on business-letter format or some phase of grammar, diction, or usage can check the reference section at the back of the book.

The letters I've received over the years from instructors, managers of all types and levels, and students lead me to feel the book has served a useful purpose. This new edition responds to many of their suggestions for change, and attempts to strengthen those areas they found most valuable.

Acknowledgments

I am indebted to Professor James H. Conley, of Eastern Michigan University, who carefully read the manuscript of this second edition and offered valuable suggestions on every section. I found his ideas and concepts for the total manuscript especially valuable. Additional views were received from Professor Michael Bartos of W. R. Harper College, Professor James M. Thompson, School of Business, San Jose State University, and Professor Antoinette McDonald of Monroe Community College. These views also proved very valuable. Mrs. Lillian Yang, assistant librarian of Crocker Library at the University of Southern California, carefully checked the section on reference sources. I am indebted to her for the care she took in bringing many up to date, adding dozens of others, and, in general, contributing her scholarly efforts in a most significant manner to this section of the book. And, of course, the suggestions given to me by my faculty colleagues throughout the nation, my students at the University of Southern California, and my many friends in industry and the companies with which I consult, have proved invaluable in adding new ideas and revising old ones.

Finally, my most sincere appreciation goes to my wife, Joan, who has contributed an untold number of hours to this edition. Her understanding, affection, and, most important, her ability to communicate appear again and again in the concepts presented. To my children, Robin and her husband Glenn Gotz; Shelley and her husband Ernest Wilkerson; and Betsy, my thanks for your understanding, your suggestions, and, above all, your love.

Norman Bruce Sigband

Contents

The Process of Communication

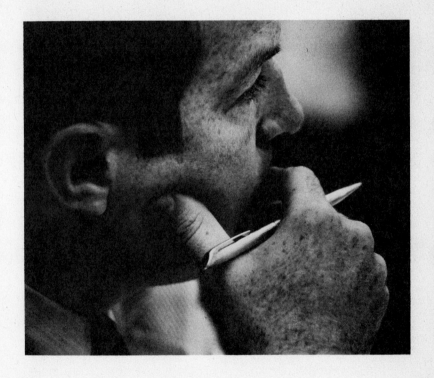

Chapter One

The Process and Problems of Communication

Informal Communication
Communication in Practice
Communication Theory
The Process of Communication
Barriers to Communication
Feedback
Nonverbal Communication

What's so important about communication? The answer is that without communication hardly anything gets done. In any large office building there are, at any moment, hundreds of different communication activities taking place. We're not aware of them, ordinarily, because we can't hear them or see them.

Let's imagine that we have cut a large office building in half. We've sliced it all the way from the television tower, which is mounted just above the 66th floor, to the third subbasement, which is 60 feet below sidewalk level. Once we have our plate glass firmly attached to the exposed side, we can tune in on dozens of different examples of "management communications."

The Lawson Corporation's vice-president of distribution is viewing a television program of an exhibition of heavy transportation vehicles. The show is taking place in Paris and the signal is being beamed from the French capital to European viewers and to a satellite in space; then to electronic receivers throughout the world. In North America, the signal is picked up by the antenna rising above the Lawson Building; and then to thousands of viewers in the United States. People in New York, Chicago, and San Francisco, as well as the corporate vice-president, will view the images only an instant later than the Parisian businessman sitting in his office on the Avenue Foch. Both men intently watch a demonstration of a new, heavy-duty, fully automatic liquid fuel-carrying vehicle. And most important, each makes a management decision to secure a demonstration of the vehicle with a view to possible purchase.

On the 63rd floor a team of Lawson employees under Department Manager Betty Walsh is putting the finishing touches on a written proposal destined for the U.S. Department of Defense. It will be in competition with proposals from four competing firms. The winning company, hopefully Lawson, will receive a $114 million initial contract for a new high-speed jet aircraft guidance system. Translated into people, it means that the 3300 individuals Lawson employs in its Fountain View plant will continue to have jobs through the next 24 months. If the contract goes to a different firm, chances are good that the Fountain View plant will be closed down when the present project, due to be terminated in four months, is completed. So even though Lawson's product may be superior, if its communication (in this case a written proposal) is poor, 3300 people and a major firm will suffer dramatically.

Just one floor below, a major report is being completed by New Products Vice-President Ernie Wilkerson. It is addressed to the Executive Committee of Lawson and recommends that the corporation move into the manufacture of luggage. Ernie and his marketing research staff have made a thorough analysis of leisure time, travel, income, age groups, types of luggage presently available, primary competitors, and a dozen other variables. Their report is thorough, their conclusions logical, and their recommendations specific.

The Executive Committee must now render a decision based on the content of that report which will, in 24 months, result in a successful and profitable new Lawson line or a three-and-one-half-million-dollar loss!

From the 58th down to the 50th floors, a dozen different departments of Lawson are housed. Executives and managers from sales, credit, marketing, personnel, industrial relations, finance, advertising, accounting, legal, engineering, and international are all busy . . . busy managing through communication.

Credit reports are being written and telephone evaluations on payment records are being made; internal memos and reports are moving vertically; the corporate annual report is being prepared in one office; and a new employee orientation manual in another. Copy is being written in the advertising department by a creative young man for the weekend newspaper ad; and down the corridor a legal brief is being prepared for a suit brought just last week against Lawson. In still another office Editor John Aspery is trying to meet the noon deadline for the Lawson monthly employee magazine. Elsewhere job descriptions are being written, a new Lawson agricultural products catalog is being prepared, and a sales manual designed. Several people are working intently on a sales brochure that will be mailed to thousands, and a new products questionnaire that will be sent to hundreds.

In room 5301 a heated meeting (still another communication medium) is taking place among representatives from production, engineering, quality control, and sales. It's a conference that was called just this morning by a vice-president to solve an unexpected but serious management problem. Almost everyone in attendance has had to shift his schedule to be present; they are all rather unprepared; facts, details, and specific information are almost completely absent; but opinions, feelings, and emotions are not. It seems to be, as two of the men have just agreed, another "typical Lawson meeting."

The personnel department is on the 55th floor. The director of that unit, Martha Rowen, is now interviewing a prospect for a senior position in the firm. In the same department, two recent college graduates are talking to personnel assistants about job opportunities within the company. And at that same moment, probably 50 different Lawson employees are involved in performance appraisal interviews at Lawson plants throughout the country.

The head of the company occupies a suite of beautifully furnished offices on the 58th floor. At the moment he is talking to and looking at (through his videophone) a member of the staff of the President of the United States. They are deep in a discussion concerning the feasibility of Lawson supplying critical production materials to a certain Communist country. What effect will such action have on Lawson? On the United States and its economic and political posture? On world affairs? Certainly this involves a management decision of the highest order.

From the 48th to the 50th floors, routine office procedures are being carried through. Hundreds of letters, memos, staff studies, proposals, and short reports are being dictated and written by managers and then processed by the secretarial staff. The three floors below are brilliantly lighted for the engineering and drafting personnel. Their blueprints and specifications typically communicate by symbols and diagrams rather than by words and sentences. But their mysterious marks on paper are vital factors in the communication network.

In the first subbasement, where the air is controlled for humidity and temperature, we find Lawson's computer, as well as the firm's teletype and dataphone equipment, which transmit and receive information almost constantly. On the basis of this information, dozens of managers will be able to work efficiently and render well-informed decisions.

And all of the communication activities are made easier and more efficient through the use of mechanical and electronic equipment. This includes electric typewriters, copying machines, photocopy equipment, computers, automatic typewriters, and many other machines.

If we step back from the Lawson Building for a minute and ask ourselves what we have observed, it is obvious that we have seen management communication in action. Managers were working toward the achievement of their objectives through face-to-face interviews, reports, letters, conferences, meetings, memos, discussions, staff studies, proposals, computer printouts, position papers, employee publications, engineering drawings, specifications, procedure manuals, telephone calls, orientation booklets, annual reports, telegrams, oral presentations, and accounting forms. All these communication activities were taking place as part of the process of management, or, in the words of the title of this book, *Communication for Management and Business.*

Informal Communication

But we haven't seen all the communication that goes on in the Lawson offices. There's also a great deal of informal and unofficial communication. This may become very important at times. For instance, several key people have heard a rumor that the company will halt production on a new product at the end of this month. The rumor is not accurate, but it has already caused anxiety among some employees. The executive vice-president hurries to send out a management bulletin that will be distributed within the hour. It contains the facts and will serve to kill the rumor.

At almost the same time, a department manager is getting a lesson in how we often communicate unintentionally—or seem to. Just two days ago he requested that four typists move into a recently vacated room across the hall from the rest of the department. His perception was that they would have more privacy, a quieter area for concentration, and far more room in which to work. They perceived it as a reprimand or an unspoken evaluation of their competence. And now one of them is saying to him, "Why have we been moved into the old printing reproduction room, separated from the department, where we can't see or work with our friends? We don't like being ostracized when we try so hard. If you don't want us to be a part of your department, we request transfers to other Lawson divisions."

What a difference in the manager's and the typists' perceptions! This calls for a decision that will set things right.

What we have seen and heard is just a small action sample of *communication for management*. Such incidents take place almost constantly in all public and private organizations.

In many respects it is unfortunate that most of us speak and write so easily. Too often we assume that simply because we *have* spoken or written, we have transmitted a message. We *may* have, but the chances are also good that we have been only partially successful, or even completely unsuccessful, and that the message hasn't gotten through. Effective communication is not always easy. It requires effort and knowledge.

Communication in Practice

We have all had the exasperating experience of realizing that we did not communicate what we thought we had. This may happen anywhere—with wives, husbands, or friends, as well as with business associates. As an example, let us eavesdrop on the discussion between an office manager, Robert Gordon, and his immediate subordinate in charge of the tabulating room, Bill Orton.

"Good morning, Bill, Come in and sit down. You remember a week ago I asked you to give me a progress report on how well your new equipment is working out; if Pete, that new employee, is working well; and if you were able to straighten out those two key-punch operators who are always bickering? This morning I checked and found that you haven't yet submitted that report, that you fired Pete, and that you still haven't spoken to the two operators. Is this all deliberate on your part, Bill? If it is, you and I had better have an understanding right here and now."

"Well, Bob, I didn't know you wanted the report right away. As for Pete, I got the idea you didn't like him, so I let him go when I found him goofing off. And the two operators don't bicker. You're all wrong about that. Maybe they disagree, but they don't cause any real trouble."

"Look, Bill, I gave you specific instructions. If you don't want to follow them, maybe I can find someone who will."

"But I do want to follow your suggestions, Bob; that's why I got rid of Pete. And you didn't say *when* you wanted the report. As for the key-punch operators, well...."

And so the discussion goes. Who is at fault? Both men? Neither one? Or does it make any difference? Yes, it does. Office procedure is upset, work routines break down, and a loyal, hard-working employee may be lost.

Actually a careful reexamination of the conversation shows clearly that there was a communication breakdown, accompanied by misunderstanding, and the harmful effect of feelings and emotions getting out of hand.[1] What did happen in the discussion above? Did Bill deliberately misunderstand? Did Bob communicate clearly? Were the words used with one meaning by one man, but understood differently by the other? And if so, why?

Perhaps we can never determine just exactly what went wrong, but we do know that barriers got in the way of the clear reception of ideas, causing confusion and errors in interpretation. These breakdowns in communication cost American industry millions of dollars each year in tangible losses; and they are also often responsible for the ill feelings and antagonism that arise among relatives, friends, and nations.

If we are to improve communication, we must understand the theory and process of communication as well as the barriers, so that we can take action, when necessary, to reduce the number of breakdowns.

Communication Theory[2]

Behavioral Theory

When we examined the Lawson Corporation, we saw many examples of verbal and nonverbal behavior. Some of the specialists in communication feel that these and almost all other behavior are really means of communication. And conversely, all forms of communication reflect the behavior of individuals.

Experts working in the behavioral sciences and related areas have contributed a great deal in recent years to the field of communication. For example, outstanding work on theories of human communication has been done by a psychiatrist. Dr. Jurgen Ruesch.[3]

People who are concerned with human communication do not focus on precisely what we say or write, but on how the persons involved *perceive and think* about the message.

Dr. Ruesch's theory of communication is based on the social situation in which individuals find themselves. Ruesch recognizes that our society has established certain behavioral patterns. In the first place, we participate in a *social situation* when people communicate with each other and their behavior is organized around a common task. Each person within that social situation assumes and carries through a *role* which is usually acceptable to him and to

---

[1] A careful study indicates that in general there is less than 50 percent understanding between supervisor and subordinate about the nature of the job the latter is supposed to be doing. Reported in A. S. Hatch, "Improving Boss-Man and Man-Boss Communication," *The Journal of Business Communication,* October 1966.

[2] For an excellent and brief discussion of the theories of communication, see K. R. Van Voorhis, "Organizational Communication: Advances Made from World War II Through the 1950s," *The Journal of Business Communication,* Summer 1974.

[3] See J. Ruesch, "Psychiatry and the Challenge of Communication," *Psychiatry,* XVII (1954).

those around him at that time.

These roles are usually agreed upon by all parties involved. In social situations, *status* is also important, but it is often designated by certain conventions, habits, and patterns in society. The company president has higher status than the foreman; the ambassador enjoys higher status in a political situation than his secretary. And in most societies there exist symbols which give us clues to status: job titles, office size and decor, uniforms, clothing, type of car, and so on. Recognition of *roles* and *status* is important, for it influences the *rules* of our verbal and nonverbal communication. The perceptive individual, aware of *roles, status,* and *rules,* constantly makes adjustments in his communication to achieve his goals.

The *rules* of communication vary from society to society. If one is to accomplish his goals, he must communicate according to the social situation and the prevailing rules. These tell him to whom he may communicate, for how long, in what way, and with what expectation of success.

Nonverbal communication also plays a vital role in transmitting messages. These cues or instructions, which derive from facial gestures, touch, or voice inflections, all help the receiver in understanding the message. The nonverbal message often communicates more forcefully than the verbal one.

Dr. Ruesch identifies various communication networks. The *intrapersonal* network is entirely within the individual and involves thinking and feeling.

There is also the *interpersonal* communication network. This links two or more persons.

A third kind of network is *group* interaction. Because of the number of people involved, it is usually more difficult to achieve effective communication with everybody.

A fourth network noted by Dr. Ruesch is *cultural.* Here there is no specific orginator or receiver of the message. Certain symbols in our society—cars, clothing, homes, morals, etc.—are part of our cultural network. It is almost impossible to correct or change the system because of its powerful and pervasive nature.

The importance of communication to the manager should be obvious. He or she, in an effort to attain organizational goals, will use communication to persuade, inform, and motivate others who play key roles in getting jobs and tasks completed.

The manager, in almost every instance, gets his or her job done through people. Managers may be skilled controllers, production supervisors, or directors of engineering, but they need people to help them achieve their objectives. The only method effective in getting other people to do what the manager thinks should be done is communication. Research indicates that monetary rewards and fear may be effective motivators, but not usually on a long-term basis. Communication, which often fulfills basic social and egoistic needs, can and does work as a positive motivator. Words of praise or of recognition; a touch or look which reflects love, encouragement, or approval, may prove to be just as truly communication as any written memorandum.[4]

[4] See David K. Berlo, *The Process of Communication,* Holt, Rinehart and Winston, 1960. Berlo's well known SMCR Model (Source, Message, Channel, and Receiver) is based on human behavior also.

Mathematical Theory

Another approach to communication theory is the mathematical one. Samuel Morse, who developed a code for use in telegraphic communication, was one of the first to apply a mathematical concept to communication. His code used dots and dashes (symbols) to stand for letters.

In 1948, Claude E. Shannon and Warren Weaver published a book called *A Mathematical Theory of Communication.* This important contribution, largely developed by Dr. Shannon at the Bell Telephone Laboratories, examined the technical problems of transmitting a message from sender to receiver. (He was concerned with the problem of electronic communication and not that of semantics.)

The message begins with an *information source,* the mind of the speaker or writer. He chooses words and organizes them into sentences to encode his message. This message is transmitted as a *signal* (sound or light waves, or marks on a paper). The signal is sent through a *channel,* but it can be garbled by *noise* (distractions, poor handwriting, static). Finally, the communicatee (man or machine) receives the message and decodes it into meaningful symbols.

The computer, which governs so much of our lives today, is based on the mathematical theory of communication.

The Process of Communication

The process of communication is a complex one involving all our senses, experiences, and feelings. When Mr. Able talks or writes to Mr. Baker, they are doing more than simply exchanging words. Let's listen to another conversation.

Assume that Able and Baker have been examining and discussing some construction plans for the past three hours. Finally Baker leans back, stretches, and says to Able, "My head is so loaded with figures and statistics that it's going in circles. Besides, the air is hot in here; what do you say we go out for a bite to eat and a cup of coffee?"

Baker has had some specific feelings that he has put into words—or encoded. Able, whose mind is still deeply involved with the building plans, listens (completely or partially) and must now receive and understand—or decode—Baker's message. But will he decode the message as Baker intended?

Baker is tired, not quite clear about the plans, and hungry. But Able is enthusiastic and wants to get the job done. As a matter of fact, he may be affronted that Baker seems to be implying that he (Able) confused him (Baker) with his discussion and thinks that is why Baker's head is "going in circles." As for the "hot air" that Baker mentions, Able's interpretation of that—in his mood—is unmistakable.

Yet Baker made a simple, sincere statement whose meaning was obvious to himself. Why, then, did Able suddenly seem angry and irritated with Baker's casual comment?

Able, of course, decoded or interpreted the message on the basis of his feelings, past experiences, thoughts, and perhaps even his desires; he interpreted not only Baker's words but also his gestures, actions, tone of voice, and their past relationship. No matter that the interpretation may not be what Baker intended; as far as Able is concerned, it *is* what Baker intended.

What Is Communication?

We can see from this that communication is not just letters, reports, telegrams, telephone conversations, and interviews. It is the action of people talking, listening, seeing, feeling, and reacting to each other, their experiences, and their environment.

When one person speaks, writes, listens, or gestures to another, there is constant action and reaction between the two. We not only interpret the words we hear; we also listen and give meaning to the voice inflection, and interpret the facial expressions of the person, the thoughts revealed in his eyes, the drumming of his fingers, and the nervous tapping of his toe on the floor. Added to these are our own internal stimuli: our emotions, feelings, experiences, interests, and other contributing factors which cause us to perceive actions and words in specific ways.

So communication is much more than talking or writing. We might define communication as the transmission and reception of ideas, feelings, and attitudes—verbally and/or nonverbally—which produce a response.

Objectives of Communication

We communicate for a purpose, and our basic objectives in communication are generally these:

1. We would like to be understood exactly as we intended.
2. We would like to secure a response to our message, and we hope that where applicable, that response will be favorable.
3. We would like to maintain favorable relations with those with whom we communicate.

Whenever we communicate with others, *some* understanding (or misunderstanding) will take place. What we wish to secure, however, is understanding of the message by the decoder as *we* understand the message. That is why the last three words in objective one above are so important. As for objective two, a response which is either positive, negative, or noncommittal tells the encoder something. Of course, he usually hopes the decoder's response (or feedback) will be positive. And finally, because we work, live, and exist in a world of associates, we hope to secure objective three.

Thus it is apparent from the above that an encoder can write or talk to a decoder and not achieve objectives one, two, or three! Or it is possible to achieve one but not two (favorable response), or three. And it is even possible to send a message in such a way so as to secure objectives one and two (favorable response), but antagonize the decoder, and not achieve three. However, our goal in *all* types of communication should be the attainment of objectives one, two, and three.

Barriers to Communication

The nonverbal external and internal stimuli play an important role in the interpretations we give to words. Sometimes, these stimuli are so strong that we interpret them instead of the words directed to us. When these factors sway our understanding to a degree that does not harmonize at all with the meaning intended by the communicator, they become *barriers* to the clear interpretation of ideas. This, of course, is what happened to our friends Mr. Able and Mr. Baker. If we become more aware of what these barriers are, maybe we can cope with them better.

Perhaps a good analogy is the physician-patient relationship. It isn't enough for the physician to state, "the patient is sick." If he is to cure the patient, he must pinpoint the trouble and treat it successfully. The same is true of the encoder. He must determine the specific barrier(s) that caused the communication breakdown and then attempt to alleviate or eliminate it. If he has an idea of some of the barriers that occur, it will be easier for him to diagnose the case and identify the problems.

Differences in perception of a situation may cause imperfect communication. Our previous experiences largely determine how we will react to specific stimuli. Viewing the same thing, individuals of different ages, cultural backgrounds, and national origins will each perceive something quite different. Each uses his learning, his culture, and his experiences to interpret what he sees. Not only does each of us see things differently from the way another person sees them, but if two of us hear a statement, we may also interpret (hear or perceive) it differently. (See Rogers and Roethlisberger, "Barriers and Gateways to Communications," in the Readings.)

Let us look at Line Foreman Anderson, his supervisor, Assistant Plant Supervisor Benton, and Development Engineer Carleton. They have just come from lunch and are walking back to their shop area. Forty feet ahead of them are seven or eight production workers who work directly under Anderson and in Benton's department. As the three men walk past, the circle of workers suddenly breaks into laughter and backslapping.

How did the foreman, assistant plant supervisor, and engineer each perceive this? Anderson, who has been having trouble securing cooperation from several of the production-line workers, hears derisive and insulting laughter. Benton, who prides himself on "running a tight ship with high morale," hears good-natured steam being let off. And Carleton, who works as an engineer with dozens of different shop groups from week to week, doesn't even hear the laughter, which came at the precise instant he reached the high point of the story *he* was telling to Anderson and Benton.

Or consider the reaction of three men to the sight of a large new machine being moved into the shop area. Worker Fenton perceives it as a threat to his job and a replacement for his skills. Production Supervisor Gable views it as an asset which will help him achieve higher production levels and thus secure his bonus. And Treasurer Holcomb perceives it as a further drain on the company's limited resources.

The point in both these examples is that effective communication cannot take place among persons when each perceives something different in what he sees and hears. Because each one mentally visualizes a different situation, they *discuss* a different situation. (The article by S. I. Hayakawa in the Readings explores these principles of semantics in greater detail.)

© 1966 Daily Mirror Newspapers Ltd., *Andy Capp* by Reggie Smythe, Courtesy of Field Newspaper Syndicate

Of course we can't hope to perceive *every* situation as the other person does, but if we make an honest effort to appreciate his point of view, we will improve the possibility of achieving effective communication. It is important to understand that we don't have to *agree*.

Lack of interest in the subject matter, on the part of either the speaker or the listener, can be a serious deterrent to the reception of the ideas presented. There are several different ways of arousing interest in readers and listeners.

One way is to use an attention-catching opening or a statement so provocative or unexpected that the members of the audience must sit up and take notice. But such gimmick devices are, at best, short-term in their overall appeal. At the other extreme, it is possible to *order* people to be interested. "I'll expect that report to be completed and submitted by 4 p.m. *today*. If it isn't, don't bother to come in to work tomorrow!" Certainly a statement like this arouses the interest of the listener in the message; in addition, of course, it arouses his animosity and antagonism, and we have lost one of our objectives of good communication: maintaining favorable relationships.

However, the most effective way to secure the reader's or listener's interest is to motivate him to *want* to pay attention. And the best way to accomplish this is to build the message around the benefits he will get if he carries through what the speaker or writer suggests. For example, to gain the interest of a group of foremen, a plant manager may point out how production will rise if they follow the suggestions he is making. This increase in production will in turn result in higher pay or recognition for the foremen. Because most of the foremen are concerned with increased pay, they probably will be interested in the communication.

Lack of fundamental knowledge can be a third barrier to the clear communication of ideas. How can you intelligently discuss a problem with those who do not have the background to understand what is being said? Certainly there will be a breakdown in the communication of ideas if a nuclear physicist attempts to explain quantum mechanics to someone with a high school education. Conversely, it is conceivable that the speaker's or writer's knowledge of his subject is superficial. This also becomes a barrier, for it is always apparent to us when we listen to someone who is, as the saying goes, only one chapter ahead of the class.

Sometimes the communicator's knowledge in a field is so thorough that he makes unconscious assumptions that the other person can't follow. He may assume that the listener has adequate background or fundamental knowledge and then try to communicate on the basis of this false premise. To overcome this barrier, determine how much knowledge of the subject the recipient of the message possesses before you speak or write to him.

This is not always easy to do. As was indicated earlier, we usually depend on some type of response—verbal or nonverbal—to indicate understanding or lack of understanding. But the response from the recipient of our message may not always be accurate.

The *emotions* of either the sender or the receiver can prove to be another obstacle in the communication of an idea. We have all been in situations where the atmosphere became so emotionally charged that reasonable discussion broke down. When any of us have deep emotional reactions—love, hate, fear, anger—we find it almost impossible to communicate coherently anything but that emotion. The lesson here is obvious; calm down before you send or receive ideas.

On the other hand, sometimes emotions can be a help in communicating. A person who is emotionally charged up or enthusiastic often finds that this quality is an asset in helping him get his message across.

The *personality* of those involved can be another barrier to communication. We are often so strongly influenced by the personality of the speaker or the writer that we may either accept or reject what he has to say without good reason. Personality is not confined to an individual, however. Sometimes an audience seems to react as if it were one person; many speakers will attest that some group or other was hostile, friendly, apathetic, disagreeable, sympathetic, or understanding. Of course our recognition of the personalities of others is often tempered by our own, and perhaps when we feel that communication has broken down because of personality, we should first examine our own—difficult as this task is—and attempt to make changes that will improve understanding.

The *appearance* of the communicator or the instrument he uses to communicate, such as the letter or report, can prove to be another critical factor. A speaker whose coat is awry, whose tie is askew, and whose general appearance is poor is not likely to arouse a favorable response in his listeners. The same is true of a business letter or a report that is typed in heavy block paragraphs, is jammed on the page from side to side and from top to bottom, and has a jagged margin, messy erasures, and few, if any, topic headings. Certainly the unkempt attire of a speaker or the careless and negligent appearance of a written message will prove to be a serious barrier to the communication of ideas. The solution here is simply correction of the fault. If the appearance of the report is poor, the business executive should have no compunction about sending it back to be retyped. The reader may be a thousand miles away from the company, and his image of the firm will be heavily influenced by the sheet of paper in his hand.

Prejudice can also seriously impede the transmission of ideas. An unreasonable bias rejects ideas without consideration. Although we sometimes think of prejudice as being confined to race, religion, and color, most of us normally encounter it in a dozen other ways. It may be a simple but strongly held viewpoint (or perception) on the part of the chief executive or it may be the classic statement of the foreman: "Well, I've been here twenty-eight years; we never tried it before, and I'm sure it won't work now."

Of all the barriers to the clear communication of ideas, bias and prejudice are probably the most difficult to eliminate. The usual answer is education, but that is a lengthy and sometimes frustrating job. Perhaps a better way to overcome deep bias is to show a person how he will benefit by following a specific course of action. People can adjust their prejudices surprisingly fast when their self-interest is at stake.

Distractions can prove to be another disturbing factor in communication. Clattering typewriters, noisy punch presses, inadequate illumination, hissing ventilation, or uncomfortable temperature conditions may be deterrents to the communication of ideas. It is most difficult for production-line workers to understand clearly what the foreman wants when they have to shout to one another over the noise of pounding machinery. Any upsetting factor which impinges upon any of our senses—visual, auditory, olfactory, or others—may well prevent the clear transmission and reception of ideas.

Poor organization of ideas may be a serious barrier to communication. Even when ideas are clearly and logically presented, it is still not always easy to assimilate them. The difficulties are compounded when thoughts are presented in a confused manner. No contractor lays a brick, and no engineer positions a steel beam without first looking at the blueprint; a surgeon makes no move without examining the laboratory reports and the X-rays; an attorney would never dare file an important case without first drawing up a careful brief; but often we begin to write or speak without bothering to organize our thoughts.

Whether the organizational framework of our message is jotted down on the back of an envelope, on a sheet of scratch paper, or carefully typed up as a formal outline, we should not attempt to communicate without knowing precisely where we are going. If the listener or reader cannot follow you easily and logically, he will simply shut off his mind. A three-minute oral presentation, a fifteen-line letter, a half-hour speech, or a thirty-page report should all be planned before they are carried through.

There is almost nothing we do, from an evening's recreation to the construction of a 20-story building, that we do not plan, except, all too often, our speaking and writing. It should not be that way.

Poor listening is perhaps one of the most serious barriers to the communication of ideas. All too often we think of communication as concerned with reading, writing, and speaking. But in fact about 60 percent of our time is spent listening.

Poor listening is often a natural result of the disparity in the time it takes to tell ideas and the time required to assimilate them. Most of us speak at the rate of about 140 words a minute, but we can assimilate approximately 500 words a minute. It is no wonder, therefore, that the listener's mind tends to wander as he moves farther and farther ahead of the speaker's ideas.

Often a listener is thinking of what he is going to say next, after the speaker has finished. Or perhaps his preconceptions are screening out much of what the speaker is saying. Listening requires an effort. If we try, we can learn to listen actively, to concentrate on what is being said, to hear the ideas beyond the words, and to appreciate the desires and needs of the speaker.

The supervisor or executive *must* listen carefully. That's part of his job. He should know that it isn't necessary to agree with a subordinate's statement or request. But it is necessary for him to show that he understands and appreciates why the employee said what he did say. Effective listening helps the administrator to control many of the activities under his jurisdiction. (See R. Nichols, "Listening Is a 10-Part Skill," in the Readings.)

The *competition for attention* in our busy society presents still another barrier. With dozens of communication media bombarding us throughout the day, we have, of necessity, become selective. As contrasted to our grandfather's eight-page newspaper, his limited circle of friends, and his crackling radio receiver, we live in a veritable torrent of sound and printed words. Sixty- and eighty-page newspapers, weekly news magazines, technical journals in our field, and dozens of reports must be read by each of us, and if we do not get to them we somehow feel guilty. And then there are meetings we must attend, friends to visit, the radio to listen to, television shows to look at, and movies to attend. The result is that we become perceptually selective; we hear and do not listen; we see and do not assimilate. This wall of defense serves us to good advantage, for there is too much communication in our world for us to take it all in; we must choose—or be chosen for.

Because of our busy society, the communicator must recognize that he is constantly competing—competing for the attention of his listeners or his readers. He must make his message so excellent, so clear, so concise, so interesting, and so compelling that the listener or reader will *want* to assimilate it.

Language itself is probably the one barrier which occurs most frequently in attempting to communicate ideas. Among the problems involved in the use of language for communication are *differences in interpretation of statements*. We have all said things that we thought were perfectly clear and simple, only to have them misconstrued completely. This happens for various reasons. Sometimes it is simply the result of misunderstanding. Or it may be due to an unconscious desire not to carry out someone's request. Or perhaps the speaker has chosen a word that conveys a different meaning than he intended. Although "fee," "salary," "wages," "payment," "stipend," and "emolument" are listed as synonymous in the dictionary, each creates a specific image in our mind. We would never pay a surgeon "wages" for an operation, or a ditchdigger weekly "fees" for his labor. As Mark Twain said, "There is as much difference between the right word and the almost-right word as between lightning and the lightning bug."

Then, too, a specific word may evoke different symbols or "pictures" in the minds of people whose backgrounds and experiences are different. What does

By permission of John Hart and Field Enterprises, Inc.

the word "pig" conjure up in the mind of a steelworker, as compared to that of a farmer or a college student? And what symbol does the word evoke when it is hurled in anger at a person?

Language uses words to convey ideas, facts, and feelings. Sometimes semantic problems arise in the interpretation of words, because their meanings are not in the words, but in the minds of the people who receive them. (See Hayakawa, "How Words Change Our Lives," in the Readings.)

Meanings of concrete words do not vary too much from one person to another. There is little possibility for confusion when we speak of pencil, or paper, or book. But as words become more abstract (democracy, honesty, happiness), they are more likely to be misunderstood. This is also true of words which carry emotional overtones in a specific society. What "liberal," "radical," "virtue," "morality," and "integrity" mean to the speaker or writer may not agree at all with the listener's or reader's concept of the same word.

Another factor to be considered under language is *inadequate vocabulary*. If our stock of words is poor and forces us to fumble and bumble as we attempt to express our ideas, our ability to communicate will be limited. It is important to build up our vocabularies so that we can express our ideas clearly, forcefully, and with facility and not be required to use a second-choice word when the *exact* word would result in a much clearer picture.

We should also make every effort to avoid *errors* in speaking and writing. Whether it is spelling, diction, or pronunciation, an error, when it is made, immediately forces the reader or listener to focus on the mistake. You know how you have been impressed by what might be called minor errors, and how they jump out of the page you are reading or the oral statement to which you are listening. Never minimize or rationalize an error, regardless of how minor; make every effort to make your language choice as correct as possible.

Remember also to choose the *proper level* of language when you communicate with others. To speak or write "above their heads" or down to them condescendingly is to invite misinterpretation, irritation, and confusion. A classic story illustrating this problem is of the plumber who wrote to the Bureau of Standards in Washington, stating that he used hydrochloric acid for cleaning out clogged drains. The Bureau wrote him: "The efficacy of hydrochloric acid is indisputable, but the corrosive residue is incompatible with metallic permanence." The plumber replied that he was glad the Bureau agreed. The Bureau tried again, this time writing, "We cannot assume responsibility for the production of noxious and toxic residue with hydrochloric acid and suggest you use an alternative procedure." The plumber again replied that he was pleased that the Bureau agreed with his findings. Finally the Bureau awoke to the fact that it was not writing at this plumber's level. Thereupon the plumber received a note which said, "Don't use hydrochloric acid. It eats hell out of the pipes."

Feedback

If there are so many barriers to the communication of ideas, how do we know when we get through . . . or, even more important, how do we know when we don't?

After all, most of us just write or speak and then assume that we have communicated what is in our minds to someone else.

Perhaps the only way to determine whether or not we have been successful is to secure a response, or *feedback*.

The technical meaning for feedback is somewhat different from the popular conception. In 1948, Norbert Wiener published a book called *Cybernetics* (a branch of science that deals with the theory of such systems as the nerve networks in animals, electronic pathways in computing machines, servo systems for the automatic control of machinery, and other information processing, transmission, and control systems).

One of the primary areas of study in cybernetics is feedback. In this context it applies to the ability of man and some machines to detect an error or deviation from what is desired in an operation, and *feed back* that error to a control mechanism, which then makes the necessary correction. If a satellite destined for the moon moves off course, the deviation is noted and fed back to the controlling mechanism for correction. A home thermostat records a temperature too low and feeds back a signal to the furnace which then operates to make a correction. Or a person's body temperature goes lower than desired; this information is fed back and his physiological control mechanism attempts to bring about the change desired.

Thus a common feature of a control system is that the output produces an effect on the input. In communication engineering this is called feedback, and a control systems engineer refers to this as a "closed loop system."

Of course the similarities of feedback in this technical concept to that in interpersonal communication are immediately apparent. We even have a common expression, "Have you closed the loop?" This obviously refers to the communicator (encoder) and whether or not he has secured a satisfactory response (feedback) from the communicatee (decoder) and thus satisfactorily closed the loop and secured understanding.

The popular meaning for feedback is the verbal or nonverbal response received from the individual to whom a message is directed. It may be a series of words; it may be a raised eyebrow, an angry expression, or a smile; it may be no response at all (which is a response indicating that the message was not heard, not understood, or not accepted). But it is only through the feedback we receive that we can know whether we have communicated our ideas.

If we ask our youngster to open the window and he does it, we know we have communicated successfully. However, if he opens the door, that incorrect response or feedback tells us that communication broke down.

When we write for our superiors, our subordinates, our colleagues, our teachers, or our students and they do not understand what we have written, they will ask us for a further interpretation. Their questions (or feedback) tell us how successful we and they have been in exchanging ideas. (See J. Fielden, "What Do You Mean I Can't Write?" in the Readings.)

But we are often not quite so fortunate in being able to secure an almost immediate response. Sometimes we speak to 50, 150, or 250 persons, or we write a report in Chicago which may be read by 20 different individuals in New York. In such instances, feedback is much more difficult to secure.

There is the further problem of trying to secure accurate feedback after we have made a presentation to a group. Why do people often say "yes" when they are asked, "Do you understand?" "Is it clear?" There are two obvious answers. One is that the communicatee (or decoder) honestly believes that he *does* understand, even though he may not. The second is that the recipient of the message is reluctant to disclose that he does *not* understand. He feels (and we must all admit to this) that he will lose face or be embarrassed by admitting his lack of comprehension. And so he says, "yes, I understand," when in truth he does not.

Every student has experienced this situation when the instructor, after his lecture, says, "Are there any questions?" How often we have been tempted to raise our hand, but as we look around the classroom, no one else has raised *his* hand. We are, therefore, reluctant to raise our own. If the teacher places faith in the feedback he received (which was "no question"), he can only assume that everyone understood the discussion. He may, however, learn differently when he grades the examination papers later.

Thus, we all depend on feedback to evaluate the clarity of our communications. This is as it should be, but we must remember to weigh the feedback for accuracy and not always trust it completely.

The communicator must keep in mind that he may not have transmitted his message. And he should design as many methods as possible to secure feedback so that he can be as certain as possible that he was successful in transmitting what was in his mind to his listener's or reader's mind.

Nonverbal Communication

It is probably no exaggeration to say that we communicate as many ideas nonverbally (and sometimes informally) as we do verbally. The way we stand, the way we walk, the manner in which we shrug our shoulders, furrow our brows, and shake our heads—all convey ideas to others. But we need not always perform an action for nonverbal communication to take place. We also communicate by the clothes we wear, the car we drive, or the office we occupy. It is true that what is communicated may not be accurate, but ideas of some kind *are* communicated. (See H. Fast, "Can You Influence People Through 'Body Language'?" in the Readings.)

Ruesch and Kees, in their book *Nonverbal Communication,* divide this area of communication into three parts: sign language, action language, and object language. Sign language is used to communicate basic ideas, such as the wave of a hand, which says "hi," or a "thumbs down" sign, which denotes non-acceptance.

Action language results from body movements which convey ideas beyond the immediate purpose of the action. We gain certain insights into an individual's personality by noting how he eats, whether he stands or not when a lady approaches, what position he takes when joining a line at a box office, etc.

We also decode object language which, according to Ruesch and Kees, includes the display of material items, either intentionally or unintentionally. These may include jewelry, coats, furniture, cars, and other tangible objects.

In the last two or three years, several books have appeared on the popular subject of "body language." The phrase is quite accurate, for indeed such things as posture, the crossing of arms or legs, a tense, arched, or relaxed seated position, a furrowed brow, a tapping heel, are all symbols in a language spoken by the body. It is to everyone's advantage to be sensitive to this nonverbal language and to interpret it as accurately as possible.

Conflict Between Verbal and Nonverbal Communication

One of the interesting aspects of communication is that two messages may be transmitted simultaneously. Quite often a verbal message is sent together with a nonverbal one. Someone may greet us with a great show of enthusiasm: "How are you? Good to see you. Come on into my office and chew the fat, you old son of a gun." But the nonverbal communication, consisting of a surreptitious but pained glance at the clock, says something else. We all know the guest who says, "Of course we want to see your slides of Europe," as he stifles a yawn and sprawls in the chair. Then there is the employee who tries to sound relaxed and comfortable when he talks to the boss, while his toe tapping the floor tells a different story.

Interestingly enough, whenever the meaning of the nonverbal message conflicts with that of the verbal, the receiver is most likely to find the former more believable. The alert receiver will almost always be able to determine when a problem exists. Most of us can discern the fearful person who truly exists behind the good-humored, back-slapping, joke-telling facade that is displayed. We somehow know quite well how dismally Betty and Joe's marriage is progressing, even though their protestations of undying love for one another are voiced loudly and clearly. The nonverbal message is usually obvious, and if it does not agree with the verbal one, the receiver quickly and almost invariably recognizes the one that is true.

[5] A discussion of a portion of the book by Ruesch and Kees may be found in Randall Harrison, "Non-Verbal Communication: Explorations into Time, Space, Action, and Object," contained in Campbell and Hepler, *Dimensions in Communication* (Wadsworth, 1965), pp. 162–63.

Media of Nonverbal Communication

Most of the nonverbal messages that we receive come to us visually. We are quick to see the hurt in someone's eyes, or another person's triumphant smile. We notice the twisting, nervous fingers in a lap, and the confidence in a posture. We also decode the message of a sudden, frightened tug at our arm when we cross in heavy traffic, or the barely noticeable touching of fingers of two people in love.

Our nose also plays an important role in nonverbal communication. What a wonderful message we decode when we walk into the cozy comfort of a home where a Thanksgiving dinner is about to be served. The aromas of a roasting turkey, dressing, and pumpkin pie require no words to transmit a message.

All in all, any message—verbal or nonverbal, formal or informal—which is received and decoded by one of our senses, can be said to be communication.

Space and Time Communicate

Does Time really talk and does Space actually speak? Of course they do, and we've all heard them. The person who arrives late for appointment after appointment seems to be telling us that we aren't very important, or that he is careless, or one of several interpretations based on our perception. And if we note Jack and Bob talking with their heads close together, we may wonder what secrets or plots are being communicated.

We have formulated rather strict patterns in America for time. A business appointment is usually kept punctually. Although we may keep someone waiting for five or ten minutes, much longer than that is usually interpreted as an affront.

If Jack is ten minutes late for an appointment with Bob, the latter's interpretation may vary according to the situation. Jack will probably apologize immediately if it is a business appointment. However, he may be quite casual about his tardiness if it takes place one afternoon on a week-long fishing trip they are taking together.

Americans are accustomed to quantifying time. "I will have this done in 30 minutes." "I'll see you at the 3 o'clock meeting." "Let's establish a six-month deadline for the project." "We'll insert a time penalty clause into the contract. The installation should be completed by December 3; for every day that is required after that, a payment of $100 will be made."

This concern with time is not so precise in other cultures, although the European and Japanese are fast approaching the North American's interpretation of time. Anthropologist Edward Hall, in his excellent and provocative book *The Silent Language,* analyzes the effect of cultural factors on the ways people communicate. (See Hall, "The Silent Language in Overseas Business," in the Readings.) The Latin American takes time more casually, and tardiness does not usually communicate the message it does in the United States. Hall points out that in some cultures, such as the Hopi, time is measured by a series of natural events, not by specific numbers of minutes or days. Time passes according to the ripening of grain, or the completion of the growth of an animal, or the winter rains.

Time certainly communicates. The office worker who is at his or her desk and begins to work promptly at 8:30 a.m. is surely communicating facts to the office manager that are in sharp contrast to what the person is saying who casually strolls in, day after day, at 8:40, 8:45 or 9 a.m.

How people use space also tells us much. As is the case with time, the utilization of space and what is communicated thereby vary from continent to continent and nation to nation.

We say this is "our property line" even though no fence exists on it; a neighbor may not encroach upon or over it. "This is the children's section of the yard, and they can mess it up as much as they like so long as they don't spoil my lawn."

In a business situation, an employee occupies a specific space where his desk, chair, and cabinets are arranged. Anyone who occupies, uses, or moves this furniture may encounter antagonism. In the conference room, the position at the head of the table belongs to the president of the company or the chairman of the meeting. If the sales manager occupies that position or decides to use the president's office, desk, and chair, he will surely communicate a message.

Space also speaks in informal situations. The man who usurps your place in the theater ticket line communicates to you. In the home, we have also laid claim to certain areas. There is the "children's play room," "Mother's kitchen," "Dad's workshop," "Grandfather's chair," "the family den," etc.

In personal communication between two people, we often find that the distance varies. Two women who are discussing routine matters of their organization may speak comfortably as they sit two to three feet distant from one another. However, if they are discussing "who would make the best president for their group," or "Betty's recent operation," or "just what *is* happening between Bob and Dorothy Campbell," the distance may be shortened considerably.

The speaking distance which is maintained in different cultures also varies. In the United States two businessmen may talk about a transaction very comfortably across the desk. However, in most of Europe and in Latin America, the distance is much closer. It is not unusual in Italy to see two men walking down a corridor in an office building, arms around each other's shoulders, talking face to face.

Time and space, as examples of nonverbal communication, certainly play an important role in our sending and receiving of ideas.

Questions for Study

Complete any of the following problems assigned. You may wish to review the chapter and note key points before attempting to solve a problem.

1. Review the article, "What's Happened to Employee Commitment" by N. B. Sigband (in the Readings section of this book), and then discuss how communication can be used to motivate personnel. You may also wish to comment on how effective *money* and *fear* are as motivators.

2. Visualize a person with whom you have some difficulty communicating effectively. Now go through the following steps recording your answers on paper:

(1) Identify the person (brother, boss, girlfriend, mother-in-law, wife, husband, etc.).

(2) State as specifically as possible the barrier(s) which make communication between you and him or her difficult.

(3) Indicate the possible solutions(s), and how you would implement them.

3. Think of a discussion that went awry you held recently with an individual. Present it as a case analysis. Who was the individual? What was the topic of discussion? Where did it take place? What specific factors caused the breakdown? Why were *those* factors the cause in this particular instance? Add any other factors which you feel are relevant.

4. Check through several secondary sources and record four different definitions of *communication* and their authors. Which one of these do you feel is most accurate and why?

5. Citizens of the United States of America frequently have a different perception of this nation than do the citizens of foreign countries. What are some of the reasons for this difference in perception? How does this difference, or how should this difference, influence our foreign policy?

6. There are a number of barriers to effective communication listed in this chapter. Can just one of these cause a breakdown in communication, or are there usually several involved almost simultaneously? Defend your answer.

7. An expression which has recently gained in popularity is "Have you closed the loop?" What connection does this statement have with our discussion of feedback?

8. Under some conditions, communication does not take place successfully even when the stated feedback from the decoder indicates it has. Can you present a situation where this might be true?

9. Many of our statesmen, columnists, and others grandly state that our civil disorders, campus unrest, high crime rate, and violence are due to "differences in perception." However, recognizing a problem does not solve it. What suggestions do you have for eliminating or alleviating the "Differences in Perception" dilemma which exists in our society?

10. The Shannon-Weaver model of communication is often said to be "linear." However, the N. Wiener approach is viewed as circular. Can you explain why? What role does "feedback" play in the latter?

11. Describe a situation in which you were recently involved where the nonverbal communication proved more important than the verbal. What was the nonverbal? How was it interpreted? What effect did it have on the individuals involved?

Complete any of the following problems assigned.

1. List and explain several informal communication messages which you have received in the last week through your senses of sight, touch, and smell.

2. List and discuss several situations in the classroom and in the typical American office which illustrate the truth of Hall's statement, "Time talks and Space speaks."

3. Is it always possible to "hear" the feelings of the speaker? What factors might prevent this?

4. What specific suggestions can you make to someone who wishes to improve his listening ability?

5. According to Ralph Nichols and other authorities in the field of listening, what are several of the important factors and habits which contribute to poor listening on the part of the decoder?

6. Carry through the following experiment in serial communication and present your findings to the class.

Secure a picture or an advertisement from a magazine. It should have several items or incidents in it as well as people involved in some activity.

Ask for four volunteers from your class, and request that three leave the room. Ask volunteer number one to remain in the room and show him and the class the picture for two to three minutes. Call volunteer two into the room and tell him to listen to what volunteer one tells the group he (volunteer one) saw, so that volunteer two may tell the group what he (volunteer two) heard.

Ask the class to record very briefly what volunteer one tells them he saw.

When volunteer one finishes telling the group what he saw in the picture, call in volunteer three so that he may listen to volunteer two. Have volunteer two tell the group what he heard volunteer one say. Ask the group to record volunteer two's statements.

Call volunteer four in so that he may listen to volunteer three tell the group what he (volunteer three) heard volunteer two say. Also ask the group to record volunteer three's comments. Finally, ask volunteer four to tell the group what he heard volunteer three say.

You may wish to distribute a form similar to the following for the group to use:

SERIAL COMMUNICATION			
Observations by Decoder One	Comments by Decoder Two	Comments by Decoder Three	Comments by Decoder Four
1. 2. 3. 4. 5. 6. 7. 8. 9. 10.			
Observations by group members on the communication process:			

At the conclusion of the experiment, indicate what specific principles in serial communication took place. Finally, read the article on serial communication by William V. Haney and compare his observations with yours.

Each of the following statements is either a quotation or a paraphrase from a book on language, semantics, or communication theory. Indicate as concisely as possible what you think the authors meant by any of the following quotations:

1. "A second principle of general semantics, non-identity, states that the word is not the thing it represents."

2. "Used correctly they [words] can cause friendliness, humor, and happiness. Used incorrectly, they can cause hatred, loss of faith, hostility, and even death."

3. "To say that we know what a word means in advance of its use is nonsense."

4. "A dictionary is an invaluable guide to interpretation, but we should remember that words do not have a *single* correct meaning."

5. "Meaning is relative to experience."

6. "The most important solution to these problems [communication problems] is to pay attention to feedback. Thus it is important to adapt communication to the receiver's interest. However, this feedback is not always to be trusted."

7. "Seldom does one bother to question the other person whether the terms used in the communication are agreed upon by both parties."

8. "Never mind what words mean. What did the speaker mean?"

9. "Semantics is an exploration rather than a science, which rewards its students with a skill rather than a body of subject matter."

10. "Some companies believe that management can exercise 'stop-go' control over information that employees receive."

11. "A piece of paper money is like a word; it has no value in itself."

12. "Speak, in order that I may see you."

13. "We must never assume that we are fully aware of what we communicate to someone else."

14. "Time talks. It speaks more plainly than words."

15. "Speakers are prisoners of their vocabularies."

16. "Nature has given to men one tongue, but two ears, that we may hear from others twice as much as we speak."

17. "It's what and how you communicate or don't communicate, that makes you what you are to others."

Chapter Two

Communication as a Tool of Management Control

Upward Communication
Downward Communication
Lateral Communication
The Grapevine
Internal Communication

Every member of management must understand that effective communication is an essential tool of good management; and that part of his job is to relay and interpret appropriate information and news, whether good or bad, to his subordinates and superiors. . . .

There is a need to inform employees about matters which affect them or their jobs, to interpret management's position on relevant issues. . . .

Lynn Townsend, former Chairman of the Board
Chrysler Corporation[1]

Whether a business, industrial, or government office is large or small, it consists of people; and whether those who operate any enterprise are many or few, they must communicate among themselves and with others to get things done. Persons at the executive level are responsible for making decisions and initiating action. For these individuals to carry out their functions effectively, they must know what is taking place throughout the company.

However, this is much easier said than done. It is very difficult to acquire a truly accurate picture of company activities, especially in organizations where there is a good distance between the men and women working on the noisy production line and the division manager seated in his walnut-paneled office (See Robert McMurry, "Clear Communications for Chief Executives," and Jay Jackson, "The Organization and Its Communications Problem," in the Readings). This distance is great not only in terms of physical space, but also in terms of social stratification and professional activities. Because of these distances and what happens to the content of a message as it travels, it is often difficult for the decision maker to know exactly what is taking place on the

---

[1] Quoted from ICIE *Reporting* (December 1964) in G. Seybold, *Employee Communication: Policy and Tools* (National Industrial Conference Board, 1966), p. 11.

worker level.

Information transmitted up or down the line is often distorted unintentionally or by design. The distortions that occur may be the result of honest but inaccurate evaluations of facts and situations, the desire to impress a supervisor, a wish to avoid embarrassment, or an effort to sidestep well-deserved blame for a mistake.

Upward Communication

Employees of all levels, except those in top management, must communicate UP. It is vital that they transmit information clearly, concisely, and accurately, so that it may be evaluated and analyzed for the purpose of making decisions. Those in charge may use such data to learn from past mistakes, to exercise better control of current situations, and to plan for future activities.

Reports

Among the most important kinds of communication to flow up are reports. These, if carefully controlled in number and content, can be invaluable to the supervisor or executive. He or she will usually receive them periodically from key subordinates, who should include in their reports important information on the activities of their sections, departments, or divisions. Reports written by several different department managers will often overlap: The sales manager will have some comments on advertising; the head of the credit department will make a statement about sales; and the production supervisor may refer to something in the personnel manager's area of responsibility. These comments may very well conflict with each other. The sales director feels that the number of credit accounts should be expanded, but the credit manager feels that "because of present conditions, open-account sales should be drastically curtailed"; the advertising department feels that an additional $10,000 should be expended on television commercials, but the controller recommends a major cut in advertising expenditures.

Indeed, it is helpful if reports from different sources within a company *are* in conflict, for the executive receiving them must make decisions that are based on as wide knowledge as possible. The action he takes may involve huge sums of money: A production line may be opened or closed, an expensive piece of equipment purchased, a contract signed, or property acquired. The correctness of the executive's decisions depends directly on the quality of the communications he receives from his subordinates; and if the information received is conflicting or overlapping, the executive can then evaluate all aspects of a given situation before making his decision.

However, if the report is unclear, incomplete, or ambiguous, or if the writer fears to recount his own mistakes or negative situations which have arisen, the actions taken or the decisions made on the basis of the report may well turn out to be incorrect and costly.

How does a firm insure that its reports are accurate and complete? Naturally, there are many ground rules, but the most important is to have policies of communication that permit negative as well as positive situations to be reported freely. This will encourage open and honest communication and help to create a climate in which, because the goal is information, people are not penalized for reporting errors or failure in their operations. (See N. Sigband, "Needed: Corporate Policies on Communication," in the Readings.)

Reports may be of two kinds: oral and written. Oral reports can be presented in formal fashion before a group, the presentation accompanied by charts, graphs, and other visual aids. Or the oral report can be as simple as a supervisor's statement: "We produced 455 units today; we will need a reorder on the cork liners for tomorrow's run."

Written reports are more various. One author has classified them according to purpose (analytical, informative, persuasive). Another writer feels that classification by type (credit, periodic, memo, examination, progress) is more accurate as a deciding factor, while still others prefer to classify them by field (engineering, marketing, management, medicine) or area of activity (research, public, annual).[2]

Suggestion Systems

There are many other possible lines of upward communication. The alert manager utilizes as many of these lines as possible, seizing every opportunity to gain information that will help him make valid and successful decisions.

One of the most popular methods of transmitting information upward is the suggestion box. Many companies solicit suggestions from all workers, and a monetary reward is usually given when the idea is used. Often the sum offered equals approximately 10 percent of the first year's savings resulting from the suggestion.

There is value in such systems, for millions of dollars are saved as a result of employee suggestions. And the psychological value an employee receives from participation in the company's production procedure is immeasurable. However, problems can arise. Sometimes the suggestion made by a worker makes a supervisor appear inefficient or incompetent because the change was not already instituted by the supervisor. Then there is the delicate task of telling someone that his suggestion has no merit and is not eligible for an award. Still another problem is the amount of money to be awarded.

In some instances the suggestion made may cause the routine of an entire work group to change, or may result in eliminating one member of the group because of a more efficient production procedure. This obviously results in lowered group morale, ill will, and antagonism. The gain made through the suggestion may be lost twice over as a result of worker resentment.

But with all these difficulties, the suggestion system often leads to improved production and more efficient methods. Employees, on the whole, enjoy a sense of participation, and it gives management another source of information.

[2] See Norman B. Sigband, *Effective Report Writing for Business, Industry, and Government* (New York: Harper & Row, 1960).

Interviews

Effective communication depends on dialogue; there must be some possibility of response, or feedback. Through face-to-face interaction, management can discover employees' ideas and goals, the level of rapport which exists, their willingness to share in and work toward the company's objectives, and their feelings about their own place in the corporate scheme.

Face-to-face encounters are as useful for downward communication as for upward, of course. The point is that communication becomes two-way rather than unidirectional.

Information is frequently forwarded up to management as a result of interviews held with past, present, and prospective employees. Interviews may be held for placement, to give information, to secure ideas, for orientation of new employees, for evaluation of employees, for a transfer in assignment, for promotion, to discipline employees or hear their complaints, and at the time of an employee's separation from the company. If these discussions are carried through openly and honestly, they may be very valuable. Certainly every manager should sit down with each subordinate periodically and communicate on a one-to-one basis. (See Waldo E. Fisher, "The Interview—A Multi-Purpose Leadership Tool," and J. M. Lahiff, "Interviewing for Results," in the Readings.)

Employee Councils

In the last few years, especially good results have been achieved with employee councils. It is exceptionally well suited to securing two-way communication between management and the work force, it results in employee recognition, and it establishes a climate for open communication.

In most firms an employee representative is elected from each department or unit. These individuals meet with management representatives on a periodic basis.

One of the ground rules is that topics which may be covered by union negotiation, such as fringe benefits, grievances, or work/compensation rules, are not reviewed. All other areas are fair game, from "Why is the soup in the cafeteria always cold?" to "Why can't the coils be ordered in 30-pound instead of 60-pound units? Handling would be much easier and safer."

A second ground rule is that answers to all questions or requests must be given at that meeting or taken up first at the subsequent conference. And still another worthwhile practice is to have minutes kept so that each item brought up is noted, as well as its disposition. These can then be distributed plant-wide.

Because a council member is elected, he is usually not reluctant to bring up sensitive issues. He is not speaking for himself but on behalf of his work group.

Of course there must be a clear understanding that management will listen even though it may not agree to approve a change. But because most people are intelligent and fair, that is usually no problem. Employees are reasonable, and if they are listened to they will usually understand a logical refusal as easily as they will an acceptance. Subject matter seems to change after the first two or three meetings. In the initial get-togethers, the employee representatives have voiced almost all their real or imaginary "gripes." By the fourth meeting, they are suggesting methods and techniques for improving production, assembly, plant layout, etc. Certainly they are as desirous of their company's success as is management.

It has been the author's experience, after sitting through many of these council meetings, that, on the whole, they really "work." The number of labor difficulties, confrontations, and strikes will usually drop where this system is used.

Of course this, like all internal communication, must be based on honesty and trust as well as effective policies if it is to be successful. (See N. Sigband, "Needed: Corporate Policies on Communication," and N. Sigband, "What Happened to Employee Commitment?" in the Readings.)

Downward Communication

People work better when they know exactly what their supervisors desire of them, what their duties, responsibilities, and privileges are. People need to know what is expected of them—perhaps not in minute detail, but certainly in general terms. For this reason management and supervisors must issue directives, and policy and procedural statements, to those in lower echelons.

How much does an employee "need to know"? The answer rests in the perception of the supervisor and the needs of the employee. Some employees react strongly and unfavorably when their desires for information go unfulfilled. Others are quite passive. On the whole, however, most people want to know and to participate, not only in company production, but also in planning, goal setting, and recruiting. (See N. Sigband, "What's Happened to Employee Commitment?" in the Readings.) Of course, the employee's assignment may limit the level of need to know. The punch-press operator who repeats the same operation hour after hour, on $12'' \times 12''$ squares of copper sheet may have a different level of need from the engineer working on long-range corporate planning of computer needs.

One business writer puts it this way:

Variations in the physical height of people occur within a limited range, and the great majority cluster within certain limits. In the same manner, variations in individual communication needs appear to vary over a certain range, but tend to cluster around a central tendency. Various studies could be brought to bear on this subject, and many more need to be made. If we had all the research information it would be nice to have, I believe we would confirm two tendencies disclosed by presently available research, and abundantly confirmed by observation.

1) The level of motivation of most people could be greatly increased through knowing more about their jobs, departments, companies, workng conditions, and their individual and group relationship to others in their departments, companies, and in other comparable companies.

2) The average supervisor is far more likely to underestimate, than to overestimate, the extent and depth of employees' interest in the enterprise, and the extent to

which additional information, properly used, can motivate a bonus for the enterprise in superior performance. . . . [3]

Employees have a need to know in two broad areas. The first is the job itself. Every employee wants to know *what* his or her task is, *how it is to be performed, how it interrelates* with other tasks to achieve the company's goals, *where* and *when* it is to be performed. Employees want to know what their duties are and what freedom they have.

The second area concerns the employees' relationship with the company, the community, and their families. They want to know *how* much insurance the company carries for them, *why* the company's stock dividends are going down, *what* management thinks about the union's demands, *how* management reacts to equal-employment laws, *where* the new plant will be built, and *what* are the company's goals and objectives.

The first of these two needs to know is easily satisfied. Printed job descriptions and on-the-job demonstration and consultation, if done conscientiously, will inform employees of the nature of their jobs. In addition, the supervisor should strive to create the kind of atmosphere in which the employees have no qualms about asking questions or requesting further explanations.

Policies of Communication

Downward communication in the larger area of need to know is not so simple. Management, when considering issues of basic interest to employees—such as strikes, benefits, layoffs—sometimes takes the view that "if we ignore it, maybe it'll go away." But it will not go away. If rumors are flying, the company will suffer. Rumor leads to uncertainty, and uncertainty to fear, and fear to inability to function efficiently. For a company to continue to function successfully, there must be mutual trust, loyalty, and interest between management and employees.

The average employee is interested in vital issues such as company goals, objectives, controversies, and sensitive issues. When the company discusses these areas, it is, in essence, saying to the employee, "We *recognize* you as an individual and a critical factor in the firm. Therefore we want to share important news with you that concerns the company, and therefore concerns you."

But how do you get all members of management to do this—to share, to discuss, to communicate? Some may and some may not. The objective, however, is to secure a consistent policy in all divisions, in all branches, in all locations of the company.

The answer is relatively simple, and that is to establish company-wide *policies of communication.*[4] Just as a firm has policies for finance, for personnel, for marketing, for credit, for sales, for expansion . . . so too should it have policies

[3] A. S. Hatch, "Improving Boss-Man and Man-Boss Communication," *The Journal of Business Communication,* October 1966, p. 27.

[4] See Norman B. Sigband, "Needed: Corporate Policies on Communications," *Advanced Management Journal,* April 1969, pp. 61–67.

for communication. Many prominent industrial leaders have noted the importance of communicating important issues to employees.

Charles B. McCoy, former chairman of the board and president of E. I. Du Pont de Nemours, has stated:

> Communication has a high priority at DuPont. Employees have a right to be informed. They should be told important news immediately, good or bad. The people who work for DuPont want to know what the enterprise is all about. They want a sense of involvement, want to be part of the organization. Therefore, they need to know about current business problems, the company's stand on such important matters as imports and pollution control, its views on issues of public importance. Employees want straightforward, honest, balanced information—not propaganda.

> Informed employees are better, more productive employees. They get more out of their work, and they do a better job for the company.[5]

William M. Allen, chairman of the board and chief executive officer of Boeing has said:

> The task of communication in business takes on larger dimensions. . . . where once it may have been concerned primarily with publications, news service, and appropriate management messages, now it must be regarded as an integral part of managing.
> The rationale for . . . meetings . . . within . . . the organization is the recognition that communication and understanding are the keys to making full use of individual capabilities. Each individual likes to feel that he is personally involved in an activity—that he is making a contribution.[6]

Lynn Townsend, former chairman of the board of Chrysler, has declared:

> Internal communication must be recognized as an essential tool of good management. . . . Employees must be well informed concerning their mutual interests in company success. . . . and about important matters which affect them or their jobs. . . . We should interpret management's position on relevant issues.[7]

In an address before the International Association of Business Communications, J. Paul Lyet, president of Sperry Rand Corporation, commented at length on the correlation he has observed between effective communications to employees of important aspects of the firm's operations and good employee relations. He emphasized that one way to save time was to take time to keep employees informed of company activities.[8]

[5] *Better Living,* Fall 1971, p. 3 (DuPont employee magazine).
[6] *Boeing Management Perspective,* July/August 1968.
[7] L. Townsend, "A Corporate President's View of the Internal Communication Function," *Journal of Communication,* December, 1965 (see Readings).
[8] J. Paul Lyet, president of Sperry Rand Corporation in an address to the National Conference of the International Association of Business Communications, St. Louis, Missouri, June 5, 1972.

American Airlines communication policy was stated this way:

The success of American Airlines, and in turn the success of its employees, is greatly dependent upon the teamwork of personnel at all levels—between staff and line, and between all functions. This teamwork will be in direct ratio to the quality of our communications.

It is therefore the policy of the company that communications will be imaginative, timely, appropriate, and free flowing—that there will be communication downward, upward, and laterally throughout the company.[9]

This policy is then spelled out at management and employee levels. Broadly speaking, the policy is to communicate with *all* employees about *all* company activities, present and projected. This program thus finds it possible to present and cover topics with strong human interest value and which are often controversial and sensitive.

Areas for Discussion. There seems to be a misunderstanding among some managers about employees' reactions to controversial issues. Some executives mistakenly believe that discussions about profits, union-management controversies, taxes, etc. have no place in company publications; that employees would resent management's treatment of such topics; that employees are not interested in the subjects or in management's point of view.

Nonsense! Intelligent employees want to hear both sides. They may actually resent being exposed only to the union viewpoint; they may feel that management is avoiding its responsibilities. Thus management must add something substantial to the "Betty is holding hands with N.R.T. from Dept. 21 and wedding bells . . ." type of chitchat, which fills so many pages in today's company publications.

From time to time, management should provide information and opinion on the following topics:

Wage and salary structures: how they are established and revised; how they compare with salary levels in the industry generally.

Benefit programs for employees: the benefits received and the important percentage they add to base pay.

Company products and how they are used by consumers and/or wholesalers; the role of such products in defense efforts, consumer use, or other activities.

Company profits, not as a flat dollar amount, but in relation to sales and job security; profits in terms of investment, replacement of equipment, and company expansion and growth; profits in terms of their value to the community, employees, and others.

Employee-management relationships: Union requests and management's viewpoint should be presented with a careful discussion of each point. Articles covering specific points of controversy and written by labor and management representatives might well appear side by side.

Analysis of strikes or work stops. Discussion of union-management negotia-

---

[9] Quoted by G. Seybold, *Employee Communication: Policy and Tools* (National Industrial Conference Board, 1966), pp. 31–34.

tions, arbitration, and rulings.

Whenever possible, representatives of labor should be permitted to present their point of view or rebuttal next to management's in an employee publication.

The company's dependence on customers, dealers, stockholders, suppliers, government agencies, community members, distributors, the general public, and the employees themselves.

The organization of the company, the various products or services it provides, the location of plants, and the number and classification of employees.

The company's short- and long-term goals.

Automation and how it will affect production and personnel.

Reductions in the work force—why they occurred and what the future holds.

Contemplated changes in products, personnel, manufacturing process, etc.

Existing rumors; the basis of the rumor should be explained and the truth told.

Taxes paid by the company and how they contribute to local, state, and federal activities.

Economic trends (inflation, lending, interest rates) and how they affect every wage earner.

Company viewpoints on controversial local and federal issues. Employees should be told frequently how important their views are; they should be encouraged to make those views known to their elected representatives.

The free enterprise system, how it works, and what it does for every citizen.

The role of organized labor and its contribution, under responsible leadership, to national growth and progress.

The opinions and activity of the company in social and cultural areas such as education, civil rights, and social welfare.

The above topics may be considered somewhat sensitive and controversial. That is no reason, however, for their not being discussed fairly, candidly, and honestly in company publications. There are many other subjects, noncontroversial but important, that should also be given attention. These include:

Employee morale
Attitudes toward jobs
The industry of which the company is a part
Promotion policies
Company and employee contributions to charity
Company competition
New company products
Company activities in research and development
Company's sources of materials and its markets
Company quality levels
Company cost reduction programs
The employee's role as a salesman for the firm's products, services, or image
Absenteeism
Safety programs
Employee's role as a recruiter
Litigation in which the company is involved
Possible mergers, sales, or diversification

In addition to the two large groups above, the following topics may be treated to the extent consistent with the employee communication policy:

Social news regarding births, marriages, anniversaries, etc.
Recognition of long-service employees and retirees
Awards received by employees and their spouses and children
News of retired employees
Employee classified ad section
Employees and their children in the service
Company celebrations, meetings, and recreation programs
Human interest accounts concerning employees

Union Relations. You can be very sure that the unions represented in your company will recognize the interests of their members. They will discuss in detail the "controversial" subjects listed above; and they will, naturally, discuss them from their own point of view. Management, in fairness to itself and to its employees, should also present its point of view.

Fred Foy and Robert Harper, in an article in *The Harvard Business Review,* said:

Both sides [management and unions] assemble their arguments. Both sides have their economists and technicians preparing the evidence. Both sides are trying to get their views before key people. But here is the reason that in the important battle for the minds of men, management so far has elected to fight with one arm tied behind it:

1) Only the unions are vigorously and effectively driving home to their members their arguments and their point of view. Week after week they pour out a flood of carefully planned and well-written articles. . . .

2) In contrast, the management publications regularly reaching the same union members fail—with only a few exceptions—to present any point of view about what management feels is good for America. Usually well-written and often beautifully printed, they cover mainly employee social news, company sport activities, and brief news reports about the company. For the most part they are conspicuously silent on such basic subjects as the profit system or on key current issues before the legislatures. This conclusion is based on an intensive study of some 700 company magazines published for employee consumption.[10]

A Cornell University study cited by Dover found that specific terms and words relating to management-labor activities were used much more frequently in union than in company communications. A sample of publications was carefully selected and studied as to economic content and terms.[11]

[10] Fred C. Foy and Robert Harper, "Round One: Union vs. Company Publications," *Harvard Business Review,* May-June 1955. (Although this study was completed in 1955, an informal survey by the author in 1974 found that Foy and Harper's research and conclusions were still valid.)

[11] C. J. Dover, *Management Communication on Controversial Issues* (Washington, D.C.: Bureau of National Affairs, Inc., 1965), p. 11.

NUMBER OF TIMES USED		
Word	In Union Publications	In Company Publications
arbitration	544	0
negotiation	1297	50
collective bargaining	906	2
strike	1364	0
wage increase	775	18
standard of living	701	38
contract	1359	101
organized labor	679	0

These figures are startling. One can only assume that these so-called sensitive areas are avoided to the same extent in face-to-face discussions.

The Cornell study concluded:

1. Economic concepts in all categories appear much more frequently in union publications than they do in company publications.

2. Union papers deal with very concrete and specific issues, while company papers are more prone to talk in economic generalities. Among the very few terms used more in company papers than in union papers were "production" (371–48); "market" (206–162); "promotion" (68–44); and "free enterprise" (25–0).

3. Union-management relationships are not so frequently treated in company papers as in union publications.[12]

There can be no doubt that management, in too many instances, has concerned itself with the prosaic, the noncontroversial, and the "safe" topics for discussion in company publications.

Foy and Harper, in their examination of union publications, found that

—the union leaders' program is carefully planned and consistent. It deals almost exclusively with "breadbasket subjects."

—communication with rank-and-file members is aided by excellent publications, which are used to promote social goals. From 45 percent to 65 percent of the space in some of these publications is allotted for this type of material.

—repetitious handling of the same subjects is extremely well done and indicates that editors and staff assistants are top-quality journalists.

In reviewing company publications, however, they determined that

—management did not counteract union activity on realistic "breadbasket" subjects such as union leaders use as levers to promote national social legislation.

—employee publications frequently take a negative approach to challenging problems—more often resorting to "sniper tactics" against the opponent's case.

—controversial subjects were avoided, but at the same time attempts were consistently made to stimulate pride in the virtues of the "American way of life." A

---

[12] Dover, p. 13.

steady reading diet of such "flag-waving" stories may prove an insult to the average worker's intelligence, for he too believes in the American way of life. The futility of communicating in this manner has been noted several times in leading business publications.

—management has the same kind of self-interest that union leaders have, but when it has used its private communications media in an attempt to influence national, state, and local domestic legislation, it has done the job so awkwardly that its employees have often been left asking "why" to a lot of questions which should have been squarely faced in public statements.

A Consistent Policy. What all this means is that firms need to have policies of communication so that employees will be informed openly, honestly, and quickly about important activities of the firm.

To have such lines of communication open and operating, it is necessary that top management accept, verbalize, and support specific policies of communication. It must do this in the same way it accepts, verbalizes, and supports company policies on personnel, finance, equal employment opportunities, or ecology.

Such policies must be based on management's desire to share information with those persons who are most in need of it and most desirous of receiving it—the employees.

If a sensitive situation exists in a company, communication will take place. If the facts are given to the employees, they will discuss those facts; if nothing is said by management, the employees will supply their own "facts." If we accept this axiom—that if something exists (or is thought to exist), it will be discussed—then it is in everybody's best interest that the company examine the situation with the employees. (See K. Davis, "Management Communication and the Grapevine," in the Readings.)

Management must be truthful with its employees. If a topic cannot be openly discussed—because of ongoing negotiations, government request, insufficient data on hand, or any other reason—employees should be so informed. Everyone is much more likely to accept a true statement of that type than some obvious "excuse" that insults one's intelligence. And nothing will lose employee loyalty and commitment faster than dishonesty or manipulation of information.

Requirements for Successful Corporate Policies of Communication. To achieve long-range success, several corporate requirements must be stated and followed:

1. That the principle of open, honest internal communication be announced and supported by the top executive with the assurance that such communication is a vital facet of good management.

2. That employees be informed of company goals, objectives, plans, and directions. This should be done in company publications, at departmental meetings, and in the one-to-one boss-worker interview.

3. That employees be informed about ongoing company activities. This should be done as quickly after the event as possible. The company newspaper, public address system, or specially convened employee meetings should be used. Nothing irritates an employee more then learning from his neighbor or a television commentator about some activity, problem, or event in which his firm is involved.

4. That employees be informed of controversial, sensitive, and negative issues. Such issues should include labor problems, minority hiring practices, a drop in sales or production, cutbacks in personnel, cancellation of contracts, court actions, a decline in profits, etc.

5. That all managers actively support the communication policies. Managers must do this in practice as well as in theory. They must also understand that it isn't a matter of choice; it's an obligation they must carry through.

6. That management learn to listen and to encourage a constant flow of honest, upward communication. That it make a real effort to listen for facts and feelings. As Drucker says, "The manager must appreciate the employees' perceptions and expectations, if communications are to be successful." (See Peter Drucker, "What Communication Means," in the Readings.)

7. That management recognize the average employee's desire to assist his or her company in the achievement of corporate goals.

8. That management recognize that good communications must be planned, organized, and carried through with the help of professional communicators. And that it is desirable to have one person in charge of internal and external communication practices. This person can see to it that communication policies are followed in a consistent fashion in all plants of the corporation, in all printed communications, and, hopefully, in all employee relations. Such a "communications manager" can bring the same consistency to his area as the personnel manager, the financial manager, and the marketing manager do to theirs.

9. That management support its policy with funds, time, and personnel.

Of course, a policy of communication does not mean that everything must be communicated to everyone. Obviously there are constraints, boundaries, and limits. National and company security must be considered, as must competition, employee morale, and the marketplace.

But once a communications policy has been structured, codified, verbalized, and practiced by top management, the employees' sense of security, fair play, openness, and credibility will rise as will their commitment to their jobs and their company.

Downward Communication Media—Putting Policies into Practice

Effective, useful, and worthwhile communication may be achieved through several media: magazines, orientation manuals, employee handbooks, annual reports, letters, bulletin boards. If they are used imaginatively and creatively, they can produce results far greater than the time and materials expended on them.

Company Magazines. Because the number of company magazines has grown so dramatically in recent years, it is hazardous even to guess how many are published and distributed today. However, it is safe to assume that almost every firm with more than a few hundred employees issues one periodically. They range all the way from slick, sophisticated magazines printed on first-grade paper stock to eight-page mimeographed affairs hastily stapled together. Most of them are published under the guidance of a company editor whose primary responsibility is the magazine. Many companies use agencies which may be part of an advertising firm, or organizations which specialize in handling company magazines.

The house magazine of today seems to fall into one of three types:

1. The most popular is the magazine that runs several feature articles on the industry of which the company is a part, the latest speech of the company president, and a story on government affairs; a fair percentage of the issue is devoted to employee activities, including weddings, births, retirements, vacations, sports, deaths, awards, and educational activities.

2. A second type is the tabloid, which may concentrate on company news, is written in a rather breezy style, and may very well have an employees' classified ad section.

3. The journal type of company magazine usually carries several articles of a broad, general nature. There is no news of employees or discussion of the day-to-day activities of the company. An attempt is made to publish only material of a fairly high level. Examples are The Western Electric Engineer, *and Standard Oil's* The Lamp.

There is a definite trend in company magazines to come to grips with topics a good deal more substantial than was the case ten years ago. Labor problems, government spending, politics, cost of living, civil rights, and other areas of common interest are being treated in many publications. It is true that the treatment is cautious, but at least these topics are being discussed.

There is probably no medium that can better carry company information than the thousands of company magazines published today in the United States. They can and should be used for informing employees in important areas and improving good will and understanding between employer and employee.[13]

Company Orientation Manuals.   The policies of most companies today are so complex, their fringe benefit programs so detailed, and their rules and regulations so varied that a printed guide to them is necessary. It is virtually impossible for a new employee to learn all he needs to know about a company in a half-hour discussion with his supervisor.

It is important for both the employer and the employees to have the details available for easy and ready reference. A small company orientation manual, carefully organized and clearly written, should contain the answers to most of the questions every employee has from time to time: What about major medical benefits? And how much does the hospitalization policy cover? How about retirement at 60? or 65? Am I entitled to free safety glasses? How about time off to vote? What about profit sharing? When do I become eligible for four weeks' vacation with pay? Does the company have a stock-buying program?

---

[13] For readers interested in this vital area of corporate communication, more information may be secured from The International Association of Business Communicators, 870 Market Street, San Francisco, California, 94102.

How about tuition refunds? What do I do about a grievance? Can I use the credit union?

This is not a booklet of company rules and regulations; it is a clear presentation of corporate policies and employee rights and privileges.

The value of such a manual is obvious. In the first place, it is a time saver for the employee. Second, everyone receives the same answer to the same question, instead of having it explained differently by different supervisors. Third, and perhaps most important, the employee manual eliminates incorrect answers. Too often a worker checks with other employees or immediate supervisors. If the question is difficult and the people who answer are depending on their memories and 25 years' experience with the firm, the information given may well be inaccurate.

A typical organization plan for an orientation manual might include company history and goals, a detailed section on employee benefits, and a careful discussion of corporate policies and practices.

It is a good idea to use a spiral binder or a loose-leaf notebook for the employee manual. Then, whenever a change takes place in vacation regulations, overtime compensation, cost-of-living adjustment, profit-sharing percentages, etc., it is not necessary to destroy all copies already printed. It is a simple task to reprint the page concerned with new information and substitute it for the outdated page.

The writing level and layout of the orientation manual should be checked very carefully. The writing style should be concise and easy to understand. Sentences should be short and words carefully chosen.

Section dividers and topic headings should be generously used. Pictures, sketches, and completed sample forms should be added where they will do the most good. If Mrs. Groweller, who works on Machine 21, wants to find out about maternity leave, she should be able to find the appropriate paragraph in a few seconds. She should not be forced to struggle through thirty pages on employee benefits before finding it. Topic headings and a good table of contents will help her find the section, and clear, concise writing will help her understand it.

Annual Reports to Employees. Several years ago quite a few of the larger corporations issued annual reports specifically for employees. In most instances they were the same (or nearly the same) as the corporate report to stockholders. To save money, the employee report was often printed in black and white only, on inexpensive paper.

However, problems sometimes arose. Employees wanted to know why their report was different from that of the stockholders, and what was being said to the stockholders that wasn't being said to the employees. As a result, few companies today issue a separate report for employees. It is really no more costly to give each employee a copy of the regular corporate report.

In those companies that do not have annual stockholders' reports, the printed annual report to employees certainly serves a useful purpose. It gives the worker an overall view of his company's activities in the preceding year, a listing of corporate goals and objectives, some mention of new processes and developments, listings of income and expenditures, and changes in personnel.

One firm that employs large numbers of recent immigrants with a Latin background has had some success with making its annual report for employees available in either English or Spanish.

Letters to Employees. Management has used letters for years in communicating orders, claims, adjustments, etc., to dealers, customers, and clients. It has used thousands in direct mail sales appeals, and dozens of different form letters to a wide variety of recipients. But it is only recently that business has learned the tremendous value of well-written letters sent to employees.

Perhaps the primary value of the letter is the personal touch it conveys. It is addressed to the employee, delivered to his home, and probably read carefully in an atmosphere that is less hurried and noisy than the shop or office. The content of the letter may well be discussed at the supper table, and thus the family is drawn into company activities and interests. What better way to build company loyalty than to involve the employee's family?

Letters have other advantages as well, not the least of which are their low cost and the speed with which they can be written, reproduced, and mailed.

Topics for Letters. Letters can cover a wide variety of topics very effectively. They can be used to welcome new employees; discuss a safety program; explain new products; announce mergers, expansions, or acquisitions; examine labor problems; discuss company profits; or simply build good will through a sincere expression of appreciation for a job well done.

North American Aviation, Inc., has used letters

> . . . not only to keep employees informed as to a specific labor situation, but also to advise them of other developments within the company. While the weekly publication, *Skywriter,* is designed to carry out this function, it is often desirable to reach employees between publication dates, and letters are then used. Additionally, we have found that letters are desirable when the subject requires lengthy explanation.[14]

Tone. Perhaps there is no aspect of a letter to an employee that contributes more to its acceptance or rejection than its tone. The letter that sounds insincere or ingratiating or pompous or dictatorial is surely doomed to failure. Because letters usually come from the top administrative officers, they are likely to be received by the employee with some skepticism in any case. If they then live up to his somewhat cynical expectations, management would have been better off never to have sent those letters at all.

Here are a couple of letters that seem to do an excellent job in tone, tact, and content:

[14] Letter to the author from Robert H. School, director, News Bureau, North American Aviation, Inc.

Dear Mr. Kelly:

Welcome to the Allied Manufacturing Company. We are
sincerely happy to have you become a member of the Allied
family. You may be sure that each of us will do everything
possible to make your stay with us pleasant and enjoyable
for many, many years to come.

Since 1959 we have been growing steadily and now have almost
8000 employees working in three different plants in the
greater Los Angeles area.

Each of these people contributes a great deal to Allied and
we know that you will also. All of us who work for the company recognize that as the company advances, so do we. For
this reason we work as a team and try to fill the needs of
our customers and take care of ourselves.

Right now we are almost at the "top of the heap" in wage
rates in the food processing industry. You and our other
employees also participate, without charge to you, in a
hospitalization program, major medical coverage, stock option plan, profit-sharing program, and paid vacations. These
are only some of the items received on the job; there are
others which you will learn about from your supervisor and
find discussed in your Allied Information Manual.

But these are only a few of the benefits you will receive
as an employee of Allied. There are paid holidays, time off
for personal affairs, an excellent company medical system,
fine recreation program, and wonderful people to work with.
I hope you won't ever hesitate to give the company the benefit of your suggestions. We need your help and advice. Just
walk in and talk to your supervisor or to me.

Within the next two weeks, you'll be spending a half day with
a Personnel Department representative who will help orient
you to all Allied activities. Begin now to think of questions to ask him. And those you have left over, bring to me.

I wish you all good fortune at Allied and I know all your
fellow employees join me in saying, "Welcome Aboard!"

Cordially yours,

Frank T. Bailey

Frank T. Bailey
President

It is important that the preceding kind of letter be individually typed and signed. A letter so personal in tone loses its value if it is mimeographed and signed by a secretary or with a rubber stamp. The following letter may, however, be mechanically reproduced, for it is obviously being sent to a large number of people.

Dear

Just a few hours ago the Board of Directors of your company voted to accept a new program: The Allied Employee Profit-Sharing Plan. I wanted you and your family to know about it just as soon as possible. A letter seemed to be the best way to tell you, and so I'm dashing this off. I'm genuinely excited about this; I hope you will be also.

What this program means is simply this: Beginning August 1, a specific percentage of the profits of the company go to the employees. As our firm grows, expands, and improves its position, we all benefit. Every single employee now has a real stake in the firm.

It is entirely possible that an employee will be able to retire from the company ten, fifteen, or twenty years from now and find that he has accumulated a very sizable sum in his Profit-Sharing Account. Such funds will make retirement all the more enjoyable.

Contributions to your fund come only from company profits; no contribution from you is required. Thus the better job we all do and the higher our profits, the faster our Fund grows.

You'll be getting a booklet very shortly which explains all the details, and we'll also have some group meetings for discussion.

I just wanted to bring this marvelous news to you today; I feel, and I'm sure you'll agree, that it is events like this that make Allied a great place to work.

Cordially yours,

Bernard Robinson

Bernard Robinson
President

Pay Envelope Inserts. The message printed on a small card or slip of paper and attached to the employee's pay check is sure to receive attention. A brief announcement, a news bulletin, or a vital piece of company information can be effectively transmitted in this way.

The message should be brief and its subject matter of importance. The pay envelope insert should be used only occasionally. If every pay check is accompanied by an insert, and the topics covered are routine, the value of this special little message is soon lost.

Bulletin Boards. In most companies, bulletin boards are used for motivational announcements (safety, zero defects program, bond drives, etc.) and for announcements of broad general interest such as approaching holidays, scheduled meetings, shift changes, and recognition of outstanding employees. If bulletin boards are strategically located and carefully handled, they can be an extremely valuable device for employee communication and team building between management and the work force. When representatives of the employee group share responsibility with management for the maintenance of bulletin boards, this medium of communication can be a strong force in the participatory process of management.

First of all, bulletin boards must be well lighted and carefully placed throughout the plant. Effective positions can be found in company cafeterias (within easy reading distance of the waiting line), in locker rooms and employee wash-up areas, next to elevators, in employee lounges, near the time clocks, and next to the vending machines.

The boards must be kept up to date. It is irritating to read the same announcement every day for months. Every message should be clean, current, and attractively mounted. Sometimes colored paper can be used as a frame or as background for an important announcement.

Some large firms use two types of boards. One of these is for the display of routine company information and employee announcements such as meetings of the stamp club, the bowling league tournament, and the retirement party. At times a section is also made available for a "classified" section listing personal items for sale or being sought. The other set of bulletin boards may have glass doors with or without a lock. On this board are displayed official company announcements. This may involve listing new corporate policies, practices, or regulations, as well as official recognition or commendation of outstanding employees.

Another way to handle this is to use one set of boards informally divided with clearly lettered headings: "News and Views" and "Official Company Announcements."

Bulletin boards are among the least expensive of all company communication devices and, if properly handled, one of the most effective.

Lateral Communication

"If someone had just bothered to tell us what was going on, we would have saved two weeks' time."

This comment, or variations of it, is not unusual in industry today. And as organizations grow bigger and more complex, it becomes more than ever necessary for management to maintain control and have knowledge of what is taking place in various divisions, sections, and departments. As individuals become increasingly specialized, they have difficulty communicating with and understanding the ideas of other specialists.

Keeping individuals and departments on the same level of activity informed is primarily the responsibility of management. This responsibility can be carried through quite easily when policies of communication have been established.

When individuals are not aware of what is taking place in a related department, unnecessary duplication of activity may result in needless expenditure of money; but money is also wasted when reports of activities are circulated to persons not concerned with the projects in question.

Here, then, strict control must be exercised. Management must decide:

1. *who is to be informed of which department's activities;*
2. *the amount of detail to be contained in such reporting;*
3. *the medium to be used for such communication.*

Management must also understand why department heads are often reluctant to communicate their activities to other department heads. Usually it is not required that the sales department know what is taking place in personnel. At times a myopic department manager may feel, "If no one quite knows all I do and how I do it, I become indispensable." And some are busy empire-building to satisfy their own ego needs. But here again, the successful manager *proves* to all department heads how each benefits from good intracompany communications and thus motivates them to carry the activity through. He or she can do this by calling the supervisors together periodically and building a climate of total participation and cooperation to achieve the goals that the entire group has selected. People appreciate knowing what is being achieved in related departments. And this knowledge can often result in suggestions which lead to more efficient production, greater economies, and better use of manpower.

The Grapevine[15]

There is another medium of communication that exists in every organization of whatever size or structure; the grapevine. It is informal, follows no set patterns of content or direction, moves in various communication networks, and comes from the informal or social organization among employees.

Most managers assume that the information flowing along the grapevine hardly reflects credit on the company, is often inaccurate, and not infrequently causes problems. These assumptions are often correct. But to ignore the grapevine, hope it will go away, or pretend it does not exist is hardly a solution. The grapevine *does* exist; it *does* carry information; and it *can* be used with benefit. (See K. Davis, "Management Communication and the Grapevine," in the Readings.)

The grapevine, if tapped wisely, can be an excellent source of information. It can tell management what activities certain individuals or groups are en-

[15] K. Davis has written widely on the grapevine and is an excellent source. See also J. W. Newstrom, R. M. Moncza, and W. Reif, "Perceptions of the Grapevine: Its Value and Influence," *The Journal of Business Communication,* Spring 1974, pp. 21–28.

gaged in, what their future plans are, and how they feel about company conditions and goals.

Some of the information in the grapevine is accurate and some is not. The wise manager sifts it all and, if he is perceptive and listens carefully, he can often discover situations that have potential for trouble, blow-up, and union difficulties. Once they are recognized, these can be discussed either with individuals or with employee groups, and the situations clarified.

The grapevine also allows people to "blow off steam." Employees cannot usually talk back to their superiors, and some of them feel better when they can talk over their problems with others rather than bottling them up. For the person who has a strong need for recognition, the grapevine serves a useful purpose. This person can be the conveyor of news of "major" importance.

The sensitive manager tries to tune in on the various grapevines existing simultaneously. But he also knows that what these rumors *say* may not be what they *mean*. The frequent rumor that shop supervisor Robinson is going to be transferred to the New Jersey plant may be a desire or a wish of many of his subordinates. Or the strong rumor that this plant is going to close down is merely a way of asking for an answer to why so many of the punch presses and milling machines are being moved out.

In almost every situation, it is unwise to ignore the grapevine. Everything in a company environment will be discussed. If management does not communicate, or does not communicate accurate information about the situation, employees will communicate what best serves their purposes or what they imagine to be the case. But silence will not exist; something will flow and management is wise to let the truth circulate rather than inaccurate and harmful rumors.

One method of working with the grapevine is to identify the "influentials" in the informal organization of the company. These individuals strongly influence the thought and actions of fellow workers. Management should talk through problems with them, asking for their suggestions and making sure these employees understand contemplated changes or new directions in the firm.

The grapevine can also be handled through an employee council. Here representatives of various departments are encouraged to ask management about the accuracy of any rumors. Many companies also have "question boxes" located around the plant. Employees are encouraged to drop questions in the boxes; a copy of the question and the company's reply are then posted on the bulletin boards.

Another method is the regular column in the company newspaper or magazine, which lists answers to the grapevine. The questions have either been heard by management or have been sent to the editor by an employee.

Still another device is to have large spikes attached to bulletin boards throughout the plant, with a sign above them: "Spike that Rumor." Employees are encouraged to hang their questions or rumors on the spike. Answers are then supplied on the bulletin boards or in a special column in the plant paper. Sometimes the plant public address system may be used if speed in handling a rumor is important.

IBM has been very successful with its "Speak Up" program, and Bank of

America has followed a similar pattern with its "Open Line." Both use a note-envelope combination. The employee writes a question on the stationery, which is also a self-seal envelope. The envelope is forwarded to the proper desk and answered. Every effort is made to protect the employee's anonymity and to direct a reply to him or her within 24 hours.

Regardless of how the grapevine is handled, the important step is to handle it. Ignoring the messages will not cause them to disappear. The grapevine is a normal and expected method of communication in the informal organization of a company.

Management must listen to the grapevine with sensitivity and perceptiveness. Careful analysis of what is said can tell management what is really behind a rumor and why it is being circulated. Not only is constructive use of the grapevine possible, but it is a necessary method for securing feedback from employees in any number of areas.

Management and Supervisory Bulletins. Many firms issue a variety of bulletins to their different management and supervisory personnel. In some companies a system has been devised of using different colors of paper for different levels and even different divisions. It is easy to see that this system can easily get out of hand. Some employees' jobs require that they see bulletins from several different departments and perhaps from more than one level. The result is that so many announcements cross their desks that soon they read none.

However, these are extreme situations which do not occur too frequently. A carefully controlled system of bulletins can prove to be an excellent way of announcing changes in policy, revisions of procedures, or information that is somewhat confidential.

Many firms feel that policies and procedures should always be communicated to employees by their immediate supervisors rather than through any company-wide announcement. In such cases, bulletins can be very effective in transmitting exactly the same information to all managers and supervisors. It is then their responsibility to communicate such information down. This obviously builds a closer relationship between supervisor and subordinate. It also strengthens the supervisor's authority, as it emphasizes his position as a source of official information.

Here, as in the case of bulletin boards, control is important. Bulletins or management letters should originate only with certain persons who occupy specific positions. They should be written carefully and edited thoroughly. Because they often change or amend company policy, they should be numbered and punched so that a file of them can easily be retained by the originator and the receiver.

It is also a good idea to use a distinctive format with perhaps a colored stripe or headline which seems to say clearly, "Here's some special news; give it your complete attention."

Rack Services. Many firms distribute to employees pamphlets covering a wide variety of topics. These are often stacked in wire racks near employee check-out points or in the company cafeteria. The booklets are free, usually pocket size (about 5" × 7"), and 8 to 12 pages long. The topics are broad and are designed to be of interest to the employee's family as well. The subjects covered are general in nature, such as safe driving, voting procedures, the future of air travel, American foreign policy, the work of the United Nations, an explanation of the operations of the stock market, or how to prepare a balanced diet.

Although some firms write, design, and produce their own pamphlets, most companies purchase theirs from organizations specializing in production of such bulletins. These are well written, cleverly illustrated, and relatively inexpensive. The purchasing company may have its name and insignia printed on the back or front if it wishes, thus adding a little personal touch to the booklet.

Perhaps the factor making this program most attractive to employees is that it is voluntary. If an employee wishes to pick up a booklet or two, they are there; if he prefers not to, he simply doesn't bother. Then, too, there is never any obvious "company sell" in the booklet to arouse his feelings positively or negatively. The booklets are there for his information and reading pleasure if he wants to take them.

Companies that use rack services have found the expenditure worthwhile, for it helps keep employees informed in economic, political, health, cultural, social, and recreational areas while building good will.

Effective Downward Communication

Each of the above media can be used successfully in a company of almost any size. Downward communication is vitally important; management must use the media creatively and wisely, but it must have policies of communication which are consistently followed. And of major importance—management must provide channels for *upward* communication. Once established, management must listen to what comes *up*, so it will then to be able to send communications *down* with some degree of confidence that those messages will be understood and (hopefully) accepted by employees. The Drucker article in the Readings makes the strong point that "downward communications can't work unless management first listens to what comes up."

Internal Communication

Every well-run organization must have a carefully supervised internal communication system. Such a system must be based on a corporate policy which not only encourages two-way communication, but bends every effort to see to it that such lines exist. These lines must carry honest information, in a timely fashion, up, down, and laterally. Where this system exists, the management functions of planning, organizing, directing, coordinating, and controlling are greatly assisted.

Questions for Study

I. Complete any of the following problems assigned. You may wish to review and note key points before attempting to solve a problem.

1. What role do reports play in the decision-making process?

2. What are the specific methods for communicating information up?

3. What factors in our changing society seem to demand that today's employee be better informed about his company's activities than the employee of 50 years ago?

4. Elect four class members to carry through research among five local companies on the firms' policies of communication to employees. At the conclusion of the research, have the four students engage in a panel discussion on the differences in the "policies," how they reflected the companies' attitudes, and whether or not there was any correlation between a company policy of communication (or lack of one) and employee attitudes.

5. Design a policy of communication for a firm that has 10,000 employees, is 12 years old, manufactures electronic components, and is located in a major urban center.

6. Secure six different company magazines. Analyze their content as to the topics covered and the relative value and interest of such topics to most employees.

7. Some research will show you that many companies have two or three different employee-orientation manuals. One of these may be for hourly personnel, one for salaried, and one perhaps for executive or administrative personnel. Why should several manuals exist (or not exist) within one firm?

8. What must the administrator keep in mind if he wishes to use pay envelope inserts most effectively?

9. Elect several class members to investigate and report to the class on the bulletin board and rack service practices of several firms.

10. Of the three directions of internal communication—up, down, and lateral—which one do you think is generally least efficient? Why?

11. Secure one or two copies of a company magazine or newspaper and an equal number of union-sponsored publications. Analyze both as to their discussion of sensitive issues such as wage rates, strikes, company earnings, legal action brought against the firm, problems of pollution or energy, etc. Are there differences in attitudes and views between the two media? Is more space devoted to any of the topics in one medium as compared to the other? (You may wish to review first, C. J. Dover, *Management Communication on Controversial Issues,* Washington, D. C., Bureau of National Affairs, Inc., 1965.)

Part Two

Listening, Speaking, Writing, and Career and Résumé Preparation

Chapter Three

Listening and Speaking in One-to-One and One-to-Group Situations

Listening—A Vital Area of Communication

The Interview—A One-to-One Relationship

**One-to-Group Presentations—
Conferences, Meetings, and Oral Reports**

Of the four areas of verbal communication—reading, writing, speaking, and listening—the manager spends the greatest proportion of his time in the latter two. Since we are often told that we must listen before we speak, let us look at listening first.

Listening—A Vital Area of Communication

Most of us spend approximately 60 percent of our work day listening. Yet we do not always listen very effectively. And because we don't listen well, we frequently encounter misunderstanding. Poor listening can be one of the biggest barriers to effective communication.

Listening is largely neglected in our educational system. Although most of our youngsters are given extensive training in how to read and write effectively, as well as instruction on how to speak competently, little, if any, time is devoted to this important aspect of communication. On one occasion or another, a teacher may admonish a class with "You'd better listen to this," or "Listen carefully," but little is ever said on *how* to listen.

We are told that we usually forget from one third to one half of what we hear within eight hours after hearing it! This alone indicates the importance of knowing how to listen. It is vital for the student whose success is dependent on how well he retains ideas, and for the manager who must know what is taking place in many areas if he is to make intelligent decisions. The salesman must listen to his customers. The parent must listen to his child. And there are several professional areas which have effective listening as their primary stock in trade: psychiatry, educational and marriage counseling, and personnel interviewing.

In this text, we are especially concerned with industry and business. And it is about this area that business leader Carl Braun said, "The problem is not one of getting men to talk. The problem is one of getting leaders to listen."

Yes, this is a problem. How do we train people to listen to what they hear?

Let us take the case of Supervisor Morrison. Joe has just approached him and reports: "Well, Mr. Morrison, I finally locked up the Carlyle Company order. Boy, was it a mess! But you said it was an emergency job, and I saw to it that it went out today—right on the button. But it was miserable. You know, I've been down here every night this week and almost all last weekend. Their specifications are ridiculous, but the order is on its way. And let me tell you, if I never see another job as tough as that, I'll be plenty happy." If Mr. Morrison should now turn to Joe and say, "Great, Joe. Now let's get to work on the Mayberry order," Morrison hasn't listened to Joe at all!

What was Joe *really* saying to Morrison? Of course, we'll never truly know, but we can be sure he was not simply saying that the Carlyle order was difficult. He was probably saying, "How about giving me a pat on the back, Mr. Morrison," or "Why do you give me all the problem jobs?" or "I hate to work nights."

If Mr. Morrison does not respond to what Joe was *not* saying, (but meaning), communication between the two men will surely break down.

You may say, "But is it Morrison's job, or is it any supervisor's job, to hear what is *not* said?" The answer is "Yes." The sensitive, concerned, and effective manager will hear what Joe really wants to say but is often inhibited from stating directly. These inhibitions may be due to ego, pride, emotions, the position we hold, or our society. But the manager, parent, husband, or friend who will make an effort to perceive the situation as the communicator perceives it will listen when he hears.[1]

Barriers to Effective Listening

One of the basic barriers to effective listening is simply the *failure to concentrate*, which in turn causes facts and ideas to be lost.

This lack of concentration may have several causes. Most of us speak, as noted earlier, at a much slower rate than what the average person can comprehend. This permits the listener to make mental excursions into other areas as he listens to the speaker. For a few seconds he thinks about that faulty car transmission; then he returns to the speaker's topic; then he is off again. This time he wonders about the football game: Will it be worth $8.50 per ticket? And again back to the speaker. But what about vacation? Two weeks in September should be O.K. And back to the speaker. But now the speaker is too far ahead; the listener has missed something vital on one of his excursions. Besides, the topic seems very complex. Oh, well, not concentrating is easier than trying to. The result is that another listener is now just hearing.

Many of us won't *work* at expending the physical and mental energy needed to listen and retain facts and ideas. Work *is* required and many of us are lazy in this area. And some of us don't listen well because *we just don't know how.*

[1] An excellent article on this topic is C. R. Rogers and R. E. Farson, "Active Listening," University of Chicago Industrial Relations Center in the Readings.

We haven't developed a technique for organizing ideas as we listen or for retaining key words or points to serve as signposts.

One's *emotions* can also cause poor listening. When the speaker makes a statement that disagrees with the listener's concepts, the latter may simply reach up into his brain and turn the communicator off. Or he may concentrate on the statement with which he disagrees as others are stated but not heard.

And the style of clothes the speaker wears (or doesn't wear), the look on his face, or the posture he assumes may cause the listener to react emotionally and tune him out. *It is this tendency to evaluate* what we see that often influences what we hear.

By Mell Lazarus, Courtesy Field Newspaper Syndicate

Listening for Facts. In listening for facts, you should first attempt to determine the theme or the thesis of the presentation. In a speech, this may be stated in the first few minutes. It will probably be noted in different words several times during the talk, and may well serve as a concluding statement.

The basic ideas should then be recognized. What are the key points in the entire talk? The alert listener will be able to recognize them, even if the speaker doesn't label each specifically. Remembering the speaker's theme, and a few key words to recall the main points, is a relatively simple and effective method in good listening.

If you listen analytically, you can recognize major ideas and separate them from minor ones. Of course this requires your full effort and concentrated attention. But effective listening is hard work.

Taking notes during the talk will also help you retain ideas and facts. And if the talk goes on for any length of time, the good listener will occasionally, but quickly, review mentally the ideas and facts which have already been cited. But you should never become so absorbed in the task of taking notes that you lose the ideas being transmitted.

The suggestions made by Ralph Nichols ("Listening Is a 10-Part Skill," in the Readings) are especially valuable for the person who wishes to improve his ability in this area of communication.

Listening for Feelings. When you listen for a person's feelings, you must be especially sensitive to what he is saying unintentionally and nonverbally. He may give special connotations to his words, and you must give the same connotations so far as you are able. You must also try to understand his ideas, feelings, and biases; you should recognize his point of view, his frame of reference, and remember his salary level, his hopes, and his desires. This can be extremely difficult, but you must try.

You must constantly listen to the message conveyed by the gestures of his hands, the tapping of his fingers, the look in his eyes, and the confusion in the lines on his brow.

If his words say, "Well, it really isn't very important to me anyway," but his posture is stiff and tight, his knuckles white, his eyes hopeful, and his forehead glistening with perspiration, you had better hear the nonverbal rather than the verbal message. For if you don't, communication between you will not be effective.

At times one may ask, "How will I know what his *feelings* are saying in what *he isn't* saying?" Sometimes you won't know unless you have lived or worked with him. For example, when a wife asks her husband, "How do you like this dress I'm wearing to the Baxters' party tonight?" she may be saying "Am I beautiful?" or "Do you love me?" or "Do you think I shouldn't have spent the money?" But because her husband has lived with her, he should know which one of these messages she is *really* sending. And the manager who works with people day in and day out should know equally well what they are saying in what they don't say!

If the listener is familiar with the situation, keeps his experiences with that person in mind, and, most important, is sensitive to the person's perceptions and expectations, then he will be able to determine, with a fair degree of accuracy, what is really being said.

How to Be a Better Listener

The business manager or executive must learn to listen both for facts and for feelings. Here is a list of suggestions that will help improve communication:

Listen actively for the main theme of the discussion and specific ideas and facts. Concentrate on what the speaker is saying; don't let your mind wander. Make mental notes on each idea and supporting fact. Remain alert; ask questions; note fallacies. Don't attempt to do something unrelated to the discussion while the speaker is talking.

Check your posture. Sit up straight and look directly at the speaker. Don't protest that you listen best when you are relaxed, hands clasped behind your head and feet propped on the desk. This may be true. But your listener may *perceive* from that posture your lack of interest and perhaps discourtesy. The result of his perception will then raise barriers to clear communication.

Listen objectively to the speaker's point of view. Try to put aside your preconceived ideas or bias on a topic. You may be correct, but nevertheless try to listen objectively. It is true that you have developed your point of view after years of experience, testing, and examination. But the speaker may have a new approach, a new concept, a new method of doing an old job that is worth putting into operation. Thus you must listen objectively.

Listen analytically to the presentation. Sometimes the speaker hasn't organized his ideas too well. He seems to be going in circles; he repeats himself, and he barely mentions a key point. He may spend eight minutes on one point, and two minutes on four others. We must recognize his five points. We, as good listeners, must organize his presentation in our minds as he talks. And we can do this if we listen analytically. Recognize the theme, then the key ideas, the supporting facts, and the necessary details. To do this requires analytical and active listening.

Listen to the speaker's meanings for words. It is almost impossible for us to give exactly the same connotation to every word as does the speaker. But we can try. If we know something of the person's background, values, and experiences, we can give meanings to words as they are intended. Of course we will never succeed completely, especially if the words are abstract or jargon (democracy, love, honesty, socialism, morals, split, far out, wild, dig, dude, man). However, we can try.

When the speaker says, "I think we ought to get on this Carlyle job right away," we must try to interpret "right away" correctly. Does it mean today? in a week? in a month? We have worked with this person for several years, and we know that he is exacting but slow and easygoing. To him, "right away" probably means in a week or two.

What does Mrs. Kelly mean when she says, "Tom is a very hard worker"? Because you know that Mrs. Kelly is an extremely conscientious employee herself and that she rarely gives praise without good reason, your connotation for "very hard worker" will probably be similar to hers.

Circumstances and environment also help us give connotations to words. The words used at a company picnic may have different connotations from the same words used in a similar statement in the conference room.

Listen to and observe the speaker's nonverbal communication. The inflection given to words often determines what meaning should be given to the statement. Our statement above, "Tom is a very hard worker," can carry several different meanings according to which word or words are emphasized, and whether the quotation is made as a question or a statement. The meaning can further change according to the facial expression which accompanies it. A simple declarative statement, "Tom is a very hard worker," carries a derisive connotation if the speaker accompanies it with a broad smile or a curled lip.

We have already talked about nonverbal communication and how important it is to decode it correctly. Of course this applies to the competent listener. He is acutely aware of the important messages that are communicated nonverbally.

Listen with empathy and with understanding. It is a communication task which requires your full energy, intelligence, and sensitivity. The results are worth the effort. Open pathways in communication are often the result, when one listens with empathy and understanding.

The Results of Good Listening[2]

In the final analysis, effective listening produces many salutary results:

1. When others note that you listen to them in a nonthreatening manner, they in turn lose some or all of the defensiveness they may have had and will usually try to understand you better by listening more effectively to you. Thus, your effective listening often results in making others good listeners.

2. Good listening permits you to secure as much information as the speaker possesses. Your careful listening will usually motivate him to cite as many facts as he is able. When you have as much information as possible, you are in a better position to make accurate decisions.

3. Effective listening usually improves relationships between people. It gives the speaker an opportunity to get ideas, facts, and hostilities off his chest. You will understand him better as you listen; he appreciates your interest in him; and friendships may thus deepen.

4. Disagreements and problems can best be solved when individuals listen carefully to each other. This does not mean that one must agree with the other's point of view; he must merely show that he *understands* the other person's viewpoint. Everyone wants understanding, and there is no better way of expressing this quality than through sensitive listening.

5. Listening may help the other person see his own problem with greater clarity. Usually when any of us are permitted to talk out a problem, we can more easily determine possible solutions.

6. Listening carefully to another will give you clues on how he thinks, what he feels is important, and why he is saying what he is saying. By understanding him better, you will be able to work better with him. Knowing that Tom is an extrovert, Jim an introvert, and that Bob needs frequent praise, leads to better understanding and thus more harmony.

If we were to summarize what the individual gains who is a good listener, we would surely list *information;* we would also list *understanding* of others and their viewpoints; we would add to these more *effective listening* on the part of others so that the listener's ideas get through; and *cooperation* from others who feel that the listener better understands them.

The Interview—A One-to-One Relationship

The interview is an invaluable instrument for receiving and giving ideas, developing attitudes, changing behavior, counseling others, and creating the will to work together.

According to function, there are several different types. However, it is quite usual that any one interview will combine two or more of the activities listed below:

Information interview: This is to supply facts, policies, and information to the interviewee.

---

[2] See also Norman B. Sigband, "Listen to What You Can't Hear," *Nation's Business,* June 1969.

Data determination interview: Used to secure data and information from the interviewee.

Appraisal interview: This is perhaps the most frequently held interview and involves an evaluation of performance.

Goal-setting interview: This is closely associated with the appraisal interview and may be a part of it. It involves discussion between the interviewer and interviewee and an attempt to set realistic job, personal, or performance goals for the latter.

Discussion or exploratory interview: Here an exchange of ideas is carried through in an effort to explore a problem, review methods or courses of possible action, or familiarize the parties with a situation.

Counseling interview: The purpose is to offer advice or counsel to someone who may be encountering personal, job, or performance problems. Obviously many interviewers are not competent to offer counsel in highly sensitive personal areas and should recognize their own limitations.

Disciplinary and grievance interviews: These are used primarily in the work situation, and when handled properly can solve minor problems while building good will.

Exit or termination interview: This is really an information interview of a specialized type. It is held with employees who are terminating their association with the firm. It is conducted by a disinterested interviewer. Through careful and nonthreatening discussion, the interviewer may secure critical and vital information concerning the firm's employer-employee relationships, the attitudes and perceptions of employees, and an individual's true reason for leaving the company.

Uses of the Interview

The one-to-one relationship has many different purposes, among which are:

Selecting new employees.
Orienting new employees to organizational policies and practices.
Explaining new company policies, procedures, goals, and directions.
Training and instructing employees.
Securing the knowledge and experience of others so that organizational objectives may be more easily attained.
Appraising employees; reviewing job performance, establishing objectives, and analyzing future potential.
Presenting and discussing company or departmental problems for the purpose of finding solutions.
Dealing with employee complaints and dissatisfaction.
Handling disciplinary or nonacceptable behavioral situations on the job.
Counseling employees in reference to family, health, or financial problems.

Differences in Interviews

Obviously each interview will be different, depending on the type of interview, the emotional needs of the parties involved, and the complexity of the topics discussed. However, to be successful, every interview must be two-way and, if at all possible, carefully planned.

It is possible, for example, that the goals of the two parties may be dissimilar or even opposite. One of the purposes of the interview would then be to find a common ground for discussion. At times the personalities of the individuals involved may be quite different, which can in itself create barriers. One way of alleviating, if not eliminating, many problems is for the interviewer to plan his interview, designate the objectives he wishes to achieve, be sensitive to the other person's needs and feelings, and listen intelligently, skillfully, and understandingly.

Planning the Interview

Too often the interview is carried through without preplanning. An unexpected problem arises, the manager immediately calls in a subordinate, and they have a discussion which results in an action plan. Sometimes their hasty decisions are good, sometimes not. Or another manager suddenly discovers that there are only two days left in which to carry through the semiannual appraisal and counseling interviews with 46 subordinates. It's true they could have been conducted anytime during June, as company policy requires, but somehow the month got away and now there are two days left. But there are 46 employees to talk to, and the ongoing work of the department to complete. Poor planning!

Almost any interview will be more successful if time is taken to establish job objectives and general methods and techniques. The experienced interviewer will plan as carefully as possible in the following areas:

Selection of purpose. In many cases, the interviewer will try to discuss too wide a variety of topics or confine the discussion to topics which are not sensitive. This is not an efficient use of time. It is true that one must be flexible during an interview, but it is also wise to plan ahead. The interviewer may wish to establish work or goal objectives with the interviewee, or reach decisions, or secure facts, or select a specific course of action.

Briefing oneself. Too many interviews reach an impasse because "I don't have the sales figures here," or "I had no idea all the data on last year's production would be needed." In almost every case, the necessary data are easily available if the interviewer simply does his "homework."

Preparation of key questions. It is often vital to get the interviewee to express himself freely. This may be done by asking the right kind of questions. But such questions often do not come quickly and easily; they, too, require preplanning. Queries such as, "How would you reorganize the operation?" or "What action do you recommend for solving the problem?" may motivate the interviewee to respond openly and freely.

Recognition of the interviewee's perceptions, expectations, and personality. Each of us responds differently. Some will be open and free with one approach; others respond better to another. A moment or two spent prior to the discussion in attempting to determine the individual's personality, perceptions, and needs, is often time very well invested.

Exploration of possible solutions. There is often more than one solution to a problem. The interviewer should examine the good and bad points of several alternatives prior to the interview.

There are other areas that the interviewer may prepare for; the point is that a communication exercise as important as an interview should always be planned.

The Interview in Action

The interviewer will certainly adapt the interview to the persons involved. However, in every instance it is important to use the tools of interviewing to their maximum effectiveness:

Questioning,
Listening,
Observing,
Evaluating.

In addition, the interviewer should attempt to:

Establish a friendly climate. When people are treated courteously, honestly, and respectfully, they usually respond positively. If the exchange is to be open, honest, and free, the climate must help to attain those goals.

Articulate the purpose of the interview. It is helpful to both parties if a common understanding is reached as to the purpose of the interview and the problems or situations to be discussed.

Secure the interviewee's input. Because the interviewer is frequently superior in rank to the person being interviewed, there is a tendency on the part of both to allow the interviewer to dominate the discussion. That is wrong. The interviewee should participate freely and thoroughly.

Question, Listen, Observe, Evaluate. These points are the keys to the successful interview. Questions should be carefully worded and should make the interviewee want to talk. And it is here that the interviewer must resist the temptation to argue, correct, explain, or pontificate. It is a time to listen—listen actively, attentively, understandingly, skillfully, and sensitively. And in listening, of course, one must also observe the nonverbal communication of the interviewee.

As a result of tactful questioning, sensitive listening, and thoughtful observing, the interviewer should now be in a position for accurate evaluating. (See Rogers and Farson, "Active Listening," in the Readings.)

Agree on action. If the interview is the kind that leads to action, then such action should be agreed on by both parties. Naturally, hasty action should not be taken. But if all angles have been covered, then a clear understanding by both parties should be reached on "the next step." And that step should be clearly verbalized and agreed to.

Terminate effectively. Too many interviews are terminated by the ringing of the interviewer's telephone or by a secretary who tiptoes in and silently points to her wristwatch. Whatever cooperative climate had existed between interviewer and interviewee is likely to be destroyed.

It is wiser to hold a short interview, expertly conducted and graciously terminated, than a longer one that is halted abruptly and discourteously.

As a one-to-one relationship, the interview can be among the most important of all the manager's communication tools. There is no better way of getting to know others—superiors, fellow workers, and subordinates. It is an excellent method for exchanging ideas, tapping the knowledge of others, and settling differences of opinion.

Interviews require time, but this is usually time well spent. It is a wise manager who finds a few minutes to meet regularly with subordinates. A good exchange will often give the manager valuable information. As for the subordinates, they have an opportunity to express themselves, and the satisfaction of having "the boss" listen to them.

If videotape equipment is available, this can be used to sharpen interviewing skills. It is a simple matter to record several interviews and then replay them for purposes of constructive criticism.

Watching and hearing oneself do an interview, one quickly perceives careless word choice, disturbing nonverbal communication, poor listening habits, and a dozen other communication patterns always apparent to the "other person" but not to ourselves. The video camera brings these into sharp focus so we may improve our next one-to-one situation.

One-to-Group Presentations— Conferences, Meetings, and Oral Reports

Conferences and Meetings[3]

How many times have you heard the following conversation at the lunch table. . . or perhaps even participated in it yourself?

"Are you supposed to go to that meeting this afternoon on new products, Joe?"
"Yup, and I can't figure out any way to get out of it. What time is it supposed to start, Ed?"
"The notice I received said it's scheduled to begin at 1 p.m. sharp."
"Yeah, and end at 3:30—dull."

Perhaps there is no corporate activity that is blamed for wasting more time and creating more antagonism, than the meeting or conference.

And yet, it need not be so.

An unorganized, unplanned, bickering conference results in frustration, antagonism, and confusion. And one doesn't need a complex mathematical formula to determine how costly it is to confine 16 people in a room every Tuesday afternoon from 1 to 3:30 p.m.

[3] This section has been summarized in N. Sigband, "How to Meet With Success," *Nation's Business,* March 1971.

But conferences should not waste money! They should not create hard feelings! They should not result in confusion!

On the contrary they can and should produce acceptable plans, worthwhile goals, profit-making decisions, and a climate that establishes the will to work together. All that is required is the formulation of a philosophy for conferences, and then attention to a three-step system for organizing them.

Management's Conference Policy. If the top personnel in the firm really believe in participative management, then they must give the conference the dignity and the recognition it deserves. Furthermore, a basic fact must be accepted and must become a part of management philosophy: The group meeting or conference, where plans are made, objectives established, and decisions reached, is an integral and vital part of the company's management procedures and decision-making process. Once that concept is accepted, the firm's meetings and conferences are on their way to success.

And what is a *successful conference?* It's a group session that participants find exciting and provocative; it's one where every member who has something to say is heard; it's one where everyone is on an equal level; it's one where decisions are reached. After such a conference participants may be heard to say, as they leave the meeting room: "Well, I personally don't agree with the way the vote went, but we *did* reach a decision on the Sunnyvale Plan, and it's on its way."

Management's attitude toward the conference is vital in securing the kind of results noted above, rather than the sour comments too often heard: "Well, that's another 2½ hours wasted"; "For the life of me, I don't know why I'm invited to those things"; and worst of all, "I'll never know why we hold these meetings; management goes its own way and never follows our suggestions anyhow."

The background to a successful meeting is management's acceptance of the fact that a conference is an important, worthwhile activity. And that the ideas, suggestions, and decisions reached at such meetings *will* be put into practice as soon as is reasonably possible.

Once this philosophy is established, following the three-step plan becomes almost a matter of mechanics.

Step One—The Preconference Period

Establish the Need. The preconference period requires a brief discussion among key personnel in which the need for the conference is clearly established. Too many meetings are called simply because "we *always* meet on Tuesdays at 1 p.m." If no useful purpose can be accomplished, a conference should not be called.

Define the Problem or Topic for Discussion. A clear statement of the problem or topic for discussion must be agreed to and set down on paper. All too often the conference leader and participants have only vague ideas of what they are to talk about. Discussion then goes in circles, and solutions or decisions are difficult to reach.

Let's not look into "Fringe Benefits with Special Attention to a Profit-Sharing Program." Instead, let's be specific: "An Analysis of Profit-Sharing Programs in Companies Similar to Ours," or "Cost of a Profit-Sharing Program to the Jono Company," or "Should the Jono Company Adopt a Profit-Sharing Program or Not?"

Defining a problem or selecting a topic usually requires careful analysis. Certainly a *symptom* of a problem should not be designated as the problem. It is true that production has slowed down, but installing faster punch presses will not solve the problem. The slowdown is only a symptom of the real problem, which may be low morale among people in the production department. That is the issue with which the conference should deal—not the possible acquisition of newer and faster punch presses.

Determine the Type of Conference. Once the need for the meeting has been agreed to, the next step is to decide what type of conference will best serve the immediate situation. The types of conferences include:

Informational, where information is provided in the same way at the same time to everyone concerned. Questions may be answered and facts explored.

Problem Solving, where questions or problems are dealt with and people concerned with them are expected to help work out solutions. This is the type of conference with which the major portion of the following discussion deals.

Training, where specific skills, concepts, or ideas are explained. There may be demonstrations and question-answer periods.

Brainstorming, where almost anything goes so long as it has to do with solving or exploring the topic or problem under discussion.

Selection of Participants. Only those individuals who are clearly and specifically concerned with the topic should be invited. Persons who occupy specific management positions should not be asked "just to keep them informed." There are easier and less time-consuming methods of informing such persons. And under no conditions should individuals be invited "who might be hurt if they are not asked."

It is important that the company policy on conferences clearly state that only those directly concerned, or who have knowledge or experience to contribute, will be asked to conferences.

Designation of the Conference Leader. A conference often "flies" or "falls" depending on the conference leader. Actually the term "leader" is a misnomer, for the best leader is one who doesn't formally lead but who acts as a catalyst, a stimulator, a moderator, or an arbitrator. The leader who talks least and stimulates most is the one who usually does the best job.

There is also good reason to advise that the highest ranking member of the group *not* be designated as the leader. When that person is in the position of conference leader, too often he or she can't forget who's boss, nor can the participants. Why not ask one of the knowledgeable people in the group to serve as the leader? Or, an idea that is gaining some popularity, have the "assistant to the president" serve as leader. And one might consider rotating leaders, so that a different individual in a common group would serve at each meeting.

But whoever is designated as the leader, an effort should be made to see that it is someone who:

> Has an ability to think quickly and clearly.
> Is analytical.
> Is impersonal.
> Is unbiased.
> Is patient.
> Is tactful.
> Is poised.
> Is self-restrained.
> Expresses himself easily.
> Possesses a good sense of humor.

And where is the saint with all these qualities to be found? Perhaps nowhere, but there is no reason why the leader can't attempt to emulate most or all of these qualities.

Designation of Topic Areas. Now that we have the specific topic, the leader, and the participants, we can move ahead and select subareas for discussion. Obviously these should be chosen with care, keeping in mind the complexity or simplicity of each point, how much discussion may be needed, and the overall time allowed for the meeting.

To list more topics than can reasonably be discussed in the time scheduled is frustrating since it means that discussion of some of them will have to be cut short.

Distribution of the Conference Announcement/Agenda. The announcement/agenda should be sent out to everyone concerned approximately 7–10 days prior to the meeting. Some of the key items to list are the following:

1. Date, time, and place of meeting
2. Topic(s) for discussion
3. Subareas for discussion
4. List of participants
5. If applicable, materials to be reviewed prior to the meeting

Here is an example of a satisfactory announcement/agenda form.

```
DATE:  February 2, 19__

  TO:  Mr. R. T. Kellogg, Production Manager

FROM:  Mr. J. M. Kean, Vice President

SUBJ:  Conference, February 15, 19__
       1:00 p.m., Lounge #2.
```

```
Topic for Discussion:

        Shall the Jono Company establish
        a Training Division?

Specific Items for Discussion:

        1.  Advantages of a training unit
            for salaried and hourly personnel.

        2.  Disadvantages of a training unit
            for salaried and hourly personnel.

        3.  Training staff required.

        4.  Cost (first 3 years).

        5.  Other business

Distribution:

        Ms. S. I. True        Ms. A. A. Able
        Mr. L. A. Strong      Mr. R. T. Kellogg
        Mr. T. M. Bird        Mr. A. B. Burton
        Mr. R. B. White       Mr. M. X. Green
        Mr. K. L. Mace        Ms. L. O. Cox
        Ms. R. J. Foreman     Mr. L. M. Gates
```

It is obvious that there are many advantages in distributing such an announcement.

1. Participants who wish to may prepare for the meeting.

2. No one can say later, "Holy smoke, if I knew we were going to discuss this aspect, I could have brought tons of statistics!"

3. Digressions can be easily and tactfully curbed by the conference leader: "That's a good point, Kellogg, but I think we will defer it until later. At the moment we are trying to tie up point number 2 on the agenda sheet."

4. All participants know who has been invited, and thus they can, if necessary, plan their strategies.

Preparation of Physical Facilities. The mechanical aspects of the meeting seem so obvious as to require no mention, yet breakdowns in this area have ruined countless meetings. What's the good of having 12 people congregate in front of the meeting room at the appointed time only to find it occupied, or locked and the key in the possession of somebody's secretary who is on her coffee break? Irritation and confusion are certain to follow as some make their way to the substitute meeting room while others drift back to their desks.

It is probably wise to go down a checklist on the physical arrangements:

1. Room set up
   Reservations for room made? Enough chairs?
   Podium needed?
2. Audiovisual materials
   Projectors? Flip charts? Mikes? Display materials?
   Tape recorders?
3. Handout materials
   Adequate number of copies for distribution?
4. Refreshments
   Coffee? Sandwiches?
5. Miscellaneous materials
   Pads? Paper? Pencils? Ash trays? Marking pens? Name cards?

These are some of the areas which should be checked out prior to the meeting. Now we're ready for the meeting itself.

Step Two—The Conference Period. A basic concept that companies must accept is that various aspects of the management of the firm, and of management development, can and should be built into the conference. Let's make this point by looking at a typical situation.

Of the six reports presented at today's meeting, three hit strongly at customer dissatisfaction with the carrier we are now using. One of the young men present, with a degree in marketing, made some thoughtful remarks on the advantages of using commercial carriers. Several of the old-timers wondered if we shouldn't transfer our entire delivery operations to a third party. The conference leader turned back to the young man, who volunteered to complete a study on this vital issue for the next meeting. A final decision on the problem is expected to be made at that time.

This certainly is more than discussion; it is management of the firm, and in the case of the young man it is also personnel development. (The reader is urged to see the excellent articles on meetings and conferences by H. Zelko as well as the one titled "Stop Misusing Your Management Meetings," in the Readings.)

If the conference is to go well, it is vital that the leader set the right climate. He must know his people and watch his time. He must be careful not to march down the list from first point to last, pushing discussion here, cutting off comments there. Rather, he must stimulate discussion so that the topics are covered while at the same time the participants feel they have made significant contributions.

Developing the technique for doing this is not really too difficult. It requires a sincere feeling on the part of the leader that the people around him, taken together, are smarter than he, possess a wealth of experience, and are as eager as he to solve the problem before the group.

Thus he begins the meeting on a positive note in which he communicates, verbally and nonverbally, his respect for each person in the room. The climate which is set in the first few minutes will either motivate the participants to contribute actively and effectively or cause them to retreat into their shells.

Someone should take notes. This may be a participant who is respected by the group (not someone who will say, "I'm invited only because I write fast") and is quite impartial. Or a secretary can be brought in. However, it may inhibit discussion if some of the participants feel that anything they say today may be known in the typing pool tomorrow.

The conference leader should be careful not to dominate the meeting physically. A leader standing at a podium that is separated from the conference tables conveys the feeling, "I'm in charge." If the conference leader sits in front of the group with space to the left and right (as in a U arrangement), this again suggests that the leader is in charge by the way the space in the room has been used. In most situations, an unbroken rectangular or oval arrangement is preferable. The conference leader need not sit at the head point; discussion may flow more easily if he takes a seat that makes him part of the team.

Perhaps the most important point for the meeting leader to keep in mind is, "Don't dominate the meeting. The less you talk and the more the participants contribute, the more successful you will be in attaining your objectives."

Securing Participation. It is wise for the leader to prepare a few meaningful questions for each topic on the agenda. Then if discussion slackens, a question can be "tossed" to the group. Sometimes a leading question can be fed to someone who has much to contribute but for some reason prefers to play the role of Silent Sam at meetings.

The leader should also step in at an appropriate moment to summarize discussion on a topic and move the group on to the next point. Otherwise a topic may be talked to death and nothing more accomplished.

The Participants. Most participants are eager to contribute, cooperate, and assist the total effort toward the group's objectives. However, there are some who occasionally cause problems and one of them may be sitting at your next meeting:

The nonstop speaker, who is enraptured by the beauty of his own voice and the brilliance of his comments. A tactful interjection that "We'll pursue that excellent point later, but right now let's get back to the topic" is usually adequate to stop him—even if only temporarily.

The chronic disagreer, who immediately says "white" if you say "black," or "yes" if you say "no." Don't try to argue with him; simply ask the other participants to react to his point of view. If the leader takes him on it may psychologically divide the meeting into two parts: the leader and the participants.

Silent Sam, who says little or nothing but does have an idea to contribute. Often he may be brought out by a carefully worded question that doesn't put him on the spot but simply seeks information. Once this is accomplished, he's on his way to making other contributions.

The Astronomer, who is fascinated by the clouds outside or the ceiling overhead. He often responds to the same technique as Silent Sam. Be careful in both cases not to draw a person into the discussion if he has little to contribute and would be embarrassed. Participation for the sake of participation is of little value.

Fumbling Francine, who has something to say but doesn't know how to say it. Be patient with her; try to let her finish, and then *very* tactfully feed back to her, as part of your discussion, the point you think she tried to make. If she accepts your rephrasing of her idea, she has made an important contribution to the meeting.

H. A. Harry, who comes to the meeting with a Hidden Agenda. Regardless of how alert the leader is, Hidden Agenda Harry will get his comment out. What he has to say is designed only to impress somebody important who is present, or to depreciate a colleague. It has little or nothing to do with the point under discussion. At times the alert conference leader can cut in and say, "We can look at that another time; at the moment we must stay with point number 2 on the agenda." At other times, he can only ignore the comment and bring the group back to the topic at hand. However, the alert conference leader will see H. A. Harry *after* the meeting to pursue the point further. Harry brought the topic up for some reason. Let's find out why. Some hidden agendas are best dealt with during the meeting, and others after.

Of course there are others who sometimes make a discussion stumble, but a little courtesy, tact, patience, and restraint on the part of the leader will usually assure a successful meeting.

Meeting Tie-Up. Everyone who leaves a meeting should feel that something has been accomplished. That feeling can often be guaranteed if the last ten minutes of the session are handled properly. During that time the discussion should be summarized and key issues brought into focus. If adequate time has been given to the topics listed and they are the type that call for a decision, a vote should be taken. Obviously not everyone can be satisfied, but most will be glad to see matters brought to a conclusion and decisions made.

It requires skill on the part of the leader not to *drive* for a decision, but to let the request for a vote come from the group. The leader has done a good job if the worst thing any of the participants say as they walk back to their desks is, "Well, I wasn't in complete agreement with the decision, but we *did* accomplish something."

Much else is involved in the conduct of a conference: the effective use of visual aids, report presentations, methods of handling debate, the use of consultants, how to handle the chairman of the board who has "just dropped in to listen quietly," and 1001 other things. But common sense, based on the principles already cited, will usually provide workable answers.

Step Three—The Postconference Period. The conference has been held, but it is not over. Its basic purpose was to hammer out another link in the chain of successful management. And the fastening of that new link to the others in the chain takes place in the postconference period.

Evaluation of the Meeting. It is now time for those who called the meeting to sit together for just five minutes to determine what the session accomplished, how the results or findings fit into overall company objectives or plans, and how the next meeting can be improved.

Distribution of Minutes. A recapitulation of the meeting should be sent to each of the participants as quickly as possible. The form used should cover the topics discussed, votes taken, and decisions reached.

```
                        MINUTES OF MEETING


        DATE:  February 16, 19__
          TO:  Mr. R. T. Kellogg, Production Manager
        FROM:  Mr. J. M. Kean, Vice President
        SUBJ:  Minutes of conference held on February 15, 19__, at
               1:00 p.m. in Lounge #2.


        Summary of Discussion:

               Item one: _____


               _____

               Item two: _____


               _____

               Item three: _____


               _____


        Assignments made:

               Ms. J. Foreman: _____


               _____

               Mr. L. M. Gates: _____


               _____


        Votes taken:

               #1 _____

               For:  10              Against:  3

               #2 _____

               For:  2               Against:  11
```

```
Distribution:

        Ms. S. I. True          Ms. A. A. Able
        Mr. L. M. Strong        Mr. R. T. Kellogg
        Mr. T. M. Bird          Mr. A. B. Burton
        Mr. R. B. White         Mr. M. X. Green
        Mr. K. L. Mace          Ms. L. O. Cox
        Ms. R. J. Foreman       Mr. L. M. Gates
```

The advantages of distributing such a form are:

1. Everyone receives the same summary of what took place. If anyone thinks he heard anything different from what is reported in the summary, he can make his views known to the secretary immediately.

2. There can be no confusion as to who was assigned to do what. Names are given and assignments spelled out. This prevents Ms. Foreman from saying three weeks after the meeting, "Well, I didn't know *I* was supposed to do that. I remember there was a suggestion that I gather statistics, but I sure don't have them for tomorrow's meeting."

3. No confusion will exist on the decisions reached and the votes taken. They will be clearly stated in black and white. Here again, Ms. Cox can hardly say three weeks later, "Well, I don't remember the vote going *that* way; I thought we agreed to wait until the next meeting before a final vote was taken on that item."

4. And finally, the minutes become a matter of record. They can be referred to by those who were absent, and reviewed by those who were present.

This postconference period is as important as the other two. It helps tie the package together and completes the job that was begun when someone said, just five weeks ago, "Well, we ought to get some additional input on this, kick it around, and then decide which way to go."

There are those who feel that the structured approach of this three-step plan has a decided disadvantage. What happens if a participant has a brilliant idea he wishes to discuss, but which has not been included on the agenda (is not part of the preplanned structure)? Will that idea be lost forever?

Certainly not!

All that is necessary is that the agenda carry an item "other business." The conference leader must then be sure that time is always saved to cover that point. In this way the advantages of both the structured and the unstructured meeting may be retained.

The conference decides which way to go—by common agreement. Voices are heard, ideas pursued, and personnel developed. A conference that is well run and democratically participated in, is an outstanding communication vehicle.

The three-step plan suggested is an excellent device for keeping lines of communication open, carrying through the process of decision making, and developing personnel.

Oral Reports and Presentations

Most managers do well in their face-to-face communications, but often their presentations before groups prove faulty. And this is a pity, for frequently a person's competence is judged on the basis of the speech that is made or the report that is presented. Too many capable people stumble and fumble when they stand before an audience. But it need not be that way if they will follow a few simple guidelines.

Background to the Presentation.   Good oral communication probably begins with the expectations on the part of the speaker, and often these expectations are much too high. Certainly the speaker usually expects more of himself than the audience does.

The audience to which the manager speaks—in business, industry, or government—does not expect a spellbinding, polished presentation. However, it does expect the speaker to be:

Knowledgeable,
Prepared,
Well organized, and
Honest.

If, in addition, the manager presents his or her ideas with force and clarity, so much the better. Good volume and enunciation help. And it is well to use visual aids to assist the audience in its understanding of the presentation.

The Formidable Four.   **Knowledgeable:** This is not usually a problem, for almost every speaker is well-informed on his own subject. But it is important to know something about related areas. And of equal importance, particularly when arguing a case, the speaker should be knowledgeable about opposing points of view.

Otherwise it is impossible to prepare effective answers and rebuttals.

Prepared: The speaker should be prepared in several different ways. Certainly he (or she) should *know his audience,* its goals, objectives, and interests. He should be sure to decide on his *purpose.* The speaker should prepare a *thesis* or core idea which will remain with the audience afterward. In preparing the presentation, the speaker should note the *limits* of the talk and avoid trying to cover too much.

Preparation should include meaningful visual aids and handout materials. And it should be sufficiently thorough so that the speaker isn't slavishly tied to notes during his delivery. Finally, the speaker should be so well prepared that he is ready to answer questions and satisfy requests for additional information.

Well organized: Perhaps this is part of being prepared. If one prepares, one usually organizes at the same time. But everyone is busy these days; probably the manager is busier than most people. The competition, both internal and external, for the manager's attention is tremendous.

Certainly one of the best ways to retain the attention of an audience is to make the presentation logical, well organized, concise, and clear. Conversely, there is no quicker way to lose an audience than with a rambling, illogical, poorly organized talk.

Honest: Probably no activity reveals a person more completely than speaking. An ancient philosopher said, "Speak that I may know you."

Somehow, some way, one's personality, knowledge, truthfulness, emotions, and self are revealed when one speaks. And because speech is so revealing of ourselves, we are ill-advised to pretend to be something we aren't. Such attempts will almost always be recognized by the audience, and the speaker will suffer in the balance.

That is why the speaker should be honest in his presentation—in his action and in his statements—if he wishes to maintain the good will of the audience. And he should also respect his audience. Finally, he should recognize the value of a straightforward, "I'm sorry, I really don't know the answer to that question" when he really doesn't know.

These qualities—being knowledgeable, prepared, well organized, and honest—are basic to an effective oral presentation.

Delivery of the Presentation.   Often a speaker places too much emphasis on his delivery. He should keep in mind, however, that his audience rarely expects him to deliver a talk with the polish of an actor or a professional speaker. They will certainly excuse a voice that is a bit high, gestures that are somewhat wooden, and a rate of speaking that is a bit rapid. If the speaker has the four qualities we have described, and also watches a few additional factors involved in the delivery of his talk, he will probably give a very satisfactory account of himself.

Choice of Words and Word Use.   A primary purpose of communication is to transfer ideas. And ideas are made up of words; therefore, the more extensive our vocabulary is, the easier the task of selecting the exact word for every meaning. Then ideas can be expressed with precision, force, and clarity.

Our choice of words must be based on the audience. Often we become so deeply involved in our own areas of specialization that we forget that our technical terms are not known to everyone. Remember, too, that certain words arouse emotional reactions which increase prejudice, build support, or evoke opposition. Words such as *strike, scab, delinquent, hippie,* or *warmonger* may cause a strong reaction among our listeners. It is one thing for a speaker to choose emotionally charged words intentionally so as better to convey his ideas. However, he should be aware that a careless choice of such words may cause listeners to tune him out. (See S. I. Hayakawa, "How Words Change Our Lives," in the Readings.)

By permission of John Hart and Field Enterprises, Inc.

Pronunciation of Words. The speaker should take care to enunciate clearly the words he chooses. Careless or sloppy enunciation is usually the result of sheer laziness in the use of mouth, tongue, and lips.

A "yeah" for a "yes," "dontchathink" for "don't you think," and "we're gonna" for "we are going," do not help the speaker in the presentation of his ideas nor in the enhancement of his image to the audience.

Volume. It is obvious that if the speaker wishes to have his ideas accepted, the audience must be able to hear him easily. If members of the group strain to hear the speaker, they will eventually find the effort too taxing and figuratively turn him off. On the other hand, if the speaker's voice is too loud, or "scratchy," or pitched too high, the audience may find that an irritation and again the speaker will lose. It really takes very little effort on the speaker's part to determine the proper volume and pitch and to maintain them.

One of the most important factors in volume is variation. A one-level presentation becomes monotonous, and it is helpful to vary the volume. However, this should not be done in a way that sounds mechanical or affected. Changes in volume should be related to the idea being presented.

Rate of Delivery. Changes in the rate of delivery, like changes in volume, help arouse audience interest and dispel monotony. The speech that is delivered too rapidly is sometimes difficult for an audience to follow. And even if an audience does comprehend easily, it is taxing for most people to stay with one who speaks extremely rapidly for more than 30 minutes or so.

On the other hand, the speaker whose words come out at a snail's pace finds that his audience becomes bored, inattentive, and even irritated.

Rate of delivery should be adjusted to the subject matter, the audience, and the speaker's personality.

Gestures and Posture. Freely motivated and natural gestures can add immeasurably to the communication of ideas. Effective nonverbal communication by means of the torso, hands, head, face, and eyes all help convey the speaker's message, mood, and attitude. But gestures must be spontaneous and natural. It is important that they not look artificial.

The speaker must also watch his posture. If he slouches or drapes himself on the lectern, the audience may feel that his ideas are as slovenly as his posture. A speaker who stands erect and is vigorous commands attention.

Eye Contact.   Eye contact, carefully and naturally maintained, helps keep the audience involved with the speaker. One way is to pick several individuals in the audience and speak directly to them. Then pick others and focus on them. Soon most of the audience begin to feel an involvement with the speaker and with what the speaker is saying.

Most of us can recall a speaker or teacher who stared out of the window, or at the floor, or glued his eyes to his notes. The speaker lost directness, and the audience, interest. But the speaker who looks at his listeners arouses their interest and captures their attention.

Evaluating the Listener.   Here, just as in the case of the written report, the speaker must adapt his content, words, visual aids, organization, and depth of presentation to the audience. Is the group made up of stockholders, salesmen, engineers, new employees, or the directors of the Frontier Corporation? Each of these groups will require a different approach.

Visual Aids.   Like the report itself, the visual aids must be prepared with careful attention to the audience. Should a complex graph be used, or would this audience prefer to view a pictogram? Would flip charts be better than slides? Slides better than transparencies? Transparencies better than handouts?

Each has its advantages. The room does not have to be darkened when transparencies are used, but the lights must be dimmed for slides. Flip charts are easy to make up and inexpensive, but will the speaker use them competently and remember to talk to his audience and not his charts?

Whatever visual aids are used, the speaker must make sure they are attractive, easy to comprehend, and clearly visible from all parts of the room. They should not be too "busy" and full of data.

Handouts.   The report may include facts, figures, statistics, or other data that require the audience to follow and study the information as the speaker talks. If these are reproduced on paper and handed around, the task of following the speaker is made easier.

The same is true of equipment, piece parts, or products. If listeners can actually feel, assemble, take apart, smell, or in some way examine the items for themselves, they will gain much more than if they only see it in the hands of the speaker 40 feet away.

There is a good time and a bad time to distribute a printed sheet or a piece of equipment. If the speaker is attempting to hold the interest of the audience, and at the same time something is being passed around, he will soon find that he is talking to himself.

Reading the Report.   When the report must cover every single point in a very precise manner, and statistics and facts must be accurately stated, it may be necessary to read it aloud. This method is not recommended unless there is no alternative. But there are ways to read a report so that it comes alive. If the speaker will familiarize himself with the content, he will know where to emphasize a key word, raise his voice, read a group of words rapidly or slowly, or gesture appropriately for an important point. Steady, slow reading can be terribly monotonous for both speaker and listener.

Speaking with Notes. The report freely given, with good eye contact and minimal reference to notes, is usually much more effective than one that is read.

The speaker can use visual aids, maintain good voice and eye contact, move freely, and gesture effectively. However, even the most experienced speaker knows the value of a few carefully prepared note cards. A quick glance at a card tells him what topic is next, when a quote should be given, and when the chart board should be referred to. No one minds a speaker using notes so long as he isn't glued to them.

Some experienced speakers prefer to eliminate note cards completely and pencil an outline discreetly on their flip charts. This is done in a hand so light that the notations are not visible to the audience.

Oral Summary of a Written Report. If the speaker is summarizing a written report, and wants to avoid overemphasizing one point and forgetting another, a good method is to make a written abstract of it. By occasionally referring to his notes he can be quite confident that no material of importance is overlooked.

Conclusion. A good presentation can be the payoff for tedious hours and days of work. Months of research, weeks of planning, and hours of writing may go into that 35-minute oral presentation.

When it is done well, the audience is often motivated to take a course of action, or convinced that the speaker's argument is sound and his recommendations valid. However, if the presentation is not done well the argument may be destined for oblivion, and the speaker with it.

Questions for Study

Complete any of the following problems assigned. You may wish to review the chapter and note key points before solving a problem.

1. In an earlier chapter, we listed as one of the barriers to effective communication, "Competition for attention." How is this barrier related to ineffective listening in this busy, complex world in which we live?

2. In listening to individuals, do you feel it is more important to hear the *facts* they transmit or the *feelings?* Or can we even say that one is more important than the other?

3. (a) List several reasons why most of us listen inefficiently. (b) It is usually easier to retain facts than to understand and appreciate feelings. Why?

4. Several major corporations, publishers, and independent counseling services offer prepared programs on Listening Improvement. Complete research, make

calls, and write several letters to secure data and sample materials. Make a report to the class on your findings. (It's most efficient if the class divides itself into 10 or 12 groups of 2 or 3 students each. Each group then investigates one program and gives a brief report and demonstration.)

5. What specific methods can you cite for listening improvement? List and explain each point.

6. Comment on the following statement: "If we don't listen to our employees, our children, or others around us, they will find someone who *will*."

7. What *specific* values accrue to the efficient listener?

8. List and discuss various types of interviews.

9. Most large companies carry through a variety of different types of interviews (recruiting, appraisal, grievance, exit, etc.). Working in teams, visit several companies and secure sample copies of the forms used. Present a report to the class. (Each team might limit itself to two firms.)

10. Insofar as the interviewer is concerned, which aspect of communication—reading, writing, speaking, listening—do you feel should be practiced most carefully and effectively? Why?

11. The text calls "Questioning, Listening, Observing, and Evaluating" tools of interviewing. Please comment on each in regard to the interview, noting the designation "tools."

12. Break into teams of two and carry through an interview in any of the following situations. If at all possible, videotape the interviews so they may be played back and constructive criticism offered. If that is not possible, set aside time at the conclusion of each interview for discussion of the comments of both interviewer and interviewee.

    1) A supervisor and a consistently late employee.

    2) A supervisor and an employee who frequently takes too much time on coffee break.

    3) A salesman and an irritated customer whose last three orders have arrived after the scheduled due date.

    4) An exit interview between a personnel director and a secretary who resigned as of this date.

    5) An interview between Manager Betty Bahr and the supervisor of Section 5, Bob Kelley. Section 5's rate of production has dropped steadily for the past three months.

13. Why do you feel there is frequent criticism of the term "conference leader"? What title(s) might be preferable? Why?

14. Split into groups of 14–17. Choose any one of the topics below, carry through research, issue a request to attend the conference, and then hold such a meeting for 40 minutes.

    At the conclusion of the meeting, hold a critique of the leader, participants, conference content, discussion, progress, and related factors.

    You may wish to ask the members of your group to simulate specific roles having opposing points of view. Representation from any of the following may be assumed: management and labor; salaried and hourly personnel; professional and nonprofessional plant employees; students and faculty; faculty and school administration; fraternity and independent representatives; etc.

1) Shall we institute a company profit-sharing program?

2) Why fraternities should (should not) be abolished.

3) Why students should (should not) have equal representation with faculty on campus committees.

4) Should the 10-minute morning and afternoon coffee breaks be abolished and the work day shortened?

5) Should an employee council be established?

6) Should employees have a voice in the distribution of company profits?

7) Should we have two separate cafeterias, one for hourly and one for salaried and administrative personnel?

8) Should our company attempt to diversify through acquisitions and merger?

9) Should a "Pass-Fail" grade designation be instituted for all undergraduate classes in place of the present A, B, C, D, F method of evaluating students?

10) Shall we hire a competent individual to edit the company magazine, or shall we engage an outside firm to carry through the complete assignment?

15. What are the three steps in the conference as designated by the text? Discuss this organizational pattern noting why you feel it is or is not logical.

16. What specific value or benefits accrue from the preparation and distribution of an agenda? List and discuss.

17. From the point of view of oral presentation, why is the statement, "Speak that I may know you" a comment on the speaker's honesty and frankness?

18. Being somewhat nervous prior to a speech seems to be common for most of us. How does being "Knowledgeable, Prepared, Well Organized, and Honest" cut that tension?

19. Make a two- to four-minute presentation on a hobby or sport activity which you enjoy. Emphasize the informational rather than the persuasive aspects of your topic.

20. Assume your audience is made of citizens who will go to the polls tomorrow to cast their votes. Attempt to convince them, in a five-minute presentation, why they should vote for the issue or candidate you suggest.

21. Assume your audience is made up of managers of your company who can accept or reject your proposal. Make a six- to ten-minute presentation in which you attempt to secure their approval. Keep in mind that they are concerned with expenditures and need "hard" proof to be convinced. You are required to use some type(s) of visual aids (flip charts, transparencies, slides, samples, etc.)

Topics which may be selected include:

1) Purchase of a new piece of equipment.

2) Instituting, abolishing, extending, or shortening the coffee break period.

3) A new employee appraisal system.

4) Introduction of a new product.

5) A new marketing plan.

6) A new recruiting system.

7) A new compensation program.

8) Any other subject of a somewhat similar (and persuasive) nature.

Chapter Four

Techniques of Planning, Organizing, and Writing

The Preliminary Plan
The Final Plan
The Process of Writing
We Communicate More Than Facts
The Writer's Job
The Parts of the Whole
Qualities of Writing Style
Editing Suggestions
The Final Product

The three activities of planning, organizing, and writing are so intimately associated that it seems logical to treat them in one chapter.

Whenever an individual faces the task of writing a report, preparing a proposal, completing a staff study, or composing a business letter, he goes through the same logical series of steps. First he *plans* the content of the communication and the objectives or goals he wishes to attain. He then *organizes* his ideas into a logical and/or psychological order so that the message may prove most effective. Finally he carries through the task of *putting those ideas on paper* so that his goals may be achieved.

Good planning and organizing are the keys to the success of a great many activities in our society. Without them it would be impossible for a space voyage to function properly, a building to be erected solidly, a surgical procedure carried through successfully, or a piece of oral or written communication presented effectively. Few activities, from baking a cake to going on a journey, take place without a plan or blueprint. But often we write or speak without following a plan; of course we should not.

How often have you thrown down a magazine, slammed shut a book, snapped off a television set, or tapped someone on the chest with a "Well, what's the point?" How often have you lost interest in an article, a report, or a speech because it seemed to be going in circles? Perhaps this was because it was not properly planned.

The Preliminary Plan

An exposition of ideas which proceeds logically and clearly is easy to follow and appreciate. It holds our attention and enables us to look for the facts that concern us. For this reason a person who wishes to transmit his ideas effectively will begin by making a plan or outline.

Normally the communicator will formulate two outlines: a tentative one which he will develop as he thinks about his problem and carries through preliminary research, and a final one from which he will write his finished paper. This latter outline will be completed after research, thought, and analysis have indicated necessary changes in the original plan.

First Steps

Before we can write even a tentative outline, we must answer several questions: What is the primary purpose of our letter, report, memo? To whom is it addressed? What are its limitations? What is its scope?

Determining Our Purpose.   First we must ask ourselves what we are aiming to accomplish. If we are replying to an inquiry letter, we must recognize that the primary purpose is to answer the inquiry, in either an informative or persuasive way, not to offer a sales appeal for the firm's new product, or dun for payment of a past due bill. When we establish the primary purpose of a communication, the organizational pattern for it begins to fall into place.

For example, a letter arrives from a customer asking for our firm's credit terms. Our purpose is simply to *inform* him of our credit terms, and we will organize our reply this way:

1. Acknowledge letter requesting credit terms.
2. Spell out our credit terms in detail.
3. Friendly close.

However, if the customer is asking for credit, and we discover that his asset-liability ratio is unsatisfactory, our purpose will be to *persuade* the customer to accept an alternative (e.g., c.o.d. instead of credit), and therefore we will organize our reply differently:

1. Acknowledge letter requesting credit.
2. Explain why it would be of benefit to the customer to improve his asset-liability ratio.
3. Offer c.o.d., explaining its advantages. (The refusal to extend credit is *implicit* in the positive statements made here.)
4. Friendly close.

By following this plan, the correspondent need not say, "Therefore we cannot . . . ," "We find it impossible . . . ," or "We must refuse. . . ." Under ordinary circumstances, if the writer first explains the reason for the refusal, a negative statement need not be made.

Identifying Our Reader.   A basic question prior to planning is, "Who is the prospective reader?" At what level shall I write? Should the discussion, charts, graphs, and related materials be presented in a simple or a complex fashion?

Is the reader one of the persons involved in financing this building project, a relatively uninterested shareholder who owns three shares of stock, or is he the consulting architect? Will this serve as a release to the newspapers for publicity purposes, or is it to be a detailed report to the board of directors? The level and amount of detail will surely differ for each.

The organizational plan may also change according to the reader. In this case, a chronological approach, which is relatively easy to follow, may be better, while in another case, a cause-and-effect order may be appropriate. More technical detail will be included in one organizational plan, and less in another; or complicated financial facts will be part of one outline but not of another. And there may be other variations reflected in the outline, concerning visual aids, financial data, and length and detail of the narrative. In this way the outline (and therefore the final paper) is designed with the reader in mind.

Defining Scope, Limitations, and Depth. The next step in building the tentative outline is to choose the major topics to be covered. These are foundation blocks upon which the entire paper will be constructed.

Let us say, for example, that our paper will be concerned with "The Marketing of Our Product in Western Europe." We may choose six major areas for examination:

Market acceptance
Competition
Advertising and sales promotion
Method of distribution
Legal restrictions
Cost of distribution

These six points may be arranged in a different order when the final paper is written, but we do know that they will be the major areas for analysis and investigation. They become the major headings in our tentative working outline.

Now we can begin to divide each one into fairly obvious subcategories:

Market acceptance
    Housewives
    The teen-age market
    Institutional purchasers
    Governmental agencies
Competition
    From similar local products
        Brand A
        Brand B
        Brand C
    From North American products
        Brand AA
        Brand BB

        Brand CC
        Brand DD
    From similar products manufactured abroad
  Advertising and sales promotion
    To the consumer
        Newspaper
        Radio
        Television
        Direct mail
        Point of sales
        Miscellaneous
    To the distributor
        Trade publications
        Direct mail
        Sales force
        Miscellaneous
  Etc.

Each of the major points has been subdivided, as indicated above, into sub-points. Those can be further divided. But the important fact to note is the method of developing an organizational plan. Always begin by listing your major topics for discussion and examination. These form the general foundation blocks of the paper. After the major areas have been identified then the writer should move to develop each into subdivisions.

It is a fairly simple matter to list the major points in an analysis. They are usually the specific questions which need to be answered. For example, let us say we are faced with a presentation on whether we should undertake to manufacture new product X. The obvious questions which arise are:

Do we have the facilities to manufacture it?
Is there a market for it?
What competition exists?
What costs will be incurred?
What advantages do we stand to gain?

Each of these questions can be easily reworded into a more succinct major topic heading, and then the subpoints under each developed. Let's try another topic for presentation. This time let us assume that we are faced with "The Advisability of Publishing and Distributing a Monthly Employee Magazine." Some of the primary questions to be answered here are: Will such a publication make a significant contribution to employee morale? What will the annual cost of such a venture be? What personnel must we secure to handle the project? What alternatives may accomplish similar ends? What are the experiences of similar industries in this area? Here again, subtopics may now be developed under each major topic. The writer should always select or identify the major topics *before* subdividing.

Before the investigator proceeds too far in his analysis and the development of his organizational plan, he should check his boundaries and limits. Certainly there is no point in his carrying through research on the first problem above in the area of "Legal restrictions" if it is not necessary. Perhaps the legal restrictions in this instance have been determined and are part of company records already. Or the legal restrictions are known to be minor and are not worth the time and effort to investigate. If an area need not be pursued, certainly time and energy should not be expended on it.

The number and content of subtopics must also be limited. There is no need to go into depth on a specific topic if it serves no purpose or may even prove detrimental by giving the reader much more than he wants on a topic. If we will only be concerned with competition from similar products manufactured in France, then let's not get involved with those manufactured in North America or Western Europe.

Limitation of the subject area is vital if the communicator (or encoder) is to get to the heart of his planning and investigation and not dissipate his efforts.

Let us say we are writing a report on "The Advisability of Constructing a New Plant in Bennington, Ohio." Our major foundation blocks for investigation are:

Labor supply available
Physical plant
Market
Source of raw materials
Financing
Community attitude
Availability of utilities
Tax structure
Transportation facilities

Now let's examine these major points and ask if we can limit the study. If there is already adequate material available in company records on "Source of raw materials" and "Community attitude," let's not waste time on research; let's just cross them out.

Our next step is to break down each of the points above into a logical series of subpoints. The number of subpoints will determine the depth of the analysis and usually the length of the presentation.

If the reader only wants to know if there are rail, air, water, and truck lines going into Bennington, that information can be covered in one paragraph.

Transportation Lines
Available to Bennington

Rail
Air
Water
Trucking

But if he wants to know which companies are involved, what the specific rates are, schedules, guarantees, history of performance, etc., this may involve 20 pages of narrative, charts, and tables based on the following outline:

Transportation Facilities
Shipment of finished products

Rail
  Santa Fe Railroad
  Mid-Continent Railroad
Truck
  Commercial trucking firms
  Company trucks
  Leased trucks
Air
  Commercial air freight
  Chartered air freight
Comparative analysis
  Cost
    Rail
    Truck
    Air
  Shipment time
    Rail
    Truck
    Air
Analyses of roads, air terminals, water and rail facilities
  Roads
    Freeways, highways, major roads
    Secondary roads
    Access roads (to plant)
  Air terminals (75 mile-radius)
    Passenger
    Freight
  Water facilities
    Ports (import-export)
    Rivers (raw material; bulk products)
  Rail facilities
    Track spurs (on company property)
      Condition
      Ownership
    Terminals
      Railroad companies involved
      Accessibility
    Receiving and shipping points
Employee transportation
  Public
    Commercial bus routes
    Rapid transit
  Private
    Individual automobiles
    Car pools
    Routes to and from residential areas
  Cost analysis

Obviously if the reader wants one level of depth and receives another, the writer is to blame for poor planning and organizing. The solution is simple: planning and organizing must be done with reference to needs and expectations, not carried through on assumptions.

Reviewing the First Steps

Let us review quickly the steps in our organizational development:

Purpose: Just what is the problem? Is it to compare two systems? Is it to analyze a situation? Is it to cite information for record-keeping purposes? Is it to sell a course of action to a prospect? To explain a technical procedure to a reader? To defend and argue for the acceptance of a procedure?

Reader: Is the reader of the message a technically oriented engineer or a business-minded member of the board of directors? Is he a potential customer or a steady account?

Limitation and Scope: Has the topic been accurately limited on the basis of the reader's needs, desires, and level? Has the depth of the research and of the report, letter, or speech been properly determined?

The tentative outline is developed, of course, as the writer carries through the steps above. At no time should he hesitate to add to or delete from the outline or change its order to a more logical form. The outline is completely flexible and should be treated as a guide to be shaped, changed, and molded as the need arises.

The Final Plan

As the writer carries through investigation in his primary and secondary sources, he will find that some of the points in his tentative outline are not logical or possible to complete. Conversely, he will discover in his sources that areas which should have been included in his tentative outline were omitted. And so he revises, changes, and polishes his tentative outline. He cuts two points here and one there; he inserts a new item here and one there. These changes are made during planning and research. The new, revised outline will frequently be quite different from the original one.

Value of an Outline

Too often we may feel that drawing up an outline or guide prior to the presentation of the report or speech is an extra and unnecessary step. "Why," we may ask, "should I go through the work? Why not just write the report or prepare the talk?"

There are several very good answers to that question:

1. If his outline is logical, the writer is assured of the logical development of his report. It is simple, for example, to move point B under IV to another section of the outline if an analysis of the organization so indicates. Think how

much more difficult it is to move that section *after* the report has been completed. And it is much easier to expand or reduce a section in the outline than in the finished report.

The example below illustrates how easy it is to make changes in the outline to secure a more logical plan.

Employee Fringe Benefits

I. Insurance Programs
    A. Hospitalization
    B. Major medical
    C. Life
II. Paid Holidays
    A. Seven specific national holidays
    B. Vacation with pay
III. Pension Plan
    A. Company retirement program
    B. Social security
IV. Miscellaneous
    A. Sick leave
    B. Annuity program (employee-sponsored)
    C. Discount purchase of merchandise
    D. Surgical coverage (employee-sponsored)

2. The length or depth of treatment of one part of the outline in comparison to the other sections can be easily evaluated. If a section is out of proportion—with either too many or too few data—it is easier to make the correction in the outline than in the finished presentation.

Employee Training at Allied Telephone

I. Employee Training in the Fairview Plant
    A. Executive training
    B. Engineering training
    C. Shop supervisory training
        1. Leadership classes for superintendents
        2. Foreman training
    D. Office personnel training
        1. Written communications
        2. Office equipment training
II. Employee Training at the Leance Plant
    A. Executive training
    B. Engineering training
        1. Electronic control systems
        2. Engineering cost control
    C. Shop supervisory training
        1. Leadership classes for superintendents
        2. Foreman training
        3. Interpersonal relations
III. Employee Training at the Stone Plant
    A. Executive training

B. Engineering training
   1. Engineering cost analysis
   2. Operations research
   3. Manufacturing processes
      a. Heat treatment of alloys
      b. Casting and molding
      c. Material joining
      d. Metal surface treatment
      e. Material cleaning
   4. Computer use
      a. Analog and digital
      b. Computer codes
      c. Programming principles
C. Shop supervisory training

It would appear, in the numbered outline above, that point B under III has been developed to an extent out of proportion to the other topics. If all the material is needed, then perhaps a new major heading should be included; if all the details are not necessary, they should be excised mercilessly. Roman numeral III will then be in better proportion to the other major headings.

3. The communicator can use the outline to check on the *completeness* of his own presentation. It is certainly simple to evaluate an outline to determine if all the necessary points have been covered; if they have not, additional items may be inserted easily. But the story is different when one must weld missing paragraphs into a completed paper.

4. The communicator can evaluate the *order of development* he employed. This is closely related to logic, as discussed above. There must be some method of logical development to any presentation: chronological, geographical, cause and effect, etc. Here again, it is easier to check the outline and correct inconsistencies than it is to rework the finished paper.

5. An outline *saves time*. This fact is obvious. As the communicator evaluates his outline, he can quickly make additions, deletions, corrections, and revisions. How much more effort is required—and how much more inconvenient it is—to take the same action on a finished paper!

In industry, time and money are frequently equated. Here is Mr. Lowell preparing to answer a letter he has just received from customer Barton. Barton has asked Lowell several specific questions: the availability of the Acme filing cabinets, what colors are in stock, the cost, possible trade-in value of the used cabinets on hand, and details on the construction of the Acme. He further wants to know why the credit of $78.50 that he requested three weeks ago has not been acted on. And, in addition, does Lowell carry the new Handy-Dollar payroll envelopes?

This is a typical business letter to which Mr. Lowell should reply *after* he has made a brief outline of what he will discuss and in what order. But does he make up a little scratch outline? Oh, no. He's much too busy. He seizes the microphone of his dictating unit and replies to customer Barton.

Unfortunately, Lowell forgets to tell Barton the price on the Acme cabinets and he neglects to comment on the $78.50 bill. Yet when Lowell's secretary brings the letter in for signing several hours after it was dictated, the dealer quickly signs it (probably without reading it), and feels that he did a good job.

But, of course, Barton is irritated with the reply he receives and is angry with Mr. Lowell. The price of the cabinets was not mentioned, so he assumes they are expensive. As a result, he places his order for $950 worth of filing cabinets with a competitor of Lowell's. In addition, he must send another letter to Lowell and again inquire about the $78.50.

Lowell, because he didn't plan his letter, has lost a sizable and profitable sale and the goodwill of Customer Barton and caused himself the needless expense of writing additional letters. Had Mr. Lowell just taken the time to formulate and check a brief outline such as the following, he would have saved time, money, and a customer.

1. Acknowledge Barton's inquiry letter of December 3
2. Indicate that Acme filing cabinets are available and are on sale
3. Cite details on Acme cabinets:
   size
   fireproof, tamperproof
   individual drawer locks
   easy roll drawers
   various colors available
   cost
4. Special price; therefore no trade-ins
5. Explain $78.50 credited on October bill (include photocopy)
6. Cite data and sales appeal on Handy-Dollar payroll envelopes
7. Offer to ship filing cabinets within 24 hours of a collect call
8. Friendly close

Using this outline, Mr. Lowell will probably dictate a letter which will be complete, concise, and courteous. It will maintain customer goodwill and increase sales.

Outline Mechanics

How you design your outline is often a matter of personal preference. Some people prefer an elaborate numbering system of Roman numerals and letters all carefully arranged on clean, white stationery; others simply indent subordinate ideas under major headings and find the back of an envelope a convenient place to write. The mechanics of organizing are personal, and most of us eventually develop our own system.

Designating Major and Minor Points.   It is always wise to arrange the items in your outline so that a glance will reveal major areas as opposed to minor ones. It is helpful to think of the most important points as the key ideas and the subordinating ones as items of substantiating evidence.

The most frequently used numbering system is the numeral-letter combination. Roman numerals are used for major points, capital letters for subtopics, and Arabic numerals and lower-case letters for smaller topics. If a further breakdown is necessary, Arabic numerals and letters enclosed in parentheses are used.

I. First Main Heading
   A. First subtopic under main heading
   B. Second subtopic under main heading
      1. First subtopic under B
      2. Second subtopic under B
         a. First subtopic under 2
         b. Second subtopic under 2
            (1) First subtopic under b
            (2) Second subtopic under b
               (a) First subtopic under (2)
               (b) Second subtopic under (2)
II. Second Main Heading

The decimal style is favored by engineers as well as others in science and technology. This system is logical, easy to use, and affords a quick method for referring to specific points.

1. First Main Heading
   1.1 First subtopic under first main heading
   1.2 Second subtopic under first main heading
      1.21 First subtopic under 1.2
      1.22 Second subtopic under 1.2
         1.221 First subtopic under 1.22
         1.222 Second subtopic under 1.22
2. Second Main Heading
   2.1 First subtopic under second main heading
   2.2 Second subtopic under second main heading
      2.21 First subtopic under 2.2
      2.22 Second subtopic under 2.2

There are other methods of outlining, such as simple indentation and the use of specialized symbols. Any system which is accurate, permits easy analysis, and works for you is the one you should use.

Ensuring Parallel Development. In designing the outline, give items of equal importance similar levels of designation under major headings. Thus if "cost of materials" is an immediate subhead to Roman numeral I, it would hardly seem possible that under Roman numeral II "cost of materials" should slip to a sub-subtopic. Points of parallel interest should be listed at similar levels in the outline.

Avoiding Overlapping of Ideas. If headings and subheadings are chosen properly, there should be little overlapping of ideas.

If a paper were written from the following outline there would surely be overlapping in the area of health and health insurance. The result would be a poorly organized, repetitious, and uninteresting analysis. However, if the outline is checked, edited, and revised, the paper that results may have merit.

An Analysis of Employee Fringe Benefits

    I. Insurance Programs
   II. Retirement Programs
  III. Blue Cross Hospitalization Plan
  IV. Employee Discount Purchase Plan
   V. Major Medical Insurance Program
  VI. Time Off with Compensation
 VII. Yearly Health Examination
VIII. Paid Holidays As Indicated in Union Contract

Using a Consistent and Logical Order of Development. Whether your communication is long or short, written or oral, simple or complex, your desire is that it be understood and accepted. This obviously requires that you analyze the content of the message, the nature of the audience, and the purpose you hope to achieve. You go through these steps to secure the most logical order of development for your message. This attribute of logic is vital, for regardless of the excellence of your word choice, the clarity of your sentences, and the appearance of the report, all will fail if the message lacks logic.

The critical businessman may well overlook a misplaced comma or a faulty phrase. But if the presentation lacks logic, the ideas then become suspect and the reader is reluctant to accept any part of the message, or he may simply "tune himself out." You have certainly read such a presentation and noted at some point that "this doesn't follow; it's not logical; I can't accept it."

Obviously we cannot hope that all we speak or write will be accepted, but when it is rejected because we *did not present it logically,* then the fault is ours.

Analysis and Synthesis. Before we design a plan for presentation, we must be sure we have recognized all or most of the important factors in the situation.

Sales of our products on the West Coast have declined very dramatically. Let's *analyze*—or identify the elements—to find out why the decline has taken place: We do not have a West Coast distribution plant; a large market for patio furniture exists on the West Coast: shipping our outdoor furniture from the Midwest is costly; freight rates for shipping have risen steadily; our West Coast customers have complained about high shipping costs; surveys show we are not competitive on price with West Coast manufacturers on similar lines. . . . Thus, we began with a condition: decreased sales. We then analyzed the situation and attempted to identify the contributing factors.

Or we may be confronted by a number of diverse elements which require *synthesis,* or "putting together," to form a logical whole or pattern: Production has declined very rapidly since the early part of June. Employees have complained about the level of illumination in the production area; a new foreman of the section took over in May; the safety equipment for the presses is slow and outdated; compensation is on a piece-rate basis; the lead man (assistant foreman) was discharged after he and the new foreman had a severe argument on June 1 . . . . Can these various facts be related or synthesized with each other into some pattern that would result in an overall theme?

Inductive Development. This is an order of development going from the particular or specific to the general. Here the writer cites details, specific events, and examples, and finally arrives at a general conclusion. We might for example explain that the quality of the product was high, the price very competitive, the service excellent, and delivery fast: all of which resulted in a year of high sales.

Deductive Development. Here the method of development is from a general statement to particulars, details, and facts. We might begin by pointing out that a firm's primary activities are dependent on communication. From here we could point out how most external transactions are based on business letters; advertising in newspapers, radio, and TV; reports to government agencies; and proposals to potential customers. Internally, communication takes place through such media as news bulletins, company magazines, management memos, interdepartmental correspondence and reports, conferences, meetings, etc.

Chronological Development. Here we should select a specific period of time and move forward with our discussion. Perhaps we would want to point out that sales in Area 3 were $80,000 in 1955; five years later they doubled; by 1965 they were over $200,000. In 1970 they reached a quarter of a million dollars and have been steadily rising since. This would all indicate that for the period 1975-80 we should make a much heavier advertising and personnel commitment, in the expectation that sales will continue to increase.

Here is a firm that is for sale. On the surface it appears to be a good buy. However, it is important for us to look at its "track record" and note its progress since its formation in 1960. What was its situation in 1950: level of sales, profit figures, number of personnel, product lines, physical plant, development activities, etc.? How did these same areas measure up five years, ten years, and fifteen years later? What trends are indicated as we come to the present? Was there a steady rise over this period of time? Was a plateau reached? Was there a strong decline? If so, in what areas? Details should be added in each of the areas (level of sales, profit figures, number of personnel, product lines, physical plant, development activities) to give unity to the report. However, the order of development of the entire report is chronological, as the message moves forward in five-year blocks from 1950 to the present.

Geographical Development. In this method we begin at one location and then move to the next. If we are analyzing sales for a corporation that has four district sales offices, and sales headquarters in New York, it would seem logical to begin with a discussion of the activities of the New York office, then go on to an examination of the Chicago office; to Waterloo, Iowa; to Denver; and finally to Los Angeles. Or we might look at warehousing facilities in Camden, Fort Wayne, and Dallas before analyzing what they should be in the new warehouse going up in San Francisco.

Spatial Development. Here the order of development moves from one logical space designation to another. In a plant, areas might be designated as administrative, manufacturing, packaging, storage, shipping, etc. If we were to examine the illumination levels (or safety hazards, or decorating schemes, or noise levels) in the entire plant, we would first discuss the aspect in one space (administrative, for example), and then go on to each of the others.

Directional Development.   Here we would simply describe the process or product as it moved in a predetermined direction. For example, the piece part must first be cleaned and sprayed. From there it goes to cutting and polishing. It is then sent to inspection, after which it is sent to production where diodes are attached. Again it is returned to inspection, after which it is sold, and taken from stock. These are the steps followed and the directions in which the item moves.

If we were to follow a state legislative bill from the time it was introduced in the house by a legislator, moving from Committee A to Committee B to the senate to the executive branch to the governor, we would be describing the direction of movement of the bill.

Simple to Complex Development.   This is a valuable method to use when we are faced with explaining a relatively involved situation to a reader who may not have a clear understanding of the fundamentals of the subject. If we begin with simple, easy-to-understand situations and gradually move to more complex areas of the same topic, the reader will be able to follow the explanation presented. If we wish to discuss a new automated production process, we might begin by explaining the fundamentals of a standard production process, then go on to the principles of a semiautomated situation, and finally to the complexity of a completely automated arrangement.

Types of Outlines

The two most frequently used outline forms are topic and sentence. In infrequent cases, a paragraph outline may be used. In addition to a list of items in topic, sentence, or paragraph form, the outline also has a title and a thesis sentence. This thesis sentence should state clearly and concisely the purpose or objective of the message.

Topic Outline.   Each entry in a topic outline consists of a few words or a short phrase. This type of outline has several advantages: The writer can jot down ideas quickly and need not bother with structuring each thought into a sentence. With a list of brief topics, the writer has little hesitation about adding several, dropping a few, or moving one from one section to another of the outline, and making other revisions as the need arises.

A disadvantage of this type of outline is that it requires a good memory. When the two- and three-word headings are examined three weeks after they were written, the writer may have quite forgotten to what the cryptic phrase "Losses—unexpected circumstances" refers. Yet when that entry was made, he knew perfectly well what he wanted to discuss under that point.

A Survey of Fringe Benefits in Industry

I. Insurance Programs
    A. Life insurance programs
        1. Executive level
        2. Other employee level
    B. Hospitalization insurance
        1. Individual
        2. Family plans
    C. Major medical plans
        1. Company-sponsored
        2. Insurance company-sponsored
    D. Surgical plans
        1. Individual
        2. Family plans

II. Vacation and Holiday Plans
    A. Vacation plans
        1. Standard vacation (specific period each year for *all* employees)
        2. Nonstandard vacation
        3. Time
            a. Weeks associated with years of company service
            b. Specific periods of time for different levels with no reference to length of service
    B. Paid holidays
        1. In conformity with union contracts
        2. As announced by the specific organization
    C. Extended leave periods (for research, travel, illness, etc.)
        1. With compensation
        2. Without compensation

III. Annuity and Pension Plans
    A. Government-sponsored (social security)
    B. Annuity programs
        1. For executives
            a. Company-employee contributions
            b. Company contributions only
        2. For other employees
    C. Pension plans
        1. Company-sponsored programs
        2. Company-employee-sponsored programs

IV. Profit-Sharing Plans
    A. Broad coverage based on net earnings
    B. Limited employee participation

Sentence Outline. In a sentence outline, each entry is a complete sentence. This requires that the writer structure his thoughts a little more carefully than with the topic outline. Ideas are stated rather completely and the danger of forgetting what an entry refers to is considerably lessened. A major disadvantage, however, is that it tempts the writer to convert his sentence outline into his report. This is sometimes done through the simple expedient of connecting the sentences with a few transitional words or phrases. Of course the results are poor since the skeleton of the outline, which shines through such a letter or report, is so apparent as to make the message rather uninteresting. However, the writer can avoid this by remembering that the outline must serve only as a guide to the writing assignment, not as an initial effort to be converted into the final paper.

Concluding Comments on Planning and Organizing

Your presentation may be a detailed and exhaustive analysis of a complex problem, a relatively routine report which will be the basis for a management decision, an ordinary business letter, a memo, a speech, an oral report, a conference discussion, or any of dozens of other communications which we are required to make in the course of a business day. But whatever it is, be sure to plan and organize it before you present it. The building which follows a carefully drawn blueprint and the communication which adheres to a logical outline are usually well-constructed products.

Always plan your communication.

The Process of Writing

Frequently during the business day, you as a manager are called upon to express your thoughts in writing. Memos, letters, reports, surveys, articles, proposals, staff studies, and a dozen other types of written presentations flow from your pen. You, like all of us, hope that each of them will be written with force and clarity. Of course, you don't expect them to be recognized as priceless examples of exposition, but you do appreciate it when your superior or one of your colleagues says, "That report of yours certainly hit the target."

Unfortunately, this doesn't happen as often as you would like; you find that writing is hard work and that what you finally achieve will very probably not be an outstanding example of business prose. (See J. Fielden, "What Do You Mean I Can't Write?" in the Readings.)

But as businessmen, we must all write, and as long as we must, let's do it as effectively as we can. Writing, like most activities from tennis to surgery, requires specific techniques, attention to detail, and hard work.

We Communicate More Than Facts

If the businessman wishes to communicate effectively, he must keep the factors of rhetoric, diction, and grammar in mind. But he must remember that, in conveying his ideas to others, he is also expressing his feelings. The listener may not interpret the message or the feeling as the speaker intended, but the communicator must be aware that the listener will react in some way.

The feelings which enter into this communication strongly influence the interpretation of the message. For example, picture two young business executives who are also good friends. They play golf together, attend plays and parties together with their wives, and generally enjoy social as well as work relations. On a particular morning while having coffee, they discuss a new advertising campaign. In the course of the conversation Bob casually comments that Bill's ideas on the presentation are "all wet." Bill, taking no offense, probably replies, "No, I'm not all wet. Here, I'll explain why I'm sure the client will accept. . . ." And so the conversation continues.

But suppose the office manager, Frank, uses the same phrase after several rather heated discussions with the tabulating room director, Marty. Marty is sure that Frank is unreasonable, unfair, and biased. Thus when Frank comments that Marty is "all wet," we can easily appreciate why Marty gets angry.

The reactions to "you're all wet" in these two cases will vary strongly because the feelings conveyed are different even though the words are the same. But this is true of almost all communication; not only are ideas conveyed, but also feelings.

In a simple written statement, such as, "We were surprised you did not understand our billing method," the writer may convey feelings to the reader not intended at all. A potential problem could have been avoided by choosing different words. A vital factor for the communicator to keep in mind is that feelings are conveyed along with facts—both in speaking and in writing.

What we have said thus far (and going back to the discussion on barriers to communication) is this: The process of sending and receiving information is a complex and difficult task. But difficult or not, this is the way individuals, groups, nations, and peoples carry through their daily activities: They must communicate. And the more effective and accurate this communication is, the better the relationship that exists in the home, in the office, on the golf course, in the United Nations, and at the summit conferences.

The Writer's Job

Many people in industry find writing a difficult task. Reports do not flow from their pens; articles and manuscripts are not created easily and quickly; the ideas for speeches do not tumble pellmell onto paper; and even the task of composing and dictating a good business letter is difficult for many.

Some people, on the other hand, are very adept at writing; their pens fly over blank paper like magic and soon excellent reports and articles are completed. They dictate long, memorable letters, quickly, clearly, and confidently. And they enjoy, and are challenged by, a good, stiff writing assignment.

But for most of us, writing is plain hard work. It would be dishonest to try to convince you otherwise; but knowledge of writing techniques and frequent practice will make you a *better* writer. You may not ever say, "Writing is easy," but hopefully you will say, sometime in your career, "Writing is a challenge and I am confident I can do a creditable job."

It is important that we recognize this principle, not to be negative, but simply to avoid becoming discouraged when we encounter difficulty in a writing assignment. No, writing is not easy; but like any task which requires work, effort, and concentration, its satisfactory completion is gratifying and rewarding.

The First Draft

Most of us do not say precisely and clearly what we mean to say in our first draft. However, there is a system we can use to achieve that final well-written communication. The system is simple. Develop a satisfactory outline. Refer to it as you write a first draft, then revise and rewrite until you are satisfied that your paper says just what you mean it to say in the manner in which you mean to say it.

Getting Ready. Before you actually begin to write, you must get ready to write. You must be in the right frame of mind, have the right atmosphere, be sure you have identified the problem correctly, and know what your purpose is, who your reader is, and what you want to say.

The Writing Environment. Once you have recognized that writing requires time and attention, make sure you have an adequate quantity of both for the job. Don't try to write an important report between meetings; don't attempt to complete that article in the midst of clicking typewriters and chattering discussions; and don't stuff the assignment into your briefcase with the intention of writing it tonight while you watch your favorite TV program.

None of these, or similar methods, usually work.

Provide a definite time and place for your writing projects. Of course, few of us are fortunate enough to have as much time as we would like, yet we must allocate a reasonable number of minutes for our required writing duties. Surely you will agree that it is foolish to work on a business or research project for days and then try to write a report on the assignment in half an hour. And yet this is often done. A manager who has carefully gathered data and conducted surveys during the past month will attempt to dash off an important report based on that information during a spare 15 minutes after lunch. If the report becomes the basis for important company decisions, the firm may suffer.

Problem, Purpose, Reader. What is the precise problem? What is my specific purpose? Who is my reader? Answering these three questions is a basic step in planning and organizing the presentation before the task of writing begins.

We have selected or been assigned a specific topic area. We have checked the topic, limited our boundaries, investigated and determined how deeply we should pursue the problem, and finally, we have drawn up an outline.

Once we have carried through our research into primary and secondary sources, we are ready to begin writing.

Thinking and Reflection. Careful, reflective thinking about all the facets of the communication is a vital step in the writing process. And yet this aspect of communication is rarely mentioned in books on writing. Perhaps it is because the authors feel it should occur continually while the executive draws up his outline, limits his topic, and does his research. And this is true: The manager *should* be thinking about his end presentation.

But at this point he needs to devote a block of time to reflection on the topic.

Just as the researcher devoted time to all his other steps, he should now allocate time to sitting and thinking. This is not random or superficial thinking. Here we are talking about reflective thinking which carefully evaluates each section of the paper. Thought is given to the logic of the design, the psychology of treating this aspect before that one, the tone of the language, the approach to use, the arguments to put forward, the complexity of treatment, the words to be chosen, how each section fits into the whole communication, and how the whole meshes into the writer's overall purpose and the company's objective. Perhaps a primary goal of reflective thinking is to attempt to recognize the reader's frame of reference and determine what arguments, facts, and methods of presentation will motivate and interest him.

To accomplish this takes time and thinking which is truly analytical and reflective. The writer can use his final outline as a guide and carefully proceed from one point to the next, weighing, evaluating, and thinking from beginning to end.

Getting It Said. After the writer has gathered all his material, tabulated and interpreted his data, carefully checked his outline, and is confident that his paper will achieve his stated purpose, he is ready to begin to write.

The writing should be done as rapidly as possible. The purpose at this stage is for the writer to get his ideas on paper. Never mind the somewhat awkward sentence, the word that doesn't quite fit the situation, the obvious repetition, and the wordy paragraph. These will be taken care of in the editing process. The most important assignment now is to get the report, article, or account down on paper.

This stage should go rapidly, for the writer has finished his research and is familiar with his material. His detailed and logical outline is there to serve as a guide, and cards are filled with vital information waiting to be transferred to paper. All that needs to be done now is to write the first draft from the materials at hand.

Editing and Revising

A primary purpose of a piece of exposition is to present data, discussions, descriptions, conclusions, and recommendations as clearly and as accurately as possible. Faulty sentence structure, confusion in ideas, negligence in word choice, or any other carelessness in presentation which impedes the free flow of ideas must be corrected. The time to make these corrections, so that the ideas in the final paper flow smoothly and easily, is in the editing process.

People who have not done a great deal of writing may be somewhat surprised at how much work there is yet to do after the first draft has been completed. That first draft, as a matter of fact, is just the beginning. The serious job of rewriting must now be undertaken.

Sometimes sentences must be reworked completely, paragraphs thoroughly revised, and entire sections reorganized. Many of the famous authors of today attest to the fact that the major portion of their time is not spent in the original composition but in revising and rewriting—again and again—the initial draft.

The interesting, easy-to-read, and completely clear piece of management writing is usually the result of writing, revising, editing, correcting, rewriting, revising, and rewriting again, and again, and again. For most of us, the task is arduous and time-consuming. However, the results are always worth the effort.

If at all possible, the communicator should take a "cooling-off" period after he completes his first draft. His awkward sentences, inaccurate words, and errors in grammar will become more apparent after a few days. If he attempts to edit his first draft immediately after writing it, he may well read into the paper what he wishes to read.

In writing the first draft, our primary goal was to get the facts down as quickly and creatively as possible. In the editing process, we must proceed more slowly, coldly, and analytically. Material which needs cutting and revising should be cut and revised—drastically and thoroughly.

The Parts of the Whole

When we communicate we attempt to transmit ideas. We select words, order them into sentences, and connect the sentences to build paragraphs. The way we handle these three elements—words, sentences, paragraphs—largely determines how effective we are in making ourselves understandable to others.

Words

It is estimated that in the English language we have well over half a million words available to us. Many of these are compound words or words borrowed from other languages. Other entirely new words come from advances in the sciences, changes in the world of recreation, and the effects of unusual activities such as war.

But in using words we find that some are suited for communicating ideas on the golf course, while others are preferable at the technical conference devoted to the use of transistors in new electronic components. Different levels of words, like different levels of dress, are designed for use in specific situations. You would not wear formal dress to a baseball game or a sport shirt and slacks to an evening wedding. Similarly, you would not ordinarily use slang and jargon in an article for the *Harvard Business Review* or highly complex technical terms in explaining the use of lasers to a Cub Scout group.

Perrin, in his excellent work *Writer's Guide and Index to English,*[1] divides words into two general groups: nonstandard and standard. The former is primarily spoken, characterized by regional colloquialisms, used in conversation but not for business or public affairs. Standard English is of three types: informal, general, and formal. Informal is more often spoken than written; it is used in informal situations and includes shoptalk and slang. General English, both spoken and written, is appropriate in almost any situation. It is commonly used in conversation and writing between friends, usual business letters,

---

[1] Porter G. Perrin, *Writer's Guide and Index to English,* 5th ed. rev. by Karl W. Dykema and Wilma R. Ebbitt (Glenview, Ill.: Scott, Foresman and Company, 1972).

newspaper features, magazine articles directed to the general public, and comments on radio and television. Formal English, according to Perrin, is more often written than spoken and is used in literary, scientific, technical, and academic writing and speaking. Perrin emphasizes that these classifications do not imply that one type of English is better than another.

Correctness.　If they are to communicate ideas effectively, words must be used carefully and correctly. There are two categories of words commonly misused: those that sound alike but have different meanings and those that are somewhat similar in sound or have the same root (see Appendix A).

Words that sound alike but are spelled differently and have different meanings (homonyms) are very common in English: where, wear, ware; bear, bare; would, wood; principle, principal; council, counsel; see, sea; bow, bough; and many others. Most people know what these words mean; the difficulty comes in spelling them. If in a business letter you write *principle* when you mean *principal*, the recipient will figure out what you mean, but he may feel that you are careless in communication and perhaps equally careless in how you handle his order or request.

Examples of the second group of misused words also abound: uninterested, disinterested; imply, infer; credible, creditable; unorganized, disorganized; incredible, incredulous. A judge on the bench should be disinterested in the case being tried before him, but surely not uninterested. When I am speaking, I imply something; when you are listening, you infer something.

The writer or speaker who uses *disorganized* when he means *unorganized,* or *healthy* when he means *healthful,* not only lessens the exactness of his statement but confuses the reader or listener, and, in the long run, helps corrupt and weaken our language.

The carpenter who uses a screwdriver when he should use a chisel will probably produce a less desirable cabinet; when we use second-rate words (our tools), we put forward ideas which have less impact because they are not expressed as they should be.

Accuracy and Precision.　Words have two distinct traits: denotation and connotation. The denotation of a word is its factual meaning or definition. Its connotation, on the other hand, is the sum of thoughts and emotions it arouses or contains. (See the article by Hayakawa, "How Words Change Our Lives," in the Readings.)

A single word may have several denotations. The word *vessel,* for example, may refer to a component in the body's circulatory system, a container for liquids, or a water-borne vehicle. As a noun, *rest* may mean repose, something used for support, a pause in music, or remainder. Yet there is little chance of confusion among these meanings; the context will make obvious which denotation is intended.

It is the connotations of words that create difficulties in communication. The word *capitalism* denotes the same thing to Americans and Soviets, but the connotations are opposite. Everybody knows what *soldier* "means"; but consider the different emotions the word arouses in a man who has been recognized as a hero, and in an individual who now lives in Canada because he left the U.S.

to avoid the draft. What different feelings do you have about the words *fat, obese, roly-poly, plump?* All have the same denotation. Manufacturers of a diet food would never say it makes you skinny; they would say it makes you slim or slender. Do you want an after-shave lotion that has a smell, a scent, a perfume, an aroma, or an odor? Yet they all have the same denotation. The picture we wish to paint can be conveyed very accurately with the words we choose for our colors.

Attention to connotation is of primary importance in business communication. We have already seen its significance in advertising; and business letters and reports are a form of advertising—for yourself and your firm. A letter over your name is your image to the recipient; if it creates unpleasant feelings it may be worse than no letter at all.

Remember *who* your reader or listener is, and choose your words with his feelings, his educational and social level, and his needs in mind.

Sentences

Writing that is clear, concise, and motivates and persuades others is effective. Such writing is based on sentences that are cogent and memorable.

In some material we read, the sentences seem to flow into each other smoothly, effortlessly, enjoyably. Other material must be read and reread, for the writing seems choppy, difficult, awkward, and stumbling.

The level of complexity probably has something to do with ease of reading, but more important is style, the way sentences are put together. What factors contribute to effective sentence structure? How does one write sentences that flow rather than stumble? There are, of course, no simple answers, but there are some directions we can follow. First, however, we should be familiar with sentence structure and classification.

Types of Sentences. There are four primary kinds of sentences. The most common is the declarative, which is a positive or negative assertion. Others are the interrogative, which asks a question; the imperative, which expresses a command or a wish; and the exclamatory. These all begin with a capital letter, end with the appropriate punctuation, and usually contain a subject and a verb.

Sentences may be formed in several ways. A simple sentence consists of one independent clause; a compound sentence consists of two or more independent clauses. A complex sentence is composed of one independent and one or more subordinate clauses; and a compound-complex sentence is made up of two or more independent clauses and at least one subordinate clause.

Variety of Sentence Structure. It is important to make writing clear and interesting. One way to do that effectively is to vary sentence structure. Paragraphs composed entirely of compound sentences are monotonous and boring; paragraphs constructed only of simple sentences are choppy, childish, and lacking in grace. However, the judicious use of a simple sentence can give writing force and impact. Complex sentences, because they are made up of independent and dependent clauses, clarify meaning and make for easier reading. Compound-complex sentences, in that they have inherent variety, also give vitality and interest to writing.

For variety within a sentence, use an occasional command, exhortation, exclamation, or question to replace the usual declarative sentence. Or why not modify the usual subject-verb sequence, beginning a sentence with a phrase or subordinate clause to give details as a lead-in to the main idea of the independent clause?

Notice the differences in the examples that follow. Compare the abruptness and unnecessary overlapping of the simple sentences, and the monotony of the compound sentences, with the smoothness and variety of the sentences on the far right.

Simple Sentences	*Compound Sentences*	*Variety of Sentence Types*
Management in any large corporation is dependent on information. This information is secured from many departments within a company. Sales, credit, production, research, advertising, and other departments forward information. This information is sent "up" to management. Often this information is in the form of reports. The information in these reports is usually gathered by each department. It is necessary that the content of these reports be accurate and complete. This is necessary because decisions are made on the basis of the content. Obviously decisions cannot be made if the reports do not contain adequate substantiating data. These data are usually statistical.	Management in any large corporation is dependent on information, and this information is received from many departments within the company. Sales, credit, production, research, advertising, and other departments forward information, and this information is then sent up to management. Often this information is in the form of reports, and this information is usually gathered by each department. It is necessary that the content of these reports be accurate and complete and this is necessary because decisions are made on the basis of the content. Obviously decisions cannot be made if the reports do not contain adequate substantiating data and these data are usually statistical.	Management in any large corporation is dependent on the information it receives from the sales, credit, production, research, advertising, and other departments. This information, which is sent "up," is usually in the form of reports. The substantiating data (usually statistical) in these reports must be accurate and complete, for decisions are made on the basis of the facts provided.

When sentences are well written, they impress, they persuade, they motivate the reader. Sentence structure that will accomplish these ends must be more than correct grammatically. It must often be dramatic and certainly imaginative.[2] Here are some good examples:

> Never before has man had such capacity to control his own environment—to end thirst and hunger—to banish illiteracy and massive human misery. We have the power to make this the best generation of mankind . . . or to make it the last. . . .

> If we fail to make the most of this moment and this momentum, if we convert our new-found hopes and understanding into new walls and weapons of hostility, if this pause in the cold war leads to its renewal and not to its end, then the shaming indictment of posterity will rightly point its finger at us all.[3]

There is, of course, a danger that the writer may write purely for the purpose of impressing the reader with catchy sentences rather than communicating ideas. This is quickly recognized as an artifice for gaining attention, and such writing soon becomes tiresome.

Revising Sentences. The best way to write, as the old saw goes, is to write. Get your ideas down in black and white; let the sentences flow from your mind to the paper.

After you have written down a complete block of ideas, go back and edit and revise the awkward and wordy sentences. As you become more critical of your own writing and more adept at revising sentences, you will find that your ability will steadily improve.

Lack of Clarity	*Improved*
Burns worked in his dad's store while attending school, and although he majored in management, I don't think he liked it.	Burns worked in his dad's store while attending school. He majored in management, but I don't think he liked the field.
To fly efficiently, a good pilot should check his plane after every flight.	If a plane is to fly efficiently, it should be checked after every flight.

Dangling	*Improved*
Arriving home late, dinner was started immediately.	Because we arrived home later than usual, we prepared dinner immediately.
Running down the sidewalk near the hospital which was a new modern building built to handle children's cases.	John ran down the sidewalk adjacent to the new children's hospital.

[2] See the Royal Bank of Canada Monthly Letter, "Imagination Helps Communication," in the Readings.
[3] From the speech of President John F. Kennedy to the United Nations, September 20, 1963.

Faulty Sentence Structure

When I first started to play tennis with John, I found that my serve was quite good. Although I had not played for six years.

When I write a report, I find that it requires a good deal of concentrated effort and work, this is, as I think of it, necessary when I do any type of writing.

Improved

When I first started to play tennis with John, I found that my serve was quite good, even though I had not played for six years.

When I write a report, I find that it requires a good deal of concentrated effort and work. This is true, as I think of it, of any type of writing I do.

Wordy and Archaic Sentence Structure

The annual report serves, by and large, two very important purposes today and the first of which is the presentation of financial information to stockholders and the second is to build company public relations in the business community at large.

You will find enclosed, as per your basic request, the report which we have taken the liberty of forwarding to you.

Improved

The annual report serves two primary functions: the presentation of financial data to stockholders and the building of company public relations in the business community.

The report that you requested is enclosed.

These examples demonstrate what can be done when a serious attempt is made to edit and revise. Improvement is not difficult; all that is necessary is a merciless blue pencil and an acceptance of nothing less than excellence in sentence structure.

Perhaps the first step in editing is to be sure the thought and ideas which you have in mind are clear. Peter Drucker in an article titled "What Communication Means" stated:

There is a very old saying among writers: "Difficulties with a sentence always mean confused thinking. It is not the sentence that needs straightening out, it is the thought behind it." In writing, people attempt, of course, to communicate with themselves. An "unclear sentence" is one that exceeds the writer's own capacity for perception. Working on the sentence—that is, working on what is normally called communications—cannot solve the problem. The writer has to work on his own concepts first to be able to understand what he is trying to say—and only then can he write the sentence.[4]

The experienced editor develops techniques to assist him. One is to evaluate a sentence by reading it aloud and listening. If it sounds awkward to the ear, it should probably be revised. Many people, when revising an awkward sentence, will scratch out a word here and move a phrase there. The usual result of this minor surgery is that some improvement takes place in the sick sentence, but it cannot usually be placed on the healthy list. Drastic surgery is often called for. Remove the sentence completely and begin again. The new version will usually say just what you mean.

And a final technique is to use your dictionary and thesaurus; don't be satisfied with the almost-right word. Search your thesaurus until you find the word which conveys *precisely* the thought you had in mind and also gives your sentence the rhythm and tone you desire.

Paragraphs

A paragraph is a group of related sentences which help advance the development of the paper. Each paragraph, though joined to the one before and the one following, develops an individual idea. Thus, carefully constructed paragraphs serve the double purpose of joining and separating. Each paragraph should develop one idea, whether that idea is explicitly stated or not. Each paragraph should add to the reader's knowledge or understanding either of the topic or of the paper itself.

The expository paragraph tells about the topic. It is linked at top and bottom with other paragraphs, but it develops, explains, illustrates, or supports a particular point. It can do this by particularization, by example, by definition of terms, by contrast and comparison, by analysis, by classification, or by narration.

The transitional or emphatic paragraph, on the other hand, assists the reader. A paragraph of transition says, "This is where we have been; that is where we're going—so get ready." The paragraph of emphasis says, "That was an important point we just passed; did you get it?"

When you rewrite your paper, be sure not only that you have chosen the right words and put those words together into clear sentences, but that those sentences are combined into logical, useful paragraphs.

[4] Peter Drucker, "What Communication Means," *Management Today*, March 1970.

Qualities of Writing Style

Most authorities, in a discussion of writing style, list the three standard qualities of rhetoric: unity, coherence, and emphasis. There are others, however, which certainly deserve more than a passing glance: consideration for the reader, clarity, liveliness, and grace.

It is a writer's style which makes his work uniquely his. This author's work is lively, his is dull, hers is persuasive, and another's is consistently entertaining. These qualities come from the heart of the composition and make up the rather indefinable quality that we label *style*.

Every communication written by a businessman should have an effective style. Of course, few executives will approach the excitement of Hemingway, the humor of Thurber, the insight of Shakespeare, or the precision of Churchill. On the other hand, their writing need not be as dull as an inventory form or as uninspired as a page of stock quotations.

Unity and Coherence

Every paragraph should develop an idea; a group of paragraphs should move a single topic forward; and the sections of the paper should all contribute to the development of the specific aspect with which the message is concerned.

Irrelevant details and materials which are not directly related to the core idea must be eliminated. Then the paper must be checked to determine if it possesses this quality of "oneness" or unity. Each sentence, each paragraph, each section must march forward toward the objective the writer hopes to achieve. If it does not, strike it out.

Coherence is attained when the ideas are logically interconnected, they smoothly follow one another, and their meaning is clear and easily comprehended. When sentences and paragraphs are connected with transitional words, phrases, and sentences, the whole body of material seems to move interestingly and coherently from one idea to another. In this way, thoughts are not isolated, but they are related to each other and all together they proceed logically toward a specific conclusion.

Transitional words assist in achieving coherence, for they connect sentences to each other. Phrases, clauses, or sentences may also be used as transitional devices between paragraphs. And in a long report or other piece of extended writing, paragraphs help bind the sections within the paper to one another.

Coherence also means clarity and accuracy in writing. This requires attention to word choice, sentence structure, and the many other areas of diction and rhetoric which make any piece of communication informative and valuable to read.

Courtesy and Consideration

In any kind of communication, oral or written, business or personal, one of the prime requisites is consideration for the recipient. Courtesy and consideration are easy to achieve, and well worth the effort involved.

In business communication, much more than common courtesy is involved. Discourtesy or thoughtlessness might mean the loss of a good customer or of a large sale. It might mean loss of prestige and status. It would almost surely mean a lessening of respect and approval for you and your company.

Basic to consideration is a knowledge of your reader. If you know who he is, what he wants, and why he wants it, you can even refuse him without offending. Remember to write in terms of "you" rather than "I." A customer is interested in *his* request or complaint, and you must be too.

It is a literary vice not to seek out the reader's interest. You may tell him what you want in impeccable language and forceful manner, but you fall short of success unless you pay attention to what he wants or can be made to desire. Your ideas must enter, influence and stick in the mind of the recipient.

As a writer, you may protest that some of the failure in communication may be blamed on the receiver, but it is your responsibility as sender to determine in advance, to the best of your ability, all potential causes of failure and to tune your transmission for the best reception.[5]

The second ingredient for a courteous business letter is "Please," "Thank you," "I'm sorry," "I'm delighted." Liberal—but not maudlin—use of these words will give your reader the feeling not only that you are polite but that you care about him.

The third ingredient in consideration goes back to knowing your reader. Use words and phrases and ideas that are on his level. If you talk over his head, he will feel unhappy, insecure, and inferior. This is no way to gain confidence. If you talk beneath him, he will be insulted. This, too, will defeat your aims.

Courtesy and consideration, then, are among the easiest attributes to achieve in communication. Their accomplishment requires from you only sensitivity and a little care.

Emphasis

At times we wish to persuade our reader to take specific action as recommended in certain segments of our writing; or perhaps we wish to bring a particular section of the paper into sharper focus. This requires that significant sections be emphasized.

There are a variety of methods that can be used by the business writer to achieve emphasis. There is the simple method of *proportion*, which involves giving more space to a key point than to items of less importance. If the writer spends four pages discussing sales and only half a page on credit, production, and research, it is obvious that he wishes to focus the reader's attention on sales.

Repetition of facts, ideas, or words also helps to emphasize what is desired. An idea may be discussed in the paper, presented factually in a table, and commented on again in a further analysis.

The thoughtful positioning or *placement* of ideas within the body of the

---

[5] The Royal Bank of Canada Monthly Letter, "Imagination Helps Communication" (see Readings).

writing may also be a device to secure emphasis. Statements made in the early portion of the presentation, or at the beginning of a section, often receive special attention.

Attention-catching words or phrases may be used to emphasize ideas. This use of dramatic words or alliterative phrases need not be limited to advertising writing; it can be used effectively in expository writing as well.

The use of *mechanical methods* has some value when the writer wishes to emphasize a particular point. Emphasis may be secured by capitalizing words, underscoring phrases, using colored inks, or inserting cartoons, sketches, and photographs. In addition, an idea or thought can be set off by itself with a dramatic amount of white space around it.

But perhaps the most effective way to emphasize a point is through *excellent writing.* One's writing should be so effective, so clear, so persuasive that the reader will remember the ideas because of the quality of the writing and not because of capitalized phrases or underscored ideas.

Securing emphasis through this method—good writing—is not easy. It requires analysis, time, and constant reference to the dictionary and thesaurus. But it is worth it, for effective writing makes an indelible impression in the reader's mind. A well-written statement may be recalled for years, while an underlined sentence may be forgotten in a few minutes.

Imagination

Imagination is important in business writing. Achieving it requires a sensitivity to words and a desire to find the exact words and combinations of words to impart not only facts but feelings. Writing that is a pleasure to read— emphatic phrases, clear and concise statements, ideas imaginatively presented—is more likely to achieve its purpose than writing that is dull, awkward, heavy-handed, and pompous.

The writer with *imagination* not only will put himself in the place of his reader but will also look for the word, the analogy, the figure that best expresses what he wants to say. He will avoid clichés and ambiguities, worn-out similes, and irritating redundancies.

Here are some examples of Winston Churchill's liveliness and grace in writing:

> Even though large tracts of Europe and many old and famous states have fallen or may fall into the grip of the Gestapo and all the odious apparatus of Nazi rule, we shall not flag or fail. We shall go on to the end, we shall fight in France, we shall fight on the seas and the oceans, we shall fight with growing confidence and growing strength in the air, we shall defend our island, whatever the cost may be, we shall fight in the hills; we shall never surrender, and even if, which I do not for a moment believe, this island or a large part of it were subjugated and starving, then our empire beyond the seas, armed and guarded by the British fleet, would carry on the struggle, until, in God's good time, the New World, with all its power and might, steps forth to the rescue and liberation of the Old.
>
> Speech to the House of Commons
> on the fall of Dunkirk, June 4, 1940

I would say to the House, as I have said to those who have joined this government: "I have nothing to offer but blood, toil, tears and sweat."

We have before us an ordeal of the most grievous kind. We have before us many, many long months of struggle and of suffering. You ask, What is our policy? I will say: It is to wage war, by sea, land and air, with all our might and with all the strength that God can give us; to wage war against a monstrous tyranny, never surpassed in the dark lamentable catalog of human crime. That is our policy.

You ask, What is our aim? I can answer in one word: Victory—victory at all costs, victory in spite of all terror, victory however long and hard the road may be . . . .
First statement to the House of Commons
as prime minister, May 13, 1940

Imagination not only requires that the writer determine the reader's interest and communicate toward that end, but he must also have the imagination to choose words that will strike a chord of response. Notice in the quotation on page 104 that the author says "tune" your transmission, not "adapt" or "design" your transmission. The word *tune* is so much more meaningful and colorful than the others, and it is much more intimately and accurately associated with the terms "transmission" and "reception." Also note the imaginative word choices below:

If you do not wish your letters to be read yawningly, write them wide awake. When a good idea strikes you . . . , ride that idea on the dead run: don't wait to ponder, criticize and correct. You can be critical after your imaginative spell subsides.[6]

Imaginative writing will have variety; this is as important in prose as it is in music. A good symphony has variety of tone and timing: the tempo is fast and slow; the sound level is high and low; the measures are strong and weak. A monotonous symphony, like a monotonous paper, is boring. In your writing, therefore, use a variety of sentence types; use a short sentence now and then for dramatic impact, an alliterative phrase for rhythm and sound. Choose words that are lively and colorful; try to use new words sometimes; put words into new combinations.

Be aware of alliteration, assonance, and consonance. Read aloud what you have written. Does it *sound* right? Does its sound echo its sense? Does the mood of the language fit the mood of the subject, of the ideas? Write so your reader will *want* to read what you have written.

Editing Suggestions

You should review your first draft several times; in each review, give special attention to a specific quality of writing. Step back, so to speak, from the paper and determine if every sentence, every paragraph, every section contributes to the theme and purpose. If any portion, whether a word or a paragraph, can be construed as being irrelevant or unnecessary, it should be cut

[6] The Royal Bank of Canada Letter, "Imagination Helps Communication" (see Readings).

without compunction.

Then check for coherence. Is there good transition between ideas? Do the sentences and paragraphs seem to be logically associated and connected? Do the sections flow into one another easily and smoothly?

What about word choice? Does every sentence say precisely what you mean it to? Do the words have the exact connotations intended? Does this phrase or that clause result in the proper picture in the reader's or listener's mind? No second-choice word or group of words is acceptable here; use your dictionary or thesaurus to find the exact words, the words that will convey the precise idea, tone, and mood. Take every opportunity to use lively words, similes, metaphors, and various figures of speech that will give your writing vitality and color.

Then check for clarity. If there is any possibility—even a slim one—that a phrase or sentence may be misinterpreted, strike it out and rewrite it so that it says precisely what you intended.

Emphasis can be achieved by proper placement of key ideas, by inserting topic and subtopic headings, and by the judicious use of detail.

Examine carefully all statistical data in your paper. Would the use of charts or graphs make your presentation clearer and easier to read? Tables, charts, diagrams, and other visuals must be used with restraint, but they are an important tool in communication. (See Chapter Twenty for a detailed discussion of visuals and how they can be used most effectively.)

What does a piece of writing look like before and after editing? Below we have a short section of the first draft of a report and the revision after editing.

```
                          ORIGINAL VERSION


    Sales for the month of June were, by and large, higher than
    they were for a similar period last year, but not appreciably
    so, at least to the extent where we might now consider sit-
    ting on "our laurels" so to speak.  As a matter of fact, the
    increase was only approximately 4.5% over last year's sales
    which were just average for the industry.

    As the reader is probably aware, our three primary lines are
    children's desks (in three different models), record cabinets
    (also in three different models), and our two different styles
    in end tables.

    Sales for this period, in all these products, have increased
    appreciably and we have found it necessary to have a corre-
    sponding increase in personnel.  As a matter of fact we have
    increased our sales personnel by two full-time men in each
    of our five sales districts for a total increase of sales per-
    sonnel of ten.  Thus with a total of 65 full-time sales person-
    nel, we have the largest staff of this type of any company in
    this field.

    But back to the discussion of sales for June of this year.
    In the area of children's desks, 365 dozen of the model 185
    were sold, 413 of the model 186, and 429 of the model 187.
    This is in contrast to 350, 395, and 405 of the models 185,
```

186, and 187 respectively in June of last year. Sales of record cabinets also went up quite dramatically but with one exception.

Record cabinet model 201 sold 215 dozen; 202 was 262 dozen; and model 203 sold 185 dozen. These figures also reflect an increase over June of last year with the exception of model 203 which dropped 65 dozen. This is difficult to explain except for the fact that Mr. Barnard of Barnard's Furniture did not like our new styling in 203 and wouldn't order one much less his usual quantity. Of course, he has extremely strong likes and dislikes which we have encountered before. However other dealers declined to order this 203 model also. As for last year's sales on record cabinets, we sold 205 dozen of 201, 251 dozen of 202, and 250 dozen of 203.

On the whole, sales of end tables were increased in June of this year over last year. See appendix one for details.

As for advertising and sales personnel, there are several comments which need discussion so that a better line of integration between sales, personnel, and advertising can be instituted. Cooperation in the past has been somewhat less than desirable.

AFTER EDITING

Sales for the month of June were approximately 4.5 percent higher than in the similar period last year. Although this is an improvement, it is not dramatic and we should make every effort to increase this figure in the future.

Sales Volume

The table which follows shows our sales for this period:

Sales Volume
(in Dozens)

Model	June 1976	June 1975
Desks		
185	365	350
186	413	395
187	429	405
Cabinets		
201	215	205
202	262	251
203	185	250
Tables		
101	760	697
102	870	791

```
The dramatic decline in sales of cabinet 203 was apparently
due to our new and rather unusual design which was not favor-
ably received.

                        Sales Personnel

To keep up with expanding sales, our personnel in this divi-
sion was increased by a total of 10 (2 per sales district).
The sales force now numbers 65 full-time men.

                 Advertising and Sales Promotion

On June 27, a meeting was held with the heads of the adver-
tising, personnel, and sales departments present. . . .
```

The edited version is much easier to read and assimilate than the wordy, unorganized original version.

Here are a few examples of edited and unedited material. Note how clarity almost always improves when material is made more concise.

Original: The Purchasing Department has a vital, basic, and important responsibility to interview all vendors who make themselves available at Company offices and examine all bids which are submitted by those firms who have been accepted and placed on the approved buyer roster. The Manual for Purchasing Agents, not the 1972 edition but the one published in 1975, contains specific recommendations on completing Request for Quotation forms.

Revised: The Purchasing Department has a responsibility to interview all vendors and examine all bids submitted by those firms listed on the approved buyer roster. The 1975 Manual for Purchasing Agents contains specific recommendations on completing Request for Quotation forms.

Original: The business executive has many duties to carry through in industry today. He is frequently called upon to make decisions involving the expenditure of funds, future corporate plans, and movement of personnel. He also must attend various meetings of a professional nature. In addition to this, he is frequently sought out as a counselor by subordinates. And on some occasions he must serve as the company's representative to community groups. These are only a few of the tasks the modern executive is expected to carry through.

Revised: Today's business executive has many duties to perform. Some of these are:

1. Decision making for the expenditure of funds, for corporate planning, and for the movement of personnel.
2. Attendance at professional meetings.
3. Counseling of subordinates.
4. Serving as the company representative to community groups.

Original: It has been requested of our organization that we offer approval of a 20-year lease arrangement of 200 acres of State property in the Del Monte area (see map enclosure) to the Michaelson Company for proper handling and development of said area. The Michaelson Company would be obliged to immediately prepare plans for a recreation area in the Del Monte area, such plans to be submitted no later than March 1. The lease would further require that a master plan be prepared for the greater Del Monte area of 500 acres (see map enclosure) and that such a master plan for a State Park be presented no later than April 15. The Michaelson Company is further required to begin actual work on the initial Del Monte area and complete all work to the satisfaction of the State Department of Recreation no later than December 1. All agreements between the Department of Recreation and the Michaelson Company are subject to acceptance by the proper state legislative committees.

Revised: The State Legal Division has been requested to evaluate a 20-year lease of 200 acres of State property in the Del Monte area (see map enclosure) to the Michaelson Company. This firm would be required:

1. To prepare plans for a recreation area in the Del Monte area to be submitted no later than March 1.

2. To prepare a master plan for the greater Del Monte area of 500 acres (see map enclosure) and submit it no later than April 15.

3. To complete all work on the initial Del Monte area to the satisfaction of the State Department of Recreation no later than December 1.

All agreements between the Department of Recreation and the Michaelson Company are subject to acceptance by the proper state legislative committees.

Gunning's Suggestions for Improving Readability.

Robert Gunning[7] offers a series of suggestions to keep in mind when writing. His points sound deceptively simple and, like most recommendations, are much easier to make than to achieve. Of course there is much more to effective composition than the points Gunning makes. Yet his list is a convenient guide against which to check your own writing.

1. Keep sentences short, on the average.

Gunning points out that there is nothing wrong with a clear forty- or fifty-word sentence, as long as it is balanced with a few that are six, eight, or ten words long. Of course, a short sentence that lacks other qualities of effective communication will have no value.

2. Use the simple rather than the complex.

If we can say, "It was difficult to free the youngster's leg from the drainpipe," why should we say, "Major difficulties of a complex nature were encountered in the process of extricating the lower left limb of the adolescent from . . . ." Write directly, simply, and to the point.

3. Select familiar words.

Use a vocabulary of words that is familiar to your reading group. In one case the best term may be *concomitant strabismus;* in another, it may be *cross-eyed.*

4. Avoid unnecessary words.

[7] *The Technique of Clear Writing* (New York: McGraw-Hill Book Company, 1952). See also Robert Gunning, *New Guide to More Effective Writing in Business and Industry* (Boston: Industrial Education Institute, 1962). Gunning is also responsible for an excellent readability index commonly called "The Gunning Fog Index."

Much of the writing done in business today is padded, wordy, and pompous. It is simple to eliminate unnecessary words and thereby improve the writing. Rather than saying, "May we take the liberty of saying that in accordance with your request, you will find enclosed Baxter drawing #305 . . . . ," it is better to state, "Enclosed is Baxter drawing #305 . . . ."

5. Use active, not passive, sentences.
Passive: A sharp drop in production was noted.
Active: Production dropped sharply.

Writing in the active rather than the passive voice results in more alive, more vivid, and more interesting prose.

6. Write as you talk.
In this recommendation, Gunning does not really want you to "write as you talk." If you did, your writing would contain a good deal of repetition, awkward phrases, and most certainly an inexcusable quantity of unnecessary words. What he is suggesting is that our writing reflect the friendly, natural tone we usually use when we talk.

Perhaps it would be more accurate to say that when we write, we should sound as though we are talking.

7. Use terms your reader can picture.
We noted earlier in our discussion that words make pictures in people's minds. When the words are concrete (chair, pen, lamp), the picture in the communicator's mind will probably be similar to that in the receiver's mind.

However, the task of securing the same picture in the minds of the sender and the receiver is more difficult when abstract terms are used. Because of this it is better to say "Please pay within three days" than to say "It is highly desirable that payment be forthcoming at your earliest convenience."

Why talk about "unavoidable exigencies which may result from the complexities of morality which infringe on the juvenile's activities" when it is easier to say "Problems of morality frequently confront today's youngsters"?

8. Relate your writing to the reader's experience.
Your writing should present material from the reader's point of view. It isn't enough to explain the company profit-sharing program; you must explain it in relation to the employee and *his* family, *his* job, *his* experiences.

9. Use variety in your writing.
Go from simple to complex sentences, from long to short statements. Choose words, from time to time, that will make your reader "sit up and take notice": "If you do not wish your letter to be read yawningly, write them wide awake." (See "Imagination Helps Communication" in the Readings.)

10. Write to express and not to impress.
Many of us feel that it is necessary, in our everyday activities, to impress someone with the importance of our job, the outstanding facts in our education, or the world-shaking impact of what we say. Skip such artificiality in writing or speaking. It fools no one. Pomposity is always recognized for what it is.

Throw out the long words, the unusual words, the pompous phrases, and the overlong sentences. They will impress no one, and they do not help express ideas.

These, briefly, are Gunning's suggestions for achieving clarity in writing.

Several of them are very closely related and appear to overlap. Furthermore, the reader may feel that Gunning reduces effective writing to a too-simple formula. But his suggestions have much to recommend them, and they can be adapted to individual needs.

The Final Product

Now that the writing and editing of the final draft have been completed, you should check one more aspect of your paper: the overall appearance.

Topic Headings

Is each new section properly headed? Will the busy reader be required to read through the 16 pages on employee fringe benefits to find the section on sick-leave pay or will he be able to find that section quickly because it is preceded by a heading?

You can assist your reader by using topic and subtopic headings. Choose your words for them carefully. Be sure these headings are concise and meaningful.

Every busy executive is delighted when he can skim through a paper and see at a glance the major and minor areas that are discussed. He can quickly note the organizational pattern (or outline) the writer had in mind and thus appreciate the method of development and emphasis. With such knowledge, he can then select the specific section or sections that require his detailed study.

The use of headings also assists the writer: he is faced with a constant reminder to deal only with the topic noted. It is difficult to digress when a guide of three or four words heads the section. Thus, topic headings serve as road markers for both reader and writer.

Below are the beginning sections of two reports. Note the advantages of the one which uses topic headings: it is visually more attractive, areas covered are immediately obvious, and the organization of the whole paper is clear. (It is also better for other reasons. Can you tell why?)

I.

A report on the activities of the personnel department must include comments in a variety of areas. For example, if we consider training which is under the direction of the Personnel Manager, we must examine shop training, office and clerical, and management training. In the case of shop training, we completed the instruction of eight groups of twenty men each. Each group met for a total of 21 hours of instruction in seven 3-hour sessions.

In the area of office and clerical training, we carried through instruction for eight groups of fifteen persons per group. Four classes were devoted to Office Procedures, and four groups received training in Written Communication. Each class met two hours a week for six weeks.

Management training was carried through on a seminar basis with each of ten groups (twenty men per group) receiving eighteen hours of instruction. Classes met for two-hour sessions once each week for nine weeks. Five groups examined the area of Human Relations, while the other five devoted their time to Management Communication.

The personnel department is also responsible for corporate safety programs and employee health care. In the case of safety, we are concerned with employee accident prevention in two areas. The first is internal or in-plant. In this area, each department (there are 32 designated departments in the company) has one man assigned as the safety officer. He holds this job for one year and receives $50.00 in extra compensation each month. He is expected to attend after-hours safety meetings, give instruction in his department, and do everything possible to protect the health of our employees. We feel this program has been successful, for in our classification of accidents into Categories I, II, and III (see Appendix One for definitions), the number has dropped in the three categories respectively to 28, 46, 150 this year as compared with 48, 72, and 190 last year.

Our external safety program is primarily concerned with our truck drivers, service men, and sales personnel. This program is under the direction of one person in the personnel office. His work has proved successful, as indicated by this year's figures of 18, 24, 38 for Categories, I, II, and III as compared to 26, 32, and 48 for last year.

Our employee health care program is divided into three areas: Preventive Medicine, Retired Employees' Health, and New Employee Medical Evaluation. In the case of the first area . . . .

II.

Personnel Department Report

The Personnel Department Report which follows covers only three areas: Training, Safety, and Employee Health.

Training

Almost 500 company personnel were involved this year in various training programs:

Shop Training. Eight groups of twenty men each were given instruction in various areas of shop activity. Each group met for three-hour periods once a week for seven weeks.

Office and Clerical Training. Eight groups of fifteen persons each met for two hours once each week for six weeks. Four groups concentrated on Office Procedures, while the other four received instruction in Written Communication.

Management Training. Ten groups of twenty men each met in seminars for two hours once a week for nine weeks. Five groups were concerned with Human Relations, while the other five studied Management Communication.

Safety Programs

The primary purpose of these programs is accident prevention and the development of safety awareness on the part of all employees. For administrative purposes, our safety program is divided into "in-plant" and external. Each of the 32 departments within the company has a designated safety officer who receives additional compensation of $50 per month for this added responsibility. His specific assignments include giving safety instruction, attendance at safety meetings, and related duties.

Our external safety program is under the direction of an assistant in the personnel department and covers truck drivers, service men, and sales personnel.

Both programs are proving successful, as the following table indicates:

REPORTABLE ACCIDENTS

Category*	1976	1975
Internal		
I	28	48
II	46	72
III	150	190
External		
I	18	26
II	24	32
III	38	48

I = minor
II = requiring medical attention
III = requiring home or hospital confinement

Employee Health Care Programs

Although this program was begun five years ago, it has proved extremely popular with our employees. It is presently divided into three areas: Preventive Medicine, Retired Employees' Health, and New Employee Medical Evaluation.

Preventive Medicine

In this particular area . . . .

White Space

It is foolish to spend a good deal of time and money on a report or letter and then economize on paper. The generous use of white space in the margins, between sections, above and below tables and charts, and on a title page adds immeasurably to the appeal of your presentation.

The well-balanced page looks inviting; the material is easy to read and easy to assimilate. This is in contrast to the appearance of a "heavy" page that has typing from the very top to the very bottom and only a half-inch margin on either side.

Appendixes, Charts, Supplements

The technical paper may require various supporting documents. To include this material in the text may upset the continuity of the discussion. This is especially true if such material is relevant to the topic but not vital. In such cases, the information should be placed in a footnote, if it is brief, or in an appendix. Sometimes a complete set of supporting documents must accompany a study; these can be placed in an appendix.

At times *extensive* tables or charts may serve their purpose better when placed at the end of a paper. Here clever fold-outs, gate folds, and lay-overs[8] can be employed.

[8] A graph reflecting trend lines may be drawn on transparent paper and so inserted that it may be laid over a related graph or chart so that contrasts are made more obvious.

Various supplements may also be made part of the whole presentation to aid in understanding. These would include sales promotion materials, statistics, company records, etc.

These are all valuable to include, but if they are not *vital* to the message being presented, they should be attached as additions to the report proper. Nothing should be permitted to interfere with the reader's understanding and assimilation of the core idea of the presentation.

Bindings, Introductory Pages, and Reproduction

Some type of binder is vital for a study, research document, or report. It is usually an important document, and a good binder helps the reader examine it, file it, or forward it to others.

The firm which issues many reports may use a standard binder; other companies may use anything from an inexpensive folder to an attractive plastic spiral affair. Here again, one should not be penny-wise and pound-foolish in his selection of a cover.

Introductory pages, such as the title page, table of contents, or list of illustrations, should be tastefully designed and meaningful in their designations.

How the paper is reproduced depends on the number of copies desired and the size of the budget available. The report writer may profit from the advice of a printing consultant. Of course, if only a limited number of copies are needed, the report should be typed. The results achieved by a competent secretary, using an electric typewriter with a contemporary type style, are invariably excellent.

Questions for Study

I. Complete any of the following problems assigned. You may wish to review the chapter and note key points before solving a problem.

1. Although most of us recognize that we should draw up a plan before we make an oral or written presentation, we often do not. Can you explain this apparent lack of logic?

2. List several factors which should be considered before designing a tentative outline.

3. What changes should be made in the following three outlines to make them more logical?

   (1) *Monthly Sales Report, TRM Corporation*
      I. Total Sales Volume
        A. Sales of Able Line
        B. Sales of Baker Line
        C. Sales of Charlie Line
      II. Sales Personnel
        A. Total number of salesmen
          1. District A
          2. District B
        B. Sales Trainees

III. Finance
    A. Stock issue
    B. Change in sales personnel compensation policies
IV. Analysis of sales accounts
    A. Over $50,000 in purchases per year
        1. Number of shipments per year
        2. Average dollar amount per sale
        3. Claim and adjustment record
    B. Over $25,000 in purchases per year
        1. Number of shipments per year
        2. Average dollar amount per sale
    C. Assignment of sales personnel

(2) *An Analysis of Training Activities, Jupiter Corporation*
  I. Basic objectives in corporate training
    A. Management training objectives
    B. Professional training objectives
    C. Skilled training objectives
    D. Training objectives of secretarial personnel and cost
  II. Organization of training department
    A. Administrative
    B. Trainers
    C. Support personnel
    D. Use of outside consultants
    E. Cost of maintaining the department
  III. Programs
    A. Supervisory management courses
    B. Shop courses
    C. Cost reduction courses
    D. Cost of maintaining the programs
  IV. Expenditures for training
    A. Direct costs of classes
    B. Indirect and overhead charges

(3) *An Analysis of Recruitment Procedures of Engineering Personnel*
  I. Campus recruitment
    A. Undergraduate engineering students
    B. Undergraduate business students
    C. Undergraduate (misc.) students
  II. Newspaper advertisement recruiting
    A. Mail résumés
    B. Responses from ads in engineering journals
  III. Recruiting through present employees
    A. Bonus methods
    B. Interview procedures for prospective personnel
    C. Disadvantages of recruiting through employees

4. Defend or attack the following statement:
"If the communicator will only take the time necessary to draw up a plan for his written or oral communication, he will, in the long run, save much time and produce a better end product."

5. Select a three- or four-page article in a professional journal and make an outline of it. How logical is it? Do you feel the author would have been wiser if he had organized his article differently? Explain.

6. What is meant by "proportion" in the outline? How is it related to "proportion" in the finished communication?

7. How can an outline be used to check on the "order of development" of a report, letter, or oral presentation?

8. Define and discuss each of the following orders of development:
   (1) Chronological
   (2) Geographical
   (3) Directional

II. Complete any of the following problems assigned. You may wish to review the chapter and note key points before solving a problem.

1. "Our words communicate more than the facts in the message." Please interpret this quotation.

2. Can you explain why some of your friends communicate their ideas easily and fluently in both writing and speaking, and others encounter major difficulties in similar tasks?

3. Review S. I. Hayakawa's *Language in Thought and Action* with special reference to his discussion of word denotation and connotation. Summarize his comments briefly and then apply his discussion in the areas of (1) race relations; (2) American foreign policy; (3) the generation gap; and (4) campus unrest.

4. Clip a column from a recent issue of a newspaper. Carefully check the author's remarks and underline key words and phrases which you feel were purposely selected to arouse some emotional reaction on the part of the reader. You may wish to discuss your interpretation of these.

5. Duplicate the assignment above, but instead of a columnist's contribution, use an advertisement from a magazine or newspaper.

6. Edit the following brief passages to improve coherence, clarity, accuracy, and conciseness:

   (1) There are many men who are not at all reluctant to tell their supervisors about their specific responsibilities and their duties.

   (2) Sometimes we can, although not in every single instance, control much of our future; we sometimes do not act (or even react) to events so that we may take full advantage of our opportunities.

   (3) The Maxwell merchandise which was shipped via a local trucking line whose services we had used on other occasions, consisted of components for our AR 232 Receiver and was designated c.o.d., although previous shipments from Maxwell had always been sent on open account.

   (4) We began our operations with three full-time and eight part-time salesmen in just 8000 square feet of space in our Ogden Avenue location. In only three years' time we had grown to a sales staff of 18. That was in 1968. It was in 1965 that we began operations on Ogden Avenue and our next move was to Villa Park where we grew to the sales staff of 18. How we managed with 8000 square feet in 1965 is hard to understand when 40,000 seemed inadequate in 1968 in Villa Park. Also in Villa Park in 1968 we had 20 part-time salesmen.

   (5) Initially we had three men serving as officers of the corporation. There was Bob Rheem who acted as head of the group and Tom Bartletti and Max Rubin our treasurer and vice president. Our treasurer had been with the company for several years before he was elected to that position, but the vice president came to us from California Electronics just three months ago. But

even though he was a newcomer to the organization, everyone seemed to like him and felt that he always acted in the best interests of the employees and the firm.

Tom Bartletti had worked in the same capacity at two or three other companies so we all seemed to feel he really knew what he was doing and as a matter of fact, he performed his job with a great degree of competency.

Which reminds me that the treasurer we had last year got our tax situation so confused that we are still trying to get a ruling on the depreciation factor on our plant which was originally disallowed.

7. Edit and rewrite the following report to improve coherence, clarity, conciseness, accuracy, and appearance.

TO: Mr. Robert Campbell, Vice President, Personnel
FROM: Mr. Jack Fargo, Training Director
SUBJECT: Review of Training Activities, January 1, 197_ to June 30, 197_

This is to report on the training activities conducted by this firm during the period January 1, 197_ to June 30, 197_ with reference only to office, sales, and management personnel and not to shop, delivery, or custodial personnel. During the period listed above, 250 office personnel, and a similar number of management personnel received training in several different courses (see below) at a cost that compares favorably with expenditures during the previous period. In the area of sales personnel, some 200 men were involved (and 9 women); however, we found that costs rose dramatically because of the extension in time of the program over the previous year and the added cost of transportation because of the opening of sales regions in New York and Chicago.

In an analysis of the course evaluations completed by students, it was found that many participants in the Advanced Shorthand class felt that for maximum benefit, several additional sessions should be considered. As a matter of fact, the feeling was to go from 6 two-hour meetings to 8. In the case of the Supervisory Management course, it was strongly recommended that all groups (we had 4 sections) be taught by Dr. Kraft rather than split between Dr. Kraft and Dr. Jackson. As for the sales training classes, it was recommended that instead of bringing the Chicago and New York regional personnel to Los Angeles for training, that we hold a sales training program in each of the three cities: Los Angeles, Chicago, and New York. This would eliminate the travel expenses of approximately 42 men from Chicago and New York to Los Angeles.

As for a breakdown in cost and other relevant data, that information follows. In the case of office personnel, we enrolled 140 secretaries in 5 shorthand classes at a cost of $2.40 per participant per class meeting as compared with a cost of $2.20 per participant per class in the previous period. In the business English classes, of which we had 5, we had 110 personnel registered. The cost was $2.90 per participant per class as compared with $2.60 in the previous period. Of the 245 Management personnel, we had a total of 100 in four Supervisory Management sections. This averaged out to $3.40 per participant per class which was up 45¢ per person from the previous 6-month period. We also had 145 men and women complete the Management Communications course. This group was broken into 7 sections and the cost was $.50 per class per participant over the $3.00 figure of July 1 to December 31, 197_ period. The 200 sales personnel were trained in 14 different sections in the Los Angeles training facility. The cost per person (which included air fare, hotel, etc.) was $10.50 per participant per class.

This is opposed to $3.75 per class per participant during the previous period. However, it should be noted that only Los Angeles-based sales personnel were trained in the previous period.

All in all, it is recommended that the training programs be continued and that the recommendations made above be followed.

8. Edit and rewrite the following material to improve coherence, clarity, conciseness, accuracy, and appearance.

An analysis of our production of the Jupiter Relay Systems for use in a variety of military and commercial applications reveals many interesting and important applications. As you may or may not recall, we began the Jupiter line with our Complete Climate unit or the CC 120 and the Bulldog B 220 line for interior assemblies. Each of these came in three capacities ranging from 300 to 400 to 500 watts. These were designated as the 3/w, 4/w, and 5/w units.

An examination of the records going back two years shows a sale of 5000 dozen of the 3/w and 5/w CC 120 units, but only 3200 dozen of the 4/w CC 120 for the same year. Certainly this hardly compared with last year's showing of 8000 and 9000 dozen of the CC 120 in the 3/w, and 5/w units respectively. The 4/w Bulldog (B 220 line) sold as many units last year (10,000) as the CC 120 in the 4/w.

Of course, the B 220 or Bulldog line consistently outsold the CC 120 model. Two years ago the 4/w hit 12,000 dozen in sales, while the 3/w and 5/w sold 15,000 and 14,000 respectively. Last year the Bulldog line dropped in sales probably because Electronics Corporation, one of our biggest customers, lost its government contract. In any event, we sold 11,000 dozen 3/w and 11,500 dozen 5/w.

Actually the sales were not the items of the greatest consideration at Jupiter. Our bigger problem was personnel and we found, probably like other companies, that we suffered from a rather critical shortage of top-flight administrative persons. However, this is not said in a deprecatory manner, but simply indicates that although a clear trend for added administrative personnel may be noted in our statistics, we have taken no specific steps or procedures to implement our Personnel Practices recommendation committee report of last January which specifically and categorically emphasized to some extent that in 10 to 14 years, 75 percent of the personnel of the Jupiter Company will retire. As an example of this, it is upsetting to note that 120, 140, 220, 360, and 570 persons retired from Jupiter in the years 1970 to 1974 in that order. Obviously the figure is now over 15 percent of our work force which is a serious matter indeed.

Chapter Five

Career Planning and Communication

Sources for Securing New Jobs
Steps Preceding the Job Search
Types and Forms of Personal Job Applications
Letter Organization
The One-Part Job Application

Many of the people you know are happy with their positions and find each working day an enjoyable adventure. But there are many others who are not, and there are some who thoroughly dislike their assignments. In addition to these there is a group of persons who have no strong feelings one way or another about their daily labors, but who are not challenged by their jobs nor working at their full potential. Often they are earning far less than they should.

Surely this is no exaggeration. A sustantial segment of the members of our society, when asked "How do you like your job?" will reply rather resignedly, "Oh, it's O.K.; nothing special of course, but it's a job. And I guess a job's a job."

And you may reply, "But if it isn't what you want, what you enjoy, why not get a new one?"

The reaction to this may be an embarrassed silence or a "Holy smokes, you don't just quit a job and go out and find a new one, you know!"

Well, of course not. None of us is inclined to "just quit," but there is much to be said for leaving a position when it proves less than satisfactory. (See P. Drucker, "How to Be an Employee," in the Readings.)

Too many people in our society remain in jobs for too many years—unhappy and dissatisfied, giving themselves and their families ulcers, bad tempers, and neuroses. The competent and hard-working person who is unhappy with his position or is insufficiently challenged should have absolutely no hesitation in attempting to secure a new job.

Peter Drucker, a leading management writer, has this to say on the subject:

To know when to quit is therefore one of the most important things—particularly for the beginner. For on the whole young people have a tendency to hang on to the first job long beyond the time when they should have quit for their own good.

120

One should quit when self-analysis shows that the job is the wrong job—that, say, it does not give the security and routine one requires, that it is a small-company rather than a big-organization job, that it is at the bottom rather than near the top, a specialist's rather than a generalist's job, etc. One should quit if the job demands behavior one considers morally indefensible, or if the whole atmosphere of the place is morally corrupting—if, for instance, only yes men and flatterers are tolerated.

One should quit if the job does not offer the training one needs. . . .

But the most common reason why one should quit is the absence of promotional opportunities in the organization. That is a compelling reason.[1]

The search for a different job may have useful results. The job hunter may learn that his present assignment is about as good as he can secure in the present job market. If so, he may well accept his job, his level, and his salary and thus overcome his feeling that he should be "doing better." Or the individual may find a more satisfying or satisfactory job.

Sources for Securing New Jobs

Although there are a variety of different sources for the job seeker, just four will be reviewed here.

For the college student, recent college graduate, or graduate student, there is probably no agency as effective (and as inexpensive) as his school placement bureau.

The placement officers are experienced in various phases of personnel testing, counseling, and evaluation; they are usually acquainted with most corporate personnel directors in their areas; and they and their staffs are dedicated to serving the needs of the student.

Hundreds of companies have their recruiters make regular calls on universities to interview prospective employees. All of this is done through the college placement services, and at no cost to the student or the college.

Employment agencies and executive placement services also provide channels to jobs for thousands of persons each year. These are commercial ventures with fees paid to the employment agency either by the individual who has secured a new position or by the firm that has hired him.

Many employment agencies perform valuable services. However, the job hunter should always be sure that he and the agency have a clear understanding on what the fee will be and precisely what obligations and responsibilities each party has. And it goes without saying that the applicant should sign an employment agency agreement only after he has carefully read the terms of the contract.

The job seeker might do well to investigate a third possible source for employment. That is his professional association's job placement services. Accounting, advertising, office management, operations research, engineering,

[1] Peter F. Drucker, "How to Be an Employee," reprinted in *Psychology Today*, 1, 10 (March 1968), 74. (See the Readings.)

and most other professional and semiprofessional groups have placement services for their members.

But one of the most effective ways of all to secure a new position is through letters of application or résumés.

Most new college graduates will secure their first full-time positions through the campus recruiters from large companies. For some, the part-time positions they already hold will become full-time.

However, it is quite possible that a position which seemed right two or three years ago is now recognized as a "dead end," lacking in challenge and unsatisfying. This, then, is the time to send out a quantity of letters and secure interviews. The letters can be prepared easily and effectively with an automatic typewriter. (See pages 127–30.)

Steps Preceding the Job Search

As with any important assignment, the job search should be preceded by careful planning and self-analysis.

Self-Analysis

First we must ask some questions about ourselves: What do I have to offer the prospective employer? What professional attributes do I possess? What are my specific capabilities? How expert am I in areas 1, 2, and 3? Do I enjoy working with others or not? How fluent am I in French? Can I handle the ABC computer? Do I like to assume responsibilities? What is my level of initiative? Do I work well with others? How well do I supervise others or take orders from others?

Peter Drucker says the prospective employee should ask himself or herself these questions concerning the job he or she takes:

1. Do you belong in a job calling primarily for faithfulness in the performance of routine work and promising security? Or do you belong in a job that offers a challenge to imagination and ingenuity—with attendant penalty for failure?

2. Do you belong in a large organization or in a small organization? Do you work better through channels or through direct contact? Do you enjoy more being a small cog in a big and powerful machine or a big wheel in a small machine?

3. Should you start at the bottom and try to work your way up, or should you try to start near the top? On the lowest rung of the promotional ladder, with its solid and safe footing but also with a very long climb ahead? Or on the aerial trapeze of "a management trainee," or some other staff position close to management?

4. Finally, are you going to be more effective and happy as a specialist, or as a "generalist," that is, in an administrative job?[2]

---

[2] Peter Drucker, op. cit.

These are just a few questions we might well ask ourselves before we begin to hunt for the job. In addition to this self-analysis, college students should also visit their campus counseling center and career and placement offices. The personnel in these offices can usually give the student excellent counsel and advice on areas of the student's competence, the future potential of many fields, salary levels, and related information.

The more we learn about the job in an interview, and the more we know about our own desires and capabilities, the more easily we can determine whether or not this position is one we would work in most efficiently and enjoyably.

Researching the Job and the Job Market

Perhaps the first item to be checked is the specific job. If our abilities permit us to apply in two or more areas, which specific type of job has the best potential in the years ahead? Should I concentrate on computers, or inventory control, or cost accounting, or auditing, or personnel management if I have the ability and knowledge in each of these areas? Of course the opportunities which become available within the company in the years ahead will also determine the job one goes into. But we can help shape our future by making specific choices early in our career.

The second area to check is the job market itself. Examine the classified ad section of local as well as out-of-town newspapers; read the "job opportunities" section of your professional journals; examine the list of "jobs available" at your college placement office; take interviews with company recruiters who visit your school; read the the job opportunity bulletins sent out by the government agencies and corporations; secure suggestions from your college professors, friends, and associates; check such books as *The College Placement Annual*. And finally, and sometimes most effectively, send out letters of application to top-level firms, and take the interviews which result.

What about the companies in which employment is available? This is a third area to research. What are the firms' futures? What are their objectives? Do they or will they participate in space-age technology? What are their earning records? Their plans for expansion? Diversification? What do the records reflect as to financial and personnel growth? What facts can be gained from their annual reports? What do knowledgeable people think about a firm? Does the company have a reputation for retaining its personnel for long periods or are there frequent changes and turnover among them?

Because our future success is intimately associated with that of the company which employs us, we should make every effort to take a position with a firm that seems to have a bright and dependable future.

Types and Forms of Personal Job Applications

Basically there are two types of applications: the *solicited* letter, in which a firm, government agency, or institution solicits your assistance through an advertisement, or an announcement; and the *unsolicited* letter, in which you send an inquiry to one or more firms, asking about job openings and requesting an interview.

If you reply to an announcement, you know an opening exists, but you will encounter competition. An interesting and inviting ad which prompts you to write will probably also bring letters from 50 to 100 other applicants. You don't face this level of competition when you mail an unsolicited letter. But, on the other hand, the company may have no immediate opening for you. This should not be a major deterrent, however. Large industrial corporations usually have dozens of persons working in management, finance, engineering, accounting, and marketing. If an opening does not exist today, there will surely be one next month, and many corporations are quite willing to hire you today for the opening which is certain to appear in the near future.

The formats for both solicited and unsolicited letters are:

One-part: Brief presentation of all necessary facts in a letter.
Two-part: Introductory and summarizing cover letter accompanied by a résumé.
Job brochure: A booklet containing a few pages outlining in detail, education, experience, membership in organizations, honors, awards, copies of letters of reference, and samples of work. This is usually used by an executive with a good deal of experience.

Let us now look at the attributes and make-up of job-seeking letters and then come back to examples of the complete message presented in various forms.

Letter Organization

The job letter, like the sales letter, attempts to sell. The latter attempts to sell a product or service, but in the job letter, the writer attempts to present the best possible picture of himself or herself.

Like the sales message, (see Chapter Twelve), the application letter can be divided into a section which attempts to *arouse the reader's interest* in the job seeker, then *describes the background* which makes the applicant eligible for the job, *continues with proof* for the statements made by citing degrees, places of former employment, and references, and concludes with a *request for an interview* (or the sale itself).

Obviously the amount of detail and the general approach differ depending on whether the letter is a cover (or covering) letter to a résumé, or an application letter for a job not accompanied by a résumé.

Arousing Interest

The prospective employer is not usually impressed with cute or clever openings, nor is he intrigued with the stereotyped "this is in reply to your ad" approach. Avoid these openings, which revolve around the writer and are dull:

On June 5 I shall receive my degree from Central College and then will be ready to take a professional position with your firm.

This is in reply to your ad which appeared in the June 27 issue of the *Daily Times.*

After many years of study and application, I have reached my goal and am now available to consider the position you have available.

The openings below are concisely worded, give the reader a quick overview of the applicant's qualifications, and indicate how the company can benefit from his or her abilities. The employer's attention is arrested when the applicant indicates his or her major attributes and how they will help the company. This is the time for the writer to use the "you" attitude sincerely and effectively.

Your recent advertisement for a college graduate with a degree in marketing and some part-time business experience seems to fit my qualifications.

A college degree in accounting, a CPA certificate, and three years' experience working directly under a corporate controller should certainly qualify me for the position you described in yesterday's *Sunday Sun.*

Ability to type, take dictation, speak intelligently to customers, clients, or patients, come up with an original idea occasionally, and be pleasant and good-humored are surely the attributes you'd like in the "Gal Friday" for whom you advertised. I have these qualities plus a good many others. Here are some details.

The three openings above have merit; they are rather fresh and original and indicate how the applicant's abilities will help the firm. For some jobs, such as advertising and copy writing, it might be advisable to inject a real "attention-getting" statement, an intriguing sentence, or a startling and clever paragraph.

The opening statement also affords a good opportunity to let your reader enjoy a capsule account of your primary selling points: experience, education, special abilities, etc.

Describing Your Abilities

In the one-part letter of application, clear and specific statements on your education, experience, leadership abilities, and awards should be made. In the two-part letter, these accomplishments are alluded to rather generally in the cover letter and specifically listed in the résumé.

The description should be written to "match" the job's requirements or the ad's demands. If experience is emphasized in the job description and you possess it, this should be treated in some detail. If education is vital or leadership qualities important, then they should be emphasized. The sample letters displayed in the pages which follow illustrate several different methods of handling these situations.

Proving Your Statements

In the description section of the application letter, your references, degrees, and former employers (all proof of your abilities) may be indicated specifically in the one-part letter, but only referred to in the cover letter of a two-part application. Here again, the specifics are listed in the résumé or data sheet.

In listing degrees it is wise to indicate specific areas of study. When noting previous employment, a brief description of duties and responsibilities should appear so that the prospective employer has some idea of what you can do. And the same is true of any activities which illustrate leadership qualities: offices held, meetings conducted, articles written, conferences attended, etc.

Securing the Interview—the Request for Action

In both the cover letter for the résumé and the one-part letter of application, the final statements are usually concerned with making arrangements for the job interview. This should *not* be a simple "If you are interested, please call me" or "If you have any questions, I shall be pleased to answer them."

Your request for an interview should be emphatic and positive, and should clearly state that you want the interview so that you can tell the prospective employer about your attributes in greater detail than appear in the letter and résumé. Perhaps an implied statement can be made indicating that what has been said in the letter is only "part of the story" (as it can only be) and that the interview is desired to expand, add, and clarify details.

May I have an interview so that we can discuss in greater detail my education, experience, and other qualifications for the position? I can be reached....

I would appreciate an opportunity to meet with you so that I can explain more completely how my experience, education, ability to work hard and take responsibility, all qualify me for the job. Please call or write ....

When can we get together? The sooner the better so that I can give you a more complete picture of how a degree in accounting, six years of responsible work as assistant to the controller, and a desire to work very hard where opportunity is unlimited can be put to use by the Cantrel Corporation.

The One-Part Job Application

Although the cover letter and résumé are much more popular and effective in today's job market, there are some individuals who prefer the simple "letter of application."

The one-part letter is usually general in nature and somewhat brief. For the individual who lacks some qualifications for the job but is eager to secure an interview, this type of letter may have some merit.

ONE-PART LETTER-RÉSUMÉ

Although this letter has a sincere, friendly approach, it omits a great many important details such as age, job objective, references, course work, etc.

18127 Oak Street
Fargo, N. Dak. 77100
July 20, 19___

Box 221 AM
Sunday Star
Denver, Colo. 86200

Dear Sir:

Your ad requests a recent college graduate who has had some experience in insurance work. My degree in management, two years with a large life insurance firm, and a sincere desire to work hard should qualify me for the position.

In June of this year I received my college degree from Illinois State University. I majored in management with a special interest in personnel. I also took as much work as my program would permit in finance and accounting.

Three years ago I held a summer job in National Insurance Company's personnel division. I continued working there during the school year (on a part-time basis, of course), and full time during the summer periods. Although my initial duties were clerical, I was soon interviewing, testing, and carrying through duties in connection with securing salaried office personnel.

Since receiving my degree I have continued working for National. However, the opportunities with this firm are somewhat restricted and I would like to associate myself with a company that offers potential for growth and advancement in management positions.

During my collegiate career I received recognition for leadership in social and academic endeavors.

I shall be pleased to meet with you, explain my background in more detail, and list work and academic references. I can meet with you at your convenience; just telephone (701) AX 2-1000, extension 201, or write to the address above.

Sincerely,

John Holmes

John Holmes

3760 Marquette Avenue
Hartford, Conn. 06100
December 10, 19__

Box 1726
Kansas City Star
Kansas City, Kans. 66100

Gentlemen:

Thorough college training in marketing and finance, ambition, and a desire to work hard are the qualities an efficient man will need to fill your position of assistant advertising manager. I am sure that after you evaluate my qualifications you will find that I am that man.

Education

In February I will receive my Bachelor of Science in Commerce degree from Hartford University. My major field of study included the following courses: principles of marketing, problems in marketing, advertising, retailing, sales management, market research, marketing seminar, and foreign marketing. Besides courses in marketing, my university training included study in such related fields as finance, management, accounting, business communications, economics, business law, and statistics.

Experience

While my experience in marketing and particularly advertising is limited to college work, an example of my ambition and ability to learn quickly is demonstrated by the job I have had for the past three years. During that time I worked for Sears, Roebuck and Co. During my employment I was promoted from a stock man to supervisor in charge of stock men. This process usually takes five years.

Personal

I am twenty-one years of age and in excellent health. I enjoy football, baseball, basketball, and bowling. I am also an active member of the Marketing Society, Society for the Advancement of Management, and the Finance Society.

Because the applicant organized carefully and used topic headings, the reader will find this letter easy to read and assimilate. However, the writer has excellent qualifications which might be better communicated in a short cover letter and easy-to-read résumé.

References

I have personally contacted the persons listed below and they have consented to offer a thorough report on my capabilities and my character.

Mr. Vernon Cates
Division Manager
Sears, Roebuck and Co.
Corporate Headquarters
Hartford, Conn. 06100

Dr. Philip Pendleton
Department of Advertising
Hartford University
Hartford, Conn. 06100

Dr. Robert E. Cantel, Chairman
Department of Marketing
Hartford University
Hartford, Conn. 06100

Mr. William B. Myers
2809 South Patterson Ave.
Chicago, Ill. 60634

I have given you all the information I believe is pertinent, but only through an interview can I tell you my entire story. Please call me at (203) 738-1212 to arrange an interview at your convenience.

Very truly yours,

Martin T. Mackay

Martin T. Mackay

ONE-PART LETTER-RÉSUMÉ

4812 North Adams Street
Boston, Mass. 02100
May 20, 19__

Box MAR 721
Boston Daily News
Boston, Mass. 02100

Gentlemen:

Next month I shall graduate from Boston College armed with a Bachelor of Science Degree in Commerce, lots of ambition, and a willingness to work hard. A position as an administrative assistant with the top qualifications you desire is just what I have been looking for. Please consider my training and background for the opening in your firm.

In this one-part letter, the reader will find some general details and some specifics. Here again a résumé accompanied by a cover letter might have been a wiser course of action. The writer obviously possesses qualifications which have not been listed.

EDUCATION--

I have attended Boston College for four years majoring in Business Education. I have a basic knowledge of business in the areas of marketing, finance, management, business law, and economics. My liberal arts background has been excellent, with special emphasis on English, including courses in business communication and report writing.

ADMINISTRATIVE SKILLS--

Dictation and accurate transcription are second nature to me. I take shorthand at better than 120 words per minute and can type accurately at the rate of 70 words per minute. While at Boston College, I took a course in office machines, in which we learned the basic skills on the comptometer, adding machines, and the automatic calculator.

WORK EXPERIENCE--

The cost of a college education is, as you know, quite expensive. I have always worked part time to help pay expenses and at the same time, I have maintained above-average grades. This has taught me responsibility as well as the ability to organize my time.

I am employed on a part-time basis by Shippey and Shippey, a legal firm, located at One North LaSalle Street, Boston. My duties include heavy dictation, complete charge of the filing system, and other secretarial duties.

From January 19____ until November 19____, I was employed by New England Insurance Company as a stenographer in their Correspondence Department. This job consisted primarily of dictation, transcription, and switchboard "relief."

May I come in for an interview to discuss my qualifications with you in greater detail? I can be reached at WAlnut 1-0771.

Very truly yours,

Ms. Jane Allen

Ms. Jane Allen

Questions for Study

Complete any of the following problems assigned. You may wish to review the chapter and note key points before solving a problem.

1. Determine the general type of position for which you would like to apply on graduation. List those sources which you feel would be effective as "leads" to possible job interviews.

2. Do a self-analysis for job purposes noting your attitudes, likes, and strong points. List the job classifications which seem to utilize those qualities.

3. For your personality and abilities, which job source do you feel will prove most valuable? Why?
   1) Newspaper ads.
   2) Company recruiters who call on colleges.
   3) Personal friends.
   4) Family connections.
   5) College placement office.
   6) Employment agencies.
   7) Listing of corporate offices in some type of reference guide.
   8) Previous part-time or full-time employers.
   9) Other.

4. For your particular attributes, why would you use or not use the "one-part" letter of application.

5. What specific advantages are there in entering the job market for the individual who is unhappy with his job? Are there any advantages even if he finds he cannot improve himself and must retain his present position?

Chapter Six

Personal Résumés and Job Communications

Résumés
Examples of Covering Letters and Résumés
Important Reminders for the Job Seeker
The Job Interview
The Follow-up Letter
Declining a Job Offer
Letters of Resignation

The personal résumé can be one of the most important items of communication you will prepare. Actually it has uses over and beyond the job search. It can be used as a substantiating document when you submit an article or a paper for publication, when you file for office, or when you apply for credit. People who ask you to lead or serve on a committee, or request that you give a speech or be a member of a panel, will find your résumé helpful.

The résumé should be looked upon as something that grows with the individual. It should be written early in your career and then revised and updated as your career progresses, your goals change, and your background becomes richer. The style, format, and layout of résumés change with the times, and yours should change also.

The next few pages will first present samples of résumés, then examples of covering letters *and* résumés. Examine them all carefully and select ideas, phrases, and a format which suit your needs and personality. Of course paragraphs should not be copied, but ideas can easily be adapted to your particular requirements.

Résumés

Robert M. Crane
1411 North Compton Avenue
Kansas City, Kans. 66100

Career   Management position in the marketing department
Objective   of a growing company. Eventual objective is to
                      become an officer in a medium-size firm.

Major   University background in business administration.
Qualifications   Experience in office management, accounting, and
                      sales.

Education   Master of Business Administration Degree,
                      Northwestern University, June 19__.

                      Courses in Marketing:
                      Marketing communications   Pricing strategy
Note the easy-to-read Marketing logistics   Market and sales
format.   Marketing planning   analysis
                                                  Retailing management

                      Courses in related fields:
                      Private enterprise   Organizational behavior
                      Policy formulation   Business communications
                      Accounting control and   Quantitative analysis
                         financial reporting   for business decision
                         I & II

                      Bachelor of Arts Degree, Missouri State University,
                      June 19__.

                      Major area: Economics
                      Minor area: Marketing

Work Experience   Gayle and Gompers Corp.
                      1414 South Jackson Road
                      Kansas City, Kans. 66100

                      Summer 19__ and 19__
                      Duties: Accounts receivable, payroll supervision,
                               routine accounting, also wrote and edited
                               technical manuals.

                      Electronic Development Company
                      101 South Madison Avenue
                      Kansas City, Kans. 66100

                      Summer 19__
                      Duties: Correspondent to customers and suppliers;
                               purchasing expediter.

```
             Other part-time and summer jobs included routine
             office work, road laborer, clerk in a law office,
             and salesman in men's clothing shop.

Personal Data   Physical details:  age, 23 years; height, 5'11";
                                    weight, 180; health, excellent.

                Hobbies:  Swimming, handball, folk music, reading.

References      Mr. Robert T. Gayle, President
               Gayle and Gompers Corp.
               1414 South Jackson Road
               Kansas City, Kans. 66100

               Dr. Henry Hale
               Professor of Marketing
               Northwestern University
               Evanston, Ill. 60200

               Mr. Michael Coffee
               Plant Manager
               Electronic Development Company
               101 South Madison Avenue
               Kansas City, Kans. 66100

               Dr. J. T. Jackson, Dean
               School of Liberal Arts
               Missouri State University
               St. Louis, Mo. 63100
```

RÉSUMÉ B

```
John T. Moore
1521 South Kensington Street
Los Angeles, Calif. 90024                    (213) 476-4220


Job Objective   A management position in the area of purchasing
               systems and procedures.  Company must afford an
               opportunity for advancement to officer level for
               qualified man.

Experience     Western Aviation Corp.
               Van Nuys, Calif. 91400   June 19__ to Present

               Title:  Staff Assistant to Vice President,
                       Materials
```

Responsible for assisting manager in development
and writing of new corporate materials directives.
Knowledge required of government procurement regulations, company procurement agreements, coordinating material policy and procedures with all
levels of division and corporate management.

The Farwell Corporation
Research Division
Whittier, Calif. 91402   May 19__ to June 19__

Title: Supervisor of Services

Staff assistant to manager of research with responsibility for operational analyses and control
of research services for branch. Work was highly
diversified and required a high level of administrative ability.

Economy Air Freight, Inc.
1515 W. Aviation Blvd.
San Francisco, Calif. 94100   May 19__ to Nov. 19__

Title: Station Manager

Responsible for all traffic and maintenance functions including handling freight movements, accepting and verifying cargo, billing and manifesting,
load planning, crew coordination, accounts payable
and receivable, and areas related to finance and
budget.

Education	Bachelor of Science Degree, June 19__
	University of Illinois School of Business Administration Major area: Management Systems
Military	Served with U.S. Air Force, May 19__ to Dec. 19__ Honorably discharged; Rank: Major Senior officer: Procurement and supply installa- tion Decorated
Personal	Age: 34 Health: Excellent Married; 2 children
References	Furnished on request.

Shirley A. Connors
1313 West Scott Street
Des Plaines, Ill. 60016

Home phone: MOnroe 6-1231
Work phone: FInancial 6-1200

JOB OBJECTIVE:

Professional position as an auditor with a CPA firm and eventual managerial capacity in such a firm.

MAJOR QUALIFICATIONS:

University education in accounting. Four years part-time experience in accounting firm. Two years assistant manager in drive-in restaurant.

EDUCATION:

Bachelor of Science degree, De Paul University's College of Commerce-- June 19__.

Courses in Accounting:

Elements	Cost Accounting
Principles	Auditing Theory
Interpretation	Auditing Practice
Intermediate Theory	Taxes I and II
Advanced Theory	Consolidations
Systems	Governmental Accounting

Courses in Related Fields:

Business Law I and II	Corporate Finance
Economics	Money and Banking
Income Determination	Business Communications
The Stock Market	Business Report Writing
Marketing Problems	Ethics

EXPERIENCE:

Martin and Allen, Certified Public Accountants
315 West Wabash Avenue
Chicago, Ill. 60604
Period from October, 19__, to June, 19__.

Duties: First Year--proofreading. Remaining three years--member of accounting staff--auditing; preparing individual and corporate tax returns, both state and federal; compiling financial statements, reports on examination and SEC 10-K reports.

Kopper Kitchen Restaurant
64 East Lake Street
Chicago, Illinois 60604
Period from September, 19__, to June, 19__.

Duties: First year--waitress. Remaining two years--assistant manager at night, supervising four persons.

Other part-time jobs: Stock person in pet shop; saxophone player in musical combo.

ACTIVITIES, HONORS, AND ORGANIZATIONS:

National Honor Society--High School
Des Plaines Library Art Club
Writer for De Paul University's Literary Magazine, "Trajectories"
Winner of De Paul University's Art Contest

PERSONAL DATA:

Physical details: Age 23; height 5 feet, 6 inches; weight 120 pounds; health excellent
Marital status: Single
Hobbies and interests: Reading, art, music, sports, and painting.

REFERENCES:

Mr. John L. Foreman, CPA   Professor Edwin T. Sloan
Audit Manager   Professor of Accounting
Martin and Allen   De Paul University
315 West Wabash Avenue   Chicago, Ill. 60604
Chicago, Ill. 60604

Mr. Harold S. Jackson   Professor Martin M. Contrant
Kopper Kitchen Restaurant, Inc.   Department of Finance
1900 East Queen Court   Northwestern University
Chicago, Ill. 60604   Evanston, Ill. 60200

Examples of Covering Letters and Résumés

Covering Letter for RÉSUMÉ D

148 West Manchester Avenue
Inglewood, Calif. 90027
April 15, 19___

General Manager
Box 121AO
Los Angeles Times
Times Square
Los Angeles, Calif. 90007

Sir:

This morning's Los Angeles Times carried your advertisement for a person with "experience in material control and a college degree." I know that my practical job experience and my educational training have prepared me for the position you have available.

For the past three years I have been employed by a small firm which manufactures children's toys. I began working for the company when it first started; because the firm "learned as it grew," I gained valuable experience in production and materials control.

In June of this year I will receive my Bachelor of Science degree from the School of Business Administration of California University, where I majored in management and minored in economics and industrial engineering. Details of my educational preparation and job experiences, as well as other information, can be found on the attached data sheet.

I feel that I can fill the job you have open. I would like an opportunity to meet with you at your convenience to discuss in detail my qualifications, salary, and possible future with your company. I can be reached any evening at 355-1933.

Sincerely yours,

Robert T. Malvey

Robert T. Malvey

Enclosure

RÉSUMÉ D

Robert T. Malvey
148 West Manchester Avenue
Inglewood, Calif. 90027

(213) 355-1933

career objective	Work as department manager with a growing manufacturing firm. Eventual position as plant manager of a sizable manufacturing organization.
major qualifications	Experience with small company involved in the manufacturing of children's toys.
	Educational background in business and in industrial engineering.
education	California University Bachelor of Science Degree in Business Administration, June 19__.

<u>Industrial Engineering Courses</u>
Production Methods
Industrial Engineering

<pre>
                          Business Courses
                          Management of Small Business
                          Industrial Management
                          Business Growth and Stabilization
                          Management Communications
                          Managerial Accounting and Cost Analysis
                          Business Finance

experience   Playtime, Inc.
                          1043 South Jefferson Street
                          Los Angeles, Calif. 90024

                          Part time: March, 19__ to present
                          Full time: Summer, 19__
                          Duties: In charge of production control,
                          materials handling, and storage.

                          Sales (representative to schools and
                          institutions)

                          McMahon Furniture Manufacturing Corp.
                          5151 South Granite Avenue
                          Los Angeles, California 90016

                          Full time: Summer of 19__
                          Duties: In charge of cocktail and coffee
                          table production (6 subordinates)

                          Westchester Standard Oil Co.
                          1515 West Fremont
                          Westchester, Calif. 90027

                          Part time: (after school) Sept. to June, 19__-19__
                          Full time: Summers of 19__-19__
                          Duties: Gas station attendant
                          mechanic
                          daily bookkeeping
                          miscellaneous sales

social activities,   Junior Member, Jonathan Club, Los Angeles
honors   Yearbook Committee, California University,
                          Fall and Spring, 19__
                          Dean's List, Fall and Spring, 19__

personal data   Age, 22   Height, 5'11"
                          Marital status, single   Weight, 195 lbs.
                          Interests, tennis,   Health, excellent
                          automotives

references   Mr. William F. McMahon
(by permission)   McMahon Furniture Mfg. Corp.
                          5151 South Granite Avenue
                          Los Angeles, Calif. 90016
</pre>

```
Dr. Martin M. Garvey
Professor of Industrial and Systems Engineering
California University
Los Angeles, Calif. 90007

Dr. M. A. Burdett
Professor
Graduate School of Business
California University
Los Angeles, Calif. 90007

Mr. Bert M. Freeman
150 Park Lane
San Francisco, Calif. 94025
```

Covering Letter for RÉSUMÉ E

```
                                    4848 North Florence Way
                                    Los Angeles, Calif. 90024
                                    May 5, 19__

Personnel Director
West Coast Food Processing Corp.
Box 10906
Palo Alto, Calif. 94300

Dear Sir:

I can help you!  Your Wall Street Journal advertisement call-
ing for "a creative, innovative individual familiar with the
Latin-American market," certainly suggests that I can.  My
Central American background, U.S. college training, and un-
inhibited creativity should definitely give your company a
long-term asset.

In four weeks I will receive my Bachelor of Science degree
from the University of California at Long Beach, where I have
majored in International Marketing and minored in Quantitative
Analysis.  The degree will complete eight years of U.S. educa-
tion ranging from private-boarding high school to university
studies.

My home is in San Jose, Costa Rica, where I was born and raised.
I was educated in the United States and have the advantage of
complete and thorough fluency in both Spanish and English as
well as an excellent understanding of both Latin and American
cultures.  With the growing influence of Latin consumers in
California, my cultural background should serve as a further
value to your company.
```

I have spent the last five summers working in Central America.
Because of the various company training programs and in-the-
field marketing experiences to which I dedicated my vacations,
I feel qualified to meet your "2-3 year professional marketing
experience" requirement. An account of these, my education,
and other information may be found on the attached résumé.

May I come in, at your convenience, and offer a more detailed
account of how I can aid your company? I can be reached during the evening at (213) 436-8160 or at the address shown
above.

Sincerely,

Ricardo Serrana

Ricardo Serrana

RÉSUMÉ E

Ricardo Serrana
4848 North Florence Way
Los Angeles, Calif. 90027

Phone: (213) 436-8160

career objective   Dedicate my resources towards researching
and improving company-consumer communica-
tion channels. Eventual objective is to
become a senior officer of a Latin American
firm which has close U.S. ties.

major
qualifications   University background in Marketing and
    Quantitative Analysis.
Fluency in both Spanish and English.
Cultural background in both the United States
    and in Latin America.
Experience in various businesses primarily
    food associated.

experience   National Tobacco Company
San José, Costa Rica

Summer of 1969
    Duties: 3-month study of Tobacco Industry
    in Costa Rica

Summer of 1971
    Duties: Marketing Representative--promotions
market surveys and analysis

Cia. Numar S.A.
(United Fruit Co.)
P. O. Box 3657
San José, Costa Rica

Summer of 1964
  Duties: 3-month training program in company's sales and distribution system

Summer of 1965
  Duties: Assistant salesman - Full salesman
  toward end of summer

Summer of 1966
  Duties: 3-month training course in company's
  marketing system

Summers 1967 and 1968
  Duties: Marketing Representative - promotions,
  merchandising, new product surveys

education   Bachelor of Science in Business
               Major--International Marketing
               Minor--Quantitative Analysis
             University of California at Long Beach, June 19__

             My marketing courses ranged from Market Analysis
             and Strategy through Consumer Behavior and
             Psychology. A lengthy list of other business
             courses provided a rounded education.

awards &   Student Body President: Benjamin Franklin High
organizations   School, Monterey,
                                     California
             President: California Association of Student
                        Councils, 19__-19__
             Cum Laude: High School and University
             Outstanding Citizenship Award - 19__

personal data   Physical details: age, 22 years; height, 5'9";
                                   weight, 150 lbs.; very healthy
                 Marital status: single
                 Hobbies and interests: Private-instrument rated
                                        pilot; swimming; soccer;
                                        traveling

references   Mr. Edward T. Brozer
             General Manager
             National Tobacco Co.
             San José, Costa Rica

```
Dr. Robert T. Hamilton
Professor of Business
Communication
University of Long Beach
Long Beach, Calif. 90800

Mr. Fernando Martinez
General Manager
Cia. Numar S.A.
San José, Costa Rica

Mr. Robert M. Ricklefs, Principal
Franklin High School
Pebble Beach, Calif. 93953
```

Important Reminders for the Job Seeker

Appearance is vital. When the prospective employer reads your letter, he should be impressed with its excellent proportion, generous use of white space, obvious organization, and easy "readability." You want him to say as he reads, "My, this is a well-organized, logical person."

Check the letter's correctness and use of English. Personnel directors feel that a college student's or graduate's letter must be completely error-free. All that is required to achieve this is editing and care. And as one employment supervisor stated:

> There is no more important letter he will ever write unless he proposes marriage by mail . . . and this job letter should be perfect. We can understand when a letter from a shop supervisor exhibits an error or two, but not when the message comes from a college-trained man. After all, if he is careless in *his* letter, what can we expect in his handling of our ledgers?

So check your letter carefully and make sure it is clear, concise, complete, and correct.

Does the covering letter have a *"you" attitude?* Have you attempted to point out how the *company* will benefit from your skill, service, and ambition? The personnel director is not particularly concerned with how his firm will give *you* experience; provide *you* with interesting and challenging situations; and offer *you* promotions and pay increases. He is interested in learning how your education, your experience, your travels can be successfully used in the advancement and progress of the firm.

> My degree in accounting and two years of part-time experience with Merril and Maxwell, CPA's, should prove of value to your company.

> If your company can use a professionally trained advertising man who has loads of energy and ambition, plus three years' experience, I'm the man for your firm.

Your covering letter and résumé should also be *specific.* The letter that is general as to what the applicant has done in the past and can do in the future usually makes little impact on the reader. We live in a world of specialization and, in professional areas especially, we like to know precisely what the job seeker can do for us.

It isn't enough to indicate that your degree is in business administration; what specific area? And there is too much left to the imagination with, "I held a management position for two years with Croxton and Croxton."

"I was the office manager of Croxton and Croxton's Southfield division," or "personnel assistant in charge of training." On the other hand, the applicant must be careful not to give the reader the impression (unless he sincerely means to) that he would only be happy doing inventory control or that he can only accomplish payroll accounting. There is certainly a middle ground that should be indicated.

And of course the letter of application should be *original.* Never copy a paragraph, and certainly not a complete letter, from any source. Anyone can find examples of clever letters in texts, paperbacks, and a dozen other sources. But you can be sure that most personnel directors have read almost all the "model" letters many times.

The Job Interview

As we all know, the letter of application will rarely result in a job offer; we hope, however, that through the letter we can secure an interview and that is the way it should be written—with the objective of securing an interview, not a job.

A job is offered only after we have "sold" ourselves at the interview, and for this reason as much time and care should be spent on that phase of job seeking as on the preparation, planning, or even writing of the letter. The half hour spent talking to the prospective employer is vital. We must give evidence of a pleasant personality, ability to communicate, knowledge of our area, our future objectives, the information we have about the company, our level of courtesy, and familiarity with topics of professional, political, and cultural interest. This requires preparation.

New York Life Insurance Company has issued an excellent booklet titled, "Making the Most of Your Job Interview." It begins with the statement:

The employment interview is one of the most important events in a person's experience, because the 20 or 30 minutes spent with an interviewer may determine the entire future course of one's life.

Yet interviewers are continually amazed at the number of applicants who drift into job interviews without any apparent preparation and only the vaguest idea of what they are going to say. Their manner says, "Well, here we are." And that's often the end of it, in more ways than one.

Others, although they undoubtedly do not intend to do so, create an impression of indifference by acting too casually. At the other extreme, a few applicants work themselves into such a state of mind that when they arrive they seem to be in the last stages of nervous fright and are only able to answer in monosyllables.

These marks of inexperience can be avoided by knowing a little of what actually is expected of you and by making a few simple preparations before the interview.

To prepare for your job interview, you might think of 20 or so questions the interviewer is likely to ask and how you will answer them. If you think that is a task which requires little thought, examine the following typical questions.[1] How would you answer them?

Tell me about yourself.

In what type of position are you most interested?

What do you know about our company?

How do you feel about your family?

Tell me a story!

How did your previous employers treat you?

What kind of boss do you prefer?

What do you think determines a man's progress in a company?

What is the source of your spending money?

What job in our company would you choose if you were entirely free to do so?

Just a quick survey of the questions above shows how important preparation is. To undertake an interview without a clear analysis of your own needs and desires, and the company's objectives, is foolhardy. (See W. Fisher, "The Interview—A Multi-Purpose Leadership Tool," and J. M. Lahiff, "Interviewing for Results," in the Readings.)

Of course, no comment is necessary concerning neat dress, erect posture, and the need to speak clearly, correctly, and completely during the interview.

The interviewee should take care not to ramble or make political hay if asked about foreign policy, national affairs, or his profession. Freedom of expression is respected, but comments should be concise and delivered in good taste.

If questioned about courses, instructors, and former employers, the applicant should remember, "If you can't say anything good about him, say nothing." The interview is not the place for disparaging others. And the job seeker should be frank and honest in all his replies about himself. A statement which is not true will surely trip him up sooner or later.

Don't be coy with the interviewer. If he offers a job and you aren't prepared to accept it at that moment, don't stall, or accept it with the mental reservation that you will turn it down if you receive a better offer that afternoon. Tell him directly that you have other interviews scheduled, and that you want to defer a decision, for the benefit of the company as well as yourself. Because the interviewer is usually a reasonable person, he will accept an honest approach of this type.

[1] The New York Life Booklet contains a list of 80 questions most frequently asked during a job interview, as reported by 92 companies. Some of those questions are listed above.

Find an opportunity during the interview to state your major attributes factually, but not boastfully.

"My extracurricular activities were somewhat limited because I had to work while attending school. My job in the bookstore helped me to pay almost 80 percent of my college expenses."

"My knowledge of Spanish is good enough for me to carry on correspondence and routine business activities with your Latin American accounts."

"I was fortunate to receive a General Bank and Trust Company scholarship as a freshman. I held it, on the basis of grades, for all four years."

Many college graduates are interviewed on campus by corporate recruiters. Others are interviewed as a direct result of the letter of application which they have submitted. In both cases, the applicants' preparation for and conduct during the discussion should be similar.

The job applicant should consider several carefully worded questions he might ask. These may be concerned with future opportunities within the firm, compensation in addition to the base salary (hospitalization, annuity funds, tuition refund plans, stock option programs, profit sharing, etc.), plans for company expansion and diversification, job duties, travel requirements, advancement policies, and a host of others.

The answers to these questions are vital to you, and will surely determine which job you choose. Furthermore, this two-way discussion gives you an opportunity to relax as the interviewer speaks. And it opens up important new avenues for discussion.

In addition to preparing questions, you should secure some information about the company. What are its primary products? Where are its plants? What is its financial history and present situation? How many employees does it have? What kind of growth picture does it reflect?

Background data can be secured from a number of sources, among which are:

The company's annual report

Thomas' Register of American Manufacturers

Moody's Manuals

Standard and Poor's Corporation Records

Dun and Bradstreet Reference Book

Poor's Register of Directors and Executives

College Placement Directory

College Placement Annual

Government booklets (for federal departments, bureaus, and divisions)

The Follow-up Letter

You would not usually send a follow-up letter as a result of an initial, brief, exploratory interview. However, if you have been interviewed at length and you are very much interested in the position, you might well consider a follow-up note. Very few persons take the time or make the effort to do this. When the interviewer receives such a letter, it is an unusual experience for him. You can be sure he will read and be impressed with it.

The written follow-up to the interview should be concise, sincere, and courteous. Basically, its purpose is to thank the interviewer for the time and effort he expended in talking to you and to review briefly your own qualifications. It should be mailed the same day, or the day following the interview.

```
                                                 May 27, 19___

Dear Mr. Cates:

Thank you very much for the time you spent with me this morn-
ing.  I found your discussion of the Fairmont Company most
interesting, and the openings you described very challenging.

You will recall that I received my commerce degree from
California State last year, acquired a CPA certificate a few
months ago, and have been employed for one year as a junior
accountant with Continental Aerospace Company.

I would certainly like an opportunity to work more extensively
in an electronic data processing position such as the one you
described.  I do hope you will call me at GR 6-4622 for further
discussion.

                              Sincerely yours,
```

```
                                              October 3, 19___

Dear Mr. Robinson:

Thank you very much for taking the time to show me Barton's
office and manufacturing facilities yesterday.  I was cer-
tainly impressed with the efficiency, friendliness, and over-
all climate of the firm.

Now that I know something about your company's directions
and objectives, I feel that my degree in industrial engineer-
ing, my two years of part-time work in motion and time study,
and my desire to work hard should all be of value to your
company.

If I can supply you with additional information on my educa-
tion and experience, I shall be happy to come in at your
convenience.  In the meantime, I hope you will consider me
favorably for the position we discussed.

                              Sincerely yours,
```

Perhaps the most important quality of the follow-up letter is sincerity. A letter that contains obviously insincere statements, or overly enthusiastic praise, will surely fail in its purpose. Keep it concise, direct, sincere, and mail it promptly after the interview.

The entire process of securing a position is a vital one; it deserves your full attention, your very careful preparation, and your maximum effort.

Declining a Job Offer

At some time an applicant may find himself in the enviable position of having more than one job offer. He may be tempted to call the interviewer's secretary and state, "Please tell Mr. Martin that I can't take the junior accountant's job after all, but I sure appreciate his asking me."

A carefully worded, courteous note will often build good will while a telephone message like the above will not. And, in addition, a note may pay important dividends for the future.

June 27, 19___

Dear Mr. Berman:

Thank you most sincerely for the time you and Mr. Cannon spent with me during our discussions during the past two weeks.

I was certainly impressed with the operations of your organization and the potential opportunities it affords its employees. However, the position does require rather extensive travel and as I indicated, this is something I would like to avoid.

On that basis, I have accepted a position with a local firm in the same capacity we discussed.

I know you will understand my position and accept my sincere appreciation for your courtesy.

Sincerely yours,

Glenn E. Robin

Glenn E. Robin

Dear Mr. Epperly:

Your courtesy and concern have made a tremendous impression
on me. I truly appreciated the time you gave me, as well as
your generosity in permitting me to fly up to your headquarters
operation in Chicago.

Although I recognize the opportunities which exist with
Fairbanks-Holly, I must also face the fact that I work better
in a small organization. I therefore feel that in fairness
to you and myself, I must decline the position you offered.

Thank you again, Mr. Epperly, for your interest in me.

Sincerely yours,

James E. Hopper

James E. Hopper

Letters of Resignation

Although it is always difficult to resign a position, it is wise to do so as
tactfully and courteously as possible. There will be discussions, of course, but
the facts set down in a letter tend to keep the record straight. In addition, it is a
good idea to have such a message in your file in the firm in the event a reference on you is requested of that company three or four years later. Such a letter may also assist those in the company who may be new or may not know
you, but must deal with a request for information on you.

October 12, 19___

Dear Mr. Dover:

Although I have found my association with Hecht and Hecht
enjoyable and challenging, I am aware of the limitations which
exist. I am sure this is true of every relatively small business.

Now that I have completed my graduate work, it is vital to me
that I put into practice the knowledge and techniques which I
studied.

Because of this I would like to terminate my employment with Hecht and Hecht at the end of this month. I hope such timing will prove convenient; if not, I will cooperate in any way possible.

I have gained much from my work here, and I hope you feel that my contributions to the firm have been significant.

Cordially yours,

John M. Powers

John M. Powers

September 15, 19___

Dear Mr. Kelly:

Carrying through marketing research for the past two years under your direction has been a rewarding, enjoyable, and challenging experience.

I found all my academic background put to good use, and the freedom to innovate (which you encouraged) a delightful situation.

Recently, however, I have been asked to head up the marketing division of a consumer products company. The opportunity is really too good to turn down. I can only hope that I will do as good a job with that firm as you do here.

On that basis, I would like to suggest that I leave at the end of the first week in October. If you feel that time is not convenient, I am sure alternative arrangements can be made.

Sincerely yours,

A direct, factual approach to a difficult situation.

Dear Mr. Rowe:

I have recently applied for and been accepted for the position of senior accountant with the Colton Carton Corporation.

On that basis I would like to resign my present position effective the last working day of this month. If it would be convenient for the firm if I stayed on the job somewhat longer or left somewhat earlier, I shall be happy to comply.

```
I have taken this step somewhat as a result of my discussion
with you last month.  You will recall we reviewed advancement
possibilities here, and you indicated that because of the
situation of excess personnel and the limited size of the com-
pany, promotion in the near future seemed unlikely.  It there-
fore seemed wise for me to accept this opportunity with Colton.

Nevertheless, I value highly my association with this company,
and wish you and the firm continued success in the future.
```

Questions for Study

Complete any of the following problems assigned. You may wish to review the chapter and note key points before solving a problem.

1. What attributes do sales and application letters have in common?

2. Under what circumstances would a two-part letter of application be superior to a one-part letter?

3. Write out six questions which you feel you should (or could) ask a campus recruiter from a corporation who would interview you.

4. Assume you were offered a specific job by an interviewer. List the job title and the salary offered. Write a follow-up letter to that interview. Indicate your interest in the position and your desire to receive a job offer.

5. Select an advertisement from the classified section of your local newspaper. Reply to the ad using a two-part letter of application. You may make no assumptions which are not accurate except that you expect to receive your college degree in six weeks, and you have successfully completed all courses leading to that degree. Clip the advertisement to your letter.

6. Send an unsolicited one-part or two-part letter of application to a firm that you would like to work for after you receive your degree. Assume your graduation will take place within two months.

7. Split into groups of five and conduct a mock job interview. Establish the job, job requirements, qualifications of the interviewee, salary level, and education and experience backgrounds necessary to secure the job. One individual should play the role of interviewer, one the job applicant, and three should act as observers.

    The interviewer and interviewee should make all necessary assumptions for the role-playing exercise. The observers should offer a carefully structured critique at the end of the interview. Roles should be rotated so that each person has an opportunity to play two or three roles in the various interviews held.

8. Make an appointment with a personnel director of a firm. Interview that person in an effort to determine what he or she feels is vital to include in the unsolicited letter of application, hints on the interviewee's conduct during the interview, and methods for securing a new position. Report your findings to the class.

9. Offer your constructive criticism of résumés A, B, and C in this chapter. Note factors that are competently done as well as those that need improvement.

10. Offer your constructive criticism of cover letters and résumés D, E, and F in this chapter. Remember to note factors that are competently done as well as those that need improvement.

Part Three

External Company Communications: The Business Letter

Chapter Seven

Writing Effective Business Communications

The Business Letter and the Company Image
Mechanics
Principles of Communication

Every company, big or small, communicates to dozens of different publics. These are all *external* to the firm: suppliers, dealers, manufacturers, customers, vendors, prospective purchasers, regulatory bureaus, government agencies, community groups, educational institutions, and on and on. Of the many types of written or printed external communications, such as newspaper and magazine advertisements, direct mail pieces, telegrams, reports, and letters, it is certainly letters which are used most frequently. Of course, communication also takes place during a salesman's presentation, a manager's phone call, or a casual discussion at lunch. However, when a record is required or facts must be stated—prices quoted, offers made, or deliveries promised—then a letter is needed.

The Business Letter and the Company Image

In many firms the business letter is the primary means of external communication. There are several reasons for this: a letter establishes a tangible record which can be used for later reference; distances can be spanned quickly at relatively small cost; the time spent traveling to another person's office and carrying through a discussion can be eliminated; and routine business matters can be completed efficiently with the help of letter guides and forms.

For example, take a large insurance company with thousands of policyowners and hundreds of agents from coast to coast. Questions about premiums, cancellations, medical bills, changes in beneficiaries, overpayments, past due accounts, conversions, reinstatements, and a thousand and one other situations arise each day. Letters flow into the home (or central) office from a variety of different sources. And replies must go out, all on the company's stationery and written by hundreds of different employees, and all contributing to the company's image.

When policyowner Mrs. Baxter of Three Forks, South Dakota, reads the letter she receives at her farm home, she has a mental picture of the company; so too does Mr. Smythe as he sits in his apartment on the 45th floor of a Chicago apartment building; and so does the corporate officer who is considering the purchase of major policies for his company. Each person, young or old, rich or poor, from the policyowner to the corporate officer, from the community member to the secretary of the state insurance commission—each one builds an image of the company on the basis of the letter he reads.

If the letter is curt, the company appears abrupt; if the letter is hackneyed, stereotyped, and dull, the company appears backward and stodgy; if the letter is discourteous or tactless, the company appears pompous and high-handed; if the letter is unattractive and sloppy, the company appears careless and negligent.

On the other hand, when the letter is clear and concise, the firm seems well organized and competent; when the letter is courteous and friendly, the company seems concerned and helpful; when the letter is attractive and neat, the company seems efficient and accurate. And so it goes: regardless of who wrote the letter, the message will reflect—to the reader—the image of the company.

The firm's manager may protest that a particular letter was carelessly written by an inexperienced, tactless new employee and is *not* an accurate reflection of company policy. But his protests will be to no avail. To the reader, the curt, overbearing, sarcastic letter *does* reflect the company. Say what you will, the image has been drawn, and good will and sales suffer.

Because the managements of many companies recognize this, they have set up training programs to improve the letter-writing abilities of their personnel. Some very large corporations have departments whose primary function is to evaluate company correspondence and train employees in letter writing. One large insurance firm holds classes, reviews correspondence, issues bulletins, and, at frequent intervals, reminds its employees of the importance of effective correspondence.

Other companies follow different patterns. Some engage outside consultants for evaluation and training purposes, and many firms subscribe to letter improvement bulletins sent out periodically by companies specializing in this service. Most firms today are aware of the importance of good company correspondence—and are doing something about raising their standards or keeping them high.

Mechanics

The training carried on for correspondents and management personnel in most organizations usually places little if any emphasis on the form and mechanics of the business letter, because these areas are considered the responsibility of the typist. However, the manager should have some familiarity with the topic. For that reason, Chapter Seventeen contains suggestions in this area.

The mechanics and form of the business letter vary considerably from one company to another. One firm requires that its employees use block form; another prefers modified block. One organization recommends identifying initials of dictator and typist, and another company omits them entirely. These minor variations in the form of the letter exist, and serve to express the individuality of companies. The "correct" form, therefore, is the one that a particular firm requires that its employees use. It is for this reason that many companies publish correspondence manuals and guides, written for their own use, which indicate their preference in letter layout, use of abbreviations, address style, signatures, and so on.

The mechanics of a business letter should be correct, but an error in typing or letter layout will not lose nearly as much good will as a tactless or sarcastic statement. Thus it is knowledge of the *principles* of business writing that is most important.

Principles of Communication

Tone

Tone, in written communication, may be said to be the quality of the person-to-person communication that comes from choice of words, topics discussed, and level of formality or informality of the message itself. Often a person will say, after reading a letter, "The tone of Acme's message was extremely friendly," or "tactful," or "impersonal," or "very positive." Our interpretation of the tone seems to depend on our reactions to the words used, the phrasing of the sentences, the order of the ideas. And this interpretation and evaluation of the tone as "friendly," "formal," "courteous," "high-pressured," then becomes the characteristic (friendly, formal, courteous, high-pressured) we tend to apply to the company as a whole.

Naturalness. There was a time when a good deal of attention was given to eliminating stiffness in business letters: hackneyed phrases, stereotyped expressions, obsolete and archaic references, and pompous statements. However, the number of letters we find today that contain such expressions is relatively few.

If you find that you sometimes use hackneyed expressions, drop them for more natural ones. It is doubtful that you use the following, or other, stereotyped expressions in speaking; why use them in writing?

As in the above	Enclosed please find
According to our records	Esteemed order
Advise	Hand you
As indicated	Hand you herewith
As per	Hereby acknowledge
At hand	Hoping to hear
At early date	In accordance with
Attached hereto	Previous to
Attached please find	Prior to
At your earliest convenience	Permit me to say
Avail yourself of this opportunity	Pursuant to

Beg to state	*Re* or *In re*
Beg to remain	Recent date
Contents duly noted	Take this opportunity
Contents noted	Trust that
Due to	We wish to state

On the other hand, the use of one or two of these in a piece of writing is certainly not bad; it is when a letter is filled with them that we receive an impression of a cold, severe, impersonal, and unfriendly company. Compare the two letters which follow. Notice that the messages are similar but the tone is not. What would your feelings be toward the companies that mailed them?

Because of the hackneyed phrases and the cold, formal tone, the reader may feel that the writer is totally unconcerned with the former's welfare.

Dear Mr. Baxter:

Received yours of the 15th and beg to state that item 204 of merchandise requested in your basic communication is out of stock and same can therefore not be shipped but will be back-ordered as per our policy.

Enclosed please find duplicate shipping ticket listing items being forwarded as per your request.

Hoping this proves satisfactory, we beg to remain,

The use of personal pronouns ("you," "we"), and courtesy ("It is always a pleasure to hear from you," "We are always eager to serve you . . .") promote a person-to-person feeling of concern.

Dear Mr. Baxter:

Your order #2146 has been received and is being processed. It is always a pleasure to hear from you.

All the merchandise you requested, with one exception, has been packaged and shipped via Midwest Fast Freight. Your order should arrive no later than January 20.

During the past month we have had an extremely heavy demand for the #204 Desk Lamps and they are temporarily out of stock. However, we are happy that they proved to be a popular and profitable item for our dealers.

We do expect a supplementary supply within 48 hours. The quantity you requested will then be sent via "special freight" and should arrive by January 26. Will this be satisfactory, Mr. Baxter? If not, please call us collect. We are always eager to serve you in every way we can.

It is true, of course, that the second letter required a little thought and probably cost the company a bit more in typing time than the first. But it is surely worth the investment. The longer letter reflects sincerity, warmth, and a natural tone that builds good will. The short one creates the impression of a company that is cold, unfriendly, and hardly concerned with going out of its way to satisfy a customer.

The Connecticut Life Insurance Company has published a booklet for its employees titled *Speak When You Write.* Its 18 pages are filled with suggestions on how to inject this natural, friendly tone into communications so that good will for the company will increase. The key perhaps is in the title—which of course should not be taken too literally. Connecticut Life does not literally mean "speak when you write." If we did write as we talked, our written communications would probably be quite wordy and repetitious. What is really meant is write as *you sound* when you talk. In this way your written communications will reflect the natural, friendly spontaneity of your spoken words.

Courtesy.   In this hurried world of ours, we sometimes overlook an opportunity to extend a little courtesy to those with whom we communicate. Letters often conclude with a phrase such as "Your merchandise was shipped on January 14." Why not add a "Thank you very much," or "Your business is always appreciated," or "We were happy we could ship this equipment immediately as you requested"? When *thank you, please, I appreciated,* or similar expressions are used in a letter—and used sincerely—they help create good will.

Positive, Not Negative; Optimistic, Not Pessimistic.   There are specific words and phrases in our vocabulary which evoke an unfavorable mental reaction which we tend to associate with the product or service to which the words refer. We have already discussed words as symbols for situations, experiences, and reactions; we know how words often make pictures in our minds. Thus, a department store does not put up a sign saying, "Complaint Department," because it would stimulate an unpleasant association. The terms "Adjustment Bureau" or "Customer Service Department," on the other hand, make the customer look forward to a helpful, favorable, and positive situation.

What would be a customer's reaction to an order form with the printed statement, "To avoid errors and mistakes in shipping, complete the order form as directed"? His immediate "picture reaction" to this sentence is obvious. He can only see his order delayed or lost, and anticipate being billed for merchandise he never received—it would be far better to tear up the order form and do business elsewhere. That is why the messages on most order forms do everything possible to stimulate a favorable reaction, a positive picture. Toward that end they may state, "Please complete the order form as requested for accurate and rapid shipment of merchandise."

What is it about these two statements which triggers different reactions? It is the words themselves. Certain words in our culture, used in a specific context, induce mental associations which are not favorable (negative), while others evoke a positive response. (See Hayakawa, "How Words Change Our Lives," in the Readings.)

Negative: We hope you won't be dissatisfied with the new All-American line.

Positive: We are sure you will be satisfied with the new All-American line.

Negative: We don't believe you will encounter trouble and difficulty in the installation of the new equipment.

Positive: For quick and efficient installation of the new equipment, please follow the directions contained in the instructional manual.

Under most conditions, it is wise to avoid words which precipitate a negative or unfavorable response. Words such as *trouble, dissatisfaction, complaint, hope, if, neglect, errors,* and *negligence* usually result in unfavorable mental associations for the product or service under discussion.

However, the negative tone is not always undesirable. It can be used to generate impact in a positive statement. This device is frequently used in advertising:

Negative problem: Have you provided for your advancing years?

Positive solution: Let us show you how enjoyable your retirement can be with Parker Protection.

Negative problem: Are you concerned that bad breath and teeth discoloration will offend those around you?

Positive solution: For sparkling teeth and mountain-fresh breath, use Glisten toothpaste every day.

The negative tone, when used in this way, certainly helps to sell many of America's products: insurance, health items, safety and personal hygiene products. But in every instance the negative tone must be handled with care, for negative symbols are much more likely to be remembered (and associated with a product) than pleasant, positive ones. This may be the reason why more and more insurance today is *not* sold as "death benefits or protection from disaster"—all negative—but for "living comfort, peace of mind, and security"—all positive.

Tact. The quality of tact in communication is certainly abstract and, as such, somewhat difficult to define. If you were to ask the man in the street, he might say that "tact is saying the right thing at the right time in the right way." But when you are trying to write a tactful letter, what is the right thing to say? when is the right time? what is the right way? It is clear that the standard definition of tact is not an adequate guide.

Like so many factors in communication, tact is intimately involved with words, their use, and their interpretation. If we say, "You failed to include the order form," or "We were surprised you did not understand the directions," or "We received your letter in which you claimed we did not ship," we are certainly being tactless. Is it because of the *denotations* of the key words, "You failed," "We were surprised," or "You claimed," or is it their *connotations?* Here we see an excellent example of how important the personal interpretation of words can be. Words which have simple, basic meanings can assume special connotations in specific contexts and result in statements which are interpreted as tactless and discourteous.

What is the answer? It's simple. Avoid words or phrases which may antagonize or embarrass. Pointing out another's error can be done so that the other person will not "lose face" if you choose the right words.

Tactless: We received your letter in which you claim we did not send. . . .
Better: Thank you for your letter concerning our shipment of December 3.

Tactless: We were surprised you did not understand the specifications we sent. . . .
Better: We are sending a more complete set of specifications for the job which we feel will. . . .

Tactless: You failed to indicate the color you preferred. . . .
Better: Please indicate the color you prefer and we will ship immediately.

Consideration—the "You" Attitude

Perhaps there is no quality in business writing that has received more attention than the "you" attitude. We discuss it, write about it, and lecture on it. Yet, it seems an elusive and a difficult concept to understand and to use.

Because of our nature and the society in which we live, our interests, activities, and goals usually center on ourselves. Most of us are impatient when *our* problems, *our* situations, *our* purchases are not examined from *our* point of view. We usually analyze the situations in which we are involved from *our* position and with *our* perceptions, and we often communicate our ideas and feelings from the same standpoint. It is easy to forget that the other person may have a position, feelings, and reactions which we have not been considering. Our decisions and actions always seem very logical to us. But how often do we ask ourselves how logical our actions are from the other person's viewpoint? (See Rogers and Roethlisberger, "Barriers and Gateways to Communication," and "Imagination Helps Communication" in the Readings.)

Essentially, a "you" attitude consists in viewing a situation from the other person's point of view. It requires a sensitivity to others, an appreciation of others, a respect for others. And this interest must be sincere, for, if it is not, the other person will be aware that it is false and resent it.

The use of the "you" attitude is most important when a difference of opinion exists. It is at precisely such times—when we are stoutly justifying and substantiating our point of view—that it is vital to appreciate the other person's.

To become aware of another's point of view will often require two attributes: sensitivity to his needs, and the ability to communicate your appreciation of his situation to him.

It must be emphasized that the "you" attitude is not necessarily *agreement*. It is quite possible to communicate a strong "you" attitude while disagreeing with the principles of the other person. People do not necessarily want us to agree with them; but they do want us to understand and appreciate their point of view. The secretary who wants a new $400 electric typewriter will be more willing to accept a "no" if her employer first indicates that he understands *why* she wants a new machine. The merchant will be more likely to accept a refusal if he is assured that his interpretation is valid but that franchise restrictions and government regulations will not permit a change in labeling.

The following letters illustrate the difference between a "you" attitude and a "we" or "I" attitude.

"We" Attitude

Dear Mr. Burling:

For several years we have shipped you and our other customers quantities of our Kentron Line from our St. Louis manufacturing plant and our Madewell Line from Chicago.

Although we have been happy to do this, you can appreciate that the cost to us for double shipping has often been excessive. This is especially true when orders are small, and our profit margin is consequently completely absorbed. Naturally no company is happy with such a situation. We certainly are not.

Beginning April 15, however, we will consolidate shipping procedures and we will forward both the Kentron and the Madewell Lines from Chicago. This will certainly save us money and will afford faster receipt of merchandise by our customers. In addition there will be less billing as well as other bookkeeping procedures for our firm to carry through.

We believe that you will agree that this new arrangement will prove wiser and more satisfactory for us as well as all concerned.

Is Mr. Burling really interested in the writer's "cost to us," "profit margin," and "save us money," or in the benefits he (Mr. Burling) will receive?

"You" Attitude

Dear Mr. Baxter:

We are happy to announce a change in our shipping procedure which will prove beneficial to you in many different ways.

For several years, as you know, we have been shipping you our Kentron and Madewell Lines from warehouses in St. Louis and Chicago respectively. Processing your order from two different cities sometimes resulted in service to you which was not always the most efficient or rapid.

Note that the tone throughout this letter seems to say, "We are completely interested in your welfare, Mr. Baxter."

```
Beginning April 15, however, our shipping will be consolidated.
All products will be shipped directly to you from Chicago.
This will result in several definite benefits to you:

    Your orders will now be filled and sent within 24 hours
    of our receipt of them.

    Shipping costs will be reduced, and the savings achieved
    will be passed on to our customers in the form of lower
    prices.

    We will maintain larger inventories so that you will enjoy
    complete selections at all times.


We are happy to add this new procedure to our list of services.
This, plus our high-quality products, sold at very competitive
prices, assures you of fast merchandise turnover and top prof-
it margins.
```

In the letter to Mr. Baxter the writer obviously has some appreciation of Mr. Baxter's point of view. He is concerned with Baxter's profits and convenience. In the letter to Mr. Burling, however, the writer has given no evidence of such appreciation. He is concerned only with his own point of view.

If a business letter has a sincere and effective "you" attitude, it needs little else, for the "you" attitude ensures that all other principles will be followed. If the writer is sincerely concerned with the reader's point of view and feelings he will be courteous in tone, his comments will be friendly and natural, he will organize his thoughts carefully, he will see to it that his letter is attractive, and make certain that his writing is clear, concise, and correct.

Effective Composition

Completeness. When facts or ideas are inadvertently omitted from business letters, we have a tendency to brush this off with "Oh, I forgot all about *that*." The result, however, is that another letter must be written to ask us about the items we omitted, and we in turn must reply again, to deal with the items we forgot about the first time. Perhaps no great harm is done in one isolated case, but if 10 percent of the letters a firm sends out are not complete, and the company mails approximately three thousand letters a week, the cost can be staggering. Not only is there the writing, typing, and mailing of unnecessary letters (at about $3.75 each), but the recipient's irritation when he finds that one of his questions was not answered is costly. The result can only be a loss of good will and, quite possibly, a customer.

Other factors are involved which are more difficult to measure. If, for example, Company Z writes to firms A, B, and C for information concerning cost, shipping dates, and guarantees on plastic widgets, and receives complete replies from firms A and B but not from C, will Z write to C and ask for shipping dates which were omitted? Not unless C's prices were significantly lower. Z will probably make a decision between A and B. Company C will not be considered because its letter was not complete.

When an industrial consultant is engaged to evaluate correspondence procedures in a company, he may begin by examining the files of incoming letters. He may find that 10 percent of the incoming letters contain such statements as "Thank you very much, but will you elaborate on . . ."; "We appreciated receiving . . . , send us additional details"; "Thank you . . . please be more explicit." These replies indicate that in many cases the original letter sent out lacked important details and required this type of follow-up to make the original communication complete.

When we communicate with others, we cannot always be sure precisely what they want, and from time to time our letters will not cover every point; however, we should avoid omitting important facts through carelessness. The key to writing letters that are as complete as we can make them with the facts at hand is simple: organize before you write.

Good Organization. Before the simplest letter is written, the writer should know precisely what topics he will cover. Some writers carefully read the letter to which they are replying and make notes in the margin or at the bottom of the page. Others find it more convenient to make notes on a piece of scratch paper, or draw up an outline of their reply. Still others prefer to outline mentally. The mechanics don't matter, so long as the writer has a guide to writing or dictating the reply letter. By checking the guide against the inquiry letter, the writer can ensure that his reply will be complete.

Here, for example, is a letter we have just taken out of its envelope. Let us read it, make an outline, and write a reply, taking care that *our* letter is as complete as we can make it.

Glen S. Robin
Robin Office Equipment Company
1414 North Jackson Avenue
Chicago, Ill. 60626

Dear Mr. Robin:

We received your recent announcement concerning the Bright-as-Day fluorescent desk lamps. They seem to be precisely what we have been looking for and we would like to have you send us two dozen charged to our account.

Your circular indicated that one free desk lamp would be included with each dozen purchased, provided the order was entered before June 1. Unfortunately it is now two weeks past that date, but we do hope that you will nevertheless send us two lamps without charge. Your announcement also indicated that the color of these desk lamps was gray; if possible we would like to get them in beige to match our office decor.

Our employees have discussed the new electric Shelley Pencil
Sharpener. It apparently saves work and produces an extremely
fine point. Do you carry this product and do you recommend
it, or do you feel that it is just another office "toy"?

What about the No. 107 Easy File cabinet which we ordered some
time ago and which you were out of stock on? Are you going
to ship this to us or are they no longer available?

Our check for last month's merchandise will be a little late
but you may expect to receive it prior to the 15th.

This is a letter to which we must reply as quickly as possible. But we should not do so unless we first organize our presentation. Let us look at the outline which we have jotted down and which we will use as a guide in replying to the above letter.

1. Acknowledge the order for lamps.
2. Explain tactfully that offer of a free lamp with each dozen no longer is available—agreement with manufacturer.
3. Comment on and promote electric pencil sharpener—recommend Efficiency Brand, not Shelley.
4. Desk lamps come only in gray, not beige.
5. Easy File cabinet due out in 30 days.
6. Sorry check will be late—discount of course is not possible.

The next step is to check the outline. Such an examination quickly shows us that point 4 should follow 2 (why break the discussion on lamps into two different segments?); that change can quickly be made. Our review also tells us that we have neglected to include a sales paragraph on the new Easy Roll typewriter tables. After those two changes have been made and the outline checked again, we are quite certain our letter will be complete and now we are ready to dictate. But under no circumstances should any communication be carried through without first making up a plan. If we do, we run the risk of writing a letter that is confused, unorganized, or incomplete. And of course, the result is costly and unnecessary correspondence.

Conciseness. It is disconcerting to read a letter which seems to ramble on and on. We must read it all because it involves a business transaction with which we are vitally concerned. But it is nevertheless irritating to plow through unending paragraphs, meaningless phrases, and unnecessary words.

Overall length is no sure guide. A letter covering a third of a page may be short but overly wordy. On the other hand, a three-page letter may be properly concise. We should strive to write business letters which do not waste words, in which every phrase, every clause, every statement says what needs to be said.

Wordy: It should be observed that not very many, in fact only 15, cases of absenteeism took place in the second month of this year, February; the very month, in fact, when the new system was begun.

Revised: Only 15 cases of absenteeism were recorded during February, the month the new system was begun.

Wordy: We found after careful investigation and research that several different organizations and companies were satisfactory, and offered programs which were designed to improve the ability of our engineers in the vital and important area of report writing.

Revised: We learned that six firms in the New York area were qualified to offer programs in report writing for engineering personnel.

Wordy: We have found that many customers of this firm have been quite concerned and upset by our new policy on deliveries. This new delivery policy requires a minimum order from each and every customer; these orders are to have a minimum dollar value of $50.

Revised: Many of our customers have become concerned about our new delivery policy which requires a $50 minimum order.

Notice how the meaning becomes clearer, understanding easier, and impact greater when unnecessary words have been dropped and phrases made shorter.

Clarity. Much confusion has been caused by lack of clarity in business communication. The sentence which can be interpreted by the reader in two different ways, or is not understood at all, is most disturbing. How should the reader interpret this statement: "If the safety bracket for the 333 Press has been completed, send it at once"? What should he ship? If he sends the press and the bracket is desired, he will have a staggering freight bill to pay. If he sends the bracket and it was the press that was wanted, time and a customer may be lost.

Everything you write, whether it is a six-line memo or a three-page letter, should be checked for clarity. If there is the slightest doubt in your mind about the clarity of what you have set down, you should immediately strike it out and rewrite it.

Diction. Statements can be clear, unified, and coherent, but yet not as accurate and precise as they should be. If you mean "thoroughly examined," you should not say "looked over"; if you mean "A proportional stratified sample was taken," you should not write "A survey was made."

Because business communication is often the basis for making decisions, precision and accuracy in diction (word choice) are very important. One or two words, carelessly chosen, may convey a thought which is far from the one desired.

Vague: Sales of the Kenwood Lumber Company have gone up during the past two or three years.

Precise: Sales of the Kenwood Lumber Company increased by 4 percent in 1975 and 8 percent in 1974 over the gross sales figures of 1973.

Vague: Quality control is assured by running tests on the mixture periodically.

Precise: Quality control of the cookie mixture is maintained by testing samples taken at 9 a.m., 1 p.m., and 3 p.m. each day.

Correctness. Careful though we may be in our writing, we sometimes make mistakes. We misspell a word, place an apostrophe incorrectly, insert the wrong punctuation mark, or use a plural instead of a singular verb. When we make such errors we should try to catch them.

It is a strange quirk of human nature that causes most people to notice that something is awry. An error in grammar or punctuation will be immediately apparent to someone else. Because the reader focuses on the error, voluntarily or not, he will necessarily give less attention to the content of the message or the letter. Some of its impact is lost. (See Fielden, "What Do You Mean I Can't Write?" in the Readings.)

And because letters are often all the recipient knows of a company, errors in basic English must diminish, to some degree, his opinion of the firm. Management must see to it, therefore, that its correspondents have mastered not only the intangibles like tact, courtesy, clarity, precision, but also the basic principles of good English. And the author of every piece of written communication should proofread it carefully before it is placed in a communication channel.

Attractiveness. The final principle has little to do with effective statement of ideas, but everything to do with communication—for communication depends as much on the nonverbal message as it does on the verbal. Your ideas may be brilliant, your statements clear, tactful, concise, accurate, and in correct English—but if those beautiful statements are thrown together haphazardly on paper, with no form or balance, the recipient will probably not even read them; if he does, it will be with prejudice. The careless erasure, the negligent strikeover, the jammed margin, the enormous, heavy 42-line block paragraph, the message poorly spaced and placed badly on the page—these reflect little credit on the company sending the letter or on the manager who signs it.

Although the handling of the mechanical aspects of the business letter, such as typing, style, and format, is the task of the secretary, the manager should have some familiarity with it (see Chapter Seventeen). And it is the manager's responsibility to see that letters going out over his name meet his standards of attractiveness.

Questions for Study

I. Revise the following sentences, eliminating phrases that are hackneyed, tactless, negative, and wordy.

1. You will not be unhappy if you decide to purchase and stock Carlin's Valves.

2. Your firm will encounter no difficulties or troubles if you decide to install our Mark III Frigid Air Conditioning system.

3. If you always include complete shipping instructions and your code number, we will be able to process your order without error.

4. We received your letter in which you claimed we did not ship your complete order on January 4.

5. We hope that you will have no difficulty installing your automatic cutter; please follow directions enclosed to avoid problems.

6. I was surprised that you did not understand our objectives in this case.

7. We know that you will appreciate our situation in this case regarding our refusal of your request for the free case of Snappettes with your dozen-case order because of your request being received almost a month after the special offer ended.

8. You neglected to include the invoice for the merchandise which was shipped on August 3.

9. You don't seem to understand that all the information requested on the credit application form is needed if we are to open a charge account for you.

10. Under ordinary circumstances we would not feel that it is necessary to request your full compliance in following the routine steps necessary in a legal situation of this sort, but to maximize your benefits and because of the fact that your child is not of legal age, we urge that all documents be completed precisely and filed according to the instructions contained in Reg. 254AT.

11. As per your valued instructions of April 28 we herewith hand you, as per your request, all necessary data for account 239.

12. May we take the liberty to inform you that henceforth we will be available for order processing on Saturdays.

II. Revise the following sentences where necessary. Eliminate phrases that are hackneyed, tactless, negative, and wordy.

1. In reference to yours of the fifth, we hand you herewith our check for $128.50.

2. It is our unbiased and considered opinion that under circumstances such as these, it would be to your best interests to pay your past due bill within a time period of 10 days.

3. We beg to state that all merchandise herewith requested is to be delivered to our place of business no later than December 10.

4. Please be advised, in reference to yours of the second, that requirements of the State of New York in this regard have been noted and will be carried through.

5. We hope you will now find it possible to place an order with us and avail yourself of the 5 percent discount being offered to special customers such as yourself.

6. Now that we have repaired your motor, we hope that you will not continue to encounter operational failures with it.

7. If you encounter problems with your Kelton unit, please call and we will do our best to alleviate the situation.

8. We were extremely sorry to learn from your letter of May 2 that the 1 h.p. motor we shipped arrived with the wrong plug attachment, a broken base, and a cracked safety shield. We are sending your replacement today.

9. It is difficult for me to understand how you arrived at your request for a $94 credit.

10. We feel very strongly, at least to some degree, that all merchandise purchased during the period previous to the opening day of the sale is not eligible nor should it receive the 2 percent discount which is explained in our sales advertisements.

III. Answer the following questions as concisely as possible.

1. Define a "you" attitude and a "we" attitude as concisely as possible.

2. Review the article "What Communication Means" by P. Drucker, (see Readings section of this book) and indicate his approach to the "you attitude." What specific relationship do his comments on "expectations and perceptions" have to the "you attitude"? How does that quality enter into his discussion of "downward communication"?

3. Review the article "Imagination Helps Communication" (see Readings section of this book) and indicate the author's approach to the "you attitude." How does the title relate to that quality? Select a sentence or two or a paragraph in the essay which you feel defines or describes the "you attitude."

4. From a semantic point of view, what happens in the process of decoding as a result of negative statements being used by the encoder? (You may wish to comment on word connotations and words as symbols.)

IV. In each pair of the statements which follow, the sentences convey essentially the same idea. Why do we feel that the one listed first in each pair is less tactful than the second, and what is the role that word connotations play in the interpretation of these statements?

1. a) "We received your letter in which you claim we did not ship."
   b) "We received your letter in which you indicated we did not ship."

2. a) "You failed to list the colors desired for the file cabinets ordered, and we therefore find it difficult to complete your request."
   b) "Your order will be shipped immediately after we hear from you as to the colors you prefer for the file cabinets listed on your Purchase Order 4-212."

3. a) "I was surprised that you did not understand our policies for customer return of merchandise."
   b) "Our customers may return merchandise for full credit on the basis of the policy printed on the reverse of all invoices."

V. "To be a good writer, one must be a severe critic of his own efforts." Assume you have written the letters which follow. Edit them carefully and then submit a completed version.

1. Mr. Robert T. Compton, President
   Apex Manufacturing Company
   4112 North 14th Street
   Chicago, Illinois 60615

   Gentlemen:

   Just three weeks ago we received six one-horsepower motors from you people on our purchase order F-121-A.

   As you probably recall, we have been purchasing motors from you for many years to run our equipment and by and large we have had no quarrel with the quality of the merchandise, although your price is sometimes out of line, until three weeks ago when we received six one-horsepower motors as per P.O. F-121-A.

   Three of the motors were immediately put into use and within two weeks, two have become inoperable. We have checked the lead, current supply, etc., and find everything in order except the motors. We believe that perhaps your manufacturing process in these two cases was faulty and you will therefore want to make proper changes.

Hoping to hear from you in the near future, we remain,

2. Caelson, Caelson, and Caelson
   Caelson Towers
   145 North Fourth Street
   New Orleans, Louisiana

   Gentlemen:

   May we take this opportunity to thank you most graciously and sincerely for placing your order for office furniture with our firm.

   All the merchandise which you requested, with one exception, has been shipped from our warehouse via Western Van Lines and should arrive within 10 days of today's date. The item in question—reception room lamp tables (2)—was temporarily out of stock, but will be shipped to you to complete the order.

   You asked about a matching coffee table for the reception room and we would suggest that at the moment you might cancel the idea. Your reception area is relatively small and to place a coffee table in it might result in a very cluttered appearance. Perhaps a slant-type wall magazine rack would be wiser to utilize for the display of periodicals. As you can see, we are much more interested in your welfare than in securing just another sale.

   And, oh yes; getting back to the lamp tables—they will be shipped in approximately two weeks of this date.

   Miss Betty Cavanaugh will stop by this coming week to talk to you about art accessories for the offices and reception areas. I'm sure you'll find her suggestions valuable as to paintings, reproductions, statuary, etc.

VI. Secure three actual business letters and submit a brief criticism of each. Substantiate your critical comments by referring to specific portions of the message or by quotations from it. Remember to note the good points as well as those which require improvement.

   Structure your comments around the following points:

1. The principles of clarity, appearance, tact, "you" attitude, tone, etc.

2. The effectiveness of the letter in achieving its intended objective in light of the reader to whom it is directed.

Chapter Eight

Inquiry and Claim Communications Requiring Action and Response

Inquiries and Requests
Orders
Claims

Although all effective business letters should have certain attributes in common—conciseness, coherence, courtesy, reader orientation, completeness, etc.—the organization of the message differs according to the type of letter. The order of points in a refusal of a claim is different from that of a grant. The make-up of a sales promotion piece is not the same as that of a collection letter. Obviously the content depends on the message to be communicated. As the content changes for the different types, so too does the organization.

As our society has become more complex, so have the services and products which are available. Frequently today a relatively simple component may be manufactured from raw materials which are secured from a dozen different sources. Often too the item itself must conform to government specifications or be interchangeable with a similar product manufactured by another firm. Thus, a company must request information, as well as order supplies, from a variety of sources. To secure the data and the raw materials often requires a great deal of correspondence, much of which is concerned with asking and answering questions. A good example of a company operating at this level is the Lockheed Corporation. This firm manufactures aircraft, ships, electronic equipment, and missile components, and engages in undersea and space research, plus many other activities. Of course, Lockheed manufactures thousands of items but it also purchases from some 20,000 suppliers. To secure the necessary materials from all these companies requires a mountain of forms and letters. The same problems are encountered by many other firms.

In this and the following chapters we shall discuss inquiries, requests, orders, claims, and collection letters—in effect, letters which require an answer or some sort of action.

Inquiries and Requests

Essentially, an inquiry asks for information. A request goes further; it asks for someone's services as a speaker, for endorsement of a product, for a free sample—in short, it requires action beyond a simple written reply.

Before you begin to write a letter of inquiry or a request, you must know, of course, exactly what your purpose is—what information or action you want. Keep in mind that you, and the recipient of your letter, are both busy. Make an outline. Include every point for which you want an answer and every point necessary to make your desires absolutely clear.

Your inquiry may be simple and brief: Who is the distributor in our area? How quickly can he ship a carload? Is a discount available? Or your inquiry may be complex and difficult: What would be involved in air conditioning our offices? What kind of market is there for our product on the West Coast? What does the Affirmative Action Program mean to us? The principle is the same— be complete, be clear, be courteous. And, particularly when the problem is a complex one, get to the point immediately. Your first sentence or two should state the subject, so that from the very beginning the receiver can identify the problem; he will not have to wade through extraneous greetings and references. He will be more likely to answer specifically and directly if you ask in the same manner.

We can see how much effort would be wasted if Office Manager Lyons sent us an inquiry in which he simply asked about air-conditioning equipment for his firm and omitted important details.

Request is vague and incomplete.

```
Dear Mr. Martin:

Because our firm is located in a Chicago Loop area which gets
very hot in the summer, we are considering air-conditioning
these quarters.

Your firm has been recommended to me by several people in the
Office Managers' Association and I am therefore writing you
for information.

We occupy an area of approximately 24,000 square feet and we
would like to have this entire space air-conditioned.  Will
you, therefore, send me information concerning the cost and
feasibility of this project?
```

If Mr. Lyons' letter were no more detailed than this, we would have to write back and ask him if he was interested in window units or central air conditioning, what was the capacity of his electrical supply lines, and about the layout of his place—several rooms, one large room, a large room with dividers? These questions might require several more letters, costing money, wasting time, and irritating people.

The following letter makes the same inquiry, but in such a way that the desired information can be provided promptly.

Dear Mr. Martin:

For some time we have been considering the feasibility of air-conditioning our offices. It is our understanding that your firm has made many installations of the type we require.

We occupy 24,000 square feet of office space on the ninth floor of the Stewart Building at 140 East Lincoln Boulevard. Because we use only a portion of the Stewart Building, it would be necessary for us to have some type of individual unit or units rather than a central system which would utilize the building's duct work. It is my understanding that our present electrical outlets are wired to accommodate almost any electrical demands placed on them.

Specifically, I would like to have your answers to the following questions:

1. How many and what type of air conditioning units would you suggest?
2. Are units available which are quiet enough so as not to interfere with office efficiency?
3. Would it be possible to have such an installation completed before the end of June?
4. Do you handle the engineering problems, as well as equipment and installation, or would it be necessary for us to secure additional professional assistance?

I am enclosing a floor plan of our offices which indicates walls, window openings, and furniture placement. I believe you will require this before you can give us an estimate of the cost of the job.

Because we would like to make a decision on this project prior to April 28, when we have an executive meeting scheduled, I would appreciate a reply from you by April 23. You may be sure that any information of a confidential nature will be respected as such.

These specific questions help the reader to make a definite response.

This insures receiving a reply in a timely fashion.

This letter of inquiry has several attributes which every letter of this type should possess:

1. Reason for inquiry, in the first or second sentence.
2. The inquiry itself, with specific questions listed.
3. Indication of the date by which a reply is needed.
4. Assurance that information will be considered confidential (if applicable).

The letter that follows includes these criteria. The reader will be able to reply intelligently because of the completeness of the material.

Dear Mr. Jameson:

As you may have heard, our firm is seriously considering the purchase of the Aero Air Craft Plant in your city. From the point of view of total space, location, physical facilities, and other attributes, this plant appears satisfactory. However, we are not quite sure whether we will find an adequate labor supply in Baseside, inasmuch as Aero has not used this plant for some eighteen months and the city itself is not very large.

We would be most grateful if you, because of your position, could inform us as to the availability of personnel in the following categories:

1. 800 unskilled production workers;
2. 35 engineers--mechanical and electrical;
3. 40 clerical personnel;
4. 35 office personnel--typists, stenographers, and miscellaneous.

In addition to this information, can you also send me data on the educational institutions in the area? Are there nearby high schools and colleges for our personnel who would be interested in night classes? What universities are available for those of our people who wish to pursue further education? Do you think it will be possible for us to fill our future needs of approximately 15-20 business and engineering graduates per year from the surrounding universities?

You may be sure that the information you give me in answer to these questions will be held in confidence, if you so desire. We request that this inquiry be kept confidential.

Inasmuch as our board of directors will meet on May 10 to make a decision concerning the possible purchase of this plant, I would appreciate a reply from you by April 28. Thank you for your assistance.

A list of specific questions helps the receiver to make a specific reply.

Assurance of confidence is often important.

In the letter above, action can be taken and an intelligent reply sent to the inquirer. And this is the objective of every letter of inquiry: to elicit an intelligent and complete reply.

The inquirer should make it as easy as possible for the recipient to reply. He can do this by listing his questions in an orderly fashion and by limiting himself to essentials; obviously it is unrealistic to ask so many questions that replying to the letter would require an unreasonable expenditure of time or money. The writer may even wish to assist the recipient of his inquiry letter by including a self-addressed envelope. And, of course, the writer must recognize when *not* to ask for information by letter: If a problem is too complex, too abstract, or too detailed, it may be necessary to set up an interview or a conference to discuss it.

Request letters follow the same pattern as inquiry letters. Because they are asking for action, however, rather than just an answer, they should be even clearer, if possible, and they should be written far in advance of the proposed date of action.

```
Dear Ms. Robertson:

We are holding a week-long workshop for our middle-management
employees, beginning October 14.  The workshop will consist
of talks and discussions on various phases of business.  The
seminars are to be led by persons prominent in each field.

We have scheduled discussion of "Corporate Communication" for
Tuesday afternoon, October 15.  We would be grateful if you
could present a 20-30 minute talk and then answer questions
for a brief period.

The meeting will begin at 1:30 p.m. in the Eagle Room of the
Mereside Hotel.  The group consists of 25 men and women.  And
will you and your husband join us for dinner afterward?

I do hope you can help us.  Will you let me know by
September 5?
```

Because the writer of the above letter is requesting a favor, he makes the project interesting; he refers to the reader as a "prominent person"; he gives all necessary details; he subtly assumes the reader will accept; and finally, he invites the speaker—and her husband—to dinner.

Orders

Because of the sheer weight of numbers, most firms today use a printed order blank or purchase order form rather than placing orders by letter; it is more efficient and less costly to use forms and blanks. Nevertheless, every order must include certain information if it is to be filled correctly; whether you use a form or a letter, you must be certain to include most or all of the following data:

1. Catalog number
2. Quantity
3. Description of merchandise (model number, size, color)
4. Unit price; total price
5. Precise identification of purchasing unit or purchaser
6. Where merchandise is to be shipped
7. How merchandise is to be shipped (rail, truck, mail)

8. Payment method (c.o.d., open account, check enclosed, etc.)
9. Delivery date desired
10. Miscellaneous information which may be included:
    a. order number
    b. date of order
    c. salesman's name
    d. information on substitutions
    e. instructions for "back order"

The businessman or consumer who writes a letter to place an order should be sure that it includes as much of the above data as possible. His primary objective is to secure the merchandise and not a reply requesting "additional information which you inadvertently omitted."

Claims

Business transactions do not always run smoothly. Regardless of how careful or efficient business organizations are, various steps in their operations will go wrong from time to time. Merchandise may be shipped to a wrong address or arrive in less than perfect condition; billing may be incorrect; details for an order may be confused; badly needed articles may be delayed; quality may not be at the level expected.

When these situations occur, a claim letter is usually sent. And because most people in industry recognize that errors do take place, the letter—if it is reasonably and properly written—will bring the desired adjustment. Claims must be handled efficiently, for in one year's time the amount of money involved can reach a very significant level.

One Los Angeles firm, as an illustration, recently found that many of its vital dollars were being drained away because of poor claim procedures. A management consulting firm found that the company had submitted some $60,000 in claims to suppliers, shippers, and dealers in one year. However, it had received only $8000 in adjustments. Investigation disclosed that the claims which were entered were incomplete and inaccurate and that follow-ups were almost nonexistent. The poor ratio of adjustments received to claims entered was the fault not of the firms to whom the requests were submitted, but of the company entering the claims.

In an attempt to improve the situation and secure a more favorable adjustment record, a brief training program was given to those persons concerned with claims. Once they began writing complete, clear, and specific claim letters, the amount of adjustments rose dramatically. It was estimated that, in the year following the initial survey of this company, adjustments received increased some $30,000 as a result of improved communication in this one area.

There are various levels of claim problems. If a transaction does not go precisely as we have requested and it is a matter of correcting a very understandable situation, we make a *routine* claim. If, however, the situation has several facets and there is a question as to who is responsible, we enter a *non-routine* claim.

Routine Claim Letters

Routine claim letters are usually associated with relatively minor situations. When the wrong quantity, size, color, or model has been shipped, a routine claim will usually correct the situation. Or perhaps an error has been made in pricing, discount privileges, or other matters of a routine nature. In such cases, all that is necessary is a clear, specific, concise letter listing the facts of the situation.

```
Dear Mr. Hollins:

Our order #415 was delivered to our warehouse this morning
via Michigan Transport Service.

All the items we requested arrived in excellent condition with
one exception.  If you will refer to our original order, you
will note that we requested your #606 fluorescent desk lamp.
Apparently, an error was made in the processing of this order,
because we received your #608 model instead of the one we
requested.

Will you kindly pick up those you sent out and substitute an
equal quantity (30) of the model #606?

Because we already have orders for several of the #606, we
would appreciate your attention to this within the next few
days.
```

Note that the writer says clearly that, with the one exception, the delivery was thoroughly satisfactory. He does not say "you made an error," but "an error was made." He mentions the demand for the product, and he assumes his claim is completely valid and will be taken care of (positive tone).

Because mistakes do happen in order filling, shipping, billing, etc., some firms have prepared form letters for routine claims which require a few blank spaces to be completed.

Nonroutine Claim Letters

In many business situations where an error occurs, the facts are not always clear-cut and obvious. The buyer may feel that he has $140 due him because the damage took place prior to his receipt of the merchandise. The seller, however, feels that it left his premises in perfect condition. Or perhaps the buyer maintains that he did not receive a case of merchandise though the seller insists that he did. These situations and a hundred others will result in nonroutine claim letters being written. They are nonroutine because there is a difference of opinion as to precisely who is at fault. But errors do occur and settlements must be made. Sometimes the adjustments are in favor of the seller; sometimes they favor the buyer. One thing is certain: the seller does not relish receiving a claim letter nor does the buyer like to write one. At the moment, however, we are concerned with the buyer and the claim he enters.

The letter he writes should be so well written that it will result in a specific answer. He hopes that that answer will be a "yes, we will credit your account." If, however, the buyer cannot secure an affirmative reply, he should strive for one that suggests a compromise. And if he can secure neither, then he should look for an answer that says "no." Of course, the "no" is not very satisfactory, but at least it tells him where he stands. He may now take his business elsewhere if he is unhappy, or accept the "no" he has received. Obviously a follow-up to a "no" will depend on the strength and size of the claim. However, one reply which the claimant should make every effort to avoid receiving is that which conveys no definite answer. Such a response is merely a brush-off or a delaying action, and it goes something like this:

> We will look into it; may we suggest that you do the same. Please be assured that this will be settled to our mutual satisfaction. Now let me call your attention to a special we are running. . . .

This type of letter is no better than none at all. Time has been wasted, and as the days and weeks go by without an adjustment, the strength and immediacy of the claim decline.

However, claim letters can be written so that they will result in a definite answer. The following outline should be generally followed in the composition of an effective claim letter:

1. An introductory statement referring precisely and specifically to the transaction.
2. A specific statement of the loss or damage incurred.
3. A specific statement of the adjustment desired.
4. A statement which will motivate favorable action.
5. A friendly close.

When the buyer is certain that his claim is correct from every point of view, and that the adjustment he is requesting is honest in every respect, then he should check his letter to be sure that the tone is positive (but not accusing), the statements specific, and the details precise. On the other hand, if he is not sure who is at fault or exactly how the damage or loss occurred, he can only write honestly and request that both parties do what is necessary to reach an equitable solution.

If his letter reflects a tone of uncertainty, the recipient will very probably seize upon that tone to delay making an adjustment. The following statements, for example, have been changed to produce a much more positive tone:

> We believe the damage took place. . . .
> The damage took place. . . .
>
> We think you did not include. . . .
> . . . was not included.
>
> It is our feeling that perhaps the loss. . . .
> The loss took place on January 10.

Just as the tone should be positive, so too should the statements of loss or damage be specific and precise. Note the contrast between the original and revised versions of the sentences below:

We suffered a considerable loss.
Our loss was $58.12.

The damage was quite extensive and we believe that. . . .
The damage was extensive and amounted to $114.52.

We imagine that it would be quite expensive for us to replace the damaged watch.
Replacement of the damaged watch would come to $85.50; this is the amount of the adjustment requested.

Sometimes the writer, in an effort to be courteous, will not be as positive and as specific as he should, lest his statement be interpreted as "pushy." It is important to be courteous, to give the reader credit for good will and care; but an element of uncertainty or vagueness may give the adjustor an opportunity to send a response that will result in delay and unnecessary correspondence. When the claim letter is framed to include the five points listed above and its tone is positive and its statements specific, the reply will usually be favorable.

The writer has been so specific that the reader must take positive or negative action.

Dear Mr. Fox:

On March 15 we received our order #207 from you. You may recall that this included a large quantity of lawn furniture, barbecue accessories, and outdoor cookware.

If you will check our original purchase order, you will find that we requested six dozen sets of your Patio Grill Sets. Three dozen were to be sent in the regular style at $2.50 each and the remainder in the deluxe at $3.50 per set.

We have just started to display this merchandise and we have found that you inadvertently sent us five dozen of the regular and only one dozen of the deluxe. However, we have been billed according to our original purchase order.

Although we are aware that claims are to be submitted within ten days of receipt of merchandise and almost five weeks have now gone by, we nevertheless feel that you will understand our position in this case and credit our account for the $24.00 which is due.

Inasmuch as this is the first claim of this nature that we have submitted in some three years of satisfactory business relations with you, we know you will handle it as we request. In the future we shall check the markings on each package to avoid such a situation.

Notice in the letter above that the writer is so specific and precise in his presentation of facts, and the tone of the letter is so positive, that it has apparently never occurred to him that the recipient might question the claim. The letter below, however, presents a contrast and certainly permits the reader to send back an equivocal reply.

Dear Mr. Wolf:

On March 28 your truck delivered the Empire Conference Table which we ordered on February 2.

Because our executive office facilities were not completely decorated at the time of delivery (as we had hoped they would be), the table was stored in our warehouse. Two days ago the painting and decorating of the conference room was completed and the table was brought in. It was at that time that we noticed a deep scratch running across the top of the table.

You may be sure that we were very upset, for we feel that the damage probably occurred prior to our receiving this piece of furniture. We do hope that you will want to make the proper adjustment in this case and we will look forward to hearing from you at your convenience.

This claim is so vague that the recipient could hardly make an adjustment even if he were inclined to.

Obviously this letter offers many opportunities for the recipient to legitimately delay taking specific action. The word "probably" will surely result in a letter asking for further investigation. Then, too, the writer did not indicate whether the table had been left with its protective wrappings on while stored, and he certainly neglected to point out what adjustment he would consider equitable. Should the table be replaced or refinished? And finally, he made no reference to former business associations which might help motivate a favorable response. Thus when he receives a reply that only suggests further investigation, he will have no one to blame but himself.

The letter which follows, like the one above to Mr. Fox, permits the recipient to answer only with a "yes" or a "no" or a compromise.

Dear Mr. Wilshire:

On June 27 we ordered 110 yards of your Superior Brand Leather at $2.10 per yard. This was requested on our purchase order #2131.

For some unexplained reason, we received our shipment from you one month after it had been entered, instead of within the usual ten days. When the merchandise arrived, we found that you had shipped us the correct quantity but in your Deluxe Espanol Brand. This was billed to us at $3.50 per yard.

This claim letter is clear, specific, and direct.

Because we were under a deadline arrangement with one of our
clients, we had no alternative except to cut this leather
and fabricate it into the furniture items (chairs) he had
ordered.

Of course, you can appreciate that our price quotations to
him were based on the cost of the Superior Brand Leather.
We, therefore, had no way of making up the $1.40 difference
per yard and could only bill him at the original price we had
quoted him. You can see that your error, though certainly
unintentional, resulted in a loss to us of $154.

Because of our long and favorable business association, we
believe that you will see the situation as we do and will want
to credit our account for one half the amount in question:
$77. May we hear from you regarding this adjustment at your
earliest possible convenience?

Here there are almost no questions the recipient can ask which would delay the adjustment. Why was the more expensive leather used without communicating with the manufacturer? Precisely what was the loss? Exactly what kind of adjustment is required? Each of these questions and others are answered and the only action the receiver of the letter can take is to send back an affirmative or negative reply.

Claims at the Consumer Level

All too often, discussions on claims situations are concerned only with those made between one company and another. But what about Joe Average who has purchased a faulty television set, automatic washer, wrist watch, automobile, or refrigerator? We frequently hear him complaining, but when asked what he has done about the situation, he responds with, "How can I fight a giant corporation like . . . ?"

The truth is that he *can* enter a successful claim against a major company. Unfortunately, he frequently suffers (and loses money) in silence. He should not. He should complain; if his letter is written as suggested above, he will probably receive the satisfaction to which he is entitled. But he must keep in mind that major corporations receive dozens of claim letters each day, of which perhaps 50 percent are legitimate. If he will write his letter specifically, courteously, and accurately, and enclose necessary substantiating data, such as bills, chances are very good that he will receive the adjustment he deserves. Certainly it would be foolish for a major American corporation to pay a television star $100,000 a week and then not take care of a faulty $20 relay switch in an automatic washer. The companies want to build good will with the American consumer; quality products and friendly service will help achieve that goal. When the consumer has difficulty, it is just as important for him to write an excellent claim letter as it is for the wholesaler.

Mr. Robert T. Farmont, President
General American Appliance Corporation
25 East Edison Parkway
New York, New York

Dear Mr. Farmont:

On March 28 I purchased a model #505 General American Refrigerator. This was secured from Star Appliance Dealers located in our city at 1511 West Marble Avenue.

You may be sure that this was not a hasty purchase. My husband and I checked several different models and examined the various companies' products carefully. We finally decided that the best and most attractive refrigerator on the market was yours, and we were delighted when it was delivered to our home.

After we had it for approximately seven weeks, we found to our disappointment that your beautiful appliance did not function as efficiently as we had been led to believe. Although the model #505 is sold as a "self-defrost" unit, it certainly did not live up to this qualification. At the end of the first three weeks we had to turn it off and chip away at the large chunks of ice which had formed in the refrigerator and freezer sections. Star Appliance Dealers sent out a repair man, but three weeks later we were again chipping away.

A second complaint to Star resulted in our being told that their guarantee period had expired and that we should get in touch with a commercial repair service.

I think that you will agree with me that a $375 refrigerator should give much better service and satisfaction than what we have experienced from your product.

We feel that you will want to see to it that this appliance is properly repaired or that we receive a new one as quickly as possible. I have always felt the General American Appliances were of excellent quality and made by a reliable firm. I know that you will want me to continue to feel this way in the future.

Note that the tone is courteous and understanding while the facts presented are clear, specific, and complete.

This letter is, like other good claim letters, specific, precise, and positive. Under ordinary conditions, it should result in favorable action.

One of the key factors is to be restrained and tactful in describing the situation and requesting an adjustment. To bluntly accuse the recipient of your letter of intentionally causing you a loss can only result in hard feelings and unfriendly relations. Every claim letter should be based on the premise that the error was completely inadvertent. No one likes being accused, and when a claim letter is unreasonable in its comments and its requests become demands, the effect on the recipient is likely to be negative.

Questions for Study

I. Offer your constructive criticism of the following inquiry, request, and claim letters. Remember to indicate which sections of the letters deserve favorable comments, as well as where improvements can be made. Be as specific as possible in your evaluations.

1. Dear Dr. Flowers:

   We have recently been talking to Mr. Robert Faverman concerning an opening we have for corporate training director. Because of your close association with Mr. Faverman at the University of California, we felt that you might be able to give us some important background information on him.

   We are especially interested, Dr. Flowers, in your opinions of Mr. Faverman in the following areas:

   1. His ability to get along with top management and "sell" them on the need for training of their personnel in necessary areas.
   2. His creative imagination in designing programs for all levels of management personnel.
   3. His instructional ability.
   4. His supervisory ability in organizing and delegating tasks to subordinate personnel in the Training Department.

   Details that you can add to the above regarding Mr. Faverman—his ability to communicate, appearance, sense of humor—will all be appreciated.

   Because of our desire to make a decision in the near future, I would appreciate your reply by June 15. Of course, all information you forward will be retained in confidence.

   Thank you very much.

2. Dear Dr. Kempton:

   The members of the Kansas City Engineering Association hold a monthly meeting which features a cocktail hour, dinner, and a speaker.

   We wonder if you would be available to be our speaker for the March meeting scheduled for the 28th at the Engineers' Club at 318 South Jackson Boulevard. We begin our "Happy Hour" at 5:30, dinner is served an hour later, and the speaker goes on at 7:30 for about a 45-minute presentation.

   Because of your research and publications in the area of cardiac conditions, it was felt that an address on "The Young Executive and Cardiac Stress" would be valuable and very timely if carefully prepared. Unfortunately our budget does not permit us to offer you an honorarium, but we can promise an excellent dinner and a responsive and interested group.

   May we count on your acceptance of our offer?

3. Dear Mr. Petre:

   Early this month we placed an order of 112 replacement chairs for our employee cafeteria.

   As you may recall, these were your model 242 but modified to include a swivel seat. We now find that after only two or three weeks' use, a sizable number of these chairs do not "swivel" easily, or at all, and are extremely noisy when people get in or out of them.

Will you arrange to pick up the faulty chairs and correct the condition or supply us with new ones? Of course we will have to have replacement chairs in the cafeteria to substitute for those you remove. Remember to bring those along. Can you make arrangements to correct this situation by the end of this month?

We were under the impression you used high-grade ball bearings, but you apparently don't.

4. Dear Mr. Carmody:

On June 15, we ordered an Excello Color TV set, model 209. This was delivered, as requested, on July 1.

Our plan was to have this unit installed in our new Employee Lounge on July 1. However, the painters and carpet men did not finish until late in July. Thus we requested and had one of your men complete the installation on August 2.

On August 25 the set "went out" and your repair man told us the picture tube was "shot" and other items needed repair. He indicated that our 30-day warranty had expired and repair costs would be $185 including labor.

Inasmuch as the set was stored from July 1 until August 2 and not removed from the carton, I think you'll agree that the set did "go out" within the 30-day warranty period. Of course it was technically in our possession for almost twice that period, but I'm sure you will appreciate our point of view and make the necessary repairs without charge. Your reputation for fair play is well known and we hope you will act favorably in this instance.

II. Complete any of the following problems assigned. You may wish to review the chapter and note key points before solving the problem.

1. It is your understanding that the Midwest Office Equipment Company has a trade-in service for typewriters. You presently have 18 manual machines in your office and would like to replace them with automatic electric models. Write to Midwest and attempt to determine if they are agreeable to a trade-in arrangement and what line or lines of automatic machines they carry. If they have brochures describing the various equipment, it would be helpful for you to review them before going further.

2. Although you have purchased cartons from National Paper Company for many years, you have never had occasion to secure any that were manufactured of fire-retardant material. You have recently received an order for merchandise to be delivered to Veterans Administration Hospitals. One of the requirements is that your product be packaged in safety cartons according to Department of Defense specification AD 108.

   Although you have checked National's latest catalog, you find no mention of the availability of fire-resistant or fire-retardant cartons. Can they manufacture their models #209 and #210 to conform to the government specifications? If so, what will they cost?

3. A communications consultant recently engaged by your firm has made several suggestions to improve internal corporate communication. One of these involved the use of plant bulletin boards. You understand that both Fullerton Manufacturing and the Freeman Corporation specialize in school and plant bulletin boards. Write a letter (a copy of which will go to both firms) inquiring about the cost of 12 units. You would like them framed in three-inch aluminum approximately 3 by 5 feet, ½ inch cork face on ½" or ¾" plywood. How much is added

to the cost when they are equipped with glass sliding doors? Is there an additional charge for locks on the doors? Do these companies have standard models? Are they less expensive and immediately available? Assume any other facts which are necessary in your letter.

4. You were recently invited on a tour of the new National Oil Corporation building. In the course of the tour, your group was told by the Management Training Director that National has made four films for use in management development programs. The training director ran about ten minutes of one titled "Building National's Corporate Image." You were very much impressed by it, and saw many communication implications in it. Write to National Oil and inquire if it would be possible to use the film in your Management Communication classes. If the film is available, you would like to show it to your classes on March 10 and 11. If the film has a "discussion guide" booklet, you would like to borrow that also.

5. You have recently received a contract from the Southern California Aerospace Corporation to manufacture the cabinets for the new commercial 1012 jet passenger aircraft. Write to Sperling Manufacturing Company and inquire if they are interested in submitting a bid on the drawer pulls or handles and locks.

   They are to be manufactured according to the specifications and design which you enclose. You will need a total of 4000 handles delivered in 1000-unit lots. The first lot must arrive in Burbank, California, no later than June 1 and the balance in 1000-unit lots every 30 days thereafter.

6. You recently purchased 24 four-drawer filing cabinets from Parker Office Equipment Company. You requested their model 405 ("All-Safe") which comes equipped with individual drawer locks, roller-bearing drawers, and two steel separators per drawer. Shortly after the cabinets arrived, your maintenance staff began to place them. However, they reported that although the cartons were stamped "Model 405," these cabinets did not have individual drawer locks. For security reasons, it is vital that 12 of the cabinets be so equipped. However, locks are not necessary on the other 12. You check Parker's invoice and find you have been charged for Model 405. Write a claim letter to the company which is 600 miles away. Determine what you wish to ask of Parker. Perhaps they can have locks installed on 12 cabinets locally? or they can pick up 12 and deliver an equal number of Model 405, or give you a reduction in price, or . . . .

7. On November 5 you purchased 500 "Sunlight" bath towel-wash cloth sets in pink, blue, and yellow from Sanford Towel Corp. These moved out of your store very briskly during the Christmas season. Since about January 10 you have had at least 15 returns and almost every day brings another claim or two. The problem is in the color of the items after washing. The wash cloths in each of the three colors are appreciably lighter than the towels after a washing. You don't know why, but you do know that many of your steady customers are upset and the situation has caused much ill will. Of course, you have taken the 210 cartons (which you have left from the original 500) off the shelf. You not only want them picked up and a credit entered, but also credit for those sets which have been returned and those which will come back in the future. It is true that Sanford has a 30-day return policy, and that applies only to unused merchandise, but in this case you feel the rule should be overlooked.

8. On October 12 you ordered 12 dozen desk pen sets from the Mitchell Company in New York, to be used as Christmas gifts to your clients. These units have an excellent quality pen mounted on a white marble base. The cost per unit, includ-

ing a 3-line message inscribed on the base, was $5.70. All 12 dozen were delivered on December 12, although Mitchell gave you a November 20 delivery date. It was at the time of the late delivery that you noted the error. On every one of the 144 sets the inscription read "Best Wishes from the Shield Company," instead of "Best Wishes from the Sheald Company."

Because you were 1200 miles from the Mitchell Company, and you wanted these delivered no later than December 20 to your clients in various parts of the country, you rushed them to a local engraver without calling Mitchell. Emory Engravers polished the word "Shield" off and engraved them correctly. This was all done within 24 hours but you had to pay a premium price because of overtime and the difficulty of the polishing job. In any event you have a bill for $216 from Emory Engravers which you feel Mitchell should pay. Write Mitchell and enter your claim.

9. On May 14 you received a shipment of furniture from Contemporary Wholesale Furniture Dealers on Order 195F. The merchandise was delivered by Contemporary. You have just taken two end tables from stock (part of order 195F). As you were about to place them in a window display, you noted that the tops of both had a series of scratches. Your stock man tells you, "I sure don't remember banging them, but you never can tell what happens. I guess they looked O.K. when they came in although I don't remember checking them in. Maybe we got them damaged from Contemporary."

You don't know who is at fault, but the possibility is good that it may be the manufacturer. Write a claim letter to Contemporary. Decide on your position before you write the letter.

10. About three months ago, you received a request from the Washington Service Group. This organization asked your railroad to sponsor a Saturday rail trip for 60 boys (from 12 to 15 years of age). The director told you that all these youngsters were from disadvantaged homes and most had never been on a train in their life.

After a great deal of effort on your part and with the hesitant approval of your superiors as well as the Commerce Commission, you arranged it.

The 100-mile round trip (which included a complimentary lunch) took place last Saturday. Although the three adults who accompanied the boys did a good job, the conductor reports one cracked sink in the men's toilet, two ripped coach seats, and two broken window shades. You know these were all inadvertent and the result of healthy spirits. Nevertheless the damage does come to $160.00, plus $80.00 for labor repair costs.

You have no alternative, as the assistant passenger agent, but to write to the Director of the Washington Service Group.

Chapter Nine

Communicating Favorable Responses to Inquiries and Claims

Answering Inquiries and Requests: Yes
Acknowledging Orders That Can Be Shipped

In the previous chapter we analyzed several types of business letters that involve inquiries and claims. Most such letters require an answer of "yes" or "no." The response says that the order can or cannot be filled, the request can or cannot be granted, the adjustment will or will not be made.

In this chapter we shall discuss the writing of a favorable response.

Answering Inquiries and Requests: Yes

Routine

When a major corporation places a double-page spread in a national magazine, it is not unusual for the advertisement to bring in one or two thousand inquiry letters: Where can I buy your television set? Is the model pictured in the lower-left-hand corner available in walnut? What are the dimensions of the set pictured in the upper center of the page? What is the address of the dealer nearest my home?

All of these inquiries should be answered, because each one represents a potential sale. But it would not be practical to answer each individually, so standard replies are prepared. These may be form letters, brochures, pamphlets, or even postcards. The form is relatively unimportant, provided the inquiry is answered completely and as quickly as possible. Further, and perhaps most important, the reply, in whatever form, should express thanks for the inquiry and interest in serving the inquirer.

Nonroutine

There are, however, many letters of inquiry or request which cannot be adequately answered with a printed form or pamphlet. A purchasing agent wants to know if a modification to an existing model is possible; a sales manager would like a price consideration on a quantity purchase; and a bookkeeper's inquiry concerns the handling of depreciation under unusual conditions. These require individual letters.

When you can answer an inquiry or grant a request, do so near the beginning of your letter. Don't leave the recipient in suspense.

Dear Mr. Hayworth:

We received your letter of May 15 in which you inquired about the recent training program conducted for our office personnel. I am happy to give you the information you requested.

The training was carried through by Communication Services located here in New York. We selected middle-management people whose job responsibilities require that they write a good many business letters and reports. The class was limited to 16 members and met for two hours each Tuesday afternoon, on company time. Twelve such sessions were held. Communication Services provided the instructor, text, and all handout material. Home assignments were given to the participants and these were evaluated by the instructor and returned to the students.

We found the program to be very valuable. Our employees enjoyed it and came away with many ideas which are clearly evident in their day-to-day writing assignments. We have scheduled a second class for this fall and we know that it will be as profitable as the one which was just concluded.

If there is any other information which you desire in this area, I should be very happy to cooperate with you.

Present a positive answer as quickly as possible.

Note how specific the reply is.

Dear Mr. Kahill:

We have received your recent inquiry concerning our research and our manufacture of the new aluminum circuit breakers, Model 101.

You will find all the technical information as well as the specifications in the enclosed technical manual. I believe you will be especially interested in pages 38 to 42 as well as the diagram in Appendix III.

If you have not seen the article by R. T. McKenzie which appeared in Science Monthly this last May, be sure to read it. Mr. McKenzie has described the results of his research, which seems related to the work you are doing. I know you will find McKenzie's article of benefit.

Although the writer was not obligated to include paragraphs two and three, they certainly help build goodwill.

```
In your letter you indicated that you were interested in the
information we are sending you from a research point of view,
with the possibility of utilizing our products in a subsequent
manufacturing process.  If we can, therefore, supply you with
quantities of our fine electronic components, we will be happy
to do so.  You will find that our quality is high and our
prices attractive.

If there is any other way in which we may assist you,
Mr. Kahill, please do not hesitate to write.
```

In these letters, a general organizational pattern was followed:

1. An introductory statement acknowledging the inquiry.
2. The grant itself.
3. Listing of the necessary information or reference to the source where it may be found.
4. A constructive suggestion, if possible.
5. A sales appeal (if applicable).
6. A friendly close.

Acknowledging Orders That Can Be Shipped

Most of the business transactions between buyer and seller are routine. Merchandise is ordered on Monday and delivered on Wednesday. These are often stock items and few if any problems ever arise. If a portion of the order is not delivered on Wednesday it will probably be sent out the following week.

However, when products are manufactured on the basis of special instructions, or are to be delivered within a limited period of time, it is usually wise for the seller to acknowledge that the order has been received. This permits a formal understanding to take place between buyer and seller so that possible problems at a future date may be eliminated. If the buyer requests a Black and Johnson Cutter, Model 304, to be delivered within 30 days, and he receives an acknowledgment of the facts of the purchase from the seller, he may then assume that understanding has taken place. However, if he receives an acknowledgment from the seller which indicates that a Model 403 cutter is being prepared for shipment, he can wire and correct the error immediately. Had the wrong cutter been shipped, both parties would have suffered. A simple acknowledgment has added to the efficiency of operations of the companies.

Many acknowledgments can be made by means of a form or guide letter; some cannot. This distinction lies largely in whether the buyer is a steady customer or a new one.

Steady Customers

Those firms that acknowledge orders from steady customers usually use postal cards, form letters, or duplicate invoices. The postal card contains only a brief message indicating the order has been received, is being processed, and will be shipped shortly. There is usually no effort made to list the items so that the buyer may verify the order as entered.

The form letter usually performs the same function as the postal card. However, it may be said to be a gesture which is a little more courteous because it travels in a stamped envelope.

The most efficient and least expensive means of acknowledgment is the duplicate invoice which is sent to the buyer. This is typed at the same time as the invoice (along with other needed copies). This duplicate of the invoice fulfills three functions: it informs the buyer that the order is being processed; it is an expression of courtesy and consideration; and it permits the buyer to check the specific details of the order.

Every now and then a personal letter of acknowledgment should be sent to steady customers, as an expression of pleasure in the business relationship. A good customer likes to know that he is not just taken for granted.

```
Dear Mr. Ryan:

This is just a short note to tell you that your order of April
28 has been received and is being shipped according to your
usual instructions.

We want you to know that your purchases, which have been made
so regularly during the past year, are always appreciated.
Of course, we haven't written you an individual letter for
each of the orders, but we want you to know that we will always
make every effort to supply you with quality merchandise at the
lowest possible prices.

If you have any special needs that we can fill, please give
us an opportunity to assist you.  We appreciate your confi-
dence in us and shall try to earn it for many years to come.
```

A letter such as this tells the customer that he has not become simply another account number to the seller. It is this kind of "unnecessary" act which helps build good will.

New Customers

Although it is obviously impossible to send a personal letter to a steady customer for every order, it is necessary to do so for a new customer. We want him to know that we truly appreciate adding his name to our customer list. This message also gives us an opportunity to tell him what some of our procedures are and to be sure that the terms of sale and payment are clearly understood.

This letter can effectively be made up as a guide letter and individually typed when the need arises. The reader should feel the red carpet has been rolled out for him, but the letter should not be so effusive as to sound insincere.

The new customer is primarily concerned with his order; this should therefore be mentioned first. Following this fact other details may be given on the company's services, policies, and practices.

Dear Mr. Dietrich:

Thank you very much for your initial order. All merchandise that you requested is in stock and will be shipped via Illinois Central Railroad on June 8. The terms of sale agreed upon will be followed through.

The merchandise which you order in the future will be shipped within three days. When bills are paid within ten days of receipt of merchandise, a profit-making 2 percent discount may be taken. In a year's time this can add up to very meaningful savings. When payment is not made within ten days, it is due, net, within thirty days.

As you probably know, Martins is extremely interested in promoting plant safety and housekeeping. Each month we publish a poster in each of these areas. We will be happy to send you a quantity for posting on your employee bulletin boards if you so desire. In addition to this, our industrial management department is at your service to answer relatively routine questions concerning storage of merchandise, movement of merchandise in the plant, and plant layout.

These are only a few of the services that we here at Martins are delighted to offer to our customers. As our relationship continues in the years ahead, you will become aware of many other services available to you and other Martins customers.

We look forward to a long and mutually satisfying relationship between you and Martins. If there is anything we can do to further that relationship, please let us know.

For further verification of the order, a duplicate of the invoice may accompany a letter such as the one above.

Making Adjustments: Claim Granted. The number of items which most firms handle today is greater than a generation ago; billing procedures are more complex; inventory controls are more difficult; handling and shipping of merchandise require more attention; and as a matter of fact, the entire process of getting goods from source to consumer requires many more steps today than it did in the past. Because there are more factors involved, there are greater possibilities for error. And errors do occur. But most businessmen recognize that such situations are likely to arise, so their claims or adjustments, when things go wrong, are tempered with patience.

Furthermore, intelligent managers are aware that a claim or a complaint can often assist by bringing attention to an area which needs improvement or change in their own firms. And in addition, they accept most claims as being legitimate and fair. There is the further fact, of course, that the people who submit claims are customers and it is upon their business that the seller's firm stands. Thus, it is important to handle quickly and courteously the claims and complaints that come in. This must be done with care and discretion so that the seller is recognized as fair; but he must be sure he does not gain a reputation for being too soft and accepting any claim, or too severe and refusing all.

Most claims are legitimate, and it is on this basis that firms usually establish a fairly generous adjustment policy. If there is a question as to the fault, companies will usually give the benefit of the doubt to the buyer. Their future business is involved, and the profits that go with that business. Certainly there will be some claims which have no merit and the seller may accept them and make an adjustment, but the individuals or firms that make such requests too frequently are sooner or later recognized and properly dealt with.

An adjustment policy is often governed by that which is accepted in the trade. Furniture manufacturers from coast to coast have agreed on a standard return privilege; appliance manufacturers have set down an industrywide repair policy; and other fields have established their ground rules. When this is done, obvious advantages are gained by the seller in an adjustment situation.

The way in which the adjustment is made is a vital factor in building or losing good will. An adjustment given grudgingly will usually do more harm than one which is refused, but carefully and courteously explained. We have probably all had occasion to request a refund that was reluctantly granted. We were interrogated and questioned and made to feel guilty about submitting the claim at all. We probably walked out of that place of business intending never to return. Had the seller, on the other hand, given us a reasonable, intelligent, and courteous refusal, we would have accepted it and more than likely he would have retained our good will. The key to granting any adjustment is to do it graciously. The following letter, although it grants the adjustment, will probably lose the account.

The tactless, writer-centered, carping tone of this letter is sure to lose a customer.

```
Dear Mr. Hoefler:

We received your letter of December 3 in which you requested
that we credit your account for $28.50 for discounts on orders
which were delivered to you in July and August.

As you may or may not know, the standard policy throughout
the furniture industry is that a 2 percent discount is granted
only when bills are paid within ten days of date of invoice.
If we did not follow this policy, and gave such discounts to
every Tom, Dick, and Harry, we would surely lose money; this
would be very bad for our company.  The discounts which you
claim you are entitled to are all for orders which you paid
late, whether you know it or not.

However, we are granting your claim and we hope this satisfies
you.  We also hope you will be more careful in the future.
```

Any adjustment which is made in a carping, grudging, and tactless manner will be resented.

Buyer at Fault

Not infrequently in business the buyer will submit a claim which is not justified, but which he honestly believes is. He may have run the machine over its rated capacity and now requests a replacement; he may return the furniture forgetting that he has overlooked the ten-day return period privilege; he may order merchandise at a special price long after the last date announced for the sale. When these claims are granted, it is purely for the purpose of building good will.

When the buyer is at fault and the claim granted, it is usually wise to structure the letter so that an explanation precedes the favorable adjustment.

Dear Mr. Milton:

We received your letter of July 5 in which you requested that we pick up the American 1/3 h.p. motor and replace it with a 3/4 h.p. unit.

We were sorry to learn that the 1/3 h.p. motor which we sold you on June 15 did not prove satisfactory. In your letter, however, you indicated that it was used to power a Jackson-Smith Industrial Saw, model #208. We checked this with our chief engineer because we are always desirous of furnishing our customers with the best and most efficient materials available.

He found that the manufacturer of this saw recommends that a 3/4 to 1 h.p. unit be used with this particular model. Apparently this was overlooked by the people in your shop and our 1/3 h.p. unit was used. Of course, we realize that incidents such as this occur and we are sending out the larger motor as you requested. However, for your satisfaction and the most efficient operation of equipment in the future, we suggest that the manufacturer's recommendations be checked and followed.

The new motor should be delivered to your warehouse no later than August 10; at that time our driver can pick up the original unit. If we can assist you in any way in the future, Mr. Milton, please call on us.

Note that the customer is tactfully told he is at fault before the grant is made. If the grant is made first, he may stop reading and thus never become aware of his error.

We stated earlier that good news should be given immediately in a business letter. This is not true, however, when granting a claim in which the buyer is at fault. If he opens his adjustment letter and finds there is an immediate grant, he may not read further to learn that he was at fault. And even when he does read the entire letter, the psychological impact of the explanation may be lost. For this reason a courteous, straightforward explanation before the grant is made, should be included which points out to the buyer how he was at fault. In most cases the following organizational structure is recommended:

1. A statement referring to the specific transaction.
2. A statement explaining tactfully and discreetly how the buyer is at fault. Care should be taken to avoid putting him in a situation where he may lose face.
3. A statement granting the claim graciously.
4. A sales appeal, if appropriate.
5. A friendly close.

This pattern was used in the letter to Mr. Milton above. Compare the effectiveness of that letter with that of the following one, where the pattern has not been followed.

He has his answer at this point; why should he continue to read?

Dear Mr. Fischer:

We are happy to tell you, in reference to your letter of April 15, that we have credited your account for $72.50.

We can understand how you felt when the merchandise you purchased was not up to the quality you expected.

However, your technicians should not have attempted to correct whatever was wrong with the #207 switching unit. This is a highly complex piece of electronic equipment and it is for this reason that we carefully seal it and place the statement on every cover which says: "To be opened by manufacturer's personnel only; call manufacturer for service."

For your best interests, we suggest that you follow our recommendations in the future.

This letter to Mr. Fischer can result in further complications. If he reads just the first paragraph, he may comment, "Boy, this was easy." And he may repeat the action which caused the claim in the first place. It is for this reason that the proper organization of such a letter is important.

Perhaps equal in importance with the organization is the tone. It should be direct, courteous, and open-handed.

Poor: Although you made the mistake, we are giving you the money.

Revised: We are pleased to make the adjustment under these circumstances.

Poor: If you had read the instructions, this would never have happened. But we are going along with you anyway.

Revised: The adjustment has been made as you requested. May we suggest that in the future the installation instructions be followed carefully for complete satisfaction.

Poor: We can't imagine why you would feel your claim is justified; nevertheless, we have credited your account.

Revised: Oversights are certainly made from time to time and on this basis we have credited your account.

Seller at Fault

When the buyer is at fault when he requests an adjustment, the seller may grant the claim, refuse the claim, or offer a compromise. When it is the seller who is at fault, however, there is no alternative: he must grant the claim.

Before Receiving a Claim. Generally the seller is not aware that he has made some mistake until the claimant tells him so. However, in those situations where the seller determines shortly after he has made a shipment that something is wrong, he should attempt to correct the error before the buyer asks for an adjustment. Maybe the seller will discover that a particular lot of merchandise has not been manufactured properly, but only after the merchandise is on its way to the customer. Or the seller may receive a justified complaint from only one of several buyers. In any of these situations, he should immediately get in touch with the other buyers who have been shipped similar faulty merchandise and offer to make proper adjustment. The seller who does make an adjustment prior to receiving claims and complaints will secure an amount of good will which no advertising can purchase. Adjustments made under these circumstances are the mark of a reliable house and the reputation gained by such action proves invaluable.

Answering Claims. The letter granting a claim when the seller is at fault is a difficult one to write. The seller must indicate that he has made an error, but in such a way that the buyer will not lose confidence in him and take his business elsewhere.

What makes this such a difficult assignment is the fact that people act like people. Although any of us will readily admit that he is likely to make an error—and does—we cannot understand how those from whom we purchase can make such "dumb and completely inexplicable mistakes." Thus when a seller does make an error in dealing with us, we often enter a claim, accept the adjustment, and then take our business elsewhere. This reaction holds true for many consumers; however, at the wholesale level the businessman does recognize that mistakes are likely to happen, and he will usually accept the adjustment in good faith.

What is the proper order of points in the letter where the seller is at fault and grants the claim? If the message opens with a grant, the reader may never read on to the explanation of how the situation occurred. He has already read the item—the grant—which is of major interest to him.

To reverse the order is also subject to criticism. After all, the buyer is primarily interested in whether he is going to receive a credit of $52.00, and he is not very much concerned with the fact that your computers suddenly began to punch holes incorrectly. Probably the situation and prospective reader should determine the order of your letter.

There is indeed a question as to whether an explanation should be included at all. A detailed discussion of what went wrong and how, may only compound the situation and erase what little confidence the customer has in us. Perhaps the best thing to do is to open by saying that we made a mistake, that we are making an adjustment, and that we will do our best to see that a similar case does not arise in the future. Of course, there are instances when an explanation will clear up a situation and will be accepted as perfectly logical and plausible. But in many situations, trying to explain how an error happened only serves to emphasize our own shortcomings.

New York Life Insurance Company had this to say in one of its *Effective Letters Bulletins:*

> Mistakes are bound to happen. As company correspondents we have the alternative of compounding the mistake or minimizing it.
>
> Considering the millions of paper operations involved in the day-to-day workings of a large company, proportionately few errors are made. But letters do go out billing a policy owner for a premium that's already been paid, billing him for the wrong amount, notifying him that his policy is lapsed when it isn't, telling him he hasn't sent a necessary form when he has.
>
> Generally, of course, management decides how such errors are to be rectified but it's the job of the correspondent to convey these decisions in language and tone that are most likely to win back the confidence of the policy owner.
>
> Let's look at an example. Say a policy owner has been billed for a previously paid premium. He writes back and says, "But I already paid it." We check, find out he's right and say:
>
>> In your letter of January 6 you claimed that the premium payment of $68.03 due on December 1 was paid by you under date of November 28. A check of our records indicated that this was not so.
>>
>> However, a further check revealed that you were correct in your assumption for the reason that a member of our clerical staff neglected to enter your payment on our books.
>>
>> We hope that this error caused you no undue concern.

Not only is this grudging—"our records revealed that this was not so," "your assumption," "UNDUE concern,"—it is also a fine example of buckpassing—"a member of our clerical staff neglected. . . ." This is a flimsy excuse at best and, anyhow, as a member of the company, the clerk's errors reflect on the company. Wouldn't it be better to say:

> You are right, Mr. Jones. We checked and found out that you did pay your premium on November 28, just as you said.
>
> Please forgive us—you can be sure we'll try to see that this doesn't happen again.

Let's take another example. A policy owner whose policy is fully paid-up receives a lapse notice regarding his policy. He writes in asking "how come?" and this is the reply he receives:

> Upon receipt of your letter of January 14, 19–, a thorough check was made of our records which bears out your statement that a lapse notice was sent you for a December premium on your above-numbered policy.
>
> You are correct in assuming that your policy is paid-up and that no further premiums are due.
>
> It is a pleasure to be of service to you.

Again no apology, just a grudging assent that he was right—for once. Why not:

> The notice you received was intended for another of our policy owners, Mr. Brown. You are perfectly right in assuming that your policy is paid-up and that no further premiums are due.
>
> I'm awfully sorry this happened, and should you receive another of these notices (we'll try to see that you don't) just ignore it.

It doesn't hurt to say "I'm sorry about this," or "I hope this didn't alarm you too much," or even a straightforward, simple, "Please forgive us." It's much easier to lose face by not apologizing than by apologizing. A customer is flesh and blood with feelings and emotions like our own. An apology, properly made, is likely to appeal to his most reasonable self.[1]

The following indicates a good organizational pattern for an adjustment letter when the seller is at fault:

1. An opening which refers to the situation and makes a grant.
2. An explanation of how the incident occurred, if such an explanation sounds reasonable. If it will only magnify a careless error, it should be omitted.
3. An attempt to regain the customer's confidence.
4. A sales appeal, if it seems appropriate.
5. A friendly close.

In the letter to Mr. Canfield below, an explanation is offered which will probably help make the entire situation more understandable to the buyer. In the second letter below, however, there is no explanation of how the incident happened, for if it were offered it would only emphasize a very careless procedure within the seller's company.

It's often wise to "get in step" with the writer (appreciate his perceptions and verbalize those to him).

```
Dear Mr. Canfield:

You had every reason in the world to be upset when your order
#509 did not arrive on July 5, as we had promised.  You were
correct in selling the higher priced Maxwell units at the sale
price you advertised for the Kolton.  We will surely take care
of the $36.50 loss which you sustained.  A credit for that
amount has been entered in your account.

As you may or may not be aware, we have two "Canfields" in
our files.  Your firm is listed as the Canfield Corporation
and is, of course, in Chicago.  The other company we carry as
Canfield's and Associates in St. Louis.  Our regular shipping
clerk is well aware of the difference and has never made a
mistake between the two.  However, he has the bad habit, like
our other employees, of requesting a vacation each year, and
his substitute mistakenly shipped your order to St. Louis.
```

[1] *Effective Letters*, "We're Sorry," January–February, 1961. Copyright, 1961, New York Life Insurance Company.

We are extremely sorry about this, Mr. Canfield, and you can
be sure that we will do everything in the future to avoid such
a situation.

I have enclosed our summer catalog and I do hope you will
give our substitute shipping clerk an opportunity to prove
his efficiency; he and I will be very pleased to receive your
order.

*It is usually wiser to end
on a reference to a positive
future than to the negative
situation in the past.*

Dear Mr. Lapidus:

Our sincere apologies for the beautiful "goof" we pulled. A
check for $28 is enclosed.

There was no excuse for our delivering your order #209 to the
wrong warehouse. Your instructions were clear and explicit,
but through our oversight, they were not followed. We are
sincerely sorry.

Our salesman in your area has sent us a note indicating your
interest in our new Empire Line. I am enclosing a bulletin
describing all of the items in this line. This is the first
release we have made on it, and I am sure that you will find
this to be a quality product at a highly competitive price.
If you will drop me a note, I can have a complete set of samples of the Empire Line to you within three days. I am sure
you will find them attractive and an excellent addition to the
stock you carry for the Junior Miss customers in your area.

*An opening like this is sure
to win the goodwill of the
reader.*

Third Party at Fault

In most transactions between buyer and seller today, a third party is involved: a shipper, carrier, broker, or storage agent. It may be that the loss or
damage involved in the claim took place while the merchandise was in the
hands of a third party. In such a situation, the seller will normally reply with a
courteous letter and extend to the buyer whatever assistance he can. If some of
his accounts are small retail merchants, he may even offer to process the claim
for them.

```
Dear Mr. Canterbury:

We were extremely sorry to hear that several of the lamps in-
cluded in order #705, which we shipped via Rapid Freight Lines,
did not arrive in satisfactory condition.

As you know, this carrier, like all others, inspects merchan-
dise before accepting it.  We have their receipt indicating
that this order was turned over to them in excellent condition.

For this reason you will probably want to get in touch with
Rapid Freight as quickly as possible and enter a claim for the
four damaged lamps.  I have enclosed two blank copies of In-
terstate Commerce Commission Form 202 which you can complete
and forward to the carrier.

If I can assist you in any other way, Mr. Canterbury, please
let me know and I will be happy to cooperate.
```

This tactful statement sets the record straight on where the fault lies.

Naturally, it is costly for the seller to get involved in a claim where he has no legal responsibility. However, the good will which may accrue to him in such circumstances will be well worth the effort expended.

Miscellaneous Adjustment Situations

Other instances arise in addition to those listed above. At times both parties can be at fault, in other cases the fault is not known, and sometimes the problem is the result of a misunderstanding. Each of these situations, and others, must be handled on its own merits and in conformity with the adjustment policy of the seller. Regardless of what the circumstances are, all such adjustment letters should carry a strong sales and good-will message.

```
Dear Mr. Dayton:

You're correct.  Your order #506 did call for six dozen ladies'
Casual Line footwear.  Why we sent you sixteen dozen (and
billed you for this number) is beyond me.

You may return them, of course, and as a matter of fact, we
will be happy to pick them up when we deliver the merchandise
which is scheduled to arrive in your store one week from today.
```

Excellent "you attitude" opening.

May I suggest, however, that you seriously consider retaining
the extra ten dozen. This line is moving far beyond our expectations and we think that you will find this merchandise
a most satisfactory sales item. Our advertising on this item
is now in full swing and a double-page spread will appear in
the June issue of the Women's Shopping Guide. We know that
this, plus the high quality of this footwear, will help increase your sales.

Naturally, we will save shipping and bookkeeping costs if you
elect to retain all of the original shipment. For your cooperation, we would like to have you deduct 5 percent from the
bill which covers this merchandise. Please call me collect,
extension 205, and let me know if this proposal is satisfactory to you.

Sometimes a claim can be adjusted through the expedient of "educating" the
customer. This may be done through courteous instructions or suggestions
which tell him how to handle the product.

Dear Mr. Huchinson:

We are as concerned as you that your new Lawn King Mower does
not give you the satisfaction you have every right to expect.
From the description of the difficulty you are having, it
seems to me that the solution and correction are relatively
simple.

You say that you turned the little knob next to the starting
control to #7 immediately before starting the motor. This is
proper and correct, but if the gas mixture is left at seven,
the motor will stall in exactly the fashion you have described.
Once the motor is turning over, the gas mixture should be reduced to #2 or #3. Try it this way and I am quite sure your
Lawn King Mower will give you the satisfaction it gives thousands of other home owners in the United States.

If however, this unit does not give you the service which you
have every right to expect, we will make arrangements to see
that an exchange is carried through for you.

The competent business manager recognizes that an equitable adjustment policy can contribute greatly to a company's image, business, and reputation.

Questions for Study

I. Please offer your constructive criticism of the following letters. Remember to indicate which sections of the letters deserve favorable comments, as well as where improvements can be made. Be as specific as possible in your evaluations.

1. Dear Mr. Blackstone:

Yes, we certainly would be happy to assist you in designing and writing your new employee orientation manual.

We were faced with the similar problem of a rapidly growing work force and vast differences in employee backgrounds; we know how difficult it is to put together a pamphlet that serves everyone.

I would strongly suggest that you use a spiral binder approach so that changes may be printed on new pages and easily inserted. And I would certainly use sketches to add humor and break the monotony of the printed page. Topic headings and an index are also helpful to the reader.

I've enclosed two copies of our latest edition. You may find them helpful for guide purposes. Please call or write, Mr. Blackstone, if I can help in any other way.

2. Dear Mrs. Gotz:

Welcome to Farmington's. The red carpet has been rolled out and our staff would like to sing you a chorus of "Glad to Have You Aboard."

Your first order (AT 303) has been processed and will leave here tomorrow in one of Farmington's bright blue trucks. You should receive your merchandise within 48 hours.

This will be true of all your future orders, Mrs. Gotz: delivery to your warehouse within seven days after your order has been received. And as our salesman indicated, payment made within ten days of receipt of merchandise assures you of an important 2 percent discount. Of course, you may take up to our maximum period of 30 days to pay your net bill.

Requests for adjustments must be made within 20 days of receipt of merchandise and returns can only be made to our driver when he has a completed yellow "Returns Authorization" form.

3. Dear Mr. MacElroy:

We received your letter inquiring about the return of one of our #2412 Electronic Heat Treating units.

We were concerned because this is one of our most reliable and widely sold items. We turned the situation over to our Chief Engineer, Mr. Karbon, who visited with your R&D Director, Mr. Jones.

After several meetings both of these men agreed that you required a unit with a top heat capacity of 1800° F. Our #2412 unit was constructed to function best at a high level of 1200° F and is so advertised and represented. Your order, however, requested the #2412 unit which we shipped.

Situations of this type do occur and for that reason we are picking up the #2412 within 10 days and giving you full credit even though it has been used.

Of course we are happy to work with you in situations like this, Mr. MacElroy. And again, I want you to know that our engineering and research staff are always available to assist you in research, design, and consulting areas. Please call on us when we can help.

4. You're right, Mr. Cutter.

   We *did* ship the wrong merchandise and we're now working to correct our error.

   We still haven't determined how we went into production on 250 large size (8″) #421 Double Lock Clamps when your Purchase Order clearly calls for the small 4″ size. But we did manufacture and deliver them, and we are certainly aware of the problem we created.

   The #420 units are now in the final manufacturing stage, and should be shipped tomorrow. Please return the #421 (8″ Double Lock Clamps) to the driver. If you find you can use these, please retain them and we will be happy to deduct 8 percent from that purchase order. This is roughly the sum we will save in accounting and handling costs.

   You may be sure, Mr. Cutter, that we will check our orders more carefully in the future.

5. Dear Mrs. Robinson:

   Now that our busy Christmas season is behind us, we have a few loose ends to gather up and apologies to make. One of these apologies is certainly due you for we did bill you for $74.00 worth of merchandise which was purchased by another Robinson family also living in Pasadena.

   I'm sure there is an explanation for this which would involve our temporary holiday help, increased volume of sales, etc., but I'm sure you're primarily interested in the correction—which has been made. And we're interested in retaining your good will—which we sincerely hope has been done.

   We have enclosed two tickets to our Winter Fun-in-the-Sun Fashion Show and Tea which is scheduled for 3:00 p.m. February 8. We do hope you and a guest will attend and enjoy viewing the latest in cruise and holiday wear.

II. Complete any of the following problems assigned. You may wish to review the chapter and note key points before solving the problem.

1. Reply to Professor John House of the Finance Department of California State College. He has requested 60 copies of your annual report for use by his two classes in Money and Banking. Unfortunately you can spare only 35 copies; perhaps he can use these in one class, collect them, and use them again in his second class.

2. The PTA of the Burnside Elementary School has requested 500 copies of your booklet "How to Keep Your Home Safe from Fire." You are not only happy to comply with the request but you can also send along one of your fire safety engineers to make a 20-minute color-slide presentation. Although your firm sells commercial and residential fire insurance, the booklets and the presentation are completely objective and contain no sales appeals.

3. Next month you will launch your annual Spring Sale which usually results in heavy sales from your steady customers. This would be a good time to send each of your retail accounts a letter acknowledging their purchases of your products (children's wear) during the previous months.

4. During the last two months your sales force has carried through an all-out campaign to secure new accounts. Your firm has been quite successful and you have secured approximately 10 to 15 new customers each week in your district.

   Prepare a letter which can be used to acknowledge a new account's initial order for golf and tennis equipment (assume brand names) and also tell them about your payment policies, your advertising assistance allowances, delivery schedules, return privileges, and special discounts for quantity purchases.

5. You have recently purchased the Bel Air Appliance Center. In most cases, the consumer makes a purchase which is delivered within 10 days to 2 weeks. You feel it would be a good idea to acknowledge the order and thank the customer for his purchase within 24 hours of the sale. Prepare such a letter keeping in mind that the expenditure of several hundred dollars for a freezer, color TV, or stereo set is usually made only after very careful consideration by the consumer.

6. Mr. and Mrs. Theodore Abbott have recently purchased a Maynard Color TV-Stereo combination from you (Bel Air Appliance Center) for $980.00. You cautioned the Abbotts about picture reception, telling them that color was critical and the picture might not be sharp and clear because their home was located in a canyon area. They assured you their aerial was mounted at the top of a nearby hill and the signal should be excellent. Two months have gone by since they purchased their set, and you have received at least 15 calls from the Abbotts. Your installer has visited them three times and assures you "they're getting the best picture possible in their location."

   Because the set is now definitely "used," you are reluctant to take it back; however, offer to do so, and give them full credit if they are not completely satisfied.

7. The Hi-Speed Corporation, a fabricator of piece parts for major aerospace companies, has made purchases from you for several years.

   They recently ordered 800 pieces of your #210B strip aluminum according to their design specifications. They were, of course, going to cut this to size and further fabricate it into a finished piece part.

   You have just received a phone call from them in which they tell you that a mistake was made. Because of the aircraft into which the part will go, the strips should have been made of your #410B titanium line. Hi-Speed indicates that it has 600 uncut pieces of the #210B on hand and would like them picked up.

   Although you decide to go along with the request, you are irritated because you will be required to stock the 600 pieces and you aren't sure how long it will take for you to dispose of them. Of course, there is a handling and shipping charge which you will have to charge against Hi-Speed.

8. Approximately eight months ago Bellview Furniture opened for business. Their initial order from you was very large, and subsequent purchases have been excellent.

   Mr. Karlton recently mentioned to your salesman that almost 100 percent of his sales are for contemporary and modern lamps and he really made an error when he secured so many of the traditional styles in that first order.

   Write Karlton and tell him if he has a quantity of those lamps in unopened cartons which are in first-class condition, you will accept their return for full credit. These are to be lamps secured only in Order 41368, of August 12 of last year.

9. Your computer equipment did it again! Campbell Can Corporation requested and received their order 4851 on September 3. It was made up of your special hi-strength coiled aluminum (catalog #202). This aluminum is used by Campbell to manufacture a specific item for the Army. For some reason an identical order was delivered on September 13. How or why it happened (a machine or human error?) seems immaterial. Offer to pick up the duplicate order and issue full credit.

10. Mr. and Mrs. Costello recently purchased a Kleen Time Vacuum Cleaner from your Chicago outlet. Unfortunately, neither the Chicago store nor warehouse had model 421 in Sunburst Yellow in stock. You called both Milwaukee and Gary

where you have other outlets. Both managers agreed to check and call you back. The Gary manager did call back and said he had the 421 and you requested that he ship it to Mrs. Costello. The Milwaukee manager apparently did not understand that he was to return your call. He shipped a 421 to Mrs. Costello also. Unfortunately, the second vacuum sweeper arrived when Mrs. Costello was not home. The driver left it with a neighbor.

Mrs. Costello is confused; she complains that she has two bills for $105.00 each and two vacuum cleaners. A letter of explanation seems to be in order.

Chapter Ten

Communicating an Unfavorable Response

The Psychology of Refusal
Reply Promptly
Acknowledging Orders When There Is a Problem
Handling Adjustments: Claim Not Granted

Saying "no" to others is never easy. Yet we must turn down requests, proposals, and even demands when circumstances do not permit us to say "yes." The task is made more difficult when the person we must refuse is someone whose good will we value highly: a spouse, a child, a brother, a friend, a customer, a subordinate, or an associate.

It makes no one deliriously happy to be told "no" to what he considered a reasonable request. We recognize that, but we also recognize that it is possible to say "no" in a manner that will maintain good will and arouse a minimum of antagonism.

The Psychology of Refusal

Let's suppose we work for a big utility company and the morning's mail brings us a message from Mrs. Crawford. This influential community member tells us she is the president of The Women's League of the Greater Council of Churches for the city. Between May 5 and 7 that organization will be sponsoring a fund-raising carnival for the crippled children's wing of the Orthopedic Hospital. Because the carnival will be held on a vacant lot, it will be necessary to bring in temporary power lines for the booths, exhibits, and rides, as well as temporary water lines. Mrs. Crawford is sure our corporation will want to contribute the necessary manpower and services.

But we must refuse. The state Public Utilities Commission does not permit us to supply services free of charge. And our liability insurance is in force only when company activities conform to the PUC regulations. Moreover, if we did this for one worthwhile group, we would have to do it for others. This would result in higher costs which would be passed on to the consumer.

If we begin by saying to Mrs. Crawford, "Sorry, we can't do it," it is likely that whatever else we have to say will not be heard or read with much understanding. She has her answer; it's a "no" to what she considered to be a very reasonable request. Her emotional response is now one of irritation, frustration, and possibly anger.

But it is often not necessary to say "no" directly. If we *explain the reason* for the refusal early in the letter or conversation, it is often not necessary to say "no" directly; Mrs. Crawford will understand. In this way, it is the reason presented which refuses the request, and not the communicator.

A statement of this type certainly "gets in step" with the reader.

A "businesslike" explanation is given.

The refusal is implied—<u>not</u> stated.

Constructive suggestions "soften" the refusal and give evidence of sincerity.

A positive and sincere offer of assistance.

```
Dear Mrs. Crawford:

We received your letter concerning your fund raising efforts
scheduled for May 5-7.  You and your organization certainly
deserve the community's highest praise for your generous ef-
forts to assist the handicapped children of Bellville.  We
are all indebted to you and your associates for your under-
standing work for such a worthwhile cause.

Although we are aware of the Public Utilities Commission's
regulations in situations of this type, we nevertheless
checked with them in reference to your specific case.  The
ruling was similar to what it was in the past; state legisla-
tion does not permit a public utility to provide services
without charge to any organization.  In addition, our liabili-
ty insurance is in force only when operations are in confor-
mity with the PUC regulations.  Thus, neither our employees
nor your patrons would be covered even if the service could
be provided.  I'm sure, Mrs. Crawford, you can appreciate our
position in this case.

May we, however, make a suggestion or two.  Mr. Robert Gaily,
President of our Employee Service Group, can list for you
several private firms that rent portable power generation
units.  He is also familiar with firms that can provide tem-
porary water and sanitation services.  Mr. Gaily has assured
me that our Employee Service Group would provide volunteers
who would man and operate the water and power services during
the carnival period.  He has also indicated that your fund
raising effort would be well publicized among our 21,000 em-
ployees.

We have an exhibit (self-contained in its own booth) titled,
"Let's Keep Our Environment Beautiful" which is available to
you.  The attendant on duty would distribute free toys and
balloons, litter bags, and cooperate in every way.

I can be reached at extension 242 and Mr. Gaily on extension
421.  We are both eager to assist you and your group in every
way possible, Mrs. Crawford, to help make this fund raising
effort completely successful.
```

If the explanation presented is a reasonable one, and the tone is friendly and sincere, most readers will probably think, "Well, I can understand their situation; I'm not happy, but I do understand." The letter to Mrs. Crawford (above), and those which follow, will usually retain the good will of their readers.

Please note that none of the letters "soft pedals" the facts. But because everyone is sensitive and dislikes being refused, the explanation and refusal are presented as courteously and as tactfully as possible.

<table>
<tr><td>

The refusal is implied.

Constructive suggestions are usually appreciated.

</td><td>

Dear Mr. Cooper:

Thank you very much for your recent inquiry concerning our management training programs here at Black Stone Steel Corporation. Your tentative plans sound excellent and we are sure that your personnel will benefit from the training which you intend to establish.

The course which we have worked out for the engineers in our Research and Development Department is the result of several years' effort. Inasmuch as some of the areas which it pursues are of a classified nature, because of either our designation or the government's, you can appreciate why it is not possible for us to send you a detailed outline of the program.

Although you did not indicate that you were interested in a training program for office personnel, I am sending you an outline of the course which we have in this area. It may be that this will prove of some value to you.

You may also wish to write to the College of Engineering State University Extension Division. They have developed an off-campus program for engineers which may be of interest to you. May I also recommend an article in the June issue of Engineering Research which described several corporate training programs for engineering development. If you have not seen it, you may wish to check it.

If there is any other way, Mr. Cooper, in which we can assist you, I do hope you will write.

</td></tr>
</table>

The refusal is implied.

Constructive suggestions are usually appreciated.

Here again the refusal is implied and a direct "no" not stated.
A careful explanation is always appreciated.

Dear Mr. Conkling:

Thank you very much for your recent inquiry concerning the Century Filing Cabinets which we sold you three years ago. You will recall that these were especially designed to be used for storage of outdated files and the cabinets themselves were relatively inexpensive.

We manufactured 5000 of these units, offered them to all our accounts, and quickly sold them. For us to go into production for the six units you require would make the price quite prohibitive.

Positive close.

In all these letters the explanation is complete and accurate. After each implied refusal a positive offer or suggestion is made. Notice that there are no statements which might arouse negative or unpleasant associations in the mind of the reader. Once the refusal is made, even if only by implication, it is not referred to again, and there are no abject apologies.

The reason for the refusal is given, the refusal is tactfully implied, and a suggestion is made by the writer in such a way that apparently the reader would be ill advised not to accept it.

Thus the organizational plan for a communication (a letter, an interview, a telephone conversation) that contains an unfavorable reply follows this basic plan:

1. An introductory statement acknowledging the inquiry.
2. An explanation of the situation which makes the refusal necessary.
3. The refusal, implied or expressly stated.
4. A constructive suggestion.
5. A sales appeal, if applicable.
6. A friendly close.

Reply Promptly

Whether you can reply favorably or unfavorably to an inquiry or request is important, but it is also vital that the inquiry be answered promptly. Too often in industry today individuals are made to wait an unreasonable time after they have made an inquiry. When questions come in concerning products or services, make every effort to reply within 24 hours. If you can tell the inquirer "yes," so much the better, but do not make him wait several days to receive a "no, we're sorry." If you let him know your decision immediately, he can then take further action to benefit himself. He may wish to accept your counter-offer or, if you cannot meet his wishes, he then has adequate time to turn elsewhere. But if he is made to wait several days, and he then receives the "no," it may then be too late for him to make other arrangements.

Of course an immediate answer should be sent to every letter we receive, but in the case of an inquiry it is especially vital that a reply go out at once.

Acknowledging Orders When There Is a Problem

Not every order which comes in can be filled completely and efficiently. There are times when all the merchandise requested is not in stock; when the order isn't clear; when the credit status of the customer is questionable; and a half dozen other situations.

Incomplete Orders

At times an order will be received that is either incomplete, indefinite, or not clear. It is usually unwise to guess at what the customer means, for if the wrong merchandise is shipped it will be returned and ill will and expense will result. An individually typed letter (below) can be used, or a form letter with "fill in" spaces.

Dear Mr. Conway:

Thank you very much for your order of March 17, #204, which arrived today. All the merchandise that you requested is in stock and will be shipped via California Freight Lines.

You may recall that you listed four dozen American Beauty two-quart cooking containers. However, you did not indicate whether you prefer these with the copper or stainless steel bottoms. If you will check your preference on the enclosed airmail card, your order will be processed precisely as you desire and shipped immediately.

I am also enclosing a flyer on our new outdoor grill line. If you wish to order a quantity of these fast-moving items, you can so indicate on the same card.

Notice in the letter above that the approach is tactful and positive. The writer did not say, "You neglected," or "You forgot to list." He simply indicated that the oversight was inadvertent and as soon as the correct information was received, the merchandise would be shipped immediately.

Merchandise Not Handled

A customer may request merchandise which the seller has never handled. This may come in as a separate order, or it may be one item in a large order.

What to do about this request? If we suggest a source of supply, we will create good will with the customer. However, there are some practical dangers inherent in this procedure. The source of supply will probably make every effort to satisfy the customer and it may be that we will lose the customer to the very source we suggested. On the other hand, business ethics almost demand that we make such recommendations.

A letter handling such a situation might follow the general outline suggested below.

```
Dear Mr. Hart:

We received your Order #202, dated January 14; all the merchan-
dise, with one exception, will be on its way to you by this
afternoon.

Although we handle all types of office supplies, we have
never stocked the Arco Filing Cabinet.  This is recognized
as an excellent unit; however, our customers' needs at this
level have always been fulfilled by the Apex Line, which we
do stock.

However, your request specifically lists your preference for
the Arco.  These may be secured from the Dearborn Office
Furniture Corporation, located in Chicago.

It has been a pleasure doing business with you, and we know
that you will be satisfied for many years to come with the
consistently high quality of merchandise we handle and the
competitive prices we offer.
```

When the merchandise requested by a customer is only related to the usual items handled, and does not compete directly with an an item in stock, it is a good deal easier to make a recommendation.

```
Dear Mr. Flynn:

Thank you for your recent note inquiring as to whether or not
we handle automobile seat covers as well as our usual line of
automotive accessories.

As you may know, we stock over 5000 parts for cars.  We have
considered putting in a line of seat covers, safety belts,
and so on, but have not as yet.

Through our own experience, we have found that the Los Angeles
Auto Seat Company is an excellent firm.  The quality of their
merchandise is high and their prices competitive.  I recom-
mend that you get in touch with them.  Ask specifically for
Mr. Kameron, who has always given us excellent service.

Enclosed you will find our latest parts catalog.  Check
through it; we know you will find many items of interest.
```

In some instances, a firm will secure the item (which it does not handle) from a supplier and forward it to its customer. This is a matter of courtesy—usually no profit is made—but a third party (who might be a competitor) is not introduced into the transaction.

Orders Which Must Be Refused

There are a variety of different reasons why orders must sometimes be refused, even when the merchandise is in stock and available for immediate shipment. A few such cases are:

1. The buyer is a poor credit risk.
2. The buyer has exceeded his credit limit.
3. Company regulations concerning a franchise or distributorship agreements would be violated.
4. Filling the order might be contrary to government regulations.
5. Filling the order would be unprofitable because of the limited quantity ordered, distances to be shipped, or modifications requested.
6. Only a limited supply is in stock, and this must be retained for steady accounts.

A direct, courteous explanation.

A positive comment listing advantages.

Note the writer does not say "if this is satisfactory"; he assumes that his suggestion is, and writes in that tone.

Dear Mr. Calloway:

Thank you for the completed order and credit application blank. Both were received today.

We have checked the credit sources which you have listed, and we find that your references speak highly of you. However, your ratio of assets to liabilities, plus the debts which you have incurred in your new location, would seem to indicate that it would be in your best interest to purchase on a cash basis.

The advantages of doing so are important. A 2 percent cash discount, low inventory, and no end-of-month bills all add up to money-making features.

Please call me collect and I will see to it that the merchandise you ordered is on its way to you, on a c.o.d. basis, almost immediately.

Dear Mr. Franklin:

We were happy to receive your request to stock the new Precision Watch line of the American Jewelry Corporation.

Some months ago we visited Indianapolis and at that time selected twelve jewelry outlets to handle the Precision Watch. Unfortunately, we did not get in touch with you. However,

we did assure each of the twelve dealers that Indianapolis
would have a maximum of one dozen franchises. In all fairness to these outlets, therefore, and in conformity with our
agreement, we can open no others at this time.

If, however, one of these twelve does not wish to retain his
franchise, we will immediately get in touch with you to determine your availability.

We certainly appreciate your interest in the Precision Line.
We have enclosed the new American Watch catalog in the hope
that you will find other nonfranchise items of interest to
you.

Dear Mr. O'Connor:

We received your request of April 30 for 2 dozen #307 kitchen
utensil sets. I have checked our files and found that this
is the first order we have had the pleasure of receiving from
you. You are, therefore, perhaps not completely familiar with
some of our operations which have been designed for our customers' benefit.

In an effort to secure shipping and office savings, we have
established $75 as the minimum amount for any order. The
savings which are thereby secured are passed on to our customers. We are sending you a copy of our general catalog via
airmail. When you check through it, I am sure you will find
many cost-saving items which your customers will want to purchase. If you will be kind enough to supplement your original
order so that the minimum figure is $75, we would be delighted
to process it immediately and ship it c.o.d.

These are a few of the acknowledgment situations which arise. Notice that
they are all handled tactfully, positively, and with a strong sales orientation.

Handling Adjustments: Claim Not Granted

The only cases in which a claim would not be granted are when the
buyer is definitely at fault (and, as we have seen, not always then) or when
there is no real "fault" but, because of government or industry regulations, the
claim cannot be granted.

When the buyer is at fault, the explanation of a refusal to grant a claim
should precede the actual refusal. Although people would not enter claims if
they did not wish them to be granted, they will understand and accept a refusal if it is presented courteously and reasonably. Such a letter should follow
this plan:

1. A statement referring to the specific transaction.
2. A statement explaining tactfully and discreetly how the buyer is at fault. Care should be taken to avoid putting him in a situation where he may lose face.
3. The refusal, either implied or expressed.
4. A sales appeal, if appropriate.
5. A friendly close.

Dear Mrs. Hardy:

We received your letter of April 15 and the package containing our Beach Fun bathing suit which you recently purchased
for your daughter.

We were, of course, concerned to learn that she did not find
the suit satisfactory and wished to exchange it for a different model. Under ordinary circumstances we do everything
possible to please our customers in the matter of adjustments,
for we recognize how important you and thousands of other
purchasers of our product are to the Beach Fun Company.

Immediately after your daughter's swim suit arrived, we sent
it to our Customer Service Department. They have indicated
to us that the garment has been worn several times. This
presents a problem, for in keeping with the statutes of this
state, garments of this type may not be restocked and sold
after they have been used. I am sure that you were not aware
of this regulation, but because of it you will understand why
we are not sending out the model you requested in exchange.

The suit you sent to us is being returned along with the addresses of several dealers who handle the Beach Fun line in
your city. We know that you will find all the latest styles
and fashions in beach wear on display in our dealers' stores.

At times the sting of the refusal may be lessened by offering some concession, a free item, or a carefully structured sales appeal. This has been done in the letter which follows.

Dear Mr. Stark:

We received your letter of December 3 concerning your request
for credit to your account for $28.50.

As you are probably aware, the discount policy throughout the
furniture field permits a 2 percent reduction when bills are
paid within ten days of date of invoice. The amount thereby
secured is passed on to our customers and represents our saving in billing and handling.

In the case of your July and August orders, with which this $28.50 discount is concerned, we have checked and found that they were inadvertently paid 18 (#209), 16 (#402), and 22 (#991) days after the discount period. This oversight in handling bills payable sometimes occurs and has certainly happened to us. Nevertheless, you will understand that in all fairness to our other accounts, as well as to our own position in this case, we cannot agree to your request.

We think you will feel as we do that this action is equitable; however, if some special circumstances are involved in your case, we will be very happy to review the facts.

I have enclosed our new brochure on the Patio Aluminum line of outdoor furniture. Our preferred customers may take a 10 percent discount from the prices listed from now through the end of the month. Why not indicate your needs on the enclosed order form and return it so that we can ship you a quantity of this high quality, excellent mark-up line of furniture.

Although these letters are refusals, the positive approach in the last paragraph or two seems to say to the reader, "Business is business; we are sorry that we must say 'no,' but we believe you will understand. Now let's continue our transactions."

Questions for Study

I. Offer your constructive criticism of the following letters. Remember to note sections of the letters deserving favorable comments, as well as to indicate where improvements can be made. Be as specific as possible in your evaluations.

1. Dear Mrs. Tedry:

I was happy to receive your letter and to learn that you are doing so many interesting things in the health sciences in your sixth-grade class.

I agree with you that your students would benefit from a visit to our hospital to see the labs, pharmacy, food preparation center, a vacant surgical room, the emergency center, and one of the patient floors. However, we do have a City Department of Health ruling to contend with: it strictly prohibits children 14 years of age or less from visiting areas where patients are confined.

Although this ruling does not apply to other areas of the hospital, I wonder how much each child would really observe if he had to compete with 30 others. And of course there is the factor of the slight disruption of hospital routine created by such a large group.

May I suggest an alternate plan, Mrs. Tedry? We have an excellent film titled, "A Complex but Gentle Giant." This tells the story of what goes on in a large, busy hospital. Although it was made by the American Nursing Council and is largely used for recruiting nurses, your students would find it very valuable and interesting. The camera gives the viewer close-ups of all types of procedures and techniques, and the commentary is excellent.

One of our staff could bring the film to your class, or you may, if you wish, use our hospital auditorium. In both cases, a competent person would be present to answer questions.

Just call me at ER2-4132, extension 259, and we can make arrangements for showing the film at a time that will suit your schedule.

2. Dear Sir:

Thank you for your recent inquiry concerning our "Travel the Wide-Wide World" display which was exhibited during the recent World Trade Fair in London.

I would be the first to agree that it is a creative and imaginative display, and we are flattered that you would like to incorporate it into your County Fair Program. However, it would be almost impossible for us to remove all our company markings and insignia from the models. Of course we recognize that you could not very well permit a display to advertise one airline without requesting other firms to participate on an equal basis.

And in addition, we have already scheduled our exhibit for the Annual Aviation Week Conference to be held in New York during the same week as your County Fair.

In any event, we are very happy that you wrote us, and we hope you will give us an opportunity to cooperate with you in some other way.

3. Dear Mrs. Gray:

Thank you for your letter of March 4. Certainly the work in which you and the other members of the Midwest Women's Association are engaged is most commendable. Your efforts in behalf of physically handicapped children are extremely important contributions to our society, and we are all indebted to you.

As you can appreciate, we receive several requests each day for contributions of our appliances to be used in fund-raising efforts. However, the number involved is prohibitive and would result in additional costs which we would have to pass on to the consumer; at the same time we would be placed in a noncompetitive position as compared to other firms.

However, we do have a plan which other organizations have found helpful. Two years ago we commissioned the famous chef, Henry Bils, to write *Favorite French Dishes.* This 300-page, hard-cover book is fully illustrated in color. We will be happy to send you 12 copies free of charge. They may be sold for a minimum of $5.00 each and the funds added to your treasury.

You should receive these within a few days; please accept them with our best wishes for the success of your Spring Fund Drive.

4. Dear Mr. Carmichael:

We were certainly concerned when we received your claim for replacement of the 12 Electro-Mark III switches you purchased on April 28.

Because we wanted to know precisely what happened to cause problems, we immediately requested one of our engineers, Mr. Costello, to visit your plant, pick up the switches, and determine how we could help.

Mr. Costello talked to your Mr. Klein and found that these switches were used in conjunction with your Double Mixer Units. These are powered by 3 h.p. motors, and it is because of this that problems arose.

All Mark III switches, as the instructions note, are rated for use with motors up to

2 h.p. only. For heavier requirements, our Mark IV and V switches should be utilized.

We are processing an order for 12 Mark V switches at a special price of $4.25 each. Please call me collect, and I will ship the switches immediately.

Our spring catalog is enclosed; I think you'll be especially interested in the automatic conveyors and the prices listed on page 21. Pick up the phone and we'll enter your request immediately.

5. Dear Mrs. Kavely:

We received the carton containing the Armstrong Toaster which you returned to us. We can appreciate your feelings inasmuch as you purchased the unit just four weeks ago.

We have checked the mechanism and found that the three ceramic plates are broken and the heating rods have been split away from the wiring. Apparently this unit was dropped or inadvertently struck by a heavy object. Perhaps you did not notice, but the exterior base is badly dented; this may have been the point of impact.

Had the malfunction been due to faulty mechanism or production, we would immediately comply with your request. However, you can appreciate our position in this case. Your toaster has been repackaged and is being returned via parcel post.

Enclosed is our new folder, "Hot Weather Recipes," which we know you will enjoy reading and using.

6. Dear Mr. Kingly:

We received the foot support brace which you returned to us.

We are sorry that it has given you no comfort during the last two months. However, we are at a loss to know what to do with the item. Surely this soiled unit cannot be returned to stock and sold again. In addition, local City Health Department rules make it impossible for us to resell an article of this type.

We are returning the brace and we know you will understand why we cannot take favorable action in this case.

II. Complete any of the following problems assigned. You may wish to review the chapter and note key points before solving the problem.

1. You have just received a request from the Bellview Children's Aid Society to use your company's parking lot area for a Fund Raising Pancake Breakfast affair. You check with your Safety Officer and he tells you that the firm's liability insurance policy does not permit the parking area to be used for "games, recreation, or social affairs." This is because of the danger of injuries which might result from accidents on the hard surface. Although you would like to cooperate, you fear that such use in violation of the policy might result in its being cancelled. Write to the Bellview Children's Aid Society and tactfully refuse. Perhaps the local park could be used instead.

2. Mr. Connory of the physics department of Jefferson High School would like to bring his Physics Club (48 members) through the electronic components department of your company. Unfortunately some of your products are classified as "secret" by the Department of Defense and tours are not permitted without official Washington clearance. Perhaps Mr. Connory would like to have his group hear an address by your Research and Development manager; that can be arranged.

3. Franklin Junior College is arranging a major affair for Saturday, November 21. There will be a beauty parade prior to the big game, half-time festivities, and other events. As a matter of fact, the governor has accepted an invitation to attend. The chairman of the program has written and asked your Chevrolet agency to supply three white convertibles for "Official Use" for that day. Arrangements for these must be made through Detroit; you don't have the cars and even if you did, you would be reluctant to take a chance on new vehicles being damaged. Your own car, a light gray convertible, may be used if the committee wishes.

4. Your research department has perfected a new method for packaging very fragile glass equipment used in outdoor signs. Very general aspects of the method were described in a recent issue of *Packaging Methods*. Several companies have written asking for specific details, and samples of the packaging materials.

   Actually the method and materials are so new and excellent that your firm plans to secure a patent and market the procedure commercially.

   Prepare one letter which can be sent to all those who have and will inquire, and tactfully refuse the request for the present time.

5. Because you are a relatively large mail-order house, you receive several hundred orders from consumers each day. About 3 percent of these orders neglect to include one or more important facts: color, size, or model of item; shipping instructions, etc. Prepare a form letter in which you acknowledge the order but request additional information necessary to process it.

6. In very few cases, in the same operation described in problem 5 above, the customer forgets to include his money although his letter or completed order form indicates that he believes that he has. Prepare another guide or form letter which acknowledges the order but refuses to fill it until the proper sum of money is received.

7. Consumers will sometimes write directly to you and request that you ship one of your appliances to them (TV set, stereo, or radio). They will even include a check at times or request c.o.d. delivery. You are a manufacturer and sell your products through some 5000 outlets of various types in the United States. Write a letter which refuses the order but encloses a booklet listing "your nearby Conroy Dealers."

8. Your weekly newspaper ads carry a brief statement inviting consumers to enjoy the convenience of a "Martin's Charge Account." As a result, you receive about 20 applications each week. One or two of these, after investigation, must be turned down. Complete a letter of refusal to the consumers involved.

9. Mr. Jarwith has purchased furniture from you for his two busy San Francisco stores for two years. During that entire period he has always paid for all merchandise on a c.o.d. basis. Although you and he have discussed an open account, he has always said, "Oh no; I pay cash or I don't buy."

   Today an order from him arrived for $1245 worth of merchandise. Attached was a note which said, "Please charge and ship immediately."

   A credit check requires at least seven days. Write and refuse to send the merchandise out immediately on a credit basis. Perhaps Jarwith can wait a week, or perhaps he will accept this order on a c.o.d. basis and charge those in the future.

10. Talbott Drugs has written you and requested one of your free "Diet for Health" signs. These are electric, automatic, and may be mounted in the diet food section of a store. Customers purchasing upwards of $1500 worth of Slim Line Diet products per month are eligible for a free sign. This is noted in your sales literature. However, Mr. Talbott's operation is small; his purchases, although steady,

never exceed $500 per month. Write and refuse Talbott's request. The signs are available to you at $79.00 each, and you secure them from White Sign Corporation.

11. Although your firm has a liberal adjustment policy, you sometimes have problems with accounts that do not abide by your policy. Claims from your accounts on damaged appliances must be entered within ten days of receipt of merchandise, and if the claim is over $25.00 it is subject to inspection.

    Barber's Appliance Outlet has made numerous claims, most of which you have accepted. However, today's letter from him tells you he received an RCA TV set from you last month (35 days ago) which he sold to a nearby bar. He said the cabinet was badly damaged, and he sold it at $50 below cost. Because the set was to be mounted above the bar for customers' viewing, the appearance of the cabinet was not very important.

    Write to Barber and note your policy. Refuse to grant the claim but remember that he has been a fairly good customer for some years.

12. Your department store handles a full line of small appliances. From time to time an individual will secure item(s) from discount outlets and attempt to return them to you for full retail price credit. To avoid this, all small appliances which you sell are identified on the base with your store insignia. This is a barely visible mark. Prepare a letter of refusal to be sent to those persons who mail an appliance in and request an adjustment even though the item was not secured from one of your stores. You should not assume that everyone who requests an adjustment does so with intent to defraud. Perhaps some individuals received such appliances as gifts and were told they had been purchased from you.

Chapter Eleven

Credit and Collection Communications

The Credit Manager
Acknowledging a Request for Credit
Acknowledging Receipt of Credit Data
Requesting Credit Information
Supplying Credit Information
Granting Credit
Refusing Credit
Collection Letters
Steps in the Collection Series
Variables in Collection Letters
Appeals Used to Motivate Payment
The Collection Letter Series
Unusual Collection Letters

Our purses and wallets bulge with plastic credit cards that can be used to finance almost everything from gasoline to the quarterly tax payments due our state and federal governments.

Around us we see credit-based skyscrapers going up like mushrooms, factories expanding in all directions, and companies spawning plant additions daily. Credit enables businessmen to carry inventories much larger than their cash resources ordinarily would permit; they are therefore in a position to secure many more sales.

Although estimates vary, it is probably accurate to state that about 50 percent of retail sales and 85 percent of wholesale and manufacturers' sales are conducted on credit.

What is credit? Credit is an estimate of the ability and the desire of the individual or company to pay debts at a later date. This ability and desire are usually weighed by the credit manager on a careful analysis of the classic C's: capital, character, conditions, and capacity.

The Credit Manager

Even the most honest man may not always be able to meet his obligations because of an oversight, a difficult business situation, or hard times. The credit manager must watch every step of the credit process to ensure maximum benefits to his company as well as to the credit user.

The manner in which he administers his department has a profound effect on the progress of the firm. If he grants credit too liberally he can overextend the resources of his company. On the other hand, if his viewpoint is very conservative, competitors will secure the accounts he was reluctant to underwrite. In such instances his firm's sales may not advance or may even decline appreciably.

Management today recognizes the need for a thorough, progressive, carefully administered and controlled credit system. In this system, the credit manager plays the dominant role—and he frequently does this through the letters and reports he writes. The purposes for which he must write letters include:

1. Acknowledging requests for credit.
2. Acknowledging receipt of credit data.
3. Requesting credit information from references furnished by applicants.
4. Sending credit information in response to requests from other credit managers.
5. Granting credit.
6. Refusing credit.

Acknowledging a Request for Credit

Companies often encourage their customers to open charge accounts or credit accounts. The obvious reason for such action is the knowledge that the customer who enjoys a credit line with a firm will usually supply most of his needs from that company. Furthermore, the mechanics of a sale are often simpler when credit, rather than cash, is the basis for the transaction.

When a customer asks that a credit account be opened, the acknowledgment should be swift and courteous.

Acknowledgement and directions.

```
Dear Mrs. Schnee:

We received your request asking that we add your name to the
list of over 200,000 Chicagoans who have charge accounts with
Conway's.

We are enclosing one of our standard forms which we would
like to have you complete and return to us within 10 days.

The information secured will, of course, be kept confidential.
```

Note that no commitment—positive or negative—is made.

We will write to you approximately two weeks after you have completed and returned the enclosed form to us.

In the meantime, please visit your nearest Conway's and take advantage of our daily specials on quality merchandise.

Dear Mr. Ragan:

Thank you for your recent request for information on a credit account with our firm. You may be sure we will be proud to add your name to our growing list of satisfied customers.

I have enclosed one of our standard application forms. Please complete and return it to us with your financial statement (certified if possible). All data received will be handled in confidence, of course.

For over four generations, Bakers has brought quality furniture to dealers throughout the United States. We are proud to sell this prestige line, and we know you will be, too.

Under separate cover I have sent you our new wholesale catalog and price list. We know you will find many items listed which you will want to include in your next order.

Dear Mr. Scott:

We appreciated receiving your order of January 14 for various items in our Atlantic Line and your request to open a credit account.

As you know, credit information is needed. Will you, therefore, complete the enclosed form or send us a copy of your most recent financial statement. Of course this will be handled in confidence.

Your order will be processed and shipped immediately after an evaluation is made. If you would like to have the merchandise immediately, we will be happy to ship it to you on a c.o.d. basis less our usual 2 percent discount. Please use the enclosed airmail return postal card to let us know your preference.

Notice that in all the letters on the preceding page the tone is optimistic and positive. In the one to Mr. Scott, for example, the statement "Your order will be processed and shipped immediately after . . ." is much better than "We will hold your order until. . . ."

Acknowledging Receipt of Credit Data

Sometimes 15 to 30 days may be required to secure the information needed to make a decision. In such cases it may be wise to let the applicant know that his request for credit is being processed. Such a letter is especially necessary if it is obvious that an unusual delay will be encountered.

Dear Mr. Kingston:

Thank you very much for sending us the completed credit application form and a copy of your financial statement.

An evaluation is now being carried through; you will hear from us just as quickly as possible.

We have already requested our salesman in your area to stop in, introduce himself to you, and leave you a copy of our latest catalog. I'm sure you will find Carl Downes to be most cooperative and eager to fill your needs for all types of Carlton Kitchen Ware.

We are certainly looking forward to a mutually satisfactory business relationship.

Requesting Credit Information

When you request information on an individual or a company that has applied to you for credit, you are basically sending out an inquiry letter. A vital attribute of such a letter is that it be easy to answer. To achieve this, the letter can be reduced to a few courteous statements with room provided for fill-ins, or else a complete form can be attached to a brief cover letter.

FOR A CONSUMER CREDIT APPLICANT:

Gentlemen:

The above-named individual has applied for a retail credit account with us.

Your comments on his financial responsibility, his credit
reputation, and his payment record with you will prove very
valuable to us.

The information you send will be kept confidential.

A stamped envelope is enclosed for your convenience. Thank
you for your cooperation.

When did applicant have an account with you?
_____
What item(s) was purchased? _____
His high credit was $_____
His payments were _____   ____   _____
                  prompt   slow   delinquent
Does he have an open account with you now? ___   ___
                                            Yes   No

Other Comments: _____
_____
_____

FOR A WHOLESALE CREDIT APPLICANT:

Gentlemen:

The _____ Company has listed your firm as one with
which they do business. We would greatly appreciate your
giving us information on your business relations with this
organization.

If you will complete the enclosed form and return it in the
envelope provided, we will be most appreciative. You may
be sure all information supplied will be kept confidential.

This form accompanied the letter above:

TO _____ Carlton Manufacturing Corp._____
CUSTOMER _____ Penway Industrial Service_____

ACCOUNT HISTORY

Sold Since _____ Terms _____
Highest Recent Credit _____
Owing on O/A _____ On Notes _____
Past Due on O/A _____ On Notes _____

```
                    MANNER OF PAYMENT

____  Discounts                ____  Pays C.O.D., customer's request
____  Prompt & Satisfactory    ____  Pays C.O.D., our requirement
____  Days slow, considered    ____  Placed for collection
        good
____  Days slow, considered    ____  Collected by attorney
        unsatisfactory



COMMENTS  _____
_____
_____

        Authorized Signature:  _____
        Date:                  _____
```

Supplying Credit Information

Quite frequently the credit manager is asked to send information on his accounts to other places of business. Usually this requires little more than completing and signing a form. At other times the request is broad and the respondent is asked to send "background credit data." Usually a brief letter, such as the following, will prove satisfactory:

```
Gentlemen:

We are happy to send you confidential credit information on
the Mary Lee Frock Shop.

   Business Relationship:  Since 1972
   High Credit:  $550
   Payment Record:  Prompt

If there are other specific data which you require, we will
attempt to cooperate in every way possible.
```

When it is necessary to return a negative evaluation, care should be exercised in the choice of words. Statements should be qualified and opinions stated tactfully. There are legal implications involved which suggest the use of discretion.

```
Gentlemen:

We received your request of January 4 for credit information
on the Campton Company.

We have had some difficulty in collecting from this firm since
they opened an account with us 18 months ago.  At the present
time all our transactions with them are handled on a C.O.D.
basis.
```

Some companies, in sending out replies of this nature, feel it is wise to omit the name of the firm on which the evaluation is made. A reference, instead, is made to the date of the inquiry.

Granting Credit

It is always easy to tell people, "Yes, you can have what you asked for." But in the credit letter, we should also attempt to build sales and good will.

The letter should also set down the terms of credit in a clear and specific manner. This is to ensure prompt and correct payment and to avoid misunderstandings (and ill will) at a later time concerning due dates, discount privileges, and related factors.

```
                  TO THE CONSUMER APPLICANT:
```

A positive opening.

Details of billing are presented.

```
Dear Mrs. Rattner:

It is a pleasure to add your name to our list of charge ac-
count customers.

We enclose two charge plates:  one for your use and one for
another member of your family.  All you need do next time you
shop at Daro's Department Stores is to select your merchan-
dise, request that it be charged, and hand the salesperson
your Daro Charge Plate.  It's that simple.

You will receive a bill between the first and the third of
each month.  Payments should be made prior to the fifteenth
of that same month.

We know you will enjoy shopping at Daro's, for every effort
is made to keep our quality high and the variety of merchan-
dise extensive.
```

Whenever you have a question concerning merchandise which
you have purchased, please do not hesitate to visit our
Customer Service Department. Our watchword is "Customer
Satisfaction" and we will do everything possible to merit
your complete confidence.

I do hope you will call on me if I can be of service at any
time in the future.

TO THE COMMERCIAL APPLICANT:

Dear Mr. Kelly:

It's a pleasure to open a credit account for your firm with
Kingsley Lumber Corporation.

Next time you give your Kingsley salesman an order, simply
say "charge it." He will be happy to do so.

All bills are payable by the 12th of the month for merchandise purchased during the previous month. Bills handled in
this manner enjoy a profit-making 2 percent discount. Net
payments are required by the 25th.

We are also pleased to offer you many other Kingsley services.
Our Consumer Sales Advisory Department representative will
visit you periodically or when you have some special problem.
And the Kingsley Display Department will supply you with
sales-building materials for your place of business and items
for direct mail distribution.

We are here to serve you and we hope you'll give us many
opportunities to do just that in the years to come.

From the letters above, it is easy to see that a pattern is followed in letters
granting credit:

1. A friendly opening.
2. The credit grant (this may very well be part of the opening).
3. A clear and specific statement concerning company credit policies and
practices (or reference to a booklet describing these in detail).
4. A brief paragraph describing other company services and designed to
build good will.
5. A friendly close.

If possible, these letters should be individually typed and signed. It isn't necessary to make each one different; they can be typed from a guide letter, but the use of the recipient's name and some personal reference is wise. This can be easily accommodated in a guide letter. (See Chapter Fourteen for a discussion of guide letters.)

Refusing Credit

It is always difficult to say "no" to people, and especially when an evaluation of the applicant's personal character is involved.

The organizational pattern for this letter is similar to that of all refusal correspondence. The key is to explain the reason for the negative action before denying the request for credit.

REFUSING THE CONSUMER CREDIT APPLICANT:

Dear Mrs. Larkin:

Thank you very much for your recent request for a charge account with Sander's Shopping Center.

We have carefully checked the information you submitted and found that you now carry several open accounts with rather heavy balances.

Rather than burden you with an additional account which will require your end-of-month attention, we suggest that you continue on a cash basis with Sander's. In this way your transactions will be completed immediately. As you know, our various service departments will be delighted to assist you.

I am enclosing our January Brochure describing our Yearly White Sale. I'm sure you'll want to take advantage of Sander's fine quality linen and bath supplies at remarkable savings.

At times the explanation for refusal is such that the applicant will only be irritated and embarrassed by the facts. However, by stating what can be done (sales for cash), you also indicate what cannot!

At times the credit manager will find that the information he secures on a consumer is so negative that to explain or mention it as a basis for the refusal would be unwise and might very well arouse antagonism. After all, how can you point out that you've checked and found Mrs. Smith to be a consistently delinquent account and an overall poor risk? In such instances it is wiser not to explain but simply to refuse tactfully. This will save face for the applicant and perhaps serve to retain his or her good will.

```
Dear Mrs. Halsted:

Thank you very much for your recent request for credit with
Wilson Women's Wear Shoppes.

We have carefully checked the information you supplied.  We
do feel that at this time you would be wiser to continue mak-
ing your purchases on a cash basis.  In this way you will be
able to take advantage of the many services cash buying af-
fords.  If, at some time in the future, you care to reapply
for a charge account, we will be delighted to again evaluate
your request.

We are enclosing two tickets for our January 20 Cruise Wear
Show.  Please bring a guest and join us at 3:00 P.M. for this
exclusive gala showing of designer fashions under the direc-
tion of Madame Blanc of Paris.  Refreshments will be served
and we know you will find the afternoon most enjoyable.
```

A refusal letter to a consumer requires extra tact, for a private individual may not be as understanding or as objective about a refusal as a company account-ant or executive.

Refusing the Commercial Credit Applicant

With business clients, the usual refusal pattern is almost invariably fol-lowed. However, it is important to project a sincere "you" attitude. Perhaps it would be to your client's advantage to use an open account for his purchases in the future, but at the moment it is your sincere and considered opinion that buying on a c.o.d. or cash-with-order basis is in his best interests. You must ex-plain your refusal and yet retain his good will. Just one or two incorrectly cho-sen words will turn your explanation into a lecture and antagonize him.

Examine the three letters which follow. The first one offers a brief explana-tion and the refusal. The second letter is a good deal more involved, and yet it carries a note of sincerity. Whether to use the first or the second type of letter will depend largely on your evaluation of the recipient and what approach he may accept or reject.

The third letter is unsatisfactory. It reflects a lecturing, pompous, "we" atti-tude that is sure to bring the irritated comment, "I asked for credit. Tell me 'yes' or 'no' but don't give me a lecture on how to run my business!"

The refusal is implied rather than stated directly. This is usually very effec-tive.

```
Dear Mr. Larson:

We received the credit information which we requested.

We have carefully evaluated the data and we are happy to tell
you that your references speak highly of you.  However, your
asset-liability ratio is such that we suggest you buy on a
C.O.D. or cash-with-order basis.
```

This will result in an immediate saving of 2 percent, the maintenance of current inventory levels, and rapid service.

Your order has been prepared and can be shipped immediately. Just call collect and we'll send the merchandise right out.

I've also enclosed a flyer describing our "special sale to special customers." Why not add a few of these items to your order when you call me?

Note positive approach here.

Dear Mr. Klein:

Thank you very much for completing and returning to us the credit information we requested.

We have carefully evaluated all the data you sent and we feel that it would be to your best interests to remain on a cash basis at this time. Let me explain the reasons for this decision and I think you'll agree with my suggestion.

Your ratio of assets to liabilities is below the generally accepted level of 2 to 1. In addition, you are just getting settled in the community and you have incurred a good many expenses through the purchase of new fixtures, remodeling costs, advertising, and heavy initial purchases.

Cash buying for the next year or so will give you the advantage of an immediate 2 percent discount, lowered inventory levels, and no end-of-month bookkeeping problems.

We sincerely believe that you will be able to build your credit rating and fill your merchandise needs through this method of buying.

Our salesman, Bob Campbell, is scheduled to call on you at the end of this week. I know you'll be interested in the specials he has on small appliances. With the wedding season fast approaching, I'm sure you will find many products that will move rapidly as gift items. Bob will explain our advertising allowances which are available and which help boost your profit margin. And of course, he will be happy to give you additional information concerning cash buying.

Please call me collect, Mr. Klein, if you have any comments or questions regarding our business arrangements. We want to work with you in every possible way.

The "tone" of this letter is "reader oriented" and the explanation thorough.

This is a good sales appeal that is "reader oriented."

An effective and positive close.

Notice that each of the three letters above has an explanation and a refusal. However, the tone differs appreciably in each letter, and will govern the reader's response—whether favorable or unfavorable.

Tactless!

Lecturing!

How many people will appreciate advice offered in this way?

Negative sales effort.

Dear Mr. Mills:

We received your letter and completed credit information forms. We have examined these and have concluded that you would benefit from buying on a cash basis.

As you are probably aware, you are thoroughly overextended at the present time. If you could secure $5000 on loan and pay off some of your bills, you would be moving in the right direction. Of course, you should not get involved with an unusually high rate of interest, for that will only increase your burden. Perhaps increasing your home mortgage might be a solution.

We also feel that the receivables which you have are probably higher than they should be. Why not tighten up on your debtors and secure cash in this manner?

We have the merchandise in stock about which you inquired.

If you want it, we can send it out C.O.D.

The credit letter is a vital one. It must be well written, for the applicant we refuse today may be a most desirable credit account in five years. Thus it is essential to secure and maintain his good will.

Collection Letters

Communication between the Sales Department and the Credit Department

Communication between the credit-and-collection department and the sales department is not as good as it should be in many companies. Too often the departments mistakenly perceive each other as rivals. Sales personnel attempt to promote maximum sales through open account buying, while the credit-and-collection department watches with a hawk's eye to make sure that such accounts don't grow to a point endangering the financial stability of the firm.

Of course, the two departments should work together, since they are both involved in sales.

The letter sent out by the credit manager establishing credit is really "selling" future business. And the primary purpose of the collection letter is to retain the account's good will (which often requires very adroit "selling") while collecting the sum due. Thus the person who writes credit-and-collection letters has significant selling and marketing responsibilities.

This means that credit-and-collection personnel must feel that they are vital to the *sales* effort of the company. Too many individuals in credit and collections perceive themselves as strict guardians of the firm's assets. That is a commendable attitude, but not when it is carried to a point that inhibits the healthy growth of the firm.

Collecting from Retail and Wholesale or Commercial Accounts

Consumer accounts that become delinquent require different types of communications from those used for the wholesale or commercial account. And the collection letter sent to the "good risk" will certainly be different in content from the one sent to the "poor risk." Because time is short and workloads are heavy, companies formulate "standard" collection letters which can be adapted to different situations. Perhaps this is why collection letters are not particularly successful; they lack the individual, personal approach. Yet how can we possibly send personal, individually typed letters to each of our 5700 delinquent retail or wholesale accounts, who owe us anywhere from $2 to $2000 each? We compromise. We begin by using a form letter, and follow this up with a more personal approach for the difficult accounts.

Credit and collection procedures for consumer accounts differ from those used for industrial, commercial, or manufacturing accounts. Naturally our approach with Mrs. Johnson, whose husband earns $9500 a year, will be different from our treatment of National Automotive Parts Company with annual sales of ten million dollars. And yet, they have factors in common: they both may be classified as "good risks"; they are both delinquent in their payments; and they are both customers whose sales and good will we wish to retain.

Classification of Risks

From our earlier discussion you will recall that, before granting credit, a company evaluates an applicant in four major areas:

His capital or financial position;
His character, based on his past, personal, and business history;
The conditions which exist at the time in his business or industry;
The capacity of the firm to do business and carry on successful operations.

After the information in the above categories is weighed, the account may be classified as a good, fair, or poor risk. Upon further evaluation, the classification is broken down into "good risk—good pay" or "good risk—poor pay," or "poor risk—fair pay," or whatever title is considered appropriate. An account may be a good risk, but for some reason he does not like to part with his money, so he is classified as a "good risk—poor pay." On the other hand, we have the new businessman who owes for his fixtures, his merchandise, his equipment, and his vehicles. Yet he makes every effort to pay his bills within the discount period so that his credit reputation will improve. Thus, at the moment, he is classified as a "fair risk—good pay."

Steps in the Collection Series

Most corporations, in dealing with delinquent accounts, divide their collection procedure into three steps: form reminders; personal letters; and finally, collection agencies or court action.

The Reminder

Shortly after a bill has become past due, most firms send out a reminder. The assumption is that the account has been overlooked and "this is just to remind you that this sum is due."

One form of reminder is a colored sticker pasted on a duplicate invoice, bearing a message such as "Please," "Past Due; Please Remit Today," "This Bill Is Now Due and Payable," "Perhaps You've Overlooked," "Just a Reminder," or "Don't Forget Us." Sometimes a rubber stamp is used. Reminders are also printed on cards, small sheets of stationery, and even on rolls of tape (in different colors to indicate different levels of urgency) which can be cut off and attached to the invoice.

Some firms have found that the most effective type of reminder is a short, sincere note written on the face of the invoice. When this is signed by the company president, treasurer, or controller, the delinquent is likely to feel the personal touch very strongly. He will surely react much more favorably to this type of appeal than to stickers, rubber-stamped messages, or reminder cards.

The Personal Letter

Most people are honest and pay their bills promptly. When they fall behind, a reminder or two will usually suffice.

But sometimes a bill remains unpaid and it is necessary to send more than a reminder to the debtor. A personal letter, or two, or three, will usually produce payment or explanation. People will generally respond when they are treated like people, and not like computer cards.

The Collection Agency or Legal Action

If a series of personal letters to a debtor does not result in payment, it will finally be necessary to turn the account over to an agency or legal firm for collection. This should be only a last resort, because it is good neither for the debtor nor for the creditor.

Variables in Collection Letters

Before we send a collection letter, we should know whether the account has been classified as a good, fair, or poor risk. And what further evaluations have been made? Is he a "fair risk—good pay"? Or perhaps a "good risk—fair pay"? On the basis of our classification, several factors in our collection actions will vary:

1. The *tone* of the letter sent to the poor risk will surely be more insistent and less lenient than that of the letter sent to the good risk; *because* he is a poor risk, we know that funds are not usually readily available to him. A more severe, insistent, and demanding tone is used in this instance.

Poor risk: We have now sent you two reminders and a letter. We have received no response concerning your delinquent account. Legal action will be started within 14 days of the date of this letter if payment of this past-due balance of $47.85 is not received.

Good risk: For over ten years you have paid your accounts promptly and taken advantage of the discount privilege. That is why your present past-due balance of $480.00 disturbs us. We know there must be a reason. Mr. Campbell of our office will be in your area on March 5, and will stop by to see you. I'm sure arrangements can be worked out.

2. The *type of appeal* may vary. Among the various types of appeals (see the discussion below), some are more adaptable to the good risk than to the poor. An *appeal to fear or self-interest* may be wiser with the poor risk than an appeal to pride.

3. Normally *more letters are sent to the good risk than the poor risk* before drastic action is instituted. Where the good risk may receive from four to seven letters, the poor risk may get two to four. The poor risk may well be delinquent to several firms and subject to many pressures. If we insist on sending him seven letters before taking action, it may be too late to recover anything. Perhaps three weeks earlier, while we were sending him letter number four, he paid what he could to creditors more insistent than we and now can make no further payments to anyone.

4. The man who has been in business for 20 years, has adequate capital, and whom we've classified as a good risk will certainly be given *more time between* collection letters than the poor risk.

5. The poor risk's account will be turned over to a collection agency or lawyer more quickly than the good risk's delinquent bill. Here again, if we are too lenient with the poor risk, we may find ourselves arranging a court date only to find that the delinquent has paid off as much as he could and has, perhaps, left town. *Time before action* may vary according to type of risk.

Appeals Used to Motivate Payment

When someone owes money to a creditor, it is not because he wants to. He has his troubles, and probably owes several creditors besides you. He has to choose what to do with his limited funds. He can choose to pay other debts, to buy more merchandise for his business, to increase his advertising in order to build up his sales . . . or to pay you.

Where should he place his limited funds to achieve maximum effectiveness? Your simple appeal, "Send it to me," may not be very effective when weighed against the insistent demands he is receiving from others. You must show him why he should pay you now—why it is to *his* benefit to do so. This is where the collection correspondent can employ the "you" attitude very effectively.

Appeals vary in strength, but they are all designed to make the debtor want to pay his bill, or to send along an explanation of why he can't pay at present and what his plans are for the future. The appeal may be to *ethics and fair play;* or to maintaining a *good credit reputation;* or to *self-interest;* or to the *saving of time and trouble;* or to *status;* or to *fear of court action;* or to a combination of these motives.

Quite frequently a collection letter will use more than one of the appeals listed above. However, the effective letter (or series of letters) emphasizes the ways the debtor benefits by paying his bill. Never, or infrequently, do the letters point out how the creditor will gain. In the examples below, note how the various appeals have been used.

An appeal to fairness.

Dear Mr. Corbett:

On March 17 we sent you order #217 as you requested it . . . we shipped it air express at our expense so that we could make the delivery date you asked for.

The order came to $574.50, due on April 15. Although we have sent you several reminders and have made two phone calls, we have not heard from you.

We know that you want to be fair about this. Therefore, will you put your check for $574.50 in the stamped envelope enclosed and return it to us immediately?

An appeal to debtor's credit reputation.

Dear Mr. Jason:

When you applied to us for a credit account, we carried through a standard credit check. We were very pleased when our inquiries brought responses which praised highly your credit reputation.

Perhaps you have merely overlooked this past-due bill of $294.50. If so, please remit the sum today. If there is some difficulty, and we can assist in any way, please let us know.

Further emphasis of the same point.

We know that it took years for you to build such a reputation and we are sure that you want to retain your outstanding rating. And so we are at a loss to explain why you have not paid or responded to the notices we have sent you.

We want to say, when someone calls us about your credit, "It's excellent!" Won't you help us maintain your fine credit reputation by sending us your check today?

Dear Mr. Lindemann:

We're not sailors, but at the moment we're at sea. We can't
understand what happened to your check for $365--an amount
which is now almost two months past due.

Surely it is in your best interest to pay this bill today.
Time can be saved and trouble avoided if you will complete
the check now and send it in.

If, on the other hand, there is some reason why you haven't
paid this balance due, we want to know about it. We've always valued your business and friendship, and we want to
retain both for many years to come.

Dear Mr. Shelley:

"Nothing seems to work," my accountant has just told me.
And unfortunately he was talking about his efforts to collect
your unpaid bill of $165.

It's a pity that he hasn't been successful, for I've had faith
in you and I've wanted to continue our pleasant business relationship. However, there seems to be little left we can do
except turn your account over to our legal department for
action.

If we don't receive your check for $165 by April 28, we'll
have to take that step. Won't you help us avoid this drastic
move? Send in your check today.

Dear Mr. Delento:

Let's recapitulate your delinquent account situation up to
this point.

On January 4 we sent you $870 worth of merchandise which when
added to your balance of $450 brought your account to $1320.

Through February, March, and April we sent you reminders and
called you regarding this past-due sum.

We have obviously done all we could to help you retain your
credit reputation. However, on May 15 your account will be
turned over to the Furniture Credit Association for collection.

```
They in turn forward the names of all delinquent accounts to
furniture manufacturers and suppliers throughout the United
States.  All Association members are then required to stop
shipments to such delinquent accounts.

You can see what this will do to your reputation and sources
of supply.  Why destroy what you've worked so many years to
build?  Please forward your check to us prior to May 15.
```

The letters above are typical of those sent out to collect from past-due accounts. The different appeals are clearly evident. Notice that few, if any, collection letters bother with a "sales appeal" unless the letter is the first or second in a series. The primary purpose is to secure money due, and any discussion which clouds that central message is usually eliminated.

However, for large corporations it is almost impossible, from the point of view of cost, to send personal letters to all delinquent accounts. Furthermore, it is usually not necessary, for a short, courteous form letter will motivate most persons to forward part or all of the sum due, or an explanation for nonpayment. Because this is true, most companies have form collection letters prepared.

Whether it is a form letter or an individually typed letter, the collection message should always:

1. Be courteous and restrained. Insults, accusations, and sarcastic comments serve no useful purpose.

2. List specific dates when payment is due or when more drastic action will be taken—and stick to these dates.

3. List the precise amount due in every letter from the first three-line reminder to the last carefully worded appeal.

4. Include a "you" attitude which clearly shows the debtor how he will gain from making the payment requested.

The Collection Letter Series

It is not very practicable to write one series of collection letters to be used for all types of risks. As noted earlier, the tone, number of letters, and other factors will differ depending on the account. For that reason it is usually wise to make up three different series, one each for good, fair, and poor risks.

The letters may be preprinted and provided with blank spaces, which can be filled in with the proper dates and amounts due. Or guide letters can be written which are bound into a folder and used as models for individually typed messages. Obviously the latter method is more effective because of the personal tone and better appearance of the letters, but they are more expensive to process.

To a Good Risk

(TWO REMINDERS HAVE BEEN SENT.)

"You're so busy you probably overlooked this matter" appeal.

```
                        LETTER ONE:

Dear Mr. Felton:

This is just to call your attention to your past-due balance
of $_____.  Perhaps you've overlooked it in the rush of
daily activities; however, we would appreciate receiving your
remittance by return mail.

Carson's prices and products were never more attractive than
at present.  Why not check your needs and get in touch with
your Carson salesman today?
```

Appeal to fair play.

```
                        LETTER TWO:

Dear Mr. Felton:

It has now been _____ days since your account for $_____
has been marked "Past Due."  We are puzzled and can only
assume that you have inadvertently overlooked this bill.

We certainly did "the right thing" in filling your requests
promptly for quality furniture at competitive prices.  They
say "Turn about is fair play"; therefore won't you do the
right thing and pay this bill today?

I've enclosed a stamped envelope for your convenience.
Please return it with your check for $_____.
```

"Maintain your fine credit reputation" appeal.

```
                        LETTER THREE:

Dear Mr. Felton:

The head of our accounting department has just been in to see
me about your delinquent account of $_____.

I must say I was surprised; there must be a very good reason
for your nonpayment.  Why don't you pick up a pen and jot a
note on the reverse side of this letter telling me what the
problem is?  We want to help in any way we can.

For some time you have been one of our valued customers and
you have enjoyed a fine credit reputation.  Surely we both
want that credit rating of yours retained.  Won't you help me
to help you by sending me a check today or an explanation for
the non-payment of your bill for $_____?
```

Credit and Collection Communications   237

LETTER FOUR:

Dear Mr. Felton:

We are at a loss to understand why you have taken no action to pay or reduce your bill of $_____ which is now _____ days past due.

We have written you several times and have received no response. You can appreciate our position, for we must now think of turning your account over to the National Furniture Wholesalers Association for collection.

We do want to avoid this for it means that your name is published and distributed industrywide as a "delinquent account." Obviously such an announcement does your credit rating almost irreparable damage.

We have no recourse except to forward your name to the Association within 15 days or by _____, 19___. Won't you help us to avoid such action by mailing us your check for $_____, or a substantial part of this sum, prior to the date indicated?

Drastic action appeal plus credit reputation appeal.

LETTER FIVE:

Dear Mr. Felton:

After several reminders and letters concerning your past-due bill of _____, we are now forced to consider taking drastic steps to collect. This means turning your account over to our attorneys for court action.

This will not be desirable for either party. For you it means the payment of not only the sum due but court costs of no inconsiderable amount, and in addition there are the time and trouble involved.

Why not save yourself all this difficulty by sending us your check for $_____? If we do not hear from you by _____ _____, your account will be turned over to McAlister, Kelley, and McAlister for legal action.

Appeal to legal action.

To a Poor Risk

(TWO REMINDERS HAVE BEEN SENT.)

LETTER ONE:

Dear Mr. Larkin:

This is to call your attention to your past-due bill for $_____.

"You simply overlooked" appeal.

It is quite possible that you simply overlooked this amount,
but we know that you want your credit record to reflect
prompt payments.

Therefore, will you send us your check today?

LETTER TWO:

Dear Mr. Larkin:

Your bill for $_____ has not been paid. We are at a loss
to understand this, for we know the merchandise and service
you received from us were satisfactory.

We must, of course, insist on payment when due. When accounts are not cleared, we send a notice of delinquency to
the Appliance Association. Our next step is legal action.

Please send us your check today.

LETTER THREE:

Dear Mr. Larkin:

Your account has now been delinquent for _____ days. You
are doubtless aware of this for we have written you several
times about this unpaid balance of $_____.

Unfortunately you leave us no reccurse unless we hear from
you by _____. If your check does not arrive by that date,
we will submit your name to the Association of Wholesale
Appliance Dealers. You will then be classified as a delinquent account and all member dealers will be so notified.

Why not avoid the stigma of such classification by sending us
your check for $_____ today?

LETTER FOUR:

Dear Mr. Larkin:

This is to inform you that we have not received any satisfactory settlement or explanation of your past-due account of
$_____.

On _____, 19___, your account will be turned over to
Mr. Thomas Shane of the legal firm of Shane and Shane,
120 South La Salle Street, Chicago, Illinois. After the
above date all communications should be made to Mr. Shane,
who will be in charge of court action to be taken against you
to collect your outstanding debt with us.

Unusual Collection Letters

There is something to be said for the imaginative collection letter. At best, collecting money is a difficult task. Sometimes the right proportions of humor, fact, and appeals to common sense—all cast in relation to the reader—work very well.

Dear Subscriber:

In Oklahoma City recently café owners opened a school to teach their waitresses to smile pleasantly.

And before you laugh, you might admit that smiling waitresses have a lot to recommend them.

Here at TIME, we've always felt the same way about "collection" letters.

We just smile pleasantly and say: "Our bill for your current subscription is enclosed."

Wonder if you wouldn't like to substantiate our faith in smiles by sending us your check, please, today?

Dear Subscriber:

Not 1001 nights but 92 days ago you again commissioned us to be your story teller. You bade us appear before you each week of the year, to bring you all the curious and exciting and significant news of all the world.

And lo, we have fulfilled your commission faithfully.

Now it is the third month since you asked us to play Scheherazade to your Sultan for another year--and still TIME arrives regularly at the appointed hour, laden with tales to inform and entertain you . . .

    Tales stranger than any fiction ever written . . .
    Tales of great heroism and man-made disaster . . .
    Tales of the magic wrought in laboratories . . .
    Wondrous tales of artists and bards and mimes.

But throughout all these 92 days and nights we have waited in vain for your check--and this is enough to make even Scheherazade lose confidence.

Please won't you reassure us by settling this small account today?

Notice in the letters on the preceding page that the level of language, the style of humor, and the type of appeals would all be acceptable to *Time-Life* readers.[1]

The following letters have also proved very effective and have been used (with variations) by many companies.

Dear Mr. Barwig:

That rubber band stapled to the top of this letter is very significant, for it has much in common with credit.

Both rubber bands and credit perform valuable functions when used correctly. But when either one is stretched too far, it breaks, with results that can prove to be disastrous.

In your case, the rubber band of credit has been stretched very thin . . . in fact we think it's close to breaking.

Let's keep the usefulness of your credit intact. Send in your check for $_____ no later than _____. Then both your credit and the rubber band will continue to function perfectly.

Dear Mr. Kranz:

That paper clip up at the top of this letter hasn't been left there by a careless stenographer.

That's Elmer our pet paper clip.

His purpose in life is to hold two pieces of paper together. But Elmer has enlarged his scope of usefulness and has accepted two very definite tasks which we've asked him to do.

    ONE . . . to hold your check for $_____ to this note
            and thus clear up your past due account and . . .
    TWO . . . by so doing, to bind the friendly relationship
            which has always existed between us.

When returning your check, don't forget to send Elmer. You know, he's our Credit Manager.

---

[1] Letters reproduced by permission of Time, Inc.

Our Side	Your Side
On March 28, we sent you a notice about your past-due bill of $_____. Since that date, we've sent you several other reminders and letters but we haven't had a reply. We are really puzzled. Surely there must be something wrong . . . the bill? our service? business conditions? a misfortune? We sincerely want to work with you but we can't if we don't know what is wrong. Won't you take a few minutes to tell us your side of the story in the attached space? Then use the stamped envelope to send us your reply. We want to work with you. Give us some help by replying today.	

Dear Mr. Farber:

You may well wonder what that piece of jig-saw puzzle is doing at the top of this letter.

Well, it's really quite simple. Our auditor has been checking our books. He finds that everything balances and is complete except for one missing item . . . your check to cover your past-due account of $_____.

Obviously, he can't finish the audit to his satisfaction without your check and I can't finish my puzzle without the missing piece.

Won't you help us both by returning your check and the jig-saw puzzle piece today?

It's conceivable that unusual collection letters may have a boomerang effect. The debtor may not take seriously the cute, clever, or funny collection letter, especially if several creditors are pressuring him at the same time. He may decide that if one of his creditors finds the situation humorous, perhaps that creditor is a logical choice for delayed payment.

Questions for Study

I. Offer your constructive criticism of the following letters. Remember to indicate which sections of the letters deserve favorable comments, as well as where improvements can be made. Be as specific as possible in your evaluations.

1. Dear Mr. Parker:

It was a pleasure to receive your request to be added to our selected list of credit accounts.

We have enclosed one of the standard credit forms used throughout the jewelry industry which we would like to have you complete and return to us. You will also note that the form requests a certified financial statement.

We look forward to working with you, Mr. Parker, as we do with our 4000 other retail accounts. We have, since 1920, instituted a variety of services designed to increase our retailers' sales: advertising campaigns, holiday tie-in store displays, contest sponsorship, counsel on direct mail, seminars on store and personnel management, and other efforts.

I have requested our salesman in your district, Joe Jemper, to stop by and introduce himself to you. Mr. Jemper will also leave you a copy of our new catalog and policy booklets.

May we ask that you return the completed forms in 10 days, Mr. Parker. You may be sure that all the data you supply will be retained in confidence.

2. Dear Mrs. Spear:

Thank you for your request to open an account with Kendry's Women's Wear.

We have enclosed one of our credit information forms; please complete and return it within 2 weeks. Of course all the data you list will be kept in confidence.

Until we have had an opportunity to evaluate the information, please continue to fill your clothing needs at Kendry's. Between January 5 and 25 we are featuring many outstanding values on cruise and vacation wear. Stop in today and shop . . . and, of course, complimentary tea and cakes are available each afternoon between 2 and 4 in our Sussex Room.

3. Dear Mr. Gotz:

It was a pleasure meeting with you last week. Your various completed forms arrived and have been evaluated. We are certainly happy to add your firm's name to our list of "Preferred Accounts."

Mr. Vern Cable is the salesman in your area. He will be calling for an appointment to meet with your canned fruit buyer. I'm sure Mr. Cable will be happy to work with your buyer in every way possible: discount privileges, lot purchases, advertising tie-ins, etc.

The enclosed card, "Credit Control at Carpenter's," will be of interest to your controller. It lists payment and discount policies as well as other information.

Please call me, Mr. Gotz, if there is anything we here at Carpenter's can do at any time.

4. Dear Mr. Roth:

It's been well over three weeks since we sent you our last reminder concerning your past-due bill.

Because you have been an excellent customer for several years, we are at a loss to understand why you have permitted your account to become delinquent.

We know you are as eager as we are to see that your fine credit reputation is retained. Please send us your check for $740 which will clear your account and maintain your excellent credit reputation. If for some reason you can't do that conveniently, please send us part of it and your comments.

We want to work with you, Mr. Roth, in every way possible.

5. Dear Mr. Fairwhether:

There's an old song that goes, "We'll take the high road and you take the low road, and we'll all meet in . . . ."

That may be acceptable for songs but not for doing business as far as we're concerned.

We want to travel on the same road with you, and we want to keep abreast. Right now, however, we seem to be on different highways.

We've been waiting patiently on the corner of Jackson and Van Buren for the $295 you owe us but you're apparently on a different road.

How about getting back on the track and clearing your past-due bill—now 60 days delinquent. We sure don't want to send a posse down the road for you, but we do want that $295.

II. Complete any of the following problems assigned. You may wish to review the chapter and note key points before solving a problem.

1. Your firm, Office Aids, sells business machines and office supplies to a large number of companies in the New York area. Prepare a letter which may be used as a guide to be sent to those firms that have applied for a credit account and have been approved. Make any reasonable assumptions concerning rules, services available, and miscellaneous factors.

2. In some instances, the company mentioned in Problem 1, Office Aids, must reject a credit applicant. Write the letter taking care of such a situation when the applicant has been found to be a poor credit risk due to very slow payments to other creditors, and in a generally unsatisfactory financial position.

3. You are the owner of Parker Fashions in Broadway, New Jersey. Assume this is a suburb of a large urban center. The population of the suburb is made up of families in upper income levels, many of whom know each other. From time to time, one of the applicants for credit must be rejected. Write such a letter, keeping in mind the individual's possible close social relationship with many of your best customers.

4. Parker Fashions advertises in the weekly *Broadway News*. The advertisement usually carries a small message at the bottom inviting charge accounts. Quite often an individual will telephone to inquire about an account. Write the letter which accompanies the blank "request for information" forms which are mailed to the applicant.

5. Sometimes you receive an order for auto parts and supplies (products which you distribute) marked, "Please charge." Many of these requests come from outlets which will be good credit risks. However, you cannot send the merchandise out on a charge basis until you have run a credit evaluation. Write the letter which will accomplish the following: (1) acknowledge the order; (2) offer to send it on a cash basis, or hold it until the evaluation is completed; and (3) request completion and return of the "request for information" forms which are enclosed.

6. Mr. Robert T. Elkins opened an account with you two years ago. His purchases of

lamps and decorative home items from you have averaged about $600 per month. He paid his bills promptly until five months ago. At that time his account stood at $940. You sent him several reminders and letters and he finally responded 21 days ago with a $250 check. However, he has made no further payment on the $690 past-due balance. Write the necessary collection letter.

7. You own a neighborhood women's dress and sportswear shop. Although you do not encourage credit accounts, some of your steady customers ask, from time to time, if they may charge a purchase. You usually agree, and payment is usually prompt. However, some accounts do not pay when they should. A further problem is that they shop elsewhere while their account with you remains delinquent. Write a letter which can be sent to such accounts; attempt to collect while retaining good will.

8. Assume you are the credit manager for a department store located in a middle-class suburb just outside of New York. Approximately 20 of your accounts each month do not pay when scheduled, although most send their checks eventually. Prepare a collection series for this group.

9. You have six salesmen who sell briefcases, attaché bags, wallets, and related items to retail outlets on the West Coast. You have relatively few delinquent accounts, but from time to time one occurs. Prepare a short reminder letter and two collection letters which can be used as models. One letter should be standard and the other quite severe.

Chapter Twelve

Sales Communication

Advantages of Direct Mail
Writing the Sales Letter
Cover Letter and Enclosure
Mailing Lists

"Do you have trouble staying awake in class? Try Professor X's course in Medieval History. It's so exciting you won't want to miss a minute."

Fortunately for our educational system, this is not the way students choose their courses. But in the business world, selling a product is as important as making it. Customers have to be persuaded that the product will serve them better than competing products, or be easier to use, or cheaper, or more exciting. Whether you're running a grocery store or a steel company, you want as many people as possible to hear about what you have to sell, and to form a favorable impression of it.

Companies use many methods of persuading the public to buy their products. You are doubtless familiar with most of them: radio, TV, letters, brochures, pamphlets, newspaper and magazine advertisements, bulletins, billboards, and others. For our purpose, we will focus on the sales letter. It is a "rifle" type of approach to the customer because it is directed at particular individuals. We select a specific prospect group—pediatricians, say, or business executives, or accountants, or registered nurses—and aim at them. This differs from the TV approach, in which we "shotgun" at thousands of viewers in the hope that an appreciable percentage of them will prove to be prospects for our product.

Advantages of Direct Mail

Selling by direct mail has proved to be an effective, inexpensive, and profitable method of doing business. When compared to radio, television, or newspaper advertising, direct mail has a number of advantages.

Two authorities in the direct mail field have the following to say about it.[1]

Here are ten advantages which direct mail offers you when your advertising needs to be personal, selective, and flexible:

1. You can be more exact in selection of and delivery to individuals or markets you wish your advertising to reach. From the list of the 'Wisest Men at $1 for 7 Names' . . . to that list right in your lap—present customers, past customers, and the people they would recommend—you can hit exactly at the market you wish.

2. You can be personal and confidential with direct mail . . . you can wrap a personal message in the secrecy of an envelope when the message is the 'between-you-and-me' type.

3. You have less competition for the reader's attention with direct mail. Because of its physical make-up, direct mail doesn't have to compete with other advertising . . . to the same degree or in the same way that display advertising does. . . .

4. You have few limits in format to restrict the creative expression of your advertising ideas. The selection of color, shape, size, and format has few restrictions except those of feasibility, practicality, and the U.S. Post Office. . . .

5. You have great flexibility in the selection and use of creative materials and reproduction processes. All forms of the graphic arts, all those elements which can give direct mail a third or fourth dimension—die cuts, folds, sound, smell—can be adapted to give you a custom-built advertising impact.

6. You can interpret your advertising story . . . with a 'reader-only' individualism, with novelty, with realism. . . .

7. You can produce direct mail as you need or want it. No publication date will make you wait for the impact of your advertising to be felt in your market. . . .

8. You can use the 'control' inherent in direct mail for research, for testing—appeals, ideas, etc.—for reaching highly selective audiences. The individual, personal qualities of direct mail are ideal for research. And . . . you can test mailings before you throw your whole advertising effort in the hopper.

9. Your timing of mailings can be accurate, exact. . . . Mail departure and arrival schedules can be obtained from your post office. This means you can have mailed material hitting at its target, as planned.

10. You can offer a complete 'reply' package so that the reader has ease of answering. With an enclosed, easily mailable, postpaid reply piece—business reply card, envelope, order blank, and the like—you can get easy, immediate action from readers.

These are some of the obvious advantages of direct mail. There are others: a sales letter will frequently penetrate (to the president's desk, for example) where other advertising media may not; it can be directed to widely separated geographic areas for much less money than it costs to send salesmen; it can introduce a product prior to the personal call; and it can accomplish a dozen other tasks for you quickly, selectively, and inexpensively.

[1] From *Planning and Creating Better Direct Mail* by J. D. Yeck and J. T. Maguire. Copyright 1961 by McGraw-Hill. Used by permission of McGraw-Hill Book Company.

Writing the Sales Letter[2]

Writing the letter which sells a product or service can be an exciting adventure. To do a good job requires vivid imagination, skill in the concepts of written communication, and the sales ability to create desire through words.

The writer must possess *imagination* so he can project himself into the reader's position and recognize the latter's hopes, needs, and desires. This is not easy, for our world usually revolves around *our* needs, *our* hopes, *our* desires. But these must be put aside, for the sales-letter writer must become the person he is attempting to sell; he must see, appreciate, understand, and feel that person's needs as though they were his own.

Imagination is also necessary to recognize new needs, new uses, new reasons why the prospect should have the product. And imagination is needed to select the words which will build a compelling picture of the product in the reader's mind.

Skill in composition is required in every communication, but in the sales letter especially. The organizational development of the letter must be logical and smooth. Persuasive point must be constructed unobtrusively on persuasive point from the introduction to the final statement which motivates the purchase of the product or service.

The sentences must be crystal clear so that they seem to flow from one idea to another. Never should the reader be required to stop and reread to understand a statement. His progress should be swift and sure and always assisted by the clarity of the statements which effortlessly move him along from one idea to another.

The word choice must be accurate and precise so that it evokes the exact response desired. There should never be a question about possible interpretations or reactions. The words should be selected so that only one response and/or interpretation may be received from them.

And the total composition which conveys the message must be concise. Today's reader does not have the time, patience, or inclination to read through three pages if the message can be contained in one.

The sales correspondent must combine his imaginative ability with his communication skill to *build desire*. His words must motivate the reader to favorable action. It can't be just a "white or blue blouse." It must be a "highly styled, easy-care blouse, fashioned in figure-flattering silk and available in Wedgwood blue or snow white." It can't be "a modern office desk." A better picture is achieved if we say, "Contemporary styling in oiled walnut or glistening mahogany to enhance your present office decor and provide your secretaries with an efficient, convenient, and attractive work area."

Initial Steps

There are several steps the sales writer must carry through before he writes his letter. He must:

[2] See also "Letters That Sell," Royal Bank of Canada, reproduced in *The Bulletin of The American Business Communication Association*, September 1974.

1. Conduct a product analysis.
2. Complete a market analysis.
3. Review the needs of the prospect.
4. Select the attribute(s) of the product which will fulfill the need.
5. Plan the presentation.

Product Analysis. The sales-letter writer must know his product intimately and thoroughly if he hopes to sell it successfully. He must know how it is made, what its components are, where the raw materials came from, what research has gone into it, what it will do, how it will do it, and a dozen other factors. He must also know a good deal about competing products which are on the market.

And knowing all this—thoroughly—he will be assisted in doing a good job of selling. Such detailed information not only permits him to talk knowledgeably about the product or service, but it also adds two vital selling factors to his presentations:

1. Sincerity and belief in his product; and
2. The ability to anticipate almost any question or objection which the prospect might raise.

A product analysis may be conducted in many ways. The sales writer may visit the company producing the product and talk with those engaged in making it. He may gather information about the quality level of the raw materials used and their sources; the production techniques employed; the quality control standards imposed; the method of operation of the product; the performance levels of the product; its design and appearance; the product's differentiating features as compared to competitive items; repair and service facilities offered; and prices and terms.

These are just some of the areas about which information can be secured. The areas examined can be used as headings on a chart, and the data entered under each head. When the writer is finished, he possesses an excellent resource chart from which to draw information for sales letters and promotion pieces.

The sales writer should also study the market analysis that has been made for the product.

Market Analysis.[3] Today most companies will bring a new product out only after very sophisticated market analysis. The sales writer does not make the market analysis himself, but he needs to know what the analysts have found out.

Thousands—sometimes hundreds of thousands—of dollars are invested in producing a product. It would be silly to spend these huge sums of money without first determining whether or not a profitable market exists. Such market analysis will determine:

[3] The *Journal of Marketing Research* and the *Journal of Marketing* are both excellent sources for research studies. The relatively new *Journal of Consumer Research* presents much valuable information on consumer response to persuasive communications.

The potential number of buyers

The present sales and acceptance of competitive products

The present buying habits and geographical concentrations of potential buyers

The likes, drives, and status symbols of the potential buyers (suburban homeowners, teen-agers, college professors, for example)

What the potential buyer wants in this product

The buyer's buying power

Under what conditions and terms the buyer will act

The short- and long-range selling potential of the product

Any possible tie-in with other products

Answers to these questions and others may be secured from secondary as well as primary sources.

Company records, earlier market studies for similar products, government statistics on buying habits, journal articles which discuss the future sales potential in various fields are only some of the secondary sources which are easily available. Primary sources of information are also extremely valuable. Interviews and questionnaire surveys of a sample of the potential buyers are frequently used. Also valuable is the personal and unobtrusive observation, at the very moment of selection, of just how or why a buyer decides to purchase one product instead of another.

Discussion with people who have had years of experience in the field—manufacturers, advertising executives, and salesmen—is also helpful.

Needs of the Buyer. The market analysis should indicate whether or not our product or service will sell and which group or groups in the population we may expect to become our buyers.

Now we must place these specific groups under the magnifying glass, so to speak, and determine what their needs and drives are and what appeals we should use to motivate them to select our product.

Psychologists tell us that most of our daily activities revolve around our efforts to fulfill our needs. These needs are usually divided into physical, social, and egoistic.

In today's society our physical needs—food, shelter, warmth, etc.—are usually met, and thus we concentrate on our social and egoistic needs. Our social needs include our desire to give and receive affection, to affiliate with others and be affiliated with, and our need to take care of others and to be taken care of (nurturance).

Unlike the social needs, which concern our relationship with others, the egoistic needs involve our relationship with ourselves. These needs may be filled by achieving recognition for something we have done, acquiring status symbols such as expensive cars or luxurious homes, occupying a position of authority, and so on.

Most of us desire or wish to secure:

Love	Saving of time
Security	Good health
Social distinction	Warmth

Comfort	Approval from others
Pleasure	Respect
Efficiency	Prestige
A position of authority	Delicious food

The specialists in consumer motivation have produced lists of human drives or motives which include from fifty to several hundred items. Of course many of these wants are offshoots of those listed above, and overlap each other.[4]

But they must be taken into account, for *consumers usually buy on the basis of the need which the product will fulfill rather than the product itself.*

The buyer of an expensive automobile may be purchasing prestige and respect rather than transportation; a woman may want from her mink coat status and position instead of warmth; instead of simple transportation, a young man may be looking for individuality, nonconformity, and distinctiveness in owning a foreign sports car; the teen-ager may be purchasing beauty and popularity rather than "just" cosmetics, soap, or clothes.

And so it goes. In the time-worn phrase: "Sell the sizzle—not the steak."

Major Appeal. In selling, it is necessary to select one or two outstanding attributes of the product or service offered—the *major appeal*—and emphasize these in the sales message. The characteristics chosen will help fulfill the needs—real or imagined—of the prospect.

This is necessary for two primary reasons. The customer doesn't have the time or inclination to examine and weigh 10 or 15 wonderful attributes of the product. He asks, "Why is it better than the other cars, autos, typewriters, shavers, or television sets on the market? Give me a short, quick answer and I'll decide for myself whether to purchase your product or not."

Second, the seller is interested in showing how his product surpasses competing items. When the seller selects and emphasizes one or two attributes which his product has, and his competitors' products do not have, he draws attention to so-called superior features rather than to attributes they have in common. But this major appeal is always based on the needs of the prospect.

Let's see how this works in practice. We have just been requested to sell prospects on the idea of coming to our appliance store to purchase the new Arctic Refrigerator-Freezer for $395. We are to mail out 50,000 letters to prospects who live in the greater Chicago area, and try to induce them to come to our downtown location.

Our refrigerator-freezer has many outstanding attributes, but our prospects are not interested in all of them. And furthermore, their needs vary. Some of them live in $80,000 to $120,000 homes in upper-class suburbs, while some live in densely populated neighborhoods. Their incomes vary from $9000 per year to $90,000. The size of families ranges from two to ten. These people are all excellent prospects but their needs and buying motives are different.

We must therefore try to adapt our appeals to our prospects' needs.

[4] Vance Packard in several of his popular books *(The Hidden Persuaders, The Status Seekers, The Pyramid Builders, The Waste Makers)* discusses the buying drives of the American consumer.

In one letter (directed to upper-income areas), our major appeal may be an automatic ice cube maker, new contemporary styling, or a new temperature-controlled butter keeper or vegetable crisper. To another group (perhaps suburban or rural), we emphasize the frost-free freezer. For the low-income group, we may focus on price, installment buying, time-payment plans, and trade-in deals. And in the letter sent to neighborhoods containing large family units, we may underscore Arctic's size, storage capacity, and efficiency. Of course, the refrigerator-freezer and its price never change, but the major appeal does.

You will find it interesting to look through newspapers and magazines and note how the advertisements for the same car, the same soap, the same cigarette, and a thousand other items change from one publication to another. The messages and appeals present various selling points of the product in an effort to match the different needs of the various buying groups. The same variations are made in sales letters.

The selection of the major appeal must be based on careful market analysis. In selling to consumers, special attention may be given to need fulfillment that is based to some degree on emotion—status, prestige, beauty, securing an attractive husband or beautiful wife, and other items of this nature. In letters sent to wholesalers, the central appeal will be more practical—it will emphasize profits, business efficiency, and rapid turnover.

The Parts of the Sales Letter

Many of those who work in the field of sales communication feel that the most effective sales letter has four parts:

Interest: Because of the tremendous competition for the attention of the prospect, the sales letter must almost instantly secure his attention and hold his interest.

Description: Once we have his interest, we must describe and explain how the product or service will fulfill his needs and result in benefits to him.

Proof: Because the marketplace gives the prospect an opportunity to select from competing products and services, we must prove why ours is superior and should be selected.

Action: And because the "pay-off" for both seller and buyer is in the sale, we must request the action that will complete the transaction.

Thus we should check every sales communication we write for IDPA: Interest, Description, Proof, and Action.

Arousing Interest. Here are some of the devices, ideas, and plans used to awaken a prospect's interest. How clever, "tricky," or unusual they should be depends on who the reader is and on the nature of the product.

But in all cases the sales correspondent should be careful that his attention-catching idea isn't a tasteless gimmick which may reflect badly on the quality of the product. And it shouldn't be so unusual that the reader's interest focuses on the attention-catching device and not on the item to be sold.

Sample of the product.   Although this can be a rather costly way of attracting attention, it is one of the most effective. Who can discard a sample swatch of cloth, slice of plastic, piece of metal, or square of rubber without first carefully examining it? Some companies have even had their letters printed on a sample of their product (wood, plastic, cardboard).

When the prospective buyer can see, feel, bend, tear, taste, or smell the actual item, he is more likely to go back to the sales letter which accompanied the sample, and read it carefully.

Photographs or sketches of the product.   Some items are too big, bulky, or in some way not adaptable for a sample. A good photograph permits the prospect to see the product and integrate it into the word picture supplied in a letter.

Gadgets and gimmicks.   Various plastic, paper, metal, cardboard, and wooden figures are used successfully. They may be reproductions of the product or some related item that ties in with the product or service offered. These may be attached to the letter, be a part of the message, or be a separate item altogether. Sometimes they are clipped or pasted to the letter, sometimes they pop up or out or fold down.

Every large city has several agencies which specialize in the sale of advertising novelties and stickers of this type.

Different openings to attract attention.   Unusual messages, type sizes, and word arrangements can be used to attract the reader's attention:

1. **Unusual offer:**
   "An Executive Briefcase at no cost to you!"
   "Four DeLuxe Safety Tires for the Price of Two!"
2. **Surprising statement:**
   "How would you like to make $80,000 per year?"
   "Here's a salesman who draws no salary."
3. **Inside address opening:**
   Here's How
   America's Teen-ager
   Can Always Score High:
4. **Vital facts about the product:**
   "Eight hours a day, seven days a week, month in and month out, Canfield Chemical Co. has used Marton hoses to transfer liquid chemicals from ships to storage facilities."
5. **Story opening:**
   "It was 3:00 a.m., January 14, when the phone next to Doc Garyl's bed rang shrilly. He reached out, instantly awake, to take in the seriousness of the message. . . . The Atlantic Flyer, bound for Florida, had just crashed into the Daily B & M Freight. . . ."
6. **Reference to prospect's problem:**
   "Are You Too Being Robbed of Your Sleep on These Hot, Sticky, Uncomfortable Nights?"

Notice in several openings above that the reference is personal: *you*. This tack immediately involves the reader, and can be accomplished with most openings.

Openings of sales letters should be positive, and so designed as to awaken in the prospect favorable associations with the product or service. And they should always be pertinent and concerned with the sales item. The reader is usually irritated if he finds that his interest has been awakened by some device that has nothing to do with the product.

Describing the Product or Service

Now that we have aroused the prospect's interest and have him reading, our next task is to describe the product carefully and show him how its purchase will benefit him.

We must not only describe the product so that he can almost see and feel it, but we must do this in such a way that he *desires* to purchase it. In our description we answer the questions of "what does it look like?" and "how is it made?"

> The Academic Briefcase is made of only number-one steer hides whose strength and durability guarantee years of wear. The heavy-duty National Zipper and triple heavy-duty nylon thread stitching add to the years of wear you will receive. The disappearing handles and Kentor Lock are valuable extras. And the four roomy interior sections provide individual compartments for your valuable papers, documents. . . .
>
> All this and impressive beauty too. The sheen, elegance, and appearance of the Academic Case have been responsible for the "Open Sesame" to many office doors. A rich golden tan or emphatic black are the two most popular executive colors. . . .

The words used to describe the product or service must evoke a real picture in the prospect's mind. Of course we can't inundate him with details but there should be enough so that he can really visualize the sales item. And the details should be presented in such a way as to add strength to the central appeal. If the letter is accompanied by an enclosure, brochure, or pamphlet, the details, sketches, and pictures can go in there. If not, they must be carefully selected and presented in the letter.

But even as he reads, the prospect asks, "What will it do for me?" "How will I benefit?" And these questions must be answered early in the letter if we are to hold him. He must be told how some need of his will be fulfilled: how the product or service will provide him with profit, prestige, comfort, security, love, beauty, economy, health, or some other thing he desires.

> Cool, pleasant, restful nights for you and your family can be yours in the warmest, most humid weather. This is what an Arctic Howe Air-Conditioning System guarantees you.
>
> A full 25 percent profit margin is secured every time you sell a Tru-Lite Lamp. And they are selling like hot cakes throughout the country as a result of unexcelled quality, competitive price, and national radio-TV-newspaper-magazine advertising. The

average furniture dealer can clear approximately $200 per week by just selling 20–25 Tru-Lite Lamps. Here is a prestige money-maker for you.

In handling the description of the product and the explanation of the prospect's benefits, it is again wise to be specific, positive, and detailed in reference to the primary selling appeal. It isn't necessary to describe the product first and then show the prospect how he will benefit. The order can be reversed or the two steps can be integrated.

Proving Your Point. But Americans are a skeptical lot and they often say, "Sounds great, but I don't believe it will do all that. Prove it!" And prove it we must if we expect the prospect to make the purchase.

A dozen different methods can be used to secure belief in what has been said. The type of proof selected will in large part depend on who the prospect is and the nature of the product. Where one person will be impressed by a testimonial from a movie star, another will only shrug.

Some of the common types of proof are:

1. *Samples.* Carefully examine the enclosed swatches of cloth—cloth that is used to tailor America's finest suits. Note the silklike quality of the Italian sharkskin, the beauty of the English tweeds, the design of the American worsted silks, and the attractiveness of the smartly styled gabardines. Each can be hand tailored to . . . .

2. *Guarantee.* And you will be happy to know that your National Stove is backed by a full 5-year guarantee on parts and service plus the National Home Makers Seal of Approval.

3. *Free trial.* Therefore, with no obligation or risk on your part, we will be happy to send you the next six issues of *National Affairs.* After you have read a few copies of this vital national news magazine . . . .

4. *Names of previous purchasers.* After your firm has received its Executive Conference Table, you will find it as useful and as attractive as have International Harvester, General Motors, Western Electric, and many other American corporations.

5. *Testimonials.* "There can be no doubt," said Martel Plant Superintendent, Bill Peterson, in a recent letter to us, "that Kelley Safety Equipment is directly responsible for our safest year on record."

"The National Briefcase," wrote Prof. L. Ryan of DePaul University, "has carried a multitude of papers and books for me and looks as attractive and impressive today as the day I purchased it almost ten years ago."

6. *"Outside" agency records.* Conclusive tests conducted by the chemistry department of Central Illinois University during the winter of 1975 indicated that every one of the Teltax cans of paint examined contained . . . . These samples of Teltax were purchased at random throughout Illinois, Michigan, and Indiana. Surely. . . .

The United States Testing Company, Inc., carefully evaluated each of our new lines and found . . . .

7. *Money-back guarantee.* We are so sure you will find the new Arctic Frozen Fruit line so tasty, delicious, and satisfactory that we promise to refund *double* the price you have paid for any item which does not meet with your complete satisfaction. All you need do is . . . .

The proof in the sales letter should be restrained, specific, and well documented. It should overcome any doubts the prospect has, and it should convince him that the product or service will be of value to him.

Although proof is normally placed after the description, it need not be. Sometimes the proof can be so startling and dramatic as to serve the twofold purpose of arousing interest and convincing the prospect to make the purchase.

Dear. Mr. Canfield:
In its first year on the market, Cartell's Drafting Lamps were purchased by the engineering divisions of U.S. Steel, General Electric, Standard Oil, Caterpillar Tractor, Zenith Radio and Television, and 1875 other leading manufacturers! . . .

Action for Sales. We have aroused the interest of our prospect through a well-written opening; we have made him want to possess the product or service through our description of it; and we have proved to him that it will give him full value. Now he must take the most important step of all—he must buy it. But most people hesitate before they buy. They think it over first. And this is to the good. Our only concern is that they may put it off until the desire or the impulse to buy disappears. Henry Hoke, editor of *The Reporter of Direct Mail Advertising,* says the two big barriers to action are (1) human inertia and (2) the competition for the reader's money.

For this reason, the "buy" section of the sales letter should reflect an appeal sufficiently strong to move the prospect to action. And, we hope, immediate action. The longer he delays, the less likely he is to act favorably.

The action does not necessarily have to be the purchase of a product. It may simply involve "purchasing" the next step. It may be sending for a brochure, agreeing to see a salesman, or accepting a demonstration.

The type and tone of the approach to use in the action section will depend on the prospect. Sometimes incentives are offered to the potential buyer so that he will act quickly:

Premiums
Special prices
Special "deals" for a limited time
Limited availability

It also helps to set the prospect in motion if you tell him *what* to do and *how* to do it.

"Cut out the coupon"
"Sign and mail"
"Check box, sign, and mail"
"Include a quarter, add your signature, and mail"

Attention catcher.	Who says, "You can't take it with you"?
	You certainly can when you have your Sportsmen's Outdoor Grill.
Description of the product.	This compact unit, made of stainless steel, is a joy to have. It folds like magic and fits into its own 16" by 16" carton with carrying handle. It unfolds in a jiffy, stands on its sturdy steel legs, and gives the outdoor chef a full 200-square-inch grill surface.
	And to top it all off, your unit comes with a spit, motor, and battery. You can roast your pheasant immediately on the slowly rotating spit and baste and season the bird to taste.
Proof	As to its acceptance, we need only cite the fact that over 100,000 have been sold since it appeared on the market last year. And it has become standard equipment for each of the 400 Colorado Mountain Rescue Patrols.
Action for the sale.	We know you will enjoy giving one of these to a friend or to yourself. They are available either with or without motor and spit. Just check your preference on the enclosed card and return it today.

Attention-catching opening.	A full 22 percent margin when you sell a set of Palmer's Patio Lights at the nationally advertised price of $6.95 per unit!
Description of the product.	Palmer's Patio Lights consist of a string of eight colored lights wired at 5-foot intervals and attached to a heavy-duty outdoor extension cord 40 feet long. There are three styles from which to choose, and you will find your customers buying one of each as they change the motif of their outdoor gatherings. The Party Line is especially popular, with the Oriental Occasion and the Hawaiian Luau running close behind.
Proof	All units are approved by the Underwriters Laboratories and sold with a money-back guarantee. You can order them in dozen lots, either in cartons of four sets of each of the three lines or packed twelve of a type to a carton.
Action for sales.	The enclosed folder describes the Palmer Patio Lights in more detail, lists prices, and tells you how you can secure three free sets for yourself when you order before June 1. Order today; you'll be happy you did.

Cover Letter and Enclosure

Most sales letters cover one page, although in some cases a sales letter of several pages has proved very successful. However, most experts, when faced with the need for a rather long, involved presentation, prefer to use a variation of the one-page sales letter.

This usually consists of a letter accompanied by a brochure, a pamphlet, or a flyer. Prospects do not object to reading through an attractively laid-out and well-written enclosure if it is concerned with a product they are seriously considering buying. However, they do object to wading through six typed pages of a sales letter. It is because of this that most people in direct mail prefer the cover letter and enclosure to the extensive sales letter.

Authorities in the field of direct mail seem to feel that the cover letter should take one of two forms:

1. A very general letter designed to arouse sufficient interest in the reader so that he will turn to the enclosure.

2. A short version of the four parts of the sales letter—interest, description, proof, and action. However, each section is treated so briefly that the total letter would be inadequate were it not for the enclosure which expands on each of the parts.

COVER LETTER AROUSING INTEREST

ENJOY--

Cool days and pleasant nights during the warmest, most uncomfortable weather Chicago has to offer.

Yes, that's what an Arctic Central Air Conditioning System
can give you at an amazingly low price. Comfort . . . Cool
comfort . . . Pleasant comfort . . . Inexpensive comfort
. . . Delightful comfort.

Those fatiguing, tiring, blistery hot days and sleepless,
perspiration-drenched nights will be gone forever once your
Arctic System is installed.

Surely the comfort of you and your family is worth just pen-
nies a day.

Examine the enclosed brochure and then return the postal
card to us. One of our expert engineers will stop by to see
you--no obligation, of course--to show you how easy and inexpensive it is to own an Arctic Air Conditioning System.

ENJOY--

Cool days and pleasant nights during the warmest, most uncomfortable weather Chicago has to offer.

Yes, that's what an Arctic Central Air Conditioning System
can give you at an amazingly low price.

The unit occupies very little space in your yard and may be
placed behind shrubs or bushes. Its operation is whisper-
quiet, thoroughly efficient, and almost completely mainte-
nance-free.

Cool, refreshing air flows through the present ductwork in
your home and provides comfortable days and restful nights.

Our expert engineers will make a scientific survey to determine the exact size unit your home requires. Then with no
fuss, muss, or bother to you, the Arctic System will be installed in one afternoon.

You may be sure you will be as satisfied as the 9400 Chicago-
land homeowners who purchased a unit last year. The Arctic
System has also been approved by the American Home Builders'
Association, and carries our five-year guarantee on parts
and services.

Examine the enclosed brochure and then return the postal
card to us. One of our expert engineers will stop by to see
you--no obligation, of course--to show you how easy and inexpensive it is to own an Arctic Air Conditioning System.

The design, color, layout, and copy of the enclosure can be as imaginative as the writer wishes. Naturally what he does will always be governed by his prospect group and his budget. The enclosure directed to the businessman will be more conservative than that sent to teen-agers. But with modern high-speed printing devices which reproduce photographs and color artwork with remarkable fidelity, the only limitations on the sales writer are money and his own imagination.

Mailing Lists

The best sales letter will not sell if it does not get into the hands of a potential buyer. It is for this reason that special attention is always given to the mailing list.

The competent sales writer examines his list of names periodically to be sure that it reflects the characteristics of a good mailing list.

1. Is each name spelled correctly?
2. Is every person a good prospect for the product or service?
3. Do all persons listed have several basic attributes in common?
4. If the list is large, has it been divided into logical divisions such as geographical location, economic level, ethnic characteristics, etc.? When this is done, different appeals can be used in different sales letters selling the same product.
5. Have all the names of persons who have moved, died, or expressed no interest in the product been removed?
6. Have names of new accounts, customers, and prospects been added?

Most firms develop their own mailing lists, which are usually made up of the names of customers. Certainly a list of this type has much to recommend it. These people have already established a friendly relationship with you, and they are sympathetic to the concept of buying through the mail.

But every firm desires to expand its sales and for this reason always adds other names to its list. One way of obtaining them is from a mailing list firm. Thousands of different lists are available, covering almost every conceivable category from clock manufacturers, blacksmiths, sculptors, and female World War II veterans to compact car dealers and bell collectors. College students are subdivided into a dozen categories—male, female, in universities or in junior colleges, at denominational schools or at public schools, by the fields they are majoring in, and by the ethnic groups they belong to. If the mailing list firm does not have a list for you in some particularly unusual field, it will compile one.

It is usually worthwhile to pay a little more to a firm that keeps its lists up to date. There is no point in buying a list, saving a few dollars, and then learning that many of the names belong to persons who have moved, died, or changed jobs.

But it isn't always necessary to buy a list. Company records are excellent sources; lists may be rented or borrowed from other merchants; and organizations—professional, social, or business—will sometimes provide a membership list.

Public rosters also offer good sources: tax rolls, vital statistics listings, auto registrations, and voters' lists.

Then there are literally hundreds of different types of directories available. Not only telephone and city directories, but directories of lawyers, doctors, manufacturers of aircraft components or auto parts or rugs, shippers, clothing dealers, building contractors, and a hundred and one other categories of professions and businesses. These provide names, addresses, and vital facts of business operations. All one needs is pencil and paper and the time to make a copy.

Davis, *Guide to American Business Directories,* lists directories in 77 different areas of activity. *Trade Directories of the World, A Guide to Foreign Business Directories,* and *Guide to American Directories for Compiling Mailing Lists* are other sources.

There are also directories of corporations such as *Moody's Investor Service, Standard and Poor's Corporation Services,* and *Thomas' Register of America Manufacturers.*

The businessman can compile a mailing list by offering a premium or a prize which requires that the prospect complete a card with his name and address.

Questions for Study

I. Offer your constructive criticism of the following letters. Remember to indicate which sections of the letters deserve favorable comments, as well as where improvements can be made. Be as specific as possible in your evaluations.

1. "It works like magic!"

   That's what thousands of persons are now saying about the Wadsworth Water Control Unit. And you will feel the same way once you start to use yours.

   Just attach it to your outdoor water outlet, connect it to your sprinkler system, pool inlet valve, or anywhere you would like a specific amount of water delivered. Just set the dial for 100 to 2000 gallons of water, and when that precise amount has run in, your Wadsworth Water Control Unit will automatically stop the flow of water. You need not be present or even at home; the Wadsworth Unit is completely automatic.

   The Unit is a precision instrument, manufactured of non-rusting aluminum to exacting specifications. Thousands have been sold in the last few years to individuals as well as hundreds of park and recreation services supervised by local, county, state, and government agencies. Supervisor Watson of the Kenton County Park Service of Ohio wrote that:

   > "The Wadsworth Unit has saved our agency thousands of dollars by cutting down on the number of men needed to supervise summer watering activities. And, in addition, we never over-water or under-water our fine flowers and grass areas."

   Once you try it, we are sure you will agree with Mr. Watson and the thousands of other satisfied Wadsworth Water Control Unit users. Just return the enclosed order form with your check or money order for $19.95 and we will have your unit on its way immediately. Of course it comes to you with a money-back guarantee in the event you're not completely satisfied . . . but we're sure you will be. Order yours today.

2. It's almost June and you're probably getting a little worried about gifts for the three bridal showers and two weddings scheduled during the coming weeks.

   Worry no more; the solution is here in Hamilton's Hardwood Boards.

   These beautiful and practical Cutting and Serving Boards have been the pride of New England housewives for three generations . . . and they're now going national.

   Constructed of alternating strips of light and dark hardwoods, carefully laminated together, they go from work counter to serving table in a jiffy. The tiny rubber base mounted at each corner assures you of not marring the finest table and the Swedish stainless steel knife attached permits the artist to carve, cut, and slice before his admiring guests.

Hamilton Hardwood Boards are available in four sizes, with or without attached knife, and range from $3.95 to $12.95 each. Of course they are sold with a money-back guarantee.

Select one for each of the parties coming up . . . and be sure you don't forget yourself. The enclosed order blank, when completed and returned to us, assures delivery of Hamilton Boards within ten days.

3. "I should really start from scratch."

If you have recently said this to yourself as you looked at your towel supply, let us spur you on with a wonderful solution.

During May only, Hubfield's is offering its regular charge account customers a full 20 percent reduction on all Hillcrest towels. These classic cotton terry towels are thick and luxurious, assuring you of years of wonderful wear.

You have four different groups to choose from: the Dundee available in four different solid colors; the Baxter in the new flower patterns; the Robinaire with its impressive crown pattern; and the Paxton for those who want the finest. They are all available in a full range of colors to match any decor. Every one of the four lines is especially priced and available either in the 12- or 18-towel sets or individually. The savings which are available in the 18-towel family sets are impressive. It's almost like getting several towels free of charge.

Go through the enclosed pamphlet soon—better yet, today. Check the pattern and color you prefer and order today. You are assured of Hubfield's quality and guarantees—but remember, time is limited.

II. Complete any of the following problems assigned. You may wish to review the chapter and note key points before solving the problem.

1. Your firm manufactures various wax products. Your leading item is dinner-table candles. These are available in various lengths and sizes and are thoroughly described in your brochure, "Caleb's Candles." Write a sales letter to be addressed to the fund-raising chairman of PTA's, church groups, private organizations, local charities, etc.

   Explain that your product can be packaged with the organization's name and insignia on each candle wrapper and that the product can be sold at bazaars, fund-raising affairs, teas, church gift shops, etc. For the next 60 days, your firm is offering a 20 percent discount over the wholesale prices listed in the brochure. The minimum order accepted under these terms is $150.00. All orders totaling $400 or more may take a 25 percent instead of a 20 percent discount. A copy of "Caleb's Candles" is to be enclosed with each letter.

2. Your firm manufactures various sport clothing. One of your lines includes bulky sweatshirts with the school name and crest imprinted. Send a sales letter to fraternity and sorority presidents offering these sweatshirts for sale. The buyer can have any sorority or fraternity name or initials imprinted (in place of the school name and crest) on the front, and any three words (maximum of 18 letters) on the back. Such statements as "Go Tigers," "We're Tops," "Follow the Leader," can be used on the back.

   The card which you enclose with your letter lists the type styles of initials available and prices. Two free shirts are available for every dozen ordered. Minimum order: one dozen. Assume prices and other necessary details.

3. Your firm has recently designed and manufactured a sign-making kit for the retail merchant. It contains patterns, letter and number templates, paper, paint, brushes, correction units, spacers, and other items.

The entire unit will permit the independent dealer to quickly make window and store posters, sales cards, counter announcements, and miscellaneous signs. All work looks professional, can be completed quickly, and should save the average merchant hundreds of dollars each year if he is now buying his signs.

Other advantages include increased sales as a result of the signs, instant availability of a sign, and crisp, fresh-looking announcements available at all times. Replacement items such as paper, paint, and brushes may be ordered from your firm at wholesale prices.

You have three kits available from $75 to $125 each.

Your sales letter should attempt to secure a request for your salesman to call to explain and demonstrate these units.

4. Secure an actual sales letter directed to a consumer (perhaps one that has come to your home) and evaluate it.

Your evaluation should be very specific and should analyze the appeals used and the way it handles the four parts: arousing interest, describing the product, proving its worth, and securing the sale. This should all be done in reference to the specific prospect to whom it was directed.

Submit both the sales letter and the criticism.

5. Complete the same assignment as in No. 4 above, but this time choose a sales promotion piece directed to a business firm.

6. Assume that you have a mailing list of 50,000 college students. Attempt to sell each of them a new high-intensity study lamp called "The Winner."

This very attractive item folds into a four-by-four-by-four-inch cube, has an extension arm that places the light source 6 inches to 16 inches from the desk top, is manufactured of unbreakable plastic, comes in ivory, white, or black, is fully guaranteed for one year, and sells for only $7.95 or two for $15.00.

Assume any other facts you feel are necessary.

7. You are the manager of the Vacation Isle Hotel in Florida. Send a sales letter and descriptive brochures to company sales managers recommending they consider the Vacation Isle as a perfect spot for high-ranking salesmen who have reached specific sales quotas.

This sales-incentive program requires the firm to send a minimum of ten salesmen and their wives in any one month during March, April, or May. All golf, swimming, tennis, and related facilities are included plus three meals each day.

Assume all necessary information that you would need as the manager of the Vacation Isle Hotel.

8. Outline a sales-letter campaign to sell the Diplomat attaché case. List four different prospect groups: college instructors, college students, businessmen, and the college and stationery store buyer. Note for your reader how the following differ for each of the four prospects: sales appeal, price, proof, and format.

Assume price, qualities, and attributes of the Diplomat and indicate which of these you would use with the different prospects.

9. Write two sales letters selling the Diplomat noted in No. 8. Direct one letter to college students, the other to business executives.

10. Complete a sales letter and sales brochure presenting the Diplomat attaché case (see problem 8) to the college bookstore buyer. Your sales enclosure should be a "dummy" with all copy written out and placed. The photos or sketches you want included should be described so that the artist or photographer knows precisely what you want. Indicate by squares or circles where in the dummy you want the art work placed.

Chapter Thirteen

Good Will and Miscellaneous Messages

Use of the Good Will Letter
Evaluation
Miscellaneous Letter Situations

The good will letter is somewhat similar to the sales letter, but instead of selling a product or a service it sells friendliness, sincerity, and good relationships.

It is the letter that doesn't *have* to be sent but *is*. It is the business letter which has as its purpose the building of good will, not selling, not inquiring, not adjusting.

In today's hectic world of business, there is seldom time (or the inclination) to carry through the extra and really somewhat unnecessary step of sending out a letter which says "thank you; we're happy to know you and feel fortunate that we can do business with you."

Many businessmen will tell you that this kind of letter is nonsense, but they are wrong. They will tell you that the customer or supplier knows that all is well—why bother to tell him? But it is human nature to want to be thanked. There are few of us who don't experience a little bit of inner excitement and self-satisfaction when someone thanks us sincerely for what we have done.

Those persons who question the value of good will letters have probably misused them or been recipients of the insincere, hard-sell type. For a good will letter to be successful, it must be sincere. There is no place in it for a strong sales pitch on products or services. On occasion one may wish to sell the idea of resuming business relations when an association has been broken off. But usually the recipient will feel irritated if the apparent good will letter turns out to have the ulterior purpose of trying to make a sale.

Some business firms feel they are sending out good will letters when they mail form letters addressed to "Dear Customer," or "Dear Occupant." They are like those people who say they don't have time to write personal letters, and instead buy ready-made greeting cards which they spend a great deal of time in signing and mailing.

How much more effective is the short, sincere, individually written letter, whether it comes from a company or from a private person!

Use of the Good Will Letter

Once the businessman is convinced of the value of good will letters, he will find numerous situations in which to use them. The two major categories are:

1. Letters which extend good wishes or thanks. These are usually sent to steady customers and are sometimes mailed in conjunction with a national holiday.

2. Letters which attempt to build good will with an account who has terminated or cut down his business relations.

To the Steady Customer

All too often, the steady customer is taken for granted; he becomes an account number. We give him special attention only when he interrupts his relationship with us. By that time, it is probably too late. The best time to thank him is when his orders are consistently coming in.

A sincere opening.

```
Dear Mr. Campbell:

Just a word to say "thanks" for giving us an opportunity to
serve you.

Here at Shelley's we always try to bring our customers the
best possible products at the lowest possible prices.  We
certainly hope we've succeeded in doing that in our business
relationships with you.

It is the steady customer, such as you, that has made
Shelley's the largest manufacturer of frames in the West.
The savings we secure through efficient operations, we pass
on to our customers . . . and we are delighted to do so,
for it is your work, effort, and cooperation that makes
Shelley's number one in the industry.  For this distinction,
we want to thank you most sincerely.

You may be sure we will continue to do everything possible
to merit your continued support and patronage.  Please call
on us when we can be of special assistance to you.
```

The writer points out benefits to the reader.

```
Dear Mr. Stone:

With the Thanksgiving season approaching, it seems to be
particularly fitting for us to say "thanks to you."

Too often most of us take our good fortune for granted . . .
but we shouldn't.  Here at Kelley's we have much to be thank-
ful for . . . the world's leading nation, good health, wonder-
ful fellow workers, pleasant plant conditions, and cooperative
customers such as yourself who keep us working month after
month.
```

Major holidays provide opportunities for goodwill letters.

The tone is sincere, direct, and effective.

```
You and hundreds of other accounts of Kelley's are respon-
sible for our present position.  For our part, we have done
everything we could to bring you the best possible paper
products at the most competitive prices.  And you have given
us your support through your steady purchases.

So we say, simply and sincerely:  Thank you for your con-
fidence in us.  We shall continue to do the best we can, and
we hope you won't hesitate to call and tell us how we can
assist you in your daily operations.
```

The letters above all have one purpose and that is to promote good will. They are simple and straightforward. However, good will letters can also be used to welcome a new account and comment on his order, attempt to increase the purchases of an old customer, or reactivate one who has terminated his relationship with us.

To the New Customer

Perhaps your salesman has been working for some time to get this account. That first order has just been shipped. Let the new customer know that not only the salesman but the company president appreciates his order.

It's usually a good idea to let the new customer know what he may expect in the way of assistance.

Note the personal touch achieved by including the customer's name in the body of the letter.

```
Dear Mrs. Melton:

Welcome to Clayton's.  We are delighted to have you as one
of our customers, and you may be sure we will do everything
possible to merit your business and good will.

Our activities have always revolved around the wishes and
demands of our customers.  You come first.  If you have some
special desires or requests on shipments, merchandise, ac-
count payments, or product modifications, let us know.  We
will work with you.

Each month our salesman will bring you window flyers and dis-
play materials.  He also will be happy to make arrangements
for you to secure our special counter and floor display cases.
And then there are traveling demonstration units which he can
schedule for your place of business.

All in all, Mrs. Melton, we are delighted to welcome you and
we want you to know that we will work with you . . . from
president to stock boy.  Just tell us how, and we'll jump
into action.
```

```
Dear Mr. Gould:

We were delighted to hear from Al Alberts that you met with
him recently and placed your first order for Miller Pipe
Products.  Thank you very much.

As Al undoubtedly told you, we pride ourselves on offering
our customers quality and service along with competitive
prices.

One of the services that we are proud of and we hope you will
use is our free drop shipments in the greater Milwaukee area.
When your customers in this area place an order for over $500
of Miller Pipe Products, we will drop it at their address if
you so direct.  And there is no shipping charge.

We also stand ready to make reasonable modifications in prod-
ucts for your special jobs; the only charge to you is our
direct labor cost.  And, in addition, we will be happy to
supply you with sales promotion material at no charge.

So, Mr. Gould, we at Miller Pipe Products stand ready to serve
you in every way possible.  We're as close to you as your
phone . . . GR 4-4200.
```

Important buying privileges are noted tactfully.

An extremely positive goodwill letter.

To the Absent Customer

The wide-awake businessman will survey his accounts periodically. When he does, he is likely to find an impressive number of customers who have become inactive. Some were excellent accounts, others mediocre. But they *were* accounts and as such added to the company's profit margin.

Why they no longer buy is relatively unimportant. It may have been a tactless comment, the personality of the salesman or truck driver, a price that proved rather high, or service that was a little slow. But the fact is, they are not customers now! The situation certainly deserves a good will letter which may bring them back.

```
Dear Mr. Palmer:

We miss you!

Yes, it's that simple.  We all miss you: our salesmen,
stock boy, shipping clerk, truck driver, and accountant.
These are some of the people at Rotel's who miss you; there
are many others.

Perhaps it's our fault that you no longer make your purchases
here.  Won't you call me collect, please, and let me know why
we haven't seen you, and I'll do my best to correct the situa-
tion.
```

This direct approach to the problem may prove successful.

The frank, open tone of the letter continues.

> We value your business and friendship and we want to keep
> them both. If your absence has been due to a Caribbean
> cruise which you took, don't bother to call. Just send your
> requests in. But if you haven't ordered because of a more
> serious reason, please phone me so that I can do everything
> possible so we may again list Palmers as one of our valued
> customers.

This letter has a rather strong negative tone ("perhaps it's our fault"). However, the frank, sincere approach may be good, for certainly we know *something* is wrong. And an open discussion may well clear the air, so that the business relationship can start over.

Here is an approach that talks to the absent customer primarily about the future.

This letter makes no mention of the fact that the customer has not been in for some time. Do you feel this approach is wise?

> Dear Mr. Palmer:
>
> Good news for you and other customers of Carlson's.
>
> Beginning on May 1 we will hit the newspapers, magazines,
> and radio commercials in an all-out summer campaign de-
> signed to increase your sales of Carlson's products.
>
> Although our advertising will emphasize our entire line, we
> will give special attention to our new Style-Bright sweaters.
> Extremely heavy newspaper and magazine exposure will place
> the Style-Bright sweater in sharp focus. Window display mate-
> rials, sample sweaters, store banners, and allowances for
> neighborhood advertising campaigns will be available for our
> accounts.
>
> We want to work with you on this and all other business activi-
> ties. Just check, on the enclosed card, the time and day
> convenient for you and our salesman will call on you.

To the "Incomplete" Customer

A surprising number of accounts may purchase only part of their needs from you. This may be because they aren't aware of how extensive your line is, or because they are satisfied with another source of supply.

If you can secure all or almost all of their business, your sales will rise appreciably though the increase in the cost of selling is only minimal. Your desire is to make better customers of them.

Naturally, if you can determine why a customer purchases only some of his products from you, you can more intelligently construct your letter. If not, a general approach, such as the following, may prove of value:

Dear Mr. Swibel:

For some time you have proved to be one of our valued customers, and we certainly appreciate your business. But we
also find that many of our best customers are not completely
familiar with the many products and services which we have
available and which can increase their profit margins.

One of our most successful policies is our "double discount
over five" arrangement. This means that our usual 2 percent
discount for payment within 10 days is doubled when the sum
paid is over $5000. This is a tremendous addition to your
margin.

We also pride ourselves on having not only a complete line
of men's and women's dress shoes, but also specialized numbers of all types: golf, tennis, bowling, safety, orthopedic,
and other hard-to-find models.

And if you haven't talked to our salesman about the New
England men's sock line, discuss it with him on his next visit.
We will supply a complete stock of fine quality socks on con-
signment together with a beautiful walnut-finish floor display case. The case harmonizes with the decor of most stores,
and the quality of the merchandise will please your customers
and add to your sales.

These are only a few of the reasons why you should look to
us for ways to increase your level of business. We want to
serve you in every way we can.

Evaluation

A good will letter program may not produce immediate, tangible results. It requires a long-range point of view. But it is valuable and worthwhile.

Check the good will letter before it goes out. Does it carry a personal pen-
and-ink signature? If it is processed, does it look neat and attractive? Is the letter always sent by first class mail? Does it have a friendly tone and a "you" attitude? And above all, is it honest and sincere?

Customers should not be taken for granted. The seller should maintain contact, and there is no better way than with good will letters.

Miscellaneous Letter Situations

Letters may serve a variety of purposes: to tell someone that he has received a promotion, to send a congratulatory message, to comment on a job
well done, and to convey condolence and sympathy. For most of these situations (and hundreds of others), the greeting card companies have developed

mass-produced messages. But how well do they achieve their objectives?

Mrs. Eileen Martinson was elected president of the 900-member Belleville City Cancer Prevention Association three days ago. Today she received seven "congratulations on your election" cards in the mail. Two are cute, two are clever, and three extol her virtues to the sky. Each is signed by a good friend. As she puts them down, she notes that the price codes on their backs indicate they cost from 25 to 50 cents each.

Mrs. Martinson also received the brief note reproduced below:

Brief, courteous, and certain to be appreciated.

```
Dear Eileen:

I was delighted to learn of your election as president of
the Belleville City Cancer Prevention Association.  The citi-
zens of Belleville are fortunate to have someone with your
dedication and leadership ability in this important post.

Many of us are well aware of how much you've already con-
tributed to the Association in the years you've spent leading
committees and serving as treasurer.

Good luck and good wishes, Eileen, on your new position as
president.

                              Cordially yours,



                              Betty Anderson
```

Which of the eight messages concerning her election will Mrs. Martinson most likely remember? Chances are good it will be the note from Betty Anderson. And the interesting fact is that Mrs. Anderson undoubtedly spent less time and effort in writing and mailing her message than did the others who had to visit card shops and make selections.

Congratulatory Letters

Because of the hundreds of situations which exist for letters of this type, it is difficult to select examples. They should all follow the same basic principles: they should be brief, deal with the primary topic only, and carry a positive, conversational tone.

Dear Cal:

This morning's paper told me of your appointment as a partner with Kells and Smith, CPA's. My sincere good wishes to you.

It hardly seems 10 years since you were a student in my senior Cost Accounting course; however, the years do fly by. In any event I recall the high level of your work at that time. I'm sure it's that type of effort which has resulted in your rapid promotions.

Good wishes for your continued success, Cal.

Congratulations, Bob,

On your recent promotion to Vice-President of Marketing of the Hopper Hotel Corporation.

When I read the announcement in this morning's Times I was delighted, for I know what an outstanding job you've done for Hopper in the years of your association with them.

I'll call within the next week or two, Bob, and perhaps we can arrange lunch and recognize your advancement in a more formal way.

Letters of Condolence

It is difficult to make suggestions on how to write this kind of letter. One person may be grateful for a brief, sincere note; another would appreciate a longer message. Perhaps the best advice is to remember who you are writing to, and write from the heart.

Dear Betty:

The tragic loss of your mother must certainly be difficult for you. She was a kind, considerate, gentle person. I well recall the many wonderful afternoons I spent at your house when we returned from school. Her interest in our classes and activities made those occasions something special.

As the years went by I know how many happy occasions you and your mother shared: your college graduation, your marriage, and then the twins. What she contributed to their growth will always be apparent to you as you watch them mature.

Memories like these, and similar ones, will help soften your recent loss of a wonderful individual. In some small way I can appreciate how deep is your sorrow.

```
Dear Bob:

I have just heard of Edith's death.  I am extremely sorry and
I offer you my deepest and most sincere sympathies.

Although our jobs have separated us by a thousand miles in
recent years, Joan and I often talk about the parties, out-
ings, and shows we enjoyed with you and Edith.  Those were
good days, which certainly got better when the boys came along.

As you look at them now and what they've accomplished, I'm
sure you have thousands of wonderful memories of Edith's con-
tributions to their growth.  And in each of them, you certainly
see something of her.

When business or pleasure takes you to the West Coast, Bob,
I do hope you will call.  We would be delighted to play host
to you for the length of your stay.
```

Questions for Study

I. Offer your constructive criticism of the following letters. Remember to indicate which sections of the letters deserve favorable comments, as well as where improvements can be made. Be as specific as possible in your evaluations.

1.   Dear Mr. Fontaine:

In the rush and hurry of daily business activities, we sometimes overlook communicating a simple "thank you" now and then. And perhaps we at the Bolton Corporation have been guilty of doing just that. Nevertheless, we are sincerely appreciative of the confidence you have placed in us.

You, and the many other dealers who handle Bolton Products, are really our bosses. We try to serve you well and bring you the finest children's wear available. And as bosses you have given us valuable help through your suggestions. Please keep them coming; we need your guidance to achieve our objectives: quality merchandise at competitive prices.

Again, our appreciation to you for your support. We shall work with you in the future in every way possible.

2.   No, Mr. Campbell,

The tiny silver whistle attached is no gag. We want you to whistle whenever you need us. And we do hope you will use it soon, for we haven't heard from you in too long a time.

As you know, we value our customers highly, and nothing pleases us more than to be whistled at . . . either in admiration or for service. So, won't you whistle soon. We promise to respond immediately with quality, service, and a smile.

3.   Dear Mrs. Fagel:

Too often today in the world of business, people, companies, and institutions have become numbers, symbols, punched cards, or printed tapes.

And too often, too, we forget that behind these impersonal identification methods are people—people who are our good friends.

So, if we may, we would like to stop the clattering machines and whispering computers to say, "Thank you, good friend Fagel, for letting us serve you during this past year. We have been delighted to fill your construction and building equipment needs." Now with another year opening before us, we will return to the high-speed business needs of today. But we won't forget our good friends for whom we are working, and if you will tell us how—from time to time—we will work harder and better to bring you exactly what you want.

II. Complete any of the following problems assigned. You may wish to review the chapter and note key points before solving the problem.

1. You have owned a large neighborhood jewelry store for several years. For some time you have noted a trend among some of your customers. A fairly large number have been shopping for gifts in the downtown centers and at discount houses. Prepare a good will letter to be sent to your entire mailing list that stresses your appreciation of their patronage as well as your service and return privileges.

2. Your corporation manufactures garden supplies which are sold through your sales staff to neighborhood hardware stores, garden shops, and miscellaneous outlets. Prepare a good will letter to be mailed at Thanksgiving time.

3. Prepare a good will letter to be sent to former customers of the men's department of Campbell's Department Store. These accounts have made no purchases from this men's department in 18 months or more.

4. Send a good will letter to all your franchise dealers who represent you as a Tasty Treat Pie Shoppe. You have 1800 franchised dealers in the United States. The letter is to arrive on the first or second day of the new year.

5. As the General Sales Manager of the Bon Ton Food Company, send a good will letter to each of your salesmen. Bon Ton has 140 salesmen operating under six division sales managers. These men have been employed by Bon Ton for anywhere from two to twenty years.

6. Your term of office as president of the Accounting Club will be up in two weeks. Prepare one good will letter to be sent to each of your four officers.

7. You are in the highly competitive furniture field. Many of your dealers purchase from several different firms. Send a good will letter to a selected group of your accounts who purchase only a limited number of items from you. Thank them for their patronage and remind them of the advantages of securing a larger variety of items from your firm.

8. You manufacture and sell hospital equipment on a national scale. You have 20 salesmen representing you. Prepare a good will letter to be directed to either the hospital administrator or the purchasing department head who has made an initial purchase from your company. Your Chicago office has a complete display of all your equipment. You also have facilities for modifying equipment to serve the special requirements of doctors or needs of patients.

Chapter Fourteen

Automation of Written Communication, Guide and Form Messages, and Dictation

Automatic Typewriters
Data Processing
Word Processing Centers
Guide and Form Letters
Hints for Efficient Dictation

Letters cost money. When we think of the time spent in drafting them, writing them and typing up clean copies, it is easy to see why so much effort has been made to increase efficiency and cut costs.[1]

The most elaborate ways of increasing efficiency involve the use of automated mechanisms such as automatic typewriters and data processing. When these are coupled with guide letters, form letters, and promotional materials such as sales brochures, time and money can be saved in impressive quantities.

Automatic Typewriters

If you want to send the same letter to a large number of people, but at the same time to personalize it, you need an automatic typewriter. This is an electric typewriter with a tape memory that will store a message and reproduce it upon command. The operator manually types the name and address of the person to whom the letter is being sent, and the typewriter takes over and completes the letter. The machine can be programmed to stop at designated points so that a name or some specific information (such as the amount past due, or the price of the product) can be manually inserted by the operator. The final effect is that of an individually typed letter.

[1] The Dartnell Corporation estimated the cost of the average business letter in 1975 to be approximately $3.70.

In addition, specific paragraphs of a letter can be stored and retrieved in almost any order you wish. The speed with which automatic typewriters work, the appearance of the finished product, and the low cost per unit make this method of communication an essential one.

Data Processing

The phrase "data processing" applies to a vast range of equipment from the business machine to the most complex computer. However, for our purposes, it means the new technique of printing letters by computer for mass distribution (sales solicitations, for example). Names and addresses all can be drawn from storage and inserted in the proper place in the opening of the letter and even at predetermined points in the body of the letter.

This use of the computer for mass mailing is steadily increasing. The cost for large batches is low, and results are reported to be good.

Word Processing Centers

A word processing center is a "systems" approach to the production of memos, letters, reports, manuals, etc. It is usually centralized, although it is possible to organize the equipment and personnel of a word processing center in several locations.

Managers who have something to be transcribed simply dial their company word processing center and dictate by phone. The message is recorded on tape or on a data card. This is then processed by an employee, using such equipment as a Magnetic Tape Selectric Typewriter, a Composer, an Executive Magnetic Card Typewriter (with proportional spacing), or a Magnetic Card Selectric Typewriter. Obviously, employees working in a center are not disturbed by telephones which they must answer, salespersons or visitors requiring direction, and a hundred other office distractions. This, together with the sophisticated recording and typing equipment available in a word processing center, enables typed materials to be produced efficiently, accurately, and rapidly.

Guide and Form Letters

The intelligent and discriminating use of form and guide letters by management can improve a firm's sales and customer relations and save thousands of dollars. There is no point in dictating a letter which must be typed (at a cost of several dollars) if a form or guide letter will accomplish the same end at a fraction of the cost.

Many companies have found it valuable to compose a series of guide letters for a variety of situations. Copies are made and complete sets are bound into a notebook or spiral binder. Each letter is numbered for easy reference. Those firms which own automatic typewriters place the same letters on tape for easy storage and use.

A copy of the notebook is then given to everyone concerned—executives and correspondents as well as the secretaries or typists who do the typing.

Let us say that Mr. Reiner has just received an initial order from a new customer, Mr. Calloway. All he need do is tell the typist to send Guide Letter #3 to Mr. Calloway, making sure to fill in the correct name, address, order number, and other details. Of course letter #3 has been carefully written, edited, and revised, and is probably better than one that Mr. Reiner would dictate off the cuff.

Or perhaps there is a type of claim which must be refused very tactfully and which arises rather frequently. The guide letter to handle it does an excellent job, and probably required several hours to write initially.

In some cases it is helpful to number the paragraphs in each guide letter. Then the dictator can ask the typist to send Mr. Dalton Guide Letter #10 but to "substitute this paragraph for paragraph #3."

The secretary types the requested guide letter from the model she has, or secures the proper tape of it for use in the firm's automatic typewriter.

Guide letters, all in all, have the following advantages:

1. They permit the use of carefully written letters for many situations.
2. They are economical.
3. A guide letter may be sent out quickly, while to prepare and write a new letter may require an extra day or two.
4. With an automatic typewriter, dozens of copies of a letter may be completed quickly and inexpensively.

Situations for Use

Guide letters work well in the following cases:

Welcome letters to new customers.

Letters to customers who have been absent for some time.

Collection letters (those sent early in the collection series).

Refusals of claims, requests for contributions of merchandise and funds, credit, and other recurring situations requiring a denial.

Letters introducing new products; explaining credit procedures, delivery, or payment methods; or making changes.

Sales letters of all types especially when tied to automatic typewriters or data processing.

Encouraging the Use of Guide Letters

Pride of authorship is a very important factor in the writing of business letters. Most persons enjoy writing them, take pride in their efforts, and often like to feel that their letters are far superior to anyone else's in the office. Because of this, many are reluctant to sign letters they haven't written.

It helps to distribute a notebook of draft copies of guide letters to those who will use them, with a request for suggestions for revision and improvement. In this way, those who sign the letters will have had something to do with their composition, and will be less reluctant to use them.

To maintain a high level of use, constantly encourage the employment of guide letters. It is important to have them revised frequently so that they will be current and applicable to everyday situations.

Form Letters

Form letters are usually reproduced in large quantities. Sales letters may be run off in lots of one hundred thousand for a large mailing. Or a hundred form acknowledgments of orders may be reproduced and used as needed.

Form letters are usually processed on high-speed printing equipment, although, as indicated earlier, automatic typewriters may be programmed to turn them out. Sometimes form letters are personalized. If the printer uses a type style that matches the company's typewriters, it is then possible to have the inside address and salutation manually typed.

The personalized letter, which looks as though it has been individually typed, may motivate people who receive it to take the action the writer requests. On the other hand, some resent the obvious attempt to deceive them.

The author's feeling is that form letters should be designed to look like form letters and nothing more. Most people recognize the need for them and accept the fact that individual letters cannot possibly be sent to a large number of prospects.

Use of Form Letters

Form letters can be used for many of the same purposes as guide letters:

Acknowledging orders.
Letters to new customers.
Basic letters in the collection series.
Acknowledging payments.
Simple claim situations.
Simple adjustment situations.
Routine inquiries.
Answers to inquiries.
Routine announcements.
Job-seeking applications.

However, their chief use is for sales promotion and follow-up. Millions of such letters are sent out annually in the United States.

Hints for Efficient Dictation

Many excellent writers and speakers are poor dictators. As one author has said, "Too many people . . . become another sort when they pick up a pen or a dictaphone. They tighten up. They become unnatural. They curdle into impersonality and choose starchy sentences. Their product is like a page printed with very old and worn out type."[2]

However, effective and rapid dictation is really quite simple if one observes a few basic procedures.

Purpose, Reader, Outline

The first step is to determine the primary purpose of the message. Is it to acknowledge an order and build good will? Is it to adjust a claim and retain the customer? Once we have our primary (and secondary) purpose in mind, we can ask the next question: Who is the reader? A consumer? A wholesaler? Has the customer been with the firm 10 days or 10 years?

The answers to these questions will largely determine the tone of the letter and the approach to be used.

Next, make a *written* outline of the points to be covered in the letter. Some find that one or two words for each point are adequate; others feel more comfortable with a phrase or sentence for each item in their outline.

When your outline is complete, study it carefully and:

Eliminate unnecessary points.
Check the sequence and move items freely until the order is logical and coherent.
Review the list for possible omissions.

But before you dictate: Do you know where the "erase" mechanism is? Are you familiar with the machine? Do you know how to give instructions to the secretary on your dictation tape? Will you be able to spell each name clearly and distinctly? Are you conscious of your secretary's transcribing speed?

It is always wise to work with your secretary and determine what dictation speed is best. Some secretaries prefer to receive format and layout instructions on the tape, while others make their own decisions.

A little practice is usually all that is needed to make you an efficient and competent dictator. However, the basis for the confidence is the blueprint from which you dictate—your outline. Once that "map" is made up logically and clearly, you need only follow it to reach your destination easily.

Questions for Study

I. Complete any of the following problems assigned. You may wish to review the chapter and note key points before solving a problem.

1. Your firm manufactures electrical appliances which are distributed nationally. Prepare a guide letter to be mailed to individuals who request free appliances which may be sold to raise funds for schools, churches, and so on. In your letter you must regretfully refuse these individual requests even though you recognize the merits of the endeavor. You receive between 25 and 50 such requests each

[2] "Imagination Helps Communication," The Royal Bank of Canada Monthly Letter, September 1960.

month. Your firm does contribute large sums to national charities on a yearly basis.

2. Prepare a guide letter to be used for new customers. This letter is to be sent after the first order has been received by one of your company's salesmen.

3. Design a guide letter to be sent to all those persons who request a replica of our new jet passenger transport. It is true that we have these replicas but we supply them to travel agents for display purposes only, and they remain our property and must be returned so that other travel agents may use them.

   As a national airline we would like very much to send them out to individuals, school classes, and various organizations, but the cost to us would be prohibitive.

4. As a local rapid transit line, we receive 15 to 30 letters each day inquiring about lost articles. We check with our central lost and found, and if the item hasn't turned up we send a letter to the individual. Prepare such a letter to be used as a guide.

5. Try to sell a guide and form letter service to the local department stores. Include two or three of your guide letters as samples.

   Point out the advantages to the store of having such a service and how economical it can be.

6. Elect a committee of students whose purpose it is to research automated office equipment for letter reproduction, as well as some of the latest solid state dictation devices. The committee should not only collect printed sales brochures for distribution to the class, but if at all possible arrange for equipment demonstrations.

Part Four

Research Techniques and Reports for Decision Making

Chapter Fifteen

Methods for Gathering Information—Secondary Sources

Secondary Sources
Books
Magazines, Journals, and Periodicals
Newspapers
Reports, Bulletins, and Brochures
Government Documents
Business and Corporation Directories
Miscellaneous Sources of Information
Guides to Secondary Research Sources

You're a young assistant vice-president of a supermarket chain. One day the president of the company calls you in and tells you he's unhappy about the way the company is training its store managers. He asks you to prepare a report on the kind of training program that will better serve the needs of the expanding chain.

Or you're the communications director for a wholesale hardware company. The management wants to cut costs by shifting from a weekly delivery schedule to a semimonthly one. You're given the job of finding out how the customers would react to the change.

Where do you begin?

If you're wise, you'll look to see what others have written on your subject. It's embarrassing to discover, after you've spent hours or days securing information on "Automobile Purchasing Habits of Young College Graduates," that somebody has already made a thorough study of the subject and that a government report is available for only 25 cents.

There's another advantage in examining what has already been published: you will soon become familiar with the broad outlines of what is known, and will then find it easier to plan your own research.

Thus the first step is to look at the secondary sources, and then move on and attempt to answer very specific questions from research in primary source materials.

Secondary Sources

Secondary sources contain information that others have recorded on your topic in books, magazines, reports, newspapers, and elsewhere. Once you have studied what others have done, you can look for additional information in primary sources—questionnaires, interviews, company records, your own observation, etc.

Secondary sources may be divided into several general categories: (1) books; (2) magazines, journals, and periodicals; (3) newspapers; (4) reports, bulletins, and pamphlets; (5) government documents; (6) business and corporation directories; and (7) miscellaneous sources. The pages which follow carry some general comments on all of these categories plus a very complete listing of useful reference guides.

Books

Many researchers working on topics of current interest feel that information found in books is likely to be out of date. That is often true, but books also may contain data available nowhere else. In addition, the time required to turn a manuscript into a book has been shortened fantastically in recent years; it can be done in two or three weeks if necessary. So don't discount the value of recently published books. Some of them are as up-to-date as periodicals.

Using the Card Catalog

Most library researchers begin by looking through the card catalog for books on their topic. Title, subject, and cross-reference cards should be checked. One disadvantage of this method is that a library may have several books that are relevant but the researcher doesn't find cards for them. Perhaps he skips the cards, or they have been misfiled, or a card was not filed under the particular topic because only a chapter or two of a book was devoted to it.

Using the Library Stacks

If the report writer can secure admission to the library stacks, he avoids the catalog problem. All he need do is determine where the books on his subject are shelved and go to that section. Naturally he asks the clerk to tell him if any have been checked out. It also happens that books on one subject may be shelved under more than one classification—all the more reason for the investigator to check several different classifications in the stacks.

Using Guides to Books

Both Journals, the above methods have obvious limitations. The researcher only discovers the books that a particular library carries on the subject, not all the books that have been published. This is why comprehensive guides to published books are so useful.

Magazines, Journals, and Periodicals

Sometimes a researcher will be told by a helpful friend, "I read an article on your topic. It appeared early this year—or maybe late last year; I don't recall the title or the name of the magazine, but it was a *great* article, concerned with the area you're investigating, and you should use it. You won't have any trouble finding it; the magazine came out about a year or so ago, was medium sized, and had a green cover!"

Where to begin? Surely not by thumbing through stacks of medium-sized magazines with green covers. Use the excellent indexes to journal articles, and the periodical guides. (See the listing in this chapter.)

Newspapers

Newspapers in this country carry tremendous quantities of valuable data of all types: statistical, political, financial, etc. But how do you find it? The answer, again, is to use an index. Only a few newspapers publish indexes (the *Wall Street Journal,* the *Christian Science Monitor,* the *New York Times*) but these will give you dates and thus lead you to the relevant issues of other newspapers.

Reports, Bulletins, and Brochures

Thousands of excellent reports, bulletins, brochures, and studies are issued each year by universities, foundations, corporations, cultural and social institutions, and professional societies and organizations. Many contain valuable information. Unfortunately, there is no overall guide that does an adequate job of indexing them. The *Vertical File Index* can prove helpful in some instances.

Government Documents

Today the United States government publishes more material than any agency in the world. Many of its publications are extremely sophisticated and of very high quality. They include technical reports, bulletins, pamphlets, and translations of foreign technical papers. Here again the appropriate reference guides (see Guides to Secondary Research Sources) can be of great assistance to the researcher.

Business and Corporation Directories

Business or trade directories carry a wide variety of information. They contain product data, sources of supply, names and addresses of individual companies, and product listings.

Corporation directories will provide you with information on the financial and manufacturing records and personnel of companies listed. Many are published annually with supplements appearing throughout the year to cover changes in personnel or operations. Job seekers will find background information in corporation directories that may be useful during employment interviews.

Listed in the section below are guides to several thousand directories. Almost every field, from Automotive Products to Wholesale Jewelers, has its own directory for foreign and national listings.

Miscellaneous Sources of Information

There are dozens of other sources of information for the researcher, including annuals and atlases. Many of them are issued by institutions, organizations, and associations. Just a few of these are the American Management Association, the Conference Board, the National Research Council, the Twentieth Century Fund, the Chamber of Commerce of the United States, and the National Association of Manufacturers.

The researcher is fortunate in having such a wide variety of guides available to him. On the other hand, the very number poses a problem. Fortunately, there are also reference guides to reference guides. Many of these are also listed below.

Guides to Secondary Research Sources

Guides to Books and Book Reviews

Books in Print. New York: R. R. Bowker Co., 1948 to date.
This guide lists books currently in print in the United States, with the exception of those on poetry, drama, fiction, juvenile fiction, and Bibles. Each book entry lists the author, title, price, and publisher. Author and title volumes. Title volume includes a list of publishers and addresses.

Cumulative Book Index: A World List of Books in the English Language. New York: H. W. Wilson Co., 1928 to date.
This index supplements the *U.S. Catalog* (see below). It lists books published in the English language throughout the world. The *CBI* is arranged by author, title, and subject. It is issued monthly (except August) with frequent cumulations. Before 1928, it was called the *United States Catalog*.

National Union Catalog. Washington D. C.: Library of Congress, Card Division, 1942 to date.
Coverage has varied through the years. At present includes works cataloged by the Library of Congress and by approximately 1000 other North American libraries. Indexed by author. Printed monthly with quarterly, annual, and quinquennial cumulations.

Paperbound Books in Print. New York: R. R. Bowker Co., 1955 to date.
This is a monthly index of currently available paperback books. This index

is cumulated quarterly with author, title, and subject headings.

Publishers' Weekly. New York: R. R. Bowker Co.

This is a weekly trade journal directed primarily to book dealers. The "Weekly Record" lists new books published. Includes price and subject of each item. Does not include government documents, subscription books, periodicals, or dissertations.

Subject Guide to Books in Print. New York: R. R. Bowker Co., 1957 to date.

Books currently in print in the U.S., as listed in *Books in Print,* are presented under some 28,000 subject heads.

U.S. Catalog: Books in Print, 4th ed. New York: H. W. Wilson Co., 1933.

This work, with its supplements, provides a complete list of American publications from 1900 to 1933. Because of the tremendous number of books that have appeared in recent years, it is doubtful that a similar work will be issued again, but it is useful for background research.

Book Reviews

Book Review Digest. New York: H. W. Wilson Co., 1905 to date.

This very valuable reference work lists books reviewed in more than 75 periodicals. For each book, quotations from a few reviews and citations to others are given. This digest appears every month (except July) and is cumulated annually. The arrangement is by author, with subjects and titles listed in the index. About 4000 books are evaluated each year.

Book Review Index. Detroit: Gale Research, 1965 to date.

This monthly publication with quarterly cumulations is very comprehensive in its coverage. It attempts to index all reviews appearing in over 200 publications. Citations are listed under the author reviewed. There are no subject entries and no digest. Supplements the *Book Review Digest.*

Guides to Periodicals and Periodical Literature

Guides to Periodicals

Katz, B. **Magazines for Libraries.** New York: R. R. Bowker Co., 1969.

An excellent guide to magazines listed under subjects. Each magazine is evaluated and described as to its strength and usefulness.

Standard Periodical Directory. New York: Oxbridge, 1964 to date. (Annual)

A subject listing of more than 53,000 U.S. and Canadian periodicals. It gives subscription rate, circulation, and basic advertising rate. Alphabetical index is provided. This work may be used to supplement the Ayer and Ulrich publications.

Ulrich's International Periodicals Directory. New York: R. R. Bowker Co. Volume I and Volume II published in alternating years, with an annual supplement to both.

A guide to some 7500 domestic and foreign periodicals. Emphasis is on periodicals published in North and South America and England. Volume I covers the fields of science, technology, and medicine; Volume II covers arts, humanities, business, and social science. Arranged by subject with author and title index. Entry includes title, publisher, address, editor, circulation; indicates whether it includes an index and book reviews, and in which major index, if any, the title appears.

Union List of Serials in Libraries of the United States and Canada, 3rd ed., 5 vols. New York: H. W. Wilson Co., 1965.

This comprehensive guide lists magazines and the libraries where they may be found. It is supplemented by *New Serial Titles,* 1956–1960, and monthly supplements.

New Serial Titles, 1956–1960. Washington: Library of Congress, 1961. 2 vols.

This supplement to *Union List of Serials in Libraries of the United States and Canada* is kept up to date by monthly and annual cumulations.

Periodical Indexes

Accountants' Index and Supplements. New York: American Institute of Certified Public Accountants, 1920 to date.

The original *Index* was published in 1920. Supplements have been published periodically from that date, generally every two years. The supplements are indexed by author, subject, and title. They list published articles, books, and government pamphlets in accounting and related fields, together with source, author, date, and title. All English language publications are indexed.

Accounting Articles. Chicago: Commerce Clearing House. 1965 to date. (Loose leaf reference)

This monthly service indexes and abstracts accounting articles appearing in journals, proceedings, and books. It contains a subject and author index.

AMA 10 Year Index of AMA Publications. New York: American Management Association.

A subject index to the publications of the AMA. Two indexes covering 1954–1963 and 1957–1966 are available. The indexes are supplemented by annual indexes for 1967 and the years following.

Applied Science and Technology Index. New York: H. W. Wilson Co., 1958 to date.

This index, like the *Business Periodicals Index,* was begun in January 1958 to replace the *Industrial Arts Index. The Applied Science and Technology Index* indexes about 226 periodicals in the fields of engineering, chemistry, physics, geology, metallurgy, aeronautics, automation, electronics, food technology, petroleum, transportation, etc. It is published monthly and cumulated annually.

Business Periodicals Index. New York: H. W. Wilson Co., 1958 to date.

This work indexes about 174 periodicals in the fields of business, finance, labor relations, insurance, advertising, office management, etc. It is published monthly except July and cumulated annually. It is the basic index for the business field. For materials prior to 1958, use the *Industrial Arts Index.*

Cumulative Index of the National Industrial Conference Board Publications. New York: National Industrial Conference Board, 1962 to date.

This valuable index, published annually, lists hundreds of classifications of NICB publications of interest to commerce and industrial managers and others. Topics range from "Absence" to "Workmen's Compensation." Description, date of publication, and price of publications are cited.

Engineering Index. New York: Engineering Index Service.

This index has been published in some form since 1884. Information concerning articles in engineering, chemistry, and physics journals is now printed on 3″ by 5″ cards and sent to subscribers. In addition, data from technical magazines, government bureaus, and research laboratories are recorded as well as abstracts of reports and reviews of books and articles. Once each year the data are cumulated in a large volume. The service is divided into 295 subject areas which may be subscribed to individually or completely.

Engineering Index Annual. New York: American Society of Mechanical Engineers, 1906 to date.

Funk and Scott Index of Corporations and Industries. Detroit: Funk and Scott Publishing Co., 1960 to date. (Weekly, with monthly and annual cumulations.)

This is a two-volume index to articles on industry as a whole, and on individual corporations. Volume I covers industries and products. Volume II is arranged by alphabetical order of companies. Articles indexed are from selected business, financial, and trade publications including brokerage house reports. For foreign companies, consult the *Funk and Scott Index International.*

Funk and Scott Index International. Cleveland: Predicasts, Inc., 1960 to date.

Similar to Funk and Scott Industries and Corporations. Section 1 covers industries and products; Section 2 covers countries (by region); and Section 3 lists companies in alphabetical order.

Index of Economic Journals. Homewood, Ill.: Richard D. Irwin, Inc., 1965.

Volume I   1886–1924   Volume IV 1950–1954
Volume II   1925–1939   Volume V   1955–1959
Volume III 1940–1949   Volume VI 1960–1963

About 115 American and foreign economic journals are indexed for English-language articles in each volume for the years given. This valuable index is divided into two sections: (1) the Author Index, where all the articles by an individual for the period covered are brought together, and (2) a Classified Index with 23 subject areas, ranging from Economic Theory to Regional Planning and Development. The 23 subject areas are further divided into numerous sub-areas for easy reference. All entries list author, title of article, journal where found, and page number.

Index of Supermarket Articles. Chicago: Supermarket Institute, 1936 to date.

Indexes articles on supermarket operations and food industry. Arranged by subject and category. A cross-reference index is provided.

Index to Labor Union Periodicals. Ann Arbor: University of Michigan, School of Business Administration, Bureau of Industrial Relations, 1960 to date.

Published monthly and cumulated annually, this work indexes articles from 50 major union periodicals; the entries usually include two or three brief descriptive sentences.

Index to Legal Periodicals. New York: H. W. Wilson Co., 1908 to date.

Industrial Arts Index. New York: H. W. Wilson Co., 1913 to 1958.

This is a cumulative index of articles which appeared in more than 200 periodicals on business, finance, applied science, and technology. It was published monthly until January 1958, when it was replaced by the *Business Periodicals Index* and the *Applied Science and Technology Index.*

International Index—A Guide to Periodical Literature in the Social Sciences and Humanities. New York: H. W. Wilson Co., 1907 to 1965.

This index was issued quarterly and cumulated every three years from 1916 to 1958, every two years from 1960 to 1964, and again in 1965, when it was replaced by the *Social Sciences and Humanities Index.*

Management Index. Ottawa: Keith Business Library, 1963 to date.

Formerly *Business Methods Index, Management Index* is published monthly except July and is cumulated annually. It is a guide to new American, Canadian, and British books, pamphlets, magazine articles, training films, maps, etc., of interest to management. It is indexed by subject, with description and price. In addition, reprints of articles are available from the publisher.

Poole's Index to Periodical Literature, 5 vols. and supplements. Boston: Houghton Mifflin Co., 1888–1908.

This index lists, under subject only, important magazine articles which appeared between 1802 and 1908. *Poole's Index* is no longer printed, but its work has been carried on by the *Readers' Guide.*

Public Affairs Information Service. New York: Public Affairs Information Service, 1915 to date.

This is a weekly subject index for current literature, primarily in political science, government, economics, and legislation. Indexes books, documents, pamphlets, and selected articles in more than 1000 periodicals. Foreign publications in English are included. Monthly, and annual cumulations are available.

Readers' Guide to Periodical Literature. New York: H. W. Wilson Co., 1900 to date.

In this invaluable reference guide, researchers working in many fields can find the names of periodicals carrying articles on their topics. *Readers' Guide* appears twice a month (except for a single issue in July and August) and is cumulated frequently. It indexes about 130 well-known and popular current periodicals. Articles are listed under title, subject, and index.

Social Science and Humanities Index. New York: H. W. Wilson Co., 1965 to date.

An author, title, and subject index to some 205 periodicals covering the fields of anthropology, area studies, economics, history, geography, political science, literature, sociology, etc. Titled *International Index* until June 1965.

Periodical Abstracts

ANBAR: Management Services. Wembley, England: ANBAR Publications, Ltd., 1961 to date.

First known as *ANBAR: Documentation Services for Management.* This British publication is arranged by a special ANBAR classification and divided into four major parts:

ACCOUNTING + DATA ABSTRACTS
MARKETING + DISTRIBUTION ABSTRACTS
PERSONNEL + TRAINING ABSTRACTS
TOP MANAGEMENT ABSTRACTS

Computer Abstracts. London: Technical Information Co., 1957 to date.

A monthly abstract arranged under 19 topics including theory, system design, programming, education, application, etc. Has a subject, author, and patent index. Books, periodical articles, U.S. government research reports, and patents are indexed.

Computer and Information Systems. New York: Cambridge Scientific Abstract Inc., 1962.

International in coverage, this publication is devoted to computer literature. Sources include periodicals, books, dissertations, government reports, etc.

International Executive. New York: Foundation for Advancement of International Business Administration, 1959 to date.

Articles on international business, reports of research by foundations and universities, book reviews, and an annotated bibliography of articles are presented here. It covers management, marketing, law, finance, accounting, banking, insurance, economic conditions, etc.

Journal of Economic Literature. Menasha, Wisc.: American Economic Association, 1963 to date.

Formerly known as *Journal of Economic Abstracts,* this quarterly journal reviews books and articles in the field of economics.

New Literature on Automation. Amsterdam: Automatic Information Processing Research Centre, 1960 to date.

Issued monthly, with text in English, Dutch, French, and German, this work contains abstracts on information processing.

Personnel Management Abstracts. Ann Arbor, Mich., Bureau of Industrial Relations, University of Michigan, 1955 to date.

A quarterly publication giving one-paragraph abstracts of articles and books in the areas of management, personnel policies, manpower, and industrial relations. Approximately 80 periodicals are indexed. Each issue has an "Index to Periodical Literature" in three sections: author, title, and subject.

Predicasts. Cleveland: Predicasts, Inc., 1960 to date.

Predicasts is divided into two sections: Forecasts, Abstracts, and Forecasts Composites. *Predicasts* presents historical data and composite short- and long-range forecasts for over 700 series. Included are general economic, and construction indicators, major materials, products, etc. *Predicasts* abstracts forecasts and good market data from articles appearing in over 500 periodicals, government reports, newspapers, and special studies. Arranged by Standard Industrial Classification code number.

Psychological Abstracts. Washington D.C.: American Psychological Association, 1927 to date. (bimonthly)

This publication provides abstracts of books, periodical articles, and reports of research in the fields of personnel and industrial psychology. Annual subject and author indexes are provided.

Selected Rand Abstracts. Santa Monica, California: Rand Corp., 1963 to date.

This guide to unclassified papers of the Rand Corporation is published quarterly with annual cumulations.

Sociological Abstracts. New York: Sociological Abstracts, Inc., 1952 to date.

This work publishes about 5000 abstracts each year. A cumulative author and subject index for 1953–1962 is available.

The ABS Guide to Recent Publications in the Social and Behavioral Sciences. American Behavioral Scientist, 1965 to date.

Books, periodical articles, pamphlets, and government publications on social sciences are listed by broad subject arrangement and alphabetical listing by author. The basic volume covers 1957–1964 bibliographies from ABS. Supplements started in 1966. Non-English language materials are included in the entries.

Guides to Reports, Bulletins, and Brochures

Alexander, Raphael. **Business Pamphlets and Information Sources.** New York: Exceptional Books, 1967.

Subject listing of pamphlets, reprints, and paperbacks in various areas of business. Includes prices, publishers, and addresses.

Gebbie House Magazine Directory. Sioux City, Iowa: House Magazine Publishing Company, 1946 to date.

This "bible" of the house magazine industry lists publications issued by over 4000 companies, associations, organizations, etc. It is published every three years.

O'Hara, Frederic J. **Over 2000 Free Publications: Yours for the Asking.** New York: New American Library, 1968.

Arranged by issuing agency and then by subjects. Publications on a variety of subjects of popular interest are listed with a general index.

Vertical File Index. New York: H. W. Wilson Co., 1932 to date.

This is a monthly descriptive list of free and inexpensive pamphlets with the prices and names and addresses of the publishers. These are grouped under subjects in the main part of the catalog with an alphabetical list of titles in the index. Includes reprints, government documents, and mimeographed material.

Guides to Newspapers and Newspaper Articles

Guides to Newspapers

American Newspapers, 1821–1936; a Union List. New York: H. W. Wilson Co., 1937.

This excellent work indicates where existing files of newspapers published in the United States from 1821 to 1936 may be found. This is a companion volume to the Union List of Serials. For earlier newspapers, consult *History and Bibliography of American Newspapers, 1690–1820* by Clarence S. Brigham.

Ayer's Directory of Newspapers and Periodicals. Philadelphia: N.W. Ayer, 1880 to date.

This directory is published annually. It contains information on circulation statistics, rates, name of publisher, size of page, politics, and other facts of some 22,000 newspapers and periodicals published in the United States, Canada, Cuba, Bermuda, and islands belonging to the United States. Population statistics are also cited.

Editor and Publisher Market Guide. New York: Editor and Publisher, 1924 to date.

> This annual publication presents market surveys for some 1500 U.S. and Canadian cities where a daily newspaper is published.

Standard Rate and Data Service.

> This service is issued in 14 parts and cites a wealth of information in the fields of publishing, consumer markets, and advertising. Information includes advertising costs, audience, and circulation figures of newspapers, U.S. business magazines, U.S. consumer magazines, Canadian newspapers, radio, and magazines, radio and television network data, films, and public transportation vehicle advertising.

Newspaper Indexes

Index of the Christian Science Monitor. Corvallis, Oregon: H. M. Cropsey, 1960 to date.

> Published monthly, with frequent cumulations.

National Observer Index. Princeton, New Jersey: Dow Jones and Company, 1970 to date.

New York Times Index. New York: New York Times Co., 1913 to date.

> This index has been issued twice a month since 1948 and is cumulated annually. News is summarized and classified alphabetically and chronologically by subject, by person, and by organization name. Each article is indexed by heading, subhead entry, date, page, and column reference. An earlier index covering 1851–1912 is now available.

The Wall Street Journal Index. New York: Dow Jones and Co., 1958 to date.

> This index is published monthly and combined into an annual. It indexes and gives synopses of *Wall Street Journal* articles for the period indicated. Only the New York edition of the *Journal* is indexed, however. It contains two parts: corporate news, and general news.

Guides to Government Publications

General Guides

Andriot, John L. **Guide to U.S. Government Statistics,** 3rd ed. McLean, Va.: Documents Index, 1961.

> All government publications which include statistical data are listed by department and issuing bureau. Description of the publication, type of statistics, and frequency of publication are included. Independent agencies, judiciary, executive, and legislative branches are also included and indexed. Detailed subject index.

Boyd, Anne Morries. **United States Government Publications,** 3d ed. rev. by Rae Elizabeth Rips, New York: H. W. Wilson Co., 1949.

> This work describes the distribution and publication of various publications issued by government agencies and departments.

Brown, Everett S. **Manual of Government Publications:** United States and Foreign. New York: Appleton, 1950.

Government publications of various countries of the world are described. Emphasis is on the United States, Great Britain, the League of Nations, and the United Nations.

Childs, James Bennett. **Government Document Bibliography in the U.S. and Elsewhere.** Washington, D.C.: Government Printing Office, 1942. Reprinted New York: Johnson Reprint Corp., 1964.

This work lists catalogs, guides, and indexes to the documents of the countries and states listed.

Jackson, Ellen. **Subject Guide to Major United States Government Publications.** Chicago: American Library Association, 1968.

Important government publications are listed under subjects such as Industries, Labor Supply, Economic Conditions, etc. A most useful section is also provided on guides, catalogs, and indexes.

Leidy, W. Philip. **A Popular Guide to Government Publications,** 3rd ed. New York: Columbia University Press, 1968.

Contains over 3000 titles of recent government publications listed under some 120 broad subject headings most likely to be of interest to the public. The title, publisher, price, and publication date are given for each item listed. A short descriptive comment accompanies most entries.

Schmeckebier, Laurence. **Government Publications and Their Use,** rev. ed. Washington, D.C.: Brookings, 1961.

Intended as a basic guide to government publications and their use. Describes the types of publications, availability, classification. Indicates what was published, when, by whom, in what form, etc.

Wynkoop, Sally. **Subject Guide to Government Reference Books.** Littleton, Colorado: Libraries Unlimited, Inc., 1972.

A general guide to the most important reference books published by government in all subject areas. Together with the biennial *Government Reference Books,* it assists in the use of government publications.

Guides to Early Government Publications

Ames, John Griffith. **Comprehensive Index to the Publications of the U.S. Government, 1881–1893,** 2 vols. Washington, D.C.: Government Printing Office, 1905. Reprinted Ann Arbor, Mich.: Edwards, 1953.

A valuable index to publications for the period noted.

Poore, Benjamin P. **A Descriptive Catalog of the Government Publications of the United States, Sept. 1774–March 1881.** Washington, D.C.: Government Printing Office, 1885. Reprinted Ann Arbor, Mich.: Edwards, 1953.

Material is arranged chronologically, giving for each document the full title, author, date, and a brief abstract of the contents.

U.S. Superintendent of Documents. **Catalog of the Public Documents of Congress and of All Departments of the U.S. for the Period March 4, 1893–December 31, 1940,** 25 vols. Washington, D.C.: Government Printing Office, 1896–1945.

This detailed work indexes all government publications, both Congressional and departmental. Listings are made under author, subject, and title. This is a very worthwhile guide.

U.S. Superintendent of Documents. **Checklist of U.S. Public Documents, 1789-1909.** Washington, D.C.: Government Printing Office, 1911.

A bibliography of publications issued by all branches of the government. Full titles, prices, and instructions for ordering are listed. An invaluable monthly reference guide.

United States Catalogs, Indexes, and Bibliographies

American Statistics Index: A Comprehensive Guide and Index to the Statistical Publications of the United States Government. New York: Congressional Information Service, 1973 to date.

Indexes all current statistical publications in print as of January 1, 1973. Principal studies and surveys published during the last decade are also included.

Andriot, John L. **Guide to U.S. Government Serials and Periodicals.** McLean, Va.: Documents Index, 1962 to date.

This publication lists items, prices, availability, and order numbers of government serials and periodicals. In addition, it gives a brief description, reason for preparation, and audience to which the item is directed. Arrangement is by branch of government, department, agency, and subagency. Includes releases, field agency publications, and miscellaneous publications. Starting with 1967 edition, to be published biannually with supplements.

Monthly Catalog of United States Government Publications, Washington D.C.: Government Printing Office, 1895 to date.

The monthly catalog is the most comprehensive list of currently issued government publications. It is arranged alphabetically by issuing authority. Index in the rear lists al entries by subject, title, and author. Each December index is cumulative for the year. February issue has an appendix for the annual Directory of U.S. Government Periodical and Subscription Publications.

U.S. Bureau of Census Catalog. Washington, D.C.: Bureau of the Census, (quarterly) 1790–1945. 1945 to date.

This work has monthly supplements and annual cumulations. The catalog is divided into a publications section and a data and tabulation section. Both are arranged by the major subject areas of general, agriculture, construction and housing, foreign trade, manufacturing and mineral industries, population, transportation, etc. Subject and geographical indexes are provided.

U.S. Department of Commerce Publications. Washington, D.C.: U.S. Department of Commerce, (annual) 1952 to date.

Lists publications of the Department from its beginning through 1950 with a subject index. It is updated by annual supplements. 1950/51 to date.

U.S. Government Research and Development Reports. Springfield, Va.: National Bureau of Standards. Clearinghouse for Federal Scientific and Technical Information, 1965 to date.

This is a semimonthly abstracting publication which lists reports of U.S. Government agencies such as Department of Defense, AEC, NASA, and others. These are not classified (as secret) and are listed under 22 categories from Aeronautics to Space Technology. Published under various titles since 1946. Basic guide to government report literature. All aspects of science and technology are covered.

U.S. Library of Congress, Processing Department. **Monthly Checklist of State Publications.** Washington, D.C.: Government Printing Office, 1910 to date.

A current bibliography of the publications of the states, territories, and insular possessions of the United States. Annual index may be used as subject index.

U.S. Superintendent of Documents. **Selected United States Government Publications.** Washington, D.C.: Government Printing Office.

This free publication, issued biweekly, lists current items of general interest, a brief description of their contents, and the price.

Wynkoop, Sally. **Government Reference Books: A Biennial Guide to U.S. Government Publications.** Littleton, Colo.: Libraries Unlimited. 1970 to date.

Bibliographies, indexes, statistical guides, and catalogs are included. Descriptive annotations accompany most entries.

Miscellaneous U.S. Government Publications

Economic Report of the President. Washington, D.C.: U.S. Office of the President, (annual) 1947 to date.

Overview of economic conditions in the U.S. supported by statistical documentation is contained in this annual report of the President to the Congress.

Handbook of Agricultural Statistics. Washington, D.C.: Department of Agriculture, (annual) 1964 to date.

This annual publication presents the more important statistics concerning agriculture and related subjects. For statistics before 1936, the *Yearbook of Agriculture* should be used.

Handbook of Basic Economic Statistics. Washington, D.C.: Economic Statistics Bureau, (monthly) 1966 to date.

Historical and current data on labor, industry, commerce, and agriculture are presented. A section on "Business Summary and Economic Highlights" in each issue is based on government sources.

Handbook of Labor Statistics. Washington, D.C.: Bureau of Labor Statistics, (annual) 1924/26 to date.

This handbook provides historical and current data for major labor statistics. For more current statistics see their *Monthly Labor Review.*

Historical Statistics of the United States, Colonial Times to 1957. Washington, D.C.: Government Printing Office, 1960.

This volume, issued by the U.S. Department of Commerce, contains innumerable facts going back to 1789 and relating to consumer activities, business, manufacturing, and national affairs.

Statistical Abstract of the United States. Washington, D.C.: Census Bureau, (annual) 1878 to date.

This is the most comprehensive summary of industrial, social, political, and economic statistics of the United States. A "Guide to Sources of Statistics" is included.

United States Government Organization Manual. Washington, D.C.: Office of the Federal Register, (annual) 1935 to date.

As the official organization handbook of the federal government, it describes the agencies of the legislative, judicial, and executive branches, and quasi-official agencies and selected international organizations. Brief histories of agencies abolished or transferred since 1933 are mentioned. Lists of governmental publications are given.

Guide to Directories and Business Directories

Guides to Directories

Angel, Juvenal, ed. **Directory of Foreign Firms Operating in the United States.** London: Simon & Schuster, 1971.

Current European Directories. Beckenham, Kent, England: CBD Research, 1969 to date.

Davis, Marjorie V. **Guide to American Business Directories.** Washington, D.C.: Public Affairs Press, 1948.

> This volume lists, under subject headings, brief descriptions of American business directories in some 77 different areas such as advertising, banking, chemicals, construction, food, insurance, and transportation. This book contains much of the information originally presented in a Department of Commerce pamphlet published in 1947.

Goodman, S. E., **Financial Market Place.** New York: R. R. Bowker Co., 1972.

Guide to American Directories. 8th ed., B. Klein, ed., Englewood Cliffs, N.J.: Prentice-Hall, Inc., 1972.

> This cross-referenced volume covers 300 major fields and describes and categorizes 3350 industrial, mercantile, and professional directories. Arranged by subject with a title index.

A Guide to Foreign Business Directories. Washington, D.C.: U.S. Bureau of Foreign Commerce, 1955.

> First published in 1931 and revised in 1939, 1948, and 1951, this guide is a good initial source for further research.

Guide to Industrial Directories. United Nations. Industrial Development Organization, 1970.

Henderson, G. P., ed., **European Companies: A Guide to Sources of Information.** 3d. ed. Beckenham, Kent, England: CBD Research, 1972.

Trade Directories of the World. Queens Village, N.Y.: Croner Publications, 1952 to date.

> This is a loose-leaf handbook listing business and trade directories in the United States and Canada. This directory is kept current through additions.

Directories

Best's Insurance Reports: Life-Health-Property-Liability. Morristown, N.J.: Alfred M. Best Co., Inc.

> U.S. and Canadian insurance companies are presented here. These publications are standard sources for financial and operating data, as well as company ratings.

Broadcasting Yearbook. Washington, D.C.: Broadcasting Publications Inc., 1958 to date.

This provides statistical information relative to TV markets. It also serves as a leading directory of TV and radio stations in the U.S. and Canada, including top personnel. Information regarding specialized directories related to the field is also provided.

Directory of American Firms Operating in Foreign Countries. N.Y.: World Trade Academy Press, 1959–1962.

Directory of Business and Financial Services. New York: Special Libraries Association, 1963.

A selective list of 1050 services, including newsletters, bulletins, reports, and other published services covering business, economics, and finance.

Directory of National Associations of Businessmen. Washington, D.C.: Government Printing Office.

This directory, published annually, lists more than 2000 national organizations, trade associations, business groups, etc., including the name, address, and chief executive officer of each group. This directory is issued through the Office of Technical Services of the U.S. Department of Commerce.

Directory of National Trade and Professional Associations of the United States. Washington, D.C.: Potomac Books, 1966 to date.

This annual publication includes names, addresses, executive officers, sizes of staffs, and memberships of approximately 3500 associations.

Directory of Non-Federal Statistics for States and Local Areas. Washington, D.C.: U.S. Department of Commerce, 1969.

Primary sources of non-federal statistical data on social, political, and economic subjects are listed here by state, county, city, and SMSA areas.

Directory of Special Libraries and Information Centers. Detroit: Gale Research Co. (2nd edition published in 1968. 3rd edition in process.)

Lists more than 13,000 special libraries in the United States and Canada alphabetically by name and address, along with a note on the special collections.

Dun and Bradstreet Reference Book. New York: Published by Dun and Bradstreet six times a year, 1859 to date.

This guide lists nearly three million business firms in the United States and Canada, indicating type of business and financial rating. Also available in separate editions by states. Not available to libraries.

Dun and Bradstreet Reference Book of Corporate Management. New York: Dun & Bradstreet, 1967 to date.

Approximately 2000 corporations with annual sales of more than $20 million and/or 1000 employees are listed in this annual. It gives biographical sketches of selected officers and directors.

Encyclopedia of Associations. 5th ed. Detroit: Gale Research, 1968 to date.

This work is in three volumes. Volume I: National Organizations of the United States, covers approximately 14,000 U.S. and some foreign associations of interest in America. Entries are arranged by subject with a good alphabetical and keyword index. Information on purpose and objectives, number of members, publications, convention data, etc., is provided for each. Volume II: Geographic and Executive Index. Volume III: New Associations and Projects.

Financial Market Place. S. E. Goodman, ed. New York: R. R. Bowker Co., 1972.

A directory of major institutions, services, and publications.

Fortune Directory. Chicago: Time, Inc., 1956 to date.

An annual publication which lists major U.S. industrial firms by sales, assets, and net profits. The geographical section lists products manufactured and the companies that manufacture them.

Foundation Directory. 4th ed. New York: Columbia University Press, 1971.

Industrial Research Laboratories of the United States. 13th ed. Tempe, Arizona: Jacques Cattell, 1970.

International Directory of Computer and Information Systems Service. London: Europa Publications, 1969.

Jane's Major Companies of Europe. London: S. Marston, 1965 to date. (Irregular)

Financial information on approximately 1000 European companies is provided.

Million Dollar Directory. New York: Dun & Bradstreet, (annual) 1959 to date.

As a companion volume to the *Middle Market Directory,* it has the same information and sections for businesses with net worth of $1 million and more. The "Top Management" section lists officers, directors, etc.

Middle Market Directory. New York: Dun & Bradstreet, (annual) 1964 to date.

This annual directory lists businesses with an indicated net worth of $500,000 to $999,999. Industrial concerns, utilities, banks and trust companies, stockbrokers, insurance companies, wholesalers, and retailers are included. It provides information on annual sales, number of employees, state of incorporation, and company officers. There are three sections listing entries alphabetically, geographically, and by SIC number.

Moody's Investor Service. New York: Moody's.

Moody's Service publishes information on various firms for the use of persons wishing to make investments. Information on officers, dividends, loans, debts, and a balance sheet are listed. Moody's Service is divided into five areas: Transportation, Industrials, Public Utilities, Banks and Finance, and Municipal and Government. Annual bound volumes supplemented by loose-leaf service. Moody's also offers other services:

Moody's Advisory Reports
Moody's Bond Record
Moody's Dividend Record
Moody's Handbook of Common Stock
Moody's Investors Advisory Service
Moody's Stock Survey

National Associations of the United States. Washington, D.C.: U.S. Office of Domestic Commerce, 1949.

A directory giving detailed information on nearly 4000 trade associations, professional societies, labor unions, farm cooperatives, chambers of commerce, better business bureaus, and other organizations which are national in scope. A detailed index in the front lists each association by name, key work, and subject.

News Front: 2500 Leading U.S. Corporations. New York: News Front, 1970.

Poor's Register of Corporations, Directors and Executives of the United States and Canada. New York: Standard and Poor's Corp. (annual), 1928 to date.

This annual directory lists the names of executives and directors of major manufacturing and investment firms. It comprises six sections:

1. The Classified Index lists corporations under SIC industry classifications.

2. The Corporation Directory lists for each company: names of officers and directors, number of employees, and principal products.

3. The Register of Directors lists key leaders in business and professional organizations, with offices, birth dates, and home addresses.

4. The Obituary section lists the deaths of executives occurring the preceding year.

5. The New Companies section lists organizations appearing for the first time in the current Directory.

6. The New Individuals section lists persons whose names appear for the first time in the current Register.

Rand McNally International Bankers Directory. Chicago: Rand-McNally. (annual) 1876 to date.

Research Center Directory. Detroit: Gale Research Co., 1968 to date.

University and other non-profit research organizations are listed. There is an alphabetical index of research centers and an institutional index.

Security Dealers of North America. New York: Standard and Poor's. (annual) 1922 to date.

A directory of investment firms in U.S. and Canada. Arranged alphabetically by state. Addresses and officers are given.

Standard and Poor's Corporation Services.

This is a loose-leaf service designed primarily for the investor. It offers current information on the structure and financial background of corporations. Additional services offered are:

The Bond Outlook	*Stock Reports Over-the-Counter and*
Industry Surveys	*Regional Exchanges*
Railroad Securities	*Listed Stock Reports*
Daily Dividend Record	*Facts and Forecasts Service*
Called Bond Record	*Listed Bond Reports*

Tax Exempt Foundations: Their Impact on Small Business. Washington, D.C.: Government Printing Office, 1968.

Over 30,000 tax-exempt foundations registered with the Internal Revenue Service are listed. Arranged by IRS District number and by name of the foundation.

Thomas Register of American Manufacturers. 10 vols. New York: Thomas Publishing Co. (annual)

A national purchasing guide listing products alphabetically, and manufacturers geographically.

Wasserman, Paul, ed. **Consultants and Consulting Organizations Directory.** 2nd ed., Detroit: Gale Research, 1973.

Miscellaneous Sources

Almanacs

The Economic Almanac. New York: National Industrial Conference Board, 1940 to date.

This biennial volume contains accurate and significant statistical data useful to persons concerned with current economic problems, often of the type not usually found in the *Statistical Abstract of the United States.* Topics include: prices, savings, consumption, labor force, foreign trade, standard of living, construction, public debt, and wages.

Exporters' Encyclopaedia. 1st ed., 1904, New York: T. Ashwell. (annual) 1904 to date.

Contains full information relative to shipments for countries all over the world.

Information Please Almanac, Atlas, and Yearbook. New York: Simon and Schuster, 1947 to date.

This almanac deals with U.S. and world events and statistics of the year issued. It contains maps, reviews of the arts, analysis of the state of the economy, and many miscellaneous statistics. It is fully indexed.

Insurance Almanac: Who, What, When, and Where in Insurance, An Annual of Insurance Facts. New York: Underwriter Printing and Publishing Co., (annual) 1912 to date.

Title varies. Directory material is included.

Troy, Leo. **Almanac of Business and Industrial Finance Ratios.** Prentice-Hall, 1971.

Financial and operating ratios for over 250 industries, both manufacturing and nonmanufacturing, are presented. Information is based on the statistics for July 1967 through June 1968.

The World Almanac and Book of Facts. New York: World-Telegram, 1868 to date.

A very thorough annual containing much valuable information concerned with the economic, social, educational, and political activities of the world.

Atlases

Columbia Lippincott Gazetteer of the World. New York: Columbia, 1962.

This geographical dictionary lists in alphabetical order the names of mountains, lakes, rivers, islands, towns, cities, and countries. For each, the location, altitude, and pronunciation are given. For cities, towns, and nations, the population, brief history, and information on industry are given.

Ginsburg, Norton, ed. **Atlas of Economic Development.** Chicago: University of Chicago Press, 1961.

This atlas contains a comparative quantitative measurement of the economic growth of the nations of the world. Its various sections, complete with detailed maps, deal with demographic data, resources, industrialization, and foreign trade.

The National Atlas of the United States of America. Washington, D.C.: U.S. Geological Survey, 1970.

Includes a general reference map section and a special map section. The economic section includes agriculture, mineral and energy resources, manufacturing, business, etc.

Oxford Economic Atlas of the World. Oxford: University Press, 4th ed., 1972.

Rand McNally Commercial Atlas and Marketing Guide. New York: Rand-McNally.

This excellent atlas is revised annually and its maps are kept up to date. The individual interested in commerce finds this especially valuable. It contains agricultural maps of the United States, population statistics, retail sales data, transportation information, and much other information in the field of marketing.

Biographical Sources

Current Biography. New York: H. W. Wilson Co., 1940 to date (monthly).

International in coverage, these collected biographies are written in a popular style based upon information from newspapers, magazines, books, and the individuals concerned. Personages included are those who have attained international fame during the period being covered.

Dictionary of American Biography. 11 vols. New York: Scribner's, 1928–1958.

This is limited to Americans no longer living who made important contributions to American life. There are around 13,000 entries. Bibliographies for further research are included.

Who's Who in America. Chicago: Marquis, 1899 to date.

The best known living men and women in the U.S. are included here. Supplemented by *Who Was Who in America* which contains biographical data on deceased individuals.

Who's Who in Banking: The Directory of the Banking Profession. New York: Business Press Inc., 1972 (3rd ed.).

Who's Who in Finance and Industry. 17th ed., Chicago: Marquis, 1972–1973.

Other Sources

A Guide to Consumer Markets. New York: National Industrial Conference Board. (annual) 1960 to date.

The most important statistical intelligence relating to the consumer is contained here. Extensive collection of graphs showing the major trends in the consumer area are provided. Major subject divisions are: Population, Employment, Income, Expenditures, Production and Distribution, Prices.

The Bibliographic Index. New York: H. W. Wilson Co., 1938 to date.

Dissertation Abstracts International. Ann Arbor, Michigan: University Microfilms, (monthly) 1938 to date.

Abstracts of doctoral dissertations. Abstracts are entered by subjects and indexed as of the date received at University Microfilms. From 1966 the publications are divided into Service "A" Humanities and Social Science; and Service "B" Science and Engineering. A cumulative index covering 1938 through 1969 is available.

Multi Media Reviews Index; the only complete guide to reviews of nonbook media, 1971. Ann Arbor, Michigan: Pierian Press, 1972.

MMRI–1971 contains some 20,000 citations of films, filmstrips, nonclassical records and tapes, transparencies, and other media forms. Review ratings are given.

State Bluebooks and Reference Publications: A Selected Bibliography. Lexington, Ky.: Council of State Governments, 1972.

Lists directories of officials, works on state government, state guides, statistical information, and legislative action.

Statistical Yearbook. New York: United Nations, (annual) 1948 to date.

This work contains major financial and economic statistics of U.N. members.

United Nations Documents Index. New York: United Nations, Dag Hammarskjöld Library, Documents Index Unit, 1950 to date.

Published monthly, with annual cumulations, this is the basic guide to current U.N. publications and documents.

United Nations Publications, 1945-1966. New York: United Nations Sales Section, 1967.

Lists all sales publications of the U.N. issued from 1945 to 1966, including sales number and price, by broad subject categories.

Wasserman, Paul, ed., **Statistics Sources.** Detroit: Gale Research Co., 3rd ed., 1971.

A guide to statistical data for the U.S. and selected foreign countries. It is arranged by subject. Governmental and nongovernmental sources are both included. However, it provides only national sources; regional or local sources are not included.

Weisenberger A. **Investment Companies, Mutual Funds and Other Types.** New York: A. Weisenberger, (annual) 1941 to date.

This is an annual compilation of historical and financial information on mutual funds and investment companies. *Mutual Funds and Statistics* is a companion volume.

Guides to the Guides

Barton, Mary Neil. **Reference Books: A Brief Guide for Students and Other Users of the Library.** Baltimore, Maryland: Enoch Pratt Free Library, 1st ed., 1938.

A brief but excellent guide to basic reference material.

Besterman, Theodore. **A World Bibliography of Bibliographies,** 4th rev. ed., 5 vols. Lausanne: Societas Bibliographica, 1966.

Bibliographies are arranged alphabetically by subject. Over 117,000 volumes are recorded. This edition is updated to 1963.

Business Books in Print, 1973. New York: R. R. Bowker Co., 1973.

This excellent reference guide lists some 31,000 items in business by author, title, and subject. It covers virtually every area of business activity, research, and history.

Cheney, Frances N. **Fundamental Reference Sources.** Chicago: American Library Association, 1971.

Coman, E. T., Jr. **Sources of Business Information,** rev. ed. Berkeley and Los Angeles: University of California Press, 1964.

A valuable text in which the first four chapters are devoted to the methodology of locating business information sources. The remaining chapters deal with sources in specific fields, such as statistics, finance, accounting, management, and personnel. Each of these subject headings is broken down in detail by type of information needed, and each periodical or text source is completely described. At the end of each chapter there is a useful summary of sources cited, and a detailed index covers the entire volume.

Courtney, W. F., ed. **Reader's Adviser.** 11th ed., New York: R. R. Bowker Co., 1969. 2 vol.

Daniells, Lorna M. **Business Reference Sources.** Boston, Massachusetts: Harvard University, Baker Library, 1971.

Financial sources, statistics for industry analysis, market research sources, international trade and economic conditions, basic U.S. statistical sources, etc.

Encyclopedia of Business Information Sources. 2 vols., Detroit: Gale Research, 1970.

A very detailed listing of business information sources. Volume one is arranged alphabetically by subject; volume two by geographical division, including foreign countries and the U.S.

Executive's Guide to Information Sources. Detroit: Business Guides Co., 1965.

This work contains a detailed listing for management reference of 2300 business and business-related subjects, with a record of periodicals, organizations, bureaus, directories, bibliographies, and other sources concerned with each topic. The subjects are arranged alphabetically.

Frank, Natalie. **Data Sources for Business and Market Analysis.** New York: Scarecrow Press, 1969.

Data sources useful in the analysis of business and economics.

Georgi, Charlotte. **Literature of Executive Management: Selected Books and Reference Sources for the International Businessman.** SLA Bibliography No. 5. New York: Special Libraries Association, 1963.

An index of books and other information sources under such headings as the philosophy of management, management of science and technology, management education and development, etc. Each entry is completely documented, with number of pages and price.

Johnson, H. W., ed. **How to Use the Business Library—with Sources of Business Information,** 4th ed. Cincinnati: South-Western Publishing Co., 1973.

A very handy and useful guide which, along with the usual subjects covered, comments on the value and availability of audio-visual aids, data processing, and materials from research foundations. The volume is recent, easy to use, and completely indexed.

Management Information Guide. Detroit: Gale Research Co.

The following handbooks have been published to present the sources of information on each subject field. Books, pamphlets, and government publications are included. They are excellent guides to information sources:

Communication in Organizations
Ethics in Business Conduct
Accounting
Public Utilities
Packaging

Public Finance
Textile Industry
American Economic and Business History
Public Relations
Commercial Law
Transportation

Computers and Data Processing
The Developing Nations
Standards and Specifications
Insurance
Food and Beverage Industries
International Business and Foreign Trade
Business Trends and Forecasting
Investment Information
Real Estate

Manley, Marian C. **Business Information—How to Find and Use It.** New York: Harper & Row, 1955.

In this thoroughly indexed book, initial chapters describe uses and applications of business information as well as ways of satisfying special informational needs. The remainder of the text provides a bibliography of various information sources concerning business and economic conditions, banking and finance, marketing and market research, plant management, communications, etc.

Murphey, Robert W. **How and Where to Look It Up—A Guide to Standard Sources of Information.** New York: McGraw-Hill Book Co., 1958.

This is an extensive and intensive work, a true laymen's guide to reference materials. Subject headings make this volume easy to use. Included are sections on annuals and almanacs, periodicals, books, directories, government publications, graphic information, and sources of bibliographic and geographic materials and information. Each chapter and subchapter includes a few pages on the uses and limitations of the materials, as well as indexed entries with very detailed descriptions. Certainly one of the most valuable of all guides to reference works. The volume is cross-indexed by subject and title.

Shores, Louis. **Basic Reference Sources.** Chicago: American Library Association, 1954.

Actually written as a textbook for research workers, this volume is valuable for its elaborate descriptions and explanations of the best use of more than 500 basic reference works, including dictionaries, encyclopedias, yearbooks, handbooks, directories, serials, indexes, and bibliographies.

Walford, Albert J., ed. **Guide to Reference Material.** 2nd ed. London: The Library Association, 1966–70. 3 vols.

Wasserman, Paul. **Information for Administrators—A Guide to Publications and Services for Management in Business and Government.** Ithaca: Cornell University Press, 1956.

A volume which describes the information and services available from such sources as government agencies, business services, periodicals, newspapers, chambers of commerce, and research organizations, as well as sources of information in local areas. The appendixes list depository libraries, bureaus of business and government research in American universities, information sources in foreign countries, etc.

White, Carl M., and associates. **Sources of Information in the Social Sciences.** Totowa, N.J.: Bedminster Press, 1964.

Sections on sociology, anthropology, psychology, economics and business, education, and political science. Bibliographic essays and annotated bibliographies on each subject.

Winchell, Constance M. **Guide to Reference Books,** 8th ed. Chicago: American Library Association, 1967.

Lists approximately 7500 reference works. It serves as a guide to bibliographies, indexes and abstracts, handbooks, annuals, directories, biographies, atlases, and serial publications. These are organized under general reference works, the humanities, social sciences, history and area studies, and pure and applied sciences. An extremely detailed author, subject, and title index locates specific items or categories. Covers material through 1964. First supplement, published 1968, covers 1965 and 1966. Supplemented biannually.

Questions for Study

I. Answer the following questions and list the reference sources from which you secured the information.

1. What articles appeared on Information Systems in the first two months of last year?

2. What books were published last year on Communications? Limit your list to five titles.

3. How many automobiles were registered in your state last year?

4. Who is the present director of the United States Department of Health, Education, and Welfare?

5. How many students are registered in your state's public university?

6. List six pamphlets or reports which have been published in the last twelve months on the topics of Presidential Impeachment, Energy Conservation, or Inflation. (Choose one topic)

7. What articles did the *Wall Street Journal* have on tariffs in the two months previous to this one?

8. Select a large corporation and give the names of its major officers.

9. List the articles on Consumerism which have appeared in any one 12-month period.

10. Indicate your major field (accounting, electrical engineering, marketing, political science, etc.), and then note a narrow subarea in the field (the auditor's statement in the corporate annual report; market segmentation for consumer products; correlations between income and literacy levels among minority populations; etc.). List journal and magazine articles on the narrow area which have appeared in any one recent 12-month period.

II. Answer the following questions and list the reference sources from which you secured the information.

1. List pertinent biographical data on the president of your school.

2. List four books which appeared in the last two years on exorcism.

3. What articles appeared in the *New York Times* last month on American Foreign Policy (limit to five)?

4. List several books (and their publication dates) which have been concerned with the assassination of John F. Kennedy.

5. How many persons were estimated to be unemployed in your state last year?

6. What libraries in a nearby urban center have files of a major journal in your primary field of interest (list journal title)?

7. How many employees work for the Lockheed Corporation? (Or select some other major corporation for the same question.)

8. What publications were issued last year by the United States Government in your major area of study (limit to five publications)?

9. Secure a directory in an area of your interest (product manufacture or professional listing) and briefly list its title and the types of information and services it offers.

10. Select a narrow subject, state it, then list the doctoral dissertations written on that topic in any one 12-month period.

Chapter Sixteen

Methods for Gathering Information—Primary Sources

Selecting the Sample
Conducting the Survey
Types of Surveys
Designing the Questionnaire
Documenting the Report

In today's busy world, most of us depend on the newspapers and radio/TV to tell us what's going on. They, in turn, get much of their information by asking questions.

"Interviews with key government officials in Washington," begins one story. "A survey of workers at the Danbury plant," runs another. A politician is disposed of with the words, "A nationwide poll showed that Throttlebottom ranked far down in the public preference."

Information obtained by asking questions is called primary information. Other kinds of primary data include company records, diaries, original reports, letters and notes, and personal observation.

The data secured from primary sources are considered "raw" because they have not been subjected to interpretation and analysis by others. The researcher may very well be the first person to analyze, evaluate, and interpret the information. No one else has added his bias to it. The researcher is free to study and evaluate the data, and, if he is in a position to do so, render a decision. He may be trying to answer the question, "If we manufacture a new sports-type car that will seat two people, sell for $4500, get 28 miles to a gallon of gasoline and look something like this, will you buy it?"

Today we secure a great deal of information on how people will react to a situation by asking them. Of course the questions need not be momentous. We may be interested in finding out whether the company's new product should be packaged in the red and blue carton or in the brown and green; whether the new plant should be built in Topeka or in Kansas City; or whether we should advertise on TV instead of on radio.

Business Week estimated some years back that U.S. corporations were spending over $200 million a year asking such questions in their market research.[1]

Selecting the Sample

When we make a survey to find out what large numbers of people are thinking or feeling, we don't try to approach everybody. To survey everybody would be too expensive, and perhaps impossible. Can you imagine asking 20 million automobile owners whether they would be interested in buying a car with the engine in back?

Instead, we take a sample of the people whose opinions we're interested in. The science of statistical sampling has advanced tremendously in recent years, and this is not the place to discuss it in detail. But if the sample is carefully selected so that it's representative of the group (or "universe") as a whole, surprisingly accurate results can be obtained from a very small sample.

The important point to remember is that the sample should be a reliable cross section of the group you're studying. If it isn't, you'll get results that are not valid. A statistician or market analyst can tell you best how to go about it. For some purposes a "random" sample may be the answer. In other cases it may be wiser to use a "stratified," "cluster," "double," "selective," or "area" sample.

Conducting the Survey

Even with a good sample and a well-planned questionnaire, a survey may fail if it is not conducted properly. Respondents to a survey are doing us a favor, and they should be treated accordingly. The investigator should be courteous at all times. He or she must also be perceptive, in order to come as close to the "real" responses as possible.

Types of Surveys

Questions are not difficult to ask; the problem is getting reliable and truthful answers. Several different methods are used to secure information from people. Basically they all involve asking them questions or presenting them with situations, securing their reactions, and then determining how they will behave in a practical situation based on their responses to the survey. Sometimes the conclusions run like this: "Of those interviewed, 53 percent preferred the smaller package, 26 percent preferred the larger, and 21 percent had no preference." Among the methods used are:

[1] *Business Week* (April 18, 1964), pp. 90–116.

Mail questionnaires
Personal interviews
Telephone interviews
Unstructured or depth interviews
Observation

The first three employ a series of questions to secure information. However, each is very different from the others and has its own advantages and disadvantages.

Mail Questionnaires

The advantages of the mail questionnaire are several. Chief among them are its low cost per response, and the ease of securing responses from a wide geographical area. Respondents can also be assured of anonymity, which helps increase the proportion of questionnaires returned. Securing answers from hard-to-see people (such as company presidents) is easier with a mail questionnaire. Also, there is no interviewer involved, whose bias may influence the answers that are given.

But there are disadvantages in the mail survey. It must be relatively brief, or people won't bother with it. Persons who feel strongly—pro or con—are the most likely to respond; thus it may not accurately reflect the attitudes of those in between. It is also difficult to know whether the intended respondent completed the questionnaire himself or some member of his office staff or family did it for him. Respondents are usually reluctant to expand on their answers in a mail questionnaire because of the effort involved. For these reasons we are never quite certain whether those who reply are really representative of our sample, and of the population at large.

Personal Interviews

Perhaps the biggest disadvantage of the personal interview technique is its cost. To use competent people as interviewers is very expensive. And even with professional interviewers, there is the risk that the interviewer's bias may influence the answers obtained. Securing data through interviewing is time-consuming as compared to a mail survey. And often the respondent, for example a housewife or a shopper, doesn't have the time or inclination to stand and chat with an interviewer.

On the other hand, an interviewer can conduct a more lengthy discussion than is usually possible by mail. He can also secure answers to questions in sensitive areas (income tax, sex, politics, religion), and bring in a reply where a mail survey may fail. Because he can choose his respondents to a certain extent, his survey usually includes a more representative sample.[2]

[2] See also, J. E. Mandel, "A Strategy for Selecting and Phrasing Questions in the Interview," *The Journal of Business Communication,* Fall 1974, pp. 17–23.

Telephone Interviews

The telephone interview has several major limitations. Questions must be brief and few in number, generally not more than three or four. Questions requiring discussion or even careful thought cannot be included, nor can any which are concerned with personal relationships. Not every telephone call will lead to an interview, since a child may answer or the person contacted may refuse to cooperate. On the other hand, telephone interviews are inexpensive, almost anyone can be called regardless of his position or office, and simple information can be secured quickly and easily.

The Depth or Unstructured Interview

We don't always answer questions truthfully. Because of the conventions of society and the inhibitions most of us have, we often answer questions as we think they should be answered. We don't want to admit that we hate our boss, dislike bridge, or find television programs a bore. We may not lie, but we evade. We reply as we think society would prefer. Naturally if the replies are not honest, the survey results cannot be valid.

Some experts believe that if you let people talk about a topic freely and easily, their true feelings will become apparent to the skilled interviewer regardless of the conventions of the society in which they live. This is the theory of depth interviewing; to set up a climate for the respondent so that he will talk freely and frankly about the topic under discussion.

"Tell me how you select a can of coffee when you shop" may produce some key information in the answer which may take 5 minutes and contain a great deal of irrelevant material.

Personal Observation

A great deal of information can often be secured simply by observing. Researchers will watch how a housewife makes a choice of one breakfast food from among 30, how she selects a cut of meat, or whether she confers with her friend before choosing a cake. Observers also secure data by watching traffic patterns, counting shoppers, noting peoples' restaurant habits, etc.

Designing the Questionnaire

Whatever type of survey is used, it is important to ask the right questions. It is often said that nothing is easier to make than a poor questionnaire, and nothing is more difficult than a good one. But there are a few rules which, if carefully followed, will greatly increase your chances of success.

Almost every detail of a questionnaire is important, even the title and introductory comments. To call it "Executive Survey" may appeal to the respondent's ego. The title "Confidential Analysis Among Our Retailers" encourages a sense of close relations between researcher and respondent. At times a very carefully worded introductory sentence or two, appealing to the respondent's professional knowledge or responsibility, his loyalty, or even his sense of humor, may motivate him to complete the survey.

The precise wording of the questions can be a significant factor in the percentage of returns received. Here are a few suggestions:

1. The order of the questions should be logical. There is no point in asking a respondent in question 3 about the ages and education level of her children, and then asking her in question 6 if she is married. If the questionnaire does not seem logical and sensible to the respondent it may be discarded.

2. Provide easy-to-answer questions early in the questionnaire. The respondent who has gone quickly and easily through the first eight questions may be reluctant to discard the questionnaire when he encounters difficulty on question number nine. This suggestion may conflict with the preceding one about following a logical order, but the researcher can only do what is most advantageous under the circumstances.

3. There should be smooth transitions between questions. This, and parallel wording, help the respondent to move easily from one question to the next.

4. Each question should be concerned with one topic only. If the respondent is faced with giving two answers to one question—and only one space is provided—he may discard the form. Or, if he does answer, his response may not give a clear indication of his preference. Consider, for example, the question: "Would you like movies on commercial air flights at a slight extra charge?" If the respondent answers "no," does it mean that he wouldn't like them even if they were free? And if he would like movies on long flights but not on short ones, how does he answer? And if he doesn't want movies at all, whether there is an extra charge or not, how does he so indicate?

5. The questionnaire should be, and should look, easy to answer. Arrange the questions so that the respondent sees clearly where to indicate his replies. There should be plenty of white space, and the numbering should be easy to follow. Choose words carefully so that everyone will understand. And provide an addressed, stamped envelope to send the questionnaire back in.

6. Certain words should be avoided—those that may provoke a biased or emotional response, and also words that may carry an undesirable connotation. These are usually abstract words (happiness, morality, democracy, communism), or words relating to politics, sex, religion, and race.

7. Clarity is of the utmost importance; eliminate all ambiguity. A question like "What type of soup do you prefer?" can only cause difficulty. One respondent will answer "hot," another "Campbell's," a third "beef noodle," a fourth "frozen," and a fifth "inexpensive." One way of handling this problem is to provide a list of alternative answers to choose among.

8. Avoid questions that "lead" the respondent to specific answers. Certainly a bias will enter into most respondents' answers if we ask, "Do you prefer General Motors cars?" "Do you usually purchase the best seats when attending a play?" "Do you always drink moderately?" "Do you prefer imported wines?" Here again, it helps if you give the respondent a list of choices from which to make a selection.

9. Do not make the respondent search his memory, or carry through computations. We can't expect an accurate answer to "In what year did you take your first jet trip?" Not many people will bother to compute the answer to "How much does your family spend each year on movies?" Questions such as these can cause the questionnaire to be tossed into the wastebasket.

10. Avoid personal questions if possible. People dislike being asked questions about their political or religious affiliation, sex habits, income, or age. A promise of anonymity may help, but it is better to avoid personal questions altogether.

11. Don't ask skip-and-jump questions. People are likely to give up in despair when confronted with "If you answered "yes" to question 4, skip questions 7 and 8 and go directly to question 9, unless you live in New York, in which case do not answer question 9."

12. Avoid questions with blanket meanings. Some words are open to a variety of interpretations. For example, the word "often" in the question, "Do you often take your wife out to dinner?" may mean once a month to some husbands and once a week to others.

Following is an example of a mail questionnaire, reprinted by courtesy of The Western Union Telegraph company.[2]

---

western union

SURVEY OF TELEGRAPH CUSTOMERS

1. FROM AN OVER-ALL POINT OF VIEW, HOW SATISFACTORY IS WESTERN UNION MESSAGE TELEGRAPH SERVICE?

    ☐ *Always Satisfactory*

    ☐ *Usually Satisfactory*

    ☐ *Frequently Unsatisfactory*

    ☐ *Usually Unsatisfactory*

    ☐ *No Opinion*

2. ON THE BASIS OF YOUR EXPERIENCE WITH MESSAGE TELEGRAPH SERVICE, WOULD YOU SAY THE QUALITY OF THE SERVICE IS PRESENTLY BETTER, ABOUT THE SAME OR WORSE THAN IT HAS BEEN IN THE PAST?

    ☐ *Better*   ☐ *About the Same*   ☐ *Worse*   ☐ *No Opinion*

3. IS YOUR ORGANIZATION OR COMPANY CURRENTLY SENDING MORE, ABOUT THE SAME NUMBER OR FEWER TELEGRAMS THAN A YEAR AGO?

    ☐ *More*   ☐ *About the Same Number*   ☐ *Fewer*   ☐ *Don't Know*

---

[2] Courtesy of Western Union Telegraph Company.

(IF FEWER TELEGRAMS) WHAT IS THE MAJOR REASON(S) FOR CURTAILING TELEGRAM USAGE?

_____

_____

_____

WESTERN UNION EFFICIENCY IN ACCEPTING TELEGRAMS

1. BY WHAT METHOD ARE TELEGRAMS **USUALLY** SENT BY YOUR COMPANY?

(Check One Method Only)

☐ *By Telephone*   ☐ *Picked Up by Western Union Messenger*

☐ *By Desk-Fax*   ☐ *By Telex Machine*   ☐ *By Teleprinter Machine*

Other Methods (please explain) _____

2. ARE YOU SATISFIED WITH WESTERN UNION'S PRACTICES IN ACCEPTING TELEGRAMS?

☐ *Always*   ☐ *Usually*   ☐ *Occasionally*   ☐ *Rarely*   ☐ *No opinion*

3. IF THERE IS ANYTHING UNSATISFACTORY ABOUT THE WAY WESTERN UNION ACCEPTS TELEGRAMS, PLEASE TELL US ABOUT IT.

_____

_____

_____

WESTERN UNION EFFICIENCY IN DELIVERING TELEGRAMS

1. AFTER WESTERN UNION ACCEPTS YOUR TELEGRAMS, ARE YOU SATISFIED WITH THE TIME IT TAKES TO DELIVER THEM?

☐ *Always*   ☐ *Usually*   ☐ *Occasionally*   ☐ *Rarely*   ☐ *No Opinion*

2. IF THERE IS ANY ASPECT OF MESSAGE DELIVERY SERVICE WHICH IS NOT SATISFACTORY PLEASE TELL US ABOUT IT.

_____

_____

_____

WESTERN UNION TELEGRAPH SERVICE IN GENERAL

1. WHAT WOULD YOU SAY ARE THE MAJOR SHORTCOMINGS OF MESSAGE TELEGRAPH SERVICE?

   (Please Comment On Any Aspect Of Service Or Your Experience With Western Union.)

   _____

   _____

   _____

   _____

2. WHAT **ONE** PARTICULAR SHORTCOMING LIMITS YOUR USAGE OF TELEGRAMS?

   _____

   _____

3. WHAT WOULD YOU SAY ARE THE **MOST** SATISFACTORY ASPECTS OF MESSAGE TELEGRAPH SERVICE?

   _____

   _____

   _____

4. IF YOU HAVE ANY OTHER SUGGESTIONS ON WHAT MIGHT INDUCE YOU TO INCREASE YOUR USAGE OF MESSAGE TELEGRAPH SERVICE PLEASE TELL US ABOUT IT IN THE SPACE PROVIDED BELOW.

   _____

   _____

   _____

   _____

   _____

   (Please feel free to use the back cover.)

   If you wish, you may fill out the following:

   *Your Name*_____ *Position*_____

   *Name of organization*_____
   And now please return this questionnaire in the stamped, addressed envelope provided. Thank you.

Below are samples of several questionnaire formats. They show alternative ways of arranging the questions. Where an attempt is being made to measure levels of attitude and feelings, a "semantic differential" is often used, as in the horizontal format of the first two examples. This permits the respondent to choose among answers ranging from one extreme to another. Placing numerical designations on the scale makes it possible to measure just how strongly the respondent feels about his or her answer. The answers from all respondents can then be charted and correlated to show how groups differ in the strength of their feelings.[3]

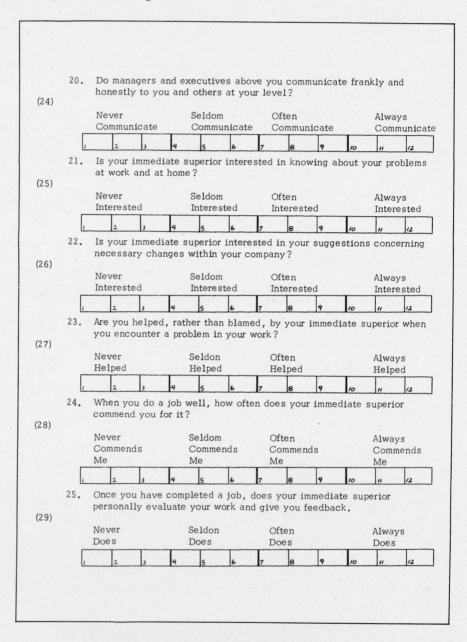

An Example of a Scaled Questionnaire (one page among several)

[3] Basic texts on research carry detailed discussions of the semantic differential.

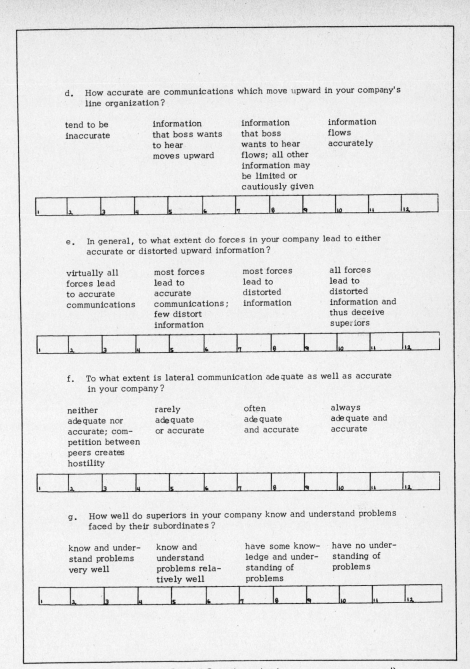

d. How accurate are communications which move upward in your company's line organization?

| tend to be inaccurate | information that boss wants to hear moves upward | information that boss wants to hear flows; all other information may be limited or cautiously given | information flows accurately |

| 1 | 2 | 3 | 4 | 5 | 6 | 7 | 8 | 9 | 10 | 11 | 12 |

e. In general, to what extent do forces in your company lead to either accurate or distorted upward information?

| virtually all forces lead to accurate communications | most forces lead to accurate communications; few distort information | most forces lead to distorted information | all forces lead to distorted information and thus deceive superiors |

| 1 | 2 | 3 | 4 | 5 | 6 | 7 | 8 | 9 | 10 | 11 | 12 |

f. To what extent is lateral communication adequate as well as accurate in your company?

| neither adequate nor accurate; competition between peers creates hostility | rarely adequate or accurate | often adequate and accurate | always adequate and accurate |

| 1 | 2 | 3 | 4 | 5 | 6 | 7 | 8 | 9 | 10 | 11 | 12 |

g. How well do superiors in your company know and understand problems faced by their subordinates?

| know and understand problems very well | know and understand problems relatively well | have some knowledge and understanding of problems | have no understanding of problems |

| 1 | 2 | 3 | 4 | 5 | 6 | 7 | 8 | 9 | 10 | 11 | 12 |

An Example of a Scaled Questionnaire (one page among several)

Q 27 Think of those instances in which you have had difficulty getting others to understand you. To what degree did each of the following conditions exist?

   a) The other person didn't have the background to understand what I was saying:

   (38)
   1 __ This happens a lot
   2 __ This happens some
   3 __ This happens very little

   b) The other person didn't listen to what I was saying:

   (39)
   1 __ This happens a lot
   2 __ This happens some
   3 __ This happens very little

   c) I didn't express myself clearly:

   (40)
   1 __ This happens a lot
   2 __ This happens some
   3 __ This happens very little

Q 28 When you request assistance from another department or branch, how frequently do you obtain that assistance in a timely fashion?

   (41)
   1 __ Always
   2 __ Usually
   3 __ Sometimes
   4 __ Not very often
   5 __ Hardly ever

Q 29 When you don't get assistance from another department or branch, which of the following happens most often?

   1 __ I am told they will help, but they don't show up
   2 __ They try to help, but can't
   3 __ I am told they have other things to do that are more important
   4 __ I am told that they don't have the personnel
   5 __ Other: _____
   _____
   _____
   _____
   (42) _____

Q 30 In general, how good are your communications with people in other departments and branches?

   (43)
   1 __ Very good
   2 __ Good
   3 __ Not too good
   4 __ Poor

Q 31 What do you think should be done to improve communications between you and people at your level in other departments and branches?

   _____
   _____
   _____
   _____
   _____
   _____ (44)

Q 32 Think of those instances in which you have had difficulty obtaining information from people in other organizations. To what degree did each of the following conditions exist?

   a) Others didn't understand what information I needed.

   1 __ This happens a lot
   2 __ This happens some
   3 __ This happens very little   (45)

   b) Others didn't understand why I needed the information.

   1 __ This happens a lot
   2 __ This happens some
   3 __ This happens very little   (46)

   c) Others didn't want to give me the information.

   1 __ This happens a lot
   2 __ This happens some
   3 __ This happens very little   (47)

   d) Others didn't communicate clearly.

   1 __ This happens a lot
   2 __ This happens some
   3 __ This happens very little   (48)

   e) Others didn't provide the information on time.

   1 __ This happens a lot
   2 __ This happens some
   3 __ This happens very little   (49)

   f) Others didn't provide enough information.

   1 __ This happens a lot
   2 __ This happens some
   3 __ This happens very little   (50)

   g) Other: _____
   _____
   _____

   1 __ This happens a lot
   2 __ This happens some
   3 __ This happens very little   (51)

An example of a checklist questionnaire (one page among several)

O P I N I O N P O L L

WHEN YOU PURCHASED YOUR PRESENT HOME, HOW
IMPORTANT WERE EACH OF THE FOLLOWING FAC-
TORS IN YOUR BUYING DECISION?
(check one level of importance for each
factor)

	low	moderate			high
	IMPORTANCE				
1-Degree of security	( )	( )	( )	( )	( )
2-Freedom from maintenance	( )	( )	( )	( )	( )
3-Closeness to work	( )	( )	( )	( )	( )
4-Degree of privacy	( )	( )	( )	( )	( )
5-Extent of recreational facilities	( )	( )	( )	( )	( )
6-Price compared to prior home	( )	( )	( )	( )	( )
7-Equity received from condo-ownership	( )	( )	( )	( )	( )

IF YOU COULD SATISFY ONLY THREE OF THE A-
BOVE FACTORS, WHICH THREE WOULD YOU CHOOSE?
(the numbers below correspond to the numbers preceding each factor above. Please
check the 3 factors you find most important.)

( )1 ( )2 ( )3 ( )4 ( )5 ( )6 ( )7

IF YOU WERE TO MOVE INTO ANOTHER CONDOMI-
NIUM, HOW IMPORTANT WOULD IT BE TO LIVE
REASONABLY CLOSE TO THE FOLLOWING LOCA-
TIONS?

	low	moderate			high
	IMPORTANCE				
1-Work	( )	( )	( )	( )	( )
2-Well stocked supermarket	( )	( )	( )	( )	( )
3-The beach	( )	( )	( )	( )	( )
4-A branch of your bank	( )	( )	( )	( )	( )
5-Facilities to play your pre-ferred sport	( )	( )	( )	( )	( )

TO WHAT EXTENT HAS YOUR PRESENT CONDOMINIUM
HOME SATISFIED THE FOLLOWING LIVING NEEDS?

	low	moderate			high
	SATISFACTION				
1-The security I desire	( )	( )	( )	( )	( )
2-The growth in equity I want	( )	( )	( )	( )	( )
3-The recreation-al facilities I need	( )	( )	( )	( )	( )
4-The price I paid for this home	( )	( )	( )	( )	( )
5-The privacy I desire	( )	( )	( )	( )	( )
6-The distance to my work	( )	( )	( )	( )	( )

PLEASE RATE THE IMPORTANCE OF HAVING AVAIL-
ABLE THE FOLLOWING RECREATIONAL FACILITIES?

	low	moderate			high
	IMPORTANCE				
1-Sauna	( )	( )	( )	( )	( )
2-Rec-Room	( )	( )	( )	( )	( )
3-Swimming pool	( )	( )	( )	( )	( )
4-Gym	( )	( )	( )	( )	( )
5-Tennis courts	( )	( )	( )	( )	( )
6-Jacuzzi	( )	( )	( )	( )	( )
7-Squash, paddle ball courts	( )	( )	( )	( )	( )

IF YOU COULD HAVE ONLY THREE (3) OF THE A-
BOVE RECREATIONAL FACILITIES, WHICH WOULD
YOU CHOOSE? (check the 3 facilities you
would most prefer.)

( )1 ( )2 ( )3 ( )4 ( )5 ( )6 ( )7

IF YOU WERE TO MOVE INTO A NEW CONDOMINIUM
WHERE THE FOLLOWING RECREATIONAL FACILITIES
ARE OFFERED, HOW OFTEN WOULD YOU USE EACH?
(please choose only one period for each facility)

	more than once a week	once a week	hardly ever	never
1-Gym	( )	( )	( )	( )
2-Tennis courts	( )	( )	( )	( )
3-Swimming pool	( )	( )	( )	( )
4-Jacuzzi	( )	( )	( )	( )
5-Squash and/or paddle ball	( )	( )	( )	( )
6-Rec Room	( )	( )	( )	( )
7-Sauna	( )	( )	( )	( )

Important LOWE'S Corporate Relations Survey

Dear Reader:

We want to make our investor relations program as inclusive and as effective as possible. Consequently, we rely on the views and opinions expressed by all recipients of our Annual Reports. You can help by taking a moment or two to complete the following questionaire. No postage is required to return it to us. As a token of our

appreciation for your time, we would like to send you our unique Lowe's Stock Market Calculator, a special slide rule for fast computation of yields, growth rates, p-e ratios, etc. Thank you for your interest and participation.

Robert L. Strickland
Senior Vice President

1. From which of the following groups does your interest in Lowe's stem? (Check more than one if applicable.)
☐ Shareholder   ☐ Financial Press
☐ Security Analyst   ☐ Mutual Fund
☐ Financial Advisor   ☐ Lowe's Employee
☐ Stockbroker   ☐ Other (specify)

2. Are you ☐ male or ☐ female?

3. In which age group would you be listed?
☐ Under 25 years   ☐ 45 to 54 years
☐ 25 to 34 years   ☐ 55 to 64 years
☐ 35 to 44 years   ☐ 65 years and over

4. When did you first become interested in Lowe's from an investment standpoint?
Within the past: ☐ Two to five years
☐ Year   ☐ Over five years
☐ One to two years

5. How did you first become aware of Lowe's? (Check one)
☐ Through my   ☐ Newspaper or
   stockbroker   Magazine Article
☐ Through a Lowe's   ☐ Other (please specify)
   employee
☐ Receiving your
   Annual Report

6. Which section of our 1972 Annual Report did you like best? (Check one)
☐ Chairman's Letter   ☐ Lowe's Sources
☐ President's Report   and Resources
☐ Audited Financial   ☐ Lowe's How
   Statements   We Grow
☐ Graphs and Charts   ☐ 16 year Review
☐ Market Dimensions   ☐ Other
                          (please specify)

7. If not already included on one of our Financial Mailing Lists, please check here if you desire to receive future mailings.
☐ Yes   ☐ No

8. How much of this Annual Report did you read?
☐ Cover to cover   ☐ Only the Highlights
☐ Almost every   ☐ Gave it a quick glance
   page   ☐ Didn't read any
☐ About half

9. My overall judgment of the report was:
☐ Excellent   ☐ Marginal
☐ Good   ☐ Poor
☐ Average   ☐ Unsatisfactory

10. If you are presently a Lowe's shareholder, are you satisfied with your investment?
☐ Satsified   ☐ Moderately
☐ Moderately   dissatisfied
   satisfied   ☐ Dissatisfied
                       ☐ No opinion

11. Based on your knowledge of Lowe's, whether shareholder or not, how would you rate the Company?
☐ Up with the   ☐ About average
   times   ☐ No opinion
☐ Behind the times

12. As a Lowe's shareholder, do you feel your comments, suggestions and inquiries receive appropriate attention?
☐ Yes   ☐ No   ☐ No opinion

13. As a Lowe's shareholder, do you feel you receive sufficient information from the Company on a regular basis to keep you adequately informed of the Company's progress and future plans?
☐ Yes   ☐ No   ☐ Not entirely

14. As a Lowe's shareholder, what is your primary investment objective by investing in Lowe's?
☐ Capital   ☐ A little of both
   appreciation   ☐ No opinion
☐ Dividend income

15. Any other comments?

_____
_____
_____
_____
_____
_____

Again, we thank you for your assistance. Please complete the following so we may send you the Lowe's Stock Market Calculator.

Name_____

Address_____

City   State   Zip Code

Lowe's Corporate Relations Survey. Reprinted by permission.

An example of a combination of cover letter and questionnaire. Note the offer of a gift (incentive) to improve response rate.

The Mail Questionnaire

We have already mentioned some of the advantages and disadvantages of mail questionnaires. They are probably used by more researchers, and certainly are better known to the public, than any of the other survey methods. In order to obtain the best results possible, it is important not only that the questionnaire be well done but also that the letter which accompanies it be well written and courteous.

The Cover Letter.   In a direct mail survey, the quality of the cover letter will strongly influence whether or not the respondent returns a completed questionnaire. A well-written cover letter may very well motivate him to check his answers more carefully, and to return the questionnaire promptly.[4]

A careful study was conducted that attempted to determine how specific characteristics of a cover letter influenced the percentage of questionnaires returned.[5] Four characteristics were tested:

1. The use of a handwritten salutation and signature to make the letter seem personal.

2. A statement designed to impress the prospective respondent with the importance or social utility of the survey.

3. An explanation of how important the prospective respondent is to the study, and the role he will play in the research by responding.

4. An appeal to the prospective respondent to help the researchers.

Sixteen types of letters were sent out, each a different combination of the four factors listed above. The results indicated that making the cover letter seem personal (1 above) was very effective in increasing the responses. Item 3, explaining the importance of the respondent, also caused the number of returns to increase significantly. The other two factors (2 and 4) seemed to have very little effect on the rate of response.

These findings seem to be substantiated by another survey in which a handwritten postscript was added to the cover letter. The postscript, which asked the prospective respondent for help and the early return of the completed questionnaire, increased the response 27 percent over cover letters without the P.S.[6]

There are many reasons why a questionnaire may not be completed and returned, and there is no way to design a survey instrument that will ensure a 100 percent response. The person who receives a questionnaire may have no interest in the topic under discussion; he may be busy; or perhaps his company does not permit him to complete such surveys. These are all understandable reasons for not completing a questionnaire. But why are so many simply discarded? The answer may lie in a poor cover letter: one that is writer-centered, pompous in tone, too demanding, or without an explanation of the survey's purpose. We know that if the recommendations below are followed, the percentage of responses will be good.

1. Keep the cover letter brief. Go over the draft with a blue pencil, striking out every extra word and phrase. The reader is in a hurry and he is busy. State what you want, why you want it, how he will benefit from giving it to you, and then stop. The cover letter should almost never be longer than one page.

2. Show the respondent the importance of his role in achieving the objective of the survey. We all want to be needed, and we like to know that we are making a contribution. Tell the respondent what the survey aims to accomplish, and why it is important. Couple this with the role of the respondent in

---

[4] See also Norman Sigband. "The Cover Letter." *Journal of Marketing*, April 1953.

[5] Arnold S. Linsky. "A Factorial Experiment in Inducing Responses to a Mail Questionnaire," *Sociology and Social Research*, IL (January 1965).

[6] George Frazier and Kermit Bird, "Increasing the Response of a Mail Questionnaire," *Journal of Marketing*, October 1958.

the survey, and you will usually involve him to the extent that he will want to help you.

3. Show the respondent how he will benefit from completing the questionnaire—the "you" attitude. Although at first this may seem almost impossible, it usually can be done after some thought. Explain the situation honestly. Perhaps you are trying to develop an improved delivery or packaging program, which will eventually bring him a better and more salable product. Or you want to improve your use of computers, so as to lower your costs and pass the savings on to him.

4. Inject a personal tone. The research cited earlier demonstrated the value of making the cover letter seem personal. This can be done with a handwritten signature, a handwritten postscript (it may be necessary to simulate this if a large mailing is planned), use of the respondent's name in the salutation and/or body of the letter, and the overall tone of the letter itself. Abandon all hackneyed and obsolete phrases. Give the letter a "conversation across the desk" tone.

5. List a due date for returning the questionnaire. Most of us tend to put things off. If we are asked to do something by a certain date, however, most of us will do it. But we have to be told. The due date should always be given in the cover letter and again in the questionnaire:

> So that we can begin our new, faster delivery service to you as quickly as possible, please return the completed questionnaire no latter than August 3.

6. Where possible, assure the respondent of confidence or anonymity. If you feel that some questionnaires will be discarded because the potential respondents do not wish to divulge confidential information, or because they fear the embarrassment of being identified, take precautions. Sometimes a simple statement will increase returns by 20 percent:

> "You may be sure that all the information you include will be kept completely confidential."

> "Of course we don't want you to sign the questionnaire; we are only interested in your answers."

7. Offer to send the respondent the results of the survey if it won't be too expensive, or won't divulge findings you would prefer to keep confidential. Most respondents are interested in or working in the field with which the study is concerned. If you tell them you will share your new knowledge by sending them a copy of your findings, this may spur them to complete the questionnaire. You can maintain their anonymity by including a postal card, addressed to you, which the respondents may return separately from the questionnaire. Or you can suggest that they "write to the address above anytime after December 3 for a copy of the survey."

These are the major factors that govern responses to questionnaire surveys. There are others, but in the sample letters given below you will notice that most of the principles listed have been included.

Courtesy of The Western Union Telegraph Company

RESEARCH INSTITUTE FOR BUSINESS ECONOMICS
UNIVERSITY OF SOUTHERN CALIFORNIA
GRADUATE SCHOOL OF BUSINESS ADMINISTRATION
UNIVERSITY PARK
LOS ANGELES 90007

                                February 5, 19__

Mr. Robert Baxter, President
Jackson Electronics Corp.
121 S. Elm Street
Los Angeles, Calif. 90007

Dear Mr. Baxter:

You will probably agree with various surveys, including those
conducted by the Harvard Business Review, which point to the
effectiveness of internal company communications as one of the

most significant factors in achieving corporate goals. This, along with the management style of those in leadership positions, are key factors in a company's success.

We have become extremely interested in the interplay between these two factors: Management styles and communication patterns. Are they separate entities or do they work together in some type of harmony?

This survey is part of a major, multi-company project which will attempt to determine correlations between the two, and if changes in one may result in changes in the other.

Because of your position, experience and knowledge, your help is needed in supplying us with data. With the information secured, we feel we can make a contribution which will prove valuable to the internal operations of many firms.

Please respond candidly and thoughtfully to each question. Do not identify yourself in any way; we are interested in your views and opinions only. Of course, all returns will be kept confidential.

Inasmuch as we are under some time constraints, may we ask that you return your completed questionnaire no later than February 28.

Thank you very much.

Sincerely,

Norman B. Sigband

Norman B. Sigband, Ph.D.
Graduate School of Business Administration
University of Southern California

TIME
INCORPORATED
NEW YORK · CHICAGO

TIME & LIFE BUILDING
541 N. FAIRBANKS CT.
CHICAGO, ILLINOIS 60611

Dear TIME Reader:

Please do us a favor.

As I mentioned in my earlier note to you, we feel it is extremely important to ask people like you, familiar with TIME, to help us learn more about our readers and their interests. Your reply -- which will help us form a composite picture -- will, of course, be completely confidential.

Because every answer is important to the reliability of the results of the survey, I hope you will send us your answers in the enclosed stamped reply envelope, today if possible.

And many thanks for your cooperation.

Sincerely,

Henry Luce III
Publisher

HL:bc
Enclosure

Letter to *Time* reader by Henry Luce III. Reprinted by permission from *Time, The Weekly Newsmagazine;* Copyright Time Inc.

<u>DAVIS RESEARCH, INC.</u>
<u>900 FOREST ST.</u>
<u>LOS ANGELES, CALIFORNIA</u>

June 3, 1975

Dear Mr. Reynolds:

May I ask you to do me a favor?

A client has requested our assistance in determining the familiarity of important people in business and industry with particular companies.

We included you in the small, scientifically selected sample to whom the enclosed confidential questionnaire is being mailed. Every answer is important to the accuracy of our survey because the sample includes only a few hundred people. I hope you will take a few moments to fill out the short questionnaire and return it in the enclosed stamped envelope.

Our client, and I, will appreciate your help.

Sincerely,

Ruth E. Martinez

Ruth E. Martinez
President

REM:tr
Enclosures

P.S. The enclosed coupon is to show our appreciation. It may
     brighten the day of a youngster you know.

Motivating the Prospective Respondent. Research directors have found that giving the prospective respondent a "reward" will usually significantly increase the percentage of completed questionnaires returned.[7] A freshly minted quarter or dime, a coupon which may be traded for a free package of the company's product, a ballpoint pen, or a crisp dollar bill ("to be passed on to your favorite charity") are some of the devices used. When using a coin, avoid saying anything like "Here is a quarter for your effort."

Sometimes these attachments to the cover letter can save the researcher a significant amount of money. If he sends out 5000 qustionnaires each of which costs 30¢ (printing, folding, postage, etc.) and receives 400 which have been completed, the cost per completed questionnaire will be $3.75. If, on the other hand, he mails 2000, each of which has a 25¢ enclosure (cost per questionnaire: 30¢ plus 25¢) and receives a response of 550, his cost will drop to $2 including the expense of the coin. Thus these premiums should be considered, but they should always be used with caution. Some prospective respondents may feel that they are unethical. And there is also the danger that the respondent who has accepted the coin or coupon may attempt to answer the questionnaire as he thinks the researcher desires, rather than as he honestly feels.

Documenting the Report

Whenever the researcher cites information that he has secured from another source, he should name the source. Usually this is done in a footnote, although it may be done in the body of the paper.

When to give credit and when not has always been a controversial point. If the statistics and information are common knowledge in the field, you should not bother with a footnote. But if the information is based on some other person's knowledge or research, and is not generally known, reference should be made. If you're not sure whether to give credit or not, then give it. This will avoid any possible misunderstanding.

But the footnote can be used for purposes other than a reference to a source. It can be used effectively to:

1. Cite information relevant to the report but not important enough to appear in the body of the report itself.

2. Cite statistics or data in support of statements made in the body of the report.

3. Cite other points of view.

4. Note differences among the authorities in the field.

5. Offer critical evaluations of major sources used—for example, a comment on the excellence of the maps in a journal article, or on the inaccuracies in a book, etc.

Usually footnotes are found at the bottom of a page and refer to statements

---

[7] Thomas R. Wotruba, "Monetary Inducements and Mail Questionnaire Response," *Journal of Marketing Research,* November 1966. See also D. P. Robin, H. W. Nash, and S. R. Jones, "An Analysis of Monetary Incentives in Mail Questionnaire Studies," *The Journal of Business Communication,* Fall 1973.

made on that page. However, some writers place the footnotes at the end of the chapter, section, or report. This makes typing easier, and also keeps the footnotes in one place for easy reference.

The form of the footnote is a matter of convention and convenience. Some researchers prefer to cite a minimum of information, since further details may be found—if needed—in the bibliography. The basic objectives in documentation are to give proper credit to a source, and to cite enough data so that the reader may find the source if he desires. If the footnote or bibliographic entry does this, it is sufficient. Preferences vary, however, so it is always wise to check with the individual for whom the paper is being written. Frequently a standard form is required.

A variety of abbreviations are used in source documentation. Most of these may be found in style manuals for research papers. Two which are frequently used are *"ibid."* and *"Op. cit."* Ibid., from the Latin *ibidem* meaning "in the same place," indicates that the source is identical to the one preceding. *"Ibid., p. 45"* means that the source is the same as the one preceding except that the page to which reference is made is now 45. *"Op. cit."* refers to a source previously cited but not immediately preceding. It is from the Latin *opere citato* meaning "in the work cited."

Suggested Footnote Forms

Alfred G. Smith, *Communication and Culture* (New York: Holt, Rinehart & Winston, 1966), p. 61.

Joseph S. Moag, "Computers, Artificial Languages, and Linguistic Behavior," *The Journal of Business Communication,* IV, 2 (March 1967), p. 49.

Ibid., p. 50. (This footnote would refer to the one immediately above.)

R. R. Aurner and M. P. Wolf, *Effective Communication in Business* (Cincinnati: South-Western Publishing Company, 1974), p. 107.

Norman B. Sigband, *Effective Report Writing for Business, Industry, and Government* (New York: Harper & Row, 1960), p. 510.

U.S. Department of Commerce, *Our Growing Population* (Washington, D.C.: U. S. Government Printing Office, 1961), p. 4.

R. Alec Mackenzie, *The Time Trap* (New York: American Managemnt Association, 1972), pp. 15–19.

Sigband *op. cit.,* p. 515. (This footnote refers back to the Sigband source listed above except to a different page number.)

Arthur L. Grey, Jr., and John E. Elliot (eds.), *Economic Issues and Policies: Readings in Introductory Economics,* 2nd ed. (New York: Houghton Mifflin Company, 1965), p. 47.

Los Angeles Times, November 6, 1974, Part II, p. 31.

Many people feel that the above footnote samples contain more material than necessary. If the place of publication, publisher's name, and date of publication also appear in the bibliographic entry, why include them in the footnote? Here is an alternative style for footnote entries:

R. Wayne Pace and Robert R. Boren, *The Human Transaction,* pp. 30–8.

R. Gist, *Marketing and Society,* p. 229.

Alfred Rappaport (ed.), *Information for Decision Making,* p. 310.

Suggested Bibliographical Forms

In the bibliography, this is the generally accepted style. Note that authors' last names are given first.

Aurner, R. R., and M. P. Wolf. *Effective Communication in Business.* Cincinnati: South-Western Publishing Company, 1974.

Grey, Arthur L., Jr., and John E. Elliot (eds.). *Economic Issues and Policies: Readings in Introductory Economics.* Second edition. New York: Houghton Mifflin Company, 1965.

McLaughlin, T. J., *et al.* (or McLaughlin, T. J., and others). *Communication.* Columbus, Ohio: Charles E. Merrill Books, Inc., 1964.

Moag, Joseph S. "Computers, Artificial Languages, and Linguistic Behavior," *The Journal of Business Communication,* IV, 2 (March 1967), 47–52.

Sigband, Norman B. *Effective Report Writing for Business, Industry, and Government.* New York: Harper & Row, 1960.

Smith, Alfred G. *Communication and Culture.* New York: Holt, Rinehart & Winston, 1966.

U.S. Department of Commerce. *Our Growing Population.* Washington, D.C.: U.S. Government Printing Office, 1961.

Questions for Study

I. Answer the following questions briefly.

1. Define the following terms as concisely as possible.

Sampling	Reliability
Universe	Random sample

2. Present a very brief paper or report on the sampling techniques used by the U.S. Census Bureau. Cite your sources of information.

3. Visit the research division of an advertising agency and determine what types of primary research it uses to secure information on consumer buying habits. Present your findings in a brief report.

4. Visit an opinion research agency and determine what types of primary research it uses to secure information on voters' political preferences. Present your findings in a brief report.

5. State the type of questionnaire survey you would use, and why, to determine:

    (1) Opinions of a specific economic group on a specific TV program.

    (2) Student opinion on the university's administrative organization.

    (3). Air passenger reaction to baggage handling.

    (4) Corporate officers' opinions of Company Profit-Sharing Programs.

    (5) The opinions of management of a specific firm on the effectiveness of that company's internal communication.

6. Secure a questionnaire and write a critique of it. Discuss:

    (1). The cover letter.

    (2) The format of the questionnaire.

(3) The questions, noting *specific* factors in *specific* questions which can be improved or have been handled very well.

7. Find an advertising agency that has used a premium of some type to motivate individuals to respond to a specific questionnaire. Write a brief report on how effective the questionnaire survey proved to be and your analysis of the results. Attempt to secure a sample of the cover letter and questionnaire and attach them to your report.

8. Using sources other than this text, present a brief report on the reliability of survey results secured from mail questionnaires. Cite sources.

9. Carry through research to explain the basis for reliability of political surveys and polls. Cite sources.

10. Secure an interview schedule (the questionnaire which the interviewer reads from) and then offer your constructive criticism of the questions noting specific factors in specific questions which can be improved or have been stated very well.

II. Offer your constructive criticism of the two cover letters which follow:

1. Dear Mr. _____ :

For some time we have wondered if we could possibly change our delivery schedule to our dealers in the Southern California area from two trips per week to one.

We are aware, of course, that you find a twice-per-week delivery convenient. However, if we can satisfy your needs through a once-per-week call, the savings which we will achieve will be very substantial. These savings can then be passed on to you and our other dealers.

However, we don't wish to influence you one way or another with our comments. Won't you please complete the enclosed questionnaire and return it before January 4 in the stamped envelope enclosed.

2. Dear Mrs. _____ :

There are cake mixes with all the ingredients and some with half the ingredients; there are mixes that require that you only open the box and pour, and abracadabra, the cake is almost done. And there are others which require mixing, stirring, rolling, and folding.

We wonder what your preferences are and we hope you will share your opinions with us. Of course our objective is to bring you Tasty Cake mixes exactly the way you want them.

The enclosed questionnaire will only take a few minutes of your time to complete and a . . . oh yes, the certificate will be accepted by your food-store manager in exchange for two free packages of Tasty Cake Mix . . . with our compliments, of course.

III. Write the cover letter and the questionnaire for each of the following problems:

1. Assume you are the manager of communications of the Gotz Corporation. In the past two months you have noticed a large number of the company's monthly magazines discarded in the employee area. There are also fewer than the usual number being picked up from the racks provided. Send a cover letter and questionnaire to the home of each employee asking him to complete and return the questionnaire. The questionnaire is designed to secure his feelings and viewpoints on the value of the company magazine. Design both the cover letter and questionnaire.

2. Design a brief questionnaire in which you attempt to secure the opinion of part-time graduate students on Saturday classes. If graduate classes were offered on Saturdays, how many students would enroll for them? Would students enroll in such classes in place of present evening classes, or in addition to them?

3. Send a questionnaire to a selected sample of homeowners in the Bellpark suburban area just outside of Chicago. Attempt to find out if the respondents would be interested in subscribing to a private home protective and patrol service if it were established. The service would cost approximately $50.00 per month. Of course it would be fully licensed by the city. Bellpark homeowners are in the upper-middle and upper economic classes.

4. Your busy travel agency has booked a good many tourist vacation trips to the Far East and Europe in the last five years. You wonder if it would be wise for you to offer a chartered trip this summer to the Near East. Send a questionnaire to a selected sample of your patrons attempting to determine how many would be interested in an inexpensive chartered trip to the Near East, and what month in the summer they would prefer to go.

IV. Complete the assignments which follow:

1. Write a careful criticism of the questionnaire used in the sample formal report in Chapter Nineteen. The questionnaire is on pages 403–11. Include in your evaluation the appropriateness of the questionnaire for its purpose; the logic and clarity of the questions; and the appearance of the questionnaire.

2. Evaluate the questionnaire below, using criteria similar to those listed in Question 1 above.

(The following questionnaire was sent to the graduating students of a large private midwestern university by an airline.)

```
        1. On the average, how many times each semester did you
           return home for visits?  _____


        2. What method of transportation did you usually use?


              _____       _____
              auto         plane


              _____       _____
              bus          rail


        3. What is the approximate distance from campus to your
           home?                        _____ miles


        4. Which mode of transportation would you have preferred
           for such trips?


              _____       _____
              auto         plane


              _____       _____
              bus          rail
```

5. Were it available, what would your reaction be to buying a booklet entitling you to four round trips in a semester for the price of three?

_____
very interested

_____
somewhat interested

_____
not interested

6. Were it available, what would your reaction be to buying a booklet entitling you to six round trips in an academic year for the price of five?

_____
very interested

_____
somewhat interested

_____
not interested

3. Evaluate the following cover letter and questionnaire. Be specific and use the criteria noted in the chapter and in Question 1 above.

Company Name
Company Address
City and State

Attn: Mr.

Dear Mr.

One of the most active lines of communication in corporations today is the grapevine, through its medium, the rumor. The problem with this informal communications network is that most often its information is inaccurate and causes uneasiness and feelings of insecurity among employees.

I am an advanced graduate student at the University of Southern California. In partial fulfillment of a course in communications, I have chosen to study the grapevine and rumor, mainly through contacting corporations directly. It is my objective to find out how companies look at this area of communications and their policies for dealing with it.

A lack of similar research material in this area recently has prompted me to contact you. I need your help, and would be very much obliged to you if you could find an opportunity to complete the enclosed questionnaire within the next ten days. A stamped, self-addressed envelope is included for your convenience.

I would like to assure you that this questionnaire is completely anonymous; please do not sign it. All the information you supply will be kept in the strictest confidence and will not be used in connection with your company's name.

I would appreciate your assistance very much.

Yours very truly,

George M. Carrick

George M. Carrick

A QUESTIONNAIRE CONCERNING CORPORATE
GRAPEVINES AND RUMORS

PLEASE COMPLETE AND RETURN BY TUESDAY,
DECEMBER 19, 19___

Note: The whole informal communications network in a company is known as the grapevine, and rumor is the speculative, unwise, or untrue message it carries.

1. Have you ever had a study done within your company to examine the presence and effects of grapevines and their rumors?

Yes ___ No ___

If yes, (a) Who did it?
        (b) How was it done?

2. With grapevines, do you attempt to:

Eliminate them completely? _____
Integrate their interests with those
of your company? _____
Let them operate at will? _____

3. Are rumors a problem in your company as a barrier to efficient operations?

Yes ___ No ___

4. Do you have any formal method for uncovering rumors and recording them?

Yes ___ No ___

If yes, please explain: _____

_____

5. Do you instruct or discuss with your supervisory personnel the dynamics of rumor and what should be done to handle it?

Yes ____ No ____

If yes, please explain: _____

_____

6. Do you try to stop

All rumors? _____
Just potentially injurious rumors? _____
None of the rumors? _____

7. What steps does your company take to prevent harmful rumors? Please explain.

(a) Through top management _____

_____

(b) Through staff employees _____

_____

(c) Through line employees _____

_____

8. What subjects do the rumors in your company seem to emphasize? Please rank in apparent descending order of importance from 1 through 9:

Union relations . . . . _____
Lay-offs . . . . _____
Pay scales . . . . _____
Processes that are designated "secret"
    or "confidential" . . . . _____
Feelings about supervisors . . . . _____
Employee transfers within company . . . . . . _____
Fringe benefits . . . . _____
Working conditions . . . . _____
Other (please specify) . . . . _____

9. Does your company have a formal procedure for dealing with rumors?

Yes ____ No ____

10. Please indicate if your company utilizes any of the following techniques for dealing with rumors:

Yes No

(a) Positive presentation of fact upon fact about the content of the rumor to all employees ____ ____

(b) Providing those whom you regard as key communicators of rumors with the true facts about the rumor ____ ____

(c) Confronting the source of the rumor
early and getting an explanation   ___ ___

(d) Requesting the help of the union   ___ ___

(e) Other (please specify)   ___ ___

11. Please indicate if your company attempts to halt
rumors from starting by practicing the following:

                                                 Yes   No

(a) Guarding against idleness and monotony
among employees   ___ ___

(b) Developing faith among employees in the
credibility and source of management's
communications   ___ ___

(c) Making rumors a topic for discussion
in supervisory training programs   ___ ___

(d) Keeping all channels of communication
open to employees for questions   ___ ___

(e) Encouraging free communication between
subordinate and superior about company
operations   ___ ___

(f) Providing supervisory personnel with
up-to-date information about the
company's future plans   ___ ___

(g) Keeping the employee who is to be
promoted, demoted, or transferred
up-to-date on the latest plans the
company has for him in the near
future   ___ ___

(h) Other (please specify)   ___ ___

Thank you very much for your time and effort in completing
this questionnaire. You may be assured that your answers and
any comments you may have added will be kept in the strictest
confidence, and in no way used with reference to your company.

V. Unscramble the following and enter footnotes for each in the order given.

1. "What's Happened to Employee Commitment?" *Personnel Journal,* pp. 132–33, February 1974, Vol. 53, No. 2, N. B. Sigband.

2. William C. Brown Company Publishers, G. M. Goldhaber, Dubuque, Iowa, 1974. *Organizational Communication,* pp. 53–5.

3. Wadsworth Publishing Company, Inc., Belmont, California, 4th Edition, *Business Communications,* W. C. Himstreet and W. M. Baty, 1973, p. 117.

4. Yale University Press, *Communication and Persuasion,* Carl I. Hovland, *et. al.,* New Haven, Connecticut, p. 105, 1953.

5. Identical reference as #2 above.

6. *The Human Transaction,* R. W. Pace and R. R. Boren, p. 73, Scott, Foresman and Company, 1973, Glenview, Illinois.

VI. Unscramble the following and enter footnotes for each in the order given.

1. Gary A. Steiner, Harcourt, Brace and World, Inc., 1964, New York, Bernard Berelson, p. 205, *Human Behavior.*

2. John W. Riley, Jr., (ed.), New York, 1963, page 150, John Wiley and Sons, Inc., *The Corporation and Its Publics: Essays on the Corporate Image.*

3. Theodore Leavitt, *Harvard Business Review,* July-August 1974, "The Managerial Merry-Go-Round," p. 122.

4. G. E. Myers and M. T. Myers, McGraw-Hill Book Company, *The Dynamics of Human Communication, A Laboratory Approach,* 1973, p. 32.

5. Vol. 16, No. 2, *Academy of Management Journal,* June 1973, M. H. Brenner and N. B. Sigband, "Organizational Communication—An Analysis Based On Empirical Data," p. 323.

6. Same reference as footnote 5.

7. *Elements of Interpersonal Communication,* J. W. Keltner, Belmont, California, 1973, Wadsworth Publishing Company, Inc., pp. 61-3.

8. Same reference as footnote 5 except p. 325.

VII. Make a bibliographic listing for all items in VI above.

Chapter Seventeen

Reports and the Decision-Making Process

Directions of Flow
Eliminating Unnecessary Reports
What to Report
The Discipline of Writing a Report
The Final Paper
Strategy of Presentation

Managers at all levels are required to make decisions. Sometimes these decisions are simple, such as a decision to hire a part-time clerk to assist in the office, or to ship merchandise via rail instead of truck. At other times a decision may involve closing down one of the company's plants and throwing 1400 people out of work, or acquiring a firm with annual sales of 12 million dollars. These decisions, major or minor, simple or complex, near-term or long-range, are arrived at after all the necessary information has been reviewed and evaluated.

The information is given to the decision maker through some form of report. The report may be written or oral, long or short, a hefty computer print-out, or a combination of several types.

Whatever its length, the report must be complete and accurate. All necessary facets of the problem or situation must be presented; all conclusions must be carefully drawn; and all recommendations must be thoroughly substantiated.

Basically, a report should be a factual, objective presentation of information. Some reports also interpret and evaluate the information given. And some not only present and interpret information, but are also persuasive in tone. However, when the purpose is other than the objective presentation of data, that fact should be stated clearly.

Most reports are part of the decision-making process. Even the short personnel status information report, issued each Monday, will eventually play a role in the quarterly action (decision) of the vice-president of personnel. The manager must insist that all reports submitted to him—written or oral, long or short—be as complete, clear, and accurate as possible. His future, that of his associates, and not infrequently that of the company, are dependent on the decisions he makes. And his decisions are dependent on the reports he receives.

Directions of Flow

A variety of reports move up to the manager. Some deal with special problems. Others are turned in by each department head at periodic intervals. The periodic reports are frequently in writing, but they may also be oral, as in an interview or a conference. The manager also receives data through informal communication: while waiting in the lunch line; in a casual chat while walking down the corridor; from the attitudes reflected by various persons in conversations and at meetings. In addition, today's manager receives data reports from the computer: sales volume, personnel turnover, inventory levels, production quantities, and a dozen other facts concerning an organization's activities. These data, when properly interpreted and evaluated, are of enormous help to the decision maker.

Reports also travel down, bringing information to every member of an organization. The data contained in these reports help guide employees and give further direction to continuing activities.[1]

And for each department or division to function most efficiently, reports should travel laterally. Certainly it helps the sales manager if he is aware of the status of production, the problems of personnel, and the plans of marketing. However, this lateral communication operates rather haphazardly in most companies. Many department heads *must* send information up because their superiors require it. The manager *must* send information down if his department is to function efficiently. But he is often too busy (or thinks he is too busy) to communicate laterally. Furthermore, his interest in other departments is usually minimal, unless something arises unexpectedly that forces him to consult with another department head. For these reasons, lateral communication does not always take place effectively.

Eliminating Unnecessary Reports

Before the astute manager begins to evaluate the quality of his reports and perhaps introduce some changes in procedure, he should first determine which reports are necessary. Most of them are vital. Industry, science, and government could not exist if they did not have competent reporting procedures.

But it often happens that too many reports are written by too many people on too many occasions. These may serve no purpose except to slow communication and decision-making in an organization. Perhaps each report was initiated by someone for a specific purpose that no longer exists; yet they are still being prepared, typed, and distributed on the first of each month.

Reports usually take careful thought, extensive research, and hours of writing time. When they are written about things that aren't very important and filed without being read, the loss in time, effort, and money is enormous.

If the manager examines the report-writing procedures in his firm, he will often find that some reports are written (and read) almost as a matter of habit.

---

[1] See P. Drucker, "What Communication Means," in the Readings, for comments on "downward communication."

For years Joe Martin, in Employee Relations, has submitted a monthly report on the participation of company personnel in social, athletic, and educational activities sponsored by the firm. It is filled with statistics, has beautiful color charts, and even contains photographs now and then. And some department chiefs are always interested to learn how many of their personnel are participating. But others have no interest in it. In fact, the report is probably not needed by most of the people to whom it is directed. But if it were compiled quarterly or even semiannually, and its distribution more carefully controlled, it might serve a valuable purpose.

Then there is the quarterly report on Fire Safety which was begun in 1959. It covers exits, the number of hand fire extinguishers, the condition of all wooden doors, and the status of the manual alarm system. The original report was requested by the city fire department following a disastrous fire in a company 40 miles away. Since that date, however, the fire department has conducted its own safety inspection of the premises every six months; iron fire doors have been installed throughout the building; the plant has an automatic alarm and sprinkler system; and the compilation of the report makes no sense whatsoever. But it keeps someone busy. It also wastes a lot of money.

Let's observe the birth, childhood, and adolescence of an unnecessary report. Initially, the executive vice-president feels that a report comparing the sales of the firm's product and changes in consumer income would be wise. Merkle is asked to prepare it. He does a good job and sends copies to the president and the three senior vice-presidents. A week later, four vice-presidents ask to receive copies. Two of them can use the report; the other two simply want their names on the distribution list.

Merkle receives several compliments. In an effort to build his own little empire in this area, he adds to the distribution list the out-of-state vice-presidents plus the board of directors. For good measure, he also adds the names of the senior people in the international division.

When the executive vice-president made his request of Merkle, he thought two monthly issues would tell him whether any correlations existed between sales and consumer income. The second issue of the report had a spiral binder and was distributed to 12 officers. The third month's copy came in three colors, with five foldouts, three supplements, and an appendix with a dizzying array of tables, charts, and pictograms.

The typical unnecessary report had now been spawned, had matured, and would probably enjoy a life span lasting until Merkle's retirement from the firm 14 years hence! Fantasy? Hardly. Perhaps enlarged a little, but not invented. The amount of time, money, and effort spent on needless reports in industry today is enormous.

Report Control

The management of every company must place "report control" high on its list of cost-saving exercises. Report requirements, including those from the computer, should be reviewed periodically. In this way some reports can be eliminated, others combined, and, where necessary, new ones initiated.

Many firms find that an efficient procedure is to conduct a report inventory each year. Reports which are necessary are continued; others dropped. Eliminating an ongoing report is obviously difficult unless the support of top management is secured, which means that the person responsible for report control must possess adequate authority. Some people in the organization are going to be unhappy when their reports are eliminated or incorporated into existing ones. Part of their work responsibility has been dropped, and they are likely to feel that their importance has been lessened. However, once an inventory policy is announced, supported, and carried through for two or three years, the task becomes routine, and—more important—valuable to the firm.

What to Report

A question that frequently arises is, "What does management want in reports?" A study was made at Westinghouse in an effort to find some answers to this question. Here is an excerpt from the article describing the study.[2]

When a manager reads a report, he looks for pertinent facts and competent opinions that will aid him in decision making. He wants to know right away whether he should read the report, route it, or skip it.

To determine this, he wants answers fast to some or all of the following questions:

What's the report about and who wrote it?

What does it contribute?

What are its conclusions and recommendations?

What are their importance and significance?

What's the implication to the Company?

What actions are suggested?

Short range? Long range?

By whom? When? How?

The manager wants this information in brief, concise, and meaningful statements. He wants it at the beginning of the report and all in one piece.

For example, if a summary is to convey information efficiently, it should contain three kinds of facts:

1. What the report is about;
2. The significance and implications of the work: and
3. The action called for.

To give an intelligent idea of what the report is about, first of all the problem must be defined, then the objectives of the project set forth. Next, the reasons for doing the work must be given. Following this should come the conclusions. And finally, the recommendations.

Such summaries are informative and useful, and should be placed at the beginning of the report.

The kind of information a manager wants in a report is determined by his management responsibilities, but how he wants this information presented is determined largely by his reading habits. This study indicates that management report reading habits are surprisingly similar. Every manager interviewed said he read the summary or abstract; a bare majority said they read the introduction and background

[2] From "What to Report" by Richard W. Dodge from *Westinghouse Engineer,* July-September 1962, Westinghouse Electric Corporation. Reprinted by permission.

Type of Report	Purpose	Who Writes It?	Who Reads It? (Distribution)	Importance to Reader				Action Taken
				Vital	Some	Little	None	
Monthly Sales Report (Computer printout attached)	To present statistical data and make comments on sales volume, sales trends, market segmentation, and related items	Sales Manager	President	✓				Report Continued
			Vice Pres. (East)	✓				
			Vice Pres. (West)	✓				
			Production Mgr.		✓			
			Personnel Mgr.		✓			
			Advertising Mgr.		✓			
			Credit Mgr.		✓			
			Transportation Mgr.			✓		
Monthly Personnel Report (Computer printout attached	To present statistical data and make comments on personnel training activities, fringe benefits, industrial relations, and recruitment	Personnel Manager	President	✓				Report Continued
			Vice Pres. (East)	✓				
			Vice Pres. (West)	✓				
			Production Mgr.		✓			
			Sales Mgr.		✓			
			Advertising Mgr.		✓			
			Credit Mgr.			✓		
			Transportation Mgr.			✓		
Monthly Safety Report	To report on plant fire equipment	Plant Manager	President		✓			Incorporate into Personnel Managers Report
			Vice Pres. (East)				✓	
			Vice Pres. (West)				✓	
			Production Mgr.	✓				
			Sales Mgr.				✓	
			Advertising Mgr.				✓	
			Credit Mgr.				✓	
			Transportation Mgr.				✓	
Fire Safety Report	To report number of plant accidents and causes	Head maintenance man	President		✓			Eliminate (city inspections held monthly)
			Vice Pres. (East)				✓	
			Vice Pres. (West)				✓	
			Production Mgr.		✓			
			Sales Mgr.				✓	
			Advertising Mgr.				✓	
			Credit Mgr.				✓	
			Transportation Mgr.				✓	

sections as well as the conclusions and recommendations; only a few managers read the body of the report or the appendix material. . . .

To the report writer, this can mean but one thing: If a report is to convey useful information efficiently, the structure must fit the manager's reading habits.

This same study indicates that several conferences should be held while the report is being written—from the initial step of problem designation to the stage of the final draft. The first conference should define the problem and the project. At this point the report writer learns just what he is to do, what kind of report is desired, and how his work relates to the decisions to be made.

A second conference should be held after the research and investigation have been completed. At this time the report writer can discuss with the manager the findings, their implications, and the evidence discovered. The manager, on the basis of his greater experience and his overall view of company activities, can suggest further investigation or additional areas to be surveyed. He may also suggest what areas should be emphasized in the report, the order of presentation, and methods of presentation.

In the third conference, the "final" outline should be reviewed. If changes in the organizational structure are needed, this is the time to make them—*before* the report is written.

And a fourth meeting should take place after the report is written. At this time the manager may suggest a distribution list, the strategy of presentation, and minor changes.

The Discipline of Writing a Report

Long or short, simple or complex, most reports follow a basic pattern. Some of the steps may be touched lightly in very short reports or even skipped, but the order is common to all. Almost anyone can write an excellent report if he will (1) simply observe the communication rules of clarity, conciseness, completeness, and accuracy discussed earlier, and (2) follow the logical series of steps given below:

Define the problem clearly and accurately
Secure a clear understanding of the purpose of the report
Identify the reader
Limit the topic
Draw up a tentative outline for the report
Define the depth or scope of the report segments
Formulate a research plan
Carry through research
   From primary sources
   From secondary sources
Tabulate the quantitative data gathered
Evaluate all material secured
Edit the data
Interpret the data

Complete a detailed outline for the report
Write a rough draft
Insert tables, graphs, visuals
Draw up supplements
Edit the rough draft
Write the final copy
Plan the presentation strategy

This plan should be carried out for every report; actually many of these steps become almost mechanical for the efficient writer. And he may even skip a few if the nature of the report or the situation permits.

Because these steps are basic to report writing, they will be discussed in detail. Several points are covered below, and the remainder will be examined in the chapters which follow.

Define the Problem

This is perhaps the most important step in researching and writing a report. It is obvious that if we identify a symptom as the problem, all the work afterward will in large measure be wasted.

Defining a problem quickly and accurately is an art that requires careful thought, critical evaluation, and mature imagination. It is not unusual for a manager to look hastily at a situation and indicate that AB is the problem, when in fact it is only a contributing factor.

For example, Manager Brickworth notes that production has dropped in Department 41. His immediate reaction to this might be to set up three additional punch presses in that department to increase production. Or to assign 12 more men to increase production. Or to increase the piece rate paid to motivate the workers to higher production. But the drop in production is not due to a shortage of punch presses or men or to inadequate pay. In this particular instance, production has declined because none of the presses is equipped with safety devices, and as a result an operator suffered a serious hand injury two months ago. All operators now work more slowly and carefully.

Once this is recognized as the problem—and solved—production will increase.

It is not always easy to identify the problem. Perhaps the manager simply knows that something is wrong: production is down, or morale is low, or sales have plummeted, or deliveries to customers are late, or pilferage has skyrocketed. But he doesn't know why. Perhaps his first inclination is to stop you in the corridor, request that you look into it, and say, "Let me have a report on the situation by Wednesday."

Obviously, the reason the manager hasn't told you precisely what problem to work on is that he doesn't know himself! All he knows is that something is wrong. And if the report writer asks him too insistently "What's the problem?" the manager may very well reply, "You're running that department; you tell *me!*" or "Forget it; I'll do it myself!"

The report writer, therefore, must often use all his tact, sensitivity, and knowledge in his effort to identify the problem. For if he does not identify it, and produces a report that deals only with symptoms, he will be the one to pay for the error.

That is why it is well for the researcher-report writer to confer with the manager before beginning his research and investigation.

Understand the Purpose

Not infrequently in business, science, or government a report will be assigned, worked on, written, and submitted—but prove unsatisfactory. The manager may very well read it and then confront the writer with, "But this isn't what I wanted at all! I wanted an *analysis* of the potential sales of this product in our Western Division, and you've given me a *comparison* of its present sales with a competing product!"

Who is at fault? The report writer? The manager who made the assignment? Both?

Actually it makes little difference whose fault it is. But we do know that money has been spent, time wasted, tempers ruffled, and the necessary job not accomplished. Had the *purpose* of the report been clearly established in the mind of the manager, and thoroughly understood by the writer, the controversy probably would not have arisen.

How, then, can the report writer and the manager be sure they both agree on the purpose of the report? Perhaps the best way is to use the same solution that is recommended above in "Defining the Problem": discussion with the manager or executive who requested the report. Once he and the report writer agree whether the purpose of the report is *informational, analytical, comparative, persuasive* (or a combination), the next step may be taken.

Identify the Reader

It is important to know for whom you are writing. On internal reports, this is usually a fairly simple task. The writer knows that the director of sales or the head of engineering will read, analyze, and act on the report; or that the report is for the information of all department heads. Special care must be taken when the report is being prepared by an expert in one area, such as engineering, for reading by a decision maker whose orientation may be finance or marketing. When the report has internal *and* external readership, or several different groups may read the report for somewhat different purposes, then the problem is more complex.

For example, a report may be intended specifically for the company's department heads, but it could also be read by the board of directors for information purposes. Or, to take an extreme example, the annual report is addressed to the stockholders, but it may be carefully read by employees, prospective investors, financial analysts, creditors, bankers, government regulatory officers, educators, investment counselors, trust and estate officers, and others.

Fortunately, the potential readers of the report are usually not too difficult to identify. Then the task becomes one of selecting the correct language level and determining the relative amounts of technical, informative, or persuasive discussion to be included.

Limit the Topic

Not infrequently a report comes along that seems to cover a tremendous topic area. But because the coverage is very wide, the depth of the examination is shallow and inadequate. This can be avoided with a little forethought. A careful discussion of the problem, the purpose, and the reader will limit the report to its proper area.

The manager who breezily asks for an "information report on the potential for a retail outlet in Centerville" may get a 90-page document which covers 18 separate areas from "population density" to "local style patterns." And it may have cost $3000 in research, writing, and reproduction time. It is true that the manager *does* want information on Centerville as a retail outlet, but he doesn't want or need data in 18 different areas. Had the topic been limited to "economic and population factors in Centerville," the report writer would not have expended time and effort on sources of raw materials, market factors, and the tax structure, and the manager would have received what he wanted.

Here we can see how vital it is to have a specific idea of the purpose of the report. If it is made clear that the purpose is to determine the income level, buying potential, present population, projected population growth, population age levels, and related factors, then perforce, the topic is limited to "Economic and Population Factors in Centerville." Social, educational, and cultural factors are ruled out, as are evaluations of Centerville's industries, transportation facilities, and tax structure. It is possible that information in these areas has already been secured or is not necessary.

Topics can be limited or narrowed by using various devices:

Limit them in time (Instead of a "Twentieth-Century Overview," the topic can be narrowed to "The Post-World War II Period.")
Limit them geographically (Instead of "An Analysis of the Rail System of the Eastern Seaboard," the topic can be narrowed to "An Analysis of the Rail System of New York State.")
Limit them by their sphere of activity within society (cultural, educational, social, political, etc.)
Limit them by area of industrial activity (marketing, production, supervision, research, etc.)

Here is an example of successive steps in limiting a topic:

An Analysis of the Automobile

An analysis of the American automobile (limited geographically)
An analysis of the sales of the American auto in New York City (limited by area of industrial activity and geographically)
An analysis of the sales of the Mustang in New York City, 1973–74 (limited by area of industrial activity, in time, and geographically)
An analysis of the social influences which motivated consumer purchase of the 1976 Mustang in Ann Arbor, Michigan, as compared with New York City (limited by all four devices)

Of course the report writer should not narrow a topic to the point where finding information becomes extremely difficult, frustrating, and discouraging.

Draw Up a Tentative Outline

The report writer has defined his problem, clarified the purpose of the report, identified his readers, and limited his topic to its proper area. Now he is ready to outline the report.

What areas should he investigate? Down what avenues should he venture?

Let's say the manager has requested a report on "the decline in sales of our Number 51 Yard-Master Power Mower." The report writer may conjecture that he should have information on:

Competitors' sales of mowers similar to the #51 Mower
Imports of piece parts for #51 Mower
Labor supply
Market acceptance of #51 Mower
Safety record of #51 Mower
Methods for handling mowing problems
Weather conditions
Pricing
Advertising and sales promotion
Servicing of #51 Mower
Reliability of #51 Mower
Production and assembly level analysis of #51 Mower
Shipping and warehousing analysis of #51 Mower
Dealer reaction and acceptance of #51 Mower

These points, when arranged into a logical order, will form a tentative outline. But they call for more thought.

Again, the best method is for the writer to talk with the manager who requested the report. He may say, "There is little point in securing information on production, assembly, shipping, and warehousing because we've checked those areas out and our data indicate the problem isn't there. In addition, we are getting all the imported piece parts we need, so don't bother with that either. However, I would suggest that you move ahead with all the rest, and you may wish to look at our export sales also."

All right. That gives us our outline. But how much does the reader want to know about each of the points in it? After all, one could write a whole book on some of them.

Establish the Depth or Scope

We don't want to do too much or too little. If our research of pricing is detailed and deep, but only an overview is needed, we will be wasting time and effort. If our examination of competition is superficial when it should have been penetrating, we will have other problems.

For example, let's take the topic noted earlier:

An analysis of the social influences which motivated consumer purchase of the 1976 Mustang in Ann Arbor, Michigan, as compared with New York City.

It would be possible to carry through a most elaborate series of market studies of consumer motivation. Thousands of dollars could be spent on interviews and questionnaire studies; we could examine the influences of status, race, and occupation on the purchase of a Mustang. But if this were not necessary, it would obviously be unwise.

Let us examine another topic, such as the availability of the labor force to support our new plant in Midvale. We could analyze the labor market in the following depth:

OUTLINE I

I. Availability of Labor
   A. Male
      Administrative
      Production
      Skilled
      Professional
      Technical
      Research
   B. Female
      Production
      Secretarial
      Stenogrphic
      Professional

II. Wage Rates
   A. Administrative
   B. Production
   C. Skilled
   D. Professional
   E. Technical
   F. Research
   G. Secretarial
   H. Stenographic

III. Labor-Management History
   A. Certified unions
   B. Strike history
   C. Arbitration results
   D. Potential problems

IV. Housing Availability
   A. Rental
   B. Home purchases
   C. Financing

V. Educational Facilities
   A. Public
      Elementary
      Secondary

Collegiate
B. Private
Elementary
Secondary
Collegiate

However, our report may not demand such depth. If the following plan is adequate, it should be our choice:

OUTLINE II

I. Availability of Labor
  A. Male
    Administrative
    Production
    Skilled
  B. Female
    Production
    Secretarial

II. Wage Rates
  A. Administrative
  B. Production
  C. Secretarial

III. Labor-Management History
  A. Strike history
  B. Potential problems

IV. Housing Availability
  A. Rental
  B. Home purchases

Our next step is to plan our research.

Formulate a Research Design and Hypothesis

Here again care must be taken. It would be easy to collect a truckload of material. But it is pointless to send out thousands of questionnaires, hold dozens of interviews, examine hundreds of company documents, and evaluate the contents of scores of articles, bulletins, reports, and pamphlets, if such effort is not required. The question to ask is, "What research design will best serve our needs, and at the same time conserve our time and funds? How can we secure the data we need with the least amount of time, money, and effort?"

We may decide, in a particular case, that our research design should include:

I. A search of company records

II. An evaluation of secondary sources

Magazines
Journals
Newspapers

III. A check of government publications
Technical reports
Translations

IV. A series of 20 interviews with company production managers

After we get into the research we may have to modify our design. Perhaps the material in the journals doesn't fill our needs, and more emphasis must be placed on interviews; or perhaps the findings presented in the government reports are so definitive, complete, and up-to-date that there is no need for a questionnaire or interview survey. But we can't be sure until we begin to use the research materials and evaluate their adequacy.

To help give direction to his research, the investigator will usually formulate a *hypothesis*. A hypothesis is a statement which may be proved or disproved as a result of the research findings. For example, we may wonder if premiums will increase the sales of our Sunshine Cake Mix by 10 percent per month as measured against monthly sales last year. Our hypothesis might then be: *Sales of Sunshine Cake Mix will rise 10 percent during 197_ as compared to 197_ when Kitchen Brite premiums are given with the product.* This is a positive hypothesis whose validity the investigator can test through research.

Because of the importance of research to the business manager, two whole chapters have been devoted to that topic. Chapters Fifteen and Sixteen review guides and indexes to information sources as well as techniques of research in primary and secondary sources.

The Final Paper

At this point, let's skip a few stages. We'll assume that the manager has carried through his research, evaluated the data, interpreted his findings, drawn up a final outline, selected his visuals, and written and edited the draft of the report.[3]

Thinking about the final draft, he recognizes that other writers will be competing with him for the attention of the reader. Every busy person has much more material to read and digest than he effectively can. We must try to make our material so attractive, so complete, so interesting, that the reader will turn to it in preference to competing material.

The best way to achieve that goal, of course, is to have something important to say and to say it effectively. But there are some rather mechanical procedures that will do a great deal to increase the attractiveness of a report:

The use of topic heads
The use of white space
The use of supplements
Good binding, format, and reproduction
A strategy of presentation

Topic Heads

Words can be frightening. It is certainly disheartening to open a report and find 14 pages of type staring us in the face—paragraph after paragraph after paragraph. We need help getting into it. We find assimilation ever so much easier when the writer puts a few signposts along the way. "Here," he might say, "is a section on Supervisory Training, and here is another dealing with Management Training, and over here is a third section covering Cost of Training."

When these signposts or topic heads are placed carefully throughout the report, they give the reader an indication of where he is going. They also save him time. Perhaps the executive vice-president wishes to review only the segment on Participants' Evaluation of Training. With topic heads throughout the report, he can find that section easily. And if the report is pulled from the file two years from today, and the reader only wishes data on Cost of Sales Training, he can find it quickly.

Notice, in the two examples that follow, how much easier it is to read the version in B than the version in A.[4]

EXAMPLE A

March 17, 197_

REPORT FOR RECORD

RE: ROAD SIGN DAMAGE STATE HIGHWAY 2
     SPECIAL REQUEST

At 11:45 a.m. on March 14, 197_, Mr. Robert Campbell, Field Superintendent, stated that the highway crews had changed all the signs on Section 33B of Highway 2 on Friday, March 13, 197_. The crews left the area, he said, at approximately 8 p.m.

On Monday, March 16, 197_, the Angeles Crest Highway Division sent a road grader to the area of the damaged signs to do some work on an access road. The operator of the road grader reported that he observed five more highway signs damaged on Highway 2. Campbell said that he had no information regarding adjoining roads with signs damaged; however, the Angeles Crest Division was dispatching a man to the scene to investigate.

---

[3] Suggestions for effective writing may be found in Chapter Four; the use of visuals in Chapter Twenty.

[4] See John Fielden's article, "What Do You Mean I Can't Write?" in the Readings for further suggestions on spotlighting sections of the report.

At approximately 12 p.m. on March 14, 197_, the writer discussed the road sign shooting problem with Mr. Bob Atkins,
Superintendent of the Angeles Crest Division. Atkins advised that the new damage occurred over the past weekend
because he personally inspected the roads in the area after
the crews completed their work at 8 p.m. on Friday,
March 13, 197_, and there was no damage to any of the signs.
Atkins felt that under the circumstances, some type of patrol should be conducted in the area and especially on week-
ends during hunting season. He said that he had been in the
area on many occasions and had observed numerous hunters in
the area.

While discussing the problem, Atkins said that he thought it
would be a good idea to run an article in the American
Rifleman Magazine because he felt that persons subscribing
to that magazine were genuine sportsmen and would be appalled
to hear of such damage and vandalism. It was his feeling that
a well written article from a member of the National Rifle
Association would be well received by the magazine and have
an impact on the magazine's subscribers. The writer advised
Atkins that the matter would be discussed with supervision
in the Special Agents Division and he would be contacted
later regarding his suggestion.

On March 16, 197_, Special Agent John Short was assigned to
patrol the area on Tuesday, Wednesday, and Friday, March 17,
18, and 20, skipping Thursday on which there is a meeting of
the Special Agents Division. Short was instructed to contact Mr. Atkins who agreed to have his senior patrolman meet
Short at the damage location and show Short the areas where
damage is most likely to occur in his opinion.

During the writer's prior conversation with Mr. Robert
Campbell, Field Superintendent, it was decided that more
warning signs should be placed on roads and at intersections
in the Angeles National Forest. Currently, there are very
few signs on this section of Highway 2.

Thomas Mann

THOMAS M. MANN
Supervisor of Criminal Investigations

TMM/bw
12-259*

REPORT FOR RECORD   March 17, 197_

Subject: Road Sign Damage, State Highway 2

Problem:
Damage to road signs on State Highway 2 as a result of rifle
fire.   (March 13 - March 16, 197_)

Background Data:
On March 13, 197_, road crews changed all the signs damaged
by rifle fire on Section 33B of Highway 2.   The crews left
the area at 8 p.m.   These facts were reported to me by Field
Supt. Robert Campbell on March 14, 197_, at 11:45 a.m.

On Monday, March 16, 197_, the operator of a road grader in
the area reported an additional 5 damaged signs on the same
section of Highway 2.

Mr. Bob Atkins, Supt. of the Angeles Crest Division, told me
that he had inspected the road shortly after the work crew
left at 8 p.m. on March 13.   Thus the damage to the 5 signs
noted above must have occurred subsequent to the first incident.

Action Taken:
Special Agent John Short was assigned to patrol the area on
March 17, 18, and 20.   Critical areas for patrol were to be
determined with the assistance of Mr. Atkins.

Action Recommended:
The following recommendations have been made:

1.   Conduct patrols in the area with special attention to
     weekends and in the hunting season.
2.   Request that an article be published in the National
     Rifle Association magazine, American Rifleman, concerned
     with elimination of vandalism as a result of malicious
     firing of rifles at private property.
3.   Place additional warning signs on the roads and at
     intersections in the Angeles National Forest.

                                   Thomas M. Mann
                                   Supervisor of Criminal Investigations

---

White Space

We all know that the appearance of a page is enhanced by using lots of
white space and arranging the material carefully. Yet it is amazing how many
times the pages of a report are solidly typed from top to bottom and side to
side, with narrow margins and heavy, block paragraphs.

Not This   **But This**

   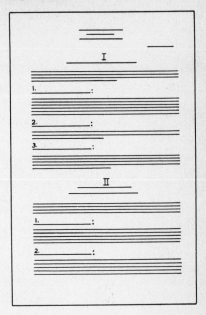

Probably this results from lack of awareness on the secretary's or manager's part. It is well worth fussing a bit over this. Keep your paragraphs short and your margins wide.

Appendixes and Supplements

Some report writers will examine a segment of their material and conclude that though it isn't relevant to the subject at hand, "it's really too good to discard." So it goes into an appendix. Sometimes, conversely, the report writer has important information which he puts into an appendix instead of the body of the report.

Of course, both methods are unwise. If the material isn't of use, discard it. If it supplements the text data and may be of value to the reader, place it in an appendix. If it is vital to the understanding of the report, then put it in the body.

When appendixes and supplements are used, they should be made as easy as possible to refer to. Use color dividers or separators so the reader may turn to the correct supplement easily. A color or number coding system may help.

Bindings, Format, Reproduction

Firms that require ongoing reports have usually found it convenient to use standard title pages and binders. It is often helpful to use one color binder for engineering, another for finance, a third for production, etc.

Most companies of any size have excellent equipment for reproducing reports, as well as mechanical devices for heavy-duty stapling or for placing reports in spiral binders. Once a system is established for reproduction and binding, distribution of reports is made easier as is their handling, storage, and retrieval.

Strategy of Presentation

All too often the report writer spends six weeks gathering information, a week evaluating it, three days writing, and—alas—only five minutes in making his presentation. He carries the report to the executive vice-president's office and quietly leaves it with him or his secretary. Or if he does talk about it to a few people, he doesn't bother to set the stage properly.

Here's how it ought to be done.

When the report—oral or written—is ready to be presented, the writer should secure a block of time for the purpose. Not just anytime, either, but the right time. And it's wise to make sure that the climate is such that the report will receive the attention it deserves.

There is a right time and a right climate for explaining the purpose of the report, what it accomplishes, and what it does not accomplish. The writer should plan the strategy of his presentation with the following considerations in mind:

Who should be present when I submit the report?

What needs to be said or explained when I submit the report?

What visual aids should I utilize at the time the report is submitted?

What advance work is needed, and with whom, before I submit the report?

The one basic principle to remember is that the end of the project is as important as the beginning. Never submit a report that has been requested for a special purpose without planning the strategy behind the presentation.

Questions for Study

I. Complete any of the following problems assigned. You may wish to review the chapter and note key points before working on the assignment(s).

1. "Decision making in the business enterprise—large or small—is almost completely dependent on reports. When those reports are not clear, complete, and accurate, the decisions reached are often faulty."
   Comment on this quotation. Note the words *clear, complete,* and *accurate.*

2. Individuals who have carried through research in the field of communications have indicated that lateral reporting is usually less complete, accurate, and effective than vertical (either up or down) reporting. Can you explain why this is so?

3. How can effective reporting contribute to management control?

4. The production of a clear, useful report is the job not only of the writer, but also of the manager who requests the report. What responsibilities does the manager have toward achieving excellence in the final report?

5. Distinguish between "limiting the topic" and "establishing the depth or scope" of a report. Why is each important?

6. Carry through an informal research project on how major reports are written in a specific firm. How is the assignment made? What steps are followed by the report writer after he receives the assignment, and what is done with the final product?

7. Compare your findings from question 6 with those of another student who examined a different firm. What are the similarities and differences and how do these factors affect operations?

8. Attempt to find a firm that conducts a report inventory on a periodic basis. Examine the method used and then submit a brief memo report on the system used. Keep your description of the procedure brief and to the point.

9. Secure permission to conduct a report inventory in a firm. Report your findings in a brief memo to the individual who arranged for you to carry through the survey.

10. Explain the difference between "problem" and "purpose" in the writing of a report.

11. "Who will be the reader of the report?" is one of the first questions that must be asked by the report writer. Explain why and indicate the specific areas of the report which will be affected by the differences in the readers.

12. Although the corporate annual report is almost invariably addressed to the stockholders, what other reader groups usually analyze this document carefully? What specific problems does this present to the report writer?

13. Limit the areas of the following so they are sufficiently narrow to serve as report topics.
    (1) Personnel Requirements in the Aerospace Industry in the 1975–77 Period
    (2) The U.S. Balance of Payments and American Foreign Policy
    (3) Growth Plans of the Jackson Corporation
    (4) Potential for New Firms in the Space Age
    (5) Corporate Cost of Fringe Benefits at the Jackson Corporation
    (6) Emerging Nations and Their Effect on the GNP of the United States
    (7) Population Boom in Latin America
    (8) Residential Construction and Population Growth
    (9) An Analysis of Employee Attitudes at the Jackson Corporation
    (10) Acquisitions and Mergers, 1970–80

14. Limit the areas of the following so they are sufficiently narrow to serve as report topics.
    (1) Student Participation in University Administration
    (2) Changes in Curriculum in the American University
    (3) The Economy and University Enrollment
    (4) Racial Unrest and Its Economic Implications
    (5) Recent Trends in the Toy Industry
    (6) Foreign Policy and the Near East
    (7) U.S. Economic Policies and the Fluctuations of the British Pound
    (8) Atomic Power: the Fuel of the Future
    (9) The Computer Programmer
    (10) The Computer and Information Storage

II. Complete any of the following problems assigned. You may wish to review the chapter and note key points before working on the assignment(s).

1. List the research design you would use for each of the following situations. Organize your presentation into "Primary and Secondary Research."

   1) Are consumers using the consumer protection information listed on foodstuffs?

   2) What percentage of Southern California stockholders read the corporate annual reports sent to them? What sections are read and to what degree?

   3) What medium of communication has the greatest impact on the food purchasing habits of consumers?

   4) How effective are appraisal interviews between supervisor and worker? (Select a limited number of firms in one industry and define "effective" in terms of goal achievement; establishing objectives; securing understanding; getting feedback, etc.)

   5) Are work problems multiplied because of communication difficulties in a firm having a work force made up of several ethnic groups?

   6) What causes differences in intensity of the grapevine in firms of similar size and offering similar products or services?

III. List a hypothesis for each of the six (or several) of the situations listed in 1 above.

Chapter Eighteen

The Short Report

The Periodic Report
The Progress Report
The Memo Report
The Letter Report
Other Written Media

Most business decisions are based on reports. If reports are to be effective, they should be accurate and precise in the data they present, clear in style, and logical and orderly in organization. A well-thought-out and clearly written report frequently brings favorable action—and focuses attention on the writer.

One young executive told the author of his frustration in suggesting a new product line to several officers in his firm. He said, "I spoke to them about it at meetings, in the corridors, on the golf course, and at lunch. I sent memos and notices, but no one ever acted favorably. One day I carefully organized a recommendation report. I worked on it, off and on, for a week. I supplied substantiating data, included visual aids, had it neatly typed and bound, and forwarded several copies, asking for a decision at the supervisors' meeting scheduled three weeks in the future. You know something? My recommendations received unanimous approval, and the product has done extremely well—and so have I. It's all the result of the report, which was read, analyzed, and evaluated."

That is what a good report always does: it turns the spotlight on the topic and the writer, and frequently gets action. It may start production lines rolling, halt expenditures on TV advertising, or even bring about a merger.

Let's examine the types of reports used most frequently in American companies. Although their purposes may differ, many of the principles of effective reports are found in all.

The Periodic Report

One of the most widely written reports in industry is the periodic report of activities. Bank cashiers prepare daily reports. Factory foremen write weekly reports. Department managers write weekly or monthly reports to their supervisors. Corporations send out annual reports to their stockholders.

Not all periodic reports are written by people. Today the computer print-out may be used as a report. If evaluations, interpretations, or recommendations must accompany the data, a series of covering comments may be attached to the print-out.

Managers commonly receive more than one report at a time. Along with the sales report for a given period may come others from production, credit, accounting, research and development, personnel, advertising, and perhaps other departments. The executive is likely to find that the reports disagree in their recommendations. The credit manager recommends that all open accounts be limited; the sales director says this is just the time to expand credit. The production manager indicates that he finally has six lines running smoothly on the new men's "long-collar style shirts with two-button, barrel cuffs." But marketing research indicates that the shorter, more conservative collar style and French cuffs will make up 90 percent of the market demand this fall. And what's more, the changeover should be made in the next seven days.

Someone has to decide among the conflicting recommendations. And that someone is the executive to whom the reports are directed. Woe unto the writer whose reports are not clearly written or are not firmly supported by statistical data!

Reports are generally composed of certain standard elements: the opening; the various sections, each with an appropriate topic heading; and the signature or initials of the writer at the end.

The report almost invariably begins with a summary of activities for the period covered. This is followed by a fairly detailed discussion of the primary topic (sales and sales volume if sent out by the sales manager; production accomplishments and problems if done by the production manager; numbers of employees, separations, and employee additions if written by the personnel manager).

The primary discussion is supported by facts and figures. These almost always include data for a previous period or periods so that current performance can be compared with past performance. The amount and depth of this information depends on what the company wants. For the monthly sales analysis, some companies will want only data on sales; others will require data on sales personnel, sales advertising, competition, sales problems encountered, and perhaps still other data. In the monthly personnel report, one firm may be satisfied with data covering the present employee level, the number added, the number dismissed, and the number separated. Another firm will want more—perhaps a careful presentation of compensation levels, training, safety, union-management relations, and so on.

Following is an example of a typical periodic report.

HAWTHORNE TOY CORPORATION
Newton, New York

Monthly Sales Report
June, 19__

TO: Robert T. Montgomery, Executive Vice President
FROM: Frank Levin, Sales Manager
DATE: July 1, 19__

Summary
Sales for the month of May have proved to be somewhat heavier than anticipated, and almost 10 percent above those of May last year.

All items in Group II (metal-mechanical) and Group III (packaged games) have sold as expected. Group IV (plastic items) has moved up to a very satisfactory level. Group V (bicycles) has declined.

Sales of all groups for November delivery are up 15 percent as compared to the same period last year.

Sales expenses have risen again this month. This has taken place in spite of new efforts to achieve economies.

Sales personnel and advertising expenditures have remained static.

Sales
Although The Toy Manufacturers Monthly for April indicated that overall toy sales should be expected to rise approximately 7 percent in May over last year's figures, our sales reflect about a 10 percent increase. This may be accounted for by our salesmen's incentive program as well as our introduction of five new items in May.

Group V figures are a cause for concern. Certainly sales in this category should reflect, as they traditionally have, increases in May over April. The reasons for our decline are not clear. However, there may be two important contributing factors:
1. Our higher price to the dealer for our entire bicycle line (as compared to our competitors).
2. Increase in advertising on the part of competitors. Hi-Flyer, for example, has purchased large blocks of TV time.

SALES VOLUME MAY, 19__ (IN DOZENS)

ITEM	MAY 19__	APRIL 19__	MAY (previous year)
GROUP I (misc.)			
A 100	5750	5700	5200
A 101	6500	6400	5800
B 300	9750	9500	8800
B 303	6700	6500	5900
GROUP II			
M 101	3150	3100	2800
M 102	2500	2500	2200
M 103	2300	2100	2000
M 104	2400	2300	2100
M 105	3500	3400	3250
M 106	3000	2850	2750
GROUP III			
G 405	8500	8450	7800
G 407	7500	7300	6500
G 408	7000	7100	6500
G 409	9500	9350	8200
G 410	3500	3400	3100
GROUP IV			
P 600-5	21,000	20,000	23,000
P 610-5	23,500	24,000	26,000
P 620-5	22,500	22,100	25,000
GROUP V (in single units)			
Whippet			
Girls'	8500	9300	9000
Boys'	12,500	14,000	14,500
Hi-Ride			
Girls'	16,000	16,000	16,500
Boys'	19,000	21,000	20,500
Speedsters			
Girls'	12,500	14,000	13,900
Boys'	16,500	17,500	18,500

Advertising Expenditures
According to Bob Carlton, Advertising Manager, expenditures
for magazine and newspaper ads were 5 percent above May of
last year. However, he indicated that we will, for the
first time, use TV spot commercials during the summer
months. An initial expenditure of $45,000 for TV will be
made in two carefully selected areas on the east and west
coasts. Sales will be observed carefully and correlations,
if any, drawn.

Sales Personnel.
The number of personnel, with the exception of trainees, has
remained stable.

SALES PERSONNEL

	MAY 19__	APRIL 19__	MAY (previous year)
Salesmen	40	38	39
Area I	20	20	22
Area II	25	23	23
Area III			
Trainees	6	3	0
Area I	3	0	0
Area II	3	1	0
Area III			

Recommendations
1. Carry through an immediate cost analysis to determine if
   wholesale prices on the Group V line can be cut 10 percent to meet competition.
2. Secure additional savings by using plastic instead of
   rubber handle grips, drop battery powered road light (as
   standard equipment) and apply two (instead of three
   coats) of enamel to the bike frame.
3. Cut all prices in Group III 15 percent when purchases
   are made in gross lots.

Note in the foregoing report that any situation which is somewhat unusual, as compared to the previous month, is explained. This is evident in the section devoted to Group V sales.

In the periodic report given above, the recommendations appear at the end. In the paper which follows, two formats (A and B) are presented: one with various recommendations noted from time to time throughout the body of the report; and the other with all recommendations listed at the end. The method used depends on the complexity of the material, who the reader is, and the company's preferred format.

AMERICAN AUTOMOTIVE ACCESSORIES COMPANY
529 South Madison Avenue
Pasadena, California 91106

MONTHLY SALES REPORT
MARCH, 19__

To: Mr. Douglas Shoemaker, General Manager
From: Harold Palmer, Sales Manager
Date: April 5, 19__

Summary

Sales are up 1.2 percent from last month and 10.7 percent
from the same period of a year ago. Net profits are up a
corresponding amount in spite of added advertising expenditures and increased personnel costs. High unit contribution
margins have enabled us to maintain our net return on sales.

While the overall sales picture looks good, the outlook for
individual product lines varies from "terrible" to "tremendous." We are passing up opportunities with great growth
potential: yet at the same time, we are continuing to carry
some product lines which should have been dropped long ago.

Inventories have taken a significant jump (4.6 percent) from
last month, but this is largely attributable to the change
in accounting procedure. Our monthly inventory turnover
ratio has improved from .70 for March, 1966, to .74 for
March, 1967.

Sales Volume

Sales volume data are presented below. Items with an aster-
isk are discussed in the following section.

	March 1975	February 1975	March 1974	% Change 3/74-3/75
Group One				
*Air Conditioners	102,000	100,000	85,000	20.0
*Heaters	23,000	24,000	37,000	(38.0)
	$125,000	$124,000	$122,000	
Group Two				
Chrome Tailpipe Extensions	22,000	22,000	25,000	(12.0)
Headlamp & Door Trim	20,000	20,000	25,000	(20.0)
Mirrors	21,000	20,000	15,000	40.0
Ski Racks	4,000	4,000	28,000	(50.0)
Miscellaneous	13,000	14,000	10,000	30.0
	$ 80,000	$ 80,000	$103,000	
Group Three				
*Stereo Tape Players	104,000	100,000	50,500	105.9
Radios	83,000	82,000	80,000	3.8
Clocks	15,000	14,000	10,000	50.0
	$202,000	$196,000	$140,500	
Total Dollar Sales	$407,000	$400,000	$365,500	

PRODUCT LINES
I. Air conditioners. Sales forecasts continued to be
    very bright.

    Recommendations:
    1. We should continue our heavy emphasis on this
        line.
    2. Truck "camper" market for air conditioners should
        be investigated

II. Heaters. Sales for auto and truck heaters are showing
     a downward trend. Analysis of past sales records in-
     dicates that this decline has continued for the past
     five years. Automotive industry statistics on cars
     sold without heaters as original equipment point out
     a far greater decline than our own sales drop. As
     automotive "no heater" sales and our heater sales have
     always shown a direct positive correlation--but with a
     three-year lag--we appear to be headed for real
     trouble in this area.

     Our salesmen report repeated inquiry about heaters for
     truck "campers." This appears to be an excellent mar-
     ket.

     Recommendation:
     We should drop standard auto heaters from our sales
     line. To replace this item, we should consider devel-
     oping a heater, or heater conversion unit, for truck
     "campers." Growth potential appears great in this
     field.

III. Ski Racks. Sales have dropped 50 percent this year.
      This decline is due to the heavy competition from the
      new rubber-plastic Hi Snow model. For the foreseeable
      future, we will not be able to manufacture a similar
      item because of our production limitations.

      Recommendation:
      We should drop this product line as soon as possible.

IV. Stereo tape players. Sales increases in this area
     have been fantastic. But--we are merely holding our
     share of the market! This is our big opportunity to
     push American Automotive Accessories into a period of
     rapid and profitable expansion. Let's not pass it up.

     Evidence continues to support the popularity of the
     4-track player over the 8-track player, particularly
     in the secondary equipment market. We should continue
     our policy of specialization on the 4-track models.

Recommendations:

1. In spite of sales gains, we should _increase_ our efforts on this product line. Increased market penetration is important. Innovation, quality, and availability of product should be of prime concern. Continued heavy advertising to let people know what we have to offer is a must.

2. Strong consideration should be given to stocking a tape library as an addition to our product line.

3. Further consideration should be given to _producing_ our own 4-track tapes from marketed stereo "33-1/3's" and 8-track tapes lacking a 4-track line. (Many "garage shop" operators have been finding this a profitable venture.)

ADVERTISING

Our first-quarter increases in advertising expenditures appear to have paid off well in added sales and profits. However, our Accounting Department feels we should cut back advertising "now that we're rolling." I'm strongly opposed to this. Coca-Cola tried cutting back advertising a few years ago--with highly negative results. And what product is better established than Coke?

Recommendation:

We should not only maintain but expand our advertising program.

PERSONNEL

While our sales have increased 10.7 percent from one year ago, our sales personnel staff has increased 250.0 percent for this same period. This situation continues to have me perplexed, but I'm holding off on any staff reduction pending (1) developments in our stereo and air conditioning product line, and (2) the results of our just-completed sales training program.

Recommendation:

Sales personnel strength should be maintained another 90 days. The personnel situation will be re-evaluated at that time.

EXAMPLE B

PRODUCT LINES

I. _Air conditioners_. Sales forecasts continued to be very bright.

II. _Heaters_. Sales for auto and truck heaters are showing a continued downward trend. Analysis of past sales records indicates that this decline has continued for the past five years. Automotive industry statistics on cars sold without heaters as original equipment point out a far greater decline than our sales drop.

As automotive "no heater" sales and our heater sales have always shown a direct positive correlation--<u>but with a three-year lag</u>--we appear to be headed for real trouble in this area.

Our salesmen report repeated inquiry about heaters for truck "campers." This appears to be an excellent market.

III. <u>Ski racks</u>. Sales have dropped 50 percent this year. This decline is due to the heavy competition from the new rubber-plastic Hi-Snow model. For the foreseeable future, we will not be able to manufacture a similar item because of our production limitations.

IV. <u>Stereo tape players</u>. Sales increases in this area have been fantastic. But--we are merely holding our share of the market! This is our big opportunity to push American Automotive Accessories into a period of rapid and profitable expansion. Let's not pass it up.

Evidence continues to support the popularity of the 4-track player over the 8-track player, particularly in the secondary equipment market. We should continue our policy of specialization on the 4-track models.

<u>ADVERTISING</u>
Our first-quarter increases in advertising expenditures appear to have paid off well in added sales and profits. However, our Accounting Department feels we should cut back advertising "now that we're rolling." I'm strongly opposed to this. Coca-Cola tried cutting back advertising a few years ago--with highly negative results. And what product is better established than "Coke"?

<u>PERSONNEL</u>
While our sales have increased 10.7 percent from one year ago, our sales personnel staff has increased 250.0 percent for this same period. This situation continues to have me perplexed, but I'm holding off on any staff reduction pending (1) developments in our stereo and air conditioning product line, and (2) the results of our just-completed sales training program.

<u>Recommendations</u>

1. <u>Air conditioners</u>:
    a. We should continue our heavy emphasis on this line.
    b. Truck "camper" market for air conditioners should be investigated.
2. <u>Heaters</u>:
    We should drop standard auto heaters from our sales line. To replace this item, we should consider developing a heater, or heater conversion unit, for truck "campers." Growth potential appears great in this field.
3. <u>Ski racks</u>:
    We should drop this product line as soon as possible.

4.   <u>Stereo tape players</u>:
   a. In spite of sales gains, we should <u>increase</u> our efforts on this product line. Increased market penetration is important. Innovation, quality, and availability of product should be of prime concern. Continued heavy advertising to let people know what we have to offer is a must.
   b. Strong consideration should be given to stocking a tape library as an addition to our product line.
   c. Further consideration should be given to <u>producing</u> our own 4-track tapes from marketed stereo "33-1/3's" and 8-track tapes lacking a 4-track line. (Many "garage shop" operators have been finding this a profitable venture.)
5.   <u>Advertising</u>:
   We should not only maintain but expand our advertising program.
6.   <u>Personnel</u>:
   Sales personnel strength should be maintained another 90 days. The personnel situation will be re-evaluated at that time.

Use of Forms for Periodic Reports.   In some companies, a standard form has been developed for the periodic report, and all that is necessary is to fill in the blank spaces. This has the obvious advantages of conciseness, the securing of the exact data desired, and a reduction in work for the department head. It also ensures that the various managers reporting, who may be stationed in different cities throughout the country, will send about the same quantity and level of information. Of course, this form may also inhibit discussion and expression of ideas on the part of the writer.

Each firm can develop its own. The form illustrated below is used by a relatively small organization in all its divisions (sales, production, personnel, finance, advertising, and administrative).

LEVERET LAMP CORPORATION
Burbank, California

Monthly Sales Report

_____
Month   Year

Complete all blank spaces.

TO:
FROM:
DATE:

<u>Sales Volume</u>

           Month   Previous   Month
                   Month

           Year   Previous
                        Year

Line AM (in dozens)
   AM 100   —————   —————   —————
   AM 200   —————   —————   —————
   AM 300   —————   —————   —————
   AM 400   —————   —————   —————

Line RT (in dozens)
   RT 100   —————   —————   —————
   RT 200   —————   —————   —————
   RT 300   —————   —————   —————

Miscellaneous Items

—————   —————   —————   —————
—————   —————   —————   —————
—————   —————   —————   —————

	Month	Previous Month	Month
	Year		Previous Year

Sales Volume (in dollars)
   Line AM $————— $————— $—————
   Line RT   —————   —————   —————
   Misc. Sales   —————   —————   —————

Inventory (in dozens)
   AM 100   —————   —————   —————
   AM 200   —————   —————   —————
   AM 300   —————   —————   —————
   AM 400   —————   —————   —————
   RT 100   —————   —————   —————
   RT 200   —————   —————   —————
   RT 300   —————   —————   —————

Miscellaneous Items

—————   —————   —————   —————
—————   —————   —————   —————
—————   —————   —————   —————

Comments and Recommendations _____
_____
_____
_____
_____
_____

                                          ———————————
                                            Signature

Have you completed all blank spaces?

The Progress Report

Some managers have to supervise half a dozen activities simultaneously. A single department may have four men carrying on research within the plant, five others engaged in a project 800 miles away for the government, and four attempting to install a new operation in a customer's plastic division. The manager must know what progress is being made on each assignment, what problems have been encountered, and when the jobs will be completed. Progress reports help the manager to maintain control by informing him as a project progresses.

Progress reports have a further value. The review of progress reports filed on projects in the past assists the manager in planning and working up cost and time estimates for similar operations contemplated for the future. The reports may tell him where problem areas existed, what to avoid, and where to focus attention. Thus they serve as a reference guide.

Every project has a beginning, a work period, and an end. Progress reports conform to this arrangement. There is an initial report, continuing reports, and a terminal statement.

The initial report should cite the background of the project, the need for it, specific goals, and who sponsors it. In addition, it should review the progress made on the assignment in the period covered by the report. Continuing reports merely recount the activities of the period, and the terminal report presents a final summary and analysis.

Most managers prefer progress reports which give them a brief background to the situation, a detailed summary of the period covered, and a statement of the work to be carried through during the next time block. Problems and obstacles encountered are usually noted in some detail, as well as recommendations for solutions.

Like the periodic report, the progress report may also be prepared by filling out a standard form. Where a firm has several teams in the field, each working on a somewhat different project, this method can be valuable, and assures a certain uniformity.

```
                 ROBIN CONSUMER RESEARCH AGENCY
                       Rockefeller Center
                       New York, New York


    Progress Report:  2

    Period Covered:  October 10, 19__ to October 24, 19__
    Date:            October 25, 19__
    Assignment:      Valley Food Centers

    Background and Review
    During the period October 1 to October 10 the entire Canton
    Valley was surveyed to determine the best locations for
    three new food marts.  Traffic surveys were taken and popu-
    lation trends analyzed.  All details and the proposed sites
    are noted in the report on this project dated October 11.
```

<u>Activities for this period</u>
Questionnaire and interview surveys were carried through in
the three areas recommended for new stores.

Details on sample size, survey validity, copies of survey
instruments, and tabulated results are all available in
appendix A for study and analysis.

A recapitulation of the findings indicates the following:

<u>FAMILY INCOME, SIZE, AND LIVING HABITS</u>

Summary of surveys, Oct. 12-19, 19__

	Average income per family	No. of children per family	No. of cars per family
Proposed Site A	$10,000	4.2	.7
Proposed Site B	$12,800	3.2	1.5
Proposed Site C	$18,500	1.5	2

<u>TYPE OF HOUSING</u>

Summary of Surveys, Oct. 12-19, 19__

	Type of Residence	Average No. of Rooms	Average Monthly Rental or Home Value
Proposed Site A	Apt.	4.5	$225.00
Proposed Site B	Apt. or home	5.	$350.00 to $375.00
Proposed Site C	Home	6.	$33,000 to $39,000 $37,000 to $48,000

<u>FAMILY EDUCATIONAL LEVEL AND USE OF LEISURE TIME</u>

Summary of Surveys, Oct. 12-19, 19__

	Educ. Grade Completed (head of house)	Use of Leisure Time				
		Read	TV	Movies	Friends	Sports
Proposed Site A	9.5		✓	✓	✓	✓
Proposed Site B	12.5	✓	✓		✓	
Proposed Site C	14.0	✓			✓	✓

PERCENTAGE EXPENDITURES OF FAMILY INCOME

(Listed in percent of income)

	Resi-dence	Food	Cloth-ing	Medi-cal	Enter-tain-ment	Trans-porta-tion	Misc.
Proposed Site A	20	20	15	15	15	10	5
Proposed Site B	20	25	12	15	12	10	6
Proposed Site C	25	16	18	15	12	10	4

Comments on findings

The survey results are quite consistent with those completed last year in the Jackson area of the state. Some of the findings, as a matter of fact, are startling in their similarity (see Appendix 3, "Comparison of Jackson and Canton Valley Findings").

Steps to be completed

The final area of research to be carried through is the survey of industry, land development and values, and community plans and direction. This will be accomplished in the period October 20 to 30. A final report will be submitted on November 2 together with recommendations.

Clarence Radke
Head, Survey Team 3

The Memo Report

More and more today, companies urge their employees to use written memos. The obvious reason for this is to avoid the distortions and misunderstandings that occur when oral statements are transferred from one person to another. An additional reason for using written memos is that their messages become a matter of record (and help fix responsibility). Also, the very act of writing forces a person to plan his communication more carefully than when he makes an "off the cuff" statement.

Many firms print slogans at the top of their memo sheets encouraging employees to write memos such as: "Write It—Don't Say It." "Put It in Writing." "If You Want It Done—Write It."

But memos may transmit more than information. They can transmit attitudes which build barriers. Some managers send out an inordinate number of

MEMO REPORT

WRITE IT — ACCEPT NO VERBAL ORDERS					
					Save Paper - Reply on This Sheet When Possible
TO	Dept./Orgn.	Bldg./Zone	Plant/Fac.	Division	Date
All Department Heads	24	T-21		Hdqrts	Nov. 13, 19____
FROM					Ext.
Sid Hammer, Exec. V.P.					
SUBJECT					
Employee nominations for Christmas Award					

Please nominate one candidate from your department for

consideration for the Annual President's Christmas Award.

Criteria for outstanding employee performance are noted

in Management Bulletin 101.

All nominations must be in no later than December 10.

interoffice memos. They fly from their desks like snowflakes, often hastily written and not even proofread. When a manager feels, "Well, it's only a memo—nothing official; I'll put my ideas down and straighten this guy out," trouble is likely to result.

A tactless directive or message will be read not only by the designated receiver but by all others who receive copies of it. Much needless antagonism results from this fact—that several people read what is addressed to only one person. Perhaps one of the phrases heard most frequently in company offices is, "Well, I don't know why he was so sore; I only sent him the memo to keep the record straight." We can understand why "he" was so upset if we keep in mind that carbons of that memo also went to his superiors and fellow supervisors.

Memoranda are important. As much care should be taken with their composition as with any other item of internal or external communication. For certain specific purposes, memos usually serve better than telephone calls or face-to-face comments.

1. To transmit *exactly* the same information to several people.
2. To put on record the information, policies, or decisions reached at a meeting or conference.
3. To confirm, as a matter of record, a decision or agreement.
4. To transmit information, policies, or directives to an individual.

The Letter Report

For many persons who are accustomed to writing or dictating business letters, completing a brief report in letter form is convenient and easy. However, there are differences between the business letter and the letter report which should be kept in mind.

The tone of the letter report is formal and objective. The writing style is factual; and it often contains substantiating data, in the form of tables and charts. The inside address, salutation, and complimentary close may be dispensed with, although letterhead stationery is used. Topic headings and subheadings are employed liberally.

```
                    J. STEVENSON MANUFACTURING COMPANY
                              101 Hilton Avenue
                              Chicago, Illinois


      October 21, 19__

      TO:       Mr. Albert Hill, Manager
                Hill, Adams and Hill, Management Consultants
      FROM:     Roberta T. Black, Personnel Director
                Stevenson Manufacturing Company
      SUBJECT:  Summary of Training Activities, 1972-74
```

You indicated that it would be helpful to your firm to learn of the training activities for employees which we carried through from 1972 to 1974. The data which follow are a summary of those activities.

Management Training, 1972-74
Personnel at the management level have been offered three specific courses. These have been well attended.

Course	Approximate No. Eligible	No. Enrolled	No. of Classes Held
Supervision and Human Relations	260	65	3
Decision Making	260	50	3
Effective Written and Oral Communication	260	85	5

Engineering Training, 1972-74
Although a number of courses have been offered to engineering personnel, the response has been very weak. Perhaps the reason for this lies in the engineering work load, which has been very heavy due to military and space orders.

Course	Approximate No. Eligible	No. Enrolled	No. of Classes
Cost Control for Engineers	350	45	3
Advances in Electronics	250	25	1
Engineering Reports	350	80	4

Clerical and Office Training, 1972-74
Response by these personnel to the training has been consistently high. However, the company has not offered as many courses as could be filled because of the high turnover of employees in these categories.

Course	Approximate No. Eligible	No. Enrolled	No. of Classes
Office Techniques and Management	425	150	6
Business Letters	300	110	6
Telephone and Filing Techniques	250	50	3

```
On the basis of your request, shop training has not been in-
cluded in this report.  However, information is available.

Instruction
Instructors for all management-level training plus the en-
gineering reports classes have been secured from outside the
company.  Most of the men used were university instructors or
professional consultants.

All other courses were taught by company personnel.

Administration
All training was carried on under the direct supervision of
the Personnel Department.  Mr. Asquith was specifically
charged with the coordination and supervision of recruitment,
assignment, and class direction.

Concluding Comments
This will give you some idea of the training which has been
carried through.  If there are any questions I can answer, I
shall be happy to do so.  I am eager to work with you on
long-range training plans for our company.
```

These are only some of the short reports which exist, and a sample of the kinds of organization and format which are found. There are many others.

Other Written Media

Aside from reports, companies use other written items that are similar in some respects. Almost every firm has a series of *policy statements* which set down guidelines for personnel, organizational segments of the company, and various activities. These guidelines usually give some indication of responsibilities as well as constraints for areas of authority and activity.

Procedural guides and *procedure manuals* are very precisely written, and give the reader specific instructions on how to carry through a designated activity or assignment. The procedural guide may be a series of 5 or 6 points while a procedure manual may be book-length.

Proposals are usually submitted to another company or a government agency in an effort to sell a product, or secure funding, or in response to a request for a proposal (RFP). Proposals are usually highly detailed and cite the precise method for product manufacture or how a service will be carried through. They usually specify the equipment to be used, the personnel who will be involved, estimated costs or expenditures, legal technicalities, and other details in which a sponsor, foundation, purchaser or purchasing agency would be interested.[1]

A good source for material in this area is Vardaman and Vardaman, *Communication in Modern Organizations,* New York: John Wiley and Sons, Inc., 1973.
See also, B. G. Rainey, "Proposal Writing: A Neglected Area of Instruction," *The Journal of Business Communication,* Summer 1974.

The length of a proposal may vary from a few pages (a research request to a foundation requesting funding) to a dozen volumes (an aerospace company proposal to the U.S. Department of Defense involving the construction of several hundred combat planes at a cost of hundreds of millions of dollars). Each proposal has to compete with several others, and the *quality of the communication itself* will often determine whether the proposal flies or falls.

The organizational format of proposals varies. However, a plan such as the following will usually prove acceptable:

1. Definition of problem
2. Purpose of research, product, or service (how it will alleviate or eliminate the problem)
3. Hypothesis
4. Research or work design
5. Work schedule (with specific dates for completion of indicated phases)
6. Funding needed or cost schedule
7. Key personnel list and their qualifications
8. How findings will be used, product sold, service implemented, or research disseminated
9. Miscellaneous such as detailed analysis or explanation of technical and management phases

Questions for Study

I. Complete any of the following problems assigned. You may wish to review the chapter and note key points before working on the assignment(s).

1. What are several key characteristics of brief reports which make them useful for decision-making purposes?

2. In large companies, monthly periodic reports are usually submitted by department or division managers. Quite often, these will disagree in some fundamental way. For example, the credit manager may recommend that the company cut back on opening new charge accounts, while the sales manager may recommend that credit be extended or the number of accounts increased. Perhaps the production manager may disagree with the marketing manager's suggestion.

   Is such disagreement harmful as far as the decision maker who reads these reports is concerned? Or are there advantages in securing several points of view?

3. Do you feel that it is more helpful to the reader if all the recommendations are presented in one section at the end of the report, or should they be presented individually at relevant points throughout the report? Why do you feel as you do?

4. What are the advantages and disadvantages of a "fill in" report form?

5. Secure two "fill in" report forms, explain their use, and offer your constructive criticism of them.

6. How do progress reports serve as control devices in the administrative process?

7. What are the specific advantages of putting very brief ideas into written memo form rather than communicating such ideas orally?

8. What are several of the important attributes of the effective memo report?

9. When copies of a memo are sent to others in a firm in addition to the addressee, the writer may have several reasons for this action. Can you list three or four such reasons.

10. What differences exist between the letter report and the business letter?

11. Secure a credit report (such as a Dun and Bradstreet report) and comment on the format and areas covered. Note the similarities and differences between it and a standard periodic report.

12. Secure (on a loan basis) a policy or procedure manual from a firm. Present a short report on it to your team members or your class.

13. Secure (on a loan basis) an outdated proposal from a firm. Present a short report on it to your team members or your class.

14. Secure from the U.S. Department of Defense the guidelines and requirements for a proposal which accompanied an RFP (Request for Proposal). Present a short report on it to your team members or your class.

II. Complete any of the following problems assigned. You may wish to review the chapter and note key points before attempting to solve the problem. You may assume any reasonable facts, data, and information which will make your report more complete.

1. Assume that you work for a real estate investment firm. You have been asked to examine two vacant pieces of commercial property, both located near shopping centers.

Write a letter report on each to your immediate supervisor. Your reports will be used as the basis for your management's decisions on whether or not to purchase one or both. To carry through this assignment, find two vacant commercial properties and do the research necessary to write the report. Your management will doubtless be interested in property size, location, traffic flow, taxes, potential use, asking price, improvements, zoning restrictions, etc.

2. Assume you own a record store which also handles a heavy line of cassette tapes and stereo equipment accessories. Mr. Dave Jablon, your major financing source, has requested a report from you on your advertising expenditures and any results you achieved from special offers or coupon deals.
   Your records reveal the following expenditures:

	Jan	Feb	March	April
Newspaper	$1,500	$1,800	$1,200	$1,400
Radio	2,700	2,500	2,500	3,500
TV	1,200	800	1,200	800
Direct Mail	400	400	400	800

Make assumptions on size of ads, time used for spot commercials on TV and radio, type, quantity, and any other data necessary.
Submit a letter report to Mr. Jablon.

3. Your firm has managed four apartment buildings for Mr. Robert Arnold for nine years. Two of the buildings include twelve apartments each, one has eight, and the other six apartments. Mr. Arnold passed away two months ago and you have received a request from the executor of Mr. Arnold's estate for information on your management services, and the buildings now part of the estate.
   Send a letter report to the executor in which you give him some information on each building, rentals, occupancy rate, management fees, taxes, expenses, and other data which you feel are relevant.

4. Assume that you are the outgoing president of a social organization. You will be graduating and leaving the university next week. The incoming president has requested a brief letter report from you giving him information on his responsibilities in several areas (to members, alumni, and the community in general), meetings, finances, recruitment, and the day-to-day factors involved.

5. Write a letter report which is an analysis of your own time allocation. Do this as accurately as possible noting all areas (scholastic, vocational, recreational, cultural, etc.). If you can make some meaningful recommendations to yourself, do so.

6. You are the manager of the Fairbanks Discount Appliance Center in Parkington. This is one of seven such outlets in the Fairbanks chain. You are permitted to donate in each 12-month period no more than $2000 worth of merchandise to local, certified fund-raising organizations.

Write a letter report to your general manager detailing your store's contributions for the 12-month period just concluded. Note items, their value, the receiving organization, and other relevant data.

7. Send a memo to each section head reminding them that the United Crusade drive only has 8 days to run and our division is $18,000 behind last year at this period.

8. Write a memo to each section head reminding him that the energy crisis is still very much with us. You may wish to make several specific recommendations for the conservation of electrical energy.

9. As head of personnel, write a memo to be directed to each employee noting a new service offered: financial planning for families. Mr. Cochran, Vice President of Imperial Bank, will be available in the personnel office each Monday and Wednesday from 4:00 p.m. to 7:00 p.m.

10. Send a memo to each of your department heads at the Easley Electronics Company reminding them to announce the annual meeting for employees. At this meeting President Easley will deliver his annual report on the company and answer questions of a broad general nature.

11. You have ten sections, each under a foreman, in your department. These foremen, in turn, supervise a total of about 220 production-line workers. Your entire department has its lunch scheduled from 11:45 a.m. to 12:45 p.m. You have noticed, however, that a large number of these men begin to leave their machines or work tables about 11:30. You have no idea if these men all come from specific sections or if there are several from every section. However, this is costly to the company and your boss has "jumped on" you twice about the early break.

Send a memo to each of your foremen, reminding them that the authorized lunch period is from 11:45 to 12:45. Of course, the time lost when an early break is taken does not help the foremen make their authorized production quotas.

12. At today's meeting of the eight division supervisors it was agreed that (1) there would be no overtime periods in March and April, (2) company tools would no longer be charged out to employees for weekend use, and (3) each employee, beginning on July 1, would have to pay $4.00 toward the cost of a pair of company-issued safety shoes when he ordered such a pair.

Write the memo to the eight supervisors in which you verify and commit to record these rules.

13. Your five foremen supervise a total of 80 men and women who manufacture lamp shades. These are made of a parchment-like heavy-weight paper, cottons, silks, and synthetic materials.

A major problem has arisen recently because of the large number of rejects resulting from dirty and greasy finger- and handprints on the shades. This is costly and unnecessary.

Employees may, if they wish, use cotton gloves which they can draw from supply at no cost. However, most insist that "gloves slow me down." Of course, eating is supposed to be done only in the cafeteria.

Send a memo to your foremen in which you ask for their help in eliminating or alleviating the problem.

14. Assume you are the District Sales Supervisor in Kansas City for Sloan Stereo products (record players, receivers, tape decks, and speakers). Write a periodic report to your general manager on sales of items, sales figures, and related data.

15. As the personnel manager of the Top Flite Toy Company, you are required to submit a monthly sales report to the general manager. In this report you comment on the sales of your three major lines of toy airplanes: fighters, bombers, and passenger jets. Each of these categories has three subgroups. Sales are reported in dozens of units sold. Figures are always compared with sales for the same month last year as well as the previous month. Because of a new Lockheed fighter which has recently proved highly successful in tactical operations, your line of toy fighters has enjoyed a tremendous upswing in sales.

Your sales force has remained relatively stable though you did add four trainees last month.

Although you do not report on sales advertising, you feel strongly that the budget for buying space in youngsters' magazines, as well as afternoon TV commercial time, should be increased by at least 20 percent to approximately $90,000 per month.

16. As the personnel director you are required to submit a periodic report each month to the corporate president. You are now writing yours for September (which always shows comparative figures for the previous month as well as the same month last year).

You include production, technical, and skilled artisans under your hourly heading. Salaried categories include clerical, administrative, and professional personnel. You report not only numbers but also salary levels.

Included in your report is training. Last month was quite active and you should list courses and programs as well as approximate cost.

Recruitment is also covered in your report, and for the first time you will include "Safety," which heretofore was submitted as a separate report by the safety director.

You will probably want to use some graphic aids to assist you in the communication of ideas.

17. Write a progress report dated today covering your work in this course. If you were issued a course outline or syllabus, you may wish to measure your progress against that. Note all areas of activity: written and oral assignments, new knowledge, readings, work on a major research project, team activities, etc.

18. Note your vocational or professional objectives and write a progress report noting your progress toward those goals.

19. If you are involved in a research project, write a progress report measured against your original research design.

20. You head a team which was assigned the task of conducting a survey of the cities of Bellplaine, Parkview, and Westwood. Your task was to interview individuals designated in a selected stratified sample to determine their reactions to compact foreign cars as compared to American compacts.

This is your first report and you have completed approximately half the survey of the first city, Bellplaine. You find, however, that interviews run an average of 22 minutes (including travel) as compared to the projected 16. This will hold you up. If your team is to stay on schedule, another person will be needed and should be assigned. Your team, under the present situation, will be in Parkview two days later than the original schedule called for. Assume all other necessary facts involved in your survey, and submit a progress report to your research director.

21.   Your firm purchased the Sun Brite Lounge Chair Company last year. One of the first tasks was the renovation of the manufacturing facility with special attention to be given to the cafeteria.

This is your second report, six weeks subsequent to the first. In these six weeks, the new loading dock has been put into shape, fluorescent fixtures wired throughout the factory area, and new furniture purchased for the cafeteria. In addition, complete stainless steel cooking facilities have been installed, and ping pong and billiard tables purchased for the lounge area. Changes have also been completed in the employee wash-up and locker areas. Labor costs for this work should be reported.

You are running about one week ahead of your schedule.

Chapter Nineteen

The Long Report

Objectives
Components
The Corporate Annual Report

The long report is written after careful investigation and research. Its style is formal and its statements carefully substantiated with facts and figures.

The subject may be a possible corporate merger, a proposed marketing plan, a corporate five-year program, the development of a shopping center, or any other matter calling for thorough and careful study.

Such study may include trends in population growth, economic analysis, sales potential, cultural contributions, ethnic considerations, national and international affairs, industrial change in a particular area, and other contributing factors.

Objectives

The objectives of the long report may be one or more of the following: to persuade, to inform, to compare, to analyze, or to argue.

The Persuasive Report

Suppose we want to convince our readers that a new 48-story apartment building to be constructed next year should be heated and air-conditioned by natural gas. We will aim our arguments at several groups: the architects, the financiers, the contractor, and probably the firm which will operate the building or sponsor it. Because these are all intelligent, analytical readers, the report must be buttressed with statistical data and information at every point. A good deal of very logical reasoning is required. The purpose is to demonstrate why the building's heating and cooling systems, as well as its kitchen equipment, should be gas rather than electric. The report must persuade through the logic of its arguments and the strength of its substantiating data, and should avoid an overly emphatic or "hard-sell" approach.

The Informational Report

As the name suggests, this type of report serves only to present data which may be used as a record, or as the basis for decision making. Perhaps the most frequent fault of such reports is overkill: they smother the subject with too much information. The scope and limitations of the topic should be carefully defined. The informational report is sometimes referred to as an "investigative" or "research" report.

The Comparative Report

When management wants to make a decision, it may call for a report comparing alternatives. Should we purchase this plant or that one? Should we introduce a new line of brushes or not? Should we open another outlet? Should we stock Product A or competitive Product B? The comparative report is primarily concerned with an evaluation and comparison of two or more products or services.

The Analytical Report

Some reports have to do with appraising a situation and sorting out the factors affecting it. For example, we may want to examine the future of our industry in relation to "Our Growth and Expansion in the Next Five Years." We state our firm's goals and objectives, and suggest strategies for reaching them. The report should examine all supportive activities within the firm such as personnel, finance, manufacturing, marketing, production, distribution, research and development, etc. It should also analyze the external environment: the market, consumerism, raw material supply, life styles and values, legal and legislative forces, energy, and so on. Typically an analytical report concludes with recommendations for specific courses of action.

The Argumentative Report

The argumentative report strongly urges a specific course of action and substantiates its recommendations with data and documentation. There is nothing subtle about this "selling job," as contrasted with the persuasive report. The writer wants the reader to follow a specific course of action, and argues for it.

Components

When a report runs to six pages or more, it covers a fairly wide area and includes a good deal of information. It is at this point that we begin to think of helping the reader assimilate the material by including a title page, a table of contents, a summary, and perhaps an appendix for statistical and/or reference data.

Some of the specific sections of the long report, in the order in which they would appear, are discussed in the pages which follow. Few reports contain all the divisions listed, although long reports usually carry a letter of transmittal, title page, table of contents, and summary.

Preliminaries

Letter of Transmittal.   A letter of transmittal almost invariably accompanies the formal report and attempts to set the stage for the reader so that he will understand why and for whom the report was prepared. It is placed at the top of the report or is clipped to the title page. It usually covers the following items (see page 383):

1. **Authorization for research.**
2. **The purpose of the project.**
3. **The limitations of the report, noting legal restrictions and the boundaries of time and funds. This can be of great help to the writer because it tells the reader what to expect and what not to expect.**
4. **A listing of certain key sources.**
5. **Reference to any finding in the report that is of particular importance or interest to the reader. Recommendations and/or acknowledgments of assistance may be included in the letter of transmittal.**

Title Page.   The title page should carry the report title, the name of the person from whom the report is written, the author's name, the name of the group or company issuing the report, and the date (see page 384).

"Cute" titles should not be used (such as Pressing Problems: Parker Garment Co.), although there is no reason why a title cannot be informative and interesting. For example, a General Electric Co. report was titled "What They Think of Their Higher Education." And an aircraft company issued one titled "Flying High: A Survey of Supersonic Aircraft."

December 22, 197_

Mr. Robert T. Mayberry, Director
Division of Consumer Affairs
City of Los Angeles
190 Hope Street
Los Angeles, Calif. 90017

Dear Mr. Mayberry:

As requested in your memo of authorization of October 20,
197_, I have completed research on the topic of "Consumer
Protection." My findings and recommendations are presented
in the attached report.

The purpose of the survey was to determine if lower and
middle socio-economic class supermarket consumers were aware
of protective agencies and legislation. The scope and depth
of the analysis was limited by constraints of time, manpower,
and finances.

The primary research sources used were interviews with:
a) supermarket consumers; b) consumer protection agencies;
and c) Los Angeles welfare offices. Secondary research information was gathered from various journal articles, books,
pamphlets, staff studies, etc.

Completing this project proved to be a challenging and
interesting experience. It is my feeling that the findings
will prove of value to the field of consumerism. If you
have any questions, I shall be happy to answer them.

Sincerely,

Ernest Wilkerson

Ernest Wilkerson

CONSUMER PROTECTION:

AN ANALYSIS OF ITS DEVELOPMENT
AND THE
RESULTS OF A CONSUMER SURVEY

Presented to

Robert T. Mayberry, Director
Division of Consumer Affairs
City of Los Angeles

Submitted by

Ernest Wilkerson

December 22, 197_

Letters of Authorization and Acceptance. The first page in government reports often cites the meeting, conference, or legislative action which authorized the appropriation of funds for the survey reported on. By clearly setting down the problem, scope, and limitations for research, the letter of authorization can prevent later misunderstanding. This letter is not usually found in business reports.

Some reports also include a letter of acceptance. Although this letter is not written often, it can be used to accept, revise, or change the terms or conditions established in the letter of authorization. It may also be used to cite times, fees, and other contractual obligations if it serves as an agreement between two companies. The letter of acceptance is part of the mechanics leading to the report's assignment and acceptance. It is usually not part of the report, although some government reports display it in an appendix.

Table of Contents. The table of contents is prepared after the report has been typed. It lists chapter or section titles and subdivisions. Page numbers are indicated for each. The headings should agree with those in the final outline.

TABLE OF CONTENTS

LIST OF FIGURES AND TABLES

List of Tables or Illustrations. Although not frequently used, an extended formal report may have a list of illustrations and the page numbers on which the tables may be found.

Foreword or Preface. Because the letter of transmittal normally "sets the stage" for the reader, a foreword or preface is not usually found in a report. When it is, it goes into some detail about the general scope and purpose of the report.

Summary. The summary, sometimes included and often referred to as a review, brief, abstract, synopsis, or digest, is designed to give the busy reader a concise overview of the entire report.

It should state the problem, the scope of the investigation, the research methods used, the key ideas in the report proper, the conclusions reached, and the course of action recommended. The writing style should be crisp, penetrating, and objective. Topic headings may be used in the summary to assist the reader further.

Body

The body of most reports can be divided into three major sections: introduction, discussion, and conclusions and recommendations.

Introduction. If the report has a letter of transmittal, a summary section, or other prefatory sections, probably a good part of the introduction has already been presented. In any event, the introduction attempts to give the reader a sufficient background for the report to be meaningful and understandable.

The introduction may include a history of the situation and a clear statement of the problem to be solved or examined. Limitations of the investigation should be noted and the purpose of the report stated. The methods of research used should be explained, and how validity or reliability of the survey was secured. If specific definitions are important to the clear understanding of the report, they may be presented at this time. The introduction may also tell the reader what the plan of presentation of the report is. If the reader is told that all statistical data may be found in the appendix, that sample questionnaires are in the body, and that this report is based on the initial study dated March 15, 19_, then he will be better able to orient himself and his thinking to the report.

INTRODUCTION

Consumer protection has been a major issue in our society in recent years. In this advanced age of mass production, fast-growing businesses, and the formation of many giant conglomerates, the consumer has been overshadowed and left almost powerless. Recently, though, through people like Ralph Nader and agencies such as the Federal Trade Commission, the consumer's rights are being brought out in the open and examined. Areas in which consumers themselves have never really been concerned are under critical investigation by some of these agencies and groups. The actual potential of consumer protection is just being tapped.

The whole area of consumerism and consumer agencies and organizations is in its infant stages with an unlimited potential for expansion. Corporations are being made aware that consumers expect certain qualities and standards to be maintained in the products they shop for, and that if these are not maintained it is the company that will pay, not the consumer. Companies are being forced to consider the social and ecological consequences of their activities. In this regard, the food industry has been given special attention.

1

Discussion. The discussion is the vital part of the report and makes up 75 to 85 percent of the total length. It is in the discussion that the investigator presents his information and his analysis and interpretation of it and points out significant facts and relationships among the data.

Throughout the discussion, the writer should assist his reader by conciseness and clarity of presentation. To this end, it is helpful to use topic and subtopic headings, and to present some of the data in easy-to-analyze tables, charts, and graphs.

CONSUMER BEHAVIOR PATTERNS (EXCERPT)

Within our society, being a good consumer has become somewhat of a science or a trade. In other words, one has to be highly educated in order to keep from getting "gypped." Businesses earn a large amount of marginal revenue from what may be called "perplexism." Everyone in a society cannot be highly educated, and "because of the diversity in the levels of education or intelligence, communication breaks down."[1]

My hypothesis is that consumers in lower and middle income groups are not aware of consumer protection legislation as it applies to the products in a supermarket. This fact can be worth money to the small businessman running the store. The owner knows that "the poor can be more easily deceived than the suburban shopper because of their deficiency in education."[2]

[Various agencies have been established to protect the rights of the consumer. These include the Better Business Bureaus and the Federal Trade Commission. But these agencies will not know about the problems if the consumer doesn't complain. And the consumer won't complain if it takes advanced education to understand the procedures for doing so.]

[1] Himstreet and Baty, "Barriers to Communication," Business Communications, 1969, p. 36.

[2] Jennifer Gross, The Supermarket Trap, p. 121.

2

EDUCATION (EXCERPTS)

Laws and regulations established to protect society are not of much value if the people they are created for are not aware of them. Laws which are not communicated to the people they serve are useless and do a disservice to them. Rights of consumers, established by laws which are never known by the consumers, can be of little help to them. The whole problem stems from the lack of consumer education, and of communication. The question is, who is supposed to educate the consumer and inform him?

[Some food chains have taken it upon themselves to inform shoppers of certain important characteristics of the products on their shelves. Some stores have established Consumer Affairs Departments to handle customer complaints and to scrutinize company policies from a consumer point of view. The interest in consumer protection has spread to schools and nonprofit organizations.]

The programs set up by the food stores and organizations are valuable and important, but they need the participation of consumers. As Margaret Dana said, people are in a "leaving" habit and not a "learning" habit today. People have put the responsibility on the producer to insure that his product is adequate. Consumers must realize that they have a joint responsibility to learn the laws and regulations governing the products for which they shop.

3

TRADE ASSOCIATIONS

The education of consumers is a job much too broad and expensive for one organization or store to handle efficiently. Large cooperative groups are needed because they have the skills and manpower to cover all aspects of consumer protection and legislation. Trade associations can provide leadership in many areas concerning buyers and sellers, such as consumer and dealer education, development of standards, and complaint handling. Associations are also large enough to keep members informed by coordinating and disseminating research. Each corporation in the association is made sensitive to consumer problems and government initiatives. A good example is the Consumer Research Institute started by the Grocery Manufacturers of America. The institute has recently been studying labeling and packaging methods that would aid the consumer. The results of the study will be issued to all food processors in an attempt to secure better labeling and packaging in food distribution. Action like this can only be fruitful if it is conducted in an open, objective way and does not simply favor the food manufacturers who finance the association's operations.

4

LABELING (EXCERPT)

Much of the research being carried on today deals with the labeling of products. Areas of particular concern are weights, percentages of ingredients, nutritional value, and unit pricing. Some chain stores have instituted consumer programs to deal with these problems.

[An important difficulty in nutritional labeling is that many consumers fail to get much advantage from it because they do not know enough about the principles of nutrition. A few companies have sought to make consumers more nutrition-conscious by providing menus adapted to particular needs.]

5

CONSUMER PROTECTION LEGISLATION (EXCERPTS)

In order for consumer protection to be effective, information must be acquired by agencies and disseminated (or communicated) to consumers. This educational function is very important if consumers are to receive prompt warning of deceptive and fraudulent practices as well as of dangerous products. Knowledge in these areas should serve to alert consumers and reduce unnecessary losses of time and money in litigation. . . .

The Consumer Protection Act of 1971

The Consumer Protection Act of 1971 was the culmination of several years of legislative development. This bill constitutes a landmark in governmental protection of consumers. For the first time, a statutory agency of the government exists to defend consumer rights and interests.

Specifically, this bill furthers the protection of consumers and provides representation of consumer interests in important areas of activity of the federal government by creating an independent Consumer Protection Agency, by giving the existing Office of Consumer Affairs statutory authority, and by establishing a Consumer Advisory Council. . . .[3]

---

[3] 92nd Congress, 1st Session, House of Representatives, Report No. 92-542, September 30, 1971, p. 2.

6

SURVEY OF LOS ANGELES AREA CONSUMERS

Although local, state, and federal agencies have worked arduously on consumer protection activities, there is some doubt that their efforts have been communicated effectively to the consumer.

In order to determine how knowledgeable and concerned the consumer is with respect to various aspects of consumerism, a research survey was carried through in the greater Los Angeles area.

7

SAMPLING METHOD

A disproportionate stratified sample[4] was taken of supermarket shoppers of the Los Angeles County Area:

White	65
Black	65
Chicano	65
Oriental	65
	260

The sample size was originally established at 400. Time and manpower constraints, however, limited the sample to 260 consumers. The universe was divided among the four ethnic groups to test the premise that awareness of consumer protection legislation was directly related to ethnic background.

The survey was directed toward consumers most affected by protective legislation--those earning less than the median income of Los Angeles County. However, because of errors in the sampling method, 22 percent of the sample consisted of consumers earning more than the median income of $215 per week ($11,196 annually).[5]

---

[4] Mildred Parten, Surveys, Polls and Samples: Practical Procedures, 1950, p. 228.

[5] U.S. Department of Commerce, 1970 Census, General Social and Economic Characteristics--California.

8

Interviewers were matched with ethnic groups (e.g., a black interviewer surveyed black consumers) and were told to choose representative sample cases from customers at supermarkets.

Depth of Survey Analysis

The assumption was made that consumers are not aware of protective legislation. The following variables, therefore, were tested to determine if they were related to consumer awareness:

1. Number of trips to the grocery store per week.
2. Amount of money spent on groceries per week.
3. Number of people in the household.
4. Interviewee's opinion about:
   a) consumer protection legislation;
   b) government involvement with consumer protection.
5. Highest level of education completed.
6. Family net income.
7. Ethnic background.
8. Age.

9

Socioeconomic class was determined solely on the family's net income. The survey addressed itself to the question of consumer awareness and did not attempt to define socioeconomic class more precisely.

HYPOTHESIS

Lower and middle socioeconomic class consumers are not aware of consumer protection legislation pertaining to the supermarket.

10

ANALYSIS OF SURVEY RESULTS

Survey results showed that consumers from the Los Angeles County Area were not aware of consumer protection.

1. Only 41.0 percent of the sample was aware of consumer protection legislation.

2. Only 30.2 percent of the sample was aware of consumer protection agencies.

When the sample was analyzed by ethnic groups, the Whites exhibited the greatest degree of awareness (approximately 50 percent--see Figures 4 and 5). However, it is felt that even this percentage reflects a very poor degree of awareness.

The percentage of Chicanos aware of laws was noticeably lower than among other minority groups. A possible reason for this is the existence of a language barrier (see Figure 4).

The consumer's awareness was not affected by his opinion of:

1. Consumer protection--96.6 percent of the sample were either very much or somewhat in favor of consumer protection.

2. Government involvement in consumer protection--96.7 percent of the sample stated that the government should either be very involved or somewhat involved in consumer protection.

11

Income Versus Awareness

   In general, consumer awareness tended to increase as
income increased.   The trend, however, was not conclusive.
(See Figures 8 and 9.)

Source of Information Versus Awareness

   59% of the sample indicated that television was a good
source for learning about consumer protection, while 25%
favored radio.

   Of those who chose television,

1.   79% were not aware of a consumer protection agency.

2.   58% were not aware of a consumer protection law.

   It can be inferred from this data that the television
medium does not effectively communicate information concerning consumer protection.

12

Conclusions and Recommendations. Conclusions and recommendations are given in most types of reports. The writer must be sure that each conclusion or recommendation is thoroughly substantiated in the body of the report. At no time should the executive who is reading the report ask, "Well, where is the evidence for this?" The evidence should be in the discussion section of the report.

Lately there has been a trend toward placing the Conclusions and Recommendations immediately after the Summary or Introduction rather than at the end of the report. This makes sense. The top executive receives reports from every division and department of his organization. These are vital if he is to have an awareness of all his firm's activities and an appreciation of the big picture. He doesn't need to know all the details, but he should be familiar with each division's broad plans. If he can get that information from the summary, conclusions, and recommendations sections of a report, then he need not plow through the entire text.

CONCLUSIONS ON SURVEY CONDUCTED

1. Consumers, in general, were found to be unaware of protective agencies and legislation.

2. Consumer awareness of codes, regulation, and laws involving consumerism can be positively correlated with higher education and income levels.

3. The sample, as a whole, was in favor of consumer protection but respondents believed that it was the responsibility of government to act in their behalf.

4. Our sample considered television the most effective medium of communication.

13

RECOMMENDATIONS BASED ON SURVEY CONDUCTED

On the basis of these conclusions, it is felt that the following recommendations are appropriate:

1. Government at local and federal levels should take a more active role in the formulation and enforcement of consumer protective legislation.

2. Consumer protection agencies should make their services known and simplify the process of entering consumer complaints.

3. Television should be used to inform the public about consumer protection agencies, laws, and regulations.

14

Addenda. After the body of the report are found the appendixes and various supplements, such as copies of questionnaires, interview schedules, diagrams, statistics, maps, and any other information related to the subject of the report that may be of interest to the reader.

APPENDIX I

PERSONAL INTERVIEW SURVEY

Interview schedule with responses
indicated (by percentage) plus
information charts and tables

15

BLACK _25%_   CHICANO _25%_   ORIENTAL _25%_   WHITE _25%_

LOCATION OF INTERVIEW _____ LOS ANGELES COUNTY _____

Hi! I'm a college student conducting a survey on laws to aid consumers who shop at supermarkets. Recently, many organizations and laws have been established to help you and me understand our rights as supermarket shoppers. I am interested in getting your opinion which will be beneficial to you in your community.

1. IN AN AVERAGE WEEK, HOW MANY TIMES DO YOU GO TO THE GROCERY STORE?

   (CIRCLE ONE)

   1-1) 1 or less 31.0%   1-5) 5   4.1%
   1-2) 2   32.8%   1-6) 6   2.2%
   1-3) 3   17.5%   1-7) More than 6   3.4%
   1-4) 4   9.0%

2. ABOUT HOW MUCH DO YOU SPEND ON GROCERIES PER WEEK FOR YOUR FAMILY?

   2-1) Less than $10   7.1%   2-6) $50 to $59   6.3%
   2-2) $10 to $19   10.8%   2-7) $60 to $69   1.1%
   2-3) $20 to $29   31.0%   2-8) $70 to $79   0.8%
   2-4) $30 to $39   34.6%   2-9) $80 and over 2.3%
   2-5) $40 to $49   16.0%

3. HOW MANY PEOPLE ARE THERE IN YOUR HOUSEHOLD?

   3-1) 1   13.8%   3-7) 7   3.0%
   3-2) 2   24.3%   3-8) 8   0.7%
   3-3) 3   26.1%   3-9) 9   0.4%
   3-4) 4   19.8%   3-10) 10   0%
   3-5) 5   9.3%   3-11) More than 10 0%
   3-6) 6   2.6%

4. DO YOU KNOW OF ANY LAWS WHICH ARE DESIGNED TO PROTECT YOU AS A CONSUMER?

16

(CIRCLE ONE)

4-1) YES   41.0%   4-2) NO   54.9%   4-3) UNDECIDED   4.1%

COMMENT _____

_____

_____

5. WHAT DO YOU THINK WOULD BE A GOOD SOURCE OF INFORMATION FOR FINDING OUT ABOUT CONSUMER LEGISLATION?

5-1) Television   59.0%   5-3) Newspaper   25.0%
5-2) Radio   4.1%   5-4) Other   11.9%

COMMENT _____

_____

_____

6. WHAT IS YOUR OPINION ABOUT CONSUMER PROTECTION LAWS?

6-1) Very much in favor of them   70.1%
6-2) Somewhat in favor   26.5%
6-3) Not in favor of them at all   1.1%
6-4) Other - explain   2.3%

_____

_____

7. ARE YOU AWARE OF ANY LEGAL CONSUMER PROTECTION AGENCIES?

7-1) Yes   If so, which agency?   30.2%
7-2) No   69.8%

COMMENT _____

_____

17

8. HOW INVOLVED DO YOU THINK THE GOVERNMENT SHOULD BE IN LEGISLATION INVOLVING CONSUMER PROTECTION?

    8-1) Very involved   72.4%
    8-2) Somewhat involved   24.3%
    8-3) Not involved at all   3.3%

    COMMENT _____

    _____

    _____

9. SOMETIMES WHEN PEOPLE SHOP, THEY BUY THINGS BY MISTAKE THAT ARE SPOILED. WHAT WOULD YOU DO IF YOU BOUGHT SOME MILK THAT WAS SPOILED?

    9-1) Complain to your store manager   76.9%
    9-2) Use the milk anyway   0.4%
    9-3) Throw it away   20.9%
    9-4) Report it to your local consumer protection agency 1.8%

    COMMENT _____

    _____

    _____

10. IT IS HELPFUL FOR CLASSIFICATION PURPOSES TO KNOW WHAT YOUR AGE GROUP IS.

    10-1) 18 and under   1.5%   10-4) 35 to 44   21.3%
    10-2) 19 to 24   17.2%   10-5) 45 to 59   20.5%
    10-3) 25 to 34   31.0%   10-6) 60 and over   8.5%

18

11. WHAT LEVEL OF EDUCATION HAVE YOU COMPLETED?

    11-1) Less than high school   10.1%
    11-2) Some high school   41.8%
    11-3) Completed high school 31.0%
    11-4) Some college   13.1%
    11-5) Completed college   4.0%

12. WHAT IS YOUR TOTAL FAMILY'S WEEKLY TAKE-HOME PAY?

12-1)	Less than $60	4.1%	12-5) $140 to $159	13.4%
12-2)	$60 to $99	4.5%	12-6) $160 to $199	9.7%
12-3)	$100 to $119	17.5%	12-7) $200 to $239	4.9%
12-4)	$120 to $139	23.5%	12-8) Over $240	22.4%

ANY ADDITIONAL COMMENTS AT ALL _____

_____

_____

_____

THANK YOU VERY MUCH FOR YOUR HELP.

13. CLASSIFICATION

    13-1) Black   65=25%
    13-2) Chicano 65=25%
    13-3) Oriental 65=25%
    13-4) White   65=25%

TOTAL SAMPLE SIZE=260

19

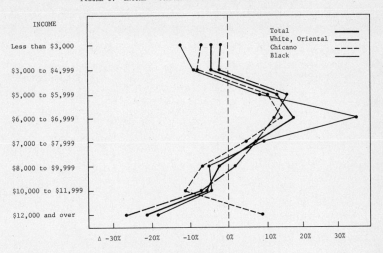

FIGURE 1: INCOME - COMPARISON OF SURVEY WITH 1970 CENSUS

This graph shows the survey's relationship to the 1970 Los Angeles
County's Census concerning income range for each ethnic group.

Δ is the percentage difference between Census figures and the survey.

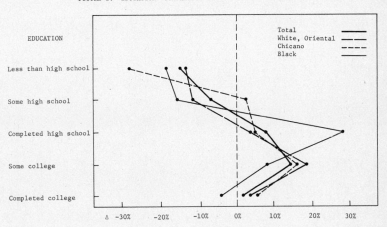

FIGURE 2: EDUCATION--COMPARISON OF SURVEY WITH 1970 CENSUS

This graph shows the survey's relationship to the 1970 Los Angeles
County Census concerning the level of education completed for each
ethnic group.

Δ is the percentage difference between Census figures and the survey.

20

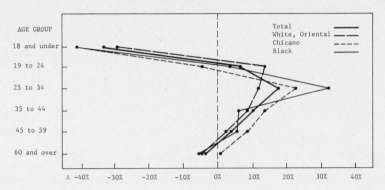

FIGURE 3: AGE - COMPARISON OF SURVEY WITH 1970 CENSUS

This graph shows the survey's relationship to the 1970 Los Angeles
County's Census concerning age categories for each ethnic group.

Δ is the percentage difference between Census figures and the survey.

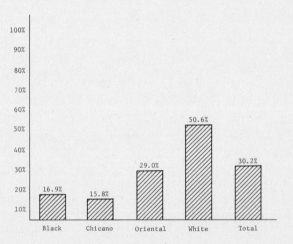

FIGURE 4: ETHNIC BACKGROUND VERSUS AWARENESS OF CONSUMER AGENCIES

21

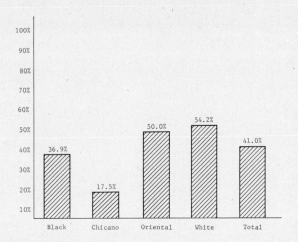

FIGURE 5: ETHNIC BACKGROUND VERSUS AWARENESS OF PROTECTIVE LAWS

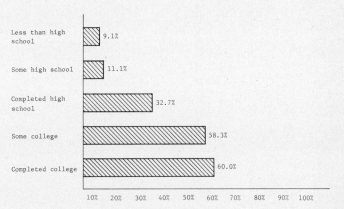

FIGURE 6: LEVEL OF EDUCATION COMPLETED VERSUS AWARENESS OF PROTECTIVE LAWS

22

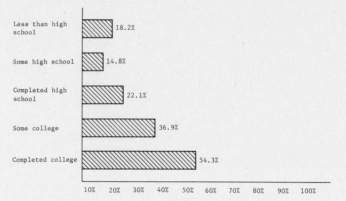

FIGURE 7: LEVEL OF EDUCATION COMPLETED VERSUS AWARENESS OF CONSUMER
PROTECTION AGENCIES

Consumer awareness increased significantly as the level of education completed increased.

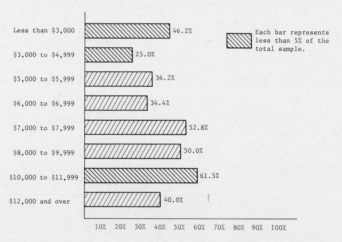

FIGURE 8: INCOME CATEGORY VERSUS AWARENESS OF PROTECTIVE LAWS

23

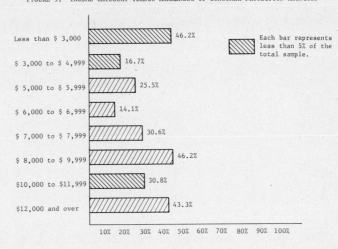

FIGURE 9: INCOME CATEGORY VERSUS AWARENESS OF CONSUMER PROTECTION AGENCIES

Less than $ 3,000   46.2%

$ 3,000 to $ 4,999   16.7%

$ 5,000 to $ 5,999   25.5%

$ 6,000 to $ 6,999   14.1%

$ 7,000 to $ 7,999   30.6%

$ 8,000 to $ 9,999   46.2%

$10,000 to $11,999   30.8%

$12,000 and over   43.3%

10% 20% 30% 40% 50% 60% 70% 80% 90% 100%

Each bar represents
less than 5% of the
total sample.

(Author's Note: Other tables and charts were included in the
original paper. These gave various data by ethnic group,
income level, and education. They have been omitted to conserve space.)

24

APPENDIX II

We reproduce here the first page of the Consumer Protection
Act of 1971. The remainder of the Act has been omitted to
conserve space.

25

CONSUMER PROTECTION ACT OF 1971

SEPTEMBER 30, 1971.—Committed to the Committee of the Whole House on the State of the Union and ordered to be printed

Mr. HOLIFIELD, from the Committee on Government Operations, submitted the following

REPORT

SECTION-BY-SECTION ANALYSIS

Section 1

The short title will be the "Consumer Protection Act of 1971."

Section 2.—Statement of findings

The Congress finds that the interests of consumers are inadequately represented and protected within the Federal Government; and that vigorous representation and protection of consumer interests are essential to the fair and efficient functioning of a free market economy.

TITLE I. OFFICE OF CONSUMER AFFAIRS

Section 101.—Establishment

An Office of Consumer Affairs is established within the Executive Office of the President to be headed by a Director and seconded by a Deputy Director, both to be appointed by the President and confirmed by the Senate. This section would give a statutory foundation to the existing Office of Consumer Affairs, established under Executive Order 11583, dated February 24, 1971.

Section 102.—Powers and duties of the Director

The Director is given the administrative powers and responsibilities ordinarily conferred upon agency heads, such as appointment and supervision of personnel, including experts and consultants, in accordance with the civil service and administrative expense laws; appointment of advisory committees; promulgation of rules necessary to carry out his functions; delegation of authority; making agreements with and obtaining the support of other Federal, State, and private agencies.

The Director is required to submit annually to the President and to the Congress a comprehensive report of activities of the Office, including recommendations for additional legislation and an evaluation of selected major consumer programs of each Federal agency.

Federal agencies, upon request of the Director, are to provide to the Office services and other support, and are to supply information to the Office as may be necessary and appropriate. Reimbursement for such assistance will be governed by existing provisions of law.

BIBLIOGRAPHY

Aaker, David A., and George S. Day, "Corporate Responses to Consumerism Pressures," _Harvard Business Review,_ November-December 1972, pp. 116-18.

Borrie, Gordon, and Aubrey L. Diamond, _The Consumer, Society and the Law,_ Great Britain: MacGibbon & Kee, Ltd., 1966, pp. 15-30, 69-81.

Boyer, Barry B., and Mary Gardner Jong, _George Washington Law Review,_ March 1972.

Dana, Margaret, "What the Consumer Expects of Product Safety," _Food Drug Cosmetic Law Journal,_ March 1972.

Directory of Government Agencies Safeguarding Consumer and Environment, Serina Press, Virginia, 1970-71, p. 7.

Engle, James F., _Consumer Behavior,_ New York: Holt, Rinehart and Winston, Inc., 1968.

Federal Trade Commission, _Consumer Alert,_ U.S. Government Printing Office, Washington, D.C., September-October 1972.

--------, _National Consumer Protection Hearings,_ U.S. Government Printing Office, Washington, D.C., November 1969.

Food and Drug Administration, "Consumer Education and Information," _FDA Papers,_ Vol. 5, No. 2, March 1971, p. 4.

--------, "FDA-FTC Liaison: Teamwork That Pays Off," _FDA Papers,_ Vol. 5, No. 3, April 1971, p. 4.

--------, "How Fares the Consumer Under FPLA?" _FDA Papers,_ Vol. 5, No. 7, September 1971, p. 12.

--------, "More Information for the Public," _FDA Papers,_ Vol. 6, No. 5, June 1972, p. 11.

--------, "Nutrient Labeling," _FDA Papers,_ Vol. 6, No. 4, May 1972, p. 4.

--------, "The Current Status of Food Regulation," _FDA Papers,_ Vol. 6, No. 2, March 1972, p. 10.

Hagedorn, Robert, and Sanford Labovitz, _Introduction to Social Research,_ McGraw-Hill, 1971, pp. 1-102.

Harnett, Donald L., _Introduction to Statistical Methods,_ Addison-Wesley Publishing Company, Massachusetts, 1972, Chapter 5.

Katona, George, _The Powerful Consumer,_ New York: McGraw-Hill Book Company, Inc., 1960.

Mansfield, Edwin, _Microeconomic Theory and Applications,_ W. W. Norton & Company, Inc., New York, 1970.

Myers, James H., and William H. Reynolds, _Consumer Behavior and Marketing Management,_ Boston: Houghton Mifflin Company, 1967.

Newman, Joseph W., _On Knowing the Consumer,_ New York: John Wiley and Sons, Inc., 1966.

92nd Congress, 1st Session, House of Representatives, _Report No. 92-542,_ September 30, 1971.

Parten, Mildred, _Surveys, Polls and Samples: Practical Procedures,_ Harper & Brothers, New York, 1950, Chapters 2, 3, 4, 6, 7, 15, 16, 17.

Peterson, Esther, "Information Labeling as a Consumer Guide," _Food Drug Cosmetic Law Journal,_ February 1972.

Sigband, Norman B., _Communication for Management,_ Glenview, Illinois: Scott, Foresman and Company, 1969, pp. 10-17, 175, 236-37.

Stanton, William J., _Fundamentals of Marketing,_ Third Edition, McGraw-Hill Book Company, New York, 1964.

U.S. Department of Commerce, Bureau of Census, _1970 Census of Population, Census Tracts, Standard Metropolitan Statistical Area, Los Angeles County, Part 1._

--------, _1970 Census of Population, General Population Characteristics--California._

--------, _1970 Census of Population, General Social and Economic Characteristics--California._

--------, _1970 Census of Population, State Economic Areas._

Vital Speeches of the Day, Vol. XXXVIII, No. 19, July 15, 1972.

Wells, Beverly H., "CRI Nutrient Labeling Research," _Food Drug Cosmetic Law Journal,_ July 1972.

Your Federal Trade Commission, What It Is and What It Does, Department of Documents, U.S. Government Printing Office, Washington, D.C., 1971.

28

The Corporate Annual Report

Perhaps the best-known example of a long report is the once-a-year summary of company activities that is issued by thousands of corporations.

Today's shareholder wants to know how "his" company is being managed. His desire for a clear, concise, and complete picture coupled with management's awareness of its public responsibility, have contributed to better and more complete reports.

The corporate annual report is no longer a drab, summary statement of company activities. Today it is usually a well-written document, divided into narrative and financial sections, and enhanced by attractive colors, excellent visual aids, and appealing format. In May 1972, *Time* magazine called it a "gold mine of information making the American investor today probably the best informed in the world."[1]

On the other hand, a recent article had this to say about readership and quality of annual reports:

"... a readership survey published in 1972 by Georgeson & Company revealed that 15 per cent of small shareholders don't read the annual reports of companies in which they own stock, while 40 per cent skim reports in five minutes or less. Fully 53 per cent said they believe annual reports were not written so the average investor can understand them.

Among professionals, annual reports fared even worse. 'In general, they don't do the job they're supposed to do,' says Dr. Abraham Briloff, professor of accountancy at Baruch College, City College of New York .... James Grant, a business writer for Time magazine, warns, 'To base any kind of money investment solely on an annual report is madness.' "[2]

More and more critical readers are requesting the firm's 10-K, which is the report that must be filed with the Securities and Exchange Commission. This report is far more detailed and complete than the annual report insofar as significant financial data are concerned. And there now are a few firms which issue to their stockholders the 10-K rather than the usual annual report.[3] However, there are those who feel the stockholder enjoys the color and photos of the annual report. If those can be retained while improving clarity, adding vital details, and increasing candor, the best of the annual report and the 10-K will be achieved.

A *Fortune* article[4] had this to say about the corporate annual report:

The exercise (of writing and producing the annual report) in a large corporation can monopolize the attention of top management and turn the staff upside down. Pub-

---

[1] *Time,* Annual Report Advertising Section, May 22, 1972.

[2] Art Detman, Jr., "Will Anyone Read Your Annual Report?" *Mainliner* (United Air Lines Magazine), March 1974, p. 25.

[3] *Ibid.*

[4] From "How's the Annual Report Coming?" by Samuel W. Bryant from *Fortune* Magazine, (January 1964). Reprinted by permission from Fortune Magazine; © 1964 Time Inc.

lic-relations men, concerned with the rounded image, find themselves arrayed against the lawyers, cautious by nature, and conservative-minded executives who are afraid of being burned by telling too much. The financial people grouse when their beloved statements are overshadowed by corporate messages and four-color photographs. Divisional vice-presidents argue for equal space (if the year's record has been a good one) or better billing. Such feuding can escalate to a very high level; the chief executive, or someone very close to him, may have to step in at a critical moment to act as arbiter, and calm the roiled waters.

Usually all the time is well spent. The annual report is of unique importance to a corporation; it is, in fact, the one chance that a company has each year formally to tell its share owners and the world at large what it has done, is doing, and plans to do. Besides being management's proud report of performance (or in some cases its *mea culpa*), the report reflects a corporation's character, creates its public image, and makes available information of interest to share owners and security analysts. What it says may have a direct bearing on the price of its securities; how it says it reflects the character of management and may well attract or repel potential customers.

Purposes of the Annual Report

The primary purpose of the annual report is to present an informative summary of company activities to stockholders, each of whom owns a share of the company and is interested in learning about the progress the firm has made during the previous year, its financial structure, its profits, its union-management relations, its expansion of facilities, its new product development, its relationship with government agencies, its long-range objectives, etc.

But today's annual report has still another purpose. It attempts to build good will among its shareholders, and sell its products, stock, and company image to others. This is one reason why corporations distribute many more reports than they have stockholders. American Telephone and Telegraph, with 2.7 million stockholders, printed 3.6 million reports in 1966. Continental Oil had 43,000 stockholders but published 93,000 copies of its 1966 report.[5]

The additional copies go to employees, educators, suppliers, government agencies, libraries, securities analysts, brokerage firms, banks, foundations, financial institutions, insurance firms, university endowment officers, financial editors of newspapers and magazines, legislators, and many others.

With this wide readership, the annual report writer is confronted with a major problem in composition. How does he adjust his style, word choice, financial data, complexity of charts, and overall content to the variety of reader levels and interests?

To accomplish a good job, the writer must weigh every word, examine every sentence, check every graph, and evaluate every page to make sure that all his readers will find the report interesting and valuable.

One author made this observation about the purpose of the annual report:

[5] Howard L. Sherman, "The Corporate Reporting Explosion in Print: Annual Reports." Speech delivered at annual report awards ceremony sponsored by *Financial World Magazine,* Hotel Commodore, New York, January 19, 1966.

"Good or bad, the annual report has become the single most important document a company publishes. A readable report can help a company's long-range profitability in a variety of ways. Besides its primary mission of helping stockholders place a proper evaluation on the company's stocks, it can help sell products and services, recruit superior personnel, improve employee relations, win the support of community leaders and government representatives."[6]

Fred C. Foy feels that it *is* possible to write an annual report that will prove interesting and valuable to two different readerships: the security analyst and the company shareholder. This can be done by providing adequate financial data and commenting on it in clear and uncomplicated language. As for company activities, they should be covered concisely and candidly in an attractive format."[7]

Content and Make-up of the Annual Report

The content of the annual report can usually be divided into three major sections: the introductory section (letter of transmittal and table of contents), the narrative portion, and the financial information.

The president or chairman's letter to the stockholder (letter of transmittal) is usually a crisply worded summary of the highlights of the year's activities. It gives the reader a bird's-eye view of the entire report and serves a purpose similar to that of the letter of transmittal in the typical formal report.

This letter should be friendly, and written from the stockholder's point of view. A stiff, formal, "boardroom" tone will build few friends among the stockholders who live on farms and in towns and cities throughout the country. This letter is the corporation to many; it is vital that it build good will.

The narrative portion of the report may discuss the company in relation to the following:

1. *Products and services.* The stockholder is interested in learning about the specific products the company handles and what services it makes available to its customers. A word should be offered on new items contemplated, future markets, advertising and marketing programs, the reactions of customers, and other areas related to the firm's products.

2. *Plants and equipment.*

3. *Employees.* The report should discuss how many employees the firm has, the benefits extended to them, payroll information, educational activities, affirmative action programs, employees in community affairs, employee health and safety records, etc.

4. *Labor relations.* A clear and frank discussion of company relations with unions should be presented. If the firm has had labor problems, strikes, or disagreements during the year, they should be discussed objectively. The stockholder will have learned of the firm's problems from newspaper articles; he deserves a clear and honest explanation of them in the report.

5. *Stockholders.* How many stockholders does the company have? How and where are they distributed? What are their interests?

[6] William H. Dinsmore, "Dear Stockholder: Everything Looks Rosy." *Harpers,* XXIII (March 1965), p. 138.
[7] Fred C. Foy, "Annual Reports Don't Have to Be Dull," *Harvard Business Review,* (Jan.-Feb., 1973).

6. *Government.* What percentage of the firm's production goes to the government? What are the future trends likely to be? What interest do federal agencies have in the company? Have investigations been completed? Are they contemplated?

7. *Community.* Some comment should be made on the firm's relations with and contributions to the community. Have employees held public office? What recognition or complaints have been directed to the company?

8. *Research and development.* Where is the firm going? Does it contemplate expanding its product line? Is it going to diversify? Will it merge with other firms?

These are only some of the areas that can be dealt with in the annual report. There are many others.

The financial information in the annual report is vital to most readers. It should be complete, objective, and presented in a style that is easily understood by the average stockholder.

The report should include a comprehensive balance sheet which permits comparison with previous years' records. As for the narrative text, the American Management Association feels that it is almost as important as the figures themselves. It can serve to amplify the statistics, to explain certain conditions, to qualify various items, and in general to throw additional light on the firm's financial picture.[8]

Howard Sherman, director of *Financial World's* annual report survey, has drawn up this list of ingredients for the well-designed report:

A minimum of twelve pages, including the cover.

Highlights, for a quick summarization of the year's results in comparison with the prior year's performance. Inclusion of percentage change figures enhances the value of this section.

An informative, easy-to-read message from the chairman and/or president.

A comprehensive narrative review of the twelve-month period just concluded. Operating and financial matters to be covered include, for example, prospects for each of the company's divisions, research and development, nature and cost of acquisitions, marketing and advertising details, sales breakdowns, and future financing plans.

A comprehensive balance sheet and profit-and-loss statement, with comparative figures for two years, and adequate footnotes.

Statement of earnings and dividends on a per share basis, for both the current and the previous year, at a minimum.

Statistical data for a sufficient number of items, preferably for ten years.

Source and disposition of funds statements.

Certification by independent public auditors.

[8] "Preparation of Company Annual Reports", American Management Association, Inc., Research Report Number 10, New York.

A high degree of technical excellence in design and typographic art so as to help the reader absorb the hard information in the quickest possible time.[9]

Presenting figures for the last five or ten years is now commonplace; longer periods are not unusual. This is vital for the serious reader who wishes to follow financial trends in the firm.

To all these criteria against which an annual report should be measured, I would add, again, the quality of clear, concise, and readable writing.

The guidelines set down by the American Management Association for good reporting are excellent: The report must be complete; it must be interesting; and it must possess clarity of expression.

Production and Distribution

Collecting information from various divisions or subsidiaries of a large corporation, securing excellent photographs, and amassing accurate statistical data is a major task in itself. It requires creative planning to wrap everything up clearly and concisely in a limited number of pages—to the satisfaction of the company's officers and stockholders.

That is why most firms make one competent person responsible for the production of the annual report. If he is wise, he prepares a timetable and holds to it: narrative explanation of the following areas is due on this date; financial data on that date; selection of photographs and drawings of graphs must be completed by this time; and presses are to roll on this date. If he fails to do this, information will trickle in, changes will be made constantly, and confusion will result.

A careful plan for the distribution of the annual reports should also be followed. Of course every stockholder receives a copy, but many other persons and groups should be considered, for, as noted earlier, the annual report can be a potent good-will builder. Among those to whom copies might be sent are:

Company employees	Community leaders
Company suppliers	Newspaper and magazine
Financial analysts	editors
Educators	Brokerage firms
Government agencies	Legislators
Bank officers	Radio and TV
University and foundation	commentators
investment officers	Libraries
Customers	Clergymen
Investment club officers	Officers of service groups

With stock ownership so widespread in America, a company that does not produce an excellent report does itself a disservice. Many firms have found that an outstanding report helps their stock sales and improves their public image.

[9] Howard L. Sherman, "Twenty-five Years of Annual Report Progress," *Financial World Magazine* (June 30, 1965), p. 69.

Questions for Study

I. Complete any of the following problems assigned. You may wish to review the chapter and note key points before attempting to solve the problem.

1. List and briefly discuss several different types of reports having different objectives.

2. Secure a persuasive and/or a comparative report. Submit it together with an evaluation noting the specific areas within the report that justify your classification.

3. Assume that you have completed a survey of the training activities of the Fairbanks Steel Corporation. You used company records going back ten years, information secured from interviews with employees, employee questionnaire surveys, and secondary sources which reported training activities of other firms. Prepare the letter of transmittal which will convey your formal report to the president of Fairbanks.

4. Assume that your instructor has requested a detailed report from you on formal and informal communication networks in an organization. You have secured your data by direct observation within the organization, structured and unstructured interviews with the personnel involved, and secondary sources. Prepare the letter of transmittal which will accompany your report.

5. Complete title pages for the reports noted in problems 3 and 4 above. Assume that both reports were completed during this month in New York.

6. Prepare a title page for a formal report concerning stock market fluctuations and apparent economic causes. The report was prepared last month by the Economics Department of your college for distribution at an Economics and Monetary Seminar that your School of Business sponsored.

7. Prepare a title page for a report which contains an analysis of the relation between educational attainment and annual income. The report was completed by the Department of Education of your state for distribution to PTAs and other groups interested in helping to reduce the number of high school dropouts.

II. Assume that you are in charge of the four-man investigation team assigned to carry through an analysis of the Department of Weights and Measures of Lyons, Illinois. Using the data in the problem below, present a formal report to the City Council of the city of Lyons, Illinois. On the basis of your findings, conclusions, and recommendations, the City Council may vote to take specific (and perhaps drastic) action concerning the organization and operations of the Department of Weights and Measures. Remember to thoroughly substantiate—with facts and figures—all your recommendations. Vague generalities and opinions (as opposed to proof) will not hold water.

You may add or delete any information which you feel will improve your report for decision-making purposes.

DEPARTMENT OF WEIGHTS AND MEASURES

This unit was established by City Ordinance in 1942 and had as its primary purpose:

The inspection of all scales, weights and measures together with the business firms using such devices. Periodic checks, on a careful sampling basis, were to be carried through to ensure that retail measuring devices (store scales, measures, and balances) ensured the consumer of full weight in all food and nonfood products. Packaged items were to be checked to ensure that printed weights and costs conformed to actual weight.

Wholesale purveyors were also to be checked (foods, coal, oil, etc.).

Miscellaneous scales (taximeters, parking lot clocks, etc.) were also to be evaluated.

Violations were subject to city legal action as set down in Lyons City Statute 21-234.

Unit Personnel Organization

At the present time the department numbers 260 personnel as compared to 180 in 1970, 160 in 1965, 110 in 1960, and 40 in 1952.

The department has one director and four assistant supervisors: consumer foods, consumer nonfoods, wholesale, and miscellaneous. They are designated Units I, II, III, and IV, respectively. Unit I has 110 inspectors, Unit II has 40, Unit III has 60, Unit IV has 20, and there is a clerical office and lab staff of 25.

Problem Areas

Although complaining citizens' letters to the Division and the Mayor have always come in, the number has increased tremendously since early 1973. Most of these accuse food store operators, both chain and independent, of short-weighting merchandise. The letter writers charge that meat and produce prepackaged items carry overcharges of 10¢ to 50¢; this is due to false listing of weights on the printed labels.

Gas station operators are also accused of having "fast" counters on pumps which charge for more gasoline than is actually delivered.

Complaints at the wholesale level and about parking lot clocks and taximeters are almost nonexistent.

Findings Within the Department

The supervisors in charge of Units I, II, III, and IV have held their positions 24, 20, 4, and 6 years respectively.

Inspectors of Units I and II are assigned to different sections of the city and as near to their own homes as possible. Some inspectors have been checking the same business establishments for many years. Unit III and IV inspectors are required to cover different areas of the city in accordance with their supervisors' directives.

All inspectors are required to complete a performance report twice each week at Headquarters. Days are staggered so that all personnel are not in the office at any one time.

Unit I has three Chief Inspectors; Unit II has one; Unit III has four; and Unit IV has one.

Your interviews within the department uncover a great deal of animosity of Units III and IV members for I and II personnel. Three or four men in Units III and IV commented bitterly on the fact that their Chief Inspectors are "rough, require 20 calls per day, and bounce anyone even suspected of taking a nickel." This is in contrast, they imply, to the men in I and II "who drive their Cadillacs to the same place, hold second full-time jobs, and fly to Hawaii every few months to spend their 'earnings.'"

Although these comments came from only a few men, the others in III and IV exhibited no great loyalty or respect for personnel in I and II.

Interviews with the supervisors led you to believe that Units I and II were "easily run," with few rules and almost no "checking on the checkers" being carried through. Units III and IV personnel were obviously closely supervised.

Your review of performance reports on file clearly indicated sloppy reporting in Units I and II, incomplete findings, lack of clarity, omission of signature and facts, and dozens of reports which would prove valueless in court action. In Units III and IV, each report was complete and signed by the inspector and his chief.

Outside the Department

Your analysis of consumer food stores revealed that several did short-weigh on meat, grocery, and produce packaged items. These purchases were, of course, made anonymously. Other personnel in the audit team disclosed that several of these same outlets had been inspected but never found in violation.

Interestingly enough, most such violations were found in very low-income, transient neighborhoods with a high percentage of Negro and Latin American residents. The same findings were determined with gasoline stations.

Interviews with store managers indicated their determination to be extremely honest, but of course, "sometimes moisture dries out and a package may lose ½ ounce or so."

Interviews with several neighborhood group officers and church officials in low-income areas determined that they had run their own surveys and found that

(1) specific independents and chains made a practice of short weight, and

(2) it was common knowledge that such stores paid off city inspectors.

Of course, this was all hearsay and no documentation or substantiation was available.

For some reason the store managers in upper income sections (Westwood, Bel Air, Prairie Palisades) reported extremely few visits by inspectors. Some indicated that they had *never* seen an inspector. Curiously enough, as many inspectors were assigned (at least on the books) to these areas as to other sections of the city.

Laboratory Procedures

The laboratory procedures seem almost completely haphazard. Packages of food and nonfood items are stacked everywhere; inspectors' labels on the items are often incomplete or nonexistent; the method of checking weights and prices is not set down; refrigerators overflow with foodstuffs; and many items approved seem to go home with inspectors rather than to public institutions as required. The lab personnel do not seem very competent.

The lab supervisor is an elderly gentleman who was transferred in from the police department after an accident which incapacitated him. "Yes, he knows his system isn't very good, but one day he's going to get some smart book man from college over, who will set up a system—maybe even new-fangled like IBM."

Expenditure of Funds

Money for the department's purchase of all over-the-counter items comes from a fund administered by the department supervisor. It is given out on signatures. The form lists only unit number, items purchased, date and signature. It does not list store, station, or place where purchase was made.

Inspector expenditures have gone up dramatically in the last 5 years:

1975	$26,540
1974	21,500
1973	16,300
1972	14,800
1971	14,200

Legal Procedures

Interviews with the city attorney and his subordinates were held. All comments in reference to the Department of Weights and Measures were negative. Cases could almost never be tried (especially at the retail level) because of extremely poor records left by inspectors or lack of clear-cut evidence. When cases were brought before the courts, inspectors frequently did not appear, their records were not available, or they were reluctant to testify.

III. Write a formal report on any one of the topics listed below or one which your instructor assigns. If you choose your own topic, you should submit the title and a brief outline for your instructor's approval.

Your instructor will designate which (or all) of the following sections should be included in your report. The approximate length may be indicated.

Cover	Body of Report
Title Page	Introduction
Letter of Transmittal	Discussion
Table of Contents	Conclusion
List of Figures	Recommendations
Preface	Appendix
Acknowledgment	Bibliography
Summary	Index

1. The Grapevine in Industrial Communications
2. Informal Lines of Communication in Industry
3. Industrial Training in Listening
4. Industrial Training in Communication
5. Industry's Attitudes Toward the Importance of Communication as a Management Skill
6. Industry's Suggestions on Collegiate Education in Communication
7. The Mathematical Theory of Communication
8. The Shannon-Weaver Communication Theory
9. Jurgen Reusch's Contributions to the Field of Communication
10. The Position of the Industrial Director of Communication
11. Research in Communication Breakdowns in Industry
12. How a Selected Group of Firms Have Attempted to Improve Vertical Communication
13. Development and Use of the Employee Orientation Manual
14. Trends in the Corporate Annual Report
15. Labor Unions' Communications to Members
16. An Analysis of Union and Management Printed Communication Media to Workers
17. The Accountant as a Communicator
18. Printed Versus Interpersonal Communications to Employees
19. What Does the Corporate "Director of Communications" Do?
20. Communications and Company Morale
21. Employee Comprehension of Company Communications
22. Do Company Communications Motivate or Antagonize the Worker?
23. What *Does* the Employee Hear When Management Speaks?
24. Information Retrieval
25. Attitude Change as a Result of Communication (among consumers; among the public in response to political situations; among students involved in campus activities)
26. An Explanation of the "Semantic Differential"
27. The Information Explosion and the Computer
28. Decision Making and Communication
29. Listening as a Management Tool
30. Can a Corporate Image be "Structured"?

IV. Complete either of the following examination reports assigned. You may wish to review the chapter and note key points before solving the problem. You may assume any reasonable facts, data, and information which will make your report more complete.

You will probably want to add visual aids to assist your reader.

1. Your firm, Westwood Furniture Corporation, has begun a program of acquisitions in an attempt to diversify and thus gain strength in areas that are extremely active. The Board of Directors has committed itself to the acquisition of firms serving the aerospace industry. By so doing, they feel that administration and control will be easier and more efficient.

   On March 1, you and three other men were each asked to "check out" a company that was under consideration. Each person is to evaluate the firm and submit a recommendation report to the Board of Directors prior to April 10. Their quarterly meeting is scheduled for the 15th, at which time decisions will be made.

   You were assigned to gather data on the Kellogg Fastener Corporation. You were in and out of the firm throughout March and you were able to watch operations, review records, and interview personnel. You have all kinds of information—most in helter-skelter form—and you're now ready to write your report.

   Kellogg manufactures several basic types of fasteners (rivets) for aircraft use. These are made of aluminum alloys and lightweight steel; a few selected types are titanium. The company is run by Mr. Albert Kellogg and his two vice-presidents (and sons), Joe Kellogg in charge of sales, and Mike in charge of production.

   The company has three primary product lines: the SR22 (hi-strength steel rivets); the AR32 (aluminum); and the TR92 (titanium). Each line has three basic models and production is measured in pounds. Models A, B, and C of AR32 have increased in production. Kellogg sold 6000 pounds of Model A in 1976 as compared to 5200 pounds in 1975. Models B and C were both up from 6000 pounds in 1975 to 8400 in the following year. In the case of the steel rivets, Models A and C rose from 9200 and 9600 pounds respectively in 1975 to 12,000 and 12,500 in 1976. However, Model B of SR22 dropped from 8500 pounds in 1975 to 6100 in 1976. This may be because the head seems to snap off under slightly greater than usual pressure.

   Perhaps the greatest potential lies with the titanium line (TR92), since each of the new supersonic planes, "air buses," and tactical aircraft uses from 400,000 to 3,000,000 titanium rivets. Of course there is much competition in the area even though demand for titanium fasteners has skyrocketed throughout the aircraft industry. Kellogg has hardly kept pace with 15,000 pounds of TR92 Model A in 1976 as compared to 13,000 in 1975. Models B and C, however, each rose from 18,000 pounds in 1975 to 24,000 in 1976.

   One of the factors that impressed you was the sales force. In 1949, when the company was founded in Hawthorne, California (where the plant is still located), Mr. Kellogg had 4 salesmen calling on the aircraft plants. Today the sales force numbers 15 under Joe Kellogg. When you asked Joe if he had tried to sell the Kellogg line to other industries (boating, shipping, truck manufacturer), he said that they keep thinking about it, "and one of these days I'm going to get a flyer out and really get involved. Surely they use our products and there's no reason why they shouldn't buy ours."

   The plant itself is about 38 years old and was used to build piston plane motors before Kellogg bought it. The water lines need replacing as does the illumination. The loading docks are very awkward and the cafeteria and so-called employee areas are in terrible condition. You estimate it would cost about $125,000 to put the 160,000-square-foot plant in decent shape. The offices are almost in the production area, and the parking facilities for the 380 employees consist of an unpaved lot next to the plant.

   The employee picture is not too good. There has been a relatively high turnover among the production workers. These are primarily of Latin American background. Since 1973 there have been 3 strikes (Local 405 of the Aerospace Union) and each strike has resulted in higher wages. Approximately 35 to 45 workers leave and are replaced each month. Many complain about the poor eating facilities, the strict supervisors, and the lack of fringe benefits.

The fastener industry on the whole is excellent. More and more fasteners are used on all types of vehicles including aircraft. Methods for their application have been improved tremendously. High-speed rivet guns and mechanical inserters permit one person to fasten two sheets of aluminum 16 feet long in 8 minutes using 96 fasteners.

Lines of authority and channels of communication at Kellogg are completely confused. The Kelloggs have no compunction about giving orders on the line and completely ignoring the foremen or lead men. Production workers often go right to supervisors or officers and skip their immediate superiors. Housekeeping in the plant is rather poor and pilferage seems high, though no specific figures on the latter are available.

The profit picture at Kellogg is excellent. In the years 1971 to 1972, the net profit rose $84,000 to $96,000. In 1973, it was $140,000; in 1974, $165,000, and in 1975, $128,000. However, in 1976 it jumped to $175,000. The price that is desired for the operation is $1,900,000 plus a 5-year contract for each Kellogg to remain in his present position at his present salary. The president now draws $55,000 per year and the heads of production and sales, $40,000 each per year. The $1,900,000 includes the site, plant, and all equipment and fixtures. Even though you're no expert in this area, you feel that figure is not at all unreasonable.

2. You have just completed a survey of the training facilities of the Jet Air Corporation on the request of the president. He felt that training within the company was fragmented, took place under different supervisors, was wasteful because it was duplicative, and was too costly.

He has asked you to prepare a report on all training within the company, the cost during each of the last two years, the number of people involved, your evaluation of the effectiveness of the various programs, and your recommendations.

You have found that there are 5 trade courses being offered for hourly personnel; 4 courses (in three different plant locations) for office personnel; and 8 different courses for management personnel.

In addition, the company runs 8 three-day seminars for engineering personnel each year.

Each year three executives are sent to the University of Southern California's Management Policy Institute, and special sessions are conducted periodically on computer use and technology.

Outside consultants and Jet Air personnel are used as instructors.

Assume all course titles, costs, test results, and data secured as a result of talking to supervisors regarding the effectiveness of the courses.

You may wish to do some research in secondary sources so that you will have adequate data to write an excellent report.

V. Complete any of the following problems assigned.

1. Although the annual report is addressed to the company's stockholders, there are many other types of readers. Name at least five additional groups that read the annual report carefully, and indicate what their primary objective is in examining corporate reports.

2. Secure two annual reports from one company; one should be current and one should have been issued at least five years earlier. Compare the following areas and note similarities and differences in the two reports.

The president or chairman's letter of transmittal
Labor relations
Employees
Government relations

3. Write a short essay on the steps, procedures, and administrative factors involved in producing an annual report. This will require primary research within a company as well as the use of secondary sources.

If two or more individuals each choose a different corporation, interesting comparisons can be drawn in oral reports or a panel discussion presented by those involved.

4. Many individuals contend that the large sums of money spent on producing elaborate and costly reports are wasteful. All the necessary information, the argument continues, could be mimeographed and the funds which would then be saved could be paid to stockholders as dividends. Do you feel that major expenditures made on costly, colorful reports are wise or wasteful? Why?

5. Survey 15 to 20 owners of common stock who receive annual reports. Design a questionnaire in which you attempt to determine what segments of the reports are read most intensively, why this is so, what action is taken (if any) as a result of the reading, how the stockholder feels toward the company, whether the reader finds it simple or difficult to understand the report, how meaningful he finds the visual aids, whether the report increases good will toward the company or not, and related questions.

When you have completed your survey, present the results in either a written or an oral report.

6. Carry through research on the *Financial World Magazine* annual report contest. Secure several annual reports which were selected for prizes this year and last, and present an analysis of their contents based on the criteria for selection established by the magazine.

Using Visual Aids

Ever since an early artist first drew pictures on the walls of his cave, men have understood the value of symbols that speak directly to the eye. Drawings, sketches, pictograms, charts, graphs, and tables are certainly not new devices for communicating ideas. Many of those early messages continue to communicate their ideas clearly and interestingly. But we are still struggling to make sense of the peculiar lettering some civilizations have left us. That is because graphic representation tells a story directly; written words do so only when we understand their key.

Beyond this, a graph or chart will sometimes convey a complex relationship much more quickly and easily than can words. Have you ever tried to read a memo that cited many different sums of money, tons of production, yearly changes in costs, or percentage differentials? We plow through such a discussion several times without understanding it. Finally we turn to making a table that will present the numbers in a more meaningful way. How much better it would have been if the writer had supplied the table himself! The assimilation of statistics is made much easier when they are presented in carefully designed tables, charts, or graphs.

Selection

One word of warning. Graphic aids should not be used just to "pretty up" a report. Their purpose is to clarify the data being presented. If they have no function, they will only confuse the reader.

Who is the Reader?

As in all phases of report writing, the writer must ask himself "Who is the reader?" before choosing the chart or graph. If the report is directed to a group of aerospace engineers, the charts, graphs, and tables can be complex. But a logarithmic chart, for example, would not be appropriate in an annual report to stockholders. An illustration fulfills its purpose only if the reader finds it clear, informative, and easy to understand.

This all seems so obvious as to require no comment. But if one looks through an annual report or a scientific journal, he will often find charts that are not in keeping with the level of the audience.

What Type of Graphic Aid Should Be Used?

A second question the report writer must ask himself is: What type of chart or table will best tell my story? At times the writer gets in the habit of using a table for one type of representation and a bar chart for another, adapting them to almost every situation. He knows them well and can use them effectively, but he runs the risk of not stretching his imagination enough to determine if there might be another, better, way to present the data. If the reader is interested in *trends,* a series of bars or a line graph may be useful. If, however, he is concerned with specifics and precise data, a table may be the answer.

Designing the Content

Not only must the report writer determine which type of graphic aid best presents his data, but he must also decide how complex or simple it should be in reference to the data and the reader. One reader will be comfortable with five different information designations on one chart: for example, solid, broken, dotted, dashed, and dot-dash lines. Another reader requires five separate charts. He doesn't have the interest, motivation, or ability to analyze a single complex visual aid. The importance of design can be seen in Tables 1 and 2 below. Both of them present the same information. But Table 1 is difficult to understand, and much more complex than it should be. Table 2 is simple in its construction and easy to interpret.

TABLE 1. SALES OF HI DEB SPORTSWEAR (LISTED IN DOZENS)

	June 1975	June 1974	June 1968	Unit Difference 1975 and 1968
Swimsuits				
Bel Air Line	225	200	250	−25
Brentwood Line	250	210	225	+ 25
Sailing Jackets				
Bel Air Line	350	330	385	−35
Brentwood Line	400	325	380	−20
Summer Blouses				
Bel Air Line	2400	2350	2150	+ 250
Brentwood Line	1250	1200	1375	−125
Summer Skirts				
Bel Air Line	300	275	285	+ 15
Brentwood Line	500	475	550	+ 50
Blazers				
Bel Air Line	950	925	760	+ 190
Brentwood Line	840	875	800	+ 40

TABLE 2. SALES OF HI DEB SPORTSWEAR (LISTED IN DOZENS)

	June 1975	June 1974	Percentage Change (approx.) June 1975 with June 1974 (Base Year)
Bel Air Line			
Swimsuits	225	200	+ 12.5%
Sailing Jackets	350	330	+ 6%
Summer Blouses	2400	2350	+ 2%
Summer Skirts	300	275	+ 9%
Blazers	950	925	+ 3%
Brentwood Line			
Swimsuits	250	210	+ 19%
Sailing Jackets	400	325	+ 23%
Summer Blouses	1250	1200	+ 4%
Summer Skirts	500	475	+ 5%
Blazers	840	875	—4%

An Example of Choice and Design

Which is the best visual aid to represent the data contained in the following excerpt from a periodic report?

Twelve of our Star-Economy gasoline stations in the Chicago area were selected to check the effectiveness of the two display stands in generating sales. For purposes of the survey, the stations were designated with numbers from 1 to 12 (see Appendix A for number and address of each station).

The test was conducted from June 5 to June 10 and the total sales for three items were recorded: "Road Safety Flares, package of 4," Unit 201; "All Purpose Med-Kit," Unit 404; and "All Purpose Wrench Kit," Unit 605.

Two different cases were used to display these three items for sale. Six of the cases were our regular 5-foot walnut with chrome trim affairs, while the other six were newly manufactured by the Greeley Company. These were only 2 feet wide, constructed of heavy cardboard, and equipped with a continuously flashing red and yellow electric blinker. Stations 1, 4, 5, 7, 9, and 10 received the 5-foot case, and Stations 2, 3, 6, 8, 11, and 12 the 2-foot case with blinkers.

Total sale of the three items during the six-day test period (Monday through Saturday) were as follows: Stores 1, 2, 3, and 4 sold 350, 820, 870, and 440 respectively. In Stores 5, 6, 7, 8, sales were recorded at 375, 950, 475, and 675 units. Sales of the same units in Store 9 were 550; Store 10, 525; Store 11, 1150; Store 12, 1050. It would certainly appear that there is a correlation between sales and type of display case. This correlation was also apparent in a similar survey conducted in Detroit early this year.

On the basis of the data given, the report writer must decide whether to present *trends* in sales, *specific sales figures,* a combination of both, or a "picture" of the information (pictogram).

A quick review of the data tells the writer that the key is to be found in the question, which display case resulted in more sales; not which station(s) had the greatest sales. If he were to present the data as in Examples 1, 5, 6, and 10 which follow he would not communicate very effectively. When the data are grouped by type of display case, as in Examples 2, 3, 4, 7, 8, and 9, the reader will see what is important right away.

SALES OF UNITS 201, 404, AND 605, JUNE 5-10.

Example 1

Station No.	Total Sales
1	350
2	820
3	870
4	440
5	375
6	950
7	475
8	675
9	550
10	525
11	1150
12	1050

(Reflects specific data, though not effectively presented)

Example 2

Station No.	5 ft. Display Case	2 ft. Display Case (Blinker)
1	350	
2		820
3		870
4	440	
5	375	
6		950
7	475	
8		675
9	550	
10	525	
11		1150
12		1050

(Reflects specific data)

Example 3

Station No.	5 ft. Display Case	2 ft. Display Case (Blinker)
1	350	
4	440	
5	375	
7	475	
9	550	
10	525	
2		820
3		870
6		950
8		675
11		1150
12		1050

Example 4

Station No.	5 ft. Display Case	Station No.	2 ft. Display Case (Blinker)
1	350	2	820
4	440	3	870
5	375	6	950
7	475	8	675
9	550	11	1150
10	525	12	1050

(Reflects specific data; well organized)

Example 5

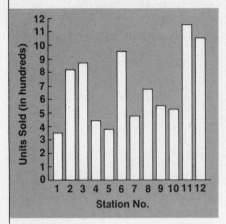

(Reflects trend but difficult to assimilate)

Example 6

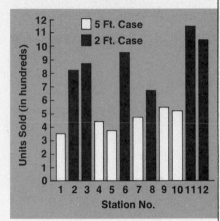

(Reflects trend but is confusing)

Example 7

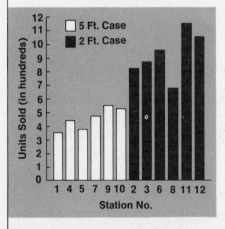

(Reflects trend; well organized)

Example 8

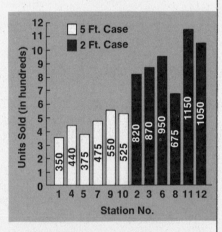

(Reflects trend and cites specific data)

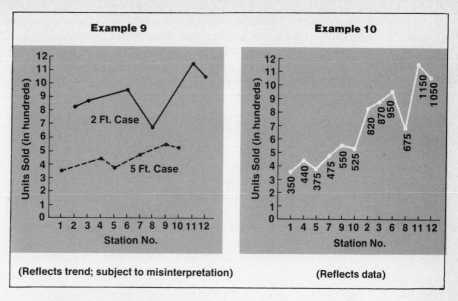

Misrepresentation

Everyone has heard the saying, "Statistics don't lie, but statisticians do." All this means is that writers who use statistics sometimes fail to present them so as to show the whole picture. Sometimes a writer will present some facts in a table, chart, or graph and omit others. The data he presents may be accurate, but the impression they create is basically misleading. The following bar chart is an example of selective omission. The casual reader might simply *assume* that sales have been climbing steadily from 1966 to 1974. However, if we examine the section which has been omitted (ostensibly to save space), we find quite a different story. Sales have *not* gone up consistently. The chart is therefore accurate but misleading.[1]

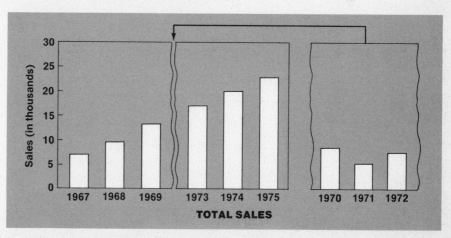

[1] There is probably nothing better available on this topic than Darrel Huff's instructive and entertaining book, *How to Lie with Statistics*. Each of us can find in it examples of misleading statistics which we have accepted—or perhaps transmitted.

Visual distortion is another way to subtly misrepresent statistics. Perhaps the first figure below is not sufficiently impressive. Why not convey it as illustrated in the second figure—or even the third? Note that the tops of the money bags are precisely at 30 and 60 on the vertical axis in each figure, but the horizontal dimension has been stretched.

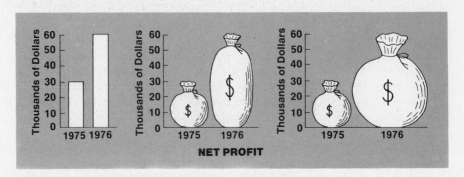

NET PROFIT

Then there are statements which *seem* to convey facts, but, like double talk, really say nothing.[2] The ad which shouts "50% bigger" but neglects to indicate "bigger than what" is an example. Or the "giant 256 sq. in. TV screen"; why "giant"? Certainly 256 sq. in. is 256 sq. in., and adjectives do not increase the size—except to the suggestible mind.

Newspaper columnist Sydney Harris had the following[3] to say about the half-truths conveyed in misleading words:

A government study of income by occupational groups shows that doctors, as a class, earn about twice as much from the practice of medicine as attorneys do from the practice of law.

But this is only another example of the danger of statistics in a void. For while the great bulk of the doctors' income comes from medicine, a similar percentage of the lawyers' income does not come from law.

Many, if not most lawyers, make as much on the side as they do from their direct law practice. They are involved in many legal deals in forming companies, buying property and "putting paper together." For their services, they are often rewarded with a piece of the action. Most lawyers get rich not from legal fees but from supra-legal connections.

Another common fallacy holds that psychiatrists—and especially psychoanalysts—are at the financial top of their profession, because they charge the patient anywhere from $25 to $50 per visit. Actually, these men rank near the bottom of the medical specialties in terms of income, as any accurate breakdown would clearly show.

A psychoanalyst sees about eight patients a day, whereas a well-equipped dermatologist can see more than eight *an hour.* At $10 a clip, the dermatologist can pull in more than $600 a day. The psychoanalyst is forced to charge so much because he gives proportionately so much more time—not to say attention—to each individual patient.

[2] Daniel Seligman, in an amusing and thought-provoking article, "We're Drowning in Phony Statistics" (*Fortune,* November 1961), identifies two varieties of misleading statements: the "meaningless statistic" and the "unknowable statistic."

[3] Sydney J. Harris, "What Statistics Don't Show," *Chicago* Daily News, April 19, 1968, page 18. © Publishers-Hall Syndicate 1968. Reprinted by permission.

Moreover, these men have perhaps double the investment in their career than most specialists have. Not only must they go through a longer regimen of study, they must also have several years of their own personal analysis—which is not deductible as an educational or professional expense.

And someone who wants to do child analysis must take an extra two years to be certified for this specialty-within-a-specialty, which may mean he is nearly 40 years old before he begins to earn more than a nominal income. . . .

The moral is that when we *read* charts, graphs, and illustrations, or interpret statements citing statistics, we should do so critically. Are the ideas conveyed to us accurate and complete? And when we *transmit* ideas through graphic aids or statistics, we should continually ask ourselves whether we are being complete and thorough.

There is probably no statistical reference more commonly used (and misused) than the term *on the average.* It is employed to designate the common characteristics or central tendency of a group.

Because "on the average" is often loosely used to mean several different things, it may be employed in one context and interpreted in another. For example, in the Dependable Car Sales Company, automobiles were sold in the quantities listed on the dates designated below:

DATE	NO. SOLD	DATE	NO. SOLD
July 1	16	July 11	6
July 2	16	July 12	5
July 5	0	July 13	7
July 6	2	July 14	8
July 7	1	July 15	4
July 8	3		

The *mean* (or arithmetical average) number of cars sold is 6.18. This figure is obtained by totaling the cars sold and dividing by the number of days. The *median* number of cars sold, 5, is the middle number in the array of daily sales arranged from high to low: 1 2 3 4 **5** 6 7 8 16. This too is an average, although quite different from the mean.

Thus "on the average" can be easily misconstrued or misused. The report writer should use it with caution, and the report reader should always question an "on the average" figure. He should determine whether the writer is referring to the mean or the median—or perhaps to some other measure of central tendency such as the *mode* (the most frequently occurring number in a group). Beyond that, he should ask how many cases were included in the sample to secure the figure.

THE WIZARD OF ID   by parker and hart

By permission of John Hart and Field Enterprises, Inc.

Tables

What would your reaction be to the following paragraphs encountered in a production report?

This month, January 1976, was an especially satisfactory one, for production increased very appreciably.

In our Model 200 line we sold 250 dozen Western in 1975 as compared to 275 dozen in 1976. This was a 10% increase. In the Tally-Ho line we had a +5% jump with 220 dozen in 1976 and only 210 dozen in the previous year. As for the Bronco Line, also in Model 200, there was a 5% decline with 380 dozen sold in 1976 and 400 in 1975.

The story is relatively similar with the model 300. The Collegiate sold 825 dozen in 1974 and 750 dozen in 1973 for a 10% increase. However, both the Fastback and the Touchdown declined. The former took a −5% (from 600 to 570) drop, and the latter suffered a decline of three percentage points when it went from 500 dozen to 485.

Now compare the above with the table below.

FANFARE PRODUCTION, JANUARY 1974 (IN DOZENS)

	January 1976	January 1975	Percentage Change
Model 200			
Western	275	250	+ 10%
Tally-Ho	220	210	+ 5
Bronco	380	400	− 5
Model 300			
Collegiate	825	750	+ 10
Fastback	570	600	− 5
Touchdown	485	500	− 3

Can there be any question that a table is far superior to a series of sentences in communicating quantitative ideas? In addition, tables have many other advantages:

1. Materials can be listed concisely.
2. Reference to specific facts can be made quickly.
3. Comparisons between and among statistics can be made easily.
4. The reader can comprehend and assimilate quantitative data listed in tables much more quickly than if the same information were presented within paragraphs in the body of the report.

Authorities in the field of visual aids classify tables in different ways. One group speaks of a *dependent* table, which does not carry a title or subtitle and is explained by the text material which follows or precedes it. The *independent* table, with its title, headnote, and explanatory comments found in the caption and/or footnote, stands by itself. Even when examined apart from the text material on the page, it conveys a clear and complete idea to the reader.

Tables are also designated as *spot, special purpose,* and *reference*. The *spot* table may be made up of a few figures, set apart from the text in some organized fashion, to make understanding easier.

FACULTY SIZE AT MIDWEST UNIVERSITY

	1976	1975	1974
Professors	110	90	62
Associate Professors	240	230	205
Assistant Professors	320	402	390
Instructors	340	320	290

The *special-purpose* table is somewhat more complex, usually contains column headings and rulings, and often carries a title.

PRODUCTION OF PRINTED CIRCUIT BOARDS (IN THOUSANDS), CIRCUIT SWITCH CORP., MANSFIELD PLANT

Year	Radio			Television		
	#101	#102	#103	#301	#302	#303
1974	150	250	90	580	300	250
1973	120	220	115	510	310	220
1972	110	220	120	420	290	205

The *reference* table usually contains a fairly large quantity of data. The table is ruled, titled, and arranged to facilitate comparisons and evaluations by the reader. It is not unusual to find government reports containing a great deal of information which has been distilled and refined into one or two excellent tables.

Checklist for Constructing Tables
- ✔ Each vertical column should be headed clearly and concisely.
- ✔ Each reference table should have a number and a title. Subtitles should be used, if necessary, to further clarify or explain the caption.
- ✔ Comparative data should be placed on a horizontal plane from left to right (the usual direction of the eyes in reading).

✔ Fractions should be noted in decimals.

✔ Standard terms should be used throughout the table (yards, meters, fathoms should all be converted to a standard unit of measure and explained in a footnote).

✔ Tables should always be designed so that reading and understanding are easy. This requires careful ruling, plenty of white space, and clear titling.

Charts and Graphs

Charts, graphs, pictograms and sketches can present information dramatically and skillfully. With a glance at a bar or line chart, the reader can determine the *trend* of an activity. For example, have sales increased? declined? remained stationary? Has the gross national product gone up? If the reader sees a tiny moneybag next to a bigger one, he will have his answer right away.

Of course, charts and pictograms do not contain the quantity of specific data a table does, but their purpose is different. They indicate trends, rather than precise data.

Pie or Circle Charts

The "pie" or circle chart is one of the most common visual aids used. It is easy to interpret, does not require extensive art work, and communicates its basic ideas with clarity and simplicity. Although each segment represents a different percentage, the total comes to 100 percent.

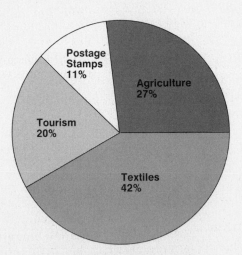

SOURCES OF ANNUAL REVENUE

The pie chart can be presented in a variety of different ways. Firms use a picture of their product to represent their "pie," and divide it into appropriate segments to represent cost of materials, salaries, depreciation, etc. The Brooklyn Union Gas Company used a flame instead of a pie to show its sources of income in 1972 (see page 439):

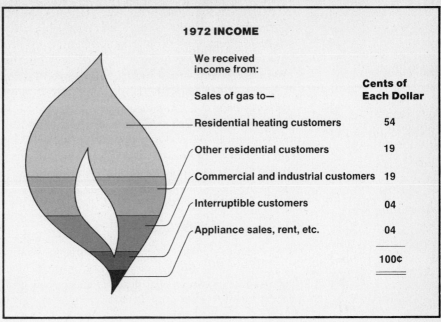

1972 INCOME

We received
income from:

Sales of gas to—	Cents of Each Dollar
Residential heating customers	54
Other residential customers	19
Commercial and industrial customers	19
Interruptible customers	04
Appliance sales, rent, etc.	04
	100¢

Courtesy of the Brooklyn Union Gas Company

A pie may contain all sorts of things, including falsehood. The report reader should beware of the "pie" which has segments labeled only in words but with no percentage figures. And he should also be skeptical of the pie that has segments numbered consecutively and explained at the bottom of the page. One of the most common ploys in the game of "lying with statistics" is the pie (or product) chart with out-of-proportion segments. Each segment in the pie chart should be identified and show the percentage it represents.

Bar Charts

The bar chart is constructed so that each point is located in reference to two variables: one a quantity of money, temperature, volume (etc.), usually indicated along the vertical axis; and the other a time, distance, load (etc.) factor, most frequently indicated along the horizontal axis.

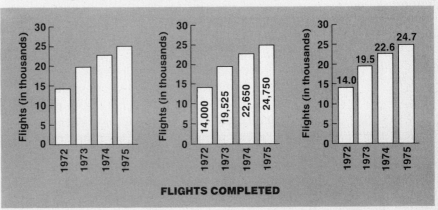

FLIGHTS COMPLETED

Bar charts may be presented either vertically (often called column charts) or horizontally; the length of the bar normally indicates quantity. Ordinarily the variation in bars should only be in length. If a bar is changed in length *and* width, to designate *two* variables, confusion in interpretation is likely to result.

Various techniques can be used to make the bar chart more interesting: bars in a seaond color, hatching effects, projective drawing, or sketches of the company's products in a stylized column form.

One of the criticisms leveled at the bar chart is that it does not reflect quantities with precision and accuracy, which is true. When the reader's eye moves from the top or end of the bar to the scale axis, it is impossible for him to determine the *exact* quantity designation. However, this can be overcome by placing the figures within the bars or at the top of each bar.

Segmented Bar Charts

The segmented bar chart is a simple variation on the pie chart. A single bar represents the total data. However, it is split into segments which are in proportion to the quantities designated. Here also the bar may be horizontal, vertical, or designed to duplicate the company's product.

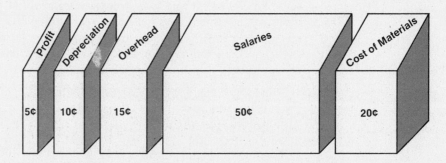

HOW THE COMPANY DOLLAR WAS SPENT IN 1975

Curve Charts

The curve chart is sometimes referred to as a line chart or line graph. The reader can quickly and easily see trends over periods of time. It is easy to make; once the various items have been plotted on the chart, it is a simple matter to connect the points with a curved line.

A further advantage of the curve chart is the large quantity of information which may be depicted on one chart. It is relatively simple to use multiple curves on one drawing to depict related data. Of course the curves are made up differently (solid, broken, dashed, dotted), so the reader can easily tell them apart.

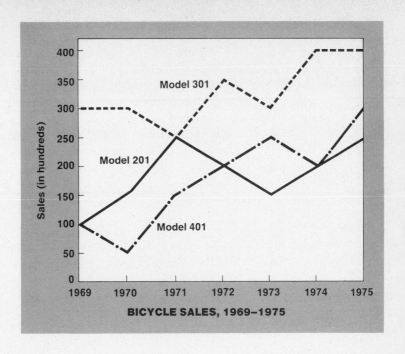

BICYCLE SALES, 1969–1975

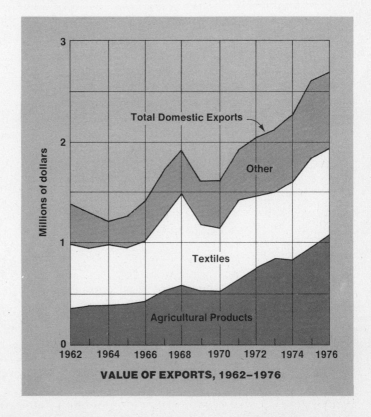

VALUE OF EXPORTS, 1962–1976

Band Charts and Component Bar Charts

The band chart is similar to the multiple curve chart except that it has shadings. Each shaded section (usually beginning at the bottom with a dark color and moving up to lighter colors) represents a quantity. The same pattern is followed with the component bar chart.

These charts should be used only to give an impression of general relationships. If the report writer wishes to give exact relationships or precise data, he should use some other visual aid.

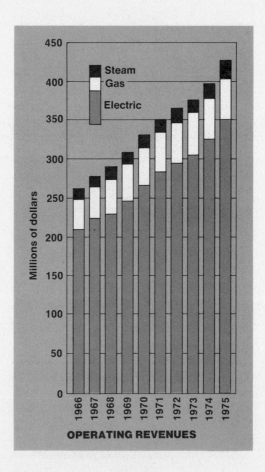

Ratio Charts

For comparisons of growth, ratio charts are often used. These are drawn on semilogarithmic paper.

On an ordinary chart, for example, a change in Army reserve strength from 3000 to 30,000 and Navy reserve strength from 10,000 to 100,000 would be difficult to represent. The major change in the large Navy figure might well force the line or bar designations off the chart completely. The same figures can be

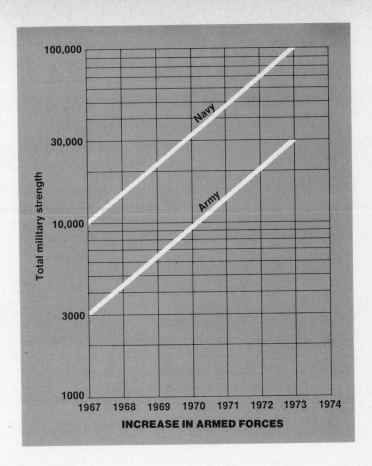

represented more compactly on a ratio chart, which telescopes quantity. Since the scale is based on percentages instead of on absolute units, it enables one to compare growth rates or percentage increases. The accompanying chart shows that the Army and Navy forces grew at exactly the same rate, each increasing by ten times.

Miscellaneous Graphic Aids

Organizational Charts

Modern organizations are so complex that it is sometimes difficult for the manager to have a clear understanding of whom he reports to and who reports to him. And every employee usually feels more comfortable when he knows precisely where he stands within the company, exactly who is his boss, and who is his supervisor's boss.

There are several kinds of organizational charts. Most common is the vertical chart shown here, which reads from top to bottom. There are also horizontal charts, which read from left to right, and circle charts that show authority

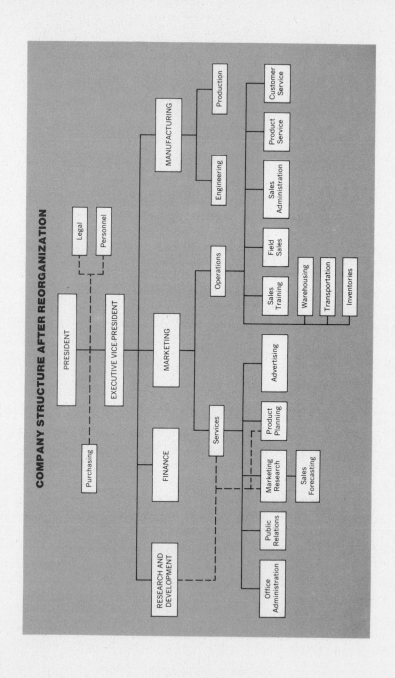

COMPANY STRUCTURE AFTER REORGANIZATION

emanating from the center. A variation of the circle is the beehive chart. In most organizational charts, solid lines indicate direct relationships and broken lines indicate indirect relationships.

Although authority and the chain of command usually differ between the real situation and what is depicted on paper, the organizational chart does serve an important purpose.

Something is needed to give an appreciation of the structure of the company, and nothing does it quite so quickly and easily as an organizational chart. At the same time, it is well to remember that the actual centers of authority in an organization usually differ from what is shown on the chart.

Flow Charts

Flow charts indicate the direction of movement of a product or a process from the initial stages to completion. Sometimes simplified drawings or symbols are used to represent stages, with arrows to indicate direction. The flow chart, flow sheet, or routing diagram can be invaluable to the new employee or anyone who wishes to gain a rapid familiarity with the sequence of activity in a process.

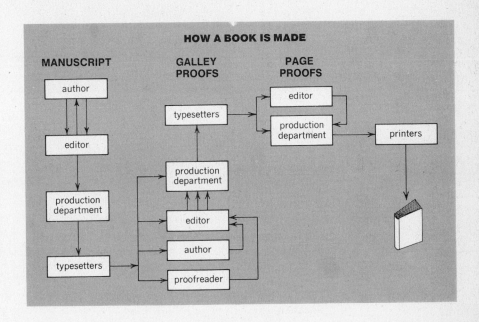

Pictograms or Pictorial Charts

The pictogram is ideal for the reader who is in a hurry, or disinclined to interpret a six-line curve chart. He can quickly see, for example, that the cost of living has gone up if little market baskets are shown marching up a chart, or that more office buildings were constructed this year than last year if five additional skyscrapers are shown on a pictogram.

The symbols, such as dollar signs, autos, homes, planes, tires, etc., should all be of uniform appearance and size. Each should represent the same quantity or dimension. The symbols should be simple and so representative that it

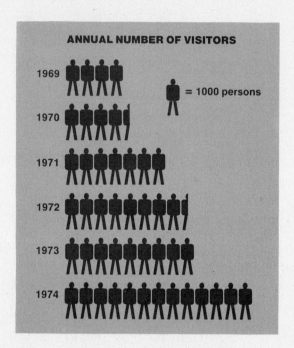

would be almost impossible for two readers to interpret them differently.

Only a limited amount of uncomplicated information can be presented in a pictogram. For data which have several facets and require thoughtful interpretation, other visual aids are preferable.

Map Charts

For representation that is dependent on geographical or spatial relationships, map charts are excellent. Symbols (trees, oil wells, people, livestock, etc.) can designate quantities, and their position on the map can indicate location.

A map drawn out of proportion to its true land areas can be used to indicate the disparate characteristics of various areas of the nation. For example, a map of the United States depicting manufacturing output will have the eastern and midwestern states drawn out of proportion so that they appear much larger than the other states.

MAJOR PRODUCT SOURCE POINTS

△ Cement & Masonry
○ Consumer Goods
■ Plywood
▼ Flooring
‹ Gypsum
□ Lumber
◖ Hardware
● Roofing
✳ Misc. Building Products
★ Appliances & Electronics

Courtesy of the Lowes Company, North Wilkesboro, North Carolina

Cutaway and Exploded Drawings

Cutaway and exploded sketches or photographs are excellent for showing the reader the component parts of a piece of equipment, as well as subsurface areas. They are usually arranged to give a perspective view. A cutaway can often convey a much clearer picture of the interior working parts of a complex mechanical device than could a 5000-word description.

An exploded diagram presents the component parts of a device. Each piece is drawn to show how it fits into, or next to, a contiguous piece. If it is a piece part, for example, each of its segments is exploded. Dotted lines are sometimes used to illustrate how the entire unit is attached to the larger mechanism.

The cutaway and exploded diagrams are most often used in technical reports. They require the services of an artist who can draw with care and precision, and can also use his imagination.

CUTAWAY DRAWING (Courtesy John Deere Company)

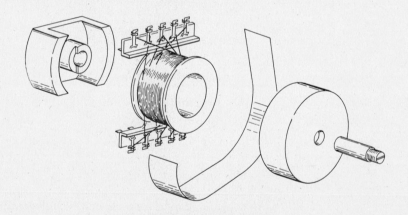

EXPLODED DRAWING

Photographs

The use of photographs in reports has increased in recent years, and with good reason. They are most persuasive as visual evidence in support of the text. If a report writer wants to indicate that a shield does not bend on impact, he can take a picture at the precise instant of impact. If he wants to prove that a cement support cracked, he can take a photo. If someone wants a view of a piece of property, he need only snap the picture and then pencil on it the width, depth, frontage, or other pertinent data. The contractor need not draw a diagram of the kitchen he is going to remodel; he snaps the room from several angles, pencils in the dimensions needed, and hours of drafting time are saved.

Another advantage of photographs is the speed with which they can be made. A Polaroid photo can be snapped and printed in minutes, in black and white or color. Photographs are also easier, less time-consuming, and less expensive to prepare than charts and graphs—although they are more expensive to reproduce in printed form. If only 10 or 20 copies of 4 or 5 pictures are needed, an industrial photo "lab" can supply them at a very nominal charge.

Placement of Illustrations

A table or chart should appear in the text if the material it presents is directly related to the topic under discussion. Any explanation, interpretation, or analysis of it should appear in the body of the report immediately before or after it. On the other hand, when tables and charts are meant only to present material which is related to text information or amplifies it—but which is not vital to it—they can be placed in an appendix or supplement.

The report writer should keep in mind the obvious danger of placing anything important in an appendix. If the reader can refer to a chart easily and quickly, he will use it. If he is required to flip back and forth between the body of the report and charts in the appendix, he may stop referring to the illustrations altogether.

At times a table or chart may be found in a footnote, but it usually seems out of place. The footnote area at the bottom of a page is not recommended for illustrations.

This chapter has presented only a few of the visual aids which can be used to help convey ideas in report writing. There are many others, such as PERT charts, schematics, block diagrams, etc. The writer who is convinced that there is some truth to the old cliché about one picture being worth a thousand words will search out the best visual aid for his particular message and his particular reader.

Questions for Study

I. Answer the following questions as concisely as possible. You may wish to review the chapter prior to completing the assignment.

1. What relationship exists between the choice of visual aid and the reader's vocation, educational level, and needs?

2. What factors govern whether the visual aid is placed in the body of the report (at the appropriate point) or in an appendix?

3. (a) Explain the difference in the meanings of the three "averages": mean, median, and mode. (b) Of what should one be careful whenever he reads or hears the term, "on the average"? Why?

4. What graphic aid(s) would you use to present *trends* most effectively?

5. Which graphic aid(s) would you consider using to describe the change in the retail cost of food between 1970 and 1976 to:
   (a) The President's Council of Economic Advisors
   (b) Readers of the daily newspaper
   (c) Fourth grade students

6. What *specific* factors should influence the report writer in his choice of a graphic aid? Please list.

7. Tables are frequently used to present extensive statistical data. What *specific* advantages do tables possess that make them especially valuable for such use?

8. Secure two annual reports and select three visual aids from each. Note, in constructive criticism, if the aids from each are consistent in their levels of communication; whether they are appropriate for the data and the reader; and related factors.

II. Present the data in the following problems in any tabular or graphic form you feel is the most appropriate.

1. Present the following data to (a) stockholders and (b) the board of directors of the same company. Each company dollar is divided as follows:

	197_	197_
Salaries	$ .38	$ .42
Cost of Materials	.40	.43
Plant Construction	.02	.02
Research and Development	.02	.01
Depreciation	.02	.01
New Profit	.04	.09
New Equipment	.03	.01
Miscellaneous	.09	.01

2. Present an organization chart of a club or society of which you are a member. If you prefer, present the organization chart of your firm.

3. The number of table model radios produced by the three plants of the Faxon Corporation has changed dramatically in the past five years. The Claremont plant produced 185,000; 140,000; 160,000; and 210,000 units between 1972 and 1975 respectively. For the same period, the Farnsworth plant turned out 95,000 for 1972 and 1973 and 110,000 and 120,000 units in 1974 and 1975 respectively.

The Colson plant produced 400,000 units in 1972 and 390,000, 420,000, and 500,000 in 1973 to 1975 respectively. In 1976 some 240,000, 140,000, and 510,000 have been produced by the Claremont, Farnsworth, and Colson plants respectively.

4. List the mean, median, and modal rates of pay for the 10-year period 1970 to 1979, on the basis of the data which follow:

1970	$230
1971	220
1972	215
1973	230
1974	230
1975	230
1976	240
1977	250
1978	310
1979	340

5. Draw a schematic or cutaway of any simple item such as a ballpoint pen, cigarette lighter, or stapler.

6. The number of homes constructed last year in the U.S. was 850,000 as compared with 1,100,000 this year. (For publication in the local newspaper.)

7. Student use of library books and periodicals for the 1975–76 year was as follows:

	Books	Periodicals
College of Engineering	210,000	95,000
College of Law	260,000	85,000
College of Commerce	210,000	98,000
College of Liberal Arts	220,000	120,000

For the period 1975–76, the figure rose 5 percent in both categories for Engineering; declined 4 percent in Law for books and 6 percent for periodicals; remained static for both groups in Commerce; and moved up 10 percent for books in the College of Liberal Arts and jumped 15 percent for periodicals.

In the statistics given above, faculty and all interlibrary loans were not included.

8. In the period 1972–76, World Wide Airlines logged 4,510; 5,000; 6,500; 7,000; and 9,000 flights in each year respectively. Payloads in passengers hit 4,500,000; 6,000,000; 8,800,000; 9,000,000; and 14,000,000 in those same years.

These figures do not include nonpaying passengers such as company officials, inspectors, and employees.

Present the data to (a) the Federal Aviation Authority and (b) Stockholders.

III. Present the data in the following problems in the tabular or graphic form which you feel is most appropriate.

1 The Lyons Corporation produced a large number of water filters in the years 1975 and 1976.

In the classification of "over 750,000 dozen," the 1975 production of the RL100, RL200, and RL300 was 800,000; 850,000; and 950,000 dozen units respectively. For the same type of units in 1976, the production was 900,000 for the RL100; 950,000 dozen for the RL200, and 1,200,000 for the RL300 unit.

In the classification of 350,000 to 750,000 dozen units, the RS300 sold 400,000 in 1975 and 510,000 dozen in 1976. For the RS400, sales rose from 310,000 in 1975 to 360,000 dozen in 1976. As for the RS500, sales dropped in 1976 to 490,000 from 550,000 in 1975.

Published figures from the competing Fargo Company indicated their overall production was 5 percent higher on all items for the same period for products almost identical to the RL Line of Lyons, but a full 20 percent less on the Lyons RS Line.

2. Salaries of seven executives, all of whom are members of the Forest Green Country Club, follow:

Mr. Shur	$ 29,000
Mr. Cates	140,000
Mr. Melton	30,000
Mr. Robinson	25,000
Mr. Arthur	27,000
Mr. Bahr	31,000
Mr. Aspery	130,000

What specific cautions would you recommend to the reader if these figures were presented as (a) mean, (b) modal, and (c) median averages?

3. The Spin-Disk Record Company has divided its sales into three categories: Popular, Classical, and Foreign. An examination of the sales of records to distributors in the United States indicated that in February of 1976, 202,000 Foreign records were sold as compared to 850,000 Pop and 350,000 Classical. In the same month of 1975, 725,000 Pop were sold, 305,000 Classical, and 140,000 Foreign. The figures for February 1976 for Pop, Classical, and Foreign were 8 percent, 6 percent, and 8 percent over the base year sales of 1970.

In Record Club sales, for February 1975, Pop sold 210,000; Classical 65,000; and Foreign numbered 30,000. This was relatively poor as compared to 1976 when sales for Foreign were 51,000; Pop, 290,000; and Classical 105,000. The contrast with the base year 1970 could not be used in this instance simply because no Record Club existed in that year.

4. ABC University is seriously considering the construction of faculty housing near the university campus. At the present time, most faculty live in homes and apartments in the greater metropolitan area of which ABC is a part.

You have just completed a survey of faculty concerning housing and you have found that:

38.5 percent would be interested in buying a new home near the university.

30.5 percent would be interested in living in a university-managed apartment building.

10 percent are undecided.

21 percent have no desire to move from their present location.

5. Our personnel recruitment efforts have encountered a few problems; however, there has been a steady rise in the number of persons secured in all four quarters last year by our Los Angeles headquarters as contrasted to the Chicago headquarters.

In Los Angeles we were able to secure 45 salaried and 320 hourly personnel in the first quarter, and 62, 60, and 40 salaried in the second, third, and fourth quarters respectively. In the area of hourly workers, we added 360, 390, and 320 in the second, third, and fourth quarters.

However, the Chicago office, with much greater needs, was able to recruit only 40, 45, 45, and 35 salaried personnel in the same calendar year in the quarters from first to fourth. The picture was somewhat different in respect to hourly employees in Chicago. In the first quarter, 450 were added to the payroll and for each of the three quarters following, 610, 650, and 550 were added, respectively.

6. Wage rates for skilled artisans in the construction industry in New York have risen from $4.50 per hour in 1972 to $4.80 in 1973 $5.50 in 1974 $5.90 in 1975 and $6.50 in 1976. This compares with California where the wage rates for the same years went from $4.90 to $5.10 to $5.75 to $6.40 and finally $6.90. In New York, this did not include hospitalization costs (of approximately 30¢ per hour in value) but it did in California. All other fringe benefits were included in the hourly rates and were essentially the same in both cities.

7. Your evaluation of college records shows that the School of Engineering awarded 850 Bachelor of Arts degrees and 290 Master of Arts degrees in 1975, and 670 Bachelors in 1974 and 550 in 1973. In 1973, 250 Masters were conferred and 210 in 1974. The School of Business Administration awarded 790 Bachelors and 410 Masters of Business Administration in 1972. These figures rose to 910 and 540 in 1973 and jumped in 1974 to 1050 Bachelors and 610 MBAs.

   The School of Liberal Arts awarded 1800 Bachelors in 1975 and 650 Masters of Arts. In 1974, the number was 1650 Bachelors and 450 Masters, and in 1973 only 290 Masters and 1750 Bachelors.

   All three schools awarded a total of 65 doctorates in 1973; 72 in 1974; and 90 in 1975. Of these figures, four were honorary in each of the three years.

8. Attempt to draw a flow chart tracing the process of registration in your school. You may do this with a specific work process at your place of employment if you prefer.

Brief Guide to Usage

In preparing a speech, writing a report, or composing a letter, all of us, from time to time, have to stop and check on the correctness of a punctuation mark, the spelling of a word, or the grammar of a sentence. Should it be "continual" or "continuous"? "Farther" or "further"? Does the question mark go inside or outside the period in this direct quotation? Should it be "who" or "whom"?

The sections which follow may be used as a quick reference guide to answer these and other common questions. There are many excellent texts and handbooks available which offer a more comprehensive discussion of the areas of diction and grammar.

Punctuation

Use a Comma:

1. To set off an introductory phrase or subordinate clause from the independent statement.

   When I entered the crowded assembly hall, I immediately noted the presence of armed guards seated in the gallery overlooking the stage.

2. Before the coordinating conjunction (*and, or, but, for, yet,* or *nor*) linking two independent clauses. If the independent clauses are very short, the comma may be omitted.

   Key management personnel in the large organization should be carefully selected, and all managers should be informed of their specific responsibilities.

   Barry shouted and Betsy turned.

3. To set off nonrestrictive (or nonessential) phrases or clauses.

   Dr. John Kelly, who taught philosophy for 25 years, received frequent commendation from students and faculty.

   The present Chairman of the Board, as you may or may not know, began as a stockboy with this firm 41 years ago.

4. To set off phrases or words in apposition.

   Mrs. Spear, fashion director for Century Clothes, was elected president of the Designers' Association.

5. To set off a name directly addressed.

   If you will write me at your earliest convenience, Mr. Barclay, I'll arrange a tour for your group.

6. To set off a mild interjection.

   Oh, I didn't want you to purchase a new one.

7. To separate adjectives in a series when they modify the same noun.

   The very contemporary design had lines and patterns of red, green, blue, yellow, violet, and white.

8. To separate words or short phrases in a series.

   The sofa was clean and uncluttered, inexpensive but not cheap, and colorful but not garish.

9. To set off a quotation from the reference source in a sentence.

   "I shall arrive in Los Angeles before midnight," said Mrs. Kelley.

10. To indicate the omission of a word or words (usually verbal).

    Buckingham Way has been renamed Washington Street; Devonshire Place, Adams Avenue; and Kavenaugh Way, Jefferson Street.

11. To avoid confusion in interpretation or to assist in reading a sentence correctly.

    That that is, is; that that is not, is not.

Use a Semicolon:

1. Between coordinate, independent clauses not joined by a conjunction.

   Mrs. Spear submitted her monthly report to the Board; it was accepted without comment.

2. Before a conjunctive adverb (*hence, however, therefore, consequently, inasmuch as*) joining two coordinate clauses.

   The girls enjoyed their vacation; however, their funds were badly depleted by the end of the second week and they had to return.

3. Before a coordinating conjunction joining two independent clauses if the clauses are very long or have commas in them.

   When the race, which has been held every year since 1925, was scheduled, we had 22 contestants; but 5 additional entrants paid their fees to the official registrar, who immediately issued a verified certificate.

Use a Colon:

1. To introduce a list, a statement, a question, a series of statements, a quotation, and in some cases, a word.

   Each man should bring the following equipment: one sleeping bag, hiking boots, rainwear, a small shovel, and heavy outdoor clothes.

2. Before or after a specific illustration of a general statement.

   In the first week he broke a turning rod, dropped a glass test kit, and tore a rubber protection sheet: he was an extremely negligent worker.

   Winter arrived with a sudden fury: the temperature dropped to 15° below zero, six inches of snow fell, and the wind howled violently.

3. Following the salutation in a business letter.

   Dear Mr. Anderson:
   Gentlemen:

Use a Dash:

1. To set off—and emphasize—parenthetical material.

   Rolsted—you know he worked for us in the 1950s—retired in June this year.

2. To indicate when the idea in a sentence has been broken off abruptly.

   Do you believe that—

3. To indicate a sudden change in thought within a sentence.

   Do you believe that—no, I'm sure you would never accept it.

4. To precede a summarizing statement at the end of a sentence.

   Magazines were everywhere, the record player was on, clothes were tossed helter-skelter, food disappeared like magic, laughter filled the air— the girls were home for the weekend.

Use Parentheses:

1. To enclose ideas not directly related to the main thought of the sentence.

   Compton's periodic reports (following the format recommended by the National Trade Council) were submitted by all department managers to the general superintendent.

2. To enclose a numerical designation of a verbal statement. This is sometimes found in legal documentation.

   The escrow deposit of five hundred dollars ($500.00) will not be refunded except through court order.

Use Brackets:

1. To enclose an explanatory comment within a quotation or to insert a correction into quoted material.

   In her article on political upsets, Sarah stated, "Martin was defeated in the election of 1956 [he was defeated in 1952] and this marked the end of 36 years of Democratic treasurers in Wade County."

Use Quotation Marks:

1. To enclose direct quotations.

   Sally said, "People don't change; their basic characteristics remain the same throughout their lives."

   "I don't agree," said Marty.

2. To enclose slang words or expressions.

   My teen-ager said it was a very contemporary styled "pad."

3. At the beginning of each paragraph and at the end of the last paragraph in a quoted passage.

4. To enclose a quotation within a quotation. The initial quotation is enclosed in double quotation marks; the quotation within that in single; and a quote within that one in double.

   Stevenson said, "If we are to live in peace, we must, as the Israeli representative has indicated, 'Appreciate the dignity of all people at all times.' "

   The professor said, "All groups have the same pleasure values, although Carter disagrees with this when he says, 'Entertainment values are not the same for all age groups; a "trip" to some is attractive; to others, repulsive.' "

5. To enclose titles of articles, chapters in a book, or any part of a whole unit such as an opera, play, book, or magazine.

   Thomas Carton wrote the article, "The Problems of International Finance," which recently appeared in *The Financial Quarterly.*

6. To enclose a question mark or exclamation point if it refers to the quotation. Place the question mark or exclamation point outside the last quotation mark if it applies to the statement as a whole.

   Dr. Martin asked, "Isn't that their usual performance?"

   Did Dr. Jameson say, "The students completed work at a very high level"?

   Did you say, "Will all of them receive their degree in June?"

   Dr. Meloan asked, "Did you write the article, 'Communication and Decision Making'?"

Kelly replied, "No, I did not, but I did submit one to *The Journal of Communication* titled, 'Is There a Relationship Between War and Words?' "

Special Note. In using marks of punctuation with quotations or quoted words or statements, remember

1. That commas and periods are almost invariably placed *within* quotation marks.
2. That semicolons and colons are almost invariably placed outside quotation marks.
3. That question marks, exclamation points, and dashes are placed within the quotation marks when they apply to the quoted material, outside when they refer to the whole statement.

Use a Hyphen:

1. To divide a word at the end of a line.
2. To form compound nouns, verbs, and adjectives.

   Mrs. Lyons was my mother-in-law.

   He got angry when he saw that I had double-spaced the letter.

   He is not a very well-known artist.

Use an Ellipsis:

1. To indicate the omission of a part of a sentence. Use three periods if the omission is within the sentence. If the omission is at the end of the sentence, use four periods.

   The transaction was completed . . . and provided for Garson to receive the car plus miscellaneous items. . . .

Use an Exclamation Point:

1. After interjections of very strong or sudden emotion.

   "I will not!" he almost shouted.

   Stop that noise!

2. See also the section on quotation marks.

Use a Question Mark:

1. After a direct, but not an indirect, question.

   Have you completed your analysis of the Compton Company case?

   He asked if we were coming.

2. A question mark is not followed by a comma, period, or semicolon when used in a quotation.

Glenn said, "Will you drive or shall I?"

3. See also the section on quotation marks.

Use a Period:

1. After a complete declarative or imperative sentence.

Effective communication is a vital management tool.

2. To indicate an abbreviation.

He worked for Kingston, Inc., for over ten years.

Use an Apostrophe:

1. To indicate the omission of one or more letters in a contraction or one or more digits in a numeral.

He hasn't been home since he graduated in '70.

2. To indicate the plural of letters, figures, or words.

Betsy received three A's and two B's on her report card.

His essay contained one sentence with three *and*'s in it.

Her *l*'s always looked like *t*'s.

She belongs to the Gay '90's.

3. To form the possessive case of nouns.

The three boys' jackets were red.

He purchased a dollar's worth of candy.

That was my aunt's coat.

The men's tools were left behind.

Note. If the word in question already ends in *s*, add only an apostrophe, if it does not, add *'s*.
The girl's coat was green.
The girls' coats were green.

Note. On the whole it is best to avoid the use of possessives with inanimate objects; e.g., *sink's top, lamp's cord*, or *chair's leg*. *Sink top, lamp cord*, and *chair leg* are standard.

Additional Uses of the Apostrophe to Indicate Possession. **1.** If two or more persons or objects own one item, possession is indicated on the last named only. If the writer wishes to indicate individual possession, an apostrophe is used with each name or object.

Robin and Shelley's car. (Robin and Shelley own one car in partnership.)

Robin and Shelley's cars. (Robin and Shelley own more than one car in partnership.)

Robin's and Shelley's cars. (Robin and Shelley each own one or more cars individually.)

2. In compound words, an apostrophe is added to the secondary or last word to indicate possession.

My brother-in-law's car was damaged in the accident (singular possessive).

My brothers-in-law's cars were all parked in front of the house (plural possessive).

3. Certain phrases involving time that seem to express possession use the apostrophe.

A month's pay was granted.

Three hours' time is not adequate for the job.

His dream was to take a four weeks' vacation in Hawaii.

4. The apostrophe is used to indicate possession with indefinite pronouns.

One's thoughts are sometimes private.

Anybody's ideas are acceptable in this brainstorming session.

5. Where an appositive is used, possession is indicated on it, rather than the basic word.

Bob Thomas the singer's coat was lost. (Because this sounds awkward, it is wiser to say *The coat of the singer, Bob Thomas, was lost.*)

6. Possession is indicated on the "junior" or "senior."

Martin Kelly, Jr.'s coat was a plaid.

Thomas Kale, Sr.'s store was sold.

7. When one-syllable words, especially names, end in *s*, and possession is to be indicated, an *'s* should be added. If the basic word has more than one syllable and ends in *s*, simply add an apostrophe after the *s*. To add an *'s* after the last *s* in the basic word (Williams') results in an awkward sound (note the difficulty of pronouncing *Mr. Williams's coat*).

Mr. Jones's car
Charles' car

Here again it would be somewhat difficult to say *Charles's car; Charles' car* is preferred.

8. Pronouns in the possessive case do *not* use the apostrophe to indicate ownership; such words are already possessive.

    The radio is hers.

    The chair is yours, but the table is ours.

    Its surface was scratched, but it's (this is a contraction of *it is,* not the possessive pronoun) really of no great importance.

Pronouns

Pronouns take the place of nouns and permit us to avoid constant repetition.

1. A basic rule for the use of pronouns is that they agree in person, number, and gender with the word to which they refer (antecedent).

    Joan gave *her* coat to the *waiter* and *he* took *it* to the check stand.

    The *boys* ran down the road to the oak tree and then *they* cut across the field.

    Shelley got *her* car from the parking lot attendant right away; the other *girls* had to wait for *theirs.*

2. Use a singular pronoun for antecedents connected by "or" or "nor." Note that the pronoun refers to one or the other antecedent singly, not to both collectively.

    Shelly or Betsy will give you her key if you arrive before noon.

    A rake or a hoe will serve no purpose if its handle is broken.

    Neither Mr. Carleton nor Mr. Frank will give you his advice without an assurance of confidence.

3. The pronoun should be plural if the antecedents are connected by "and."

    The car and the train blew their horns simultaneously.

    Barnes and Blackwell gave their briefcases to the messenger.

4. When two antecedents are simply different names for the same person, the pronoun is singular.

    The professor and conference leader received a scroll for his efforts.

5. When two antecedents refer to different persons, the pronoun is plural. Usually the second name is preceded by "the."

The professor and the conference leader received scrolls for their excellent contributions.

6. When two or more antecedents are closely associated by usage or practice, a singular pronoun is used.

Tea and toast has its place in a convalescent's diet.

7. Antecedents nouns take either a singular or plural pronoun, according to the sense of the sentence or the idea to be conveyed.

The jury reached its verdict (one verdict coming from one jury).

The jury put on their hats and coats and left for home.

8. Antecedents involving both genders usually take a masculine pronoun. For precision, however, a separate pronoun for each gender should be used.

Each graduate will receive his degree at commencement.

Each graduate will receive his or her degree at commencement.

9. The words which follow, when used as antecedents, should take singular pronouns. More and more frequently, however, many of them are being interpreted as plural.

anybody	everybody	somebody
neither	someone	nobody
either	none	any
each	everyone	one
		another

Neither of the men paid *his* bill.

Everybody in the room has *his* own opinion.

None of the boys had *his* paper completed.

Note that the sentences above really say, *Neither one of the men; Every single body in the room; No one of the boys.*

Personal Pronouns

The choice between *I* and *me, she* and *her, they* and *them* sometimes causes confusion. Each explanation which follows includes the standard grammar rule as well as a short-cut method. To begin, let us review the pronouns in the objective and subjective cases.

	Singular	*Plural*
Subjective or nominative case	*I, you, he, she, it*	*we, you, they*
Objective case	*me, you, him, her, it*	*us, you, them*

Nominative Case.   1. A pronoun takes the nominative or subjective case when it serves as the subject of a sentence or a clause.

Betty, Dorothy, and I (not *me*) have made arrangements for the party.

Short-cut method: Would you say, "*I* have made arrangements" or "*me* have made arrangements"? Certainly you would choose the former. Therefore the sentence must be "Betty, Dorothy, and *I* have made arrangements for the party."

Mr. Kelly and I (not *me*) were selected.

Short-cut method: Would you say, "*I* was selected," or "*me* was selected"? Certainly you would choose "I was selected." Therefore the sentence must be "Mr. Kelly and *I* were selected."

2. A pronoun completing the meaning of a connective verb or predicate complement (*am, is, are, was, were, be, been,* or *will be*) should be in the nominative case.

It was *he* who was selected.

I believe it is *she* who should receive the award.

3. When the pronoun is the subject of an implied verb, the nominative or subjective case should be used.

He is quicker than I (not *me*).

Short-cut method: Would you say, "He is quicker than *me* am quick," or "He is quicker than *I* am quick"?

He did more for the Church than they (not *them*).

Short-cut method: Would you say "He did more for the Church than *they* did for the Church" or "He did more for the Church than *them* did for the Church"?

Objective Case.   A pronoun in the objective case is chosen when it is the object of a verb or a preposition or when it serves as an indirect object.

He mailed the books to Bob, John, and me (not *I*).

Short-cut method: Would you say, "He mailed the books to *I*" or "He mailed the books to *me*"? Certainly it is the second; therefore the sentence must be "He mailed the books to Bob, John, and *me.*"

He called Miss Johnson, Miss Short, and me (not *I*).

Short-cut method: Would you say, "He called *I*" or "He called *me*"? Obviously the second sounds better; therefore, the sentence must be "He called Miss Johnson, Miss Short, and *me.*"

Relative Pronouns

Some of the more frequently used relative pronouns are *who, whom, which, what,* and *that.* The two that are often confused are *who* and *whom.* However, informal usage seems to be accepting *who* for *whom* more and more.

*Subjective case—**Who***
Who, like personal pronouns in the subjective case, is used as the subject of a sentence or a clause.

Miss Costello is a girl who (not *whom*) I am sure will do well.

Short-cut method: Would you say, "I am sure *she* will do well" or "I am sure *her* will do well"? Certainly "*she* will do well" sounds better than "*her* will do well." Inasmuch as *she* and *who* are both in the same case, the sentence must be "Miss Costello is a girl *who* I am sure will do well."

*Objective case—**Whom***
Whom, like the personal pronouns in the objective case is used as the object of the verb or preposition or an indirect object.

The soldier whom (not *who*) she loved has been sent overseas.

Short-cut method: Would you say, "She loved *he*" or "she loved *him*"? Obviously "she loved *him*" sounds better than "she loved *he.*" Because *whom* and *him* are both in the same case, the sentence must be "The soldier *whom* she loved has been sent overseas."

Miss Colgate is the girl to whom (not *who*) we gave the award.

Short-cut method: Would you say, "We gave the award to *she*" or "we gave the award to *her*"? The second choice is preferable and because *her* and *whom* are both in the objective case, the sentence must be "Miss Colgate is the girl to *whom* we gave the award."

Whoever and *Whomever*
Whoever is in the subjective case and *whomever* is the objective case. Their use follows the same principles as for *who* and *whom.*

The company will award contracts to whomever (not *whoever*) they find acceptable.

Short-cut method: Would you prefer "They find *they* acceptable" or "they find *them* acceptable"? The second choice is better and because *them* and *whomever* are in the same case, the sentence must be "The company will award contracts to *whomever* they find acceptable."

Mrs. Taylor, Miss Jones, and whoever (not *whomever*) else is selected will vacation in England.

Short-cut method: Would you say, "*She* is selected" or "*her* is selected"? Certainly it would be "*she* is selected" and because *she* and *whoever* are in the same case, the sentence must be "Mrs. Taylor, Miss Jones, and *whoever* else is selected will vacation in England."

Capitalization

1. Capitalize the first letter in the opening word in a sentence, a direct quotation, or each line of verse.

   He was an outstanding student.

   Mr. Boynton said, "Effective communication is the executive's primary management tool."

   My heart leaps up when I behold
     A rainbow in the sky:
   So was it when my life began;
   So is it now I am a man:
   So be it when I shall grow old,
     Or let me die!

   The Child is father of the Man;
   And I could wish my days to be
   Bound each to each by natural piety.

2. Titles associated with names are capitalized.

   Senator Birmingham
   President Adams
   Aunt Anna
   Commissioner Baxter

3. Names of national groups, races, languages, or similar designations are capitalized.

   French
   Israelis
   Canadians
   English

4. Names of holidays, days of the week, holy days, and months of the year begin with a capital letter.

   Veterans' Day
   Wednesday
   Good Friday
   Rosh Hashanah
   June

5. Capitalize the first letter in words which designate names of historical periods, treaties, laws, government departments, conferences, commissions, and so on.

   Renaissance
   Clayton Act
   United States Supreme Court
   Bill of Rights

6. Capitalize the first letter in words which refer to names, national or international organizations, or documents.

> House of Representatives
> Drug Council of the International Medical Association
> World Council of Churches

7. Capitalize the first letter of a word referring to a deity, a Bible, or other religious reference sources.

> The Bible, the Koran, and the Torah . . .
> Allah
> God, Lord, and Almighty
> the Congregation of the Missions
> To those persons who know He will . . .

8. The first letter of each important word is capitalized in titles of magazines, books, essays, plays, and so on. Short prepositions, articles, and adverbs in such titles are not, except as first word.

> *Journal of Business Communication*
> *An Analysis of Government Taxation*
> *The Taming of the Shrew*
> *The Decline and Fall of the Roman Empire*
> *My Fair Lady*

9. Capitalize a general term that is part of a name: Santa Fe Railroad

> Southern College of Arts and Sciences
> Baptist Church
> New Horizons Psychedelic Temple

10. Although words which refer to directions are not capitalized, words which are derived from directional terms are. Names of specific geographical areas or directional terms which have reference to parts of a nation or the world are also capitalized.

> A path directly northwest of the tower.
> Far East
> Wild West
> Orient
> a Southerner

Words Frequently Confused

Accent: to stress or emphasize; a regional manner of speaking.
Ascent: a rising or going up.
Assent: to agree; agreement.

Accept: to receive, to give an affirmative answer to.
Except: to exclude; to leave out; to omit.

Access: admittance or admission.
Excess: surplus or more than necessary.

Accidentally:
Incidentally: in both these cases, the "ly" ending is added to the adjective forms, *accidental* and *incidental,* and not the noun forms, *accident* and *incident.*

Ad: abbreviation for *advertisement.*
Add: to join; to unite; to sum.

Adapt: to accustom oneself to a situation.
Adept: proficient or competent in performing a task.
Adopt: to take by choice; to put into practice.

Advice: counsel; a recommendation (noun).
Advise: to suggest; to recommend (verb).

Affect: to influence (verb).
Effect: result or consequence (noun).
Effect: to bring about (verb).

Aggravate: to increase; to intensify; to make more severe.
Irritate: to exasperate or bother.

All ready: prepared.
Already: previously.

All right: completely right.
Alright: an incorrect usage of *all right.*

Allusion: a reference to something familiar.
Illusion: an *image* of an object; a false impression.
Delusion: a false belief.

Almost: nearly; only a little less than.
Most: an informal use of *almost;* correctly, it means greatest in quantity or the majority of.

Altar: a place to worship or pray.
Alter: to change.

Altogether: completely or thoroughly.
All together: in a group; in unison.

Alumnus (sing.): male graduate.
Alumni (pl.)
Alumna (sing.): female graduate.
Alumnae (pl.)

Among: refers to three or more.
Between: refers to two only.

Amount: quantity without reference to individual units.
Number: a total of counted units.

Anxious: upset; concerned about a serious occurrence.
Eager: very desirous; anticipating a favorable event.

Anyone: any person in general.
Any one: a specific person or item.

Assay: to evaluate.
Essay: to try or attempt.
Essay: a literary composition.

Balance: as an accounting term, an amount owed or a difference between debit and credit sums.
Remainder: that which is left over; a surplus.

Bank on: informal expression for "rely on."

Bazaar: an establishment that sells merchandise.
Bizarre: eccentric in style or mode.

Being as, being that: should not be used for *since* or *because.*

Beside: by the side of.
Besides: in addition to.

Biannually: two times a year.
Biennially: every two years.

Borne: past participle of *bear* (to carry, to produce).
Born: Brought into existence.

Breach: an opening; an infraction of a law; a broken promise.
Breech: part of a firearm.

Calculate: to determine by mathematical process. Dialect for "think" or "expect."

Can: refers to ability or capability.
May: refers to permission.

Callous: not sympathetic; hardened.
Callus: hardened area of skin.

Canvas: a coarse type of cloth.
Canvass: to solicit; survey.

Cannon: large gun.
Canon: a law; church official.

Capital: a seat of government; money invested; a form of a letter.
Capitol: a government building.

Carat: unit of weight generally applied to gem stones.
Caret: mark showing omission.
Carrot: vegetable.
Karat: unit for measuring the purity of gold.

Cease: to halt or stop.
Seize: to grasp or take possession.

Censer: an incense pot.
Censor: a critic.

Sensor: an electronic device.
Censure: to find fault with or to blame.
Criticize: to evaluate; to examine.

Cereal: any grain.
Serial: arranged in successive order.

Choir: organized group of singers.
Quire: measure of paper.

Cite: to quote from a source.
Sight: act of seeing; object or scene observed.
Site: a place, such as "building site."

Coarse: composed of large particles; unrefined.
Course: a direction of progress or a series of studies.

Collision: a clashing of objects.
Collusion: a conspiracy or fraud.

Command: to direct or order; an order.
Commend: to praise or laud.

Complacent: satisfied, smug.
Complaisant: obliging.

Complement: that which completes or supplements.
Compliment: flattery or praise.

Complexioned: refers to skin coloring or appearance.
Complected: dialect for "complexioned."

Confidant: one who may be confided in.
Confident: positive or sure.

Consensus of opinion: redundant; *consensus* means "general opinion."

Contact: meeting of surfaces. Frequently misused as a verb to mean "to ask," "to call," "to consult," or "to inform."

Continual: taking place in close succession; frequently repeated.
Continuous: no break or letup.

Council: an assembly of persons.
Counsel: to advise; advice; an attorney.
Consul: a resident representative of a foreign state.

Councillor: a member of a council.
Counselor: a lawyer or adviser.

Core: a center.
Corps: a body of troops; a group of persons in association.
Corpse: a dead body.

Credible: believable or acceptable.
Creditable: praiseworthy or meritorious.
Credulous: gullible.

Critic: one who evaluates.
Critique: an analytical examination of.
Criticism: an evaluation.

Currant: fruit.
Current: timely; motion of air or water.

Data:
Criteria:
Phenomena: The plural forms of *datum, criterion,* and *phenomenon.* Sometimes used as singular, collective nouns.

Deal: informal use for a business transaction; use instead "sale," "agreement," "plan."

Deceased: dead.
Diseased: infected.

Decent: correct; proper.
Descent: going from high to low.
Dissent: disagreement.

Decree: a proclamation of law.
Degree: difference in grade; an academic award.

Defer: to delay or put off.
Differ: to disagree.

Deference: respect.
Difference: unlikeness.

Depot: a storehouse for merchandise or goods.
Station: a place for passengers, a regular stopping place.

Deprecate: to express disapproval of.
Depreciate: to lessen in value because of use and/or time; to belittle.

Desert: a reward or punishment.
Desert: to abandon.
Desert: a barren geographical area.
Dessert: a course at the end of a meal.

Different from:
Different than: either may be used, although American usage prefers "different from."

Differ from: to stand apart because of unlikeness.
Differ with: to disagree.

Disapprove: not to accept.
Disprove: to prove wrong.

Disburse: to make payments; to allot.
Disperse: to scatter.

Discomfit: to frustrate; to disconcert (verb).
Discomfort: distress; not comfortable (noun).

Discreet: prudent; good judgment in conduct.
Discrete: separate entity; individual.

Disinterested: neutral; not biased.
Uninterested: not concerned with; lacking interest.

Disorganized: disordered.
Unorganized: not organized or planned.

Dual: double or two.
Duel: a contest between two antagonists.

Dying: in the process of losing life or function.
Dyeing: changing the color of.

Each other: refers to two.
One another: refers to more than two.

Either:
Neither: refers to one or the other of two. With "either" use "or"; with "neither" use "nor."

Elicit: to draw forth, usually a comment.
Illicit: unlawful; illegal.

Eligible: acceptable; approved.
Illegible: impossible to read or decipher.

Elusive: difficult to catch.
Illusive: deceptive.

Emerge: to come out.
Immerge: to plunge into, immerse.

Emigrate: to travel out of one country to live in another.
Immigrate: to come into a country.
Migrate: to travel from place to place periodically.

Eminent: outstanding; prominent.
Imminent: impending, very near, or threatening.
Immanent: inherent.

Enthuse: a colloquialism meaning "to show enthusiasm."

Envelope: container for a communication.
Envelop: to surround; cover over or enfold.

Erotic: sexually arousing.
Erratic: unpredictable, irregular.
Exotic: foreign.
Esoteric: of interest only to a select few.

Exceptional: much better than average; superior.
Exceptionable: likely to cause objection; objectionable.

Expansive: capable of extension or expansion.
Expensive: costly.

Expect: informal use of "suppose" or "think."

Extant: living or in existence.
Extent: an area or a measure.

Extinct: no longer living or existing.
Distinct: clear, sharply defined.

Facet: a small surface of a cut gem stone; aspect of an object or situation.
Faucet: a spigot.

Facilitate: to make easier.
Felicitate: to greet or congratulate.

Faint: to lose consciousness (verb); feeble, weak (adjective).
Feint: to pretend or simulate; a deceptive movement.

Farther: refers to geographical or linear distance.
Further: more; in addition to.

Fate: destiny.
Fête: to honor or celebrate (verb); a party (noun).
Feat: an act of unusual skill.

Faze: to disturb, discomfit, daunt.

Fiancé:
Fiancés (pl.): the man to whom a woman is engaged to be married.

Fiancée:
Fiancées (pl.): the woman to whom a man is engaged to be married.

Flair: natural ability.
Flare: a signal rocket; a blazing up of a fire.

Formally: according to convention.
Formerly: previously.

Freeze: to turn solid because of low temperatures.
Frieze: ornamentation along the top edge of a wall, sometimes on hung fabric.

Genius: unusual and outstanding ability.
Genus: a grouping or classification, usually on a biological basis.

Grisly: ghastly; horrible; very bad.
Grizzly: a subspecies of bear.

Hale: free from defect, healthy.
Hail: precipitation that has frozen.
Hail: to greet or call out.

Healthful: giving or contributing to health.
Healthy: having health.

Hoard: to collect and keep; a hidden supply.
Horde: a huge crowd.

Holey: having perforations or holes.
Holy: sacred, saintly.
Wholly: entirely; completely.

Human: pertaining to man.
Humane: kindly, considerate.

Immunity: safety from infection; exemption from regulation.
Impunity: freedom or exemption from punishment.

Imply: to hint at or to allude to in speaking or writing.
Infer: to draw a conclusion from what has been said or written.

In: indicates location within.
Into: indicates movement to a location within.

Incite: to stir up.
Insight: keen understanding; intuition.

Incredible: extraordinary; unbelievable.
Incredulous: skeptical; not believing.

Indignant: angry.
Indigenous: native to an area or country.
Indigent: needy; poor.

Individual: refers to a single item.
Party: a festive occasion; legal reference to a group or single person.

Ingenious: clever, resourceful.
Ingenuous: frank, honest, free from guile.

In regards to: incorrect; use "in regard to" or "as regards."

Inside of: informal use for "within" as "inside of five minutes."
Outside of: informal use for "except" or "besides" as "outside of those three members . . . ."

Irregardless: nonstandard for "regardless."

Its: a possessive singular pronoun.
It's: a contraction for "it is."

Later: refers to time; the comparative form of *late*.
Latter: refers to the second named of two.

Learn: to acquire knowledge.
Teach: to impart knowledge.

Less: smaller quantity than, without reference to units.
Fewer: a smaller total of units.

Let: to permit.
Leave: to go away from; to abandon.

Lie, lay, lain: to recline.
Lay, laid, laid: to place.

Likely: probable.
Liable: legally responsible.
Apt: quick to learn; inclined; relevant.

Load: a burden; a pack.
Lode: a vein of ore.

Loath: reluctant; unwilling.
Loathe: to hate; to despise; to detest.

Locate: informal for "settle"; "to make one's residence."

Lose: to cease having.
Loose: not fastened or attached; to set free.

Magnate: a tycoon; important official.
Magnet: a device that attracts metal.

Marital: used in reference to marriage.
Marshal: an official; to arrange.
Martial: pertaining to military affairs.

Maybe: perhaps (adverb).
May be: indicates possibility (verb).

Medal: a badge of honor.
Mettle: spirit or temperament.
Metal: a mineral substance.
Meddle: to interfere.

Miner: an underground laborer or worker.
Minor: one who has not attained legal age; of little importance.

Moral: a principle, maxim, or lesson (noun); ethical (adjective).
Morale: a state of mind or psychological outlook (noun).

Nice: pleasant, agreeable; finely drawn, subtle, as in "nice distinction."

Notable: distinguished.
Notorious: unfavorably known.

Observance: following or respecting a custom or regulation.
Observation: act of seeing; casual remark.

Off of: informal use for "off."

Oral: by word of mouth.
Verbal: communication in words whether oral or written.

Ordinance: a local law.
Ordnance: military weapons; munitions.

Peak: top of a hill or mountain; topmost point.
Peek: a quick look through a small opening.

Peal: sound of a bell.
Peel: to strip off.

Percent: should be used after a numeral (*20 percent*).
Percentage: for quantity or where numerals are not used (a larger *percentage*).

Persecute: to subject to harsh or unjust treatment.
Prosecute: to bring legal action against.

Personal: private; not public or general.
Personnel: the staff of an organization.

Plaintiff: the complaining party in a lawsuit.
Plaintive: sorrowful; mournful.

Plane: to make smooth; a tool; a surface.
Plain: area of level or treeless country; obvious, undecorated.

Practical: not theoretical; useful, pragmatic.
Practicable: can be put into practice (not used in reference to people).

Precedence: priority.
Precedents: cases that have already occurred.

Proceed: to begin; to move; to advance.
Precede: to go before.

Principal: of primary importance (adjective); head of a school; original sum; chief or official.
Principle: a fundamental truth.

Provided: on condition; supplied.
Providing: supplying.

Quite: almost; entirely; positively.
Quiet: without noise.

Real: actual, tangible; also slang for "very" or "extremely."

Recent: newly created or developed; near past in time.
Resent: to feel indignant.

Respectfully: with respect or deference.
Respectively: in order named.

Resume: to begin again.
Résumé: a summing up.

Right along: informal for "without interruption" or "continuously."

Rise: to move upward; to ascend (rise, rose, risen).
Raise: to elevate; pick up (raise, raised, raised).

Salvage: to save (verb); material saved from a fire, shipwreck, etc. (noun).
Selvage: edge of cloth.

Sit: to be seated.
Set: to put in position (set, set, set).

Sometime: at one time or another.
Sometimes: occasionally.

Spoonfuls, carfuls, shovelfuls: the plural forms of *spoonful, carful, shovelful.*

Stationary: not moving; fixed.
Stationery: writing paper or writing materials.

Statue: a carved or molded three-dimensional reproduction.
Stature: height of a person; reputation.
Statute: a law.

Straight: direct; uninterrupted; not crooked.
Strait: narrow strip connecting two bodies of water; a distressing situation.

Than: used in comparison (conjunction): "Joe is taller than Tom."
Then: relating to time (adverb): "First he ran; then he jumped."

Their: belonging to them (possessive of *they*).
There: in that place (adverb).
They're: a contraction of the two words *they are.*

To: preposition: "to the store."
Too: adverb: "too cold."
Two: number: "two apples."

Toward:
Towards: indentical in meaning and used interchangeably; *toward* is preferred.

Veracity: truthfulness.
Voracity: ravenousness; greed.

Vice: wickedness.
Vise: a clamp.

Waive: to give up; relinquish.
Wave: swell of water; a gesture.

Ways: procedures; also slang for distance.

Weather: climate or atmosphere.
Whether: an alternative.

Who's: a contraction of the two words *who is.*
Whose: possessive of *who.*

Your: a pronoun.
You're: a contraction of the two words *you are.*

Expressing Numbers

Should numbers be expressed in figures or words in written communication? To help solve this question, a number of general rules have been established.

1. When several numbers are used in one sentence and they are all above ten, use figures. If they are below ten, write them out. If a sentence begins with a number, write it out. However, it is usually wiser to revise the sentence.

   We shipped 75 chairs, 90 tables, 32 lamps, and 32 pictures.

   You have requested two rugs, three TV sets, and eight area rugs.

   Seventy-five chairs, 90 tables, 32 lamps, and 32 pictures were shipped on December 3.

   On December 3 we shipped 75 chairs, 90 tables, 32 lamps, and 32 pictures.

2. When numbers are below ten, write them out; when they are above, use numerals. When some above and some below are used in one sentence, follow one pattern for consistency. Round numbers over ten are usually written out.

   He owned three shares of A.T.&T., seven shares of Sears, and fifty-five shares of Zenith.

   The scouts consumed 8 pies, 7 chickens, 8 quarts of milk, and 32 bottles of soda.

   He made two great throws, one of sixty feet and the other of fifty-five.

3. When two numbers are used in different contexts in the same sentence, one should be written out and the other indicated in numerals.

   The thirty-man team canvassed more than 50,000 homes.

4. When one number immediately follows another, express the smaller in words, the larger in numerals.

   He purchased five 59-cent notebooks for use in his spring quarter classes.

5. Place a comma between two unrelated numbers when they immediately follow each other.

   In 1975, 95 supersonic aircraft should be available for commercial use.

Dates.
1. Write out the month when expressing a date.

   June 27, 1979
   27 June 1979

It is strongly recommended that numerals for both month and day not be used. Although North American custom is to place the month first and then the day, the reverse is true in many countries of the world. Confusion in interpretation can thus easily result.

1–4–78   Preferred: January 4, 1978
3/7/78   Preferred: March 7, 1978 or 7 March 1978

2. Only use *nd, rd, st,* or *th* with the day of the month when that day precedes the month or stands by itself.

She became engaged on the 4th of January.

In your order of the 2nd, you did not list the colors desired.

Your shipment of the 1st was lost in transit.

Please mail your check by March 28.

Addresses.

1. Street numbers should always be expressed as numerals except one, which should be written out.

One East Wilshire
10 North Roscomare Road
215 South Kansas Street
2157 South Topeka Avenue

2. Use words for streets from one to ten inclusive; use numerals for streets after eleven. The letters *nd, rd, st,* or *th* may be used with numerals.

2115 West Fifth Avenue
1115 West Tenth Street
210 North 19th Street
400 East 121st Avenue

3. When a number is used as a street name, use a dash to separate it from the street number only if a street direction is not included.

210–10th Street
2100–7th Avenue
2111 West 45th Street
205 North 41st Street

Amounts of Money.

1. All sums of money, domestic or foreign, should be presented in figures.

Johnson paid $155.60 for the merchandise.

It is difficult for me to convert £275 into dollars.

2. For sums of less than a dollar, follow the figure with the word *cents* or with the cent sign (¢); the preferred alternative is to use the dollar sign with a decimal point.

> It cost 25 cents.
> It wasn't worth 65¢.
> Tom paid $.75 for the ball.

3. When expressing even or round sums of money, do not use the decimal and zeros.

> His payment was $275 dollars.

4. In legal statements the numerals should be enclosed by parentheses and the sum written out.

> A firm offer for the car of seven hundred forty dollars ($740) is hereby made.

Decimals and Fractions.

1. When a decimal fraction begins with a zero, do not place a zero before the decimal. If the decimal fraction begins with a whole number, precede the decimal with a zero.

> .04683
> 0.1746

2. Simple fractions are written out. When whole numbers and fractions make up one unit, a decimal may or may not be used.

> It took him one half hour.
> It was 25.5 feet long.
> It was 25½ feet long.

Miscellaneous Quantities, Units, and Measurements.

1. Distance: Use numbers unless the amount is less than a mile.

> We were one third of a mile from the house.

> It is 9 miles to Kingston and 350 miles from there to Prampton.

2. Financial quotations: Use numerals.

> American Telephone and Telegraph hit 56⅞ this afternoon.

3. Arithmetical expressions: Use numerals.

> Multiply 70 by 44 and you will have the area of the house in square feet.

4. Measurement: Use numerals.

> The land produced approximately 95 bushels per acre.

> He quickly found that 15 kilometers did not equal 16 yards.

5. Specific numbers: Use numerals.

The engine number was 4638147.

Write for Training Manual 255.

6. Time: Use numerals except when the word *o'clock* is used.

The plane leaves at 7:17 P.M.
He is due to arrive at ten o'clock.

7. Dimensions: Use numerals with either x or *by*.

The room measured 10x15 ft.

The trim size of the annual report was 8½ by 11 in.

8. Age: Use numerals except where approximations are used.

She became 21 and got engaged on the same day.

I would say that he's about seventy years old.

For your information, Bob is exactly 3 years and 6 months old today.

9. Government units: Write out such expressions as congressional units or districts.

He served in the Eighty-seventh Congress and represented the Tenth Congressional District of the state.

10. Book or magazine references: Major units or divisions are indicated by Roman numerals; minor units by Arabic numbers.

He found the reference in Volume XX, number 4, of the *Journal of Communications*.

You will find Figure 4 next to Table 7 on page 83 of Section 4.

Business Letter Style and Format

The Sections of the Business Letter

The business letter is usually divided into six major parts: the heading, which includes the letterhead and the date; the inside address; the salutation; the body; the complimentary close; and the signature.

	Heading
	Inside address
	Salutation
	Body
	Complimentary close
	Signature

The Heading

The heading of the business letter contains the letterhead and the date. The former is given a good deal of attention by most firms because it contributes to the company image.

The letterhead that shouts at us with oversize pictures of the product, unattractive sketches of the plant, or "call us day or night" statements, does not usually convey the best image of the company. However, the firm which utilizes a relatively simple, dignified letterhead, designed carefully and with good taste, conveys an image of competence and efficiency.

There are many specialists and advertising agencies to assist the businessman in designing a new letterhead or revising the one he has used for years. And this revision is necessary, for styles in letterheads change as does the company image. Certainly outmoded type styles or a picture of a 25-year-old car or office machine in the letterhead design will not contribute to a very favorable impression of the company. *Printer's Ink* magazine had this to say about the letterhead design and the message it conveys:

> In addition to identifying the sender, letterheads convey, both liminally and subliminally, an image of the company. The great mass of mail sent out by the average company gives its letterhead a significant role to perform in its sales-promotion and public-relations programs.

Many of the large paper corporations will also assist in letterhead revision. Their staff artists will draw up a new letterhead or send out letterhead kits which contain sample designs of letterheads and different grades and colors of stationery, graph paper, and directions for a "do-it-yourself" approach.

The trend in letterhead designs today is toward simplicity and clean-cut type faces that reflect dignity and good taste. Reproductions of products or office buildings or factories, if included, are usually small and very well executed, so they will not detract from the overall letterhead "message" or from the letter itself.

Many firms are also using the empty space along the bottom of the page. A listing of the cities in which the company has outlets or plants, small pictures of the firm's products, or even the company address can be included. The type should be small and distinct, and the layout in balance with the information at the top of the stationery.

In addition to being attractive, meaningful, and in good taste, the letterhead should answer the questions of *who, where,* and *what.* The "who," of course, is the name of the company presented exactly as the firm wishes to be identified. This includes the precise abbreviations ("Corp." or "Inc.") and designations ("Furniture manufacturers" or "Manufacturers of furniture").

The "where" includes street address, city, state, zip code number, telephone number, cable address, and other items of this nature.

The "what" tells the reader the nature of the company's operations. It is disconcerting to receive a letter from the R. T. Cronin Corporation at 102 East Adams Street in Los Angeles and not be able to determine whether the firm manufactures kitchen appliances or conducts national surveys.

The date should be written out using either of the following methods:

January 4, 1979
4 January 1979

It is recommended that the date not be typed as 1/4/79 or 1–4–79 even in intracompany memos. Many persons feel that this exhibits a distinct lack of courtesy. But a more important reason for avoiding this method is to eliminate the possibility of confusion or misinterpretation. Although most North Americans would read 4/7/79 as April 7, 1979 this would not be true in Europe and among most Latin Americans who would read it as July 4, 1979.

The Inside Address:

The inside address should be sufficiently complete to ensure accurate and rapid delivery of the letter. The information in the inside address should duplicate the address on the envelope.

The data for the inside address are usually drawn from the letterhead of the piece of correspondence being answered. Exact company designations and titles (as they appear in the letterhead) should be followed for the inside address.

The recipient's name in the inside address should be preceded by his title—*Mr., Mrs., Dr., General, Reverend,* etc. If the individual occupies a supervisory office, both his title and area of responsibility can be indicated.

```
Dr. Lester Jameson, Director
Medical Research Department
Cicero Clinics
3148 North Cicero Avenue
Chicago, Illinois 60606
```

If the initials which designate degrees mean the same as the person's title, both title and initials should be used.

```
Incorrect:
    Dr. Robert Clock, M.D.
    Dr. Roberta Mann, Ph.D.

Correct:
    Dr. Robert Clock
    Robert Clock, M.D.

    Dr. Roberta Mann
    Roberta Mann, Ph.D.
```

Words in the inside address, such as *street, north* and *avenue* should not be abbreviated unless the company specifically requires such action. On the whole, the use of abbreviations should not be encouraged for the inside address.

Street numbers should always be written in numerals with the exception of *one.* Street names should be written out from First to Tenth streets. After that, numerals should be used. The zip code should follow the state. The examples on page 480 illustrate these recommendations.

```
Dr. Albert Fine, Director          Ms. Joan Star, Manager
Conrad Research Center             Personnel Department
Conrad General Hospital            Foods, Inc.
1007 West 63rd Street              One East 95th Street
Los Angeles, California 90024      Cincinnati, Ohio 45216


Reverend Peter Jackson             John T. Kasper, Ph.D.
Lutheran Central Church            Department of Management
7 South Ninth Avenue              Illinois State University
New York, New York 10010           Springfield, Illinois 62704


Rabbi Herman Schaalman             Thomas L. Lamp, M.D.
Temple Emanuel                     Allerton Medical Center
5959 North Sheridan Road           17 North Bolton Avenue
Chicago, Illinois 60626            Columbus, Ohio 43227
```

The Salutation

Every effort should be made to use the recipient's name in the greeting or salutation. Almost everyone responds much more actively and sincerely to his name than to *Dear Occupant, Dear Friend, Dear Sir* or *Dear Purchasing Agent*.

Many firms have expended large sums of money to have a personally typed inside address and/or salutation added to thousands of form letters before mailing. It is felt (usually with reason) that the form letter receives a much better reaction from the reader because of the added personal touch.

When individual letters are typed and the name of the recipient is not known, it is customary to use *Dear Sir* or *Dear Madame* in the singular, and *Gentlemen* or *Ladies* in the plural. *My Dear Sirs, Dear Sirs,* and *Mesdames* are all considered obsolete.

Many individuals, in an effort to add a more friendly and informal tone to their letters, and to give some significance to the opening, use a "salutation phrase" instead of a salutation. These might be *Thank you, Mrs. Klay; We were happy, Mr. Conway; Enclosed, Mrs. Finer, you will find; Your order, Ms. Fay, was sent.* These phrases appear, in the letter, in place of the salutation.

These are certainly different and do attract attention. Some authorities argue that they may be too different and therefore resented by the recipient. However, they can be used with certain readers very effectively. And in sales writing they may well serve a very useful purpose.

The Body

Any discussion of the "body" of the letter must, perforce, be concerned with the type of letter (sales, credit, collection, etc.) under consideration. From the point of view of appearance and format, however, the body should be attractively centered, broken into relatively short paragraphs, and surrounded by plenty of white space.

The Complimentary Close

The standard forms used in most letters are *Yours truly, Truly yours, Sincerely, Sincerely yours, Yours sincerely,* and to a lesser extent, *Cordially* or

Cordially yours. As in the case of the salutation, attempts have been made to make the complimentary close more meaningful and personal. Some companies close their letters with phrases such as *Buy Arctic Freezers Today, See Your Arctic Dealer, Arctic for Quality, Arctic Is Yours Truly, Soft Glo for the Best in Lighting,* or *Truly a Fine Product.*

When such phrases are chosen with care and discretion, they often produce excellent results. However, the letter writer should not reach too far for an interesting close. What may be clever to him might be interpreted by the reader as much too cute. Some firms compose a close, use it on all letters for two weeks, and then switch to a new one. In effect most persons will not see the same one repeated under this system.

The Signature

This section of the letter is handled in a variety of ways. In most firms the signature has three or four parts, with the trend toward the latter number. The four-part signature includes the name of the company, the signature of the writer, his typed name, and his title. If the signature has only three parts, the name of the company (which appears in the letterhead) is omitted.

The use of the words *per* or *by* in front of the signed name is obsolete and should be discouraged.

Sometimes one will find initials placed immediately below the signature. This is done when the secretary signs the writer's name and adds her own initials. However, this practice is often interpreted by the reader in a rather poor light. He may be irritated that the writer apparently could not find fifteen seconds to sign his own name, but had a secretary do it for him. This is understandable and therefore every effort should be made by the writer to sign every letter he sends out.

Of course it is possible that the writer could have dictated the letter in the morning and then have left on a business trip. In such case, he obviously would not have been available to sign the letter when it was ready for his signature. However, the fact is that most people resent what the initials below a signature seem to imply.

Yours truly,

CAIN PRODUCTS CO.

John Kingly

John Kingly
Sales Manager

JK/js

Sincerely yours,

Robert Blake

Robert Blake
Superintendent

RB:ks

```
                                     Truly yours,

                                     LOOP LAMP COMPANY

                                     William Key

        WK/vt                        William Key, Manager
```

```
                                     Sincerely,

                                     BAINE, INC.

                                     Roberta Baine

        Roberta Baine/mt             Partner
```

Other Factors in the Mechanics of the Business Letter

The Attention Line

Frequently we find that one person in a company with which we are doing business gives us excellent service. Mr. Kelly, for example, is aware that we prefer to have our merchandise shipped via Star Freight Lines; that our terms are always C.O.D.; that we like to have our items individually wrapped and packaged, etc. Thus, in order to have Kelly handle our requests, we send our communications to his *attention*. If we send the letter directly to him, and he has left the company, it is very possible that the envelope will be *returned* to us or *forwarded* to him. However, if the letter is sent to his *attention* and he has left the company, the communication will normally be opened and processed by his successor.

The position of the attention line varies, although it usually appears in one of the following places:

```
Belmont Steel Company
1122 West Ninth Street
Belmont, Indiana  60397

Gentlemen:              Attention of Mr. Keelton, Treasurer
```

```
Belmont Steel Company
1122 West Ninth Street
Belmont, Indiana  60397

Attention of Mr. Keelton, Treasurer

Gentlemen:
```

```
Belmont Steel Company
1122 West Ninth Street
Belmont, Indiana  60397

                    Attention of Mr. Keelton, Treasurer

Gentlemen:
```

Many firms use an abbreviation for *attention; Attn:* or *Att.,* and the pattern followed in the inside address is repeated on the envelope.

The Subject Line

The subject line is another device used to speed handling or retrieval of correspondence from files. In addition, it can eliminate much of the first paragraph if it is worded carefully. Its position, like the attention line, varies according to company preference.

```
Kelvyn Clock Company
1515 West Granby Street
Springfield, California 92077

Gentlemen:          Subject:  Your order #2136


Betsy B. Ice Cream
1000 West Nevada Avenue
Boulder, Colorado  80303

                    Subject:  Your invoice #201,
                              January 7, 1979

Gentlemen:
```

This *subject* line, like a *file number, or in reply refer to file number*_____, can save time and increase office efficiency.

Identifying Initials

For many years it was customary to place the dictator's and typist's initials in the lower-left-hand section of the business letter. However, in recent years the trend seems to be toward omitting them. With the name of the writer in the signature section, it is obvious who dictated the letter, and if the letter was completed in a typing pool or even by a secretary, the value of having her initials on the letter seems questionable.

On the other hand, many firms follow the practice carefully, especially when all letters from a department are signed by one man even though any one of six people may have done the dictating. In this instance, the dictator's initials are used and, of course, do not match the signature of the department head. The initials serve to identify the person who actually wrote the letter.

Some of the accepted variations in handling identifying initials are shown below. Note that both a slash mark and a colon are acceptable separators.

```
JS/rt      MRL:AO
LT/MR      TTA:bm
```

Enclosure Line

The enclosure notation is usually placed immediately below the identifying initials and serves as a reminder that some item such as a check, invoice,
or reprint has been included in the envelope along with the letter.

Either the word *Enclosure* is typed or the abbreviation *Encl.* If only one enclosure is included, no numeral is used; if more than one item goes with the
letter, the number of different items is indicated. Some firms and most federal
government agencies identify each enclosure so that when one is withdrawn, it
can be easily identified.

```
BM:rt                          LMS/rd
Encl.                          Enclosures 3

GM/tl                          LM:ML
Encl. 3                        Enclosure
     1. Birth certificate
     2. Visa
     3. Letter of reference
```

Carbon Copies

Obviously if a letter is sent to Mr. Robert Blackstone, a copy of that letter should ordinarily not be forwarded to anyone else; the contents of a business letter are a private matter between the writer and addressee. It is easy to
understand how offended Mr. Blackstone might become if another person indicated, through a comment or a note, that he was aware of information which
had been contained in a letter sent by Acme Products to Blackstone.

To avoid such a situation, and because it is also a matter of ethics, we tell
Mr. Blackstone that a copy of this letter addressed to him was sent to Mr.
Clayton. The device of *cc:* (carbon copy) is used.

```
DM/ts
cc: Mr. Clayton

LT/sa
cc: Mr. Clayton
    Credit Department
```

Some firms will sometimes employ the initials *bc* or *bcc* which stands for
blind copy or *blind carbon copy*. This is typed only on the copy and not on the
original letter and tells the reader of the carbon copy that Mr. Blackstone is
not aware that a copy has been sent to a second party.

Punctuation

The terms *open* or *closed* punctuation refer to end-of-line punctuation in the inside address, complimentary close, and signature. Almost all correspondence today uses open punctuation for it saves typing time and therefore money. One frequent variation found in open punctuation is the comma after the complimentary close.

Closed punctuation:

    Mr. Robert T. Scott,
    Morrell and Company,
    1515 West Ohio Street,
    St. Louis, Missouri 63125.

    Dear Mr. Scott:

    _____
    _____
    _____

                             Yours very truly,

Open punctuation:

    Mr. Robert T. Scott
    Morrell and Company
    1515 West Ohio Street
    St. Louis, Missouri 63125

    Dear Mr. Scott:

    _____
    _____
    _____

                             Yours very truly,

Part Five

Readings in Communication

S. I. Hayakawa

How Words Change Our Lives

The end product of education, yours and mine and everybody's, is the total pattern of reactions and possible reactions we have inside ourselves. If you did not have within you at this moment the pattern of reactions which we call "the ability to read English," you would see here only meaningless black marks on paper. Because of the trained patterns of response, you are (or are not) stirred to patriotism by martial music, your feelings of reverence are aroused by the symbols of your religion, you listen more respectfully to the health advice of someone who has "M.D." after his name than to that of someone who hasn't. What I call here a "pattern of reactions," then, is the sum total of the ways we act in response to events, to words and to symbols.

Our reaction patterns—our semantic habits, as we may call them—are the internal and most important residue of whatever years of education or miseducation we may have received from our parents' conduct toward us in childhood as well as their teachings, from the formal education we may have had, from all the sermons and lectures we have listened to, from the radio programs and the movies and television shows we have experienced, from all the books and newspapers and comic strips we have read, from the conversations we have had with friends and associates, and from all our experiences. If, as the result of all these influences that make us what we are, our semantic habits are reasonably similar to those of most people around us, we are regarded as "well-adjusted," or "normal," and perhaps "dull." If our semantic habits are noticeably different from those of others, we are regarded as "individualistic" or "original," or, if the differences are disapproved of or viewed with alarm, as "screwball" or "crazy."

Semantics is sometimes defined in dictionaries as "the science of the meaning of words"—which would not be a bad definition if people didn't assume that the search for the meanings of words begins and ends with looking them up in a dictionary.

If one stops to think for a moment, it is clear that to define a word, as a dictionary does, is simply to explain the word with more words. To be thorough about defining, we should next have to define the words used in the definition, then define the words used in defining the words used in the definition . . . and so on. Defining words with more words, in short, gets us at once into what mathematicians call an "infinite regress." Alternatively, it can get us into the kind of run-around we sometimes encounter when we look up "impertinence" and find it defined as "impudence," so we look up "impudence" and find it defined as "impertinence." Yet—and here we come to another common reaction pattern—people often act as if words can be explained fully with more words. To a person who asked for a definition of jazz, Louis Armstrong is said to have replied, "Man, when you got to ask what it is, you'll never get to know," proving himself to be an intuitive semanticist as well as a great trumpet player.

"How Words Change Our Lives" by S. I. Hayakawa. © 1958 by Curtis Publishing Company. Reprinted (in slightly different form) from *Symbol, Status, and Personality* by permission of Harcourt Brace Jovanovich, Inc.

What Semantics Is About

Semantics, then, does not deal with the "meaning of words" as that expression is commonly understood. P. W. Bridgman, the Nobel-prize winner and physicist, once wrote, "The true meaning of a term is to be found by observing what a man does with it, not by what he says about it." He made an enormous contribution to science by showing that the meaning of a scientific term lies in the operations, the things done, that establish its validity, rather than in verbal definitions.

Here is a simple, everyday kind of example of "operational" criticism. If you say, "This table measures six feet in length," you could prove it by taking a foot rule, performing the operation of laying it end to end while counting, "One . . . two . . . three . . . four . . ." But if you say—and revolutionists have started uprisings with just this statement—"Man is born free, but everywhere he is in chains!"—what operations could you perform to demonstrate its accuracy or inaccuracy?

But let us carry this suggestion of "operationalism" outside the physical sciences where Bridgman applied it, and observe what "operations" people perform as the result of both the language they use and the language other people use in communicating to them. Here is a personnel manager studying an application blank. He comes to the words "Education: Harvard University," and drops the application blank in the wastebasket (that's the "operation") because, as he would say if you asked him, "I don't like Harvard men." This is an instance of "meaning" at work—but it is not a meaning that can be found in dictionaries.

If I seem to be taking a long time to explain what semantics is about, it is because I am trying, in the course of explanation, to introduce the reader to a certain way of looking at human behavior. Semantics—especially the general semantics of Alfred Korzybski (1879–1950), Polish-American scientist and educator—pays particular attention not to words in themselves, but to semantic reactions—that is, human responses to symbols, signs and symbol-systems, including language.

I say *human* responses because, so far as we know, human beings are the only creatures that have, over and above that biological equipment which we have in common with other creatures, the additional capacity for manufacturing symbols and systems of symbols. When we react to a flag, we are not reacting simply to a piece of cloth, but to the meaning with which it has been symbolically endowed. When we react to a word, we are not reacting to a set of sounds, but to the meaning with which that set of sounds has been symbolically endowed.

A basic idea in general semantics, therefore, is that the meaning of words (or other symbols) is not in the words, but in our own semantic reactions. If I were to tell a shockingly obscene story in Arabic or Hindustani or Swahili before an audience that understood only English, no one would blush or be angry; the story would be neither shocking nor obscene—indeed, it would not even be a story. Likewise, the value of a dollar bill is not in the bill, but in our social agreement to accept it as a symbol of value. If that agreement were to break down through the collapse of our Government, the dollar bill would become only a scrap of paper. We do not understand a dollar bill by staring at it long and hard. We understand it by observing how people act with respect to it. We understand it by understanding the social mechanisms and the loyalties that keep it meaningful. Semantics is therefore a social study, basic to all other social studies.

It is often remarked that words are tricky—and that we are all prone to be deceived by "fast talkers," such as high-pressure salesmen, skillful propagandists, politicians or lawyers. Since few of us are aware of the degree to which we use words to deceive ourselves, the sin of "using words in a tricky way" is one that is always attributed to the other fellow. When the Russians use the word "democracy" to mean something quite different from what we mean by it, we at once accuse them of "propaganda," of "corrupting the meanings of words." But when we use the word "democracy" in the United States to mean something quite different from what the Russians mean by it, they are equally quick to accuse us of "hypocrisy." We all tend to believe that the way we use words is the correct way, and that people who use the same words in other ways are either ignorant or dishonest.

Words Evoke Different Responses

Leaving aside for a moment such abstract and difficult terms as "democracy," let us examine a common, everyday word like "frog." Surely there is no problem about what "frog" means! Here are some sample sentences:

"If we're going fishing, we'll have to catch some frogs first." (This is easy.)

"I have a frog in my throat." (You can hear it croaking.)

"She wore a loose, silk jacket fastened with braided frogs."

"The blacksmith pared down the frog and the hoof before shoeing the horse."

"In Hamilton, Ohio, there is a firm by the name of American Frog and Switch Company."

In addition to these "frogs," there is the frog in which a sword is carried, the frog at the bottom of a bowl or vase that is used in flower arrangement, and the frog which is part of a violin bow. The reader can no doubt think of other "frogs."

Or take another common word such as "order." There is the *order* that the salesman tries to get, which is quite different from the *order* which a captain gives to his crew. Some people enter holy *orders*. There is the *order* in the house when mother has finished tidying up; there is the batting *order* of the home team; there is an *order* of

ham and eggs. It is surprising that with so many meanings to the word, people don't misunderstand one another oftener than they do.

The foregoing are only striking examples of a principle to which we are all so well accustomed that we rarely think of it; namely, that most words have more meanings than dictionaries can keep track of. And when we consider further that each of us has different experiences, different memories, different likes and dislikes, it is clear that all words evoke different responses in all of us. We may agree as to what the term "Mississippi River" stands for, but you and I recall different parts of the river; you and I have had different experiences with it; one of us has read more about it than the other; one of us may have happy memories of it, while the other may recall chiefly tragic events connected with it. Hence your "Mississippi River" can never be identical with my "Mississippi River." The fact that we can communicate with each other about the "Mississippi River" often conceals the fact that we are talking about two different sets of memories and experiences.

Fixed Reactions to Certain Words

Words being as varied in their meanings as they are, no one can tell us what the correct interpretation of a word should be in advance of our next encounter with that word. The reader may have been taught always to revere the word "mother." But what is he going to do the next time he encounters this word, when it occurs in the sentence "Mother began to form in the bottle"? If it is impossible to determine what a single word will mean on next encounter, is it possible to say in advance what is the correct evaluation of such events as these: (1) next summer, an individual who calls himself a socialist will announce his candidacy for the office of register of deeds in your city; (2) next autumn, there will be a strike at one of your local department stores; (3) next week, your wife will announce that she is going to change her style of hairdo; (4) tomorrow, your little boy will come home with a bleeding nose?

A reasonably sane individual will react to each of these events in his own way, according to time, place and the entire surrounding set of circumstances; and included among those circumstances will be his own stock of experiences, wishes, hopes and fears. But there are people whose pattern of reactions is such that some of them can be completely predicted in advance. Mr. A will never vote for anyone called "socialist," no matter how incompetent or crooked the alternative candidates may be. Mr. B-1 always disapproves of strikes and strikers, without bothering to inquire whether or not this strike has its justifications; Mr. B-2 always sympathizes with the strikers because he hates all bosses. Mr. C belongs to the "stay sweet as you are" school of thought, so that his wife hasn't been able to change her hairdo since she left high school. Mr. D always faints at the sight of blood.

Such fixed and unalterable patterns of reaction—in their more obvious forms we call them prejudices—are almost inevitably organized around words. Mr. E distrusts and fears all people to whom the term "Catholic" is applicable, while Mr. F, who is Catholic, distrusts and fears all non-Catholics. Mr. G is so rabid a Republican that he reacts with equal dislike to all Democrats, all Democratic proposals, all opposite proposals if they are also made by Democrats. Back in the days when Franklin D. Roosevelt was President, Mr. G disliked not only the Democratic President but also his wife, children and dog. His office was on Roosevelt Road in Chicago (it had been named after Theodore Roosevelt), but he had his address changed to his back door on 11th Street, so that he would not have to print the hated name on his stationery. Mr. H, on the other hand, is an equally rabid Democrat, who hates himself for continuing to play golf, since golf is Mr. Eisenhower's favorite game. People suffering from such prejudices seem to have in their brains an uninsulated spot which,

when touched by such words as "capitalist," "boss," "striker," "scab," "Democrat," "Republican," "socialized medicine," and other such loaded terms, results in an immediate short circuit, often with a blowing of fuses.

Alfred Korzybski, the founder of general semantics, called such short-circuited responses "identification reactions." He used the word "identification" in a special sense; he meant that persons given to such fixed patterns of response identify (that is, treat as identical) all occurrences of a given word or symbol; they identify all the different cases that fall under the same name. Thus, if one has hostile identification reactions to "women drivers," then all women who drive cars are "identical" in their incompetence.

Korzybski believed that the term "identification reaction" could be generally used to describe the majority of cases of semantic malfunctioning. Identification is something that goes on in the human nervous system. "Out there" there are no absolute identities. No two Harvard men, no two Ford cars, no two mothers-in-law, no two politicians, no two leaves from the same tree, are identical with each other in all respects. If, however, we treat all cases that fall under the same class label as one at times when the differences are important, then there is something wrong with our semantic habits.

Another Definition of General Semantics

We are now ready, then, for another definition of general semantics. It is a comparative study of the kinds of responses people make to the symbols and signs around them; we may compare the semantic habits common among the prejudiced, the foolish and the mentally ill with those found among people who are able to solve their problems successfully, so that, if we care to, we may revise our own semantic habits for the better. In other words, general semantics is, if we wish to make it so, the study of how not to be a damn fool.

Identification reactions run all the way through nature. The capacity for seeing similarities is necessary to the survival of all animals. The pickerel, I suppose, identifies all shiny, fluttery things going through the water as minnows, and goes after them all in pretty much the same way. Under natural conditions, life is made possible for the pickerel by this capacity. Once in a while, however, the shiny, fluttery thing in the water may happen to be not a minnow but an artificial lure on the end of a line. In such a case, one would say that the identification response, so useful for survival, under somewhat more complex conditions that require differentiation between two sorts of shiny and fluttery objects, proves to be fatal.

To go back to our discussion of human behavior, we see at once that the problem of adequate differentiation is immeasurably more complex for men than it is for pickerel. The signs we respond to, and the symbols we create and train ourselves to respond to, are infinitely greater in number and immeasurably more abstract than the signs in a pickerel's environment. Lower animals have to deal only with certain brute facts in their physical environment. But think, only for a moment, of what constitutes a human environment. Think of the items that call for adequate responses that no animal ever has to think about: our days are named and numbered, so that we have birthdays, anniversaries, holidays, centennials, and so on, all calling for specifically human responses: we have history, which no animal has to worry about; we have verbally codified patterns of behavior which we call law, religion and ethics. We have to respond not only to events in our immediate environment, but to reported events in Washington, Paris, Tokyo, Moscow, Beirut. We have literature, comic strips, confession magazines, market quotations, detective stories, journals of abnormal psychology, bookkeeping systems to interpret. We have money, credit, banking, stocks, bonds, checks, bills. We have the complex symbolisms of moving pictures, paintings, drama, music, architecture and dress. In short, we live in a vast human dimension of which the lower animals have no inkling and we have to have a capacity for differentiation adequate to the complexity of our extra environment.

Why Do People React As They Do?

The next question, then, is why human beings do not always have an adequate capacity for differentiation. Why are we not constantly on the lookout for differences as well as similarities instead of feeling, as so many do, that the Chinese (or Mexicans, or ballplayers, or women drivers) are "all alike"? Why do some people react to words as if they were the things they stand for? Why do certain patterns of reaction, both in individuals and in larger groups such as nations, persist long after the usefulness has expired?

Part of our identification reactions are simply protective mechanisms inherited from the necessities of survival under earlier and more primitive conditions of life. I was once beaten up and robbed by two men on a dark street. Months later, I was again on a dark street with two men, good friends of mine, but involuntarily I found myself in a panic and insisted on our hurrying to a well-lighted drugstore to have a soda so that I would stop being jittery. In other words, my whole body reacted with an identification reaction of fear of these two men, in spite of the fact that "I knew" that I was in no danger. Fortunately, with the passage of time, this reaction has died away. But the hurtful experiences of early childhood do not fade so readily. There is no doubt that many identification reactions are traceable to childhood traumas, as psychiatrists have shown.

Further identification reactions are caused by communal patterns of behavior which were necessary or thought necessary at one stage or another in the development of a tribe or nation. General directives such as "Kill all snakes," "Never kill cows, which are sacred animals," "Shoot all strangers on sight," "Fall down flat on your face before all members of the aristocracy," or, to come to more modern instances, "Never vote for a Republican," "Oppose all government regulation of business," "Never associate with Negroes on terms of equality," are an enormous factor in the creation of identification reactions.

Some human beings—possibly in their private feelings a majority—can accept these directives in a *human* way: that is, it will not be impossible for them under a sufficiently changed set of circumstances to kill a cow, or not to bow down before an aristocrat, to vote for a Republican, or to accept a Negro as a classmate. Others, however, get these directives so deeply ground into their nervous systems that they become incapable of changing their responses no matter how greatly the circumstances may have changed. Still others, although capable of changing their responses, dare not do so for fear of public opinion. Social progress usually requires the breaking up of these absolute identifications, which often makes necessary changes impossible. Society must obviously have patterns of behavior; human beings must obviously have habits. But when those patterns become inflexible, so that a tribe has only one way to meet a famine, namely, to throw more infants as sacrifices to the crocodiles, or a nation has only one way to meet a threat to its security, namely, to increase its armaments, then such a tribe or such a nation is headed for trouble. There is insufficient capacity for differentiated behavior.

Furthermore—and here one must touch upon the role of newspapers, radio and television—if agencies of mass communication hammer away incessantly at the production of, let us say, a hostile set of reactions at such words as "Communists," "bureaucrats," "Wall Street," "international bankers," "labor leaders," and so on, no matter how useful an immediate job they may

perform in correcting a given abuse at a given time and place, they can in the long run produce in thousands of readers and listeners identification reactions to the words—reactions that will make intelligent public discussion impossible. Modern means of mass communication and propaganda certainly have an important part to play in the creation of identification reactions.

In addition to the foregoing, there is still another source of identification reactions; namely, the language we use in our daily thought and speech. Unlike the languages of the sciences, which are carefully constructed, tailor-made, special-purpose languages, the language of everyday life is one directly inherited and haphazardly developed from those of our prescientific ancestors: Anglo-Saxons, primitive Germanic tribes, primitive Indo-Europeans. With their scant knowledge of the world, they formulated descriptions of the world before them in statements such as "The sun rises." We do not today believe that the sun "rises." Nevertheless, we still continue to use the expression, without believing what we say.

Erroneous Implications in Everyday Language

But there are other expressions, quite as primitive as the idea of "sunrise," which we use uncritically, fully believing in the implications of our terms. Having observed (or heard) that *some* Negroes are lazy, an individual may say, making a huge jump beyond the known facts, "Negroes are lazy." Without arguing for the moment the truth or falsity of this statement, let us examine the implications of the statement as it is ordinarily constructed: "Negroes are lazy." The statement implies, as common sense or any textbook on traditional logic will tell us, that "laziness" is a "quality" that is "inherent" in Negroes.

What are the facts? Under conditions of slavery, under which Negroes were not paid for working, there wasn't any point in being an industrious and responsible worker. The distinguished French abstract artist Jean Hélion once told the story of his life as a prisoner of war in a German camp, where, during the Second World War, he was compelled to do forced labor. He told how he loafed on the job, how he thought of device after device for avoiding work and producing as little as possible—and, since his prison camp was a farm, how he stole chickens at every opportunity. He also described how he put on an expression of good-natured imbecility whenever approached by his Nazi overseers. Without intending to do so, in describing his own actions, he gave an almost perfect picture of the literary type of the Southern Negro of slavery days. Jean Hélion, confronted with the fact of forced labor, reacted as intelligently as Southern Negro slaves, and the slaves reacted as intelligently as Jean Hélion. "Laziness," then, is not an "inherent quality" of Negroes or of any other group of people. It is a *response* to a work situation in which there are no rewards for working, and in which one hates his taskmasters.

Statements implying inherent qualities, such as "Negroes are lazy" or "There's something terribly wrong with young people today," are therefore the crudest kind of unscientific observation, based on an out-of-date way of saying things, like "The sun rises." The tragedy is not simply the fact that people make such statements; the graver fact is that they believe themselves.

Some individuals are admired for their "realism" because, as the saying goes, they "call a spade a spade." Suppose we were to raise the question "Why should anyone call it a spade?" The reply would obviously be, "Because that's what it is!" This reply appeals so strongly to the common sense of most people that they feel that at this point discussion can be closed. I should like to ask the reader, however, to consider a point which may appear at first to him a mere quibble.

Here, let us say, is an implement for digging made of steel, with a wooden handle. Here, on the other hand, is a succession of sounds made with the tongue, lips and vocal cords: "spade." If you want a digging implement of the kind we are talking about, you would ask for it by making the succession of sounds "spade" if you are addressing an English-speaking person. But suppose you were addressing a speaker of Dutch, French, Hungarian, Chinese, Tagalog? Would you not have to make completely different sounds? It is apparent, then, that the common-sense opinion of most people, "We call a spade a spade because that's what it is," is completely and utterly wrong. We call it a "spade" because we are English-speaking people, conforming, in this instance, to majority usage in naming this particular object. The steel-and-iron digging implement is simply an object standing there against the garage door; "spade" is what we *call* it—"spade" is a *name*.

And here we come to another source of identification reactions—an unconscious assumption about language epitomized in the expression "a spade is a spade," or even more elegantly in the famous remark "Pigs are called pigs because they are such dirty animals." The assumption is that everything has a "right name" and that the "right name" names the "essence" of that which is named.

If this assumption is at work in our reaction patterns, we are likely to be given to premature and often extremely inappropriate responses. We are likely to react to names as if they gave complete insight into the persons, things or situations named. If we are told that a given individual is a "Jew," some of us are likely to respond, "That's all I need to know." For, if names give the essence of that which is named, obviously, every "Jew" has the essential attribute of "Jewishness." Or, to put it the other way around, it is because he possesses "Jewishness" that we call him a "Jew"! A further example of the operation of this assumption is that, in spite of the fact that my entire education has been in Canada and the United States and I am unable to read and write Japanese, I am sometimes credited, or accused, of having an "Oriental mind." Now, since Buddha, Confucius, General Tojo, Mao Tse-tung, Syngman Rhee, Pandit Nehru and the proprietor of the Golden Pheasant Chop Suey House all have "Oriental minds," it is hard to imagine what is meant. The "Oriental mind," like the attribute of "Jewishness," is purely and simply a fiction. Nevertheless, I used to note with alarm that newspaper columnists got paid for articles that purported to account for Stalin's behavior by pointing out that since he came from Georgia, which is next to Turkey and Azerbaijan and therefore "more a part of Asia than of Europe," he too had an "Oriental mind."

Improving Your Semantic Habits

Our everyday habits of speech and our unconscious assumptions about the relations between words and things lead, then, to an identification reaction in which it is felt that all things that have the same name are entitled to the same response. From this point of view, all "insurance men," or "college boys," or "politicians," or "lawyers," or "Texans" are alike. Once we recognize the absurdity of these identification reactions based on identities of name, we can begin to think more clearly and more adequately. No "Texan" is exactly like any other "Texan." No "college boy" is exactly like any other "college boy." Most of the time "Texans" or "college boys" may be what you think they are: but often they are not. To realize fully the difference between words and what they stand for is to be ready for differences as well as similarities in the world. This readiness is mandatory to scientific thinking, as well as to sane thinking.

Korzybski's simple but powerful suggestion to those wishing to improve their semantic habits is to add "index numbers" to all terms, according to the formula: A_1 is not A_2. Translated into everyday language we can state the formula in such terms as these: Cow_1 is not cow_2; cow_2 is not cow_3; $Texan_1$ is not $Texan_2$; $politician_1$ is not $politician_2$; ham and eggs (Plaza Hotel) are not ham and eggs (Smitty's Café); socialism (Russia) is not socialism (England); private enterprise (Joe's Shoe Repair Shop) is not private enterprise (A.T.&T.). The formula means that instead of simply thinking about "cows" or "politicians" or "private enterprise," we should think as factually as possible about the differences between one cow and another, one politician and another, one privately owned enterprise and another.

This device of "indexing" will not automatically make us wiser and better, but it's a start. When we talk or write, the habit of indexing our general terms will reduce our tendency to wild and woolly generalization. It will compel us to think before we speak—think in terms of concrete objects and events and situations, rather than in terms of verbal associations. When we read or listen, the habit of indexing will help us visualize more concretely, and therefore understand better, what is being said. And if nothing is being said except deceptive windbaggery, the habit of indexing may—at least part of the time—save us from snapping, like the pickerel, at phony minnows. Another way of summing up is to remember, as Wendell Johnson said, that "To a mouse, cheese is cheese—that's why mousetraps work."

Carl R. Rogers and F. J. Roethlisberger

Barriers and Gateways to Communication

Communication among human beings has always been a problem. But it is only fairly recently that management and management advisers have become so concerned about it and the way it works or does not work in industry. Now, as the result of endless discussion, speculation, and plans of action, a whole cloud of catchwords and catch-thoughts has sprung up and surrounded it.

The following two descriptions of barriers and gateways to communication may help to bring the problem down to earth and show what it means in terms of simple fundamentals. First Carl R. Rogers analyzes it from the standpoint of human behavior generally (Part I); then F. J. Roethlisberger illustrates it in an industrial context (Part II).

Part I

It may seem curious that a person like myself, whose whole professional effort is devoted to psychotherapy, should be interested in problems of communication. What relationship is there between obstacles to communication and providing therapeutic help to individuals with emotional maladjustments?

Actually the relationship is very close indeed. The whole task of psychotherapy is the task of dealing with a failure in communication. The emotionally maladjusted person, the "neurotic," is in difficulty, first, because communication within himself has broken down and, secondly, because as a result of this his communication with others

has been damaged. To put it another way, in the "neurotic" individual parts of himself which have been termed unconscious, or repressed, or denied to awareness, become blocked off so that they no longer communicate themselves to the conscious or managing part of himself; as long as this is true, there are distortions in the way he communicates himself to others, and so he suffers both within himself and in his interpersonal relations.

The task of psychotherapy is to help the person achieve, through a special relationship with a therapist, good communication within himself. Once this is achieved, he can communicate more freely and more effectively with others. We may say then that psychotherapy is good communication, within and between men. We may also turn that statement around and it will still be true. Good communication, free communication, within or between men, is always therapeutic.

It is, then, from a background of experience with communication in counseling and psychotherapy that I want to present two ideas: (1) I wish to state what I believe is one of the major factors in blocking or impeding communication, and then (2) I wish to present what in our experience has proved to be a very important way of improving or facilitating communication.

Barrier: The Tendency to Evaluate

I should like to propose, as a hypothesis for consideration, that the major barrier to mutual interpersonal communication is our very natural tendency to judge, to evaluate, to approve (or disapprove) the statement of the other person or the other group. Let me illustrate my meaning with some very simple examples. Suppose someone, commenting on this discussion, makes the statement, "I didn't like what that man said." What will you respond? Almost invariably your reply will be either approval or disapproval of the attitude expressed. Either you respond, "I didn't either; I thought it was terrible," or else you tend to reply, "Oh, I thought it was really good." In other words, your primary reaction is to evaluate it from *your* point of view, your own frame of reference.

. . . Although the tendency to make evaluations is common in almost all interchange of language, it is very much heightened in those situations where feelings and emotions are deeply involved. So the stronger our feelings, the more likely it is that there will be no mutual element in the communication. There will be just two ideas, two feelings, two judgments, missing each other in psychological space.

I am sure you recognize this from your own experience. When you have not been emotionally involved yourself and have listened to a heated discussion, you often go away thinking, "Well, they actually weren't talking about the same thing." And they were not. Each was making a judgment, an evaluation, from his own frame of reference. There was really nothing which could be called communication in any genuine sense. This tendency to react to any emotionally meaningful statement by forming an evaluation of it from our own point of view is, I repeat, the major barrier to interpersonal communication.

Gateway: Listening with Understanding

Is there any way of solving this problem, of avoiding this barrier? I feel that we are making exciting progress toward this goal, and I should like to present it as simply as I can. Real communication occurs, and this evaluative tendency is avoided, when we listen with understanding. What does that mean? It means to see the expressed idea and attitude from the other person's point of view, to sense how it feels to him, to achieve his frame of reference in regard to the thing he is talking about.

Stated so briefly, this may sound absurdly simple, but it is not. It is an approach which we have found extremely potent in the field of psychotherapy. It is the most effective agent we know for altering the basic personality structure of an individual and for improving his relationships and his communications with others. If I can listen to what he can tell me, if I can understand how it seems to him, if I can see its personal meaning for him, if I can sense the emotional flavor which it has for him, then I will be releasing potent forces of change in him.

Again, if I can really understand how he hates his father, or hates the company, or hates Communists—if I can catch the flavor of his fear of insanity, or his fear of atom bombs, or of Russia—it will be of the greatest help to him in altering those hatreds and fears and in establishing realistic and harmonious relationships with the very people and situations toward which he has felt hatred and fear. We know from our research that such empathic understanding—understanding *with* a person, not *about* him—is such an effective approach that it can bring about major changes in personality.

Some of you may be feeling that you listen well to people and yet you have never seen such results. The chances are great indeed that your listening has not been of the type I have described. Fortunately, I can suggest a little laboratory experiment which you can try to test the quality of your understanding. The next time you get into an argument with your wife, or your friend, or with a small group of friends, just stop the discussion for a moment and, for an experiment, institute this rule: "Each person can speak up for himself only *after* he has first restated the ideas and feelings of the previous speaker accurately and to that speaker's satisfaction." . . .

If, then, this way of approach is an effective avenue to good communication and good relationships, as I am quite sure you will agree if you try the experiment I have mentioned, why is it not more widely tried and used? I will try to list the difficulties which keep it from being utilized.

Need for Courage. In the first place it takes courage, a quality which is not too widespread. I am indebted to Dr. S. I. Hayakawa, the semanticist, for pointing out that to carry on psychotherapy in this fashion is to take a very real risk, and that courage is required. If you really understand another person in this way, if you are willing to enter his private world and see the way life appears to him, without any attempt to make evaluative judgments, you run the risk of being changed yourself. You might see it his way; you might find yourself influenced in your attitudes or your personality.

This risk of being changed is one of the most frightening prospects many of us can face. . . .

Heightened Emotions. But there is a second obstacle. It is just when emotions are strongest that it is most difficult to achieve the frame of reference of the other person or group. Yet it is then that the attitude is most needed if communication is to be established. We have not found this to be an insuperable obstacle in our experience in psychotherapy. A third party, who is able to lay aside his own feelings and evaluations, can assist greatly by listening with understanding to each person or group and clarifying the views and attitudes each holds. . . .

Size of Group. . . . Thus far all our experience has been with small face-to-face groups—groups exhibiting industrial tensions, religious tensions, racial tensions, and therapy groups in which many personal tensions are present. . . . What about trying to achieve understanding between larger groups that are geographically remote, or between face-to-face groups that are not speaking for themselves but simply as representatives of others? . . .

Yet with our present limited knowledge we can see some steps which might be taken even in large groups to increase the amount of listening *with* and decrease the amount of evaluation *about*. To be imaginative for a moment, let us suppose that a therapeutically oriented international group went to the Russian leaders and said, "We want to achieve a genuine understanding of your views and, even more important, of your attitudes and feelings toward the United States. We will summarize and resummarize these views and feelings if necessary, until you agree that our description represents the situation as it seems to you."

Then suppose they did the same thing with the leaders in our own country. If they then gave the widest possible distribution to these two views, with the feelings clearly described but not expressed in name-calling, might not the effect be very great? It would not guarantee the type of understanding I have been describing, but it would make it much more possible. We can understand the feelings of a person who hates us much more readily when his attitudes are accurately described to us by a neutral third party than we can when he is shaking his fist at us.

Faith in Social Sciences. But even to describe such a first step is to suggest another obstacle to this approach of understanding. Our civilization does not yet have enough faith in the social sciences to utilize their findings. The opposite is true of the physical sciences. During the war when a test-tube solution was found to the problem of synthetic rubber, millions of dollars and an army of talent were turned loose on the problem of using that finding. If synthetic rubber could be made in milligrams, it could and would be made in the thousands of tons. And it was. But in the social science realm, if a way is found of facilitating communication and mutual understanding in small groups, there is no guarantee that the finding will be utilized. It may be a generation or more before the money and the brains will be turned loose to exploit that finding.

Summary

In closing, I should like to summarize this small-scale solution to the problem of barriers in communication, and to point out certain of its characteristics.

I have said that our research and experience to date would make it appear that breakdowns in communication, and the evaluative tendency which is the major barrier to communication, can be avoided. The solution is provided by creating a situation in which each of the different parties comes to understand the other from the *other's* point of view. This has been achieved, in practice, even when feelings run high, by the influence of a person who is willing to understand each point of view empathically, and who thus acts as a catalyst to precipitate further understanding.

This procedure has important characteristics. It can be initiated by one party, without waiting for the other to be ready. It can even be initiated by a neutral third person, provided he can gain a minimum of cooperation from one of the parties.

This procedure can deal with the insincerities, the defensive exaggerations, the lies, the "false fronts" which characterize almost every failure in communication. These defensive distortions drop away with astonishing speed as people find that the only intent is to understand, not to judge.

This approach leads steadily and rapidly toward the discovery of the truth, toward a realistic appraisal of the objective barriers to communication. The dropping of some defensiveness by one party leads to further dropping of defensiveness by the other party, and truth is thus approached.

This procedure gradually achieves mutual communication. Mutual communication tends to be pointed toward solving a problem rather than toward attacking a person or group. It leads to a sit-uation in which I see how the problem appears to you as well as to me, and you see how it appears to me as well as to you. Thus accurately and realistically defined, the problem is almost certain to yield to intelligent attack; or if it is in part insoluble, it will be comfortably accepted as such.

This then appears to be a test-tube solution to the breakdown of communication as it occurs in small groups. Can we take this small-scale answer, investigate it further, refine it, develop it, and apply it to the tragic and well-nigh fatal failures of communication which threaten the very existence of our modern world? It seems to me that this is a possibility and a challenge which we should explore.

Part II

In thinking about the many barriers to personal communication, particularly those that are due to differences of background, experience, and motivation, it seems to me extraordinary that any two persons can ever understand each other. Such reflections provoke the question of how communication is possible when people do not see and assume the same things and share the same values.

On this question there are two schools of thought. One school assumes that communication between A and B, for example, has failed when B does not accept what A has to say as being fact, true, or valid; and that the goal of communication is to get B to agree with A's opinions, ideas, facts, or information.

The position of the other school of thought is quite different. It assumes that communication has failed when B does not feel free to express his feelings to A because B fears they will not be accepted by A. Communication is facilitated when on the part of A or B or both there is a willingness to express and accept differences.

As these are quite divergent conceptions, let us

explore them further with an example. Bill, an employee, is talking with his boss in the boss's office. The boss says, "I think, Bill, that this is the best way to do your job." Bill says, "Oh yeah!" According to the first school of thought, this reply would be a sign of poor communication. Bill does not understand the best way of doing his work. To improve communication, therefore, it is up to the boss to explain to Bill why his way is the best.

From the point of view of the second school of thought, Bill's reply is a sign neither of good nor of bad communication. Bill's response is indeterminate. But the boss has an opportunity to find out what Bill means if he so desires. Let us assume that this is what he chooses to do, to find out what Bill means. So this boss tries to get Bill to talk more about his job while he (the boss) listens.

For purposes of simplification, I shall call the boss representing the first school of thought *"Smith"* and the boss representing the second school of thought *"Jones."* In the presence of the so-called same stimulus each behaves differently. Smith chooses to *explain;* Jones chooses to *listen.* In my experience Jones's response works better than Smith's. It works better because Jones is making a more proper evaluation of what is taking place between him and Bill than Smith is. Let us test this hypothesis by continuing with our example.

What Smith Assumes, Sees, and Feels

Smith assumes that he understands what Bill means when Bill says, "Oh yeah!" so there is no need to find out. Smith is sure that Bill does not understand why this is the best way to do his job, so Smith has to tell him. In this process let us assume Smith is logical, lucid, and clear. He presents his facts and evidence well. But, alas, Bill remains unconvinced. What does Smith do? Operating under the assumption that what is taking place between him and Bill is something essen-

tially logical, Smith can draw only one of two conclusions: either (1) he has not been clear enough, or (2) Bill is too damned stupid to understand. So he either has to "spell out" his case in words of fewer and fewer syllables or give up. Smith is reluctant to do the latter, so he continues to explain. What happens?

If Bill still does not accept Smith's explanation of why this is the best way for him to do his job, a pattern of interacting feelings is produced of which Smith is often unaware. The more Smith cannot get Bill to understand him, the more frustrated Smith becomes and the more Bill becomes a threat to his logical capacity. Since Smith sees himself as a fairly reasonable and logical chap, this is a difficult feeling to accept. It is much easier for him to perceive Bill as uncooperative or stupid. This perception, however, will affect what Smith says and does. Under these pressures Bill comes to be evaluated more and more in terms of Smith's values. By this process Smith tends to treat Bill's values as unimportant. He tends to deny Bill's uniqueness and difference. He treats Bill as if he had little capacity for self-direction.

Let us be clear. Smith does not see that he is doing these things. When he is feverishly scratching hieroglyphics on the back of an envelope, trying to explain to Bill why this is the best way to do his job, Smith is trying to be helpful. He is a man of goodwill, and he wants to set Bill straight. This is the way Smith sees himself and his behavior. But it is for this very reason that Bill's "Oh yeah!" is getting under Smith's skin.

"How dumb can a guy be?" is Smith's attitude, and unfortunately Bill will hear that more than Smith's good intentions. Bill will feel misunderstood. He will not see Smith as a man of goodwill trying to be helpful. Rather he will perceive him as a threat to his self-esteem and personal integrity. Against this threat Bill will feel the need to defend himself at all cost. Not being so logically articulate as Smith, Bill expresses this need, again, by saying, "Oh yeah!"

What Jones Assumes, Sees, and Feels

Let us leave this sad scene between Smith and Bill, which I fear is going to terminate by Bill's either leaving in a huff or being kicked out of Smith's office. Let us turn for a moment to Jones and see what he is assuming, seeing, hearing, feeling, doing, and saying when he interacts with Bill.

Jones, it will be remembered, does not assume that he knows what Bill means when he says, "Oh yeah!" so he has to find out. Moreover, he assumes that when Bill said this, he had not exhausted his vocabulary or his feelings. Bill may not necessarily mean one thing; he may mean several different things. So Jones decides to listen.

In this process Jones is not under any illusion that what will take place will be eventually logical. Rather he is assuming that what will take place will be primarily an interaction of feelings. Therefore, he cannot ignore the feelings of Bill, the effect of Bill's feelings on him, or the effect of his feelings on Bill. In other words, he cannot ignore his relationship to Bill; he cannot assume that it will make no difference to what Bill will hear or accept.

Therefore, Jones will be paying strict attention to all of the things Smith has ignored. He will be addressing himself to Bill's feelings, his own, and the interactions between them.

Jones will therefore realize that he has ruffled Bill's feelings with his comment, "I think, Bill, this is the best way to do your job." So instead of trying to get Bill to understand him, he decides to try to understand Bill. He does this by encouraging Bill to speak. Instead of telling Bill how he should feel or think, he asks Bill such questions as, "Is this what you feel?" "Is this what you see?" "Is this what you assume?" Instead of ignoring Bill's evaluations as irrelevant, not valid, inconsequential, or false, he tries to understand Bill's reality as he feels it, perceives it, and assumes it to

be. As Bill begins to open up, Jones's curiosity is piqued by this process.

"Bill isn't so dumb; he's quite an interesting guy" becomes Jones's attitude. And that is what Bill hears. Therefore Bill feels understood and accepted as a person. He becomes less defensive. He is in a better frame of mind to explore and reexamine his own perceptions, feelings, and assumptions. In this process he perceives Jones as a source of help. Bill feels free to express his differences. He feels that Jones has some respect for his capacity for self-direction. These positive feelings toward Jones make Bill more inclined to say, "Well, Jones, I don't quite agree with you that this is the best way to do my job, but I'll tell you what I'll do. I'll try to do it that way for a few days, and then I'll tell you what I think."

If I have identified correctly these very common patterns of personal communication, then some interesting hypotheses can be stated:

(a) . . . Jones has a better map than Smith of the process of personal communication.

(b) The practice of Jones's method . . . depends on Jones's capacity and willingness to see and accept points of view different from his own, and to practice this orientation in a face-to-face relationship. This practice involves an emotional as well as an intellectual achievement. It depends in part on Jones's awareness of himself, in part on the practice of a skill.

(c) . . . Most educational institutions train their students to be logical, lucid, and clear. Very little is done to help them to listen more skillfully. As a result, our educated world contains too many Smiths and too few Joneses.

(d) The biggest block to personal communication is man's inability to listen intelligently, understandingly, and skillfully to another person. This deficiency in the modern world is widespread and appalling. In our universities as well as elsewhere, too little is being done about it.

Peter Drucker

What Communication Means

Communication in management has long been a central concern of students and practitioners in all institutions—business, the military, public administration, hospital administration, university administration and research administration. In no other area have intelligent men and women worked harder or with greater dedication than psychologists, human relations experts, managers and management students have worked on improving communications in our major institutions. The trickle of books on communications has become a raging torrent. A recent bibliography prepared for a graduate seminar on communications ran to 97 pages: a recent anthology contained articles by 49 different contributors.

Yet "communications" has proved as elusive as the unicorn. Each of those 49 contributors has a different theory of communications which is incompatible with all the others. The noise level has gone up so fast that no one can really listen any more to all that babble about communications. But there is clearly less and less "communicating." The so-called communications gap within institutions and between groups in society has been widening steadily—to the point where it threatens to become an unbridgeable gulf of total misunderstanding.

In the meantime, there is an "information explosion." Every professional and every executive suddenly has access to data in inexhaustible abundance. But what must be done to make this cornucopia of data add up to information, let alone to knowledge? The one thing clear so far is that no one really has an answer. Despite "information theory" and "data processing," no one yet has actually seen, let alone used, an "information system," or a "data base." The one thing we do know, however, is that the abundance of information changes the communications problem and makes it both more urgent and even less tractable.

There is a tendency today to give up on communications. In the psychology of management, for instance, the latest fashion is the T-group, with its "sensitivity training." The avowed aim is not communications, but "self-awareness." T-groups focus on the "I" and not on the "Thou." A decade or two ago the rhetoric stressed "empathy"; now it stresses "doing one's thing." However needed self-knowledge may be, communication is needed at least as much (if indeed self-knowledge is possible without action on others—that is, without communications). So whether or not T-groups are sound psychology and effective psycho-therapy, their popularity attests to the failure of attempts at communications.

A good deal has been learned about information and communications. However, most of it has not come from the work on communications to which so much time and energy has been devoted. It has been the by-product of work in a large number of seemingly unrelated fields, from learning theory to genetics and electronic engineering. Equally there is a lot of experience—though mostly of failure—in a good many practical situations in all kinds of institutions. Although commu-

Abridged and adapted from Chapter 38 in *Management: Tasks, Responsibilities, Practices* by Peter F. Drucker. Copyright © 1974 by Peter F. Drucker. By permission of Harper & Row, Publishers, Inc. and William Heinemann Ltd.

nications may never be understood, there is now some knowledge about communications in organizations—or "managerial communications."

This knowledge leads to some surprising conclusions for managers—for instance, that the traditional downward communication in companies and other organizations does not and cannot work: that the human relations approach of "listening" to surbordinates does not work, either: that more and better information does not solve, but worsens, the communications problem: that almost no computer today is being used properly. The honest, sincere efforts which have been made to "communicate" in management have no validity. To understand why this is so requires an understanding of the knowledge and experience which have been gained by study of psychology and perception.

Mastery of communications, even in organizations, is still far away. But at least we increasingly know what does not work and, sometimes, why it does not work. Indeed most of today's brave attempts at communication in organizations—whether business, trade unions, government agencies, or universities—is based on assumptions that have been proven to be invalid, and therefore these efforts cannot have results. But now, perhaps, what might work can be anticipated. The four fundamentals of communication have been learned, mostly through doing the wrong things—that communication is *perception*, that it is *expectation*, that it is *involvement* and that it is *not* information. Information presupposes functioning communications, but they are totally different things.

An old riddle asked by the mystics of many religions—the Zen Buddhists, the Sufis of Islam, or the Rabbis of the Talmud—goes: "Is there a sound in the forest if a tree crashes down and no one is around to hear it?" The right answer is "no."

There are sound waves. But there is no sound unless someone perceives it. Sound is created by *perception*. Sound is "communication." This may seem trite; after all, the mystics of old, too, always answered that there is no sound unless someone can hear it. Yet the implications are great.

First, it is the recipient who communicates. The so-called "communicator" only "utters." Unless there is someone who hears, there is no communication, only noise. The communicator cannot communicate"; he can only make it possible, or impossible, for a recipient—or rather "percipient"—to perceive.

Perception, moreover, is not logic. It is experience, and always part of a "total picture." The gestures, the tone of voice, the whole environment, not to mention the cultural and social relations, cannot be dissociated from the spoken language. In fact, without them the spoken word has no meaning and cannot communicate. The same words—for example, "I enjoyed meeting you"—will be heard as having a wide variety of meanings. Whether they are heard as warmth or as icy cold, as endearment or as rejection, depends on their setting—say, the tone of the voice or the occasion. By themselves, without being part of the total configuration, the words have no meaning at all. To paraphrase an old saying, "one cannot communicate a word; the whole man always comes with it."

But men can only perceive what they are capable of perceiving. Just as the human ear does not hear sounds above a certain pitch, so human perception does not perceive what is beyond its range of perception. A man may hear physically, or see visually, but he cannot accept what he hears or sees. It cannot become communication. The teachers of rhetoric have known this for a very long time—though the practitioners of communications tend to forget it again and again. In

Plato's *Phaedrus* Socrates points out that one has to talk to people in terms of their own experience, to use carpenter's metaphors when talking to carpenters, and so on. One can only communicate in the recipient's language or altogether in his terms. And the terms have to be experience-based. It therefore does very little good to try to explain terms to people. They will not be able to receive them if they are not terms of their own experience.

The connection between experience, perception, and concept formation—that is, understanding—is infinitely subtler and richer than any earlier philosopher imagined. But one fact is proven. Percept and concept in the learner, whether child or adult, are not separate. We cannot perceive unless we also conceive. But we also cannot form concepts unless we can perceive. To communicate a concept is impossible unless the recipient can perceive it, that is, unless it is within his perception.

There is a very old saying among writers: "Difficulties with a sentence always mean confused thinking. It is not the sentence that needs straightening out, it is the thought behind it." In writing, people attempt, of course, to communicate with themselves. An "unclear sentence" is one that exceeds the writer's own capacity for perception. Working on the sentence—that is, working on what is normally called communications—cannot solve the problem. The writer has to work on his own concepts first to be able to understand what he is trying to say—and only then can he write the sentence.

In communicating, whatever the medium, the first question has to be: "is this communication within the recipient's range of perception? Can he receive it? The most important limitations on perception are usually cultural and emotional rather than physical. That fanatics are not convinced by rational arguments has been known for thousands of years. But it is not argument that is lacking.

Fanatics do not have the ability to perceive communication which goes beyond their range of emotions. To conceive them, their emotions would have to be altered. In other words, no one is "in touch with reality," if that means complete openness to evidence. The distinction between sanity and paranoia does not lie in the ability to perceive, but in the ability to learn, in the ability to change emotions on the basis of experience.

As Mary Parker Follett realized 40 years ago, a disagreement or a conflict is likely not to be about the answers, or indeed about anything ostensible. In most cases, it results from incongruity in perceptions. What A sees so vividly, B does not see at all. And, therefore, what A argues has no pertinence to B's concerns, and *vice versa*. Both, Follett argued, are likely to see reality. But each is likely to see a different aspect of reality. The world, and not only the material world, is multidimensional. Yet men can only see one dimension at a time. We rarely realize that there could be other dimensions, and that something that is so obvious to us and so clearly validated by our emotional experience, has other dimensions, a back and sides, which are entirely different and which, therefore, lead to entirely different perception.

There is an old story about the blind men and the elephant, in which every one of them, upon encountering this strange beast, feels part of the elephant's anatomy, his leg, his trunk, his hide, and reports an entirely different conclusion, each one held tenaciously. This is simply a story of the human condition. And there is no possibility of communication until this is understood and until he who has felt the hide of the elephant goes over to him who has felt the leg and feels the leg himself. There is no possibility of communications, without first knowing what the recipient, the true "communicator," can see—and why.

Men perceive, as a rule, what they expect to

perceive. They see largely what they expect to see, and hear largely what they expect to hear. That the unexpected may be resented is not the important thing—though most of the work on communications in business or government thinks this is so. What is truly important is that the unexpected is usually not received at all. It is neither seen nor heard, but ignored. Or it is misunderstood—that is, mis-seen as the expected or misheard as the expected.

The human mind attempts to fit impressions and stimuli into a frame of expectations. It resists vigorously any attempts to make it "change its mind"—to perceive what it does not expect to perceive, or not to perceive what it expects to perceive. The human mind can, of course, be altered to the fact that what it perceives is contrary to its expectations. But this first requires understanding of what it expects to perceive. The mind then requires an unmistakable signal—"this is different"—that is, a shock which breaks continuity. A gradual change, in which the mind is supposedly led by small, incremental steps to realize that what is perceived is not expected, will not work. It will rather reinforce the expectations and make it even more certain that what will be perceived is what the recipient expects to perceive.

Before we can communicate, we must therefore know what the recipient expects to see and to hear. Only then can we know whether communication can utilize his expectations—and what they are—or whether there is need for the "shock of alienation," for an "awakening" that forces the recipient to realize that the unexpected is happening.

Communication, in fact, always makes demands. It always demands that the recipient becomes somebody, do something, believe something. It always appeals to motivation. If, in other words, communication fits in with the aspirations, the values, the purposes of the recipient, it is powerful. If it goes against his aspirations, his values, his motivations, it is likely not to be received at all, or at best, to be resisted. Of course, at its most powerful, communication brings about "conversion"—a change of personality, of values, beliefs, aspirations. But this is the rare event, and one against which the basic psychological forces of every human being are strongly organized.

All through history, the problem has been how to glean a little information out of communications—that is, out of relationships between people, based on perception. All through history, the problem has been to isolate the information content from an abundance of perception. Now, all of a sudden, there is the capacity to provide information, both because of the conceptual work of the logicians, and because of the technical work on "data processing" and "data storage"—especially, of course, because of the computer and its tremendous capacity to store, manipulate and transmit data.

Now, there is the opposite problem from the one mankind has always been struggling with, the problem of handling information *per se,* devoid of any communication content.

The requirements for effective information are the opposite of those for effective communication. Information is, for instance, always specific. We perceive a "configuration" in communications, but we convey specific individual data in the information process. Information is, above all, a principle of economy. The fewer data needed, the better the information. And an overload of information—anything much beyond what is truly needed—leads to a complete information blackout.

At the same time, information presupposes communication. Information is always encoded. To be received, let alone to be used, the code must be known and understood by the recipient. This requires prior agreement or communication. At the very least, the recipient has to know what the data relate to. Are the figures on a piece of computer tape the height of mountain tops or the cash balances of banks? In either case, the recipient has to know what mountains or banks are, to get any information out of the data.

Communications, finally, may not be dependent on information. Indeed, the most perfect communications may be purely "shared experiences," which are not based on any logic. Perception has primacy rather than information.

The foregoing summary of what has been learned is, of course, a gross over-simplification, which glosses over some of the most hotly contested issues in psychology and perception. No one, it might be said, could possibly be surprised at the statements made. They say what "everybody knows." But whether this is true or not, it is not what "everybody does." On the contrary, the logical implications for communications in organizations of these apparently simple and obvious statements are at odds with current management practice.

For centuries managers have attempted communication "downwards." This cannot work, no matter how hard and how intelligently they try. It cannot work, first, because it focuses on what the manager wants to say. It assumes, in other words, that the utterer "communicates"—when in fact, communication is the act of the recipient. The emphasis has been put on the emitter, the manager, the administrator or the commander, to make him capable of being a "better communicator." But all that can be communicated downwards are commands, that is, pre-arranged signals. Nothing connected with understanding, let alone with motivation, can be communicated downwards. This requires communication upward, from those who perceive to those who want to reach their perception.

This does not mean that managers should stop working on clarity in what they say or write. Far from it. But it does mean that *how* they say something can come only after they have learned *what* to say. And this cannot be found out by "talking to." "Letters to the Employees," no matter how well done, will be a waste unless the writer knows what employees can perceive, expect to perceive and want to do. They are a waste unless they are based on the recipient's rather than the emitter's perception.

But "listening" does not work either. The theory of Elton Mayo was that instead of starting out with what "we," that is, the executive, wants to "get across," the executive should start out by finding out what subordinates want to know, are interested in, are (in other words) receptive to. To this day, this human relations prescription of "listening," though rarely practised, remains the classic formula. Of course, "listening" is a prerequisite to communication. But it is not adequate, and it cannot work by itself. Perhaps the reason why it is not being used widely, despite the popularity of the slogan, is precisely that, where tried, it has failed.

"Listening" first assumes that the superior will understand what he is being told. It assumes, in other words, that the surbordinates can communicate. It is hard to see, however, why the subordinate should be able to do what his superior cannot do. There is no reason for assuming he can, or to believe that "listening" results any less in misunderstanding and communications failure than does talking. In addition, the theory of "listening" does not take into account that communications is involvement. It does not bring out the subordinate's preferences and desires, his values and aspirations. It may explain the reasons for misunderstanding. But it does not lay down a basis for understanding.

Again, "listening" is not wrong, any more than the futility of downward communications furnishes any argument against attempts to write well, to say things clearly and simply, and to speak the language of those addressed rather than one's own jargon. Indeed, the realization that communications have to be upwards (or rather that they have to start with the recipient, rather than the emitter), which underlies the concept of "listening," is absolutely sound and vital. But listening is only the starting point.

More and better information does not solve the communications problem, does not bridge the communications gap. On the contrary, the more the information, the greater is the need for functioning and effective communication. In the first place, the more impersonal and formal the information process is, the more it will depend on prior agreement on meaning and application, that is, on communications. In the second place, the more effective the information process, the more impersonal and formal will it become, the more it will separate human beings and thereby require separate, but also much greater efforts, to re-establish the human relationship, the relationship of communication. The effectiveness of the information process will depend increasingly on the ability to communicate; in the absence of effective communication—as today—the "information revolution" cannot really produce information. All it can produce is data.

Perhaps more important, the test of an information system will increasingly be the degree to which, by freeing human beings from concern with information, it frees them for work on communications. The test of the computer, in particular, should increasingly be how much time it gives executives and professionals on all levels for direct, personal, face-to-face relationships with other people. It is fashionable today to measure the "utilization" of a computer by the number of hours it runs during one day. But this is not even a measurement of the computer's efficiency. It is purely a measurement of input. The only measurement of output is the degree to which availability of information enables human beings **not** to control—not to spend time trying to get a little information on what happened yesterday.

The only measurement of this, in turn, is the amount of time that becomes available for the job which only human beings can do, the job of communication. By this test, almost no computer today is being used properly. Most of them are being misused, to justify spending even more time on control rather than to relieve human beings from controlling by giving them information. The reason for this is quite clearly the lack of prior communication, of agreement and decision on what information it needed, by whom and for what purposes, and what it means operationally.

The "information explosion" is the most impelling reason to go to work on communications. The frightening communications gap all around us—between management and workers; between business and government; between faculty and students, and between both of them and university administrations; between producers and consumers, and so on—may well reflect in some measure the tremendous increase in information without a commensurate increase in communications.

In terms of traditional organization communications we thus have to start upwards. Downward communications cannot work and do not work. They come *after* upward communications have been successfully established. They are reaction rather than action; response rather than initiative. Nor is it enough to "listen." The upward communications must first be focused on something that both recipient and emitter can perceive, focused on something that is common to both of them. And second, they must be focused on the motivation of the intended recipient. They must, from the beginning, be informed by his values, beliefs, and aspirations.

One example—but only an example—is found in the promising results in one organization. Here communication started with the demand by the superior that the subordinate think through and present to the superior his own conclusions as to what major contributions to the organization—or to the unit within the organization—the subordinate should be expected to provide and should be held accountable for. What the surbordinate then comes up with is rarely what the superior expects. The first aim of the exercise is precisely to bring out this divergence in perception between superior and subordinate. But the perception is focused, and focused on something that is real to both parties. To realize that they see the same reality differently is in itself already true communication.

Second, in this approach, the intended recipient of communication—in this case the subordinate—is given access to experience which enables him to understand. He is given access to the reality of decision-making, the problems of priorities, the choice between what one likes to do and what the situation demands, and above all, the responsibility for a decision. He may not see the situation in the same way the superior does—in fact, he rarely will or even should. But he may gain an understanding of the complexity of the superior's situation, and above all of the fact that the complexity is not of the superior's making, but is inherent in the situation itself.

Finally, the communication, even if it consists of a "no" to the subordinate's conclusions, is firmly focused on his aspirations, values and motivation. It starts out with the question: "what would you *want* to do?" It may then end up with the command: "this is what I tell you to do." But at least it forces the superior to realize that he is over-riding the desires of the subordinate. It forces him to explain, if not to try to persuade. At least, he knows that he has a problem—and so does the subordinate.

A similar approach has worked in another organizational situation in which communication

has been traditionally absent: the performance appraisal, and especially the appraisal interview. Performance appraisal is today standard in large organizations (except in Japan where promotion and pay go by seniority, so that performance appraisal would serve little purpose). Most people want to know "where they stand." Indeed, one of the most common complaints of employees in organizations is that they communicate not being appraised and are not being told whether they do well or poorly.

The appraisal forms may be filled out. But the appraisal interview in which the appraiser is expected to discuss his performance with a man is almost never done at all. The exceptions are a few organizations in which performance appraisals are considered a communications tool rather than a rating device. This means specifically that the performance appraisal starts out with the question, "what has this man done well?" It then asks: "and what, therefore, should he be able to do well?" And then it asks: "and what would he have to learn or to acquire to be able to get the most from his capacities and achievements?"

This, first, focuses on specific achievement. It focuses on things which the employee himself is likely to perceive clearly and gladly. It also focuses on his own aspirations, values and desires. Weaknesses are seen as limitations to what the employee himself can do well and wants to do, rather than as defects. The proper conclusion from this approach to appraisal is not the question: "what should the employee do?", but "what should the organization and I, his boss, do?" A proper conclusion is not: "what does this communicate to the employee?" It is: "what does this communicate to both of us, subordinate *and* superior?"

Perhaps these small examples illustrate conclusions pointed to by past experience with communications—which is largely an experience of failure—and past work in learning, memory, perception and motivation. The start of communications in organization must be to get the intended recipient to try to communicate himself. This requires a focus on the impersonal but common tasks, as well as on the recipient himself. It also requires the experience of responsibility. Perception presupposes experience. Communication within organization therefore, presupposes that the members of the organization have the foundation of experience to receive and perceive. The artist can convey this experience in symbolical form: he can communicate what his readers or viewers have never experienced. But ordinary managers, administrators, and professors are not likely to be artists. The recipients must, therefore, have actual experience themselves and directly, rather than through the vicarious symbols.

The traditional defence of paternalism has always been "it's a complex world; it needs the expert, the man who knows best." But paternalism really can only work in a simple world. When people can understand what Papa does, because they share his experiences and his perception, then Papa can actually make the decisions for them. In a complex world there is need for a shared experience in the decisions, or there is no common perception, no communications, and therefore neither acceptance of the decisions, nor ability to carry them out. The ability to understand presupposes prior communication. It presupposes agreement on meaning.

There will be no managerial communication or any kind of communication, in sum, if it is conceived as going from the "I" to the "Thou." Communication only works from one member of "us" to another.

Jay M. Jackson

The Organization and Its Communications Problem

Business executives, I am told, are very similar to other people: they have communication problems, too. They are concerned, of course, about better understanding among all persons. They are interested in overcoming barriers to communication between members of the public and their own particular industry. They are especially concerned. or should be, about problems of communication within an organization, since business administration by its very nature is a collective enterprise, and people in this profession must spend their days in organized groups, or organizations.

First, I want to discuss some characteristics of all organizations that create communication problems. Second, I shall present some conclusions based on recent research findings regarding the forces which determine the flow of communication in an organization. Next I shall consider the consequences of communication in a number of conditions that often exist within an organization. Finally, I shall attempt to indicate that what we call problems of communication are often merely symptomatic of other difficulties between people.

Characteristics of Organizations

What is it about organizations that seems to make communication especially difficult? An organization may be considered a system of overlapping

"The Organization and Its Communications Problem" by Jay M. Jackson. Reprinted by permission of the publisher from *S.A.M., Advanced Management Journal*, February © 1959 by S.A.M., a division of American Management Associations.

and interdependent groups. These groups can be departments located on the same floor of a building, or they can be divisions scattered over the face of the earth. Other things being equal, people will communicate most frequently to those geographically closest to them, even within a relatively small organization. Spatial distance itself can thus be a barrier to communication.

Each one of the subgroups within an organization demands allegiance from its members. It has its own immediate goals and means for achieving them. It distributes tangible or intangible rewards to members of the group, based on their contribution to these objectives. When any particular communication is sent to a number of subgroups in an organization, each group may extract a different meaning from the message, depending upon its significance for the things the group values and is striving to accomplish.

The groups in an organization often represent different subcultures—as different, for example, as those inhabited by engineers, accountants, and salesmen. Each occupational or professional group has its own value system and idealized image, based on its traditions. These are guarded jealously, since to a considerable degree they give the members of that group their feelings of identity. Other groups in an organization, based on experience, age, sex, and martial status, have to varying degrees similar tendencies. Each develops along with its peculiar value system a somewhat specialized system of meanings. What is required to communicate effectively to members of different groups is a system of simultaneous translation, like that employed by the United Nations. This simultaneous translation must be taking place both within the sender and the receivers of a communication.

It is also characteristic of organizations that persons are structured into different systems of relationships. A work structure exists: certain persons are expected to perform certain tasks together with other persons. An authority structure exists: some people have responsibility for directing the activities of others. The status structure determines which persons have what rights and privileges. The prestige structure permits certain persons to expect deferential behavior from others. The friendship structure is based on feelings of interpersonal trust.

These systems of relationships overlap but are not identical. Each has an important effect upon communication in an organization, by influencing the expectations people have regarding who should communicate to whom about what in what manner. Now, how often do people openly and freely discuss these matters and come to agreement? Since these areas involve ranking of persons and invidious distinctions, they are commonly avoided. Yet disagreements and distorted perceptions about questions of relationship in an organization are the source of many communication difficulties.

What intensifies these communication problems is the fact that relationships among persons in an organization are in a continual state of flux. Personnel losses, transfers, promotions and replacements are occurring. Decisions about new policies and procedures are being made, and often modify people's relationships. Some people are informed about changed relationships before others; some are not informed at all. Although it is common practice to communicate decisions to all the persons who are affected by them, the problem is often to determine who are the relevant persons. Unless we are extremely sensitive to the social structure of our organization, it is likely that we

shall restrict communication too narrowly. The restrictive communication of decisions about change, however, can be extremely disruptive to any consensus people have about their relationships to one another, and thus can create for them problems of communication.

The Flow of Communication

Any solution of a communication problem must be based on analysis of the particular situation in which the problem occurs, and an application of general principles about communication. It is possible, on the basis of findings from research, to formulate a number of principles about the forces in an organization which direct the flow of communication.

You may have heard at one time or another that communication flows downward all right in an organization; the problem is to get communication from below. This is only partially true. In fact, any generalization that communication flows down, up, or across, is equally false. Communication is like a piece of driftwood on a sea of conflicting currents. Sometimes the shore will be littered with debris, sometimes it will be bare. The amount and direction of movement is not aimless, nor unidirectional, but a response to all the forces—winds, tides and currents—which come into play.

What forces direct communication in an organization? They are, on the whole, motivational forces. People communicate or fail to communicate in order to achieve some goal, to satisfy some personal need, or to improve their immediate situation. Let us examine briefly some of the evidence from research which supports this statement.

A study was made of the communication patterns among the personnel of a medium-sized government agency.[1] Everyone was included in the research, from the director to the janitor. It was found that people communicated far more to members of their own subgroups than to any other persons. They also preferred to be communicating to someone of higher status than themselves, and tried to avoid having communication with those lower in status than themselves. The only exception to this tendency was when a person had supervisory responsibilities, which removed his restraints against communicating with particular lower status persons. When people did communicate with others of the same status level in the organization, there was a strong tendency for them to select highly valued persons, and to avoid those they thought were making little contribution.

Let us see if we can find a principle which explains these results. The formal subgroupings in an organization are usually based upon joint work responsibilities. There are strong forces, therefore, to communicate with those whose work goals are the same as one's own. A supervisor can accomplish his work objectives only by having relatively frequent contact with his subordinates: and he probably would like to have more contact than he has. The people in an organization who are most valued for their ability to contribute are those who acan give the best information and advice. People seek them out. These findings all seem to point to the same conclusion:

1. *In the pursuit of their work goals, people have forces acting upon them to communicate with those who will help them achieve their aims, and forces against communicating with those who will not assist, or may retard their accomplishment.*

In the midst of one study of a housing settlement,[2] a rumor swept through the community and threatened to disrupt the research. The investigators turned their attention to this rumor and were able to trace its path from person to person. They were trying to understand the forces which led people to communicate. Later on they tested their understanding by deliberately planting a rumor in an organization and again tracing its path by the use of informants.[3] They concluded that people will initiate and spread rumors in two types of situation: when they are confused and unclear about what is happening, and when they feel powerless to affect their own destinies. Passing on a rumor is a means of expressing and alleviating anxiety about the subject of the rumor.[4]

Let us consider one more fact before we draw a general conclusion from these findings. Studies in industry, in a hospital, and in a government agency all yield the same result: people want to speak to higher status rather than lower status persons.[5] Why are there these strong forces on people to direct their communication upwards? Higher status persons have the power to create for subordinates either gratifying or depriving experiences. These may take the form of tangible decisions and rewards, or perhaps merely expressions of approval and confidence. Lower status persons need reassurance about their superiors' attitudes, evaluations, and intentions towards them. We can conclude that:

2. *People have powerful forces acting upon them to direct their communication toward those who can make them feel more secure and gratify their needs, and away from those who threaten them, make them*

[1] Jay M. Jackson, *Analysis of Interpersonal Relations in a Formal Organization*, Ph.D. Thesis, University of Michigan, 1953.
[2] Leon Festinger, Dorwin Cartwright, *et al.*, "A Study of a Rumor: Its Origin and Spread," *Human Relations*, 1948, 1, pp. 464–486.

[3] Kurt Back, Leon Festinger, *et al.*, "The Methodology of Studying Rumor Transmission," *Human Relations*, 1950, 3, pp. 307–312.
[4] For an illustration of this in a hospital setting, see: Jay Jackson, Gale Jensen, and Floyd Mann, "Building a Hospital Organization for Training Administrators," *Hospital Management*, September, 1956, p. 54.
[5] See Elliott Mishler and Asher Tropp, "Status and Interaction in a Psychiatric Hospital," *Human Relations*, 1956, 9, pp. 187–206; Jay Jackson, *Analysis of Interpersonal Relations in a Formal Organization*, Ph.D. Thesis, University of Michigan, 1953; Tom Burns, "The Directions of Activity and Communication in a Departmental Executive Group," *Human Relations*, 1954, 7, pp. 73–79.

feel anxious, and generally provide unrewarding experiences.

People's needs largely determine content of their communication to others of different status. There is evidence that subordinates will often be reluctant to ask supervisors for help when they need it, because this might be seen as a threatening admission of inadequacy.[6] And superiors tend to delete from their communications to subordinates any reference to their own mistakes or errors of judgment.[7] I am sure that these findings are in accord with the experiences that many of us have had in organizations.

A third principle which helps us understand the flow of communication is this:

3. *Persons in an organization are always communicating as if they were trying to improve their position.*

They may or may not be aware of their own behavior in this respect. But the evidence indicates that they want to increase their status, to belong to a more prestigeful group, to obtain more power to influence decisions, and to expand their authority. It has been said that talking upwards is a gratifying substitute for moving upwards. Persons in an organization who are attracted to membership in a particular department or group will feel inclined to direct much more communication in that direction than will those who do not want to belong to it. If they are excluded or barred from membership and their desire to belong persists, they will increase their communication even further, as if this represented a substitute for actually moving into the desired group.[8]

In a study of the role relationships of three types of professionals who work together in the mental health field[9]—psychiatrists, clinical psychologists, and psychiatric social workers—it was found that the direction, amount, and content of their communication to one another could be predicted largely from two factors. These were: their perception of the other professions' power relative to their own; and how satisfied they were with their own power position compared to that of the other groups. The general principle that forces act on persons to communicate so as to improve their relative position in the organization seems to be supported by all these findings.

The Consequences of Communication

Recent research also has something to tell us about the consequences that communication will have when various conditions exist within an organization. Again we find that it is not possible to state that a particular type of communication will always have the same effect, without specifying the conditions in which the generalization will hold true. At the present time, however, the evidence from research appears to warrant four general conclusions.

1. *The effect of any particular communication will depend largely upon the prior feelings and attitudes that the parties concerned have towards one another.*

Findings from a number of different studies support this statement. During World War II, hostile attitudes and negative stereotypes existed between the inhabitants of a housing project for industrial workers and members of the surrounding community. An action research project was under-

---

[6] Ian Ross, *Role Specialization in Supervision*, Ph.D. Thesis, Columbia University, 1957.

[7] This finding is from an unpublished study of a public utility company by Alvin Zander.

[8] Experimental evidence exists for this statement in: Jay Jackson and Herbert Saltzstein, *Group Membership and Conformity Processes* (Ann Arbor: Research Center for Group Dynamics, University of Michigan, 1956), p. 89; see also: Harold Kelley, "Communication in Experimentally Created Hierarchies," *Human Relations*, 1950, 4, pp. 39–56.

[9] Zander, A., Cohen, A. R., and Stotland, E., *Role Relations in the Mental Health Professions* (Ann Arbor: Institute for Social Research, University of Michigan, 1957).

taken to increase contact between these two groups of people.[10] It was found, however, that after increased contact the attitudes and feelings of these people had become polarized: those that were initially positive became more positive, and those that began by being negative became even more negative. The effect of stimulating greater contact could have been predicted only from a knowledge of the pre-existing attitudes and feelings.

In another study of the communication patterns in a large organization, it was found that increased communication did make people more accurate about others' opinions, but only when they initially trusted one another and already were in considerable agreement.[11] When people are in disagreement or do not trust one another, an increase in communication will not necessarily lead to greater understanding.

It was found in another study that frequent communication among personnel made working for the organization either more or less attractive for them. The mediating factor was whether or not the persons who were in constant communication valued each others' contribution to the work of the organization.[12]

2. *The effect of any particular communication will depend upon the pre-existing expectations and motives of the communicating persons.*

Executives of a large organization were asked to indicate on a checklist how much time they spent with each other, and the subject of their interaction.[13] In one-third of the answers they were in disagreement about the subject of their communication. For example, one reported that he had been discussing personnel matters with another; the latter thought they had been discussing questions of production. When these executives differed, each assumed that the problem with which he was personally most concerned was what they had really been talking about.

The subjects of this study were men with an engineering background. They consistently overestimated the amount of time executives spent on production matters and underestimated the amount of time spent on personnel problems. The impressions their communication made upon them had been shaped by their own goals and motives.

From this and other studies it seems clear that the consequences of communication are limited by people's interest in achieving certain effects, and lack of concern about achieving others. They will be inclined to remember and feel committed to those decisions which are consistent with their own expectations and motives.

3. *The effect of a superior's communication with a subordinate will depend upon the relationship between them, and how adequately this relationship satisfies the subordinate's needs.*

Communication between superior and subordinate often has consequences which neither of them anticipates nor welcomes. It is especially difficult to avoid problems of misinterpretation or ineffectiveness in this area.

In one organization it was found that some employees who received frequent communication from their supervisor became more accurately informed about their supervisor's real attitudes; but this was not true for other employees who also had constant contact with their supervisor.[14] The difference was traced to whether or not a supervisor said he trusted his subordinates. When he did not trust them, he was more guarded in what he said to them, revealing less of his true feelings.

[10] Leon Festinger and Harold Kelley, *Changing Attitudes Through Social Contact* (Ann Arbor: Research Center for Group Dynamics, University of Michigan, 1951).
[11] Glen Mellinger, "Interpersonal Trust as a Factor in Communication," *Journal of Abnormal and Social Psychology*, 1956, 52, pp. 304–309.
[12] Jay Jackson, *op. cit.*
[13] Tom Burns, *op. cit.*

[14] Glen Mellinger, *op. cit.*

A lack of trust between superior and subordinate can thus act as a barrier to the creation of mutual understanding.

We have discussed how people's need for security directs their communication toward higher status persons in an organization. A study was conducted in a public utility company,[15] where it was possible to vary experimentally the kind of communication supervisors gave their subordinates. People became anxious and threatened in response to two different conditions: when communication from their supervisor was unclear, and when the supervisor was inconsistent in what he said from one time to another.

We have also pointed out that the persons in an organization tend to communicate as if they were constantly attempting to improve their positions. This is consistent with the finding that the experienced employees in an organization resent close supervision,[16] since it implies that their power and prestige are less than they want them to be.

The study of the senior staff members in a British engineering plant, referred to earlier, led to the discovery of a process of "status protection." When these men received instructions from their superiors, they often treated them as merely information or advice. In this manner they in effect achieved a relative improvement in their own position in the authority structure, by acting as if no one had the right to direct their activity.

Thus the findings from laboratory and field research point unequivocally to the supervisor-subordinate relationship as one of the crucial factors determining the effect of a supervisor's communication to subordinates. Another major factor is whether or not the subordinate stands alone in his relationship to the supervisor, or belongs to a group of peers in the organization.

4. *The effect of a superior's communication with a subordinate will depend upon the amount of support the subordinate receives from membership in a group of peers.*

An experimental study has demonstrated the remarkable effect of belonging to a group of equals on a subordinate confronted by a powerful and directive superior.[17] Being a member of a group decreased a person's feelings of threat and freed him to disagree with his supervisor and make counterproposals. The person who had the moral support of membership in a group reacted to his supervisor's communication with less defensive and more problem-oriented behavior.

There is a considerable body of evidence, too, that a group acts as a source of "social reality" for its members, providing them an opportunity to validate their ideas and opinions.[18] When communication from a superior is directed to a group as a whole rather than to isolated individuals, it is likely that more accurate transmission of information will be achieved.

Problems of Communication Are Often Symptomatic

From our discussion thus far, I think it should be clear that what we call communication problems are often only symptomatic of other difficulties which exist among persons and groups in an organization. To summarize what has been said or implied, I should like to point to four problems which people in organizations must solve in order to overcome barriers to communication.

[15] Arthur Cohen, "Situational Structure, Self-Esteem, and Threat-Oriented Reactions to Power." A chapter in Dorwin Cartwright, *et al., Studies in Social Power* (Ann Arbor: Research Center for Group Dynamics, University of Michigan, 1959).

[16] This finding is from an unpublished study by Jay Jackson, Jean Butman, and Philip Runkel of the communication patterns and attitudes of employees in two business offices.

[17] Ezra Stotland, "Peer Groups and Reaction to Power Figures." A chapter in Dorwin Cartwright, *et al., Studies in Social Power* (Ann Arbor: Research Center for Group Dynamics, University of Michigan, 1959).

[18] See, for example, Jay M. Jackson and Herbert D. Saltzstein, "The Effect of Person-Group Relationships on Conformity Processes," *The Journal of Abnormal and Social Psychology* (in press).

1. *The problem of trust or lack of trust.* Communication flows along friendship channels. When trust exists, content is more freely communicated, and the recipient is more accurate in perceiving the sender's opinion.

2. *The problem of creating interdependence among persons: common goals and agreement about means for achieving them.* When persons have different goals and value systems, then it is especially important to create mutual understanding about needs and motives.

3. *The problem of distributing rewards fairly,* so that people's needs are being met, and so that they are motivated to contribute to the over-all objectives of the organization. Nothing can be so restrictive of the free flow of ideas and information, for example, as the feeling that you may not obtain credit for your contribution.

4. *The exceedingly important problem of understanding and coming to common agreement about the social structure of the organization.* I can think of nothing which would facilitate more the free and accurate flow of communication in an organization than consensus about questions of work, authority, prestige, and status relationships.

Robert N. McMurry

Clear Communications for Chief Executives

As one retiring chief executive said to his successor, "Yesterday was the last day you heard the truth from your subordinates." In many companies, often despite feverish efforts to improve internal communications, top executives are almost totally insulated from what is actually taking place in their enterprises. The intelligence they receive, including formal reports, is all too often incomplete or, at best, slanted.

Of equal concern, *not all chief executives are temperamentally capable of accepting and assimilating information which happens to conflict with their personal values and predilections.*

Consequently, undertakings of great magnitude and of critical significance to the integrity of the business are often entered into on the basis of incomplete, inadequate, or incorrect information. Without knowing it, the chief executive is in the perilous situation of the shipmaster who blindly sails uncharted shoals. He is unaware of the seriousness of his situation until confronted with catastrophe itself. It is probable that this is a not infrequent cause of the failure even of small, presumably well-integrated businesses. It certainly often contributes to the fact that, as a rule, the chief executive who is a professional manager and not a proprietor has the least job security of anyone in his organization.

In order to assist the chief executive in solving his predicament, I shall attack the communication problem point-blank by examining:

* The barriers which fault the chief executive's

knowledge of "what's going on" in the middle and lower echelons of his organization.
* The sources of error which hinder his ability bto communicate effectively with subordinates.
* The major remedies needed to improve his "intelligence," to help him to see himself, his staff, his employees, and his organization as a whole.
* The reorganization steps that should be taken to improve the overall function of his organization.
* The personal conflicts which must be overcome if he is to establish clear, comprehensive, and valid channels of communication with his people at all levels.

Upward Failures

The top business manager is often lulled into a false sense of security regarding communication flows. His first and most egregious error is to assume that his supervisory hierarchy provides a clear channel of vertical communication, either upward or downward, and that lateral interdepartmental communication is equally reliable. Actually, most levels of supervision are less communication *centers* than communication *barriers*. In addition, many company functions, such as production and sales, are frequently less inclined to be cooperative *allies* than to be bitter *rivals* for power, recognition, and executive favor; hence, communication between them is often poor. Both are prolific *sources* of information, but this does not mean that the intelligence which they provide is complete, accurate, objective, or generally valid and useful.

Misleading Information

In fact, much information provided the chief executive by his subordinates is either unintentionally or willfully and maliciously inaccurate. There are a number of reasons for this:

• No subordinate wishes to have his superiors learn of anything which *he* interprets to be actually or potentially discreditable to him. Hence, he consciously and intentionally endeavors to screen everything that is transmitted upward, filtering out those items of information which are potentially threatening.

• He learns what his superiors desire to hear. Hence, he becomes adept not only at avoiding the unpleasant, but also at "stressing the positive." Though the individual subordinate may consciously be entirely sincere and accountable, his personal anxieties, hostilities, aspirations, and system of beliefs and values almost inevitably shape and color his interpretation and acceptance of what he has learned and is expected to transmit.[1]

• Each subordinate is often desirous of impressing the top manager with the superiority of *his* contributions to the enterprise—and, by the same token, of the pitiful inadequacy of the contributions of his rivals in other divisions and departments of the company. *Special pleading* of this nature is often most seriously misleading. How can the chief executive know which protagonist is telling the truth? In most instances, he cannot be sure. If he depends solely upon his own judgment, he will probably be wrong at least as often as he is right.

• Another source of error arises from the fact that the position of chief executive is one for which there is often substantial competition and rivalry. Hence, the incumbent is not always surrounded and supported by allies and friends, despite his staff's frequent servility, obsequiousness, and dramatic protestations of loyalty. While most

[1] See my article, "Conflicts in Human Values," *Harvard Business Review* (May–June 1963), p. 130.

subordinates would hesitate to give their chief executive a final push into the abyss, many are not at all reluctant to sit by and let him stumble into it blindly.

• Finally, and from the viewpoint of upward communications of the greatest consequence, there is the inability of many chief executives to comprehend and accept valid information even when it is brought to their attention. No wonder top managers are seldom told "the whole truth and nothing but . . ." by their subordinates.

Resulting Errors

In effect, the typical chief executive is the prisoner of his position communications-wise. He is largely insulated from the everyday realities of the enterprise he leads. It is not surprising that under these conditions the top manager makes a number of costly, sometimes even fatal, errors. These principally appear as:

• The acceptance of misinformation concerning what is actually happening within the business on a day-to-day basis.

• The institution and perpetuation of ill-advised policies and practices.

• Loss of contact with and misinterpretation of customer, public, and employee attitudes toward the firm.

• Failure to have a reality-centered control on executive wishful thinking concerning the present state of the enterprise and its future outlook.

Downward Deficiencies

The foregoing failures are in no sense limited to upward communications. Many chief executives believe that their supervisory hierarchies—supplemented by printed material, such as the house organ, bulletin boards, letters to the employees' homes, and occasional addresses by company executives—suffice as channels to convey messages to company personnel. It is assumed, moreover, that as long as the message, whatever its content, is clear, concise, well illustrated, and dramatically presented, its reception will be satisfactory. This, unfortunately, is not always true. There is much more to communication than merely the cogent presentation of a message. If the communication is not understood, believed, and regarded as having a positive value for its recipients, it will fail in its mission. The over-estimation of the effectiveness of the communication media employed is one of the greatest sources of managerial error in dealing with customers, personnel, and the public.

Feedback Missing

Chief executives repeatedly fail to recognize that for communication to be effective, it must be two-way: *there has to be feedback to ascertain the extent to which the message has actually been understood, believed, assimilated, and accepted.* This is a step few companies ever take (perhaps because they fear to learn how little of the message has actually been transmitted).

Thus, the chief executive frequently is in every sense isolated; he is not only denied access to valid information about what is transpiring below him in his enterprise, but his facilities for communication downward (with other than a few of his immediate associates) are severely circumscribed. As a result, he is often forced to make major decisions on the basis of unreliable intra-company intelligence. Furthermore, his orders to those in the lower echelons may be distorted or even blocked at any supervisory level in between.

It is not surprising, in consequence, that even an able, experienced, and well-qualified chief executive not infrequently finds himself unable to cope with the problems such conditions create. This is especially true where the executive has been brought in from the outside and lacks immediate, personal knowledge of conditions. Under such circumstances, he is almost totally at the mercy of his subordinates in the area of communications.

Executive's Dilemma

Not only are many top executives unaware of what transpires within their organizations; they are even less well informed concerning the competence and potential of their key personnel. Ironically, many think they know their subordinates well, and may even have strong personal likes and dislikes for certain individuals. The difficulty here is that these attitudes are often simply the results of *impressions* which have little or no inherent validity.

Few, if any, businesses today have any genuinely reliable *measures* of the inherent competence and quality of performance of their top, middle, and first-line managements. (Particularly sensitive are research, development, and engineering groups.) Most merit rating programs are subject to some 16 sources of error (see Exhibit I).

Much of the operating inefficiency and internecine strife that plague many firms arises in part from the top manager's failure to be properly apprised of what is actually taking place in the organization. Often he knows neither how well suited each member of top, middle, and first-line management is to his job assignment nor the nature and extent of the consequences of his subordinate's maladaption to his job where this exists. . . .

Labor Trouble

Many of the effects of inadequate communication are self-evident. If the company's top manager is unaware of what is happening in the lower echelons or has been deliberately misled, is unable to communicate effectively with his subordinates, or must work through and with a staff of whose competence and true level of performance he knows little, it is to be assumed that he will be operating under a severe handicap. Such a situation can hardly be prevented from having an adverse effect on over-all morale, productivity, and, ultimately, profits.

Less clearly evident, however, is the fact that *failures of communication, in conjunction with weak and incompetent first-line supervision, are the prime cause of much chronic, intractable labor trouble.* This accounts for the phenomenon of the employer who has excellent working conditions, pays premium wages, and offers exceptional fringe benefits, yet has continual labor unrest.

Because of vertical communications failures, incredibly bad conditions are often permitted by the top manager to exist for long periods of time. Consider this glaring example:

A manufacturing plant employed women to assemble casters. The women worked on a moving assembly line, while the components they used were stored in metal containers which rested on the floor beside them. Their complaint of several years' standing was that rats nested in the containers and bit their fingers when they reached in to obtain the component parts. Yet top management was never told.

This kind of phenomenon becomes of even greater significance in the light of the contributions of first- and second-line supervision to workers' distrust of—and hostility toward—company leadership. To most hourly rated employees, *the foreman is management:* the attitude toward him reflects the attitude toward the company as a whole.

Diminishing Competence

Just because its workings are usually concealed by inadequate communications, and so its effects are not recognized, many businesses are, to a greater or lesser extent, victims of what I call McMurry's Law of Diminishing Competence. It postulates that in any supervisory hierarchy *weakness begets greater weakness.* By this I mean that if a supervisor is weak (overly passive, dependent, submissive, or indecisive), his subordinates will tend to be even weaker. In other words, such an anxious individual cannot tolerate as a subordinate anyone who is as strong or stronger than he. Furthermore, this phenomenon tends to repeat itself at each level down the supervisory hierarchy.

Ingrown Ineptitude. If the organization is a "tall" one (i.e., has many intermediate supervisory levels), and the chief executive is weak and uncertain, his inadequacies will be multiplied and elaborated at each supervisory echelon. The outcome may be, and often is, unbelievable incompetence and ineptitude in the lower levels of supervision. Since weak supervision is, on the one hand, the prime source of poor employee morale, because it is never supportive and is often both erratic and punitive, numerous organizations harbor built-in guarantees of continuing labor unrest. On the other hand, many of these passive and weak individuals are intelligent, knowledgeable, and consummate company politicians. Hence, they are highly skilled at concealing or rationalizing their shortcomings and preventing them from being revealed to their supervisors.

Concretized Cliques. When the supervisory hierarchy has a substantial infusion of weak incompetents, self-perpetuating cliques tend to be formed. Such persons habitually staff their departments in their own images. Strength of character and superior competence are regarded by such supervisors as contraindications for acceptance. In consequence, where promotions take place largely from within—as is the practice in many companies—little control is exercised over the influence of the Law of Diminishing Competence. Not only does management as a whole come to be ingrown and blindly conforming, but strong, decisive managerial candidates are actively excluded from acceptance and promotion.

Atrophied Attitudes. The result, over the years, is the formation of a rigid and sterile bureaucracy such as is typical of government agencies. Many of the more competent, decisive, and aggressive individuals, being denied advancement up the management ladder, leave or become union officers. Nevertheless, so completely is even strong top management often isolated from the reality of what is taking place in the organization that it is practically never aware of the steady deterioration of morale and efficiency.

Allegiance to Strength

The qualifications of first- and second-line supervision are important from another point of view in the determination of the character of labor relations. This is true because of the operation of a second phenomenon, which I call McMurry's Law of Allegiance to Strength. In effect, this postulates that where two agencies—for example, the company acting through the foreman and the union acting through the steward or business agent—are competing for employee allegiance and loyalty, the one with the strongest, most aggressive, and decisive representative will nearly always win out. This is due to a simple truism: the stronger and more aggressive of the two will, if all other factors are even, be able to accomplish more for his followers than his less dynamic counterpart. Solely on the ground of self-interest, most employees will give their allegiance to the leader who can demonstrably win the most for them.

Self-Reliant Supervision. Hence, the winning of employee allegiance by the chief executive is less a matter of providing benefits and recreational and feeding facilities than it is of instituting strong, competent supervision. In this connection, it must be warned that the supervisor chosen must be *innately* strong and self-reliant—*these qualities cannot be inculcated by admonition or training.* The supervisor either has them or he does not. If he has them, they can be enhanced by training him in the skills of dealing with people; if the person does not have them, he should not be in a supervisory position. Since few executives have any valid measures for assessing their supervisors' attributes, in practice few have any means of knowing to what extent their supervisors are actually qualified for the positions they hold. Oddly enough, weakness in management shows itself very clearly to those who recognize the overt signs.

Major Remedies

But this dilemma of the chief executive is not insoluble. There are three essential things which the astute chief executive can, and *must,* do if he is to establish clear, comprehensive, and valid channels of communication with his people at all levels.

1. *He should recognize the primary dangers to good communication, if he is to improve his "intelligence" in the military sense.*

2. *He should systematically and comprehensively inventory every member of his management and supervisory staff.*

3. *He should periodically conduct an employee poll or morale survey which will provide him with a comprehensive overview of the human realities of his organization.*

Recognizing Dangers

The establishment of clear channels of communication throughout all levels of the organization hinges on the chief executive's recognition of these primary dangers:

• The tendency on his own part to perceive only "what he wants to see."

• The faulty medium of his supervisory hierarchy for both upward and downward communication.

• The inadequacy of most current supervisor and executive appraisal programs.

• The fallacious standards used in selecting candidates for promotion.

• The limited facilities for employee grievance drainage because of fear of supervisors and distrust of the personnel department.

• The possibility of chronic and legitimate employee dissatisfaction caused by company conditions, policies, and practices.

• The weaknesses of many supervisors, including some who are highly rated by upper management, which deteriorate morale, efficiency, and productivity.

• The risk of employee misunderstanding, disbelief, or refusal to accept a factual statement of company policies and the reasons behind them.

Norman B. Sigband

Needed: Corporate Policies on Communications

Almost every company of reasonable size has developed philosophies on a wide variety of corporate activities: finance, personnel, management, expansion, market selection, growth, acquisition, and others. And these philosophies have been translated into company policies which are needed and vital. They give direction and establish boundaries for a firm's activities.

But the one activity in which a firm engages to carry out the policies of the organization is, of course, communication. But how many firms have a philosophy for that?

The answer is, "very few."

It is true that every organization communicates with its customers, suppliers, government agencies, vendors, dealers, and community members outside the firm. And every individual communicates with superiors, subordinates and colleagues within the organization. And this communication carried on through so many different channels, utilizes various media: reports, letters, conferences, meetings, interviews, discussions, mass media advertisements, sales promotion, goodwill literature, and others.

But is there a policy—even a broad one—which governs all these communications? which gives them some uniformity? some consistency? some direction?

Very, very rarely.

But if there were, company relationships—

"Needed: Corporate Policies on Communications" by Norman B. Sigband. Reprinted by permission of the publisher from *S.A.M., Advanced Management Journal,* April © 1969 by S.A.M., a division of American Management Associations.

internal and external—would improve tremendously. Action on similar problems would be fairly consistent, anxiety among employees would lessen, and directions would be more clearly defined, for the policy would be established.

Let's look at the fictitious Robinson Corporation. It has plants in New York, Chicago, and Los Angeles. Its consumer kitchen-ware products are sold in thousands of stores. On any given day, the Robinson Corporation receives at its three central offices several dozen letters from consumers which are concerned with:

1. Routine inquiries, requests, and acknowledgments which pose no problems,
2. Unsatisfactory merchandise purchased,
3. Requests for contributions of money or merchandise for charity affairs,
4. Pointed questions on civil rights activities,
5. Use of company equipment or facilities for community activities.

It is true that the three locations have a company correspondence manual which tells the stenographer *how* to set up the letter, and to use a modified instead of a full block form, whether to spell out or use a numeral for "Ninth Street," and even guide letters to follow for frequently recurring situations. But nowhere has the company told the manager what the philosophy of communication is which will govern the content and tone of the replies in those situations where tact and discretion are vital. These are the factors which determine whether goodwill will be retained or lost with the external publics.

Or even more serious, let's look at the communications within the plants of the Robinson Corporation in New York, Chicago, and Los Angeles. In one week's time there are questions from employees on:

1. The rumor concerning lay-offs
2. An acquisition of a firm
3. A change in production procedure
4. Equipment ordered which may or may not displace 50 people
5. The promotion or transfer of Frank Adams
6. A possible profit-sharing program

And on and on.

What is the philosophy which tells the manager how to communicate on these issues? Should he explain what the firm hopes to achieve with the new acquisition, piece of equipment, or different production method? The manager in New York may choose to discuss the three areas as honestly as he can; the one in Chicago may partially explain two of the areas, but say nothing about the third because "it's not the employees' business anyway." And the person in charge in Los Angeles feels that all the topics are "hot" and discussion at this time wouldn't be wise—"so we will discuss none." The result in this case is that the rumor mill takes over to explain the situations and fulfill everyone's need to know.

In any one of the three situations above, we see that the result may very well be unhappy, uninformed, and disgruntled employees. And this may lead to strikes, grievances, work slowdowns, and at the least, poor morale. It is obvious, of course, that three managers of different divisions in *one plant* may take exactly the same diverse actions as our supervisors above who were located in New York, Chicago, and Los Angeles.

If the Robinson Corporation had a Philosophy of Communications, however, and it had been translated into policies, the managers would and could communicate on these issues using similar rationales, frameworks, and points of reference.

Because so many firms have no philosophy of communication on vital issues, they communicate

in areas which are pleasant but innocuous—marriages, engagements, retirements, promotions, vacations, and the state of that firm's industry today. And because there is no philosophy on how to deal with Foreman Johnston's complaints, Supervisor Cameron decides that he just won't sit down with him at all, and attempt to reach a solution. "Frankly," he may well say to himself, "I don't know what the company philosophy is on this. It's probably safer to say nothing." "And I wonder how far I should have gone in that Salary and Promotion Committee meeting today? With all those section chiefs there, I had a good opportunity to talk about . . . but maybe I was just as well off saying nothing at this time. I might have talked myself into trouble."

When firms have no philosophy of communications we almost invariably have as a result:

1. Little or no discussion on controversial issues (labor problems, salaries, promotion, layoffs, etc.),
2. Different ways of handling similar issues throughout the organization,
3. Continued discussion on superficial and surface topics to the exclusion of items of real importance to individuals in and outside the firm.

Foy and Harper in an article some years ago found in their research of company publications addressed to employees that:

"Management did not counteract union activity among employees on realistic "breadbasket" subjects such as union leaders' use as levers to promote national social legislation.

"Controversial subjects were avoided, but at the same time, attempts were consistently made to stimulate pride in the virtues of the American way of life. A steady reading diet of such flag waving stories may prove an insult to the average worker's intelligence for he too believes in the American way of life."

Foy and Harper go on to say, "In too many companies the 'sweetness and light' concept seems to govern. This *can* be unrealistic. This *can* be misinterpreted. Too often the policy seems to be one of ducking controversial issues in employee publications, presumably on one or more of the grounds that employees (a) wouldn't read such material, (b) wouldn't believe it, and (c) would resent it. We don't believe any one of those three reasons has a shred of validity."[1]

My contention is that if a firm had a mature, responsible philosophy of communications, effective communications to employees *would* take place in company publications.

But let's look at another facet of superior-subordinate communication. Robert N. McMurry has this to say about the accuracy and flow of internal management level communications:

"The top manager is often lulled into a false sense of security regarding communication flows. His first and most egregrious error is to assume that this supervisory hierarchy provides a clear channel of vertical communication, either upward or downward, and that lateral interdepartmental communication is equally reliable. Actually, most levels of supervision are less communication centers than communication barriers. In addition, many company functions, such as production and sales, are frequently less inclined to be cooperative allies than to be bitter rivals for power, recognition, and executive favor; hence, communication between them is often poor. Both are prolific sources of information, but this does not mean that the intelligence which they provide is complete, accurate, objective, or generally valid and useful."[2]

"The foregoing failures are in no sense limited to upward communications. Many chief executives believe that their supervisory hierarchies—supplemented by printed material, such as the house organ, bulletin boards, letters to the employees' homes, and occasional addresses by company executives—suffice as channels to convey messages to company personnel. It is assumed, moreover, that as long as the message, whatever its content, is clear, concise, well-illustrated, and dramatically presented, its reception will be satisfactory. This, unfortunately, is not always true. There is much more to communication than merely the cogent presentation of a message. If the communication is not understood, believed, and regarded as having a positive value for its recipients, it will fail in its mission. The over-estimation of the effectiveness of the communication media employed is one of the greatest sources of managerial error in dealing with customers, personnel, and the public."[3]

Here, again, an effective philosophy of communications would assist in achieving a climate where information would move freely. Fear, ambitions, emotions, ego, and status, might assume secondary positions so that information might move truthfully and frankly up, down, and laterally within a firm.

And when this is accomplished properly, one's "Need to Know" is fulfilled and his anxieties, insecurities, and fears lessened.

What a Philosophy of Communication Is Not

A company-wide philosophy of communication does not exist where:
• There is obvious fear to communicate openly and freely with superiors, others on the same level, and even subordinates,
• Employee appraisal and performance interviews are perfunctory, innocuous, non-existent or formalties held every 6 months that accomplish little,
• Meetings and conferences are information and decision *giving* sessions rather than those which encourage, promote, foster, and seek good two-

[1] Fred C. Foy and Robert Harper, "Round One: Union vs. Company Publications," *Harvard Business Review,* May-June 1955.

[2] Robert N. McMurry, "Clear Communication for Chief Executives," *Harvard Business Review,* March-April 1965, p. 131.

[3] *Ibid.,* p. 132.

way communication where no holds are barred and differences of opinions are encouraged,

• Company publications are concerned primarily with engagements, retirements, the company picnic, and stories on such "safe" topics as vacation planning, the value of education, the importance of voting, etc.,

• Lateral communication is so poor that one department head may not be familiar at all with what is taking place in other departments or divisions . . . and has no desire to learn,

• Rumors fly constantly and the grapevine flourishes wildly. Morale is low and employees are concerned primarily with their own goals, needs, and aims and have little or no knowledge or appreciation of the company's.

But a different climate exists in a company where a workable, viable, and honest philosophy of communication has been established and put into practice.

What a Philosophy of Communication Is

To be effective a philosophy of communication must:

1. Be timely.
2. Be honest.
3. Recognize employees' need to know.
4. Reflect integrity.
5. Be structured cooperatively.
6. Be truthful.

It is no error, mistake, or accident that the quality of truth appears in points 2, 4, and 6, above, for this is vital. We must have candor and frankness if we are to achieve our goals of a constant flow of truthful communication moving in all directions.

To be effective, a philosophy of communication must be based on management's desire to:

Keep employees informed about corporate activities,

Explain sensitive and controversial employer-employee situations,

Counsel and discuss with each employee his progress and position in the firm,

Open lines of communication so that all individuals feel free to consult with others about problems, issues, plans, failures, and goals,

Establish a climate where failure is accepted, ideas of all types explored openly, where communication is encouraged under all conditions, and fears are lessened,

Underwrite with funds, time, and personnel such a program.

To achieve these ends, management must develop its own philosophy. And this philosophy will differ according to the company's goals and objectives, what its publics are, and the composition of its own labor force. However, a sample philosophy, which is *published*, *distributed*, and *practiced* might include the following points:

1. Inform all employees about on-going activities of the company.

2. Inform employees about company goals, objectives, plans, and directions.

3. Inform employees of the various facets of negative, sensitive, and controversial issues.

4. Encourage and foster a steady flow of two-way communications.

5. Assurance that all employees will meet periodically with their superiors for performance and job appraisal and discussion.

6. To hold meetings which will explore important areas and where free expression is encouraged.

7. To communicate important events and situations as quickly as possible to all employees.

When a philosophy such as this is established, a policy will evolve. This then permits *all* managers in *all* of the company's plants to recognize their boundaries. They know what, when, and how completely they may communicate with their subordinates.

A corporate philosophy of communication is

not, however, a license to communicate everything to everyone. Obviously, there are constraints, there are boundaries, there are limits. Surely there are instances of labor problems, cancellation of orders, and cut-backs in budget, which must be evaluated very carefully, before a decision is reached on how much to say about the situation at "this" time. For a firm to communicate everything without first thinking and selecting is no more commendable than the individual who puts his mouth in gear before checking his thoughts. Judgment must be used.

There also are certain areas which are confidential either because of company or national security. These cannot be discussed. But if employees are told *why* an area is secret, they will accept such a statement. They have been told why they can't be told, and this fulfills the need to know.

An effective philosophy of communication is a commitment to a long range plan for informing others, for opening channels and lines of communication, and for securing a free flow of ideas among people. It is structured on honesty and a respect and sensitivity for others. Once committed to a philosophy of communication, a firm must practice it in every single one of its relationships. It's a commitment which builds a feeling among personnel of security, fair play, and openness.

Putting Philosophy into Action

Obviously recording and distributing such a philosophy is not enough. It must be practiced, and practiced honestly and completely. Here are some of the media and devices:

An employee council with an elected representative from each division or segment of the company. This council is permitted to meet periodically with representatives of management. Employee representatives may ask any questions on any issue. Management's representatives are required to answer immediately or secure a reply within 24 hours. And, conversely, management must be permitted to ask and receive answers from the employees' representatives.

Periodic meetings of department heads to keep lateral communication flowing and staff personnel informed.

Periodic and carefully planned one-to-one discussions between individuals and their superiors to explore ideas, attitude, and feelings; appraise job performance; and secure suggestions, grievances, and opinions.

Conferences and meetings which would permit individuals at various levels to occupy the leadership position. The highest ranking individual at a meeting would certainly not be the conference leader, but the man who would be expert in motivating and encouraging free and open discussion.

Company publications which discuss topics of vital interest to employees: wages, union demands, contracts lost, business secured, profit outlook, new products, competition, company plans, etc.

Representation on committees of personnel from various levels and departments throughout the company.

A Final Word

A philosophy is not drawn up on Monday, distributed on Tuesday, and accepted and practiced on Wednesday and thereafter.

It is an air, a climate which is formulated, accepted and practiced from the president on down. It is based on honesty and a belief in the concept that employees are as interested in the activities, progress, and growth of the firm as is management. And that their desire to advance the goals of the firm are as sincere as is management's.

Thus, next time your firm is drawing up philosophies and policies for personnel, finance, acquisition, and growth, add *communications*.

Once added, see that it is practiced. And once practiced, you will see fears of personnel diminished, harmful jockeying lessened, detrimental empire building slowed, and cliques dissolved. As the lines of communication open and flow freely among all levels within a firm, a climate grows that permits administrative wheels to turn more smoothly, production wheels to hum more efficiently, and profit wheels to spin more rapidly.

Lynn A. Townsend

A Corporate President's View of the Internal Communication Function

At this Conference, most of your attention is focused on the particular area of employee and management communication. While this is only a part of the *total* problem of human communication, it's an important part. And any progress made in this field—in Chrysler or in any other business organization—is, in fact, a constructive development of significant proportions.

Your program planners have asked that I give you my views on the requirements for effective internal communication in a large company. Based on our experience with the Chrysler program, I have listed eight such requirements.

Eight Requirements for Effective Internal Communication

1. Requirement number one is: *Internal communication must be recognized as an essential tool of good management.*

There is a particular need for every manager to understand that good communication is a way to achieve corporate objectives; it's a way to build better teamwork; it's a way to *make* money—not just a way to spend it.

For example, Chrysler did not start a communication program at a time when sales and profit were high. Board Chairman George Love and I—

From *Journal of Communication*, XV (December 1965) 208–215. Based on speech given at the convention of the International Council of Industrial Editors in San Francisco, June 24, 1965. Reprinted by permission.

along with other Chrysler executives—made the initial decision to invest in a substantial communication program in early 1962—a time when Chrysler's sales and profit were at a very *low* ebb.

Chrysler's policy on employee and management communication reflects this approach. It states, in part:

"The Corporation recognizes that employee attitudes and resulting performance are improved when employees are well informed about the affairs of their company and how such company matters affect them as individuals . . ."

In Chrysler, therefore, we see effective communication as an important motivating force.

It can help managers become better leaders.

It can develop constructive attitudes. It can make employees feel they are working *with* a company—not just *for* it.

It can build employee confidence in management.

Good communication can achieve better quality and safety records, increased production, and reduction of waste and spoilage. It can improve corporate-wide performance in United Fund drives, and similar worthwhile campaigns. It can lessen employee resistance to changing technology. It can persuade employees to buy and boost the products made by their company.

In short, one of the reasons we *have* an internal communication program in Chrysler is because we see it as an important contributing factor to profit and progress.

2. Requirement number two is: *Employees must*

be well informed concerning their mutual interests in company success.

Chrysler's OBC[1] research confirmed my belief that employees want to be well informed about *their* stake in company success—and about important matters which affect them or their jobs. This imposes some specific *responsibilities* on management. We should communicate on the subject of basic economics; about how private business operates in a free society; about the role of profit; technological change, and high quality standards; about cost reduction and other elements essential to *pleasing the customer* and protecting jobs. We should interpret management's position on relevant issues. We should try to persuade employees to take actions which will best serve the long-range mutual interests of themselves and their company.

Chrysler's written communication policy puts substantial emphasis on this fact of mutual interest.

I welcome every opportunity to talk with production employees at Chrysler, and I have been impressed over and over again with how well they understand that their personal objectives are directly related to the success of the company . . . and vice versa. During a visit to one of our assembly plants, for example, a production employee expressed appreciation for a message from me that had been printed in *Chrysler Views.* The subject of that message was *corporate profit,* and why it's important to employees.

On another occasion, as I was leaving the executive garage late one evening, I noticed a group of second-shift employees on their lunch break. They were standing outside, looking through the windows at an early model of our Chrysler Turbine car. I invited them in, and showed them how the turbine engine works. In the spirited discussion which followed, it was clear that these employees understood that the future status of this car was mighty important to *them,* personally.

3. Requirement number three is: *Individual managers must actively support the corporate communication effort.*

The organization structure in large companies is simply too complex to handle the full communication load. So, it's a very bad mistake to assume that oral communication which comes from the top will ever get filtered through the many organizational layers in its original form.

I know for a fact—because I have checked it out myself—that there are far too many barriers to the free flow of information. And, in many cases, these barriers are created by individual managers.

A manager must *not* view corporate information as his personal province—as something to parcel out to a favored few.

Managers at various levels must not create separate islands of communication autonomy and programming; they must cooperate with the total corporate communication effort, and help build higher levels of corporate-wide loyalty and understanding.

Managers also must resist communication inertia. By that I mean the tendency to be passive about information, or the failure to understand that active, individual effort is needed to keep information flowing.

To assure the cooperation of individual managers, Chrysler's written communication policy states:

"It is desirable that a policy be established to guide managers in establishing throughout the Corporation the climate and the channels necessary to maintain a consistent, two-way flow of effective communication—communication which will *not* depend on varying interpretations by managers of its desirability—or on other extraneous factors . . ."

[1] An earlier, three-hour presentation outlined the details of Chrysler's "Operation Better Communication" program—a comprehensive internal communication effort involving oral, visual and written communication channels, continuing research measurement techniques, a headquarters Communication Department, and approximately 25 plant-level Communication Coordinators.

What the policy is saying here is that individual managers *do not have the luxury of deciding whether communication is desirable.* They are being reminded that *part of their job* is to communicate regularly with subordinates and superiors—and to actively support the corporate-wide communication program.

4. Requirement number four is: *Substantially greater emphasis must be put on communication planning and measurement.*

I am astonished at how often managers assume that communication can be effective on a haphazard basis. Managers agree that quality, or finance, or engineering, are functions which require planning and measurement. Why, then, should communication be left to chance—unplanned, unorganized, uncontrolled, unmeasured?

It's my guess that this problem exists because a planned communication program usually requires radical changes—including a change in traditional management thinking. Admiral Rickover once commented that nothing unusual is ever accomplished in the usual way. And it's my belief that a corporate communication program, because it affects every department in the company, requires substantial innovation.

The old way—in Chrysler as well as many other companies—was to hire a couple of editors, bury them someplace out of sight in the organization, and say to them: "Get out your publication on time, don't print anything controversial, and, above all, don't make anybody mad." Beyond that, the *existing organization structure* was to be relied on to carry the communication load.

But I believe a communication program should be a great deal *more* than just getting out a publication. Every major management decision should be accompanied by a communication plan. Who is to do the communicating? How much credibility does the announcing source have?

What is to be said, when, and through what channels? What is the desired audience? What is the *purpose* of the communication? How will results be measured?

These are the questions which need answers. These are the challenges which require substantial innovation in program planning and results measurement.

I am aware of the limitations on precise measurements of the effects of communication. But you heard this morning about Chrysler's communication research. And I believe this approach is substantially superior to the traditional, seat-of-the-pants measurement methods.

5. The fifth requirement is: *Top management must establish a good communication climate.*

I have frequently observed that good communication is man-made. By this I mean that the communication patterns in a given plant, department, group, or division inevitably reflect the communication behavior of the man in charge.

If the boss is silent and uncommunicative, his subordinates are apt to be the same. If the boss takes a negative attitude toward the corporate communication program, those who report to him will likely feel the same way.

What's true at the plant or department level is also true at the corporate level. I would counsel any company which wants to improve internal communication to start in the office of the chief executive.

It is the top man who first must establish the right communication climate. It is he who should initiate and take an active part in the total communication program. It is he who must make clear that such an investment is not an on-again, off-again proposition—not a first-cut item when budgets get tight—not a process that can be assigned to staff people and forgotten.

I am fully aware that what I *personally* do is a major factor in Chrysler's communication effort. For example, when a company development of top importance is pending, I do my best to notify our internal communication people in time. They can then use internal channels to pump out the information *before* our people hear the news on the radio, or from some other outside source.

In short, the chief executive must himself set the example if he desires substantial credibility and communication effectiveness. He must first be honest with himself. He must not merely give lip service to the idea of communication.

6. Requirement number six: A *long-term investment in professional talent and communication programming must be made.*

To improve communication in any large organization is a tough and complex job. Internal communication needs are not easily met. It is essential, therefore, that management make a long-range investment in people and in communication programming.

It seems to me that many managers practice a double standard when it comes to communication. They wouldn't think of turning over the maintenance of a half-million-dollar machine to an unskilled person. They would certainly avoid entrusting the direction of a complicated engineering process to a person without an engineering background.

But these same managers will too often assign the internal communication function to an untrained individual. Good organizational communication requires skill with the techniques of communication, and depth experience in directing the flow of information.

As I see it, the job of establishing adequate communication programming begins only when professional communication talent is put in place. Someone recently called to my attention a thoughtful article by Robert Vivian, written some years ago in the magazine *The Communicator*. The author's key point was stated as follows: "In any corporate communication program, the one indispensable ingredient is professional talent."

So, it is management's responsibility to create a *new* kind of job—one which appears on too few corporate organization charts. This job is commu-

nication programming. It involves planning and measurement. It involves the direction of the work of creative people; the required research and training; the all-important salesmanship which is needed to help line managers understand the importance of communication—and how they can apply it.

To the degree that your elected officers of ICIE have honored me with the Communicator of the Year award, you have, of course, honored the professional people who have filled these kinds of jobs in Chrysler since Operation Better Communication was launched. Many of these people, as you know, are members of your own organization.

7. Requirement number seven: *Management must recognize its responsibility to listen as well as to speak.*

Perhaps the most common deficiency in corporate communication programs today is an inadequate *upward* flow of information. The large-company organization structure has many built-in obstacles to the free flow of information upward—and these obstacles must be overcome.

An individual manager is too often reluctant to give his boss the *bad* news. And poor listening habits by individual managers frequently discourage subordinates. If the boss is not a good listener, those who report to him will soon stop *trying* to communicate with him.

Chrysler's communication policy specifically calls for the establishment of a formal upward communication program. It instructs all managers to create and maintain a receptive climate for the upward transmission of employee ideas, suggestions and opinions. It identifies employee ideas and opinions as an important corporate asset.

But upward communication remains one of our toughest problems. We are using surveys, the employee suggestion plan, and other techniques you heard about this morning. But we still have a long way to go in this part of our effort.

It would be well, perhaps, for all of us who are associated with large companies to heed the counsel of a wise man—given to us many centuries ago. He said: "Nature has given man two ears and one mouth, so he may *hear* twice as much as he speaks."

8. The last of the eight requirements that I have listed is: *Managers must recognize the desire of employees to help their company, and the power of communication to tap this great potential.*

In the presentation on OBC you heard this morning, Mickey Dover[2] reported the research results which showed how production employees overwhelmingly indicated a desire to help the business go better. The fact that employees feel this way did not surprise me. However, I believe many managers have a tendency, first to *underestimate* the willingness of employees to help the business—and, second, to underrate the power of good communication to turn this latent desire into constructive action.

I believe strongly that there's great *potential* for greater productivity here. If we can learn how to communicate more effectively with employees—how to motivate them—how to show them it's in *their* interest to do *more* than they are now doing—the results will be of truly great significance.

Recommended General Approach to Internal Communication

Before concluding my remarks, let me be responsive to a request that I summarize a recommended *general* approach to internal communication effectiveness—a course of action that any large-company president might consider.

Specific needs vary, of course, from company to company. But I would offer the following general recommendations:

First, see to it that professional communication talent is put in place, and that preliminary research is done to determine specific communication strengths and weaknesses. Issue a written policy on internal communication which defines program purposes. Bring together the written, oral, and visual communication tools in a newly created communication department. Adopt specific plans and programs to encourage better upward, downward, and horizontal flow of information. See to it that the line and staff organizations work closely together in properly fulfilling their vital roles.

Make it known to all concerned that the formal communication program has the benefit of the support and personal participation of the chief executive. Encourage the communicators to do the *selling* job so important to winning the continuing support of all levels of management. And last, but certainly not least, measure communication progress—as carefully and objectively as possible.

[2] C. J. Dover, Manager of Communication, Chrysler Corp., Detroit, Mich.

Gary Gemmill

Managing Upward Communication

The problem of upward communication appears to be endemic to superior-subordinate relationships. It is a common observation that subordinates in their relationship with superiors often conceal and distort their real feelings, problems, opinions, and beliefs because they fear disclosure may lead superiors to punish them in some way. Decisions by subordinates not to disclose such information results in a superior being unaware of how his actions affect them. This lack of feedback may prevent him from changing his managerial style or from correcting misperceptions on their part. Similarly, he is put in a position where he is unable to share knowledge with them that might lead to improvements in their performance. Perhaps most important, however, from a manager's perspective, is that this lack of communication may cut him off from some essential information.

Given that concealment and distortion by subordinates can be costly, is there anything a superior can do to lessen it? Is it possible for him to lower the probability that subordinates will conceal or distort their communication with him? If it is possible, what must he do in his relationship with subordinates? How can he manage their upward communication?

Why Subordinates Distort Their Upward Communication

An understanding of the factors that lead subordinates to distort upward communications is a pre-

requisite for managing it. One frequently cited reason for such concealment and distortion is that subordinates believe their superior may penalize them in some way for disclosing their real opinions, feelings and difficulties. Stated in a propositional form:

If a subordinate believes that disclosure of his feelings, opinions, or difficulties may lead a superior to block or hinder the attainment of a personal goal, he will conceal or distort them.

According to this proposition, a subordinate enters an organization with such personal goals as moving upward as fast as possible, achieving stable or increasingly higher earnings, or doing work that leads to growth in his abilities. In pursuit of these goals, he evaluates contemplated actions in terms of how he believes they will facilitate their attainment, attempting to avoid actions he believes may hinder. At various levels of personal awareness, he may conceal or distort his opinions, difficulties, or feelings when he believes disclosure may lead a superior to do something to block or hinder attainment of his goals.

For example, if he receives a salary increase he considers unfair, he tells his superior it is more than fair because he is afraid that by expressing disappointment he may injure his promotion prospects. He may believe the superior would consider him an ingrate or interpret his remark as an insult to his managerial proficiency and hold it against him when his name comes up for promotion. This belief, however, may not be grounded in reality since the superior may not actually attach a penalty to the expression of disappointment. But if the subordinate believes there may be one, it is sufficient for him to distort his feelings to avoid the possibility that the superior might react to disclosure by blocking or hindering the attainment of his personal goal of upward mobility. This may be done consciously. In some situations, however, the subordinate may not be fully aware that he is distorting the feedback to his boss.

The Origins of Disclosure Beliefs

Subordinates acquire beliefs about the types of information to avoid disclosing to superiors from many sources. For example, subordinates who have worked for a superior for a number of years may instruct new subordinates that careerwise, it is unwise to express ideas for improvements to him. They may even cite a case where a subordinate was purportedly penalized by him for rocking the boat. While the belief may lack an objective basis, if the new subordinates accept it, the probability that they will disclose ideas for improvement is reduced.

Some beliefs are undoubtedly founded in general social norms or corporate "folklore." For example, "subordinates should not display emotions in the presence of superiors" or "subordinates should never question the decisions of superiors." If subordinates have internalized such a norm, the probability is great that they will make decisions not to disclose their feelings or criticisms of decisions handed down to them. Indeed, they may even consider it legitimate for a superior to reprimand them if they make such disclosures. ·

Some beliefs originate in a subordinate's direct observation of types of disclosures that he perceives his superior dislikes. For example, when he disagrees with a superior who becomes emotionally upset and defensive he may say to himself: "I shouldn't have disagreed with him even though he told me he wanted me to feel free to do so. It's obvious he is upset by it. He may hold it against me when my name comes up for promotion or a new assignment. I'd better play it safe in the future and

refrain from voicing my opinions." Rightly or wrongly, he considers the superior's reaction to disagreement to be a threat. He perceives the superior as being capable of blocking attainment of his personal goals and acts in a way to avoid it.

Where subordinates have not directly or indirectly acquired beliefs about the types of disclosures that may be penalized, they frequently operate on an uncertainty principle. When they are unable to predict if a superior will reward or penalize disclosure, to avoid the risk of a penalty they make a decision not to disclose. When in doubt, they say nothing.

Empirical Studies of Upward Communication

There are a number of empirical studies that offer support for the proposition that subordinates make decisions not to disclose their feelings, opinions, and difficulties because they are afraid that their superior may punish them in some way for doing so. Vogel, in a study of approximately 2,000 employees in 8 companies, found that almost a majority of them believed that if a subordinate told his immediate superior everything he felt about the company, he would probably get into a "lot of trouble," and that the best way to gain promotion was not to disagree very much with a superior.[1] This study, however, identifies only the prevalence of these beliefs and not how or where they were acquired.

Read, in a study of fifty-two superior-subordinate pairs in three companies, found that the accuracy with which subordinates disclosed their difficulties to superiors was negatively related to their desire for upward mobility.[2] The greater the

[1] A. Vogel, "Why Don't Employees Speak Up?" *Personnel Administration*, May-June, 1967.
[2] W. Read, "Upward Communication in Industrial Hierarchies," *Human Relations*, Vol. 15, 1962, pp. 3-15.

desire of subordinates for upward mobility, the less likely they were to accurately disclose their difficulties to their superiors. The amount of inaccuracy in the upward communication, however, was affected by the perceived influence of the superior over their careers and how much they trusted him not to hold disclosures against them in considering promotion. The greater his perceived influence over their careers and the lower their trust in him, the more inaccurate their upward communication of difficulties. Read points out, however, that even when subordinates trust their superiors not to hold disclosures against them or block mobility, high mobility aspirations militate against disclosure.

Blau and Scott in a study of agents in a federal law enforcement agency found that the agents were reluctant to take their work-related problems to superiors even though they were officially expected to do so.[3] They believed that exposure of problems might be interpreted by superiors as a lack of independence, resulting in a low rating. Perceiving the possibility of a goal block by superiors, they decided not to disclose their difficulties in order to avoid it.

Argyris has also found that subordinates often conceal their feelings, opinions, and difficulties from superiors because they are fearful that they may be penalized in some way for such disclosure.[4] He suggests that one of the primary reasons for lack of disclosure is that many organizations place a high reward value on rational-technical aspects of behavior and discourage or penalize emotionally based behavior. When, for example, a subordinate expresses feelings in a dis-

cussion, the superior tells him to keep his feelings out of it. The subordinate thus learns not to disclose his feelings to avoid a career penalty of being labeled as too "emotional."

Managing Upward Communication

The important question remains: What, if anything, can a superior do to lessen the probability that subordinates will conceal or distort their real feelings, opinions, and difficulties when communicating with him? Unfortunately, there has been little if any research directed to this question. Thus, the intent here is to conceptually examine factors that would appear to have a significant role in managing upward communication.

It seems clear that an awareness that subordinates tend to filter upward communication is a necessary condition for lessening it. Given awareness, diminishing the probability would seem to require a change in their perception of penalties for disclosure. The crux of the problem is establishing a relationship where they feel they will not be penalized by the superior for disclosure. Is it possible for a superior to create such a climate? If so, how can he do it?

Changing the Basis of Perceived Penalties

If the superior's control over the personal goals of subordinates were decreased, their fear of receiving a penalty for disclosure would undoubtedly decrease. It is perhaps unrealistic, however, to expect this to be a feasible alternative, given the type of organizational structure prevalent in our society. It is a fact of organizational life that a superior has a fairly high degree of control over the

[3] P. M. Blau and W. R. Scott, *Formal Organizations,* San Francisco: Chandler, 1962, pp. 128-134.
[4] A. C. Argyris, "Interpersonal Barriers to Decision-Making," *Harvard Business Review,* Vol. 44, March-April 1966, pp. 84-97.

means of satisfying the personal goals of subordinates. He can often, for example: fire, layoff, block promotion, block salary increase, or hold back developmental assignments if he doesn't like what he hears from a subordinate. Even though he may claim there is no penalty for disclosure, and, in fact, can refrain from applying one, as long as the subordinate believes there may be one, or believes he can't hold back a penalty even though he wants to, he in all probability will refrain from disclosure.

Eliciting Disclosure Decisions Through Rewards

While it may not be feasible to create a situation in which a superior lacks control over the personal goals of subordinates, it may be possible for a superior to improve the chances of openness by rewarding incidences of disclosure. Stated in a propositional form:

The more a superior rewards disclosure of feelings, opinions and difficulties by subordinates, the more likely they will be to disclose them.

To create a relationship in which subordinates perceive disclosure as rewarding or not threatening, a superior can begin by telling them he expects them to have problems and disagreements and that he would like them to disclose them.

Obviously, simply telling them that they should feel free to discuss their feelings, opinions, and difficulties is not enough. They want to know if such actions on their part will, in fact, be rewarded or punished. Here, again, words by the superior to the effect that there will be no penalty are not sufficient to bring about a decision to disclose. Subordinates realize there is often a difference between what a superior says he wants to hear and what he

actually wants to hear. The problem from their viewpoint is one of determining if he means what he says. How would he really react to disclosure? What types of disclosure can he tolerate? If he didn't like what I said, would he hold it against me?

These questions deal with the subordinate's perception of the consistency between the superior's words and actions. Are his actions consistent with his statement? It is a common belief in our culture that actions speak louder than words. Thus, it is perhaps not surprising that subordinates test out the consistency of a superior's words and actions by observing how he actually reacts to disagreements, expression of emotions, or reports of difficulties. If his response is a hostile or a demeaning one, they may conclude that there is a penalty for disclosure, even though he tells them there is not. In short, they may feel that his actions contradict his statements of the behavior he says he really wants, and they give priority to his actions. Because of the perceived penalty for disclosure, they learn to conceal their problems and disagreements from him.

At a minimum then, managing upward communication requires a superior to reinforce verbally stated expectations of leveling with actions that lead subordinates to view disclosure as a rewarded response or, at least, a response that does not result in a perceived penalty or threat. When subordinates make decisions to disclose, the superior must act in such a way that they will find the situation rewarding or at a minimum nonthreatening. Sometimes this means that he must act contrary to his natural inclinations. Any expression of hostility or impatience will be perceived by subordinates as a threat or a perceived penalty which will seal off disclosure in the future. To increase the probability of future disclosure, he must reward instances of disclosure, since rewarded responses tend to be repeated while unrewarded ones tend to be eliminated.

To further increase the probability of disclosure by subordinates, a superior may use himself as a disclosure model in his relationship with them or his own superior. When talking with them, he makes a practice of disclosing his feelings, opinions, and difficulties, demonstrating that he practices what he preaches. Stated in a propositional form:

The more a superior discloses his own feelings, opinions and difficulties to subordinates and his superior, the more likely subordinates will be to disclose theirs.

Such modeling would tend to reinforce his verbally stated desire for disclosure, thereby increasing the probability of disclosure.

To sum up, managing upward communication involves building a relationship with subordinates in which disclosure is encouraged and rewarded. It must be a supportive relationship—one in which subordinates feel that the superior will not take advantage of them if they fully speak their minds. For full disclosure to occur they must know that they can express their feelings, difficulties, and opinions without fear of reprisal. They must look upon the superior as a source of help rather than as an all powerful judge.

Norman B. Sigband

What's Happened to Employee Commitment?

In recent months, journal articles, corporate president's speeches, and the business press have expressed their concern with the lack of employee commitment that is evident, the increasing worker alienation from the job which is apparent, and the individual's search for recognition which is obvious. These three areas are closely related.

Commitment (or lack of it) certainly influences the others. If the employee is not committed, he will not do the kind of job which results in recognition. This in turn often leads to alienation, which in itself leads to still less commitment and so the circle goes 'round and 'round.

D. S. Sherwin, in an article in the *Harvard Business Review*, feels that lack of commitment by employees is behind much of the behavior blamed for high costs and poor services. As a result, executives try to change behavior, personality, and attitudes through various training methods which have little value.[1]

Sherwin makes the vital point that commitment, far from being something that has to be created in employees, is a natural, psychological need which already exists. And like the needs of affection, affiliation, recognition, achievement, responsibility, etc., every man strives to have it fulfilled.

Many employees in our busy, impersonal, highly competitive industrial complex feel they do not receive the recognition they deserve; the personal boss/man relationships they desire; the responsibility they want. And as a result, many employees' commitment to the job is marginal, their alienation from the company and their superiors increases, and their cry for recognition grows stronger. This last named is all around us as we watch the young men's hair curl thickly, beards sprout luxuriantly, and clothes shout loudly. The girls are no different as they move from mini minis to maxi maxis. From raggle taggle blue jeans to smartly styled casual wear. From the tightly controlled up and out to the loosely designed bra-less down and out. Anything seems to go as the individual shouts, "Recognize me as a person; give me your attention."

And those employees whose commitment level is low and job alienation high, seek recognition (or personal need fulfillment) elsewhere. Their comments reflect their inner feelings: "No one in management cares; the job I do is unimportant. I'm only a 'clock number' and I receive as much attention as a number. But if I receive no recognition on the job, I'll find it elsewhere. It may be in my after-work hours which I devote to skiing, painting, classes, or social or religious organizations. These supply me with the recognition I deserve and need. And as a matter of fact, if you won't talk to me, if you won't listen to me, I'll get someone who will *make* you talk or listen—the union." But to many employees becoming involved in a union/management dialogue is not the answer and they would prefer not "to hassle" it on the job. They secure their recognition from "outside" activities. The job is only a *means* to those activities.

It is this negative situation which is nibbling away at corporate drive, enthusiasm, and profits. It is apparent by the moans and groans as another work week begins, by the extended coffee breaks, by the rise in employee pilferage, and by the "Thank God it's Wednesday and only two days to go" statement voiced by too many workers.

And the company suffers!

But it need not be this way if companies will use the simple and most effective device available for satisfying needs, increasing commitment, and eliminating job alienation.

The answer lies in effective and sincere manager/worker communication in a climate of high trust and credibility. Research studies tell us that well informed employees are usually satisfied employees;[2] that where communication lines are open and operating, company goals are more easily achieved.

And management doesn't argue that point. On the contrary, there is much evidence to support it:

Charles B. McCoy, Chairman of the Board and President of DuPont, stated:

Communication has a high priority at DuPont. Employees have a right to be informed. They should be told important news immediately, good or bad.

The people who work for DuPont want to know what the enterprise is all about. They want a sense of involvement, want to be part of the organization. Therefore, they need to know about current business problems, the company's stand on such important matters as imports and pollution control, its views on issues of public importance. Employees want straight-forward, honest, balanced information—not propaganda.

Informed employees are better, more productive employees. They get more out of their work, and they do a better job for the company.[3]

William M. Allen, Chairman of the Board and Chief Executive Officer of Boeing, said:

The task of communication in business takes on larger dimensions . . . Where once it may have been concerned primarily with publications, news service, *and appropriate management messages, now it must be regarded as an integral process of managing.*

The rationale for . . . meetings . . . within . . . the organization is the recognition that communication and understanding are the keys to making full use of individual capacities. Each individual likes to feel that he is personally involved in an activity—that he is making a contribution.[4]

Several years ago, Lynn Townsend, President of Chrysler, stated that:

Internal communication must be recognized as an essential tool of good management and employees must be well informed concerning their mutual interests in company success.[5]

Here we have a peculiar situation. The worker wants to be communicated with so he may be informed, so that he will be "part of the action." Being informed gives him recognition, satisfies a need.

And top management says he should be informed; it knows that an informed worker is a happier worker, a more productive worker.

Where, then, is the problem?

Obviously, if those at the top and the bottom want communication to flow, and it often doesn't, the fault may very well be found in middle management. But investigation shows us that most middle managers *want* to communicate with subordinates, although too often they aren't sure about:

1. What areas they can communicate on,
2. How much they can reveal, and
3. Whether or not they can or should become involved in a discussion of controversial or sensitive issues

And so we see the "man in the middle" caught in this communication dilemma because he has no parameters, no boundaries, no communication policies to guide him.

This is not the case in almost every other area in

which he operates. He has policies and procedures which tell him how much he can appropriate for this action; what he can pay for these skills; who to call if this piece of equipment breaks down; where to turn to secure approval for this requisition.

But he often doesn't know how much he can tell his subordinates on, say, a new corporate objective—or for that matter, if he can talk about it at all!

The answer is simple. Just as the manager has policies to guide him on most of his work activities, so, too, he should have policies of communications that will help him in his interpersonal relations.

Sharma and Carnahan have recently pointed out that the "man in the middle" has had his authority reduced and his task made more difficult. Improved communication, they feel, will improve this situation.

Downward communication should be used to provide task directions, job rationale, organizational goals, procedures and practices, feedback to . . . subordinates. Upward communication should be used to encourage subordinates to express ideas, attitudes, feelings about job, performance, organizational policies, and similar matters.[6]

Establishment of Policies

The first step in the total process is top management's recognition that it has policies in almost every area of corporate activity—finance, personnel, marketing, promotions, purchasing, etc.,— and it must also have policies on communication.

The policies themselves must be based on management's recognition of the employees' need to know and the importance of fulfilling that need.

Furthermore, management must structure these policies on integrity and honesty, draw them up cooperatively, and be responsive to legitimate questions. And of most importance, these policies must be verbalized and fully supported by the chief executive and his staff.

Guidelines for Policies of Communication

To be successful, policies of communication must be based on management's desire to:

1. Keep employees informed of company goals, objectives, and plans.

2. Inform employees of company activities in the market place.

3. Tell employees about various facets of negative, sensitive, and controversial issues.

4. Encourage, if not require, every manager and supervisor to meet with his subordinates on a weekly, if not a daily basis for open, honest two-way communication on job related situations.

5. Communicate important events and decisions as quickly as possible to all employees.

6. Establish a climate where innovation and creativity are encouraged, and employees are rewarded for trying and succeeding, but not penalized for trying and failing.

7. Have every manager and supervisor discuss with each of his subordinates, the latter's progress and position in the firm.

When such guidelines are accepted and practiced by top management as company communication policy, the firm's climate will improve. Of course, it must be practiced consistently and mitment. managers must understand that they don't have the *privilege* of communicating important information to subordinates, but the *obligation* and *responsibility* to do so. Those managers who consciously or unconsciously build their empires by not telling anyone anything, must recognize that such walls must come down.

Limitations

However, it is important for employees to understand that corporate policies of communication are not a license to tell everybody everything! There are constraints, there are boundaries, and there are limits. Certainly information which would harm a firm's competitive advantage in the market place would be restricted, as would items concerned with security, national defense, and some facets of labor problems. And, of course, those items which are just being reviewed for analysis and subsequent decision making, would not be presented to all the firm's employees.

However, when it is thought advisable, employees should be told they can't be told for legitimate reasons. What this obviously says to the employees is, "We know you are frustrated because you haven't been told what is taking place in this particular situation. We appreciate the need you have to know, but here is the reason for restricted communication."

Obviously, no one is happy when he is told he can't be told. On the other hand, management has partially satisfied the need to know by recognizing it, talking about it, and offering a legitimate, honest explanation.

Putting Policies into Practice

Recording, announcing, and distributing such policies is not enough. They must be practiced, and practiced honestly and completely. Here are some of the ways in which the policies may be implemented:

1. An employee council with elected or appointed representatives from each division or segment of the company. This council meets periodically with management representatives. Except for clearly noted restricted areas, all questions, suggestions, complaints, and problems may be aired. Responses should be given immediately or within 24 hours by either management or employee representatives.

2. Frequent periodic and carefully planned one-to-one meetings between subordinate and superior to explore ideas, attitudes, and feelings; appraise job performance; listen to suggestions and complaints; evaluate achievement of an individual's objectives; and discuss the employee's role in the company's attainment of its goals.

3. Company publications which go light on trivia, and discuss topics of vital interest to employees: wages, union demands, contracts awarded or lost, goals achieved, new products, competition, profit picture, and company plans.

4. Conferences and meetings that permit an open, honest interchange of ideas and opinions. Such meetings should encourage the type of participation which lets the employees become involved in some of the decision making process of the company.

5. Periodic meetings of department heads to keep *lateral* communication flowing and staff personnel informed.

Communication policies are not formulated on Monday, written down on Tuesday, practiced on Wednesday and all problems solved thereafter. It is true that they must be formulated, they must be published, and they must be practiced, but it takes time for the results to become apparent.

To be successful they must be articulated and supported by all members of the management team from the president down. The policies must be based on honesty and a belief in the concept that the employees are as interested in the activities, progress, and growth of the firm as is management, and that every employee has a need to be committed to the achievement of the company's goals.

Policies of communication almost force information to flow between superior and subordinate. Such communication gives the employee the recognition he needs and helps to secure his commitment and eliminate the alienation which causes problems for everyone.

References

1. Douglas S. Sherwin, "Strategy for Winning Employee Commitment," *Harvard Business Review,* June 1972.

2. R. H. Migliore, "Improving Worker Productivity Through Communicating Knowledge of Work Results," *Human Resource Management,* Summer 1970;

M. Brenmer and N. Sigband, "Organizational Communication— An Analysis Based on Empirical Data," *Academy of Management Journal,* May 1973.

3. *Better Living,* Fall 1971, p. 3 (DuPont employee magazine publication).

4. *Boeing Management Perspective,* July/August 1968, p. 203.

5. L. Townsend, "A Corporate President's View of the Internal Communication Function," *Journal of Communication,* Dec. 1965.

6. J. M. Sharma and G. R. Carnahan, "Resolving the Middle Management Dilemma," *Personnel Administrator,* March-April 1973.

William V. Haney

Serial Communication of Information in Organizations

An appreciable amount of the communication which occurs in business, industry, hospitals, military units, government agencies—in short, in chain-of-command organizations—consists of serial transmissions. *A* communicates a message to *B; B* then communicates *A*'s message (or rather his *interpretation* of *A*'s message) to *C; C* then communicates his interpretation of *B*'s interpretation of *A*'s message to *D;* and so on. The originator and the ultimate recipient of the message are separated by "middle men."

"The message" may often be passed down (but not necessarily all the way down) the organization chain, as when in business the chairman acting on behalf of the board of directors may express a desire to the president.[1] The message begins to fan out as the president, in turn, relays it to his vice presidents; they convey it to their respective subordinates; and so forth. Frequently a message goes up (but seldom all the way up) the chain. Sometimes it travels laterally. Sometimes, as with rumors, it disregards the formal organization and flows more closely along informal organizational lines.

Regardless of its direction, the number of "conveyors" involved, and the degree of its conformance with the formal structure, serial transmission is clearly an essential, inevitable form of serial communication in organizations. It is equally apparent that serial transmission is especially susceptible to distortion and disruption. Not only is it subject to the shortcomings and maladies of "simple" person-to-person communication but, since it consists of a series of such communications, the anomalies are often compounded.

This is not to say, however, that serial transmissions in organizations should be abolished or even decreased. I wish to show that such communications can be improved if communicators are able (1) to recognize some of the patterns of miscommunication which occur in serial transmissions; (2) to understand some of the factors contributing to these patterns; (3) to take measures and practice techniques for preventing the recurrence of these patterns and for ameliorating their consequences.

I shall begin by cataloguing some of the factors which may influence a serial transmission.[2]

[2] During the past three years I have conducted scores of informal experiments with groups of university undergraduate students, business and government executives, military officers, professionals, and so on. I would read the message (below) to the first "conveyor." He would then give his interpretation to the second conveyor who, in turn, would pass along his interpretation to the third, etc. The sixth (and final) member of the "team" would listen to the message and then write down his version of it. These final versions (examples later) were collected and compared with the following original:

"Every year at State University, the eagles in front of the Psi Gamma fraternity house were mysteriously sprayed during the night. Whenever this happened, it cost the Psi Gams from $75 to $100 to have the eagles cleaned. The Psi Gams complained to officials and were promised by the president that if ever any students were caught painting the eagles, they would be expelled from school."

[1] I place quotation marks around "message" to indicate that what is conveyed is not static, unchanging, and fixed. Despite their absence with later uses of the word, the dynamic nature of the "message" should be kept in mind.

Motives of the Communicators

When *B* interprets *A*'s message to *C* he may be influenced by at least three motives of which he may be largely unaware.

1. *The Desire to Simplify the Message.* We evidently dislike conveying detailed messages. The responsibility of passing along complex information is burdensome and taxing. Often, therefore, we unconsciously simplify the message before passing it along to the next person.[3] It is very probable that among the details most susceptible to omission are those we already knew or in some way presume our recipients will know without our telling them.

2. *The Desire to Convey a "Sensible" Message.* Apparently we are reluctant to relay a message that is somehow incoherent, illogical, or incomplete. It may be embarrassing to admit that one does not fully understand the message he is conveying. When he receives a message that does not quite make sense to him he is prone to "make sense out of it" before passing it along to the next person.[4]

3. *The Desire to Make the Conveyance of the Message as Pleasant and/or Painless as Possible for the Conveyor.* We evidently do not like to have to tell the boss unpleasant things. Even when not directly responsible, one does not relish the reac-

tion of his superior to a disagreeable message. This motive probably accounts for a considerable share of the tendency for a message to lose its harshness as it moves up the organizational ladder. The first line supervisor may tell his foreman, "I'm telling you, Mike, the men say that if this pay cut goes through they'll strike—and they mean it!" By the time this message has been relayed through six or eight or more echelons (if indeed it goes that far) the executive vice president might express it to the president as, "Well, sir, the men seem a little concerned over the projected wage reduction but I am confident that they will take it in stride."

One of the dangers plaguing some upper managements is that they are effectively shielded from incipient problems until they become serious and costly ones.

Assumptions of the Communicators

In addition to the serial transmitter's motives we must consider his assumptions—particularly those he makes about his communications. If some of these assumptions are fallacious and if one is unaware that he holds them, his communication can be adversely affected. The following are, in my judgment, two of the most pervasive and dangerous of the current myths about communication.

1. The Assumption That Words Are Used in Only One Way

A study indicates that for the five hundred most commonly used words in our language there are 14,070 different dictionary definitions—over twenty-eight usages per word, on the average.[5] Take the word *run,* for example:

---

[3] On an arbitrary count basis the stimulus message used in the serial transmission demonstrations described in footnote 2 contained twenty-four "significant details." The final versions contained a mean count of approximately eight "significant details"—a "detail loss" of sixty-five percent.

[4] The great majority (approximately ninety-three percent) of the final versions (from the serial transmission demonstrations) made "sense." Even those which were the most bizarre and bore the least resemblance to the original stimulus were in and of themselves internally consistent and coherent. For example:

"At a State University there was an argument between two teams—the Eagles and the Fire Gems—in which their clothing was torn."

"The eagles in front of the university had parasites and were sprayed with insecticide."

"At State U. they have many birds which desecrate the buildings. To remedy the situation they expelled the students who fed the birds."

[5] Lydia Strong, "Do You Know How to Listen?" *Effective Communication on the Job,* ed. Dooher and Marquis (New York, 1956), p. 28.

Babe Ruth scored a *run.*
Did you ever see Jesse Owens *run?*
I have a *run* in my stocking.
There is a fine *run* of salmon this year.
Are you going to *run* this company or am I?
You have the *run* of the place.
Don't give me the *run* around.
What headline do you want to *run?*
There was a *run* on the bank today.
Did he *run* the ship aground?
I have to *run* (drive the car) downtown.
Who will *run* for President this year?
Joe flies the New York-Chicago *run* twice a week.
You know the kind of people they *run* around with.
The apples *run* large this year.
Please *run* my bath water.

We could go on at some length—my small abridged dictionary gives eighty-seven distinct usages for *run.* I have chosen an extreme example, of course, but there must be relatively few words (excepting some techincal terms) used in one and in only one sense.

Yet communicators often have a curious notion about words *when they are using them,* that is, when they are speaking, writing, listening, or reading. It is immensely easy for a "sender" of a communication to assume that words are used in only one way—the way he intends them. It is just as enticing for the "receiver" to assume that the sender intended his words as he, the receiver, happens to interpret them at the moment. When communicators are unconsciously burdened by the assumption of the mono-usage of words they are prone to become involved in the pattern of miscommunication known as *bypassing.*

A foreman told a machine operator he was passing: "Better clean up around here."

It was ten minutes later when the foreman's assistant phoned: "Say, boss, isn't that bearing Sipert is working on due up in engineering pronto?"

"You bet your sweet life it is. Why?"

"He says you told him to drop it and sweep the place up. I thought I'd better make sure."

"Listen," the foreman flared into the phone, "get him right back on that job. It's got to be ready in twenty minutes."

. . . What the foreman had in mind was for Sipert to gather up the oily waste, which was a fire and accident hazard. This would not have taken more than a couple of minutes, and there would have been plenty of time to finish the bearing.[6]

Since we use words to express at least two kinds of meanings there can be two kinds of bypassings: denotative and connotative. Suppose you say to me, "Your neighbor's grass is certainly green and healthy looking, isn't it?" You could be intending your words merely to denote, that is, to point to or to call my attention, to the appearance of my neighbor's lawn. On the other hand, you could have intended your words to *connote,* that is, to imply something beyond or something other than what you were ostensibly denoting. You might have meant any number of things: that my own lawn needed more care; that my neighbor was inordinately meticulous about his lawn; that my neighbor's lawn is tended by a professional, a service you do not have and for which you envy or despise my neighbor; or even that his grass was not green at all but, on the contrary, parched and diseased; and so forth.

[6] *The Foreman's Letter,* publication of the National Foreman's Institute (New London, Connecticut).

Taking these two kinds of meanings into account it is clear that bypassing occurs or can occur under any of four conditions:

1. *When the sender intends one denotation while the receiver interprets another.* (As in the case of Sipert and his foreman.)

2. *When the sender intends one connotation while the receiver interprets another.* A friend once told me of an experience she had years ago when as a teenager she was spending the week with a maiden aunt. Joan had gone to the movies with a young man who brought her home at a respectable hour. However, the couple lingered on the front porch somewhat longer than Aunt Mildred thought necessary. The little old lady was rather proud of her ability to deal with younger people so she slipped out of bed, raised her bedroom window, and called down sweetly, "If you two knew how pleasant it is in bed, you wouldn't be standing out there in the cold."

3. *When the sender intends only a denotation while the receiver interprets a connotation.* For a brief period the following memorandum appeared on the bulletin boards of a government agency in Washington:

> Those department and sections heads who do not have secretaries assigned to them make take advantage of the stenographers in the secretarial pool.

4. *When the sender intends a connotation while the receiver interprets a denotation only.* Before making his final decision on a proposal to move to new offices, the head of a large company called his top executives for a last discussion of the idea. All were enthusiastic except the company treasurer who insisted that he had not had time to calculate all the costs with accuracy sufficient to satisfy himself that the move was advantageous. Annoyed by his persistence, the chief finally burst out:

"All right, Jim, all right! Figure it out to the last cent. A penny saved is a penny earned, right?"

The intention was ironic. He meant not what the words denoted but the opposite—forget this and stop being petty. For him this was what his words connotated.

For the treasurer "penny saved, penny earned" meant exactly what it said. He put several members on his staff to work on the problem and, to test the firmness of the price, had one of them interview the agent renting the proposed new quarters without explaining whom he represented. This indication of additional interest in the premises led the agent to raise the rent. Not until the lease was signed, did the company discover that one of its own employees had, in effect, bid up its price.[7]

2. The Assumption That Inferences Are Always Distinguishable From Observations

It is incredibly difficult, at times, for a communicator (or anyone) to discriminate between what he "knows" (that is, what he has actually observed—seen, heard, handled) and what he is only inferring or guessing. One of the key reasons for this lies in the character of the language used to express observations and inferences.

Suppose you look at a man and observe that he is wearing a white shirt and then say, "That man is wearing a white shirt." Assuming your vision and the illumination were "normal" you would have made a statement of *observation*—a statement which directly corresponded to and was corroborated by your observation. But suppose you now say, "That man bought the white shirt he is wearing." Assuming you were not present when and if the man bought the shirt that statement would be *for you a statement of inference*. Your statement went *beyond* what you observed. You inferred that the man bought the shirt; you did not observe it. Of course, your inference may be correct (but it

[7] Robert Froman, "Make Words Fit the Job," *Nation's Business* (July 1959).

could be false: perhaps he was given the shirt as a gift; perhaps he stole it or borrowed it, etc.).

Nothing in the nature of our language (the grammar, spelling, pronunciation, accentuation, syntax, inflection, etc.) prevents you from speaking or writing (or thinking) a statement of inference *as if* you were making a statement of observation. Our language permits you to say "Of course, he bought the shirt" with certainty and finality, that is, with as much confidence as you would make a statement of observation. The effect is that it becomes exceedingly easy to confuse the two kinds of statements and also to confuse inference and observation on nonverbal levels. The destructive consequences of acting upon inference as if acting upon observation can range from mild embarrassment to tragedy. One factual illustration may be sufficient to point up the dangers of such behavior.

The Case of Jim Blake

Jim Blake, 41, had been with the Hasting Co. for ten years. For the last seven years he had served as an "inside salesman," receiving phone calls from customers and writing out orders. "Salesman," in this case, was somewhat of an euphemism as the customer ordinarily knew what he wanted and was prepared to place an order. The "outside salesmen," on the other hand, visited industrial accounts and enjoyed considerably more status and income. Blake had aspired to an outside position for several years but no openings had occurred. He had, however, been assured by Russ Jenkins, sales manager, that as senior inside man he would be given first chance at the next available outside job.

Finally, it seemed as if Jim's chance had come. Harry Strom, 63, one of the outside men, had decided in January to retire on the first of June. It did not occur to Jenkins to reassure Blake that the new opening was to be his. Moreover, Blake did not question Jenkins because he felt his superior should take the initiative.

As the months went by Blake became increasingly uneasy. Finally, on May 15 he was astonished to see Strom escorting a young man into Jenkins' office. Although the door was closed Blake could hear considerable laughing inside. After an hour the three emerged from the office and Jenkins shook hands with the new man saying, "Joe, I'm certainly glad you're going to be with us. With Harry showing you around his territory you're going to get a good start at the business." Strom and the new man left and Jenkins returned to his office.

Blake was infuriated. He was convinced that the new man was being groomed for Strom's position. Now he understood why Jenkins had said nothing to him. He angrily cleaned out his desk, wrote a bitter letter of resignation and left it on his desk, and stomped out of the office.

Suspecting the worst for several months, Blake was quite unable to distinguish what he had inferred from what he had actually observed. The new man, it turned out, was being hired to work as an inside salesman—an opening which was to be occasioned by Blake's moving into the outside position. Jenkins had wanted the new man to get the "feel" of the clientele and thus had requested Strom to take him along for a few days as Strom made his calls.[8]

Trends in Serial Transmission

These assumptions,[9] the mono-usage of words, and the inference-observation confusion, as well as the aforementioned motives of the communicators, undoubtedly contribute a significant share of the difficulties and dangers which beset a

[8] The names have been changed.
[9] For a more detailed analysis of these assumptions and for additional methods for preventing and correcting their consequences, see William V. Haney, *Communication: Patterns and Incidents* (Homewood, Ill.: 1960), Chs. III, IV, V.

serial transmission. Their effect tends to be manifested by three trends: omission, alteration, and addition.

Details Become Omitted

It requires less effort to convey a simpler, less complex message. With fewer details to transmit, the fear of forgetting or of garbling the message is decreased. In the serial transmissions even those final versions which most closely approximated the original had omitted an appreciable number of details.

> There are Eagles in front of the frat house at the State University. It cost $75 to $100 to remove the paint each year from the eagles.

The essential question is, perhaps, which details *will be retained?* Judging from interviewing the serial transmitters after the demonstrations these aspects will *not* be dropped out:

A. Those details the transmitter wanted or expected to hear.

B. Those details which "made sense" to the transmitter.

C. Those details which seemed important *to the transmitter.*

D. Those details which for various and inexplicable reasons seemed to stick with the transmitter—those aspects which seemed particularly unusual or bizarre; those which had special significance to him; etc.

Details Become Altered

When changes in detail occurred in the serial transmissions it was often possible to pinpoint the "changers." When asked to explain why they had changed the message most were unaware that they had done so. However, upon retrospection some admitted that they had changed the details in order to simplify the message, "clarify it," "straighten it out," "make it more sensible," and

the like. It became evident, too, that among the details most susceptible to change were the qualifications, the indefinite. Inferential statements are prone to become definite and certain. What may start out as "The boss seemed angry this morning" may quickly progress to "The boss was angry." . . .

It became obvious upon interviewing the serial transmitters that bypassing (denotative and connotative) had also played a role. For example, the "president" in the message about the "eagles" was occasionally bypassed as the "President of the U.S." and sometimes the rest of the message was constructed around this detail.

> The White House was in such a mess that they wanted to renovate it but found that the cost would be $100 to $75 to paint the eagle so they decided not to do it.

Details Become Added

Not infrequently details are added to the message to "fill in the gaps," "to make better sense," and "because I thought the fellow who told it to me left something out." . . .

An interesting facet about serial transmission is that the three trends—omission, alteration, and addition—are also present when the "message" is pictorial as opposed to verbal. . . .

Correctives

Even serial transmissions, as intricate and as relatively uncontrolled communications as they are, can be improved. The suggestions below are not sensational panaceas. In fact, they are quite commonplace, common sense, but uncommonly used techniques.[10]

1. *Take notes.* Less than five percent of the serial transmitters took notes. Some said that they

[10] Most of these suggestions are offered by Irving J. and Laura L. Lee, *Handling Barriers in Communication* (New York, 1956).

assumed they were not supposed to (no such restriction had been placed upon them) but most admitted that they rarely take notes as a matter of course. In the cases where all transmitters on a team were instructed to take notes the final versions were manifestly more complete and more accurate than those of the non-notetakers.

2. *Give details in order.* Organized information is easier to understand and to remember. Choose a sequence (chronological, spatial, deductive, inductive, etc.) appropriate to the content and be consistent with it. For example, it may suit your purpose best to begin with a proposal followed by supporting reasons or to start with the reasons and work toward the proposal. In either case take care to keep proposals and reasons clearly distinguished rather than mixing them together indiscriminately.

3. *Be wary of bypassing.* If you are the receiver, query (ask the sender what he meant) and paraphrase (put what you think he said or wrote into your own words and get the sender to check you). These simple techniques are effective yet infrequently practiced, perhaps because we are so positive we know what the other fellow means; perhaps because we hesitate to ask or rephrase for fear the other fellow (especially if he is the boss) will think less of us for not understanding the first time. The latter apprehension is usually unfounded, at least if we can accept the remarks of a hundred or more executives questioned on the matter during the last four years. "By all means," they said almost to a man, "I *want* my people to check with me. The person who wants to be sure he's got it straight has a sense of responsibility and that's the kind of man (or woman) I want on my payroll."

Although executives, generally, may take this point of view quite sincerely, obviously not all of them practice it. Querying and paraphrasing are *two-way* responsibilities and the sender must be truly approachable by his receivers if the techniques are to be successful.

This check-list may be helpful in avoiding by-passing:

Could he be denoting something other than what I am?

Could he be connoting something other than what I am?

Could he be connoting whereas I am merely denoting?

Could he be merely denoting whereas I am connoting?

4. *Distinguish between inference and observation.* Ask yourself sharply: Did I *really* see, hear, or read this—or am I guessing part of it? The essential characteristics of a statement of observation are these:

A.   It can be made only by the observer. (What someone tells you as observational is still inferential for you if you did not observe it.)

B.   It can be made only during or *after* observation.

C.   It stays with what has been observed; does not go beyond it.

This is not to say that inferential statements are not to be made—we could hardly avoid doing so. But it is important or even vital at times to know *when* we are making them.

5. *Slow down your oral transmissions.* By doing so, you give your listener a better opportunity to assimilate complex and detailed information. However, it is possible to speak *too* slowly so as to lose his attention. Since either extreme defeats your purpose, it is generally wise to watch the listener for clues as to the most suitable rate of speech.

6. *Simplify the message.* This suggestion is for the *originator* of the message. The "middle-men" often simplify without half trying! Most salesmen realize the inadvisability of attempting to sell too many features at a time. The customer is only confused and is unable to distinguish the key features from those less important. With particular respect to oral transmission, there is impressive evidence to indicate that beyond a point the addition of de-

tails leads to disproportionate omission. Evidently, you can add a straw to the camel's back without breaking it, but you run the decided risk of his dropping two straws.

7. *Use dual media when feasible.* A message often stands a better chance of getting through if it is reinforced by restatement in another communication medium. Detailed, complex, and unfamiliar information is often transmitted by such combinations as a memo follow-up on a telephone call; a sensory aid (slide, diagram, mock-up, picture, etc.) accompanying a written or oral message, etc.

8. *Highlight the important.* Presumably the originator of a message knows (or should know) which are its important aspects. But this does not automatically insure that his serial transmitters will similarly recognize them. There are numerous devices for making salient points stand out as such; for example, using underscoring, capitals, etc., in writing; using vocal emphasis, attention-drawing phrases ("This is the main point . . . ," "Here's the crux . . . ," "Be sure to note this . . ."), etc., in speaking.

9. *Reduce the number of links in the chain.* This suggestion has to be followed with discretion. Jumping the chain of command either upward or downward can sometimes have undesirable consequences. However, to the extent that it is possible to reduce or eliminate the "middlemen," the message becomes progressively less susceptible to aberrations. Of course, there are methods of skipping links which are commonly accepted and widely practiced. Communication downward can be reduced to person-to-person communication, in a sense, with general memos, letters, bulletins, group meetings, etc. Communication upward can accomplish the same purpose via suggestion boxes, opinion questionnaires, "talkbacks," etc.

10. *Preview and review.* A wise speech professor used to say: "Giving a speech is basically very simple if you do it in three steps: First, you tell them what you're going to tell them; then you tell them; then, finally, you tell them what you've told them." This three-step sequence is often applicable whether the message is transmitted by letter, memo, written or oral report, public address, telephone call, etc.

Summary

After the last suggestion I feel obliged to review this article briefly. We have been concerned with serial transmission—a widespread, essential, and yet susceptible form of communication. Among the factors which vitiate a serial transmission are certain of the communicator's motives and fallacious assumptions. When these and other factors are in play the three processes—omission, alteration, and addition—tend to occur. The suggestions offered for strengthening serial transmission will be more or less applicable, of course, depending upon the specific communication situation.

An important question remains: What can be done to encourage communicators to practice the techniques? They will probably use them largely to the extent that they think the techniques are needed. But *do* they think them necessary? Apparently many do not. When asked to explain how the final version came to differ so markedly from the original, many of the serial transmitters in my studies were genuinely puzzled. A frequent comment was "I really can't understand it. All I know is that I passed the message along the same as it came to me." If messages were passed along "the same as they came," of course, serial transmission would no longer be a problem. And so long as the illusion of fidelity is with the communicator it is unlikely that he will be prompted to apply some of these simple, prosaic, yet effective techniques to his communicating. Perhaps a first step would be to induce him to question his unwarranted assurance about his communication. The controlled serial transmission experience appears to accomplish this.

Edward T. Hall

The Silent Language in Overseas Business

With few exceptions, Americans are relative new-comers on the international business scene. To-day, as in Mark Twain's time, we are all too often "innocents abroad," in an era when naiveté and blundering in foreign business dealings may have serious political repercussions.

When the American executive travels abroad to do business, he is frequently shocked to discover to what extent the many variables of foreign behavior and custom complicate his efforts. Although the American has recognized, certainly, that even the man next door has many minor traits which make him somewhat peculiar, for some reason he has failed to appreciate how different foreign businessmen and their practices will seem to him.

He should understand that the various peoples around the world have worked out and integrated into their subconscious literally thousands of behavior patterns that they take for granted in each other.[1] Then, when the stranger enters, and behaves differently from the local norm, he often quite unintentionally insults, annoys or amuses the native with whom he is attempting to do business. For example:

In the United States, a corporation executive knows what is meant when a client lets a month go by before replying to a business proposal. On the other hand, he senses an eagerness to do business if he is immediately ushered into the client's office. In both instances, he is reacting to subtle cues in the timing of interaction, cues which he depends on to chart his course of action.

Abroad, however, all this changes. The American executive learns that the Latin Americans are casual about time and that if he waits an hour in the outer office before seeing the Deputy Minister of Finance, it does not necessarily mean he is not getting anywhere. There people are so important that nobody can bear to tear himself away; because of the resultant interruptions and conversational detours, everybody is constantly getting behind. What the American does not know is the point at which the waiting becomes significant.

In another instance, after traveling 7,000 miles an American walks into the office of a highly recommended Arab businessman on whom he will have to depend completely. What he sees does not breed confidence. The office is reached by walking through a suspicious-looking coffee-house in an old, dilapidated building situated in a crowded non-European section of town. The elevator, rising from dark, smelly corridors, is rickety and equally foul. When he gets to the office itself, he is shocked to find it small, crowded, and confused. Papers are stacked all over the desk and table tops—even scattered on the floor in irregular piles.

The Arab merchant he has come to see had met him at the airport the night before and sent his driver to the hotel this morning to pick him up. But now, after the American's rush, the Arab is tied up with something else. Even when they finally start talking business, there are constant interruptions. If the American is at all sensitive to his environment, everything around him signals, "What am I getting into?"

Before leaving home he was told that things

"The Silent Language in Overseas Business" by Edward T. Hall from *Harvard Business Review*, May-June 1960 © 1960 by the President and Fellows of Harvard College; all rights reserved.

[1] For details, see my book, *The Silent Language* (New York, Doubleday & Company, Inc., 1959).

would be different, but how different? The hotel is modern enough. The shops in the new part of town have many more American and European trade goods than he had anticipated. His first impression was that doing business in the Middle East would not present any new problems. Now he is beginning to have doubts. One minute everything looks familiar and he is on firm ground; the next, familiar landmarks are gone. His greatest problem is that so much assails his senses all at once that he does not know where to start looking for something that will tell him where he stands. He needs a frame of reference—a way of sorting out what is significant and relevant.

That is why it is so important for American businessmen to have a real understanding of the various social, cultural, and economic differences they will face when they attempt to do business in foreign countries. To help give some frame of reference, this article will map out a few areas of human activity that have largely been unstudied.

The topics I will discuss are certainly not presented as the last word on the subject, but they have proved to be highly reliable points at which to begin to gain an understanding of foreign cultures. While additional research will undoubtedly turn up other items just as relevant, at present I think the businessman can do well to begin by appreciating cultural differences in matters concerning the language of time, of space, of material possessions, of friendship patterns, and of agreements.

Language of Time

Everywhere in the world people use time to communicate with each other. There are different languages of time just as there are different spoken languages. The unspoken languages are informal; yet the rules governing their interpretation are surprisingly *ironbound*.

In the United States, a delay in answering a communication can result from a large volume of business causing the request to be postponed until the backlog is cleared away, from poor organization, or possibly from technical complexity requiring deep analysis. But if the person awaiting the answer or decision rules out these reasons, then the delay means to him that the matter has low priority on the part of the other person—lack of interest. On the other hand, a similar delay in a foreign country may mean something altogether different. Thus:

In Ethiopia, the time required for a decision is directly proportional to its importance. This is so much the case that low-level bureaucrats there have a way of trying to elevate the prestige of their work by taking a long time to make up their minds. (Americans in that part of the world are innocently prone to downgrade their work in the local people's eyes by trying to speed things up.)

In the Arab East, time does not generally include schedules as Americans know and use them. The time required to get something accomplished depends on the relationship. More important people get fast service from less important people, and conversely. Close relatives take absolute priority; nonrelatives are kept waiting.

In the United States, giving a person a deadline is a way of indicating the degree of urgency or relative importance of the work. But in the Middle East, the American runs into a cultural trap the minute he opens his mouth. "Mr. Aziz will have to make up his mind in a hurry because my board meets next week and I have to have an answer by then," is taken as indicating the American is overly demanding and is exerting undue pressure. "I am going to Damascus tomorrow morning and will have to have my car tonight," is a sure way to get the mechanic to stop work, because to give another person a deadline in this part of the world is to be rude, pushy, and demanding.

An Arab's evasiveness as to when something is going to happen does not mean he does not want to do business; it only means he is avoiding unpleasantness and is side-stepping possible commitments which he takes more seriously than we do. For example:

The Arabs themselves at times find it impossible to communicate even to each other that some processes cannot be hurried, and are controlled by built-in schedules. This is obvious enough to the Westerner but not to the Arab. A highly placed public official in Baghdad precipitated a bitter family dispute because his nephew, a biochemist, could not speed up the complete analysis of the uncle's blood. He accused the nephew of putting other less important people before him and of not caring. Nothing could sway the uncle, who could not grasp the fact that there is such a thing as an *inherent* schedule.

With us the more important an event is, the further ahead we schedule it, which is why we find it insulting to be asked to a party at the last minute. In planning future events with Arabs, it pays to hold the lead time to a week or less because other factors may intervene or take precedence.

Again, time spent waiting in an American's outer office is a sure indicator of what one person thinks of another or how important he feels the other's business to be. This is so much the case that most Americans cannot help getting angry after waiting 30 minutes; one may even feel such a delay is an insult, and will walk out. In Latin America, on the other hand, one learns that it does not mean anything to wait in an outer office. An American businessman with years of experience in Mexico once told me, "You know, I have spent two hours cooling my heels in an executive's outer office. It took me a long time to learn to keep my blood pressure down. Even now, I find it hard to convince myself they are still interested when they keep me waiting."

The Japanese handle time in ways which are almost inexplicable to the Western European and particularly the American. A delay of years with them does not mean that they have lost interest. It only means that they are building up to something. They have learned that Americans are vulnerable to long waits. One of them expressed it, "You Americans have one terrible weakness. If we make you wait long enough, you will agree to anything."

Indians of South Asia have an elastic view of time as compared to our own. Delays do not, therefore, have the same meaning to them. Nor does indefiniteness in pinpointing appointments mean that they are evasive. Two Americans meeting will say, "We should get together sometime," thereby setting a low priority on the meeting. The Indian who says, "Come over and see me, see me anytime," means just that.

Americans make a place at the table which may or may not mean a place made in the heart. But when the Indian makes a place in his time, it is yours to fill in every sense of the word if you realize that by so doing you have crossed a boundary and are now friends with him. The point of all this is that time communicates just as surely as do words and that the vocabulary of time is different around the world. The principle to be remembered is that time has different meanings in each country.

Language of Space

Like time, the language of space is different wherever one goes. The American businessman, familiar with the pattern of American corporate life, has no difficulty in appraising the relative importance of someone else, simply by noting the size of his office in relation to other offices around him:

Our pattern calls for the president or the chairman of the board to have the biggest office. The executive vice president will have the next largest, and so on down the line until you end up in the "bull pen." More important offices are usually located at the corners of buildings and on the upper floors. Executive suites will be on the top floor. The relative rank of vice presidents will be reflected in where they are placed along "Executive Row."

The French, on the other hand, are much more likely to lay out space as a network of connecting points of influence, activity, or interest. The French supervisor will ordinarily be found in the middle of his subordinates where he can control them.

Americans who are crowded will often feel that their status in the organization is suffering. As one would expect in the Arab world, the location of an office and its size constitute a poor index of the importance of the man who occupies it. What we experience as crowded, the Arab will often regard as spacious. The same is true in Spanish cultures. A Latin American official illustrated the Spanish view of this point while showing me around a plant. Opening the door to an 18-by-20-foot office in which seventeen clerks and their desks were placed, he said, "See, we have nice spacious offices. Lots of space for everyone."

The American will look at a Japanese room and remark how bare it is. Similarly, the Japanese look at our rooms and comment, "How bare!" Furniture in the American home tends to be placed along the walls (around the edge). Japanese have their charcoal pit where the family gathers in the *middle* of the room. The top floor of Japanese department stores is not reserved for the chief executive—it is the bargain roof!

In the Middle East and Latin America, the businessman is likely to feel left out in time and overcrowded in space. People get too close to him, lay their hands on him, and generally crowd his physical being. In Scandinavia and Germany, he feels more at home, but at the same time the people are a little cold and distant. It is space itself that conveys this feeling.

In the United States, because of our tendency to zone activities, nearness carries rights of familiarity so that the neighbor can borrow material possessions and invade time. This is not true in England. Propinquity entitles you to nothing.

American Air Force personnel stationed there complain because they have to make an appointment for their children to play with the neighbor's child next door.

Conversation distance between two people is learned early in life by copying elders. Its controlling patterns operate almost totally unconsciously. In the United States, in contrast to many foreign countries, men avoid excessive touching. Regular business is conducted at distances such as 5 feet to 8 feet; highly personal business, 18 inches to 3 feet—not 2 or 3 inches.

In the United States, it is perfectly possible for an experienced executive to schedule the steps of negotiation in time and space so that most people feel comfortable about what is happening. Business transactions progress in stages from across the desk to beside the desk, to the coffee table, then on to the conference table, the luncheon table, or the golf course, or even into the home—all according to a complex set of hidden rules which we obey instinctively.

Even in the United States, however, an executive may slip when he moves into new and unfamiliar realms, when dealing with a new group, doing business with a new company, or moving to a new place in the industrial hierarchy. In a new country the danger is magnified. For example, in India it is considered improper to discuss business in the home on social occasions. One never invites a business acquaintance to the home for the purpose of furthering business aims. That would be a violation of sacred hospitality rules.

Language of Things

Americans are often contrasted with the rest of the world in terms of material possessions. We are accused of being materialistic, gadget-crazy. And, as a matter of fact, we have developed material things for some very interesting reasons. Lacking a fixed class system and having an extremely mobile population, Americans have become highly sensitive to how others make use of material possessions. We use everything from clothes to houses as a highly evolved and complex means of ascertaining each other's status. Ours is a rapidly shifting system in which both styles and people move up or down. For example:

The Cadillac ad men feel that not only is it natural but quite insightful of them to show a picture of a Cadillac and a well-turned-out gentleman in his early fifties opening the door. The caption underneath reads, "You already know a great deal about this man."

Following this same pattern, the head of a big union spends an excess of $100,000 furnishing his office so that the president of United States Steel cannot look down on him. Good materials, large space, and the proper surroundings signify that the people who occupy the premises are solid citizens, that they are dependable and successful.

The French, the English, and the Germans have entirely different ways of using their material possessions. What stands for the height of dependability and respectability with the English would be old-fashioned and backward to us. The Japanese take pride in often inexpensive but tasteful arrangements that are used to produce the proper emotional setting.

Middle East businessmen look for something else—family, connections, friendship. They do not use the furnishings of their office as part of their status system; nor do they expect to impress a client by these means or to fool a banker into lending more money than he should. They like good things, too, but feel that they, as persons, should be known and not judged solely by what the public sees.

One of the most common criticisms of American relations abroad, both commercial and governmental, is that we usually think in terms of material things. "Money talks," says the American, who goes on talking the language of money abroad, in the belief that money talks the *same*

language all over the world. A common practice in the United States is to try to buy loyalty with high salaries. In foreign countries, this maneuver almost never works, for money and material possessions stand for something different there than they do in America.

Language of Friendship

The American finds his friends next door and among those with whom he works. It has been noted that we take people up quickly and drop them just as quickly. Occasionally a friendship formed during schooldays will persist, but this is rare. For us there are few well-defined rules governing the obligations of friendship. It is difficult to say at which point our friendship gives way to business opportunism or pressure from above. In this we differ from many other people in the world. As a general rule in foreign countries friendships are not formed as quickly as in the United States but go much deeper, last longer, and involve real obligations. For example:

It is important to stress that in the Middle East and Latin America your "friends" will not let you down. The fact that they personally are feeling the pinch is never an excuse for failing their friends. They are supposed to look out for your interests.

Friends and family around the world represent a sort of social insurance that would be difficult to find in the United States. We do not use our friends to help us out in disaster as much as we do as a means of getting ahead—or, at least, of getting the job done. The United States systems work by means of a series of closely tabulated favors and obligations carefully doled out where they will do the most good. And the least that we expect in exchange for a favor is gratitude.

The opposite is the case in India, where the friend's role is to "sense" a person's need and do something about it. The idea of reciprocity as we know it is unheard of. An American in India will have difficulty if he attempts to follow American friendship patterns. He gains nothing by extending himself in behalf of others, least of all gratitude, because the Indian assumes that what he does for others he does for the good of his own psyche. He will find it impossible to make friends quickly and is unlikely to allow sufficient time for friendships to ripen. He will also note that as he gets to know people better, they may become more critical of him, a fact that he finds hard to take. What he does not know is that one sign of friendship in India is speaking one's mind.

Language of Agreements

While it is important for American businessmen abroad to understand the symbolic meanings of friendship rules, time, space, and material possessions, it is just as important for executives to know the rules for negotiating agreements in various countries. Even if they cannot be expected to know the details of each nation's commercial legal practices, just the awareness of and the expectation of the existence of differences will eliminate much complication.

Actually, no society can exist on a high commercial level without a highly developed working base on which agreements can rest. This base may be one or a combination of three types:

1. Rules that are spelled out technically as law or regulation.
2. Moral practices mutually agreed on and taught to the young as a set of principles.
3. Informal customs to which everyone conforms without being able to state the exact rules.

Some societies favor one, some another. Ours, particularly in the business world, lays heavy emphasis on the first variety. Few Americans will conduct any business nowadays without some written agreement or contract.

Varying from culture to culture will be the circumstances under which such rules apply. Americans consider that negotiations have more or less ceased when the contract is signed. With the Greeks, on the other hand, the contract is seen as a sort of way station on the route to negotiation that will cease only when the work is completed. The contract is nothing more than a charter for serious negotiations. In the Arab world, once a man's word is given in a particular kind of way, it is just as binding, if not more so, than most of our written contracts. The written contract, therefore, violates the Moslem's sensitivities and reflects on his honor. Unfortunately, the situation is now so hopelessly confused that neither system can be counted on to prevail consistently.

Informal patterns and unstated agreements often lead to untold difficulty in the cross-cultural situation. Take the case of the before-and-after patterns where there is a wide discrepancy between the American's expectations and those of the Arab:

In the United States, when you engage a specialist such as a lawyer or a doctor, require any standard service, or even take a taxi, you make several assumptions: (a) the charge will be fair; (b) it will be in proportion to the services rendered; and (c) it will bear a close relationship to the "going rate."

You wait until after the services are performed before asking what the tab will be. If the charge is too high in the light of the above assumptions, you feel you have been cheated. You can complain, or can say nothing, pay up, and take your business elsewhere the next time.

As one would expect in the Middle East, basic differences emerge which lead to difficulty if not understood. For instance, when taking a cab in Beirut it is well to know the going rate as a point around which to bargain and for settling the charge, which must be fixed before engaging the cab.

If you have not fixed the rate *in advance*, there is a complete change and an entirely different set of rules will apply. According to these rules, the going rate plays no part whatsoever. The whole relationship is altered. The sky is the limit, and the customer has no kick coming. I have seen taxi drivers shouting at the top of their lungs, waving their arms, following a redfaced American with his head pulled down between his shoulders, demanding for a two-pound ride ten Lebanese pounds which the American eventually had to pay.

It is difficult for the American to accommodate his frame of reference to the fact that what constitutes one thing to him, namely, a taxi ride, is to the Arab two very different operations involving two different sets of relationships and two sets of rules. The crucial factor is whether the bargaining is done at the beginning or the end of the ride! As a matter of fact, you cannot bargain at the end. What the driver asks for he is entitled to!

One of the greatest difficulties Americans have abroad stems from the fact that we often think we have a commitment when we do not. The second complication on this same topic is the other side of the coin, i.e., when others think we have agreed to things that we have not. Our own failure to recognize binding obligations, plus our custom of setting organizational goals ahead of everything else, has put us in hot water far too often.

People sometimes do not keep agreements with us because we do not keep agreements with them. As a general rule, the American treats the agreement as something he may eventually have to break. Here are two examples:

Once while I was visiting an American post in Latin America, the Ambassador sent the Spanish version of a trade treaty down to his language officer with instructions to write in some "weasel words." To his dismay, he was told, "There are no weasel words in Spanish."

A personnel officer of a large corporation in Iran made an agreement with local employees that American employees would not receive preferential treatment. When the first American employee arrived, it was learned quickly that in the United States he had been covered by a variety of health plans that were not available to Iranians. And this led to immediate protests from the Iranians which were never satisfied. The personnel officer never really grasped the fact that he had violated an ironbound contract.

Certainly, this is the most important generalization to be drawn by American businessmen from this discussion of agreements: there are many times when we are vulnerable *even when judged by our own standards*. Many instances of actual sharp practices by American companies are well known abroad and are giving American business a bad name. The cure for such questionable behavior is simple. The companies concerned usually have it within their power to discharge offenders and to foster within their organization an atmosphere in which only honesty and fairness can thrive.

But the cure for ignorance of the social and legal rules which underlie business agreements is not so easy. This is because:

- The subject is complex.
- Little research has been conducted to determine the culturally different concepts of what is an agreement.
- The people of each country think that their own code is the only one, and that everything else is dishonest.
- Each code is different from our own; and the farther away one is traveling from Western Europe, the greater the difference is.

But the little that has already been learned about this subject indicates that as a problem it is not insoluble and will yield to research. Since it is probably one of the more relevant and immediately applicable areas of interest to modern business, it would certainly be advisable for companies with large foreign operations to sponsor some serious research in this vital field.

A Case in Point

Thus far, I have been concerned with developing the five check points around which a real understanding of foreign cultures can begin. But the problems that arise from a faulty understanding of the silent language of foreign custom are human problems and perhaps can best be dramatized by an actual case.

A Latin American republic had decided to modernize one of its communication networks to the tune of several million dollars. Because of its reputation for quality and price, the inside track was quickly taken by American company "Y."

The company, having been sounded out informally, considered the size of the order and decided to bypass its regular Latin American representative and send instead its sales manager. The following describes what took place.

The sales manager arrived and checked in at the leading hotel. He immediately had some difficulty pinning down just who it was he had to see about his business. After several days without results, he called at the American Embassy where he found that the commercial attaché had the up-to-the-minute information he needed. The commercial attaché listened to his story. Realizing that the sales manager had already made a number of mistakes, but figuring that the Latins were used to American blundering, the attaché reasoned that all was not lost. He informed the sales manager that the Minister of Communications was the key man and that whoever got the nod from him would get the contract. He also briefed the sales manager on methods of conducting business in Latin America and offered some pointers about dealing with the minister.

The attaché's advice ran somewhat as follows:

1. "You don't do business here the way you do in the States; it is necessary to spend much more time. You have to get to know your man and vice versa.

2. "You must meet with him *several times* before you talk business. I will tell you at what point you can bring up the subject. Take your cues from me. [Our American sales manager at this point made a few observations to himself about "cookie pushers" and wondered how many payrolls had been met by the commercial attaché.]

3. "Take that price list and put it in your pocket. Don't get it out until I tell you to. Down here price is only one of the many things taken into account before closing a deal. In the United States, your past experience will prompt you to act according to a certain set of principles, but many of these principles will *not* work here. Every time you feel the urge to act or to say something, look at me. Suppress the urge and take your cues from me. This is very important.

4. "Down here people like to do business with men who *are* somebody. In order to be somebody, it is well to have written a book, to have lectured at a university, or to have developed your intellect in some way. The man you are going to see is a poet. He has published several volumes of poetry. Like many Latin Americans, he prizes poetry highly. You will find that he will spend a good deal of business time quoting his poetry to you, and he will take great pleasure in this.

5. "You will also note that the people here are very proud of their past and of their Spanish blood, but they are also exceedingly proud of their liberation from Spain and their independence. The fact that they are a democracy, that they are free, and also that they are no longer a colony is very, very important to them. They are warm and friendly and enthusiastic if they like you. If they don't, they are cold and withdrawn.

6. "And another thing, time down here means something different. It works in a different way. You know how it is back in the States when a certain type blurts out whatever is on his mind without waiting to see if the situation is right. He is considered an impatient bore and somewhat egocentric. Well, down here, you have to wait much,

much longer, and I really mean *much, much* longer, before you can begin to talk about the reason for your visit.

7. "There is another point I want to caution you about. At home, the man who sells takes the initiative. Here, *they* tell you when they are ready to do business. But, most of all, don't discuss price until you are asked and don't rush things."

The Pitch

The next day the commercial attaché introduced the sales manager to the Minister of Communications. First, there was a long wait in the outer office while people kept coming in and out. The sales manager looked at his watch, fidgeted, and finally asked whether the minister was really expecting him. The reply he received was scarcely reassuring, "Oh, yes, he is expecting you but several things have come up that require his attention. Besides, one gets used to waiting down here." The sales manager irritably replied, "But doesn't he know I flew all the way down here from the United States to see him, and I have spent over a week already of my valuable time trying to find him?" "Yes, I know," was the answer, "but things just move much more slowly here."

At the end of about 30 minutes, the minister emerged from the office, greeted the commercial attaché with a *doble abrazo*, throwing his arms around him and patting him on the back as though they were long-lost brothers. Now, turning and smiling, the minister extended his hand to the sales manager, who, by this time, was feeling rather miffed because he had been kept in the outer office so long.

After what seemed to be an all too short chat, the minister rose, suggesting a well-known café where they might meet for dinner the next evening. The sales manager expected, of course, that, considering the nature of their business and the size of the order, he might be taken to the minister's home, not realizing that the Latin home is reserved for family and very close friends.

Until now, nothing at all had been said about the reason for the sales manager's visit, a fact which bothered him somewhat. The whole set-up seemed wrong; neither did he like the idea of wasting another day in town. He told the home office before he left that he would be gone for a week or ten days at most, and made a mental note that he would clean this order up in three days and enjoy a few days in Acapulco or Mexico City. Now the week had already gone and he would be lucky if he made it home in ten days.

Voicing his misgivings to the commercial attaché, he wanted to know if the minister really meant business, and, if he did, why could they not get together and talk about it? The commercial attaché by now was beginning to show the strain of constantly having to reassure the sales manager. Nevertheless, he tried again:

"What you don't realize is that part of the time we were waiting, the minister was rearranging a very tight schedule so that he could spend tomorrow night with you. You see, down here they don't delegate responsibility the way we do in the States. They exercise much tighter control than we do. As a consequence, this man spends up to 15 hours a day at his desk. It may not look like it to you, but I assure you he really means business. He wants to give your company the order; if you play your cards right, you will get it."

The next evening provided more of the same. Much conversation about food and music, about many people the sales manager had never heard of. They went to a night club, where the sales manager brightened up and began to think that perhaps he and the minister might have something in common after all. It bothered him, however, that the principal reason for his visit was not even alluded to tangentially. But every time he started to talk about electronics, the commercial attaché would nudge him and proceed to change the subject.

The next meeting was for morning coffee at a café. By now the sales manager was having difficulty hiding his impatience. To make matters worse, the minister had a mannerism which he did not like. When they talked, he was likely to put his hand on him; he would take hold of his arm and get so close that he almost "spat" in his face. As a consequence, the sales manager was kept busy trying to dodge and back up.

Following the coffee, there was a walk in a nearby park. The minister expounded on the shrubs, the birds, and the beauties of nature, and at one spot he stopped to point at a statue and said: "There is a statue of the world's greatest hero, the liberator of mankind!" At this point, the worst happened, for the sales manager asked who the statue was of and, being given the name of a famous Latin American patriot, said, "I never heard of him," and walked on.

The Failure

It is quite clear from this that the sales manager did not get the order, which went to a Swedish concern. The American, moreover, was never able to see the minister again. Why did the minister feel the way he did? His reasoning went somewhat as follows:

"I like the American's equipment and it makes sense to deal with North Americans who are near us and whose price is right. But I could never be friends with this man. He is not my kind of human being and we have nothing in common. He is not *simpatico*. If I can't be friends and he is not *simpatico*, I can't depend on him to treat me right. I tried everything, every conceivable situation, and only once did we seem to understand each other. If we could be friends, he would feel obligated to

me and this obligation would give me some control. Without control, how do I know he will deliver what he says he will at the price he quotes?"

Of course, what the minister did not know was that the price was quite firm, and that quality control was a matter of company policy. He did not realize that the sales manager was a member of an organization, and that the man is always subordinate to the organization in the United States. Next year maybe the sales manager would not even be representing the company, but would be replaced. Further, if he wanted someone to depend on, his best bet would be to hire a good American lawyer to represent him and write a binding contract.

In this instance, both sides suffered. The American felt he was being slighted and put off, and did not see how there could possibly be any connection between poetry and doing business or why it should all take so long. He interpreted the delay as a form of polite brush-off. Even if things had gone differently and there had been a contract, it is doubtful that the minister would have trusted the contract as much as he would a man whom he considered his friend. Throughout Latin America, the law is made livable and contracts workable by having friends and relatives operating from the inside. Lacking a friend, someone who would look out for his interests, the minister did not want to take a chance. He stated this simply and directly.

Conclusion

The case just described has of necessity been oversimplified. The danger is that the reader will say, "Oh, I see. All you really have to do is be friends." At which point the expert will step in and reply:

"Yes, of course, but what you don't realize is that in Latin America being a friend involves much more than it does in the United States and is an entirely different proposition. A friendship implies obligations. You go about it differently. It involves much more than being nice, visiting, and playing golf. You would not want to enter into friendship lightly."

The point is simply this. It takes years and years to develop a sound foundation for doing business in a given country. Much that is done seems silly or strange to the home office. Indeed, the most common error made by home offices, once they have found representatives who can get results, is failure to take their advice and allow sufficient time for representatives to develop the proper contacts.

The second most common error, if that is what it can be called, is ignorance of the secret and hidden language of foreign cultures. In this article I have tried to show how five key topics—time, space, material possessions, friendship patterns, and business agreements—offer a starting point from which companies can begin to acquire the understanding necessary to do business in foreign countries.

Our present knowledge is meager, and much more research is needed before the businessman of the future can go abroad fully equipped for his work. Not only will he need to be well versed in the economics, law, and politics of the area, but he will have to understand, if not speak, the silent languages of other cultures.

Ralph G. Nichols

Listening Is a 10-Part Skill

White collar workers, on the average, devote at least 40 per cent of their work day to listening. Apparently 40 per cent of their salary is paid to them for listening. Yet tests of listening comprehension have shown that, without training, these employes listen at only 25 per cent efficiency.

This low level of performance becomes increasingly intolerable as evidence accumulates that it can be significantly raised. The component skills of listening are known. They boil down to this:

Learning through listening is primarily an inside job—inside action on the part of the listener. What he needs to do is to replace some common present attitudes with others.

Recognizing the dollar values in effective listening, many companies have added courses in this skill to their regular training programs. Some of the pioneers in this effort have been American Telephone & Telegraph Co., General Motors Corporation, Ford Motor Company, The Dow Chemical Company, Western Electric Co., Inc., Methods Engineering Council of Pittsburgh, Minnesota Mining & Manufacturing Co., Thompson Products, Inc., of Cleveland, and Rogers Corp. of Connecticut.

Warren Ganong of the Methods Engineering Council has compared trainees given a preliminary discussion of efficient listening with those not provided such discussion. On tests at the end of the courses the former achieved marks 12 to 15 per cent higher than did the latter.

"Listening Is a 10-Part Skill." Copyright © 1957 by Nation's Business. The Chamber of Commerce of the United States from *Successful Management* by Ralph Nichols. Reprinted by permission of Doubleday & Company, Inc., World's Work Ltd. and the author.

A. A. Tribbey, general personnel supervisor of the Wisconsin Telephone Company, in commenting on the results of a short conference course in which effective listening was stressed, declared: "It never fails to amaze us when we see the skill that is acquired in only three days."

The conviction seems to be growing that upper-level managers also need listening skill. As Dr. Earl Planty, executive counselor for the pharmaceutical firm of Johnson & Johnson puts it: "By far the most effective method by which executives can tap ideas of subordinates is sympathetic listening in the many day-to-day informal contacts within and outside the work place. There is no system that will do the job in an easier manner. . . . Nothing can equal an executive's willingness to hear."

A study of the 100 best listeners and the 100 worst listeners in the freshman class on the University of Minnesota campus has disclosed 10 guides to improved listening. Business people interested in improving their own performance can use them to analyze their personal strengths and weaknesses. The 10 guides to good listening are:

1. Find Area of Interest

All studies point to the advantage in being interested in the topic under discussion. Bad listeners usually declare the subject dry after the first few sentences. Once this decision is made, it serves to rationalize any and all inattention.

Good listeners follow different tactics. True, their first thought may be that the subject sounds dry. But a second one immediately follows, based on the realization that to get up and leave might prove a bit awkward.

The final reflection is that, being trapped anyhow, perhaps it might be well to learn if anything is being said that can be put to use.

The key to the whole matter of interest in a topic is the word *use*. Whenever we wish to listen efficiently, we ought to say to ourselves: "What's he saying that I can use? What worth-while ideas has he? Is he reporting any workable procedures? Anything that I can cash in, or with which I can make myself happier?" Such questions lead us to screen what we are hearing in a continual effort to sort out the elements of personal value. G. K. Chesterton spoke wisely indeed when he said, "There is no such thing as an uninteresting subject; there are only uninterested people."

2. Judge Content, Not Delivery

Many listeners alibi inattention to a speaker by thinking to themselves: "Who could listen to such a character? What an awful voice! Will he ever stop reading from his notes?"

The good listener reacts differently. He may well look at the speaker and think, "This man is inept. Seems like almost anyone ought to be able to talk better than that." But from this initial similarity he moves on to a different conclusion, thinking "But wait a minute. . . . I'm not interested in his personality or delivery. I want to find out what he knows. Does this man know some things that I need to know?"

Essentially we "listen with our own experience." Is the conveyer to be held responsible because we are poorly equipped to decode his message? We cannot understand everything we hear, but one sure way to raise the level of our understanding is to assume the responsibility which is inherently ours.

3. Hold Your Fire

Overstimulation is almost as bad as understimulation, and the two together constitute the twin evils of inefficient listening. The overstimulated listener gets too excited, or excited too soon, by the speaker. Some of us are greatly addicted to this weakness. For us, a speaker can seldom talk for more than a few minutes without touching upon a pet bias or conviction. Occasionally we are roused in support of the speaker's point; usually it is the reverse. In either case overstimulation reflects the desire of the listener to enter, somehow, immediately into the argument.

The aroused person usually becomes preoccupied by trying to do three things simultaneously: calculate what hurt is being done to his own pet ideas; plot an embarrassing question to ask the speaker; enjoy mentally all the discomfiture visualized for the speaker once the devastating reply to him is launched. With these things going on subsequent passages go unheard.

We must learn not to get too excited about a speaker's point until we are certain we thoroughly understand it. The secret is contained in the principle that we must always withhold evaluation until our comprehension is complete.

4. Listen for Ideas

Good listeners focus on central ideas; they tend to recognize the characteristic language in which central ideas are usually stated, and they are able to discriminate between fact and principle, idea and example, evidence and argument. Poor listeners are inclined to listen for the facts in every presentation.

To understand the fault, let us assume that a man is giving us instructions made up of facts A to Z. The man begins to talk. We hear fact A and think: "We've got to remember it!" So we begin a memory exercise by repeating "Fact A, fact A, fact A. . . ."

Meanwhile, the fellow is telling us fact B. Now we have two facts to memorize. We're so busy doing it that we miss fact C completely. And so it goes up to fact Z. We catch a few facts, garble several others and completely miss the rest.

It is a significant fact that only about 25 per cent of persons listening to a formal talk are able to grasp the speaker's central idea. To develop this skill requires an ability to recognize conventional organizational patterns, transitional language, and the speaker's use of recapitulation. Fortunately, all of these items can be readily mastered with a bit of effort.

5. Be Flexible

Our research has shown that our 100 worst listeners thought that note-taking and outlining were synonyms. They believed there was but one way to take notes—by making an outline.

Actually, no damage would be done if all talks followed some definite plan of organization. Unfortunately, less than half of even formal speeches are carefully organized. There are few things more frustrating than to try to outline an unoutlineable speech.

Note-taking may help or may become a distraction. Some persons try to take down everything in shorthand; the vast majority of us are far too voluminous even in longhand. While studies are not too clear on the point, there is some evidence to indicate that the volume of notes taken and their value to the taker are inversely related. In any case, the real issue is one of interpretation. Few of us have memories good enough to remember even the salient points we hear. If we can obtain brief, meaningful records of them for later review, we definitely improve our ability to learn and to remember.

The 100 best listeners had apparently learned early in life that if they wanted to be efficient note-takers they had to have more than one system of taking notes. They equipped themselves with four or five systems, and learned to adjust their system to the organizational pattern, or the absence of one, in each talk they heard. If we want to be good listeners, we must be flexible and adaptable note-takers.

6. Work at Listening

One of the most striking characteristics of poor listeners is their disinclination to spend any energy in a listening situation. College students, by their own testimony, frequently enter classes all worn out physically; assume postures which only seem to give attention to the speaker; and then proceed to catch up on needed rest or to reflect upon purely personal matters. This faking of attention is one of the worst habits afflicting us as a people.

Listening is hard work. It is characterized by faster heart action, quicker circulation of the blood, a small rise in bodily temperature. The overrelaxed listener is merely appearing to tune in, and then feeling conscience-free to pursue any of a thousand mental tangents.

For selfish reasons alone one of the best investments we can make is to give each speaker our conscious attention. We ought to establish eye contact and maintain it; to indicate by posture and facial expression that the occasion and the speaker's efforts are a matter of real concern to us. When we do these things we help the speaker to express himself more clearly, and we in turn profit by better understanding of the improved communication we have helped him to achieve. None of this necessarily implies acceptance of his point of view or favorable action upon his appeals. It is, rather, an expression of interest.

7. Resist Distractions

The good listeners tend to adjust quickly to any kind of abnormal situation; poor listeners tend to tolerate bad conditions and, in some instances, even to create distractions themselves.

We live in a noisy age. We are distracted not only by what we hear, but by what we see. Poor listeners tend to be readily influenced by all manner of distractions, even in an intimate face-to-face situation.

A good listener instinctively fights distraction. Sometimes the fight is easily won—by closing a door, shutting off the radio, moving closer to the person talking, or asking him to speak louder. If the distractions cannot be met that easily, then it becomes a matter of concentration.

8. Exercise Your Mind

Poor listeners are inexperienced in hearing difficult, expository material. Good listeners apparently develop an appetite for hearing a variety of presentations difficult enough to challenge their mental capacities.

Perhaps the one word that best describes the bad listener is "inexperienced." Although he spends 40 per cent of his communication day listening to something, he is inexperienced in hearing anything tough, technical, or expository. He has for years painstakingly sought light, recreational material. The problem he creates is deeply significant, because such a person is a poor producer in factory, office, or classroom.

Inexperience is not easily or quickly overcome. However, knowledge of our own weakness may lead us to repair it. We need never become too old to meet new challenges.

9. Keep Your Mind Open

Parallel to the blind spots which afflict human beings are certain psychological deaf spots which impair our ability to perceive and understand. These deaf spots are the dwelling place of our most cherished notions, convictions, and complexes. Often, when a speaker invades one of these areas with a word or phrase, we turn our mind to retraveling familiar mental pathways crisscrossing our invaded area of sensitivity.

It is hard to believe in moments of cold detachment that just a word or phrase can cause such emotional eruption. Yet with poor listeners it is frequently the case; and even with very good listeners it is occasionally the case. When such emotional deafness transpires, communicative efficiency drops rapidly to zero.

Among the words known thus to serve as red flags to some listeners are: mother-in-law, landlord, redneck, sharecropper, sissy, pervert, automation, clerk, income tax, communist, Red, dumb farmer, pink, "Greetings," antivivisectionist, evolution, square, punk, welsher.

Effective listeners try to identify and to rationalize the words or phrases most upsetting emotionally. Often the emotional impact of such words can be decreased through a free and open discussion of them with friends or associates.

10. Capitalize on Thought Speed

Most persons talk at a speed of about 125 words a minute. There is good evidence that if thought were measured in words per minute, most of us could think easily at about four times that rate. It is difficult—almost painful—to try to slow down our thinking speed. Thus we normally have about 400 words of thinking time to spare during every minute a person talks to us.

What do we do with our excess thinking time while someone is speaking? If we are poor listeners, we soon become impatient with the slow progress the speaker seems to be making. So our thoughts turn to something else for a moment, then dart back to the speaker. These brief side excursions of thought continue until our mind tarries too long on some enticing but irrelevant subject. Then, when our thoughts return to the person talking, we find he's far ahead of us. Now it's harder to follow him and increasingly easy to take off on side excursions. Finally we give up; the person is still talking, but our mind is in another world.

The good listener uses his thought speed to advantage; he constantly applies his spare thinking time to what is being said. It is not difficult once one has a definite pattern of thought to follow. To develop such a pattern we should:

• *Try to anticipate what a person is going to talk about. On the basis of what he's already said, ask yourself: "What's he trying to get at? What point is he going to make?"*

• *Mentally summarize what the person has been saying. What point has he made already, if any?*

• *Weigh the speaker's evidence by mentally questioning it. As he presents facts, illustrative stories and statistics, continually ask yourself: "Are they accurate? Do they come from an unprejudiced source? Am I getting the full picture, or is he telling me only what will prove his point?"*

• *Listen between the lines. The speaker doesn't always put everything that's important into words. The changing tones and volume of his voice may have a meaning. So may his facial expressions, the gestures he makes with his hands, the movement of his body.*

Not capitalizing on thought speed is our greatest single handicap. The differential between thought speed and speech speed breeds false feelings of security and mental tangents. Yet, through listening training, this same differential can be readily converted into our greatest asset.

Carl R. Rogers and Richard E. Farson

Active Listening

Section One—the Meaning of Active Listening

One basic responsibility of the supervisor or executive is the development, adjustment, and integration of individual employees. He tries to develop employee potential, delegate responsibility, and achieve cooperation. To do so, he must have, among other abilities, the ability to listen intelligently and carefully to those with whom he works.

There are, however, many kinds of listening skills. The lawyer, for example, when questioning a witness, listens for contradictions, irrelevancies, errors, and weaknesses. But this is not the kind of listening skill we are concerned with in this booklet. The lawyer usually is not listening in order to help the witness adjust or cooperate or produce. On the other hand, we will be concerned with listening skills which *will help* employees gain a clearer understanding of their situations, take responsibility, and cooperate with each other.

The kind of listening we have in mind is called "active listening." It is called "active" because the listener has a very definite responsibility. He does not passively absorb the words which are spoken to him. He actively tries to grasp the facts and the feelings in what he hears, and he tries, by his listening, to help the speaker work out his own problems. . . .

Reprinted by special permission. Industrial Relations Center, University of Chicago. August 1975.

Active listening does not necessarily mean long sessions spent listening to grievances, personal or otherwise. It is simply a way of approaching those problems which arise out of the usual day-to-day events of any job.

To be effective, active listening must be firmly grounded in the basic attitudes of the user. We cannot employ it as a technique if our fundamental attitudes are in conflict with its basic concepts. If we try, our behavior will be empty and sterile and our associates will be quick to recognize this. Until we can demonstrate a spirit which genuinely respects the potential worth of the individual, which considers his rights and trusts his capacity for self-direction, we cannot begin to be effective listeners.

What We Achieve by Listening

Active listening is an important way to bring about changes in people. Despite the popular notion that listening is a passive approach, clinical and research evidence clearly shows that sensitive listening is a most effective agent for individual personality change and group development. Listening brings about changes in people's attitudes toward themselves and others, and also brings about changes in their basic values and personal philosophy. People who have been listened to in this new and special way become more emotionally mature, more open to their experiences, less defensive, more democratic, and less authoritarian.

When people are listened to sensitively, they tend to listen to themselves with more care and make clear exactly what they are feeling and thinking. Group members tend to listen more to each other, become less argumentative, more ready to incorporate other points of view. Because listening reduces the threat of having one's ideas criticized, the person is better able to see them for what they are, and is more likely to feel that his contributions are worthwhile.

Not the least important result of listening is the change that takes place within the listener himself. Besides the fact that listening provides more information than any other activity, it builds deep, positive relationships and tends to alter constructively the attitudes of the listener. Listening is a growth experience. . . .

Section Two—How to Listen

Active listening aims to bring about changes in people. To achieve this end, it relies upon definite techniques—things to do and things to avoid doing. Before discussing these techniques, however, we should first understand why they are effective. To do so, we must understand how the individual personality develops.

The Growth of the Individual

Through all of our lives, from early childhood on, we have learned to think of ourselves in certain, very definite ways. We have built up pictures of ourselves. Sometimes these self-pictures are pretty realistic but at other times they are not. For example, an over-age, over-weight lady may fancy herself a youthful, ravishing siren, or an awkward teenager regard himself as a star athlete.

All of us have experiences which fit the way we need to think about ourselves. These we accept. But it is much harder to accept experiences which don't fit. And sometimes, if it is very important for us to hang on to this self-picture, we don't accept or admit these experiences at all.

These self-pictures are not necessarily attractive. A man, for example, may regard himself as incompetent and worthless. He may feel that he is doing his job poorly in spite of favorable appraisals by the company. As long as he has these feelings about himself he must deny any experiences which would seem not to fit this self-picture, in this case any that might indicate to him that he is competent. It is so necessary for him to maintain this self-picture that he is threatened by anything which would tend to change it. Thus, when the company raises his salary, it may seem to him only additional proof that he is a fraud. He must hold onto this self-picture, because, bad or good, it's the only thing he has by which he can identify himself.

This is why direct attempts to change this individual or change his self-picture are particularly threatening. He is forced to defend himself or to completely deny the experience. This denial of experience and defense of the self-picture tend to bring on rigidity of behavior and create difficulties in personal adjustment.

The active-listening approach, on the other hand, does not present a threat to the individual's self-picture. He does not have to defend it. He is able to explore it, see it for what it is, and make his own decision as to how realistic it is. And he is then in a position to change.

If I want to help a man reduce his defensiveness and become more adaptive, I must try to remove the threat of myself as his potential changer. As long as the atmosphere is threatening, there can be no effective communication. So I must create a climate which is neither critical, evaluative, nor moralizing. It must be an atmosphere of equality and freedom, permissiveness and understanding, acceptance and warmth. It is in this climate and this climate only that the individual feels safe enough to incorporate new experiences and new values into his concept of himself. Let's see how active listening helps to create this climate.

What to Avoid

When we encounter a person with a problem, our usual response is to try to change his way of looking at things—to get him to see his situation the way we see it, or would like him to see it. We plead, reason, scold, encourage, insult, prod—anything to bring about a change in the desired direction, that is, in the direction we want him to travel. What we seldom realize, however, is that, under these circumstances, we are usually responding to *our own* needs to see the world in certain ways. It is always difficult for us to tolerate and understand actions which are different from the ways in which *we* believe *we* should act. If, however, we can free ourselves from the need to influence and direct others in our own paths, we enable ourselves to listen with understanding, and thereby employ the most potent available agent of change.

One problem the listener faces is that of responding to demands for decisions, judgments, and evaluations. He is constantly called upon to agree or disagree with someone or something. Yet, as he well knows, the question or challenge frequently is a masked expression of feelings or needs which the speaker is far more anxious to communicate than he is to have the surface questions answered. Because he cannot speak these feelings openly, the speaker must disguise them to himself and to others in an acceptable form. . . .

Passing judgment, whether critical or favorable, makes free expression difficult. Similarly, advice and information are almost always seen as efforts to change a person and thus serve as barriers to his self-expression and the development of a creative relationship. Moreover, advice is seldom taken and information hardly ever utilized. The eager young trainee probably will not become patient just because he is advised that, "The road to success in business is a long, difficult one, and you must be patient." . . .

Interestingly, it is a difficult lesson to learn that positive *evaluations* are sometimes as blocking as negative ones. It is almost as destructive to the freedom of a relationship to tell a person that he is good or capable or right, as to tell him otherwise. To evaluate him positively may make it more difficult for him to tell of the faults that distress him or the ways in which he believes he is not competent.

Encouragement also may be seen as an attempt to motivate the speaker in certain directions or hold him off rather than as support. "I'm sure everything will work out O.K." is not a helpful response to the person who is deeply discouraged about a problem. . . .

What to Do

Just what does active listening entail, then? Basically, it requires that we get inside the speaker, that we grasp, *from his point of view,* just what it is he is communicating to us. More than that, we must convey to the speaker that we are seeing things from his point of view. To listen actively, then, means that there are several things we must do.

Listen for Total Meaning

Any message a person tries to get across usually has two components: the *content* of the message and the *feeling* or attitude underlying this content. Both are important, both give the message *meaning.* It is this total meaning of the message that we try to understand. For example, a machinist comes to his foreman and says, "I've finished that lathe set-up." This message has obvious content and perhaps calls upon the foreman for another work assignment. Suppose, on the other hand, that he says, "Well, I'm finally finished with that damned lathe set-up." The content is the same but the total meaning of the message has changed—and changed in an important way for both the foreman and the worker. Here sensitive listening can facilitate the relationship. Suppose the foreman were to respond by simply giving another work assignment. Would the employee feel that he had gotten his total message across? Would he feel free to talk to his foreman? Will he feel better about his job, more anxious to do good work on the next assignment?

Now, on the other hand, suppose the foreman were to respond with, "Glad to have it over with, huh?" or "Had a pretty rough time of it?" or "Guess you don't feel like doing anything like that again," or anything else that tells the worker that he heard and understands. It doesn't necessarily mean that the next work assignment need be changed or that he must spend an hour listening to the worker complain about the set-up problems he encountered. He may do a number of things differently in the light of the new information he has from the worker—but not necessarily. It's just that extra sensitivity on the part of the foreman which can transform an average working climate into a good one.

Respond to Feelings

In some instances the content is far less important than the feeling which underlies it. To catch the full flavor or meaning of the message one must respond particularly to the feeling component. . . .

Note All Cues

Not all communication is verbal. The speaker's words alone don't tell us everything he is communicating. And hence, truly sensitive listening requires that we become aware of several kinds of communication besides verbal. The way in which a speaker hesitates in his speech can tell us much about his feelings. So too can the inflection of his voice. . . . We should also note such things as the person's facial expressions, body posture, hand movements, eye movements, and breathing. All of these help to convey his total message.

What We Communicate by Listening

The first reaction of most people when they consider listening as a possible method for dealing with human beings is that listening cannot be sufficient in itself. Because it is passive, they feel, listening does not communicate anything to the speaker. Actually, nothing could be farther from the truth.

By consistently listening to a speaker you are conveying the idea that: "I'm interested in you as a person, and I think that what you feel is important. I respect your thoughts, and even if I don't agree with them, I know that they are valid for you. I feel sure that you have a contribution to make. I'm not trying to change you or evaluate you. I just want to understand you. I think you're worth listening to, and I want you to know that I'm the kind of a person you can talk to."

The subtle but most important aspect of this is that it is the *demonstration* of the message that works. While it is most difficult to convince someone that you respect him by *telling* him so, you are much more likely to get this message across by really *behaving* that way—by actually *having* and *demonstrating* respect for this person. Listening does this most effectively.

Like other behavior, listening behavior is contagious. . . . Just as one learns that anger is usually met with anger, argument with argument, and deception with deception, one can learn that listening can be met with listening. Every person who feels responsibility in a situation can set the tone of the interaction, and the important lesson in this is that any behavior exhibited by one person will eventually be responded to with similar behavior in the other person. . . .

Testing for Understanding

Because understanding another person is actually far more difficult than it at first seems, it is important to test constantly your ability to see the world in the way the speaker sees it. You can do this by reflecting in your own words what the speaker seems to mean by his words and actions. His response to this will tell you whether or not he feels understood. A good rule of thumb is to assume that one never really understands until he can communicate this understanding to the other's satisfaction. . . .

Section Three—Problems in Active Listening

The Personal Risk

To be effective at all in active listening, one must have a sincere interest in the speaker. We all live in glass houses as far as our attitudes are concerned. They always show through. And if we are only making a pretense of interest in the speaker, he will quickly pick this up, either consciously or unconsciously. And once he does, he will no longer express himself freely.

Active listening carries a strong element of personal risk. If we manage to accomplish what we are describing here—to sense deeply the feelings of another person, to understand the meaning his experiences have for him, to see the world as he sees it—we risk being changed ourselves. . . .

For the supervisor, the courage to take another's point of view generally means that he must see *himself* through another's eyes—he must be able to see himself as others see him. To do this may sometimes be unpleasant, but it is far more *difficult* than unpleasant. We are so accustomed to viewing ourselves in certain ways—to seeing and hearing only what we want to see and hear—that it is extremely difficult for a person to free himself from his needs to see things these ways. . . .

Hostile Expressions

The listener will often hear negative, hostile expressions directed at himself. Such expressions are always hard to listen to. No one likes to hear hostile action or words. And it is not easy to get to the point where one is strong enough to permit these attacks without finding it necessary to defend himself or retaliate. . . .

Out-of-Place Expressions

In any face-to-face situation, we will find instances of this type which will momentarily, if not permanently, block any communication. In business and industry any expressions of weakness or incompetency will generally be regarded as unacceptable and therefore will block good two-way communication. For example, it is difficult to listen to a supervisor tell of his feelings of failure in being able to "take charge" of a situation in his department because *all* administrators are supposed to be able to "take charge."

Accepting Positive Feelings

It is both interesting and perplexing to note that negative or hostile feelings or expressions are much easier to deal with in any face-to-face relationship than are truly and deeply positive feelings. This is especially true for the businessman because the culture expects him to be independent, bold, clever, and aggressive and manifest no feelings of warmth, gentleness, and intimacy. He therefore comes to regard these feelings as soft and inappropriate. But no matter how they are regarded, they remain a human need. The denial of these feelings in himself and his associates does not get the executive out of the problem in dealing with them. They simply become veiled and confused. If recognized they would work for the total effort; unrecognized, they work against it.

Emotional Danger Signals

The listener's own emotions are sometimes a barrier to active listening. When emotions are at their height, when listening is most necessary, it is most difficult to set aside one's own concerns and be understanding. Our emotions are often our own worst enemies when we try to become listeners. . . .

Listening to Ourselves

To listen to oneself is a prerequisite to listening to others. And it is often an effective means of dealing with the problems we have outlined above. When we are most aroused, excited, and demanding, we are least able to understand our own feelings and attitudes. Yet, in dealing with the problems of others, it becomes most important to be sure of one's own position, values, and needs.

The ability to recognize and understand the meaning which a particular episode has for you, with all the feelings which it stimulates in you, and the ability to express this meaning when you find it getting in the way of active listening, will clear the air and enable you once again to be free to listen. That is, if some person or situation touches off feelings within you which tend to block your attempts to listen with understanding, begin listening to yourself. It is much more helpful in developing effective relationships to avoid suppressing these feelings. Speak them out as clearly as you can, and try to enlist the other person as a listener to your feelings. A person's listening ability is limited by his ability to listen to himself.

Section Four—Active Listening and Company Goals

"How can listening improve production?"

"We're in business, and it's a rugged, fast, competitive affair. How are we going to find time to counsel our employees?"

"We have to concern ourselves with organizational problems first."

"We can't afford to spend all day listening when there's a job to be done."

"What's morale got to do with production?"

"Sometimes we have to sacrifice an individual for the good of the rest of the people in the company."

Those of us who are trying to advance the listening approach in industry hear these comments frequently. And because they are so honest and legitimate, they pose a real problem. Unfortunately, the answers are not so clear-cut as the questions.

Individual Importance

One answer is based on an assumption that is central to the listening approach. That assumption is: the kind of behavior which helps the individual will eventually be the best thing that could be done for the group. Or saying it another way: the things that are best for the individual are best for the company. This is a conviction of ours, based on our experience in psychology and education. The research evidence from industry is only beginning to come in. We find that putting the group first, at the expense of the individual, besides being an uncomfortable individual experience, *does* unify the group. In fact, it tends to make the group less a group. The members become anxious and suspicious.

We are not at all sure in just what ways the group does benefit from a concern demonstrated for an individual, but we have several strong leads. One is that the group feels more secure when an individual member is being listened to and provided for with concern and sensitivity. And we assume that a secure group will ultimately be a better group. When each individual feels that he need not fear exposing himself to the group, he is likely to contribute more freely and spontaneously. . . .

Listening and Production

As to whether or not listening or any other activity designed to better human relations in an industry actually raises production—whether morale has a definite relationship to production is not known for sure. There are some who frankly hold that there is no relationship to be expected between morale and production—that production often depends upon the social misfit, the eccentric, or the isolate. And there are some who simply choose to work in a climate of cooperation and harmony, in a high-morale group, quite aside from the question of increased production.

A report from the Survey Research Center[2] at the University of Michigan on research conducted at the Prudential Life Insurance Company lists seven findings relating to production and morale. First-line supervisors in high-production work groups were found to differ from those in low-production work groups in that they:

1. Are under less close supervision from their own supervisors.
2. Place less direct emphasis upon production as the goal.

3. Encourage employee participation in the making of decisions.
4. Are more employee-centered.
5. Spend more of their time in supervision and less in straight production work.
6. Have a greater feeling of confidence in their supervisory roles.
7. Feel that they know where they stand with the company.

After mentioning that other dimensions of morale, such as identification with the company, intrinsic job satisfaction, and satisfaction with job status, were not found significantly related to productivity, the report goes on to suggest the following psychological interpretation:

People are more effectively motivated when they are given some degree of freedom in the way in which they do their work than when every action is prescribed in advance. They do better when some degree of decision-making about their jobs is possible than when all decisions are made for them. They respond more adequately when they are treated as personalities than as cogs in a machine. In short if the ego motivations of self-determination, of self-expression, of a sense of personal worth can be tapped, the individual can be more effectively energized. The use of external sanctions, or pressuring for production may work to some degree, but not to the extent that the more internalized motives do.

The Survey Research Center has also conducted studies among workers in other industries. In discussing the results of these studies, Robert L. Kahn writes:

In the studies of clerical workers, railroad workers, and workers in heavy industry, the supervisors with the better production records gave a larger proportion of their time to super-

[2] "Productivity, Supervision, and Employee Morale," *Human Relations,* Series 1, Report 1 (Ann Arbor, Mich.: Survey Research Center, University of Michigan).

visory functions, especially to the interpersonal aspects of their jobs. The supervisors of the lower-producing sections were more likely to spend their time in tasks which the men themselves were performing, or in the paper-work aspects of their jobs.[3]

Maximum Creativeness

There may never be enough research evidence to satisfy everyone on this question. But speaking from a business point of view, in terms of the problem of developing resources for production, the maximum creativeness and productive effort of the human beings in the organization are the richest untapped source of power still existing. The difference between the maximum productive capacity of people and that output which industry is now realizing is immense. We simply suggest that this maximum capacity might be closer to realization if we sought to release the motivation that already exists within people rather than try to stimulate them externally.

This releasing of the individual is made possible first of all by sensitive listening, with respect and understanding. . . .

[3] Robert L. Kahn, "The Human Factors Underlying Industrial Productivity," *Michigan Business Review*, November 1952.

G. L. Clements, president of Jewel Tea Co., Inc., in talking about the collaborative approach to management says:

> We feel that this type of approach recognizes that there is a secret ballot going on at all times among the people in any business. They vote for or against their supervisors. A favorable vote for the supervisor shows up in the cooperation, teamwork, understanding, and production of the group. To win this secret ballot, each supervisor must share the problems of his group and work for them.[4]

The decision to spend time listening to his employees is a decision each supervisor or executive has to make for himself. Executives seldom have much to do with products or processes. They have to deal with people who must in turn deal with people who will deal with products or processes. The higher one goes up the line the more he will be concerned with human relations problems, simply because people are all he has to work with. The minute we take a man from his bench and make him a foreman he is removed from the basic production of goods and now must begin relating to individuals instead of nuts and bolts. People are different from things, and our foreman is called upon for a different line of skills completely. His new tasks call upon him to be a special kind of person. The development of himself as a listener is a first step in becoming this special person.

[4] G. L. Clements, "Time for 'Democracy in Action' at the Executive Level," an address given before the A.M.A. Personnel Conference, February 28, 1951.

Keith Davis

Management Communication and the Grapevine

Communication is involved in all human relations. It is the "nervous system" of any organized group, providing the information and understanding necessary for high productivity and morale. For the individual company it is a continuous process, a way of life, rather than a one-shot campaign. Top management, therefore, recognizes the importance of communication and wants to do something about it. But what? Often, in its frustration, management has used standard communication "packages" instead of dealing situationally with its individual problems. Or it has emphasized the means (communication techniques) rather than the ends (objectives of communication).

One big factor which management has tended to overlook is communication *within its own group.* Communication to the worker and from the worker is dependent on effective management communication; and clearly this in turn requires informal as well as formal channels.

The Grapevine

A particularly neglected aspect of management communication concerns that informal channel, the grapevine. There is no dodging the fact that, as a carrier of news and gossip among executives and supervisors, the grapevine often affects the af-

fairs of management. The proof of this is the strong feelings that different executives have about it. Some regard the grapevine as an evil—a thorn in the side which regularly spreads rumor, destroys morale and reputations, leads to irresponsible actions, and challenges authority. Some regard it as a good thing because it acts as a safety valve and carries news fast. Others regard it as a very mixed blessing.

Whether the grapevine is considered an asset or a liability, it is important for executives to try to understand it. For one thing is sure: although no executive can absolutely control the grapevine, he can *influence* it. And since it is here to stay, he should learn to live with it.

Perspective

Of course, the grapevine is only part of the picture of communication in management. There is also formal communication—via conferences, reports, memoranda, and so on; this provides the basic core of information, and many administrators rely on it almost exclusively because they think it makes their job simpler to have everything reduced to explicit terms—as if that were possible! Another important part of the picture is the expression of attitudes, as contrasted with the transmission of information (which is what we will be dealing with in this article). Needless to say, all these factors influence the way the grapevine works in a given company, just as the grapevine in turn influences them.

In this article I want to examine (a) the significance, character, and operation of management communication patterns, with particular emphasis on the grapevine; and (b) the influence that various factors, such as organization and the chain of procedure, have upon such patterns. From this analysis, then, it will be possible to point up (c) the practical implications for management.

As for the research basis of the analysis, the major points are these:

1. *Company studied*—The company upon which the research is based is a real one. I shall refer to it as the "Jason Company." A manufacturer of leather goods, it has 67 people in the management group. . . .

2. *Methodology*—The methods used to study management communication in the Jason Company are new ones. Briefly, the basic approach was to learn from each communication recipient how he first received a given piece of information and then to trace it back to its source. Suppose D and E said they received it from G; G said he received it from B; and B from A. All the chains or sequences were plotted in this way—A to B to G to D and E—and when the data from all recipients were assembled, the pattern of the flow of communication emerged. . . .

Significant Characteristics

In the Jason Company many of the usual grapevine characteristics were found along with others less well known. For purposes of this discussion, the four most significant characteristics are these:

1. *Speed of transmission*—Traditionally the grapevine is fast, and this showed up in the Jason Company.

For example, a certain manager had an addition to his family at the local hospital at 11 o'clock at night, and by 2:00 p.m. the next day 46% of the whole management group knew about the event. The news was transmitted only by grapevine and mostly by face-to-face conversation, with an occa-

sional interoffice telephone call. Most communications occurred immediately before work began, during "coffee hour," and during lunch hour. The five staff executives who knew of the event learned of it during "coffee hour," indicating that the morning rest period performed an important social function for the staff as well as providing relaxation.

2. *Degree of selectivity*—The grapevine here showed that it could be highly selective and discriminating.

For example, the local representative of the company which carried the employee group insurance contract planned a picnic for company executives. The Jason Company president decided to invite 36 executives, mostly from higher executive levels. The grapevine immediately went to work spreading this information, but it was carried to *only two of the 31 executives not invited.* The grapevine communicators thought the news was confidential, so they had told only those who they thought would be invited (they had to guess, since they did not have access to the invitation list). The two uninvited executives who knew the information were foremen who were told by their invited superintendent; he had a very close working relationship with them and generally kept them well informed.

Many illustrations like the above could be gathered to show that the grapevine can be discriminating. Whether it may be *counted on* in that respect, however, is another question. . . .

3. *Locale of operation*—The grapevine of company news operates mostly at the place of work. . . .

The significance of at-the-company grapevines is this: since management has some control over the work environment, it has an opportunity to influence the grapevine. By exerting such influence the manager can more closely integrate grapevine interests with those of the formal communication system, and he can use it for effectively spreading more significant items of information than those commonly carried.

4. *Relation to formal communication*—Formal and informal communication systems tend to be jointly active, or jointly inactive. Where formal communication was inactive at the Jason Company, the grapevine did not rush in to fill the void (as has often been suggested[1]); instead, there simply was lack of communication. Similarly, where there was effective formal communication, there was an active grapevine.

Informal and formal communication may supplement each other. Often formal communication is simply used to confirm or to expand what has already been communicated by grapevine. . . .

Spreading Information

Now let us turn to the actual operation of the grapevine. How is information passed along? What is the relationship among the various people who are involved?

Human communication requires at least two persons, but each person acts independently. Person A may talk or write, but he has not *communicated* until person B receives. The individual is, therefore, a basic communication unit. That is, he is one "link" in the communication "chain" for any bit of information.

The formal communication chain is largely determined by the chain of command or by formal procedures, but the grapevine chain is more flexible. There are four different ways of visualizing it, as Exhibit I indicates:

1. *The single-strand chain*—A tells B, who tells C, who tells D, and so on; this makes for a tenuous chain to a distant receiver. Such a chain is usually in mind when one speaks of how the grapevine distorts and filters information until the original item is not recognizable.

2. *The gossip chain*—A seeks and tells everyone else.

3. *The probability chain*—A communicates randomly, say, to F and D, in accordance with the laws of probability; then F and D tell others in the same manner.

4. *The cluster chain*—A tells three selected others; perhaps one of them tells two others; and then one of these two tells one other. This was virtually the only kind of chain found in the Jason Company, and may well be the normal one in industry generally.

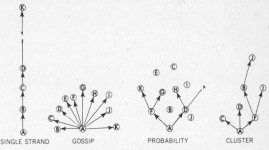

SINGLE STRAND   GOSSIP   PROBABILITY   CLUSTER

EXHIBIT I. TYPES OF COMMUNICATION CHAINS

Active Minority

The predominance of the cluster chain at the Jason Company means that only a few of the persons who knew a unit of information ever transmitted it—what Jacobson and Seashore call the "liaison" individuals.[2] All others who received the information did not transmit it; they acted merely as passive receivers.

For example, when a quality-control problem occurred, 68 percent of the executives received the information, but only 20 percent transmitted it. Again, when an executive planned to resign to enter the insurance business, 81 percent of the executives knew about it, but only 11 percent passed

[1] For example, see National Industrial Conference Board, *Communicating with Employees,* Studies in Personnel Policy, No. 129 (New York, 1952), p. 34.

[2] Eugene Jacobson and Stanley E. Seashore, "Communication Practices in Complex Organizations," *The Journal of Social Issues,* VII, 3 (1951), p. 37.

the news on to others. Those liaison individuals who told the news to more than one other person amounted to less than 10 percent of the 67 executives in each case. . . .

The above findings indicate that if management wants more communication, it should increase the number and/or effectiveness of its liaison individuals. This appears to be a large order, but it is entirely possible. Liaison individuals tend to act in a predictable way. If an individual's unit of information concerns a job function in which he is interested, he is likely to tell others. If his information is about a person with whom he is associated socially, he also is likely to tell others. Furthermore, the sooner he knows of an event after it happened, the more likely he is to tell others. If he gets the information late, he does not want to advertise his late receipt of it by telling it to others.

In other words, three well-known communication principles which are so often mentioned in relation to attitudes also have a major influence on the spread of information by liaison individuals:

1. Tell people about what will affect them (job interest).

2. Tell people what they want to know, rather than simply what you want them to know (job and social interest).

3. Tell people soon (timing).

Organizational Effects

The way an organization is divided horizontally into organizational levels and vertically into functions, such as production and sales, obviously has effects on management communication, for it cuts each company's over-all administrative function into small work assignments, or jobs, and sets each management person in certain relationships to others in his company.

Horizontal Levels

Organizational levels are perhaps the more dramatic in effect because they usually carry authority, pay increases, and status. From the communication point of view, they are especially important because of their number. In a typical firm there are usually several management levels, but only one or two worker levels; furthermore, as the firm grows, the management levels increase in number, while the worker levels remain stationary.

Communication problems are aggravated by these additional levels because the chain of communication is lengthened and complicated. Indeed, just because of this, some companies have been led to try to reduce the number of intermediate management levels. Our concern here is with the patterns of communication among individuals at the different levels.

At the Jason Company, executives at *higher* levels communicated more often and with more people than did executives at *lower* levels. In other words, the predominant communication flow was downward or horizontal. When an event happened at the bottom level, usually the news did reach a high level; but a single line of communication sufficed to carry it there, and from that point it went downward and outward in the same volume and manner (cluster chain) as if it had originated at the top.

Accordingly, the higher an executive was in the organizational hierarchy (with the exception of nonresident executives), the greater was his knowledge of company events. This was true of events which happened both above his level and below his level. Thus, if the president was out of town, a greater proportion at the fourth level knew of it than at the sixth level. Or—and this is less to be expected—if a foreman at the sixth level had an accident, a larger proportion of executives at the third level knew of it than at the fourth level, or even than at the sixth level where the accident happened. The more noteworthy the event, of course, the more likely it was to be known at upper levels—but, in a company of this size, it had to be quite trivial indeed before it failed to reach the ears of top executives.

The converse follows that in terms of communications transmitted and received the sixth and lowest level of supervision, the foreman level, was largely isolated from all other management. The average foreman was very hesitant to communicate with other members of management; and on the rare occasions when he did, he usually chose someone at his own level and preferably in his own department. Members of this group tended to be the last links in management communication, regardless of whether the chains were formal or informal.

A further significant fact concerns the eight departmental superintendents at the fourth level. Six of them supervised foremen directly; two others, with larger departments, each had a single line assistant between him and his foremen. The two who had line assistants were much more active in the communication chains than were the six others; indeed, all but one of the six appeared to have little to do with their foremen except in a formal way.

Perhaps the clue is that, with increased organizational levels, those at the higher (and hence further removed) levels both recognize a greater need for communication and have more time to practice it!

Functional Groups

Functionalization, the second important way in which an organization is "cut up," also has a significant impact on communication in management. The functions which are delegated to a manager help to determine the people he contacts, his relationships with them, his status, and, as a result, the degree to which he receives and trans-

mits information. More specifically, his role in communication is affected (a) by his position in the chain of command and (b) by his position in the chain of procedure, which involves the sequence of work performance and cuts across chains of command, as when a report goes from the superintendent in one chain of command to the chief engineer in another chain of command and to the controller in still another.

In the Jason Company the effects of functionalization showed up in three major ways:

1. *Staff men "in the know"*—More staff executives than line men usually knew about any company event. This was true at each level of management as well as for the management group as a whole. For example, when the president of the company made a trip to seek increased governmental allotments of hides to keep the line tannery operating at capacity, only 4 percent of the line executives knew the purpose of the trip, but 25 percent of the staff men did. In another case, when a popular line superintendent was awarded a hat as a prize in a training program for line superintendents, within six days a larger proportion of the staff executives than of the line executives knew about this event.

The explanation is not just that, with one staff executive to every three line executives, there were more line executives to be informed. More important is the fact that the *chain of procedure* usually involved more staff executives than line executives. Thus, when the superintendent was awarded his hat, a line executive had approved the award, but a staff personnel executive had processed it and a staff accounting executive had arranged for the special check.

Also the staff was more *mobile* than the line. Staff executives in such areas as personnel and control found that their duties both required and allowed them to get out of their offices, made it easy for them to walk through other departments without someone wondering whether they were "not working," to get away for coffee, and so on—

all of which meant they heard more news from the other executives they talked with. (In a larger company staff members might be more fixed to their chairs, but the situation in the Jason Company doubtless applies to a great many other businesses.)

Because of its mobility and its role in the chain of procedure, the staff not only received but also transmitted communications more actively than did the line. Most of these communications were oral; at least in this respect, the staff was not the "paper mill" it is often said to be. It seems obvious that management would do well to make conscious use of staff men as communicators.

2. *Cross-communication*—A second significant effect of functionalization in the Jason Company was that the predominant flow of information for events of general interest was between the four large areas of production, sales, finance and office, and industrial relations, rather than within them. That is, if a production executive had a bit of news of general interest, he was more likely to tell a sales, finance, or personnel executive than another production executive.

Social relationships played a part in this, with executives in the various groups being lodge brothers, members of the same church, neighbors, parents of children in the same schools, and so on. In these relationships the desire to make an impression was a strong motivation for cross-communication, since imparting information to executives outside his own area served to make a man feel that the others would consider him "in the know." Procedural relationships, discussed earlier, also encouraged the executives to communicate across functional lines.

Since communications tended not to stay within an area, such as production, they tended even less to follow chains of command from boss to subboss to sub-sub-boss. Indeed, the chain of command was seldom used in this company except for very formal communications. Thus Exhibit II reproduces a communication chain concerning a

quality control problem in production, first brought to the attention of a group sales manager in a letter from a customer. Although it was the type of problem that could have been communicated along the chain of command, the exhibit shows that, of 14 communications, only 3 were within the chain of command and only 6 remained within one functional area—sales—where the information was first received.

The fact that the chain of command may affect management communication patterns less than procedural and social influences—which has shown up in other companies too[3]—means that management needs to devote considerably more attention to the problems and opportunities of cross-communication.

3. *Group isolation*—The research in the Jason Company revealed that some functional groups were consistently isolated from communication chains. Also, there were other groups which received information but did not transmit it, and thus contributed to the same problem—the uneven spread of information through the company. Here are three examples at the foreman level illustrating different degrees of failure to participate in the communication process and different reasons for this failure:

a. The foremen in one group were generally left out of communication chains. These men were of a different nationality from that of the rest of the employees, performed dirty work, and worked in a separate building. Also, their work fitted into the manufacturing process in such a way that it was seldom necessary for other executives to visit their work location.

b. Another group often was in a communication chain but on the tail end of it. They were in a separate building some distance from the main manufacturing area, their function was not in the main manufacturing procedure, and they

[3] See Carroll L. Shartle, "Leadership and Executive Performance," *Personnel* (March 1949), pp. 377-378.

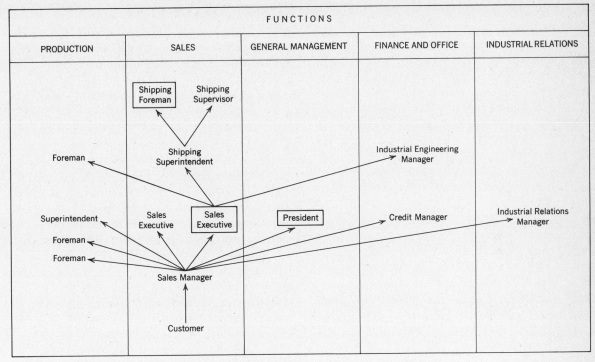

Exhibit II. Communication Chain for a Quality Control Problem

usually received information late. They had little chance or incentive to communicate to other executives.

c. A third group both received and transmitted information, but transmitted only within a narrow radius. Although they were in the midst of the main work area, they failed to communicate with other functional groups because their jobs required constant attention and they felt socially isolated.

In sum, the reasons for group isolation at the Jason Company were: geographical separation; work association (being outside the main procedures or at the end of them); social isolation; and organizational level (the lower the level of a group, the greater its tendency to be isolated).

Obviously, it is not often feasible for management to undertake to remove such causes of group isolation as geographical or social separation. On the other hand, it may well be possible to compensate for them. For example, perhaps the volume of formal communication to men who happen to be in a separate building can be increased, or arrangements can be made for a coffee break that will bring men who are isolated because of the nature of their work or their nationality into greater contact with other supervisors. In each situation management should be able to work out measures that would be appropriate to the individual circumstances.

Conclusion

The findings at the Jason Company have yet to be generalized by research in other industries, but they provide these starting points for action:

1. If management wants more communication among executives and supervisors, one way is to increase the number and effectiveness of the liaison individuals.

2. It should count on staff executives to be more active than line executives in spreading information.

3. It should devote more attention to cross-communication—that is, communication between men in different departments. It is erroneous to consider the chain of command as *the* communication system because it is only one of many influences. Indeed, procedural and social factors are even more important.

4. It should take steps to compensate for the fact that some groups are "isolated" from communication chains.

5. It should encourage further research about management grapevines in order to provide managers with a deeper understanding of them and to find new ways of integrating grapevine activities with the objectives of the firm.

6. "Ecco analysis," the recently developed research approach used at the Jason Company, should be useful for future studies.

If management wants to do a first-class communication job, at this stage it needs fewer medicines and more diagnoses. Communication analysis has now passed beyond "pure research" to a point where it is immediately useful to top management in the individual firm. The patterns of communication that show up should serve to indicate both the areas where communication is most deficient and the channels through which information can be made to flow most effectively.

In particular, no administrator in his right mind would try to abolish the management grapevine. It is as permanent as humanity is. Nevertheless, many administrators have abolished the grapevine from *their own minds*. They think and act without giving adequate weight to it or, worse, try to ignore it. This is a mistake. The grapevine is a factor to be reckoned with in the affairs of management. The administrator should analyze it and should consciously try to influence it.

Peter F. Drucker

How to Be an Employee

Most of you graduating today will be employees all your working life, working for somebody else and for a pay check. And so will most, if not all, of the thousands of other young Americans graduating this year in all the other schools and colleges across the country.

Ours has become a society of employees. A hundred years or so ago only one out of every five Americans at work was employed, i.e., worked for somebody else. Today only one out of five is not employed but working for himself. And where fifty years ago "being employed" meant working as a factory laborer or as a farmhand, the employee of today is increasingly a middle-class person with a substantial formal education, holding a professional or management job requiring intellectual and technical skills. Indeed, two things have characterized American society during these last fifty years: the middle and upper classes have become employees; and middle-class and upper-class employees have been the fastest-growing groups in our working population—growing so fast that the industrial worker, that oldest child of the Industrial Revolution, has been losing in numerical importance despite the expansion of industrial production.

This is one of the most profound social changes any country has ever undergone. It is, however, a perhaps even greater change for the individual young man about to start. Whatever he does, in all likelihood he will do it as an employee; wherever he aims, he will have to try to reach it through being an employee. . . .

Abridgement of "How to Be an Employee" by Peter Drucker from *Fortune Magazine, (May 1952) p. 126.* Reprinted by permission of author.

Being an employee is . . . the one common characteristic of most careers today. The special profession or skill is visible and clearly defined; and a well-laid-out sequence of courses, degrees, and jobs leads into it. But being an employee is the foundation. And it is much more difficult to prepare for it. Yet there is no recorded information on the art of being an employee.

The first question we might ask is: what can you learn in college that will help you in being an employee? The schools teach a great many things of value to the future accountant, the future doctor, or the future electrician. Do they also teach anything of value to the future employee? The answer is: "Yes—they teach the one thing that it is perhaps most valuable for the future employee to know. But very few students bother to learn it."

This one basic skill is the ability to organize and express ideas in writing and in speaking.

As an employee you work with and through other people. This means that your success as an employee—and I am talking of much more here than getting promoted—will depend on your ability to communicate with people and to present your own thoughts and ideas to them so they will both understand what you are driving at and be persuaded. The letter, the report or memorandum, the ten-minute spoken "presentation" to a committee are basic tools of the employee.

If you work as a soda jerker you will, of course, not need much skill in expressing yourself to be effective. If you work on a machine your ability to express yourself will be of little importance. But as soon as you move one step up from the bottom, your effectiveness depends on your ability to reach others through the spoken or the written word. And the further away your job is from manual work, the larger the organization of which you are an employee, the more important it will be that you know how to convey your thoughts in writing or speaking. In the very large organization, whether it is the government, the large business corporation, or the Army, this ability to express oneself is perhaps the most important of all the skills a man can possess.

Of course, skill in expression is not enough by itself. You must have something to say in the first place. The popular picture of the engineer, for instance, is that of a man who works with a slide rule, T square, and compass. And engineering students reflect this picture in their attitude toward the written word as something quite irrelevant to their jobs. But the effectiveness of the engineer—and with it his usefulness—depends as much on his ability to make other people understand his work as it does on the quality of the work itself.

Expressing one's thoughts is one skill that the school can really teach, especially to people born without natural writing or speaking talent. Many other skills can be learned later—in this country there are literally thousands of places that offer training to adult people at work. But the foundations for skill in expression have to be laid early: an interest in and an ear for language; experience in organizing ideas and data, in brushing aside the irrelevant, in wedding outward form and inner content into one structure; and above all, the habit of verbal expression. If you do not lay these foundations during your school years, you may never have an opportunity again.

If you were to ask me what strictly vocational courses there are in the typical college curriculum, my answer—now that the good old habit of the "theme a day" has virtually disappeared—would be: the writing of poetry and the writing of short stories. Not that I expect many of you to become poets or short-story writers—far from it. But these two courses offer the easiest way to obtain some skill in expression. They force one to be economical with language. They force one to organize

thought. They demand of one that he give meaning to every word. They train the ear for language, its meaning, its precision, its overtones—and its pitfalls. Above all they force one to write.

I know very well that the typical employer does not understand this as yet, and that he may look with suspicion on a young college graduate who has majored, let us say, in short-story writing. But the same employer will complain—and with good reason—that the young men whom he hires when they get out of college do not know how to write a simple report, do not know how to tell a simple story, and are in fact virtually illiterate. And he will conclude—rightly—that the young men are not really effective, and certainly not employees who are likely to go very far.

The next question to ask is: what kind of employee should you be? Pay no attention to what other people tell you. This is one question only you can answer. It involves a choice in four areas—a choice you alone can make, and one you cannot easily duck. But to make the choice you must first have tested yourself in the world of jobs for some time.

Here are the four decisions—first in brief outline, then in more detail:

1. Do you belong in a job calling primarily for faithfulness in the performance of routine work and promising security? Or do you belong in a job that offers a challenge to imagination and ingenuity—with the attendant penalty for failure?

2. Do you belong in a large organization or in a small organization? Do you work better through channels or through direct contacts? Do you enjoy more being a small cog in a big and powerful machine or a big wheel in a small machine?

3. Should you start at the bottom and try to work your way up, or should you try to start near the top? On the lowest rung of the promotional ladder, with its solid and safe footing but also with a very long climb ahead? Or on the aerial trapeze of "a management trainee," or some other staff position close to management?

4. Finally, are you going to be more effective and happy as a specialist or as a "generalist," that is, in an administrative job?

Let me spell out what each of these four decisions involves:

The decision between secure routine work and insecure work challenging the imagination and ingenuity is the one decision most people find easiest to make. You know very soon what kind of person you are. Do you find real satisfaction in the precision, order, and system of a clearly laid-out job? Do you prefer the security not only of knowing what your work is today and what it is going to be tomorrow, but also security in your job, in your relationship to the people above, below, and next to you, and economic security? Or are you one of those people who tend to grow impatient with anything that looks like a "routine" job? These people are usually able to live in a confused situation in which their relations to the people around them are neither clear nor stable. And they tend to pay less attention to economic security, find it not too upsetting to change jobs, etc. . . .

The difference is one of basic personality. It is not too much affected by a man's experiences; he is likely to be born with the one or the other. The need for economic security is often as not an outgrowth of a need for psychological security rather than a phenomenon of its own. But precisely because the difference is one of basic temperament, the analysis of what kind of temperament you possess is so vital. A man might be happy in work for which he has little *aptitude;* he might be quite successful in it. But he can be neither happy nor successful in a job for which he is *temperamentally* unfitted.

You hear a great many complaints today about the excessive security-consciousness of our young people. My complaint is the opposite: in the large organizations especially there are not enough job opportunities for those young people who need challenge and risk. Jobs in which there is greater emphasis on conscientious performance of well-organized duties rather than on imagination—especially for the beginner—are to be found, for instance, in the inside jobs in banking or insurance, which normally offer great job security but not rapid promotion or large pay. The same is true of most government work, of the railroad industry, particularly in the clerical and engineering branches, and of most public utilities. The bookkeeping and accounting areas, especially in the larger companies, are generally of this type too—though a successful comptroller is an accountant with great management and business imagination.

At the other extreme are such areas as buying, selling, and advertising, in which the emphasis is on adaptability, on imagination, and on a desire to do new and different things. In those areas, by and large, there is little security, either personal or economic. The rewards, however, are high and come more rapidly. Major premium on imagination—though of a different kind and coupled with dogged persistence on details—prevails in most research and engineering work. Jobs in production, as supervisor or executive, also demand much adaptability and imagination.

Contrary to popular belief, very small business requires, above all, close attention to daily routine. Running a neighborhood drugstore or a small grocery, or being a toy jobber, is largely attention to details. But in very small business there is also room for quite a few people of the other personality type—the innovator or imaginer. If successful, a man of this type soon ceases to be in a very small business. For the real innovator there is, still, no more promising opportunity in this country than that of building a large out of a very small business.

Almost as important is the decision between working for a large and for a small organization. The difference is perhaps not so great as that between the secure, routine job and the insecure, imaginative job; but the wrong decision can be equally serious.

There are two basic differences between the large and small enterprise. In the small enterprise you operate primarily through personal contacts. In the large enterprise you have established "policies," "channels" of organization, and fairly rigid procedures. In the small enterprise you have, moreover, immediate effectiveness in a very small area. You can see the effect of your work and of your decisions right away, once you are a little bit above the ground floor. In the large enterprise even the man at the top is only a cog in a big machine. To be sure, his actions affect a much greater area than the actions and decisions of the man in the small organization, but his effectiveness is remote, indirect, and elusive. In a small and even in a middle-sized business you are normally exposed to all kinds of experiences, and expected to do a great many things without too much help or guidance. In the large organization you are normally taught one thing thoroughly. In the small one the danger is of becoming a jack-of-all-trades and master of none. In the large one it is of becoming the man who knows more and more about less and less.

There is one other important thing to consider: do you derive a deep sense of satisfaction from being a member of a well-known organization— General Motors, the Bell Telephone System, the government? Or is it more important to you to be a well-known and important figure within your own small pond? . . .

You may well think it absurd to say that anyone has a choice between beginning at the bottom and beginning near the top. And indeed I do not mean that you have any choice between beginner's jobs and, let us say, a vice presidency at General Electric. But you do have a choice between a position at the bottom of the hierarchy and a staff position that is outside the hierarchy but in view of the top. It is an important choice.

In every organization, even the smallest, there are positions that, while subordinate, modestly paid, and usually filled with young and beginning employees, nonetheless are not at the bottom. There are positions as assistant to one of the bos-

ses; there are positions as private secretary; there are liaison positions for various departments; and there are positions in staff capacities, in industrial engineering, in cost accounting, in personnel, etc. Every one of these gives a view of the whole rather than of only one small area. Every one of them normally brings the holder into the deliberations and discussions of the people at the top, if only as a silent audience or perhaps only as an errand boy. Every one of these positions is a position "near the top," however humble and badly paid it may be.

On the other hand the great majority of beginner's jobs are at the bottom, where you begin in a department or in a line of work in the lowest-paid and simplest function, and where you are expected to work your way up as you acquire more skill and more judgment.

Different people belong in these two kinds of jobs. In the first place, the job "near the top" is insecure. You are exposed to public view. Your position is ambiguous; by yourself you are a nobody—but you reflect the boss's status; in a relatively short time you may even speak for the boss. You may have real power and influence. In today's business and government organization the hand that writes the memo rules the committee; and the young staff man usually writes the memos, or at least the first draft. But for that very reason everybody is jealous of you. You are a youngster who has been admitted to the company of his betters, and is therefore expected to show unusual ability and above all unusual discretion and judgment. Good performance in such a position is often the key to rapid advancement. But to fall down may mean the end of all hopes of ever getting anywhere within the organization.

At the bottom, on the other hand, there are very few opportunities for making serious mistakes. You are amply protected by the whole apparatus of authority. The job itself is normally simple, requiring little judgment, discretion, or initiative. Even excellent performance in such a job is unlikely to speed promotion. But one also has to fall down in a rather spectacular fashion for it to be noticed by anyone but one's immediate superior.

There are a great many careers in which the increasing emphasis is on specialization. You find these careers in engineering and in accounting, in production, in statistical work, and in teaching. But there is an increasing demand for people who are able to take in a great area at a glance, people who perhaps do not know too much about any one field—though one should always have one area of real competence. There is, in other words, a demand for people who are capable of seeing the forest rather than the trees, of making over-all judgments. And these "generalists" are particularly needed for administrative positions, where it is their job to see that other people do the work, where they have to plan for other people, to organize other people's work, to initiate it and appraise it.

The specialist understands one field: his concern is with technique, tools, media. He is a "trained" man; and his educational background is properly technical or professional. The generalist—and especially the administrator—deals with people; his concern is with leadership, with planning, with direction giving, and with coordination. He is an "educated" man; and the humanities are his strongest foundation. Very rarely is a specialist capable of being an administrator. And very rarely is a good generalist also a good specialist in a particular field. Any organization needs both kinds of people, though different organizations need them in different ratios. It is your job to find out, during your apprenticeship, into which of those two job categories you fit, and to plan your career accordingly.

Your first job may turn out to be the right job for you—but this is pure accident. Certainly you should not change jobs constantly or people will become suspicious—rightly—of your ability to hold any job. At the same time you must not look upon the first job as the final job; it is primarily a train-ing job, an opportunity to analyze yourself and your fitness for being an employee.

In fact there is a great deal to be said for being fired from the first job. One reason is that it is rarely an advantage to have started as an office boy in the organization; far too many people will still consider you a "green kid" after you have been there for twenty-five years. But the major reason is that getting fired from the first job is the least painful and the least damaging way to learn how to take a setback. And whom the Lord loveth he teacheth early how to take a setback.

Nobody has ever lived, I daresay, who has not gone through a period when everything seemed to have collapsed and when years of work and life seemed to have gone up in smoke. No one can be spared this experience; but one can be prepared for it. The man who has been through earlier setbacks has learned that the world has not come to an end because he lost his job—not even in a depression. He has learned that he will somehow survive. He has learned, above all, that the way to behave in such a setback is not to collapse himself. But the man who comes up against it for the first time when he is forty-five is quite likely to collapse for good. For the things that people are apt to do when they receive the first nasty blow may destroy a mature man with a family, whereas a youth of twenty-five bounces right back.

Obviously you cannot contrive to get yourself fired. But you can always quit. And it is perhaps even more important to have quit once than to have been fired once. The man who walks out on his own volition acquires an inner independence that he will never quite lose.

To know when to quit is therefore one of the most important things—particularly for the beginner. For on the whole, young people have a tendency to hang on to the first job long beyond the time when they should have quit for their own good.

One should quit when self-analysis shows that the job is the wrong job—that, say, it does not give the security and routine one requires, that it is a small-company rather than a big-organization job, that it is at the bottom rather than near the top, a specialist's rather than a generalist's job, etc. One should quit if the job demands behavior one considers morally indefensible, or if the whole atmosphere of the place is morally corrupting—if, for instance, only yes men and flatterers are tolerated.

One should also quit if the job does not offer the training one needs either in a specialty or in administration and the view of the whole. The beginner not only has a right to expect training from his first five or ten years in a job; he has an obligation to get as much training as possible. A job in which young people are not given real training—though, of course, the training need not be a formal "training program"—does not measure up to what they have a right and a duty to expect.

But the most common reason why one should quit is the absence of promotional opportunities in the organization. That is a compelling reason.

I do not believe that chance of promotion is the essence of a job. In fact there is no surer way to kill a job and one's own usefulness in it than to consider it as but one rung in the promotional ladder rather than as a job in itself that deserves serious effort and will return satisfaction, a sense of accomplishment, and pride. And one can be an important and respected member of an organization without ever having received a promotion; there are such people in practically every office. But the organization itself must offer fair promotional opportunities. Otherwise it stagnates, becomes corrupted, and in turn corrupts. The absence of promotional opportunities is demoralizing. And the sooner one gets out of a demoralizing situation, the better. There are three situations to watch out for:

The entire group may be so young that for years there will be no vacancies. . . .

Another situation without promotional opportunities is one in which the group ahead of you is uniformly old—so old that it will have to be re-

placed long before you will be considered ready to move up. Stay away from organizations that have a uniform age structure throughout their executive group—old or young. The only organization that offers fair promotional opportunities is one in which there is a balance of ages.

And finally there is the situation in which all promotions go to members of a particular group—to which you do not belong. Some chemical companies, for instance, require a master's degree in chemistry for just about any job above sweeper. Some companies promote only engineering graduates. . . . Or all the good jobs may be reserved for members of the family. There may be adequate promotional opportunities in such an organization—but not for you.

On the whole there are proportionately more opportunities in the big organization than in the small one. But there is very real danger of getting lost in the big organization—whereas you are always visible in the small one. A young man should therefore stay in a large organization only if it has a definite promotional program which ensures that he will be considered and looked at. . . .

But techniques do not concern us here. What matters is that there should be both adequate opportunities and fair assurance that you will be eligible and considered for promotion. Let me repeat: to be promoted is not essential, either to happiness or to usefulness. To be considered for promotion is.

I have only one more thing to say: to be an employee it is not enough that the job be right and that you be right for the job. It is also necessary that you have a meaningful life outside the job.

I am talking of having a genuine interest in something in which you, on your own, can be, if not a master, at least an amateur expert. This something may be botany, or the history of your county, or chamber music, cabinetmaking, Christmas-tree growing, or a thousand other things. But it is important in this "employee society" of ours to have a genuine interest outside of the job and to be serious about it.

I am not, as you might suspect, thinking of something that will keep you alive and interested during your retirement. I am speaking of keeping yourself alive, interested, and happy during your working life, and of a permanent source of self-respect and standing in the community outside and beyond your job. You will need such an interest when you hit the forties, that period in which most of us come to realize that we will never reach the goals we have set ourselves when younger—whether these are goals of achievement or of worldly success. You will need it because you should have one area in which you yourself impose standards of performance on your own work. Finally, you need it because you will find recognition and acceptance by other people working in the field, whether professional or amateur, as individuals rather than as members of an organization and as employees.

This is heretical philosophy these days when so many companies believe that the best employee is the man who lives, drinks, eats, and sleeps job and company. In actual experience those people who have no life outside their jobs are not the really successful people, not even from the viewpoint of the company. I have seen far too many of them shoot up like a rocket, because they had no interests except the job; but they also come down like the rocket's burned-out stick. The man who will make the greatest contribution to his company is the mature person—and you cannot have maturity if you have no life or interest outside the job. Our large companies are beginning to understand this.

That so many of them encourage people to have "outside interests" or to develop "hobbies" as a preparation for retirement is the first sign of a change toward a more intelligent attitude. But quite apart from the self-interest of the employer, your own interest as an employee demands that you develop a major outside interest. It will make you happier, it will make you more effective, it will give you resistance against the setbacks and the blows that are the lot of everyone; and it will make you a more effective, a more successful, and a more mature employee.

You have no doubt realized that I have not really talked about how to be an employee. I have talked about what to know before becoming an employee—which is something quite different. Perhaps "how to be an employee" can be learned only by being one. But one thing can be said. Being an employee means working with people; it means living and working in a society. Intelligence, in the last analysis, is therefore not the most important quality. What is decisive is character and integrity. If you work on your own, intelligence and ability may be sufficient. If you work with people you are going to fail unless you also have basic integrity. And integrity—character—is one thing most, if not all, employers consider first.

There are many skills you might learn to be an employee, many abilities that are required. But fundamentally the one quality demanded of you will not be skill, knowledge, or talent, but character.

Harold P. Zelko

When You Are "In Conference"

Whether we like it or not, the conference is one of today's major communication tools in management and supervision. Bringing a group of people together who share common work goals and experiences accomplishes many objectives at one sitting such as: To inform, explain, and instruct; to analyze and discuss problems; to make decisions; and to afford opportunity for participation and recognition.

The conference for years has been a major vehicle of top and middle management; but it is fast becoming a very useful tool for all supervisors. The average supervisor finds himself attending a conference, usually called by his immediate superior, perhaps more times as a member than as a leader. But, regardless of which role you are in, you can make yourself more effective by following a few suggestions.

We are not sure whether group decisions reached in conference are always better than those you can make yourself. Nor do we advocate that all problems requiring decisions should be taken up in conference. A good manager has to use his best judgement as to when this will be most valuable. We do know, from many research studies, that when individuals have an opportunity to participate and to be a part of decisions and policies which they will later have to carry out, they will execute the decision more effectively and with more desire and enthusiasm.

During World War II, in a book called *The Production Conference,* Jack Wolff pointed out numerous examples of how conferences can best solve problems arising in the work scene, chiefly because the men doing the actual work have the most knowledge and best judgement about the problems that confront them.

Good conferences do not just happen. They require careful planning, good leadership, and good participation. As a leader, you have certain responsibilities which start way before the actual conference takes place. As a member, you again must assume responsibilities both to prepare yourself and in your actual participation. Too many conference members take the attitude that it is all up to the leader to see that it is a good conference, and that they can just sit back and let him "sweat it out." This is far from true, and probably more conferences fail because of this attitude and the consequent poor participation that results than for any fault of the leader.

Conference Planning

There is a systematic way of going about the planning for a good conference. The leader or person calling the conference has most to do in good planning. It is a mistake to do this at the last minute or to hurriedly call your people together "for a few minutes" and then proceed to hold them for two hours. Conferences should start and end on time, with a specific time limit indicated in the agenda. Here are the major steps in conference planning:

1. *Know the purpose of the conference.* Is it to solve a problem, make a decision, give instructions

"When You Are 'In Conference'" by H. P. Zelko. Reproduced by permission from the June 1965 issue of *Supervision.* Copyright 1965 by the National Research Bureau, Inc., Burlington, Iowa.

or information, or perhaps a combination of all of these?

2. *Analyze the group.* Even though you meet with this group regularly and think you know them, you must consider their relationship to the particular subjects to be taken up. How much do they know about them? What is their degree of interest? What is their attitude, and what are the issues that may come up on particular problem-solving objectives?

3. *Plan the agenda.* This is basically a listing of the major subjects to be taken up. But it is not enough simply to decide that something should be put on the agenda. In what sequence should the subjects be taken up? How much time on each? To what extent will the group participate on each? Importance of the subject, complexity, amount of information at hand, attitude of the group, and whether the purpose is to convey information about it or solve a problem are all factors to consider in determining the answers to some of these questions.

4. *Notify persons to attend.* This is usually done by sending a copy of the agenda to all participants sufficiently in advance so they can prepare. It is even better to ask the members for suggestions in planning the agenda. Many managers do this at the conference the week before, assuming regularly held conferences. And there is a great deal of evidence of the value of conferences held regularly, say once a week, so that the group members look forward to coming at a specific time each week and a feeling of participation and group teamwork is developed.

5. *Make a working outline for leading.* This is an extention of the agenda which the leader should prepare for his own use in leading the conference. It shows major areas, questions, sub-questions, material to be offered for consideration, use of visual aids where desirable; and other details.

6. *Arrange room facilities.* Too often all of us have walked into a conference room where the tables are not neatly arranged, chairs are in all sorts of positions, ash trays are still filled, dust is on the furniture, blackboard is not clean, and other indications of untidiness are obvious. These are simply not conducive to a good conference, nor is a hurried attempt to make things look neat the proper answer.

The best conference arrangement is for a group of about 10 or 12 to sit face-to-face around an oblong or oval table, usually with the leader at the head. If the group members know each other, it is not necessary to have name cards, but these add to the feeling of belonging with the group and are an asset even for groups that meet regularly. A pad and pencil should be at each place. A clean blackboard or chart easel should be near the leader's position. Whatever source materials, such as reports, memos, or other items necessary to develop a subject, are to be used should all be considered in advance and brought into the conference room before the start. Temperature and clear air are factors that should be given continuous consideration throughout the conference.

The *participant* should also plan for attending a conference. First, he should assume a responsibility for contributing to the agenda if the leader gives him this opportunity. And if the leader does not, he should still try to offer suggestions tactfully. Once he receives the agenda, the participant should analyze his own present knowledge and understanding of subjects to be taken up.

He should gather information and plan to bring necessary sources into the meeting. He should then analyze his own present attitudes and points of view regarding problems to be taken up and their solutions. While doing this, he should consider the probable attitudes of other participants and how they may affect the ultimate outcome or decision to be reached.

If there is a strong opinion or solution he feels will be proposed by others and he wishes to show the weakness of such a proposal, he should do some thinking and research so that he can properly refute the other position and also back up his own.

Planning for the participant should also include consideration of the leader's position and what problems are likely to remain as the leader's own responsibility for decision, as well as those which the leader is probably going to let the group decide. A good member should realize that the leader, who is usually his superior, has a basic responsibility for making decisions which frequently compels him to make them himself, even though he has sought the opinion of the group.

Within the conference itself, the participant member has many factors to consider for best participation, as we point out in the next section.

Leading and Participating

Having pointed out some of the essentials for both leader and participant in planning for a conference, let's look at what both should do in the actual conduct of the conference.

Leadership involves the major functions of guiding, stimulating, and controlling the discussion. To accomplish these, a leader should have certain essential qualities including an attitude of open-mindedness and group-centeredness rather than being dogmatic and self-centered. He must be pleasant and animated in his manner, tactful in handling comments of members, a good listener, and a good speaker. These do add up to a big order.

Guiding the conference means primarily to see that the purpose is accomplished through covering the agenda. There are two chief purposes which usually apply to each item on the agenda: To convey information or instruction, and to solve a problem or reach a decision. If an item on the agenda requires that the leader explain, instruct, and inform the group, he needs to plan for this and perhaps make a brief "speech" on the subject.

There is nothing wrong with this, as long as information giving is the goal and purpose. He should be sure that he first motivates the group by pointing out the significance and importance of this material to them; then he should arrange the main body of the information into clear points, in logical sequence, with appropriate material for support of each. He should then allow questions to be raised for clarification by group members.

A more difficult process of guiding is when the objective is problem-solving. Here the sequence should be that of first motivating and arousing interest in the problem at hand; thorough analysis of the problem by finding out its source, importance, complexity, and effects before turning to the next step; consideration of possible solutions before evaluating them, so that as many possibilities as possible are brought before the group; analysis and evaluation of proposed solutions in order to arrive at the best solution; and the determination of the best course of action, usually in the form of making a decision and planning for its execution.

But, as already pointed out, leaders are not necessarily obliged to let the group do this fully or to make the decision at the conference. As long as he is honest and sincere, the leader should explain the extent to which he can let the group do this. Studies have shown that over 60 percent of managers who hold problem-solving conference discussions return to their offices and make the decision themselves, based on the group's suggestions as much as possible.

Stimulating means the constant attempt on the part of the leader to keep his group interested, motivated, and desirous of participating. His primary tool for doing this, in addition to his own manner and attitude, is the use of questions. It has been generally determined that questions thrown out to the group as a whole, called "overhead" questions, are best and give all in the group equal opportunity to participate. If no one speaks up, the question should be made more clear or more precise.

Sometimes the leader resorts to "direct" questions to particular members, but in so doing he should be quite sure that the member wants to respond. He should also know whether his question seeks information or factual material or seeks opinion or attitude in the reply. He should try to arouse interest in participating among silent members, yet he must realize that it is not possible to get an even distribution of participation.

Controlling involves those methods and techniques necessary to accomplish the purpose of the meeting. Time is our greatest enemy, and if there are several items on the agenda, some of a problem-solving nature which usually take more time (most agendas are mixed in the inclusion of informational and instructional subjects and problem-solving subjects), the leader is sometimes obliged to work toward ending a discussion and moving on to the next item.

We should not be too critical of a leader who does this as long as he tries his best to be "democratic" in considering the group. Another aspect of control is the leader's ability to select one solution from a group that has been proposed for more detailed analysis and evaluation. By making this selection, this solution may have more chance of becoming the ultimate decision; but someone has to do this.

Control also involves the sometimes difficult job of handling those members who talk too much at the expense of others. First, we must realize that all members will not talk an equal amount, as already pointed out. Next, we have found through research that the talkative member is not necessarily bad. He may well be the most valuable and contribute the most factual and useful information.

Nor is it necessary to get all silent members to talk. Conferences need good listeners; and sometimes the more silent member who contributes

only a few remarks may have stimulated others to contribute, and his own few remarks may be more valuable than if he had talked many more times but with less substance.

Leaders must also realize that there are many reasons why a person does not want to contribute, including a lack of confidence, lack of knowledge, or even one's not feeling well. He should thus be cautious about asking direct questions to silent members.

Still another important tool of control is the use of internal summaries and transitions by the leader. He should always make clear just where the group is at a given time, when a new topic is taken up, and what the reason is for taking it up. While this kind of control is a part of the leader's guiding function and is primarily a leadership responsibility, members should be alert to ask questions and even to supply suggested transitions when the leader fails to do this.

Sometimes a leader may allow the group to stay on a point too long, or he may neglect to move toward an important area of the subject. In this case, a member should help supply functions of leadership, as long as he does this tactfully and appropriately and does not give indication that he wants to "take over" the management of the conference.

Participating in a conference has been the subject of much research in recent years, and we have learned more about the member's responsibilities and functions. We used to devote most of our attention to the leader, and most writing in the field of conference process is about leadership. But studies of what and how people interact in conferences have led us to conclude that there is much that the average participant can do to make the conference more effective, to improve his own participation, and even to enjoy conferences. After all, we do attend perhaps ten or a hundred conferences for every one that we lead.

The primary areas of concern for improving yourself as a participant member of a conference are these: What should your attitude be? How much do you need to know about group process, as well as the group itself? When, how much, and how should I participate?

Attitude toward anything starts from within and is based partly on logical, partly on emotional, and partly on environmental factors. The primary requisite of proper attitude in a conference is that of openmindedness and consideration for others.

Then it is important to avoid negative feelings about the conference as a useful tool of supervision and management. It is quite easy to think of the positive values of conference process. These include opportunities for benefiting from knowledge and opinions of others, for accumulating maximum information from the backgrounds and experiences of your co-workers, for feeling a part of a policy or decision under which you will be working, for developing a better understanding and appreciation of your co-workers and the teamwork that can be developed among you, and for the opportunity to express and communicate your own thoughts to others.

Knowledge on your part of *group process* and how groups function will both help you develop the right attitude and make you a better participant. You should know the basic steps in the problem-solving process, as described above. You should be aware of the problems and responsibilities of the leader, so that you can be more understanding of his methods of leadership and also be helpful in contributing positively toward helping him achieve the conference goals.

You should realize that every other member sitting around the table with you is an individual who is different from you. He has his own personal problems, his own self-centeredness (which all of us should try to avoid in favor of being more "you-centered"), and his own way of thinking which may be different from yours. The goal of your development as a good conference member should include a constant study of other people, including a consideration of our basic drives, prejudices, emotions, and logical thought process.

Your own actual participation boils down to how good a communicator you are. For human communication involves: First, a consideration of the other people involved; second, a realization that communication is always an interacting process and not just a one-way transmittal; third, an attempt to put your message into clear organization and language adapted properly to others; fourth, the use of support and evidence to back up and to clarify your position; fifth, a sense of proper timing which includes a consideration of the setting and place where the communication takes place; and sixth, speaking up with a proper degree of projection, animation, sincerity, directness, and other qualities of a good speaker.

Then to all these we must add the qualities of good listening which include open-mindedness, alertness, sensitivity to others, motivation to try to understand others, and an attempt to think logically and apply what is being said.

The timing of participation and the length of remarks you make are factors that can affect your value as a participant. Studies have shown that if you participate early in a conference, you will establish yourself with the group and may gain their respect so that they will welcome future comments.

If you prolong the period of time before you start to participate, this tends to lead toward the group being less inclined to accept your future comments. It also tends to keep you silent as a group member for the longer you wait for your first comments the more satisfied you become to remain silent.

Of course this does not mean that the group does not need silent members and good listeners, as we have already pointed out. An animated, alert listener contributes a great deal. But listening alone will keep within you valuable information or opinion that should be offered so that the group can consider your contributions.

It is also wise to talk a number of different times than to try to say all you have on your mind at one time. Speak only to the point at hand, and do not fall into the pitfall of becoming a "chain" talker where one thought leads to another, and you don't know when to stop. Remarks of about one minute in length are usually sufficient at one time, or perhaps up to two minutes at most.

Sometimes it is necessary to be quite alert in making your remarks at the most effective time in relation to what has been said by others. You may find that several people want to speak as soon as the present participant is finished, so you must follow his words carefully and come in with your response almost with split-second timing. The slow and less alert person may want to say something but finds himself going all the way through a conference saying nothing because he does not maintain this constant alertness.

Your participation also requires that you be considerate and understanding of what the leader is trying to do and accomplish as the purpose of the conference, at any given time. If you keep most of the above principles in mind, you will realize constantly that the accomplishment of the conference goals requires the consideration of many things, not just your own personal desires.

Conclusion

We can conclude, then, that the conference is here to stay as one of management's most fundamental tools of communication. Its primary purposes are to achieve communication downward through explanations, information, and instruction; to solve problems and arrive at decisions through cooperative interaction to the extent that this can best be done in the given instance; and to afford a maximum medium for participation and exchange of ideas for all who attend.

In both leading and participating in conferences, you should follow these suggestions of careful planning and preparation and then use the principles and tools we have discussed. Supervisors at all levels of management will find themselves attending more and more conferences in this age of teamwork and the application of democratic group process to business.

Stop Misusing Your Management Meetings

Your meetings are not an activity in themselves. They are a tool—a communications tool for getting action results in the plant. Plenty has been written about meetings. Much of it critical of the meeting as a time waster, a social event, a private soapbox, or an opportunity to dilute individual responsibility. But the meeting is potentially one of your most effective and productive management devices, if you understand its dynamics and exploit its possibilities.

Following are 10 rules to help you focus on the meeting process. If you understand and practice them, your meetings will be smoother. And you should notice an improvement in your action results in the plant:

1. Plan to Solve a Problem—Not to Hold a Meeting

The cost of a meeting—in wages and salaries alone—can be terrific. So don't waste time drifting. Plan. Know why you want to call a meeting. Ask yourself:
• What's the problem?
• What are the related facts?
• How can we solve the problem?

Too often we think we're planning when we're finding a good meeting place, checking on time and availability of members, and setting the date. But this is scheduling, not planning. The time you spend asking yourself hard questions—not about

From "Stop Misusing Your Management Meeting" from *Factory*, April 1960. Reprinted by special permission of *Modern Manufacturing* (formerly *Factory*), April 1960. Copyright McGraw-Hill, Inc.

the meeting but about the problem—can be a real money saver.

2. Use the Meeting as a Tool

There are good and bad reasons for calling a meeting—and you should know the difference. The basis for your use of meetings (or your neglect of them) may be worth questioning. A meeting is only one of several communications tools. Other tools are often just as good or better. Telephones, for instance. Or memos. Or private conversations.

A meeting may also be used as an escape or excuse. Ask yourself these questions from time to time:
• Is a meeting really necessary to accomplish this task?
• Could I get this job done at some other meeting, later?
• Am I calling this meeting to get some listeners and increase my own sense of importance? To get other people to do my homework for me? To pass the buck on responsibility?

Here are some good occasions for calling a meeting:
• When you must be sure your message will be understood. Most managers have experimented rather widely with written communications and are aware of the limitations of this one-way method.
• When you want to get subordinates' reactions and stimulate two-way communications. By himself, a subordinate is bound to tell you what he thinks you want to hear. In a meeting, he'll gang up with others and tell you the facts.

- When you need more facts or expert opinions.
- When you need creative new ideas, approaches, and solutions. The clash of ideas in a group can often produce superior solutions.
- When you must depend on others to carry out decisions. It's well known that people support what they help create.
- When you want to build better teamwork. Don't restrict meetings to crises. Members need to feel they have a part in the creation and growth of their organization.

3. Pick Each Member as a Resource

Think twice before you flip the switch to call your "kitchen cabinet" into a meeting. When you've got a problem, "Smith," "Jones," and "Green" may first come to your mind. The reason you call them may be that they are the smartest, quickest, and best informed members of your organization. Or is it because they can do you the most good in your future? Or because they usually agree with you? You should make sure you have good reasons for calling in these men.

But, depending on the problem, there are compelling reasons why you should call in various other kinds of people, without regard for their rank, age, position, or even whether you like them or not:
- The idea man. Maybe not all his ideas are good, but they may stimulate thinking.
- The company's informal "communicator." He seems always to know everything that's going on throughout the shop.
- The compromiser, who can help smooth things over.
- The technical expert.
- The man who should give his "blessing" to the project. He has informal power.
- The guy who has all the facts.
- A key member of the department that might block this project.

Representatives from interested groups (foremen or unions) who could help sell the project.

But it's important to be clear about what happens to a meeting each time you add a new member. According to communications experts, you're not merely ADDING to the complexity of the group—you are MULTIPLYING its complexity. A good rule of thumb is this: Use all the people you need as resources. But make it the minimum number.

4. See Your Meeting as Others See It

When your members are with you—really going along with what you're trying to do in a meeting—the job is easy. But you can't assume this will happen automatically. Too often the members have other purposes in attending your meeting. They have other goals in mind. And they may work at cross-purposes to your meeting goals unless you do something about them—both before and during the meeting.

Before the meeting you might take these steps:
- Send the members the problem in advance. Ask them to do some thinking about it. Ask for plans, approaches, and possible holes in your plan.
- Distribute a tentative agenda. Ask for comments or additions to it. Be sure you acknowledge contributions when you meet.
- Brief members on the meeting and ask them to take action beforehand, such as preparing statistics or getting a few reactions to an idea.

Don't assume that announcing the agenda beforehand will eliminate conflicting interests at the meeting. Deal with them again at the start of the meeting. One way of handling this, especially in regular staff meetings, is through the use of "agenda budgeting." Here's a good procedure for budgeting an agenda:
- Use chart pad or blackboard to list agenda items you've selected for the meeting.

- Ask members for additional items they'd like to have covered.
- Help the group decide what priorities to give each item, labeling them, for example, as: urgent; important, today; important, this week; individual attention.
- Work with the group to budget time to be spent on each item.
- Review and revise time budgets during the meeting.

You may find that this joint agenda setting may take six or seven minutes. But this time spent in getting squared away for even an hour-long meeting is a worthwhile expenditure in "getting your people with you."

5. Don't Tolerate Late Attendance, Interruptions, Etcetera

To set up ground rules, do these things before the meeting:
- Give at least 48 hours' notice of time and place. Impossible? You'd be surprised how often it can be done. And the number of "emergencies" somehow decreases.
- Tell how long the meeting will last. How can you tell? Once you start predicting, you'll become more and more accurate. Many men can tell within minutes.
- Tell exactly why the meeting is called. A good reason can make a lot of difference in the attitudes of those attending.
- Tell what the meeting is expected to accomplish. Don't say, "To discuss a new product." That's too vague. Say: "To set up production schedules for Model 7A."
- Tell each man why he's invited and what he's expected to do. Don't hamstring people with rigid assignments, but suggest beforehand: "Jones, would you be ready to look at this in terms of possible production snags?" "Rogers, would you just listen in? You'll be facing this problem next year."

And here's what you can do at the meeting:
- Insist on prompt attendance. And always be on time yourself for your own and others' meetings.
- Don't allow phone interruptions. Have calls held for answering at breaks or right after meetings.
- Have the meeting room checked beforehand for ventilation, quiet, paper, and pencils.
- Arrange the seating to fit the meeting.

6. Share the Responsiblity for Starting Out Right

The more important the meeting, the more concerned you may become about starting it off well. But the more concerned you get, the more likely you are to start off wrong. Why? First, because you're worried. And probably taking all the responsiblity on yourself. You're not thinking about letting the other members share this responsibility. So they're not thinking about how they can help.

A second trap is related to the first. Maybe you're over-prepared. In your concern for the job, you forget to consider the feelings of these other members.

Much depends on your faith in the group's ability to solve problems, and your willingness to let them take the bull by the horns. There are a number of specific things you can do to avoid these two traps:
- Be sure everyone clearly understands the long-range objectives—where this meeting fits into the larger picture.
- Restate just what the meeting is for.
- Tell each person (again) just why he is there.
- Inform everybody of the meeting plan before you work on the agenda.

But don't be a mother hen. It's easy to over-plan what each member should do. After a general briefing, let members be flexible about how they participate.

7. Change Your Leader Style to Fit the Type of Meeting

Meetings fall generally into five major categories. For each category you'll find one style of chairmanship is usually best:

• Meetings for information giving—Addressing civic groups and explaining directives call for autocratic leadership because it's from you to them with no need for reactions.

• Meetings for information collecting—Interviewing employees, hearing union committee opinions, and getting reports call for shared leadership because lots of participation is important to get the facts. Members stimulate each other.

• Meetings for decision making—Planning a cost reduction program or setting up a work schedule calls for shared leadership because each member can perform useful functions, and follow-up is needed.

• Decision-selling—Getting acceptance of new organization set-up passed down by the front office calls for autocratic and shared leadership. Autocratic with regard to the decision, shared with regard to carrying it out. Again, commitments to action are needed.

• Meetings for problem-solving—Helping each other find the best ways to handle subordinates calls for shared leadership because it requires flexibility and the use of all resources available.

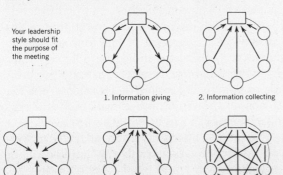

Your leadership style should fit the purpose of the meeting

1. Information giving
2. Information collecting
3. Decision making
4. Decision selling
5. Problem solving

A meeting is a group of individuals interacting with each other in some pretty complex ways to try to get a job done. So it is vital that they stick together as a group and develop teamwork en route to the goal. What's more, most meetings don't reach the ultimate goal *at the meeting,* but later on, in actions back on the job. If a member is not really on the team during the meeting, he's less likely to do his share in carrying out the decision afterwards. So hold the group together.

Some aids to this objective:
• Help quiet members participate.
• Compliment the group on the progress it is making.
• Relieve the tension with a joke or story.
• Mediate arguments.

8. Harness Many Skills to Get Good Decisions

Studies of the way decisions are made in meetings reveal that many groups, often at high levels, do a distressingly poor job of decision-making. To test your performance, keep tabs on the movements of decision-making meetings through these five phases:
• Pinning down the problem.
• Collecting information.
• Finding alternative solutions.
• Testing alternatives.
• Determining action.

Of course no meeting group is likely to proceed logically and systematically from the first to the last phase. But if your group jumps almost immediately to the last phase without further defining and redefining the problem, or concerning itself about facts, it will be behaving immaturely—the way many groups do in meetings.

Here are some factors that often tend to block good decisions—ask yourself if they affect your meetings:
• Grabbing at the first few alternatives suggested

on the assumption they're the only ones.
• Jumping to a decision without testing it.
• Asking people to make a decision without data.
• Failing to *build in* an action commitment.
• Placing decision reponsibility too high.
• Having the leader state his position too soon.
• Failing to take an experimental attitude. This is from a fear of failure—"Let's not take chances."

Below are six functions, all necessary parts of the decision-making process at your meetings. Ask yourself questions like these:

1. Defining the problem—How well was the information assembled? Was the importance of the problem really understood?

2. Clarifying—Was questioning encouraged? Were members asked to help clarify the problem?

3. Keeping discussion on the beam—Were members concerned about staying on the subject? Were temporary digressions permitted?

4. Summarizing—Who did the summarizing? Did he come in at the right time?

5. Testing consequences of the emerging decision—How did we know when we were ready for a decision? What checks were made on the decision's realities?

6. Decision-making—How was the decision made: Majority vote? Consensus? Silent consent?

9. Diagnose and Treat the Hidden Agendas

Long experience confirms the fact that even the best of people—when you get them together—do not always work logically or react intelligently. Below are some useful clues to this mystery. Dr. Leland P. Bradford, director of the National Training Laboratories, claims it results from a meeting's "Hidden Agendas."

"Groups work simultaneously and continuously on two levels," says Dr. Bradford. "One level is formally labeled. . . . This is the obvious, advertised purpose for which the group meets.

"Unlabeled, private, covered, but deeply felt and very much the concern of the group, is the other level. Here are the conflicting motives, desires, aspirations, and emotional reactions of the group members . . . problems which, for a variety of reasons, cannot be laid on top of the table—the Hidden Agendas."

Groups work hard on either or both of these agendas. A group may have been working hard on its surface agenda and getting nowhere. Suddenly it starts to move efficiently on its appointed job and quickly reaches a conclusion. Explanation: The group had to work on its hidden agenda and get it out of the way before it could go to work on its real job.

Some typical hidden agendas:

• The plant manager has a hip-pocket solution to the production-line problem being discussed. He wants the production planning committee to buy his solution. He waits his chance to slip it into the discussion. But meanwhile his mind is closed to everything else.

• The sales manager is in a meeting to discuss quality problems. Some of the problems are caused by errors in specifications made in the engineering department, which is managed by his best friend. Although he's not present, the engineering manager is an "invisible member" of the meeting.

• When a new committee is formed, even among people who know each other, each individual is concerned with his place in the group. Each wants to know what's expected of him and how far he should move. And depending on how important the group is to him, this need for respect or position or power will be more or less intense. Hidden agendas are almost always at work in these opening moments of a new committee's first meeting.

You need to be equally aware of the effect hidden agendas of various kinds may have on you in the leading role.

Hidden agendas often relate to you and your leadership. A man may compete with you (often without realizing it) for influence over the others. He may feel hostile to all leaders. He unconsciously may be dependent on you, need to lean on you. Another may support you because you have power to aid a special interest of his.

The group itself may have a hidden agenda in relation to you, the leader. (Ask yourself: Are you *really* its leader?)

Finally, of course, you may have your own hidden agendas. One of these may be your (carefully hidden) desire to box the ears of a subordinate. Another may be a hip-pocket solution to the problem at hand. Still another may be your need to maintain leadership at any cost.

Here are several ways of approaching hidden agendas:
• Be alert to their presence.
• Keep in mind that the meeting operates at two levels. Don't always expect top-speed action on the surface task assigned. Other problems of personalities may be gnawing at each other underneath.
• Make people comfortable enough to bring out their hidden agendas. Encourage them to talk it over.
• Don't force discussion of a sub-surface problem that can't really be faced at the moment.
• Don't get angry or discipline the members for their hidden agendas. They can't help them—don't even know they have them.
• Help members develop ways of handling hidden agendas just as they handle surface agendas—by resolving the problem.

Hidden agendas are neither good nor bad. They're simply part of the game. But we need to be conscious of them and deal with them the way we deal with the surface problems. They're every bit as *real.*

10. Build a Bridge from the Meeting to the Goal

You want results, not meetings. You want results in terms of decisions carried out, actions taken, things done. Unless a meeting produces results afterwards—no matter how successful it seemed to be at the time—the meeting failed.

Too often what you're going to do afterward isn't planned until the meeting is over—then it's too late. Follow-up should be:
• Planned before meeting.
• Planned during meeting.
• Re-planned before the end of the meeting in terms of action.

Planning *follow-up* at the start of planning *the meeting* happens automatically if you are really viewing the meeting as a means, not an end. In this case you'll be looking at the ultimate goal and considering how the meeting will help move toward that goal.

A common method for planning follow-up is through minutes of the meeting. These minutes are often a colossal bore and practically useless because either too little or too much is recorded. Don't boil them down until the content is boiled away, and don't keep volumes of word-for-word notes. The key to the problem lies in making a distinction between meeting content and meeting procedures. Get on-the-spot highlights of what the meeting produces, not what goes on.

Follow-up action taken only at the close of the meeting may be too little and too late. Often a group makes a decision, sighs, "Thank Heaven that's done!" and files out of the conference room under the impression that the meeting goal has been reached. Far from it. You've merely made a decision.

The second phase of the problem is "How to get the action carried out successfully?" You're safer if you can create for yourself a mental picture of two meetings in one. The first meeting makes the decision, the second plans to carry it out. Possible approaches:

A.   Test its consequences ...
• What does it mean?
• How does it relate to other projects and policies?
• Is the decision possible? Is it realistic?
• How about cost, time, people to carry it out?
• What are the possible effects on other departments, customers, suppliers, the community?

B.   Test understanding and member commitment ...
• Is everyone clear about what this means?
• Is each one willing to go along?
• Are there any other concerns or misgivings?
• Does anyone see major pitfalls?

C.   Plan next steps ...
• Who does what?
• Who will coordinate?
• How about follow-up reports or meetings?
• What schedule of time, place, and people?

Follow-up that commits members to action and builds a bridge from the meeting to the goal is the final focal point for getting payoff from your meetings. But this payoff will also depend upon everything else we've been talking about.

One point in closing ...

While all these rules can be useful to you, don't expect them to produce results in your meetings without a good deal of practice. They require, also, the development of skills—not only your own, but also those of the other members who participate.

Waldo E. Fisher

The Interview—a Multi-Purpose Leadership Tool

One common denominator characterizes the work of members of management: they all spend a lot of time solving problems. These problems will vary with the functions that are performed, but basically most of them deal with one or more production essentials: people, products, methods, markets, finances, equipment, and machines.

To solve these problems many management tools must be used. High on the list of these tools is the interview. It is surprising how often talking things over with others will suggest the solution to a problem or help to determine a course of action.

The Business Value of the Interview

Because the interview is an effective instrument for getting and giving information and for winning acceptance of ideas, it is an indispensable communication device. It is invaluable in changing and developing attitudes and behavior and in creating the will to work together. It is also of primary importance in handling the following functions:
- Selecting new employees and inducting them into the organization in a manner which will make them effective members as quickly as possible.
- Presenting a point of view and tapping the experience of other persons.

From "The Interview—a Multi-Purpose Leadership Tool" by Waldo E. Fisher © Mary Reynolds Fisher 1966, published by Industrial Relations Center, California Institute of Technology, June 1966.

- Explaining company policies, rules, regulations, complex orders, and innovations.
- Coaching and training employees.
- Reviewing employee peformance on the job and helping ambitious and able employees to prepare themselves for greater responsibility.
- Handling complaints and grievances.
- Dealing with disciplinary situations.
- Counseling individuals confronted with personal problems affecting their work.

When it is realized (1) that in the final analysis an organization is a group of people who perform functions and activities essential to its successful operation and (2) that the interview is an invaluable instrument in selecting, training, appraising, developing, promoting, and counseling people, the importance of this instrument to management stands out clearly. For these reasons, management personnel should be fully aware of the nature and values of the interview and become proficient in its use.

What Interviewing Involves

Ideally, an interview is a friendly and informal conversation between two people on a subject that they both want or need to explore. To be effective the interview should be planned, and the conversation conducted, as a two-way process. How much planning will be required and how much talking each person should do will depend on (1) the purpose of the interview and (2) the personalities of the participants.

Planning may be used to advantage in all types of interviews but is especially important when counseling and solving problems. Similarly, the distribution of the interviewing time between the participants will vary with the purpose depending, for example, on whether the interviewer is explaining company policies or standards or helping the interviewee to improve his performance or to change his attitudes or behavior.

Personality will also affect the distribution of time. An outgoing and well-informed interviewee who has considerable self-confidence and has no reason to be suspicious will usually talk freely with little or no encouragement, while one who is by nature taciturn or who is uninformed or unsure of himself will need to be drawn out and will be likely to place the burden of carrying the conversation on the interviewer.

In many interviews two sets of goals may be involved—those of the interviewer and those of the interviewee. These goals may be complementary, unrelated, or diametrically opposed. Irrespective of the goals, the function of the interview is to find a common ground for discussion which will facilitate a meeting of the minds of the participants.

Because the goals sought in the interviewing process vary in difficulty of attainment and because people differ greatly in capacities, interests, and temperament, no simple formula can be prescribed for conducting successful interviews. The competent interviewer will formulate clearly the things he wants to accomplish, plan his approach carefully, strive to be sensitive to human responses, and develop interviewing skills by applying accepted interviewing principles and utilizing correct methods.

Types of Interviews

It may be helpful to attempt a classification of the kinds of interviews used in business situations. It should be recognized that the suggested categories cannot have hard and fast outlines since much overlapping will occur in actual practice. With this limitation in mind, the following classification is submitted:

Informative interview: The purpose of this type is to supply facts, opinions, policies, methods, and similar information to the interviewee.

Fact-finding interview: Here the interviewer is seeking information and advice which the interviewee, because of his training and experience, is in a position to offer.

Exploratory interview: The purpose in this instance is to obtain the opinions and judgment of the interviewee with respect to problems to be studied, programs to be introduced, methods to be utilized, or courses of action to be followed. This type of interview is sometimes used in resolving conflicting interests.

Appraisal interview: This type of interview is used in evaluating a person's suitability for employment with a company or his performance and behavior on the job in order to determine whether he should be considered for transfer, discharge, additional training, a merit increase, or promotion.

Counseling interview: The primary purpose of this type of interview is to deal with organizational problems involving people or personal problems affecting performance and working relationships: grievances, disciplinary cases, training and development, performance reviews, and personal problems of the interviewee that affect efficiency and teamwork.

The above classification is functional in nature, having been based on the primary purposes for which interviews are held. It is recognized that many interviews, especially in counseling, may require two or more of these functions in achieving the desired objectives. It will be observed that no separate category has been designated for problem solving. Actually problems, while occurring most frequently in counseling interviews, may arise during all kinds of interviews. Stating a topic in the form of a question tends to place it in the category of a problem.

Preparing for the Interview

The interview will be far more effective if time is taken to think through beforehand the objective sought and the methods by which the desired results can best be attained. The plan, however, should be general—not a detailed blueprint—and should be only a guide to be modified as circumstances require. Some of the principles and steps to keep in mind are:

1. Keep Your Goal in Mind

Defining the purpose of the interview will give it direction, maximize results, and minimize irritations and wasted time and effort. The interviewer should contemplate the approach to use, the areas to cover, the information needed, the key and lead questions to ask, and possible solutions if a problem is involved.

What the interviewer will want to achieve will depend on the type of interview to be held: whether the principal goal is fact-finding, giving information, exploring possible courses of action, or appraising or counseling employees. Regardless of the type, it will be helpful to speculate beforehand about the specific things that are to be accomplished.

2. Adapt the Interview to the Individual's Personality and Needs

Because each person is a distinctive combination of traits, capacities, needs, attitudes, and aspirations, the interviewer should strive to utilize the approach and methods best suited to the personality and needs of the interviewee. The approach and method to be used will vary depending on the degree to which the individual is, let us say, mentally keen or slow, friendly or antagonistic, responsive or indifferent, emotionally disturbed or well-adjusted.

3. Bring Together Needed Information

The interviewer frequently will require pertinent information for his own use or to present to the interviewee. How does one decide what kind of information is to be compiled? Most interviews that are held in a business situation will be related to the factors often described as "The Six M's of Management": men, methods, machines, markets, materials, money. If the interviewer will speculate about the facts, policies, and programs related to each of these factors and which have a bearing on his problem, he will be likely to recognize the information that he will need. Most of this material is available in company records.

4. Develop Key and Lead Questions

In most interviews the principal task of the interviewer will be to get the individual to explore the subject under examination or tell why he responds, feels, or believes as he does, or prod him to make a decision or encourage him to solve a problem. These objectives can best be achieved by means of key and lead questions.

The key or primary questions set the pattern or structure of the interview and introduce and invite discussion of the broad areas covered by the interview. The lead or secondary questions draw out the interviewee by stimulating him to think and encouraging him to talk about the area opened up by the key question.

5. Explore Possible Solutions If a Problem Is Involved

When the topic under examination is a personal or organizational problem, the interviewer will find it helpful to speculate about possible solutions or courses of action that might be taken. The results of his speculation should not, as a general rule, be submitted by him during the interview. As we shall see later, such action often defeats the purpose of the interview. Its real value, as is also that of the key and lead questions, is to help the interviewer to think his way through the problem and enable him to guide the conversation into constructive channels.

The interviewer who has prepared for an interview will know what he hopes to accomplish, what he wants to talk about, how he will open the conversation, what questions to use to move toward his goal and get the interviewee to talking, and what courses of action to explore.

The Impromptu Interview

It will not always be possible to prepare for an interview. There will be matters that cannot wait such as when an employee comes with a grievance or personal problem that needs immediate attention. In that event, the interviewer will have to take the preparatory steps as he carries on the interview. He will want to obtain an understanding of the problem and so will help the interviewee to state it clearly. He will also get what facts he can from the interviewee but will recognize that additional facts may be needed especially if another employee is involved. Under these circumstances, the final decision will have to await further investigation.

The interviewer who plans for important interviews from day to day will adjust himself quickly to the needs of the impromptu interview and will pull out of his experience the key and lead questions and the possible solutions required to meet the situation.

Conducting the Interview

At the outset, it should be recognized that, because the personalities of those who participate in it vary greatly and the uses to which it is put are many, the interviewing process must be flexible. The interviewer, therefore, will want to utilize those principles and methods that he finds are best suited to his personality and to the situations with which he must deal. In particular, he will want to use the basic interviewing tools: interrogation, listening, observation, and evaluation. The following analysis presents the interviewing steps, to the extent that it is possible, in the order in which they are normally taken.

1. Create the Right Setting and Put the Interviewee at Ease

The atmosphere must be conducive to a friendly and free exchange of ideas and experiences. What is needed is a relationship between the participants that will bring about mutual understanding, confidence, and participation.

Attitudes play an important part in bringing about this relationship. Experience has shown that most people respond positively to friendliness, courtesy, and to being accepted as equals. They want others to recognize their worth as persons and to respect their desire to be worthwhile. There still is no better way to achieve this relationship than to treat the interviewee as one would like to be dealt with under similar circumstances.

Because the interview is usually prearranged, it tends to become a formalized process. The skillful interviewer tries to overcome this tendency by putting the interviewee at ease. He makes it a point to be cordial and informal. He quickly finds a common ground for exchanging pleasantries and experiences having to do with mutual friends, events of current interest, or activities related to the purpose of the interview. But setting the tone and getting started should not become a time-consuming process which infringes on the business of the interview or even makes the interviewee less at ease.

2. Supply Pertinent Information

Early in the process, the interviewee should be given a clear understanding of why he is being interviewed. It is often helpful to review the events leading to the interview. Moreover, information that is needed by the participant to facilitate exploration of the subject under consideration should be presented early so as to avoid backtracking or interruptions to the smooth flow of ideas. The nature of the information to be presented will be determined in planning the interview.

3. Secure Interviewee Participation and Cooperation

The normal tendency of the non-professional interviewer is to dominate the interview. Except in the informative interview, the objectives sought are best attained if the interviewee is encouraged to do most of the talking by a friendly, observing, and responsive person who seldom interrupts.

a. Interrogation

This interviewing tool is especially helpful in getting the interviewee to participate. The role of key and lead questions in accomplishing this goal was discussed in the section on preparing for the interview. It may be helpful to point out that the "Why" questions are of especial significance since they often reveal the motives behind people's attitudes and behavior or the factors that have led to the selection of particular policies, programs, or courses of action.

b. Listening

Once the interviewee begins to talk, a second interviewing tool, listening, becomes important. There is a temptation to listen with only half one's mind, the other half speculating about other aspects of the interviewing process or even about unrelated things. The successful interviewer listens with an open mind, tries to comprehend the full meaning of what is being said, separates facts from opinions, evalutes the pertinent remarks, and tries to fit them into an overall pattern.

Some of the things said by the interviewee may run contrary to the interviewer's experience and convictions. He will be tempted to enter into an argument or to set the interviewee "straight in his thinking." Such action often satisfies his ego, but it uses up valuable time and energy and delays or may even preclude a successful interview. Interruptions on the part of the interviewer should be held to a minimum; they should be used primarily to encourage the interviewee to continue telling his story or to guide the conversation into more meaningful channels.

4. Observation

Observation is used throughout the entire interview but is of particular importance when the interviewee is relating his experiences and impressions.

Much can be learned about a person from the way in which he tells his story or reacts to a given situation. Facial expressions, postures, and gestures throw light on what is said. The tone of voice, a glint in the eye, flushed cheeks, clenched hands, a smile, a nod of the head, and other behavioral responses help to reveal personality traits and serve as red or green lights that indicate how the interview is progressing. But important as mannerism, responses, and the spoken word are, they are no substitutes for an understanding of the anxieties, needs, goals, and loyalties that motivate the individual.

5. Evaluation

The next step is to relate to each other the facts, responses, and traits revealed by the interviewee's words and behavior, and to determine their importance and place in the overall picture. Evaluation will go on throughout the interview, but the final appraisal must wait until interrogating, listening, and observing have had a chance to take place. Evaluation is necessary in order to form a reliable opinion as to the value of advice or counsel; to decide if an applicant should be hired, an employee retained, or how a person can be utilized more effectively; and to determine the best approach for helping an individual to develop himself or solve a perplexing problem.

6. Work Out a Program of Action When the Situation Demands It

In certain types of interviews, notably performance reviews and counseling interviews generally, the participants often will find it desirable to work out a program of action. Experience has established the fact that any program or solution developed by the interviewee under the skillful guidance of the interviewer has a much better chance of being accepted and carried out than one that is made for him. When the interviewee helps to evolve the program, he will be more likely to have a greater sense of responsibility for it and more of a will to make it work.

7. Terminate the Interview

In closing the interview, the salient points covered and particularly any agreements reached should be summarized. If a program of action has been formulated, the interviewer will want to review the specific things the interviewee agreed to do and the actions he himself offered to take. Should a follow-up interview be needed, a date should be set or the responsibility for arranging it assigned. The interview should be closed on a friendly note and a feeling of accomplishment when that is possible.

The Problem Employee

From time to time, those who must work with or direct people will have to interview individuals with problems which prevent them from carrying out their duties and responsibilities as they should. How much help the interviewer can give such individuals will depend on the mental condition of the interviewee and the understanding and interviewing skill of the supervisor. The non-professional interviewer is not qualified to deal with deep-seated personal and emotional maladjustments. These conditions require psychotherapy and should be referred to the medical department.

But there are many problems of a less severe nature with which a supervisor will have to deal. In this class will fall difficulties involving grievances, discipline, motivation, status, and adjustments to changes in output standards, methods of production, materials, machines, working conditions, and especially people. In dealing with these problems (particularly when emotions are involved), it is of little help to admonish, exhort, issue ultimatums, or hand down programs of action. A different approach and more refined interviewing methods are needed.

Professional counselors have developed some basic principles and techniques that should be of material help in dealing with these situations.[1] The problem employee frequently must be dealt with in performance reviews. A brief discussion of this type of interview, therefore, may be useful.

Performance Reviews

Performance reviews are usually conducted as part of an employee appraisal program. Their immediate purpose is to let the employees know their supervisor's evaluation of how they are doing their work, how they can do it better, what their strengths and weaknesses are, and, if they are able

and willing, how they can develop themselves and move up in the organization. Unless it is done well, this type of interview may boomerang and hurt instead of help personal relations.

The interviewer should keep in mind that in the final analysis he is trying to help the employee (1) become a more effective member of his team and (2) prepare himself for greater responsibility in the organization. Since most employees have a strong desire to be worthwhile and dislike criticism, it is well to begin with a positive emphasis by calling attention to traits in which the employee stands high or has shown recent improvement or to attitudes and incidents which reflect desired performance. Credit should also be given for aspects of his work that merit praise.

The interviewer will then want to shift to the employee's weaknesses and show how they affect his work and that of his fellow employees. Because no one likes to have his shortcomings enumerated, criticism should be resorted to only when it will be helpful and then used gently, tactfully, and constructively with emphasis on what the employee has or has not done rather than what he is or is not. Moreover, such criticism should be supported with observed examples and factual information.

The interviewer should not be disturbed if the interviewee disagrees with his appraisal. There may be a good explanation for unsatisfactory performance; circumstances inside or outside the organization may account for it. Differences of opinion have the advantage of disclosing misunderstandings or situations that need attention; so instead of trying to prove that the interviewee is wrong, it is far better strategy for the interviewer to ask him why he feels as he does and how he would remedy the situation. Such an approach will get him to think positively, help him to clarify his thinking, and often lead him to a solution of his problem or a program of self-improvement.

Generally speaking, in dealing with problem employees, the interviewer should seek to establish a personal relationship which will encourage

---

[1] An excellent presentation of the role of the interview in counseling will be found in Carl R. Rogers, *Counseling and Psychotherapy* (Boston: Houghton Mifflin Company, 1942), especially pp. 11 to 47 and pp. 115 to 131.

and enable the interviewee to look carefully at his problem, analyze the reasons that lead him to feel and act as he does, and work out his own solution to it with the minimum of help. The interview should be a listening post and the interviewer a friend. Ask leading questions. Try to understand the meaning of what has been said. Respond sympathetically when appropriate. Restate and summarize from time to time the things that have been said to encourage the interviewee to continue his narrative. Refrain from making judgments by word or actions. These techniques help the interviewee (1) to feel as well as think his way through his difficulty and (2) to try his hand at developing a workable solution.

Check List for Appraising an Interview

1. *Opening of Interview*
   a. Was the setting of the interview conducive to obtaining the best results?
   b. Was the interviewer, himself, at ease?
   c. Did the interviewer appear as well prepared as possible?
   d. Did the interviewer put the interviewee at ease?
2. *Main Part of Interview*
   a. Did the interviewer demonstrate an awareness of the interviewee and let him participate to the fullest?
   b. Did the interviewer and the interviewee seem to jointly think their way through the problem under consideration?
   c. Did there seem to be a logical development as the interview progressed?
3. *Termination of Interview*
   a. Was there a mutual understanding of the decision and of who would do what and when, etc.?
   b. Was the interview terminated on a friendly, constructive note?

4. *Overall Rating*
   a. Did the interviewer seem to be skilled in interviewing?
   b. Any additional comments?

Concluding Remarks

What has been said about the interview—its nature, purposes, principles, and procedures—should have made it clear that interviewing is an art and not a formalized process. A knowledge of principles and techniques is a basic requirement for successful interviewing, but an understanding of people and skill in the use of these techniques are far more important. As we all know, skill—whether it is in interviewing, writing, painting, or athletics—is not only a matter of understanding but of practice.

The procedures outlined here to promote successful interviewing may have seemed involved and time consuming. But we must remember that people are exceedingly complicated beings. It would be a disservice to infer that they can be dealt with by a simple set of rules and procedures. Effective human relationships will always require a flexible approach supplemented by as much understanding, skill, experience, and wisdom as can be acquired.

The many pressures which characterize the work environment may make it seem hard to adhere to the approach recommended. But the results achieved by following these recommendations will make for more satisfying human relationships, better morale, and better employee performance which in turn should help increase output, improve service, and lower operating costs.

James M. Lahiff

Interviewing for Results

The stereotype of the typical businessman has long been a well-dressed, self-assured individual whose workday was a melange of conferences. Today's version may differ somewhat in hair style and clothing, and may, as likely as not, be a woman; however, the workday continues to be envisioned in the same way. As with most stereotypes both descriptions are somewhat removed from reality, especially in regard to the workday. For most businessmen report that they spend more time in face-to-face interaction with only bone or two others than in conferences.

Until recently the interview, the face-to-face exchange of information between two or more persons, had been neglected. It had been assumed that anyone who can carry on a conversation has the ability to conduct an interview and for that reason much more attention had been devoted to training individuals in public speaking and conference techniques, two formats whose importance is magnified by the high visibility of the participants. Since most interviews are held in private with no audience in attendance, scant attention has been accorded it.

A perusal of the recent research on the subject of interviewing should convince the skeptical that the interview has "come of age" for it has attracted the attention of a multitude of researchers representing many different disciplines. When one considers the many occupations which require considerable interviewing, it is surprising that public recognition was so slow in focusing on it.

"Interviewing for Results" by James M. Lahiff from *Readings in Interpersonal Communications* by Huseman, Logue, and Freshley, eds., 1973. Reprinted by permission of Holbrook Press, Inc.

Many regard the communication process and the interview process as one and the same. While it is true that the elements in any model of the communication process are readily identifiable in the interview process there are some differences, differences which dictate that the interview be recognized as a unique communication event.

The interview process transcends all of the unique situational variables which may affect it accidentally rather than substantially. For this reason regardless of the environment in which an interview may be conducted the basic components remain the same. It is these components, and the influence which they exert in an interview, which make the interview distinctive. The universality of these components renders this consideration of the process equally meaningful to anyone, regardless of occupation, who engages in interviews. These major components are control, objectives, questions, situational instability, crucial junctures, and receiver involvement.

Control

In this era when it is fashionable to construct a "game plan" prior to taking action one might interpret control as suggesting aggressiveness and domination. . . . The interviewer who exerts control, however, does not try to retain possession of the discussion nor does he monopolize it. Instead he seeks to draw out the desired kinds of information by keeping the interviewee on the track by reinforcing responses of a desirable nature and by inhibiting the others.

The amount of control exerted by the interviewer will determine the efficiency with which the interview is completed as well as the amount of extraneous information which will be introduced. When conducting a survey with the intent to quantify the results, the interviewer would exert more control than if he were seeking to learn why an employee, formerly reliable, has suddenly begun to shirk his duties.

A good interviewer is able to recognize in a situation the amount of control that is necessary. He is able to maintain the proper balance between control and flexibility. In any interview situation control is most recognizable in the areas of subjects discussed and in the phrasing of the questions.

Objectives

It is not enough for the interviewer to be aware of his objectives. He must transmit this information to the interviewee. Once armed with the information the interviewee has more insight into the direction to be taken by the interviewer and he can then organize his responses accordingly. Without a clear perception of objectives the interviewee is often handicapped in responding simply because he doesn't understand the purpose of the interview and hence doesn't know the kind of information that is being sought. Oftentimes it is the interviewer's lack of clarity rather than the interviewee's unwillingness to cooperate which results in an aborted interview. . . .

Questions

The correlation between appropriate questions and a successful interview cannot be overemphasized. Most authorities on the subject regard the question as the most important tool which the interviewer has. If the verb is the motor of the sentence, as has been preached by untold numbers of grammar teachers, the question is the motor of the interview.

While it is inaccurate to regard an interview as nothing more than a series of questions and answers, it is the questions which largely determine the route to be followed to the goal as well as how many detours may be encountered enroute. The lack of adequate planning of questions by the interviewer is one of the most frequent causes of inferior interviews. . . .

Crucial Junctures

By crucial junctures is meant those moments in an interview when the next response of the interviewer will largely determine whether its continuance will be productive or not, whether vital data will be elicited or if tangential information will be forthcoming. When speaking to a group, the individuality of the members reduces the import of crucial junctures. Each person's innate individuality insures that not all group members will recognize the same point as being critical and, therefore, eventual success with a group is rarely determined by the leader's recognition of certain moments as vital.

In an interview, however, crucial junctures acquire additional significance. Since all of the interviewer's efforts are usually directed at one person and since the response of that one person determines achievement for the interviewer it is mandatory that the interviewer learn to recognize those all-important moments.

While some interviewers claim to be able to know in advance, on the basis of the type of interview it is, when and how the crucial junctures will surface, many interviews are mishandled because the interviewer did not recognize what the interviewee had perceived as a crucial juncture. The interviewer may be faced with such a crisis when he least expects it. According to Holm an interviewer must anticipate where he will encounter resistance and be prepared to cope with it when it does arise.[1] It is not enough to do this and to then assume that the interviewee will be a model of cooperativeness and will perceive as junctures exactly what you had anticipated that he would.

The veteran interviewer can attest to the knack that interviewees seem to have to say and do the unexpected. It is this erratic tendency which helps keep the interviewer "honest" and cognizant of the elusive human element which makes each of us unique. How often could the nurse who conducts pre-examination interviews with the doctor's patients expect a patient to respond with "Once, in Oklahoma," to her routine inquiry of "Sex?" Rarely, but it did happen once. The point is that the unexpected does occur in the most mundane of interviews and a skillful interviewer does not allow it to deter him from accomplishing his purpose. Whether the moment is severe enough to be termed a crucial juncture or simply a "temporary inconvenience" the interviewer should not be caught unaware.

Receiver Involvement

In few communication formats is greater involvement expected of a participant than in an interview. When a public speaker holds forth on some weighty subject there is usually little active participation by members of the audience nor is it customarily expected of them. In a conference attended by ten it is more than likely that most of the ten will actively participate although none will ordinarily be expected to participate to the extent that the leader will. It is only in the interview that approximately equal participation is expected of both parties.

The necessity of stimulating involvement in the interviewee places a unique burden upon the interviewer. While this is viewed as desirable for any communicator, it is only an actual requisite in an interview. The professional interviewer secures this involvement in a variety of ways, the most obvious being through the use of appropriate questions.

Much of the interviewer's effectiveness in involving the interviewee is dependent upon the climate the interviewer establishes. Some of the determinants of climate are the attitude of both participants, the interviewer's willingness to listen, his receptiveness to new ideas, and probably most overlooked, his patience. Although the interviewer cannot establish the climate by himself, the obligation is mainly his. If the interviewee feels the climate to be satisfactory he will be more likely to cooperate and will most likely allow himself to become involved to the fullest extent possible. . . .

Types of Interviews

It is difficult to place interviews in general categories. They tend to defy the laws of categorization because of the numerous variations possible. Interviews are often classified into three types: information-getting, information-giving, and problem-solving. The difficulty with such categories is that it is implied, especially in the first two, that the interview is a unilateral, rather than a reciprocal, event. Never is this true. Because interviews are so diverse in nature they can be more clearly identified on the basis of specific purpose.

Employment Interview

Today's newspapers and journals can easily lead the uncritical reader to the conclusion that man will soon be able to vacation most of the year while the softly humming computers do his work for him. While no one can deny the widespread changes brought about by advanced technology, there are some human activities which remain relatively untouched by it all, love-making and interviewing to mention two of them. Since there is already a plethora of literature on the former, we will concentrate on the latter. . . .

While the main goal of the employment interview is to determine a person's suitability for employment, it is not the only goal. As important as securing relevant information from the interviewee is, it is equally important that enough information be transmitted to him so that he will have an accurate picture of the job. It seems likely that certain companies which have a high rate of personnel turnover could alleviate the problem somewhat by paying more attention to the way in which their interviewers describe the vacant positions. Especially when labor is scarce have interviewers been known to glamorize those positions which they are trying to fill. While this ploy often results in the rapid filling of the position, a less desirable result is that the new employee, upon recognizing the disparity between the interviewer's description and the actual job, grows frustrated equally rapidly, and before long, is seeking a different job.

The third goal of the employment interview is to create and to maintain goodwill for the company. The employment interviewer is often an individual's sole contact with a company. His importance as a practitioner of public relations is inestimable. It is the interviewer who provides the interviewee with an image of the company. . . .

Counseling Interview

The time when payment for services was thought to be the extent of an employer's obligation to his employees is long gone. Today, findings in the behavioral sciences have resulted in considerable expansion of the parameters of the obligation. It is now recognized that it is impossible to disassociate your personal life from your work and that personal problems often cause and intensify problems on the job.

The counseling interview is directed at personal problems. Emphasis on industrial counseling appears to be growing as does the incidence of personal problems which affect one's work. A recent survey in England found mental illness to be the second fastest growing cause of absence from work after sprains and strains, and that more days were lost due to that than to the common cold and influenza together. Some of the most frequently reported causes of such stress among executives are inability to cope with sudden change, failure to accept thwarted ambitions, promotions to jobs beyond one's capacity. Such problems of course are not restricted to executives nor are other common ones such as marital discord and fear about one's impending retirement.[2] These are the kinds of problems which are regularly dealt with in the counseling interview. In addition to problems of that nature many business organizations today are attempting to deal with some problems which had once been considered the sole province of the doctor, alcoholism and drugs.

The Labor-Management Services Department of the National Council on Alcoholism reports the presence of a minimum of four million men and women in the U.S. work force who suffer from this disease. Each employee costs a company at least $1500 to $2000 a year because of absenteeism and health plan claims related to the illness.[3] Since two out of three alcoholics who are willing to accept treatment can be rehabilitated, employers often attempt to initiate the treatment of such employees through the counseling interview.

In a 1970 survey of fifty New York companies,

conducted by the New York Chamber of Commerce, only five reported no incidence of drug abuse on company premises. Most of these companies have also noticed a sharp increase in absenteeism, turnover, and theft. A significant share of these problems is reportedly attributable to drug abuse by employees. Many firms now provide counseling for users as well as for those employees who, while not users, are considered to be susceptible by virtue of their age and peer group. In either of these problems, alcoholism or drug abuse, the counseling provided by the employer is usually of a preliminary nature with its main goal being to motivate the individual to seek professional assistance.

While managers must often conduct counseling interviews, there are other occupations which make even greater use of them. Many social workers, for example, devote a large part to counseling interviews.[4] . . .

Regardless of the situation in which the counseling interview is being conducted, it is important that the interviewer strive to create a climate in which understanding will flourish. Such a climate is most likely if the interviewer: 1) secures the trust of the interviewee, possibly through the assurance that the information the interviewee provides will remain confidential; 2) maintains a permissive atmosphere, one in which the interviewee will feel free to introduce any subject into the discussion without fear of offending, alienating, or embarrassing the interviewer; 3) is nondirective in approach so that the interviewee, rather than the interviewer, will determine the subjects to be considered; 4) is nonevaluative in words and demeanor. Some authorities consider the tendency to evaluate to be the main barrier to communication.[5] The interviewer should accept what the interviewee says, without any indication of approval or disapproval; 5) empathizes with the interviewee. Empathy is the ability to understand and identify with another. An empathic interviewer is able to sense the feelings and personal meanings of the interviewee as though he himself were experiencing them.

Work Appraisal Interview

The work appraisal interview is one in which an employee meets with a superior for the purpose of discussing the quality of the employee's performance on the job. In many organizations these interviews are conducted on a regular basis, often annually or semi-annually. In recent years, however, there has been a move toward making such appraisals a continuous process rather than scheduling them simply on the basis of the calendar. In too many organizations, appraisals are conducted primarily because it is the organization's policy and little attempt is made to make it a helpful experience for the interviewee.

The appraisal interview is normally conducted by an employee's immediate superior, the person who is probably in the best position to evaluate him. One of the most common problems encountered in this type of interview is defensiveness by the interviewee. A technique sometimes employed to overcome this is to invite the interviewee to appraise himself and to then express disagreement or agreement with his findings as he states them. This mutual involvement will facilitate a more rational discussion of the on-the-job problems which the employee experiences.

Employees often criticize the traditional appraisal format because of the tendency of the interviewer to dwell upon negative information. Considerable research has verified that this emphasis is true in regard to the selection interview,[6] and there is little reason to doubt its applicability to the appraisal interview also.

It is important that the interviewer remember the desirability of providing some positive feedback also, for the appraisal interview has several purposes, none of which will be accomplished by devoting the interview to a recitation of the employee's faults. Besides the obvious purpose of discussing job performance, the interviewer also seeks to inspire the interviewee to improve it, and one route to accomplishing this is by letting the employee know that his efforts are recognized and appreciated by the employer.

Employees are often unaware of the standards by which they are being measured. It is part of the interviewer's task to inform the employee of the standards and of their meaning. It is not uncommon for the employees to question the applicability of the standards to their individual job duties and the interviewer should remain open-minded and responsive to this subject. Since many organizations measure all employees, or at least large numbers of them, by the same standards, these complaints are frequently well-founded. . . .

The key to successful appraisal interviewing is the ability to involve the interviewee in open two-way communication. Such involvement is a prerequisite for his acceptance of the evaluation and for the establishment of goals for the future which, if they have been mutually agreed upon, should result in improved performance.

Disciplinary Interview

Of the numerous roles played by a manager, one of the least enjoyable, but most important, is that of the disciplinary interviewer. Goethe's advice to "Treat people as if they were what they ought to be and you help them to become what they are capable of being," is laudable and deserving of consideration. Unfortunately it is not always feasible. There comes a time when the manager must attempt to correct some behavior or attitude of a subordinate. Some of the most common reasons for such interviews are habitual tardiness, wasting time, and doing work improperly.

When conducting a disciplinary interview, objectivity is of maximum importance. Since the recognition of the need for this type of interview is often accompanied by anger and frustration (i.e., you are "mad as hell"), it is often necessary to defer the interview until you have had a chance to simmer down. It is impossible to be both angry and objective at the same time.

While the temptation may be great to preach to the interviewee, it must be subjugated to the intent to get his side of the story. . . .

At the conclusion of the interview, the employee should know where he stands, not just in general but specifically. If the interview is to be followed by some action the interviewee should be made to understand what it will be. If there are several courses of action, perhaps an appeal process is one of them, they should be clearly explained to him. Disciplinary interviews are not intended to strengthen friendships, however, neither must they disrupt the working relationship between the two parties. Used effectively, the disciplinary interview will result in a more efficient organization, as well as in a clearer perception by individuals of the roles expected of them.

Probably the most extreme type of disciplinary interview is that which results in firing the employee. As with the more common types of disciplinary interview, it is not to be conducted in the heat of anger. . . .

The interviewer should be prepared to explain the termination process and its effect on such things as the company's insurance plan and retirement benefits. The employee might possibly raise the question of whether or not the company would serve as a job reference for him. Since this is of the utmost importance to the employee, the interviewer should be completely honest in his response and tell him exactly what he feels can be said in his behalf. Since this interview is usually regarded as equally unpleasant by both parties, if the interviewer is prepared and decisive, neither party will wish to prolong it.

Exit Interview

An exit interview is one which is ordinarily conducted by a representative of the personnel department and an employee who is voluntarily leaving his job. The purpose of the interview is to learn the person's reasons for leaving. The rationale behind the exit interview is that if an organization learns the causes of employee turnover it will be able to remedy the problem.

As the expense of training new employees grows and as it becomes increasingly difficult to find satisfactory employees, exit interviews are receiving considerable attention at many companies. . . .

In the exit interview the interviewer is confronted with a number of unique obstacles to frank disclosure of reasons for leaving the job. A feeling of suspicion on the part of the interviewee is one of them. It is natural for him to wonder why, all of a sudden, has the company gotten interested in his thoughts and feelings. Another obstacle is presented by the interviewee's desire, often unspoken, to get a favorable recommendation from his employer. Another possible explanation for the interviewee's hesitancy to give reasons is his wish to keep a "foot in the door" by departing on a pleasant note and hence making it possible to return to this employer should his plans for the new job go awry. It is the interviewer's task to overcome these obstacles and determine the interviewee's real reasons for leaving.

Considering the above obstacles, it is obvious that the interviewer must secure the trust of the interviewee. How does the interviewer allay the suspicions of the interviewee? If the organization has regularly shown interest in the attitudes and suggestions of its employees, this task will be much easier than otherwise. Early in the interview it is sometimes possible to facilitate communication by sincerely explaining to the interviewee that the information he provides you with will in no way influence any employment references which he may seek in the future from the company. A brief discussion of the type of recommendation he would receive at any rate might result in cooperation.

One of the pitfalls of the exit interview is the ease with which it can be transformed from an open exchange of information to one which is conspiratorial and clandestine in tone. The motives of the interviewer should be beyond question and the appeal made by him should be directed at the highest motives of the interviewee—his unique ability to provide helpful information, and his altruism in providing it.

Information-seeking Interview

The kinds of interviews which fall within this broad category differ markedly one from the other. An interview conducted by the U.S. Census Bureau is a prime example of this type as are the numerous kinds of opinion polls with which we are all familiar.

When structuring this kind of interview, one must determine definitely the kind of information being sought. If a large number of interviews are to be conducted it is advisable to run a pilot study. In the pilot study you will conduct a small number of interviews in order to determine how well the respondents understand the questions and to insure that you are eliciting the kind of information which you are seeking. On the basis of the findings in the pilot study one is usually able to adapt the interview plan so as to increase understanding. It is important that all of the interviews be conducted in a uniform manner in order to reduce the influence of the variation in interviewing style. . . .

Persuasive Interview

We are all veterans of many persuasive interviews. As consumers many of the product choices we reach are arrived at through an interview with a salesperson. While few of us conduct persuasive interviews as a part of our occupation, as a salesperson does, we still engage in a considerable number in our business life as well as in our social activities.

Whether you are seeking a covert response, such as tacit agreement that your candidate is the only man for the office, or an overt response, such as getting a friend to cosign a bank note for you, the persuasive process is the same. A key to effective persuasive interviewing is to appeal to the interests of the interviewee. The interviewer must show the interviewee how he will benefit from making the desired decision. Since the interests and wants of the interviewee can only be learned through appropriate questions it follows that success in persuasive interviewing is contingent upon the framing of the questions.

Phases of the Interview

There are six distinct phases into which the interview process may be divided. To consider these phases as distinct does not mean that they are separate from what precedes and follows, since an interview is a continuous process, but that the thrust of the interviewer's strategy differs at each stage. The phases follow in their usual sequence.

1. Preliminary Planning

In most cases this is the only phase which is truly separated from the others, for an effective interviewer, like any effective strategist, does his planning prior to the event itself. In the planning phase the interviewer determines the specific purpose of the interview, exactly what he wants to accomplish, and then predicts what action he must take to accomplish this purpose with the interviewee(s) with whom he will be meeting. The more he can learn about the interviewee the more accurate his prediction is likely to be.

On the basis of his knowledge of the interviewee and of the purpose of the interview the interviewer then makes two crucial decisions: a) the amount of structure he will provide in the interview, and b) the kinds of questions he will employ.

The interviewer will usually provide a high degree of structure if he is seeking very specific information or if he is going to conduct a number of interviews and wishes to insure uniformity in the questions he will ask. An interview in which all of the questions have been written out in advance would be highly structured.

The kinds of questions to be asked are usually determined by the nature of the interview. An interview conducted for the U.S. Census Bureau would probably be comprised of closed questions, those which call for a specific response. The office manager, seeking to learn the extent of an employee's involvement with drugs, will probably rely on more open-ended questions in the expectation that the free response format will stimulate the interviewee to expound upon the subject.

2. Clarification of Purpose

In many instances when a person is called in for an interview he believes that he knows the reason for it. Sometimes he is right, other times grievously wrong. A common mistake by interviewers, however, is to assume that the interviewee is aware of the reason. It is not uncommon for a person to participate in a thirty-minute counseling interview and to then depart still not knowing the purpose of it. Even at the risk of belaboring the obvious, the interviewer should always prevent this unnecessary problem by simply stating his purpose.

3. Preview of Topics

After the interviewer has clarified the purpose of the interview, the interviewee is usually asking himself "What kind of information is he going to want?" Unfortunately in most interviews the question goes unanswered and the interviewee must wait from one question to the next in order to realize what the interviewer is getting at. Therein lies one of the main faults of most interviewers. By failing to give advance notice early in the interview of topics to be covered, the interviewer misses the opportunity to provide some direction for the interviewee and thereby help him organize his thoughts. This advance notice will usually increase the interviewee's trust in the interviewer. . . .

4. Motivation of Interviewee

Since few interviewees are materially rewarded for their efforts and since it is common for the interviewee to be apprehensive about the interview it is usually necessary for the interviewer to provide some motivation. The greater the threat felt by the interviewee, the more the interviewer must motivate him to insure his cooperation. Another factor which will dictate the necessary level of motivation is the effort which the interviewee must expend to participate in the interview. The interviewer for the man-on-the-street radio program need usually provide little motivation to learn

how you feel about taxes since there would be little threat involved. The interviewer seeking interviewees for an hour long in-depth interview will have to provide some sort of motivation as will the interviewer seeking data of a very personal nature.

5. Body of the Interview

It is in this phase that the interviewer must pursue his preconceived plan with the intent of accomplishing the purpose of the interview. In most interviews the interviewer's main function is to ask questions, the sequence of which is determined by the type of information he is seeking. When asking questions, one should group them on the basis of the topics you had previewed for the interviewee in the third step of the interview sequence. By organizing your questions in this manner, you are providing continuity which will facilitate the exchange of relevant information.

While the interviewer's main function is to ask questions, it is not his only function. He will also be expected to answer the questions raised by the interviewee, whenever one arises, rather than wait until the end of the interview.

6. Summary of Conclusions

By the close of the interview, a great deal of information will probably have been exchanged. In most interviews a fair amount of this information is irrelevant. Sometimes, especially in poorly planned interviews, there is redundancy in the information discussed. . . .

The irrelevancies plus the redundancies plus unanticipated interruptions may combine to blur the conclusions arrived at. For this reason, it is important for the interviewer to summarize the conclusions he feels were reached in the interview. If the interviewee perceives the conclusions somewhat differently he can raise his objections immediately and the two parties can mutually clarify whatever discrepancy there is. It often happens that such a summary is overlooked and the interview ends with the parties unaware that such differences exist. . . .

It has been the purpose of this article to illuminate the process of interviewing. To that end we have investigated those components which characterize this format of communication. The most common types of interviews have been analyzed and the phases which are common to all of the types identified. The causes of distorted information were also considered.

All that remains to be done is to assure the reader that should he religiously follow all of the advice included herein he will never err as an interviewer. Such assurance will not be forthcoming, however, for two reasons: 1) Since there are exceptions to every rule, blind allegiance to rules is a mistake, and 2) Because we are dealing with fellow human beings whose most interesting frailty is their unpredictability. It is for these reasons that the study and practice of interviewing is difficult and challenging, but rarely boring.

Notes

[1] James N. Holm, *Productive Speaking for Business and the Professions* (Boston: Allyn and Bacon, 1967), p. 230.

[2] Iain Carson, "What Are the Causes of Executive Stress?" *International Management,* (January 1972), 16.

[3] From *Industrial Relations News,* November 13, 1971, as quoted in "Notes and Quotes" No. 390, December 1971, a newsletter published by Conn. Genl. Ins. Co.

[4] Margaret Schubert, *Interviewing in Social Work Practice* (New York: Council on Social Work Education, 1971), 30–37.

[5] Robert L. Kahn and Charles F. Cannell, *The Dynamics of Interviewing* (New York: John Wiley & Sons, 1957), 7.

[6] See W. Crissy and J. Regan, "Halo in the Employment Interview," *Journal of Applied Psychology,* 45 (1961), 97–103. B. Springbett, "Factors Affecting the Final Decision in the Employment Interview," *Canadian Journal of Psychology,* 12 (1958), 13–22. B. I. Bolster and B. M. Springbett, "The Reaction of Interviewers to Favorable and Unfavorable Information," *Journal of Applied Psychology,* 45 (1961), 97–103.

Julius Fast

Can You Influence People Through "Body Language"?

The bus was crowded when Peter boarded it and he found himself close to very pretty girl. Peter enjoyed the bus ride and admired the girl; in fact, he couldn't keep his eyes off her. Staring at her, he noticed that she had light blue eyes and dark brown hair, a pleasant combination.

His innocent enjoyment was shattered when the girl turned to him angrily before she left the bus and said loudly, "You should be ashamed of yourself!"

"What did I do?" Peter asked the driver in honest bewilderment. "I only looked at her."

"It takes all kinds . . ." the driver shrugged, but did he mean Peter or the girl? Peter spent a miserable evening wondering just what he had done that was wrong. He would have known what was wrong if he understood some of the rules of body language. Peter violated a very basic law. He looked at the girl beyond the proper looking time.

For every situation there is a proper looking time, a definite period during which you are allowed to meet and hold someone's eyes. In an elevator the time is so brief that it can hardly be considered looking at all. Your eye catches that of a stranger and you look away at once. In a crowded bus, a subway or train, you can look a little longer. But go beyond the proper time—some 10 seconds—and you violate the unwritten but rigid code of body language and take the chance of getting into the same situation that embarrassed Peter.

"Can You Influence People Through 'Body Language'?" by Julius Fast. Reprinted from November 1970 issue of *Family Cirlce* Magazine. © 1970. The Family Circle, Inc.

The girl Peter admired interpreted his stare as insolent or arrogant or insulting in the same way that a cripple interprets the stares of the curious. If we have any consideration, we look only briefly at a cripple or a deformed person, pretending not to look at all.

We look at celebrities in the same way, taking care not to catch their eyes, not to stare at them with too curious a look.

The unwritten laws of body language allow a longer time for staring when we talk to someone, but it is still a limited time. In all conversations we look away frequently and break eye contact. Only a lecturer or a politician addressing an audience can hold eye contact as long as he wishes.

Just what are these unwritten laws of body language? For that matter, just what is body language? Are the rules learned or are they acquired instinctively? Do we all know them, or are they something we must learn? If so, how do we learn them?

These questions have intrigued psychologists ever since they discovered that we communicate with more than the words we speak. Words are only one part of communication. How we use those words is another part. Are our voices loud, angry, overbearing, confident, soft, shy? The quality of a voice can communicate as much as the words. The same words can be tender, mocking, sarcastic or angry, depending on how they are said. We can signal our own authority by talking in a loud, overbearing way. We can use the same words to signal our humility by talking softly and hesitantly. But even beyond voice communication, there are the messages our bodies send out constantly. Sometimes the body message reinforces the words. Sometimes the messages are sent with no accompanying words and we speak in body language alone.

But what gestures make up body language? Most of us are familiar with the common hand gestures. Some people cannot talk without using their hands. They reach out as they explain, almost shaping the words, emphasizing and exaggerating and punctuating with their hands. Other people hardly use their hands at all when they talk. How people use their hands and whether they use them depends on their cultural background. Italians are great hand movers. So are Russians and Latin Americans. Englishmen are stingy about their hand movements; they appear as more controlled and rigid in their behavior.

In the United States, almost any type of hand movement can be found because we have a mixture of cultures. American etiquette books tell us that waving the hands and gesticulating is ill-mannered and distasteful. It is "unrefined." Refined behavior is always tight and formal. True etiquette can be equated with control and discipline. It can also be equated with an Anglo-Saxon, over-controlled culture. But our cultural mix in the last century has been too much for books of etiquette.

It is just this cultural mix in America that makes some men more eloquent than others. When body language is used to emphasize the spoken language, to reinforce it, the man who cannot use it is crippled. Too many politicians, awkward with their hands, have learned this to their sorrow. Many have had their images revamped by a re-education in body language.

A man who uses hand movements when he talks appears freer, more open and more honest to an audience than a controlled nonmover. At certain times, however, a limited amount of hand movement indicates things like solidity, reliability and confidence.

A good politician knows this instinctively and matches his hand movements to the image he wishes to project. Former President Johnson was apparently taught the proper hand movements because his image was too distant and withdrawn. There was a period, before he learned the gestures, when he appeared awkward and uncomfortable.

It seems obvious that President Nixon has had his body language changed and tailored to match his new image. He does not come across now as the same man who lost the election to John Kennedy in 1960, and the change is largely due to a more controlled, but not nearly so stiff, body movement.

Fiorello H. La Guardia, New York City's mayor in the '30s and early '40s, used to campaign in English, Italian, and Yiddish. When he spoke Italian he had one set of hand gestures, another set for Yiddish and still a third for English. Each language demanded its own set of body-language gestures.

But body language is more than hand movements. The eyes play a large part, too. Try holding a fellow pedestrian's eyes a bit longer than the proper time. You create an awkward situation and often the only solution is to smile and offer a casual remark, "How are you?" or "Nice day." You may find yourself in conversation with a complete stranger.

The eyes give hidden signals as well as obvious ones. Scientists have found that the pupils dilate unconsciously under pleasant circumstances. Show a man a naked lady, or show a woman a pretty baby, and their pupils dilate. Do the pupils also dilate when a man has a good hand at poker? If so, then perhaps the "natural" poker player is one who unconsciously reads this body-language sign.

What of the rest of the body? Does it also send out unconscious signals?

It does, and the fact that these signals are unconscious means that they are beyond our control. We are not aware that we are sending them out and, therefore, they are more honest than words. It is easy to lie with our voices. but murder to lie with our bodies.

Actors are the exception to this rule. They are trained to lie with their bodies. Recently I talked to Lily Tomlin, who plays a number of characters on "Laugh-In." One of them, a telephone operator, is a masterpiece of body language. The operator torments a customer as she plucks at her breast and twists her face and body. Discussing her movements I told Miss Tomlin that the breast-touching indicated loneliness and introversion; the foot-twisting, self-satisfaction.

"That's what she is," Miss Tomlin agreed. "Lonely and yet self-satisfied with what she is doing. The gestures? They just came naturally once I knew the character."

This is an unconscious adoption of body-language gestures by an actress who first created the character, then lived it and, in living it, naturally used the right body-language gestures.

In addition to the messages we send with our bodies, we also use the space around us to communicate. All of us have our own territories—comfortable distances that we like to keep between us and our friends. We stay closer to people we love, farther away from strangers. When a stranger intrudes on our territory—comes too close to us—we may find it uncomfortable. If the intruder is a wife or husband or lover, we may like the intrusion. It tells us, "I care for you. I love you."

Parents often use space to dominate a child. By looming over him, a parent proves her superiority. The child feels the parent as overpowering and himself as helpless. On the other hand, a parent can draw a child into the circle of her arms and by forcibly invading his space, communicate love and warmth. To do this more easily, the parent may kneel down to the child's level and do away with the looming quality of an adult-child encounter.

Teachers, too, can take a tip from body language in relating to their pupils. The teacher who sits behind a desk is placing an obstacle, the desk, between herself and her pupils. In body language she's saying, "I am your superior. I am here to teach you. You must obey me."

Many educators feel that this is an important and necessary attitude to establish if any "real" teaching is to be done. Other teachers, however, try to do away with the barrier of a desk. They perch on the edge of it and have nothing between them and their students. Still others feel that this is an elevated position, putting the teacher above the student and creating resistance to the teacher. They prefer a position in the center of the room, surrounded by the students, some of whom must turn in their seats to face the teacher.

"This," a teacher once explained to me, "puts me in the center of things. I never sit in a student's seat because I'd be too low. I'd be no better than a student, and a teacher has to be better or why be a teacher? I sit on a student's desk in the center of the room. I'm one of them and yet still a teacher. You'd be amazed at how well they respond."

She is using space to communicate a body-language message. "I'm one of you. I'm on your side even though I'm your teacher."

Which method is most efficient? It's hard to say, except that each teacher must adopt the method that works best for her. If her body language is restricted and tight, sitting on a student's desk may seem simply an affectation—false and unnatural.

The use of desk as a protective device is familiar to everyone who has watched the Johnny Carson show. Carson uses a desk to separate himself from his guests and to achieve a certain formality. David Frost, when he interviews a guest, does away with a desk and sometimes even does away with chairs, sitting on the stage steps with his guest and using territorial invasion and touch to communicate closeness and warmth. Frost's interviews have a different quality from Carson's because of this different use of space. Perhaps not better, but surely more personal.

The quality of an interview depends not only on the body language of the interviewer, but on his personality as well, and every personality has its own characteristic body-language gestures, even as each culture has its own gestures. We shake our heads up and down for "yes." In India they use the same gesture for "no." To really understand a person's body language we must understand something of their personality, as well as something of their cultural background.

But there are some gestures, such as smiles, that seem to cut across cultural lines. In America there are many common gestures in spite of our cultural mix. Arm-crossing and leg-crossing are two of them. If someone is trying to persuade us and we cross our arms tightly, it is often a sign of resistance. Crossed legs can also be a sign of resistance. When a woman crosses them tightly at the knees and at the ankles, sort of intertwining them, it may indicate resistance to sexuality or a tight, closed personality.

Women in pants tend to give better clues to their emotions by the positioning of their legs. They can sprawl out comfortably. If they sit with open laps they may indicate acceptance, not only sexually, but also intellectually. The well-organized woman may tend to run her legs parallel—as orderly as her life. But I say "tend" because these are still just tendencies. With a skirt, parallel legs are simply a model's pose. Girls are taught in charm schools that this is more graceful. They

area also taught the proper arm-crossing.

If all this is true, can we ever really tell anything from a person's body language? Can we use it to control other people or to interpret the true meaning of the messages they send?

We can. We can learn certain tricks of domination to control a situation. We can arrange to be higher than our subordinates, or we can allow our boss to be higher than we are. We can be aware that we dominate our children when we hover over them, that certain facial gestures should be matched to main body gestures for a smoother appearance—but these are tricks and rather superficial. The real value of body language lies in the insight it can give to our behavior.

Are we tight and rigid about life in general? Our body language can give us a clue to how we are acting and allow us to change our behavior for the latter. How a woman sits next to a man on a couch contains a dozen clues to her personality. Does she use her arms as a barrier? Does she cross her legs away from him? Does she turn her body toward him?

How we react to other people's zones of privacy, and how strong our territorial needs are, give other clues. Do we feel uncomfortable when people are close to us? Are we afraid of touching, of being touched? If we are, it might be a sign of our own insecurity, our own fear of revealing ourselves. Understanding this can allow us to take the first step toward dropping the barriers that stand between us and the world.

Only when these barriers begin to fall is it possible to realize not only our own potential as human beings, but the potential of the entire world around us.

John Fielden

"What Do You Mean I Can't Write?"

What do businessmen answer when they are asked, "What's the most troublesome problem you have to live with?" Frequently they reply, "People just can't write! What do they learn in college now? When I was a boy . . . !"

There is no need to belabor this point; readers know well how true it is. *HBR* subscribers, for example, recently rated the "ability to communicate" as the prime requisite of a promotable executive.[1] And, of all the aspects of communication, the written form is the most troublesome, if only because of its formal nature. It is received cold, without the communicator's tone of voice or gesture to help. It is rigid; it cannot be adjusted to the recipients' reactions as it is being delivered. It stays "on the record," and cannot be undone. Further, the reason it is in fact committed to paper is usually that its subject is considered too crucial or significant to be entrusted to casual, short-lived verbal form.

Businessmen know that the ability to write well is a highly valued asset in a top executive. Consequently, they become ever more conscious of their writing ability as they consider what qualities they need in order to rise in their company.

They know that in big business today ideas are not exchanged exclusively by word of mouth (as they might be in smaller businesses). And they know that even if they get oral approval for something they wish to do, there will be the inevitable "give me a memo on it" concluding remark that

will send them back to their office to oversee the writing of a carefully documented report.

They know, too, that as they rise in their company, they will have to be able to supervise the writing of subordinates—for so many of the memos, reports, and letters written by subordinates will go out over their signature, or be passed on to others in the company and thus reflect on the caliber of work done under their supervision.

Even the new data-processing machines will not make business any less dependent on words. For while the new machines are fine for handling tabular or computative work, someone must write up an eventual analysis of the findings in the common parlance of the everyday executive.

Time for Action

Complaints about the inability of managers to write are a very common and justifiable refrain. But the problem this article poses—and seeks to solve—is that it is of very little use to complain about something and stop right there. I think it is about time for managers to begin to do something about it. And the first step is *define what "it"—what good business writing—really is.*

Suppose you are a young managerial aspirant who has recently been told: "You simply can't write!" What would this mean to you? Naturally, you would be hurt, disappointed, perhaps even alarmed to have your *own* nagging doubts about your writing ability put uncomfortably on the line. "Of course," you say, "I know I'm no stylist. I don't even pretend to be a literarily inclined person. But how can I improve my writing on the job?

"What Do You Mean I Can't Write?" by John Fielden from *Harvard Business Review*, May-June 1964. © 1964 by the President and Fellows of Harvard College; all rights reserved.
[1] See also C. Wilson Randle, "How to Identify Promotable Executives," *HBR* (May-June 1956), p. 122.

Where do I begin? Exactly what is wrong with my writing?" But nobody tells you in specific, meaningful terms.

Does this mean that you can't spell or punctuate or that your grammar is disastrous? Does it mean that you can't think or organize your thoughts? Or does it mean that even though you are scrupulously correct in grammar and tightly organized in your thinking, a report or letter from you is always completely unreadable; that reading it, in effect, is like trying to butt one's head through a brick wall? Or does it mean that you are so tactless and boorish in the human relations aspect of communication that your messages actually build resentment and resistance? Do you talk "down" too much or do you talk "over your reader's head"? Just what do you do wrong?

Merely being told that you can't write is so basically meaningless and so damaging to your morale that you may end up writing more ineffectually than ever before. What you need to know is: "What are the elements of good business writing? And in which of these elements am I proficient? In which do I fall down?" If only the boss could break his complaint down into a more meaningful set of components, you could begin to do something about them.

Now let's shift and assume that you are a high-ranking manager whose job it is to supervise a staff of assistants. What can you do about upgrading the writing efforts of your men? You think of the time lost by having to do reports and letters over and over before they go out, the feasibility reports which did not look so feasible after having been befogged by an ineffectual writer, the letters presented for your signature that would have infuriated the receiver had you let them be mailed. But where are you to start?

Here is where the interests of superior and subordinate meet. Unless both arrive at a common understanding, a shared vocabulary that enables them to communicate with one another about the writing jobs that need to be done, nobody is going to get very far. No oversimplified, gimmicky slogans (such as, "Every letter is a sales letter"; "Accentuate the positive, eliminate the negative"; or "Write as you speak") are going to serve this purpose. No partial view is either—whether that of the English teacher, the logician, or the social scientist—since good business writing is not just grammar, or clear thinking, or winning friends and influencing people. It is some of each, the proportion depending on the purpose.

Total Inventory

To know what effective business writing is, we need a total inventory of all its aspects, so that:

• Top managers can say to their training people, "Are you sure our training efforts in written communications are not tackling just part of the problem? Are we covering all aspects of business writing?"

• A superior can say to an assistant, "Here, look; this is where you are weak. See? It is one thing when you write letters that you sign, another when you write letters that I sign. The position and power of the person we are writing to make a lot of difference in *what* we say and *how* we say it."

• The young manager can use the inventory as a guide to self-improvement (perhaps even ask his superior to go over his writing with him, using the writing inventory as a means of assuring a common critical vocabulary).

• The superior may himself get a few hints about how he might improve his own performance.

Such an inventory appears in Exhibit I. Notice that it contains four basic categories—*readability, correctness, appropriateness,* and *thought.* Considerable effort has gone into making these categories (and the subtopics under them) as mutually exclusive as possible, although some overlap is inevitable. But even if they are not completely exclusive, they are still far less general than an angry, critical remark, such as, "You cannot write."

EXHIBIT I. WRITTEN PERFORMANCE INVENTORY

1. READABILITY

Reader's Level
- [ ] Too specialized in approach
- [ ] Assumes too great a knowledge of subject
- [ ] So underestimates the reader that it belabors the obvious

Sentence Construction
- [ ] Unnecessarily long in difficult material
- [ ] Subject-verb-object word order too rarely used
- [ ] Choppy, overly simple style (in simple material)

Paragraph Construction
- [ ] Lack of topic sentences
- [ ] Too many ideas in single paragraph
- [ ] Too long

Familiarity of Words
- [ ] Inappropriate jargon
- [ ] Pretentious language
- [ ] Unnecessarily abstract

Reader Direction
- [ ] Lack of "framing" (i.e., failure to tell the reader about purpose and direction of forthcoming discussion)
- [ ] Inadequate transitions between paragraphs
- [ ] Absence of subconclusions to summarize reader's progress at end of divisions in the discussion

Focus
- [ ] Unclear as to subject of communication
- [ ] Unclear as to purpose of message

2. CORRECTNESS

Mechanics
- [ ] Shaky grammar
- [ ] Faulty punctuation

Format
- [ ] Careless appearance of documents
- [ ] Failure to use accepted company form

Coherence
- [ ] Sentences seem awkward owing to illogical and ungrammatical yoking of unrelated ideas
- [ ] Failure to develop a logical progression of ideas through coherent, logically juxtaposed paragraphs

3. APPROPRIATENESS

A. Upward Communications

Tact
- [ ] Failure to recognize differences in position between writer and receiver
- [ ] Impolitic tone—too brusk, argumentative, or insulting

Supporting Detail
- [ ] Inadequate support for statements
- [ ] Too much undigested detail for busy superior

Opinion
- [ ] Adequate research but too great an intrusion of opinions
- [ ] Too few facts (and too little research) to entitle drawing of conclusions
- [ ] Presence of unasked for but clearly implied recommendations

Attitude
- [ ] Too obvious a desire to please superior
- [ ] Too defensive in face of authority
- [ ] Too fearful of superior to be able to do best work

B. Downward Communications

Diplomacy
- [ ] Overbearing attitude toward subordinates
- [ ] Insulting and/or personal references
- [ ] Unmindfulness that messages are representative of management group or even of company

Clarification of Desires
- [ ] Confused, vague instructions
- [ ] Superior is not sure of what is wanted
- [ ] Withholding of information necessary to job at hand

Motivational Aspects
- [ ] Orders of superior seem arbitrary
- [ ] Superior's communications are manipulative and seemingly insincere

4. THOUGHT

Preparation
- [ ] Inadequate thought given to purpose of communication prior to its final completion
- [ ] Inadequate preparation or use of data known to be available

Competence
- [ ] Subject beyond intellectual capabilities of writer
- [ ] Subject beyond experience of writer

Fidelity to Assignment
- [ ] Failure to stick to job assigned
- [ ] Too much made of routine assignment
- [ ] Too little made of assignment

Analysis
- [ ] Superficial examination of data leading to unconscious overlooking of important pieces of evidence
- [ ] Failure to draw obvious conclusions from data presented
- [ ] Presentation of conclusions unjustified by evidence
- [ ] Failure to qualify tenuous assertions
- [ ] Failure to identify and justify assumptions used
- [ ] Bias, conscious or unconscious, which leads to distorted interpretation of data

Persuasiveness
- [ ] Seems more convincing than facts warrant
- [ ] Seems less convincing than facts warrant
- [ ] Too obvious an attempt to sell ideas
- [ ] Lacks action-orientation and managerial viewpoint
- [ ] Too blunt an approach where subtlety and finesse called for

Furthermore, you should understand that these four categories are not listed in order of importance, since their importance varies according to the abilities and the duties of each individual. The same thing is true of the subtopics; I shall make no attempt to treat each of them equally, but will simply try to do some practical, commonsense highlighting. I will begin with readability, and discuss it most fully, because this is an area where half-truths abound and need to be scotched before introducing the other topics.

Readability

What is *readability?* Nothing more than a clear style of writing. It does not result absolutely (as some readability experts would have you believe) from mathematical counts of syllables, of sentence length, or of abstract words. These inflexible approaches to readability assume that all writing is being addressed to a general audience. Consequently, their greatest use is in forming judgments about the readability of such things as mass magazine editorial copy, newspaper communications, and elementary textbooks.

. . . It does not make much difference whether the sentences are long or short; if the reader does not have the background to understand the material, he just doesn't. And writing specialized articles according to the mathematical readability formulas is not going to make them clearer.

Nevertheless, it is true that unnecessarily long, rambling sentences are wearing to read. Hence you will find these stylistic shortcomings mentioned in Exhibit I. The trick a writer has to learn is to judge the complexity and the abstractness of the material he is dealing with, and to cut his sentences down in those areas where the going is especially difficult. It also helps to stick to a direct subject-verb-object construction in sentences wherever it is important to communicate precisely. Flights of unusually dashing style should be re-served for those sections which are quite general in nature and concrete in subject matter.

What about paragraphs? The importance of "paragraph construction" is often overlooked in business communication, but few things are more certain to make the heart sink than the sight of page after page of unbroken type. One old grammar book rule would be especially wise to hark back to, and that is the topic sentence. Not only does placing a topic sentence at the beginning of each paragraph make it easier for the reader to grasp the content of the communication quickly; it also serves to discipline the writer into including only one main idea in each paragraph. Naturally, when a discussion of one idea means the expenditure of hundreds (or thousands) of words, paragraphs should be divided according to subdivisions of the main idea. In fact, an almost arbitrary division of paragraphs into units of four or five sentences is usually welcomed by the reader.

As for jargon, the only people who complain about it seriously are those who do not understand it. Moreover, it is fashionable for experts in a particular field to complain about their colleagues' use of jargon, but then to turn right around and use it themselves. The reason is that jargon is no more than shop talk. And when the person being addressed fully understands this private language, it is much more economical to use it than to go through laborious explanations of every idea that could be communicated in the shorthand of jargon. Naturally, when a writer knows that his message is going to be read by persons who are not familiar with the private language of his trade, he should be sure to translate as much of the jargon as he can into common terms.

The same thing holds true for simplicity of language. Simplicity is, I would think, always a "good." True, there is something lost from our language when interesting but unfamiliar words are no longer used. But isn't it true that the shrines in which these antiquities should be preserved lie in the domain of poetry or the novel, and not in business communications—which, after all, are not baroque cathedrals but functional edifices by which a job can be done?

The simplest way to say it, then, is invariably the best in business writing. But this fact the young executive does not always understand. Often he is eager to parade his vocabulary before his superiors, for fear his boss (who has never let him know that he admires simplicity, and may indeed adopt a pretentious and ponderous style himself) may think less of him.

Leading the Reader

But perhaps the most important aspect of readability is the one listed under the subtopic "reader direction." The failure of writers to seize their reader by the nose and lead him carefully through the intricacies of his communication is like an epidemic. The job that the writer must do is to develop the "skeleton" of the document that he is preparing. And, at the very beginning of his communication, he should identify the skeletal structure of his paper; he should, in effect, frame the discussion which is to follow.

You will see many of these frames at the beginning of articles published in *HBR,* where the editors take great pains to tell the reader quickly what the article is about and what specific areas will come under discussion during its progress. In every business document this initial frame, this statement of purpose and direction, should appear. Furthermore, in lengthy reports there should be many such frames; indeed, most major sections of business reports should begin with a new frame.

There should also be clear transitions between paragraphs. The goal should be that of having each element in a written message bear a close relationship to those elements which have preceded and those which follow it. Frequently a section should end with a brief summary, plus a sentence or two telling the reader the new direction of the article. These rather mechanical signposts, while frequently the bane of literary stylists, are always of valuable assistance to readers.

The final aspect of readability is the category that I call "focus." This term refers to the fact that many communications seem diffuse and out of focus, much like a picture on a television screen when the antennas are not properly directed. Sometimes in a report it seems as if one report has been superimposed on another, and that there are no clear and particular points the writer is trying to make. Thus the burden is put on the reader to ferret out the truly important points from the chaos.

If a writer wants to improve the readability of his writing, he must make sure that he has thought things through sufficiently, so that he can focus his readers' attention on the salient points.

Correctness

The one thing that flies to a writer's mind when he is told he cannot write is *correctness.* He immediately starts looking for grammar and punctuation mistakes in things that he has written.

But mistakes like these are hardly the most important aspects of business writing. The majority of executives are reasonably well educated and can, with a minimum of effort, make themselves adequately proficient in the "mechanics" of writing. Furthermore, as a man rises in his company, his typing (at least) will be done by a secretary, who can (and should) take the blame if a report is poorly punctuated and incorrect in grammar, not to mention being presented in an improper "format."

Then what is the most important point? Frequently, the insecure writer allows small mistakes in grammar and punctuation to become greatly magnified, and regards them as reflections on his education and, indeed, his social acceptability. A careless use of "he don't" may seem to be as large a disgrace in his mind as if he attended the company banquet in his shorts. And in some cases this is true. But he should also realize (as Exhibit I shows) that the ability to write *correctly* is not synonymous with the ability to write *well*. Hence, everyone should make sure that he does not become satisfied with the rather trivial act of mastering punctuation and grammar.

It is true, of course, that, in some instances, the inability to write correctly will cause a lack of clarity. We can all think of examples where a misplaced comma has caused serious confusion—although such instances, except in contracts and other legal documents, are fortunately rather rare.

A far more important aspect of correctness is "coherence." Coherence means the proper positioning of elements within a piece of writing so that it can be read clearly and sensibly. Take one example:

Incoherent: "I think it will rain. However, no clouds are showing yet. Therefore, I will take my umbrella."

Coherent: "Although no clouds are showing, I think it will rain. Therefore, I will take my umbrella."

Once a person has mastered the art of placing related words and sentences as close as possible to each other, he will be amazed at how smooth his formerly awkward writing becomes. But that is just the beginning. He will still have to make sure that he has placed paragraphs which are related in thought next to one another, so that the ideas presented do not have to leapfrog over any intervening digressions.

Appropriateness

I have divided the category *appropriateness* into two sections reflecting the two main types of internal business communications—those going upward in the organization and those going downward. This distinction is one that cannot be found in textbooks on writing, although the ideas included here are common-place in the human relations area.

There is an obvious difference between the type of communication that a boss writes to his subordinate and the type that the subordinate can get away with when he writes to his boss (or even the type that he drafts for his boss's signature). I suspect that many managers who have had their writing criticized had this unpleasant experience simply because of their failure to recognize the fact that messages are affected by the relative positions of the writer and the recipient in the organizational hierarchy.

Upward Communications

Let us roughly follow the order of the subtopics included under upward communications in Exhibit I. "Tact" is important. If a subordinate fails to recognize his role and writes in an argumentative or insulting tone, he is almost certain to reap trouble for himself (or for his boss if the document goes up under the boss's actual or implied signature). One of the perennially difficult problems facing any subordinate is how to tell a superior he is wrong. If the subordinate were the boss, most likely he *could* call a spade a spade; but since he is not, he has problems. And, in today's business world, bosses themselves spend much time figuring out how to handle problem communications with discretion. Often tender topics are best handled orally rather than in writing.

Two other subtopics—"supporting detail" and "opinion"—also require a distinction according to the writer's role. Since the communication is going upward, the writer will probably find it advisable to support his statements with considerable detail. On the other hand, he may run afoul of superiors who will be impatient if he gives too much detail and not enough generalization. Here is a classic instance where a word from above as to the amount of detail required in a particular assignment would be of inestimable value to the subordinate.

The same holds true for "opinion." In some cases, the subordinate may be criticized for introducing too many of his personal opinions—in fact, often for giving any recommendation at all. If the superior wishes the subordinate to make recommendations and to offer his own opinions, the burden is on the superior to tell him. If the superior fails to do so, the writer can at least try to make it clear where facts cease and opinions begin; then the superior can draw his own conclusions.

The writer's "attitude" is another important factor in upward communications. When a subordinate writes to his boss, it is almost impossible for him to communicate with the blandness that he might use if he were writing a letter to a friend. There may be many little things that he is doing throughout his writing that indicate either too great a desire to impress the boss or an insecurity which imparts a feeling of fearfulness, defensiveness, or truculence in the face of authority.

Downward Communications

While the subordinate who writes upward in the organization must use "tact," the boss who writes down to his subordinates must use "diplomacy." If he is overbearing or insulting (even without meaning to be), he will find his effectiveness as a manager severely limited. Furthermore, it is the foolish manager who forgets that, when he communicates downward, he speaks as a representative of management or even of the entire company. Careless messages have often played an important part in strikes and other corporate human relations problems.

It is also important for the superior to make sure that he has clarified in his own mind just what it is he wishes to accomplish. If he does not, he may give confused or vague instructions. (In this event, it is unfair for him to blame a subordinate for presenting a poorly focused document in return.) Another requirement is that the superior must make sure that he has supplied any information which the subordinate needs but could not be expected to know, and that he has sufficiently explained any points which may be misleading.

Motivation is important, too. When a superior gives orders, he will find that over the long run he will not be able to rely on mere power to force compliance with his requests. It seems typically American for a subordinate to resent and resist what he considers to be arbitrary decisions made for unknown reasons. If at all possible, the superior not only should explain the reasons why he gives an order but should point out (if he can) why his decision can be interpreted as being in the best interests of those whom it affects.

I am not, however, suggesting farfetched explanations of future benefits. In the long run, those can have a boomerang effect. Straight talk, carefully and tactfully couched, is the only sensible policy. If, for example, a subordinate's request for a new assignment has been denied because he needs further experience in his present assignment, he should be told the facts. Then, if it is also true that getting more experience may prepare him for a better position in the future, there is no reason why this information should not be included to "buffer" the impact of the refusal of a new assignment.

Thought

Here—a most important area—the superior has a tremendous vested interest in the reporting done by his subordinates. There is no substitute for the thought content of a communication. What good is accomplished if a message is excellent in all the other respects we have discussed—if it is readable, correct, and appropriate—yet the content is faulty? It can even do harm if the other aspects succeed in disguising the fact that it is superficial, stupid, or biased. The superior receiving it may send it up through the organization with his signature, or, equally serious, he may make an important (and disastrous) decision based on it.

Here is the real *guts* of business writing—intelligent content, something most purveyors of business writing gimmicks conveniently forget. It is also something that most training programs shortchange. The discipline of translating thoughts into words and organizing these thoughts logically has no equal as intellectual training. For there is one slogan that is true: "Disorganized, illogical writing reflects a disorganized, illogical (and untrained) mind."

That is why the first topic in this section is "preparation." Much disorganized writing results from insufficient preparation, from a failure to think through and isolate the purpose and the aim of the writing job. Most writers tend to think as they write; in fact, most of us do not even know what it is we think until we have actually written it down. The inescapability of making a well-thought-out outline before dictating seems obvious.

A primary aspect of *thought*, consequently, is the intellectual "competence" of the writer. If a report is bad merely because the subject is far beyond the experience of the writer, it is not his fault. Thus his superior should be able to reject the analysis and at the same time accept the blame for having given his assistant a job that he simply could not do. But what about the many cases where the limiting factor *is* basically the intellectual capacity of the writer? It is foolish to tell a man that he cannot *write* if in effect he simply does not have the intellectual ability to do the job that has been assigned to him.

Another aspect of thought is "fidelity to the assignment." Obviously the finest performance in the world on a topic other than the one assigned is fruitless, but such violent distortions of the assignment fortunately are rare. Not so rare, unfortunately, are reports which subtly miss the point, or wander away from it. Any consistent tendency on the part of the writer to drag in his pet remedies or favorite villains should be pointed out quickly, as should persistent efforts to grind personal axes.

Another lapse of "fidelity" is far more forgivable. This occurs when an eager subordinate tends to make too much of a routine assignment and consistently turns memos into 50-page reports. On the other hand, some subordinates may consistently make too little of an assignment and tend to do superficial and poorly researched pieces of work.

Perhaps the most important aspect of thought is the component "analysis." Here is where the highly intelligent are separated from those less gifted, and those who will dig from those who content themselves with superficial work. Often subordinates who have not had the benefit of experience under a strict taskmaster (either in school or on the job) are at a loss to understand why their reports are considered less than highly effective. Such writers, for example, may fail to draw obvious conclusions from the data that they have presented. On the other hand, they may offer conclusions which are seemingly unjustified by the evidence contained in their reports.

Another difficulty is that many young managers (and old ones, too) are unsophisticated in their appreciation of just what constitutes evidence. For example, if they base an entire report on the fact that sales are going to go up the next year simply because one assistant sales manager thinks so, they should expect to have their conclusions thrown out of court. They may also find themselves in difficulty if they fail to identify and justify assumptions which have been forced on them by the absence of factual data. Assumptions, of course, are absolutely necessary in this world of imperfect knowledge—especially when we deal with future developments—but it is the writer's responsibility to point out that certain assumptions have been made and that the validity of his analysis depends on whether or not these assumptions prove to be justified.

Another serious error in "analysis" is that of bias. Few superiors will respect a communication which is consciously or unconsciously biased. A writer who is incapable of making an objective analysis of all sides of a question, or of all alternatives to action, will certainly find his path to the top to be a dead end. On the other hand, especially in many younger writers, bias enters unconsciously, and it is only by a patient identification of the bias that the superior will be able to help the subordinate develop a truly objective analytical ability.

Persuasiveness

This discussion of bias in reporting raises the question of "persuasiveness." "Every letter is a sales letter of some sort," goes the refrain. And it is true that persuasiveness in writing can range from the "con man" type of presentation to that which results from a happy blending of the four elements of business writing I have described. While it would be naive to suggest that it is not often necessary for executives to write things in manipulative ways to achieve their ends *in the short run*, it would be foolish to imply that this type of writing will be very effective with the same people (if they are reasonably intelligent) *over the long run*. Understandably, therefore, the "con man" approach will not be particularly effective in the large business organization.

On the other hand, persuasiveness is a necessary aspect of organizational writing. Yet it is difficult to describe the qualities which serve to make a communication persuasive. It could be a certain ring of conviction about the way recommendations are advanced; it could be enthusiasm, or an understanding of the reader's desires, and a playing up of them. One can persuade by hitting with the blunt edge of the axe or by cutting finely with the sharp edge to prepare the way. Persuasion could result from a fine sense of discretion, of hinting but not stating overtly things which are impolitic to mention; or it could result from an action-orientation that conveys top management's desire for results rather than a more philosophical approach to a subject. In fact, it could be many things.

In an organization, the best test to apply for the propriety of persuasiveness is to ask yourself whether you would care to take action on the basis of what your own communication presents. In the long run, it is dangerous to assume that everyone else is stupid and malleable; so, if you would be offended or damaged in the event that you were persuaded to take the action suggested, you should restate the communication. This test eliminates needless worry about slightly dishonest but well-meaning letters of congratulation, or routine progress reports written merely for a filing record, and the like. But it does bring into sharp focus those messages that cross the line from persuasiveness to bias; these are the ones that will injure others and so eventually injure you.

Conclusion

No one can honestly estimate the billions of dollars that are spent in U.S. industry on written communications, but the amount must be staggering. By contrast, the amount of thinking and effort that goes into improving the effectiveness of business writing is tiny—a mouse invading a continent. A written performance inventory (like Exhibit I) in itself is not the answer. But a checklist of writing elements should enable executives to speak about writing in a common tongue and hence be a vehicle by which individual and group improvement in writing can take place.

By executives' own vote, no aspect of a manager's performance is of greater importance to his success than communication, particularly written communication. By the facts, however, no part of business practice receives less formal and intelligent attention. What this article asserts is that when an individual asks, "What do you mean I can't write?"—and has every desire to improve—his company owes him a sensible and concrete answer.

Michael J. Reiter

Reports That Communicate

Modern accounting reports range far beyond the textbook classifications of balance sheet, income statement, and annual report. Much emphasis is being placed on preparation of reports that are highly analytical and interpretive. Today's accountant must be more than a gatherer of figures, more than an allocator of costs. Today's accountant must be a "management accountant." That is, he must have not only highly developed accounting skills and knowledge of accounting principles but also a far greater insight into the overall functioning of the business than ever before.

To meet the needs of modern business, management is challenging the accountant to produce more reports, bigger reports, and better reports. The greatest challenge lies not in gathering the varied data, not in analyzing for hidden trends, but rather in being able to transmit this data with all its pertinent meanings to management. Liken the accountant to the football spotter. From his vantage point the spotter watches the game. He sees a weakness in the opposing backfield. This information in the hands of his quarterback may mean the difference between victory and defeat. He picks up his telephone and relays the information to the bench. But on the bench the coach hears only static. There has been no communication. The key play is lost.

In this same way a business play can also end in a loss. For the accountant to have the information and be aware of a trend is not enough. To be able to communicate rather than just present is becoming a good accountant's prime skill. If he has this ability, he can increase the effectiveness of a management group by giving it the best tools possible with which to do its work.

Scope of Accounting Reports

Accounting reports can be divided into three major groups or types: statistical reports, financial reports, and narrative reports. Under the heading of statistical reports we find reports on such facts as units produced, number of complaints versus sales, and waste. The financial report group includes reports of receivables, budget reports, and, that statesman of the accounting world, the annual report. The final group includes the research report and variance explanations.[1]

Accounting reports for management could instead be divided on a frequency basis—into periodic reports of performance and special reports for planning and policy making. The periodic reports, such as budget reports, monthly statements, and sales reports, have become fairly fixed in form and content through accounting convention and company policy. Most organizations have standardized these reports to the point of presenting them on printed forms. Although this practice may sacrifice some communication effectiveness, the volume of periodic reports necessitates some degree of standardization.

[1] C. E. Redfield, *Communication in Management* (Chicago: University of Chicago Press, 1958), p. 164.

Pyramid Structure

The essential feature of periodic reports is that each is a supporting part of the report at the next higher level. Such an integrated system permits management by exception. A division manager can see which area of his organization—production, sales, or advertising—is causing a deviation. The production manager can pinpoint an off-budget department, and the general foreman can locate the specific part of the plant where the deviation occurs. In each instance the individual can direct his attention to the persons or operations at fault and initiate corrective action promptly.

Special reports are designed to give detailed information on specific operations or problems about which management decisions must be made. The special report should expand or supplement data that may be found only in part in various periodic reports. Special reports may be required to give comparisons of performance data other than those comparisons generally used. These reports deal as much in "how" and "why" as they do in "how much."

Many long-range planning decisions, for expansion or for changes in product mix, for example, cannot be made on the basis of the information given in the periodic reports. The special studies required to obtain the needed data must be thorough, and their presentation must be highly communicative. In selecting the format and reporting style the accountant must take into consideration the end use of the report, the complexity of the problem being studied, and the needs and temperament of the person who will receive it.[2]

Problems of Reception

All of us, whether accountants, engineers, or managers, tend to assume that when we report data we have gathered or state even a simple opinion it will be understood exactly as we meant it. Modern-day research in the field of communication clearly disproves this normal assumption.

Claude E. Shannon in 1948 presented a paper entitled "A Mathematical Theory of Communication" that laid the groundwork for the modern-day study of information theory or communication theory. This new field of study has shown us how much, or perhaps how little, we actually do communicate with our fellow man. Its theories, although enlightening, do not solve our communication problems for us. They do, however, point out the areas of difficulty and strongly emphasize the need for skill in the art of communicating with others.

Communication theory provides, in the "bit," a universal measure of the amount of information we can pass on to someone else. It tells us how many of these "bits" can be sent per second over different channels, be the channel oral or visual. Communication theory shows us how to state, or "encode," messages efficiently and how to avoid errors in transmission. This last is of great value to us; how to say what we mean.[3]

Communication theory tells us that the amount of information conveyed by a message is directly related to the receiver's uncertainty about what the source of the message will say. Here is an example: If you see what is obviously a one-dollar bill and a man tells you it is a one-dollar bill, the amount of information conveyed is negligible. If you see what looks like some kind of engine and are told its type, use, and other particulars, the

---

[2] W. C. Himstreet and W. M. Baty, *Business Communications* (Belmont, California: Wadsworth Publishing Co., 1964), p. 319.

[3] J. R. Pierce, *Signals, Symbols and Noise* (New York: Harper & Row, 1961), pp. 1–9.

amount of information conveyed is greater. The amount of information transmitted, then, depends in part on how uncertain the receiver is of what he will receive.

Of what value are these abstract theories and generalizations to the accountant who must write a report? How can an accountant apply such concepts as "transmitter," "receiver," and "noise" to his work? How can he better communicate?

Know the "Noises"

The first step to better communication through reports is to know what "noises" cause poor reports. These "noises" may be personal traits, lack of communication skills, or outside distortions. Accountants of one major company were accused by a top executive of "using a pattern of rubber-stamp expressions. They write badly and their reports are complicated, obscure, and tiresome."[4] Such a comment is not one that an accountant should be proud of. Yet it does point up a common "noise" in the form of shopworn expression and poor writing style.

"Noise" can take various forms. For example, you are a sales manager whose orders are not being filled because of production processing problems. You receive a report that reads like a technical dictionary. Buried somewhere in the "noisy" verbiage may be the length of time required for solution of the problem and the anticipated level of production until then, the facts you need to know. Yet you may tire long before you reach the page on which they are hidden. You are a victim of "noise." Another common example of "noise" is the qualified sentence: "Production is good, all things considered" or "Costs were fairly low, despite minor scrap problems."

Such distortions often result from accountants'

lack of training in basic report writing. Many times such training on the high school and college level is relegated to the few courses in English that everyone is obliged to take. Courses in the field of accounting tend to deal with method and cover reporting only in terms of standardized forms. With more special reports to be done, the managerial accountant finds that not only are the figures important but so are the narrative comments on those figures.

Fear of authority and the "cover-up" attitude also produce distortions. Just how detailed should an accountant's analysis be? Information may well be lost because of fear of uncovering a skeleton in someone's business closet.

Distortion can also occur on the receiving end. The mere quantity of reports received may have become more important to the receiver than what the reports say; he rates a job by the poundage of paper produced. Or a manager may look upon a periodic report not as information on performance but as a prescription for conduct. This is especially likely to occur with budgets and variance reports. The tendency is to change performance so as to have a better report without trying to get at the real cause of a variance.

The managerial accountant, as "transmitter," must tune himself to perform his reporting function well. Of prime importance is his ability to put himself in the place of the manager or executive who will use the report. The accountant must be able to envisage what the report is supposed to do. He must be aware of the problem involved, be it expansion or new products or whatever. He must detail the narration of his report to answer as many as possible of the foreseeable questions. The scope of his study must be such that all factors involved in and affected by the decision management will make are completely covered.

To achieve this high degree of problem orientation, the accountant must have a close working relationship with both the receiver of the report and those from whom background information

[4] P. Douglass, *Communication Through Reports* (Englewood Cliffs, New Jersey: Prentice-Hall, Inc., 1957), p. 379.

and primary data are obtained. He must think in the frame of reference of the receiver. Semantic issues must be settled before the narrative section of the report is written. When the narrative discusses overhead, asset, or discount, will the executive reading the report include the same items under these headings as the accountant who writes the report? To avoid confusion the accountant must become an extension of the person requesting the report.

Assuming that you have the requisites of a good "transmitter" and that you are alert to possible distortion factors, you have only to pick the proper "signals." Your "signals" will consist of the format used for data tables and charts, the key segments of the analysis narrative, and, most important, the words and style used.

Data tables may be large or may be in small segments, each dealing with one cost segment or area of the report. The prime requisite here is to keep tables in meaningful order and readable. Charts may run the gamut from line charts through bar graphs to pie segment charts, depending on which will best convey the significance of the data presented. Clutter should be avoided. Charts and graphs should be easy to interpret and clearly labeled.

Words and style are of great importance, particularly in the special reports. A foundation of good grammar is essential for good reports. Another handy tool is an unabridged dictionary. Reports such as accountants prepare cannot be polished by the average secretary.

The standard writing techniques for tone setting, proper flow, emphasis, and phrasing are as basic to accounting reports as to any other writing. Reader attention will be held if the basic principles are followed. Brevity and conciseness are also essential. Many an important fact is lost in a mass of verbiage. The use of new and different words and phrases will give life to reports. The same old worn-out statements can be an anesthetic rather than a stimulant to action.

Guideposts to Good Reports

A good report is not a matter of chance but almost a work of art. All of the rules in the many books written about reporting can be summed up in six key words. Good reports should possess *clarity*. They are clear and concise, are written in good style, and are easy to read. Good reports have *consistency*. They stay in the problem area and do not deviate. Meanings and terms do not change in midreport. Good reports display *adequacy*. They are complete in all respects. Coverage is not slipshod. Good reports possess *timeliness*. Their data and interpretation are in the light of present circumstances and practices. Good reports have *adaptability*. They show recognition of the possible different viewpoints on the problem at hand by presenting data to analyze these views. And, lastly, a good report has *interest*. Gone are the rubber-stamp phrases and mire of useless words. The report takes and holds the reader's attention. It not only shows but it also tells.

The managerial accountant, in properly fulfilling his reporting function, displays skills in composition, human relations, general business knowledge, and communication as well as accounting. He *must* communicate the necessary information in the proper manner so as to achieve the best end result. He must be a dynamic part of the decision making team.

The Royal Bank of Canada

Imagination Helps Communication

The Basic Skill in every profession and in most businesses is the ability to organize and express ideas in writing and in speaking.

No matter how clever an engineer may be technically, or an executive managerially, or a research man creatively, he does not show his worth unless he communicates his ideas to others in an influential way.

Language is the most momentous product of the human mind. Between the clearest animal call of love or warning or anger, and man's most trivial word, there lies a whole day of creation—or, as we would say it today, a whole chapter of evolution.

A business man is not called upon to present the elegance of a wit, a novelist or a poet. He must express himself accurately, clearly and briefly, but he need not denude his language of beauty and appeal.

The purpose of the writer is to communicate effectively. He needs a feeling for writing the right thing in the right way at the right time: not a barebones recital of facts, unless in a specification or legal document, but a composition of words which will convey his meaning and his sentiment.

This requires use of imagination, which is the cornerstone of human endeavour. John Masefield, the Poet Laureate, wrote: "Man's body is faulty, his mind untrustworthy, but his imagination has made him remarkable."

Writing imaginatively cannot be taught. It can be studied in examples—the writings of Defoe, Shakespeare, La Fontaine and Jules Verne show what can be done, but not how to do it. In this, writing is on a par with art and the product of an artisan's hands. The painter can no more convey the secret of his imaginative handling of colour than the plumber can teach that little extra touch he gives a wiped joint. All three, writer, artist, artisan, have secrets springing from within. After learning the principles, they go on to produce their works inspired by the dignity of accomplishment due to their gifts.

Look at the drama built into small events by choice of words and use of imagination: Defoe gave us Crusoe recoiling from the footprint in the sand; Homer gave us Achilles shouting over against the Trojans and Ulysses bending the great bow; and Bunyan gave us Christian running from the tempter with his fingers in his ears. None of these was an epic event, but by their mastery of putting imagination into their communication these writers painted scenes which stirred us in the reading and linger in our memories.

A good piece of writing, whether it be a novel or a business letter does three things: it communicates a thought, it conveys a feeling, and it gives the reader some benefit.

The Writer's Tools

What are the writer's tools? A wide range of language, for variety and to avoid the commonplace; active verbs, to keep the action moving; similes, which make words paint a thousand pictures; metaphor and parable, to make meanings clear; and rhythm, which contributes to smooth, easy reading.

"Imagination Helps Communication" from *The Royal Bank of Canada Monthly Letter, XLI*, 7 (September 1960). Reprinted with permission of The Royal Bank of Canada.

To these tools, the writer adds imagination, always being careful to bring it within the scope of facts. Art in writing must not be used as an escape from reality.

This sort of writing is not so simple a thing as fluency, which soap-box orators have in abundance. It is not so simple a thing as grammatical exactitude, which can be hammered into boys and girls by a teacher.

But when it is properly done, imaginative writing is very powerful. Look at Cyrano de Bergerac in the drama by Edmond Rostand. The hero was valiant and romantic, but very sensitive regarding the size of his nose. This sensitivity prevented his making his court to the beautiful Roxane, but he wrote ardent letters to her for a handsome and stupid friend. The power of the written word won Roxane's love for his friend by proxy.

Good writing needs to be appropriate to the occasion, the purpose, the reader and the writer. It must not be too pompous for its load, or hesitant about what it seeks to do, or beneath the intelligence of the reader, or too arrogant for the writer's position.

Writing is only serviceable and good with reference to the object for which it is written. You say: "That is a beautiful dress"; but let the dress slide from the model's shoulders and lie in a heap on the floor, and what is it? A heap of material. Its virtue resides in its fittingness to its purpose.

What is written imaginatively in the daily work of office and industry will get desired results. If the writer looks further, what is written with imagination will live on when this Atomic Age is ancient history. Why? Because imagination is the one common link between human minds in all ages.

Imagination in writing finds expression through the use of accurate and illuminating equivalents for thoughts. You may show your imagination by dealing with something unfamiliar; by calling to attention a commonplace fact that is generally overlooked; by bringing into view familiar things in new relationship; or by drawing together relevant thoughts in a nosegay tied with your own ribbon.

An imaginative writer can look out upon the sprawling incoherence of a factory or a city or a nation or a problem and give it intelligible statement.

Something About Style

The style in which you write is the living embodiment of your thought, and not merely its dress.

When you put words together you convey not only your purpose in writing but your character and mood, both of which are important to your reader's understanding.

Let the occasion dictate the manner of your writing. Sometimes a manly rough line, with a great deal of meaning in it, may be needed, while a different set of circumstances demands the lubrication of sweet words. A blinding light is not always the best illumination: the delicate colours in moss-covered rock are enhanced by overcast, misty air.

Knowledge of techniques does not give the writer this discrimination. Technique is always a means and not an end. If we allow rules to govern our writing we become tongue-tied by authority. As Rembrandt remarked to someone who was looking closely into one of his paintings, seeking the technique, "pictures are intended to be looked at, not smelled."

We do not find ourselves tripping over technique in the inspired paragraphs of great literary works. Think of the forcefulness, the meaning, the simplicity of expression, in Lincoln's Gettysburg address, in Churchill's "fall of France" radio broadcast. Then contrast the great golden phrases of political campaigners, rising from nothing and leading to nothing: words on words, dexterously arranged, bearing the semblance of argument, but leaving nothing memorable, no image, no exaltation.

At the other end of the scale are those who write speeches and letters stodgily. Too many people who are nice people at heart become another sort when they pick up a pen or a dictaphone. They tighten up. They become unnatural. They curdle into impersonality and choose starchy sentences. Their product is like a page printed with very old and worn-out type. In the vivid prose which marked some seventeenth century writers, James Howell wrote: "Their letters may be said to be like bodies without sinews, they have neither art nor arteries in them."

A letter in which something significant is attempted—a sale, a correction, a changing of opinion, the making of a friend—cannot be written in a neutral and bloodless state of mind.

In letter writing, imagination must supply personal contact. When you call in your stenographer to write a letter you are entering into a personal relationship with the reader. He is no longer a statistic in a mass market. He and you are human beings talking things over.

Most business communications have lucidity rather than emotion as their aim, but none except those which are frankly and openly mere catalogues can afford to exclude humanity. There should be some in-between space in your letters, some small-talk between the important ideas, some irrelevancies which temper the austerity of business.

The Reader's Interest

No matter what your letter is about, the reader will want to know: "How does this affect me?"

It is a literary vice not to seek out the reader's interest. You may tell him what you want in impeccable language and forceful manner, but you fall short of success unless you pay attention to what he wants or can be made to desire. Your ideas must enter, influence and stick in the mind of the recipient.

As a writer, you may protest that some of the failure in communication may be blamed on the receiver, but it is your responsibility as sender to determine in advance, to the best of your ability, all potential causes of failure and to tune your transmission for the best reception.

Granted, something must be expected of the reader. Every writer is entitled to demand a certain amount of knowledge in those for whom he writes, and a certain degree of dexterity in using the implements of thought. Readers who demand immediate intelligibility in all they read cannot hope to go far beyond the limitations of comic strip language.

However, the writer is bound to eliminate every possible obstacle. He must not grow away from people. He must anticipate their questions. Let the salesman stand at a bargain counter and listen to what goes on in the minds of prospective customers. He will see women who spend ten minutes examining socks advertised at 35 cents a pair—do they stretch? are they washable? will they stay soft? are they tough enough to wear long? Those women are not up on the plateau of bulk sales, but down where a nickel counts.

That is the imagination of preparation. Then comes the imagination of expression. The most important demand of customers is for friendliness in those who seek to do business with them. A man may pride himself upon being an efficient, logical person, unswayed by sentiment in business matters, but at some stage in his every business deal there is a spark of emotional appeal and response.

You need to study your audience and then write what you want them to understand in the form that is most likely to appeal to them. Any other course is like the childish custom of writing a letter to Santa Claus and burning it up the chimney.

Give Imagination Wings

If you do not wish your letters to be read yawningly, write them wide awake. When a good idea strikes you for a letter, ride that idea on the dead run: don't wait to ponder, criticize and correct. You can be critical after your imaginative spell subsides.

The search for the exact word should never so usurp the writer's attention that the larger movements of thought on which the letter's argument depends are made to falter and so lose their fire. The first draft of a piece of writing should be done at white heat. The smoothing and polishing may follow later.

Some degree of novelty must be one of the materials in every instrument which works upon the mind.

By "novelty" it is not meant that the letter should be artificial. Great art consists in writing in an interested and straightforward way.

A good writer is not always original. You cannot hope to reproduce in your own words how Keats felt as he listened to the nightingale singing. It is far better to copy his ode. Mr. Churchill could not help it, even if he did not desire it, when his "blood, toil, tears and sweat" echoed Garibaldi, or when his first speech as Prime Minister, declaring it to be his policy "to make war," echoed Clemenceau's "Je fais la guerre." Shakespeare took his plots wherever he could find them, from older plays, English chronicles and Plutarch's *Lives*. His originality consisted in the skill with which he made a story over and covered the skeleton with the living flesh of his language.

If a man has vision and sympathy—ingredients of imagination—and adds sincerity, he will be able to beautify the familiar and illumine the dingy and sordid. Montaigne, one of the world's great essayists, said: "I gather the flowers by the wayside, by the brooks and in the meadows, and only the string with which I bind them together is my own."

Variety in expression is as necessary to a piece of written matter as it is to an attractive bouquet. Monotony in a letter is like a paralyzing frost.

The Greeks knew this: they set off the loveliness of roses and violets by planting them side by side with leeks and onions. Some fastidious or critical people may complain of unevenness in your writing because it is not sustained at a peak. But there is no one more tiresome than the man who is writing always at the top of his voice.

Use Words Honestly

The effort to bring up the highlights must not bind us to our obligation to be moderate. To be dynamic and forceful we don't need to give the impression of breathlessness. Strong words lose their force if used often. Don't say "the roof is falling in" when you mean that a crack in the ceiling needs patching. If you habitually term a dull party "a disaster" what have you left that is vivid enough to cover your feelings about an earthquake?

From the moment that a writer loses his reverence for words as accurate expressions of his thoughts he becomes second-rate. Even experienced writers testify to their constant search for the right word.

Follow the spirit of what you are saying in the way you write it. Sometimes you will use little, jolting, one-syllable words; in another composition your meaning and feeling may be conveyed better in cascading syllables like Milton's, or in earthy words that fit the urgency of the occasion.

There is no better way to learn the feeling of words than through reading poetry. The use of synonyms so necessary in poetry gives us a grasp of language and readiness in its use. Exercise your imagination by looking up wide choices of words meaning the same thing, in varying shades of strength and attractiveness. A handy book to have on your desk is *A Dictionary of English Synonyms* by Richard Soule (Little, Brown, and Company, Boston).

Be careful to use qualifying words only where they contribute something to the sense you wish to convey. An excessive use of qualifiers vitiates the force of what you write.

Correct modification is an essential of perceptive accuracy, but every modification means a deflection in the reader's flow of understanding.

To test this, take some magazine which professes to popularize news events, and strike out every adjective and adverb which seems dispensable: note how much more authoritative and less tinted by opinion the items appear.

The business man should test business reports and letters by asking "What omission of fact or skimping of research or expression of prejudice does this adjective cover up?"

Pictures in Words

Our writing creates pictures in the reader's mind. We use metaphors to sharpen and extend the reader's understanding of our ideas by presenting him with images drawn from the world of sensory experience: "She has roses in her cheeks; he has the heart of a lion." If we say that a brook is laughing in the sunlight, an idea of laughter intervenes to symbolize the spontaneous, vivid activity of the brook.

In 240 words of a single soliloquy of *Hamlet*, Shakespeare gives us these imaginative phrases, now part of our everyday language: to be or not to be, the law's delay, the insolence of office, the undiscover'd country from whose bourne no traveller returns, the slings and arrows of outrageous fortune, 'tis a consummation devoutly to be wish'd, there's the rub, shuffled off this mortal coil, conscience doth make cowards of us all.

Metaphors are not confined to poetic writing: they occur in science and business writing, too: the flow of electricity, the stream of consciousness, the thinking machine, getting at the root of the problem, falling into error, indulging in mental gymnastics.

Local colour is an element in imaginative writing. Your highlights and your expressive phrases do not have to come from the classics. A good writer, even on the most prosaic of topics, will mix his own mind with his subject. True imagination, no matter how strange may be the regions into which it lifts its head, has its roots in human experience. What arises in your writing from what you have been through will be more vivid than what you glean from the writings and experience of others.

Background for Imagination

If the imagination is to yield any product useful to the writer, it must have received material from the external world. Images do not spring out of a desert.

The writer will train his mind to roam, to seek food, to experience events. He will read widely, observing words at work in a multitude of combinations.

A library has evocative power. Merely to sit within view of good books draws out the goodness in one. A library has driving power, too: it challenges us to convey meanings and feelings as these writers did.

The books in an executive's office should not consist solely of directories, almanacs, *Canada Year Book,* and the like. In literature are recorded all the thoughts, feelings, passions, and dreams that have passed through the human mind, and these can play their part in the efficiency of the letter writer today. Even on the battlefield, Napoleon had in his tent more than three hundred volumes ranging through science, art, history, poetry, travels, romance and philosophy.

To do all that has been suggested takes time. It requires preparation, practice and participation: preparation through reading and study, practice through revising and rewriting, and participation through putting something of yourself into every letter.

We must get out of the vicious system whereby we spend a forenoon verifying the price to be quoted to a customer, while refusing to spend two minutes in reconstructing a clumsy sentence in the letter we write him. To be slovenly and feeble is not only discourteous to the persons we address but bad business, because it leaves the door open for misunderstanding.

If you are going to describe an event or a product, do not be content with black marks on white paper: at least stipple in the background and use some colour in the foreground.

It is necessary, too, to be in earnest. Many people dream away their lives, talking of the writing they mean to do, and in the end they fall asleep, still babbling of the green fields of literature.

If you make only average grades in your letters when you could with a little effort top the class, you are bound to be disappointed with yourself. The writing of letters, business or personal or professional, is no mean ministry. It deserves the best that can be given it, and when it is rightly done it absorbs the mind wholly.

Why not be one of the knowledgeable elite instead of one of the conforming average?

They are probably best who, having a subject on which they wish to express themselves, sit down to write about it in a loving way. As Cyrano de Bergerac described his genius: "I have but to lay my soul beside my paper, and copy!"

The Royal Bank of Canada   Letters That Sell

Everyone writes letters that sell, and every letter has as its purpose the selling of something: goods, services, ideas or thoughts.

Someone may say that a family letter has no such purpose, but consider this: a letter telling about the children seeks to promote a favourable impression of their welfare and happiness; a letter telling about illness is designed to gain sympathy; the letter that says nothing but "I hope you are well" is selling the idea "I am thinking of you."

Family letters are usually rambling letters. They would be improved both in their readability and their informativeness if they adopted some of the principles that are used to sell goods and services. Business building letters, on the other hand, could with advantage incorporate some of the friendly informality of family letters.

Salesmanship of any kind is basically a person moving goods by persuading another person that he needs them, or winning that person's support or approval of an idea or a plan.

Some non-commercial type sales letters are those that champion good causes, such as community welfare or health standards or national unity. They seek to influence the thinking of individuals or groups.

It is not a simple task to compose a letter designed to sell. Like any other product of value, it calls for craftsmanship. There are techniques to be learned, techniques of conveying ideas, propositions, conclusions or advice appealingly and purposefully.

"Letters That Sell" from *The Royal Bank of Canada Monthly Letter*, Vol. 55, No. 5 (May 1974). Reprinted with permission of The Royal Bank of Canada.

In the Beginning

In creating a letter to sell something we need to begin by thinking about the person to whom we are writing. A lawyer studies his opponent's case just as sharply as his client's; the manager of a baseball or hockey team analyzes the qualities, good and bad, of members of the opposing team.

The writer must anticipate and answer in his letter questions that will occur to the reader: What is this about? How does it concern me? How can you prove it? What do you want me to do? Should I do it?

People buy goods or services because these will give them a new benefit or will extend or protect a benefit they already have, so the writer needs to translate what he offers into owner benefits.

The proffered benefits must be accessible and adapted to the reader's position, environment and needs. No letter is likely to sell sun-bonnets to people who live beyond the Arctic Circle or baby carriages to bachelors. We may classify a potential customer as a man, woman, company or institution that will have use for a product or service, has sufficient money to pay for it, and in whom a desire for possession may be created.

The reader's interest: that is the guiding star in sales letter writing. See his interests, his angle, and accommodate your stance to them. A simple precaution against sending a letter to the wrong person is to ask yourself what use you would have for the commodity if you were in the reader's place.

It is a good rule to spend more time thinking about the reader than about what you have to say. Otherwise you may become wrapped up in the virtues of your product so that you forget that the decision to buy rests with your prospect.

The self-interest of the person to whom you write is a major factor to consider in successful sales communication. When you remember it you give the impression that you have singled out this reader as being an important individual, and that is an excellent introduction.

It is not to be expected that the writer of letters that sell will know every person to whom he writes, but he must know certain facts: approximate income and age, occupational level, his business, and things like that. Then he is able to slant his sales points accurately toward the reader's needs, interests and purchasing power.

Know Your Product

The reader's attention should be attracted to the product or service, not to the grand style or picturesque phraseology of your letter. When you catch a person's attention you are focusing his consciousness on something. Concentrate on your commodity. The best magnet to draw and hold attention is what you say about the product, showing it to be useful and the means of fulfilling a desire.

It is no small accomplishment to analyse and marshal into order the facts about a product so as to win the thoughtful consideration of a person who has plenty of other things on his mind.

In purchasing almost any sort of commodity the buyer has a choice between what you are offering and what others are selling. Your sales job is to show the superiority of your product. Tell why what you offer is necessary or desirable, what it will accomplish in your reader's business, and how it can be fitted into his present layout and his plans. Do not content yourself with telling about the article as it sits on display: picture it in use in the reader's home or factory.

Your letter needs to convey the assurance that you are telling the truth about your goods. It is not a sensational offer that makes a letter convincing, but the feeling that the reader can depend upon what is said. He should feel assured that he will be buying what he thinks he is buying. Customer dissatisfaction caused by misleading sales talk can cause shock waves that affect the whole selling organization.

Let Your Personality Show

Make your letter sound friendly and human: put your personality on paper. Your letter is you speaking. Some of the features in your personality that you can display are: friendliness, knowledge, keen-mindedness, trustworthiness and interest in the prospect's welfare.

What you have in your mind about the good quality, appearance and usefulness of your product has to be communicated to your reader so as to arouse his interest, create a desire to possess, and induce him to buy.

Communication is not the easiest thing in the world to attain in writing, in art, or in music. Dr. Rollo May wrote in *Man's Search for Himself:* "We find in modern art and modern music a language which does not communicate. If most people, even intelligent ones, look at modern art without knowing the esoteric key, they can understand practically nothing."

It is not enough to write something so that it can be read. The degree to which communication occurs depends upon the degree to which the words represent the same thing for the reader as they do for the writer.

The recipient of a letter that is not clear is likely to blame its opacity on the lack of intelligence of the writer.

The art of composing sales letters is not one to be mastered by minds in which there is only a meagre store of knowledge and memories.

The art consists in having many mental references and associating them with new thoughts. Consider a poem. Its theme will likely have arisen from a single event, but the images used in its construction will have been drawn from the total life experience of the poet.

Put some flavour into your letters so that they taste good. Your letter will not be like anyone else's. That is a virtue, just as being an individual is a virtue in conversation. Who wishes to be a carbon copy of a textbook letter or to parrot phrases that other people use?

Practise talking on paper as if you were on the telephone. First write down the imagined questions asked by the person on the other end of the line and then your answers, given in simple, direct and pleasing words. To humanize your letters in this way with the natural idiom of conversation does not mean that you use cheap slang or clever verbal stunting.

Show Some Style

The style in which you write is not a casual feature of your letter. It is vital to your reader's understanding of what you are saying to him. It is not your job to please the reader's sense of the aesthetic, but to tell and explain plainly what is necessary to introduce your goods or your idea to his favourable attention. This may be done in a way that has grace and comeliness.

Never "talk down" to a reader. Make him feel that he knows a great deal, but here is something he may have missed. There is a big difference, when trying to build business, between making a suggestion and preaching a sermon.

It is highly important in writing a letter to sell something that it should be appropriate. Whatever your writing style may be, it will fit the occasion if it gives this particular correspondent information that will be useful to him, conveys to him a feeling of your interest in him and his business, and assures him of your goodwill.

Besides being grammatically correct, language should be suitable. At one extreme of unsuitability is the language that is too pompous for its load, and at the other is the language of the street which belittles the receiver's intellectual level.

Your words should be the most expressive for their purpose that the language affords, unobstructed by specialty jargon, and your sentences should be shaken free of adjectives—the most tempting of forbidden fruit to a person describing something.

Properly chosen words will convey your appreciation of the addressee as a person, and such friendliness is contagious. Some people are afraid to be friendly in their letters. They fear they will be thought of as "phonies" who have disguised themselves as Santa Claus for the occasion. Being friendly and showing it should not raise this scarecrow. It would be a grave mistake, indeed, for any of us to indulge in flowery language foreign to our natural talk: but it is no mistake at all to incorporate in our letters the warm, personal language that comes naturally to us in person-to-person social contacts.

Letter writing invites us to use the same etiquette as we use in courteous conversation. We look at the person with whom we are talking, converse on his level of understanding, speak gently, and discuss matters he considers important or interesting.

What the reader of your letter will notice is not its normal courtesy, but the extra touch that demonstrates care and understanding, a genuine interest in the reader's wants, a wish to do what is best for him, and the knowledge you show of how it can be done.

Everyone who writes a letter has a moral as well as a business reason to be intelligible. He is placing his reader under an obligation to spend time reading the letter, and to waste that time is to intrude upon his life plan.

There is an eloquence of the written as well as of the spoken word. It consists in adapting a statement to the receptive system of the reader so that he will have maximum help against confusion, against mistaking what is incidental from what is fundamental. A familiar device to use in this effort is to relate the new commodity you are offering to something that is familiar.

Use Suitable Formulas

There are formulas you may wish to make use of. Your letter must conform in some respects to what letters are expected to be. This does not mean pouring all letters into the same mould. Within the accepted pattern you are free to develop your talent for expression.

Skill is needed in the use of formulas. A form letter reveals itself to the reader and gets short shrift. It is possible to make use of the form as a guide to what points to cover, and then speak your piece on paper in a natural way.

Here are three formulas for letters. The first may be called the sales formula, the second the logical formula, and the third the rhetorical formula.

1. Get attention, provoke interest, rouse desire, obtain decision. Attention is curiosity fixed on something; interest is understanding of the nature and extent of what is new and its relationship to what is old; desire is the wish to take advantage of the proffered benefits; decision is based on confidence in what the writer says about his goods.

2. This is summarized: general, specific, conclusion. You start with a statement so broad and authoritative that it will not be disputed; you show that the general idea includes a specific idea; the conclusion is that what has been said about the general idea is also true of the specific.

3. This is very simple: picture, promise, prove, push. You write an attractive description of what you are selling; you promise that it will serve the reader well in such-and-such a way; you give examples of the commodity in use, proving that it has utility and worth; you urge the reader to take advantage of the promised values.

Selling Needs Ideas

Selling is done with ideas, so never throw away an idea even if it is of no use at the moment. Put it into your idea file where it will rub against other ideas and perhaps produce something new. The file is like an incubator. Thoughts and fancies you put into it will hatch out projects and plans.

Imagination helps in this operation. A correspondent of ordinary ability may never write anything that is not absolutely accurate and yet fail to interest his readers. This is a real weakness: to be perfect as to form but lacking in imagination and ideas.

Imagination should be given priority over judgment in preparing your first draft of a letter designed to sell. Then put reason to work: delete what is unnecessary, marshal your sentences into logical form so that your ideas advance in an orderly way; revise your words so that your thought is conveyed exactly as you wish it to be.

When you tell the advantages of your product or service or idea, and show how it will fill a need in the reader's life or job, in clear, truthful words placed in easily understood sentences brightened by ideas and imagination, you have done a good job of writing a sales letter.

Desire of the reader to do what you want done is created, just as in conversation, by both rational and emotional means, by proof and by persuasion, by giving reasons. Some goods and some buyers need nothing more than facts. An office manager buying pencils or pens for his staff will respond to an informative, factual, statistical sales letter. He is already sold on the idea of using pencils and pens, so you do not have to coach him about their usefulness: in fact, you may lose a sale if you give the impression of "teaching grandmother to suck eggs." What is needed is to catch his attention, give pertinent information about your product, and show him why buying from you will be profitable to him.

Try to make the information you give really enlightening. Comparing something unknown with something already known makes it possible to talk about the unknown. The analogy (like that between the heart and a pump) can be used as an aid in reasoning and in explaining or demonstrating.

The Soft Sell

The tone of a letter designed to sell something should be persuasive rather than insistent. It should seek to create a feeling of wanting, or at least an urge to "let's see."

People do not want to be told how to run their affairs, but anyone who shows them how to do things more economically or faster or better will find keen listeners. Soft sell gives the prospect credit for knowing a good thing when it is shown him, and acknowledges his right to make up his own mind.

The soft sell is recognition of the Missouri mule in human nature. Try to push a mule and he lashes out with his heels. Try to pull him by the halter rope and he braces his legs and defies you to budge him. "In the old cavalry," says A. C. Kemble in *Building Horsepower into Sales Letters,* "they said all it took to get a mule working for you was to recognize that he was an individualist who hated nagging and needed a chance to make up his own mind about things."

One hears a lot in advertising circles about "appeal." It is, according to the dictionary, "the power to attract, interest, amuse, or stimulate the mind or emotions."

Obviously, when you wish to influence someone you must take into account the kind of person you are addressing and what you want him to do. Your appeal must touch his feelings, needs and emotions. It strengthens your position if you can relate your own experience to that of the person you are addressing and write your message around the overlap of that experience.

The sort of mistake to be avoided with great care is slanting your appeal in a way that runs counter to the feelings of those whom you wish to influence.

It has been found in recent years that the advertising messages addressed to older people *as* older people did not win the desired response. In travel, for example, only a very small minority who want or need a sheltered situation are attracted by the semi-custodial "trips for the elderly."

The Swiss Society for Market Research decided that "to sell anything to the over-65 age group it is important to keep one concept in mind: most senior citizens are vigorous and independent. Don't try to reach them with a head-on approach to the senior market. It probably won't work."

Writing a letter that pleases the recipient is not enough: it must be designed to lead to action. Do not fear to be explicit about what you want. Coyness in a letter is not attractive, and it exasperates the reader. Answer the reader's questions: "What has this to do with me?" and "Why should I do what this person is asking me to do?"

You may answer these questions and encourage a purchase by appealing to emotional motives like pride, innovation, emulation, or social prestige; or to rational motives like money gain, economy, security, timesaving or safety.

Read Your Letter Critically

Imagine your letter to be your garden upon your return from vacation. You have to get into it and prune, clean up, tie up, and trim the edges.

Read the letter as if you were the recipient. How does it strike you? What can be added to attract attention? Is there anything irrelevant in it? Read the letter aloud to capture the conversational rhythm.

If you are not satisfied, do not crumple up the paper on which your draft is written. Try rearranging the paragraphs, the sentences, the words. Give the letter a new twist. Change the shape of your appeal. Delete anything that is distracting.

Be careful when trying to shorten a letter that seems to be too long. While a letter should be as short as possible, consistent with clearness and completeness, it is not the length that counts, but the depth. Since clearness and brevity sometimes get in the way of each other, remember that the right of way belongs to clearness. It will make a good impression if you find occasion to write: "I can be quite brief because this letter deals with a topic already well known to you."

The end of your letter, like the end of your pencil, should have a point. It should answer the reader's natural question: "So what?"

Follow Through

Do not let your customer forget you. When you produce a piece of copy that hits the bull's-eye, that is not the time to sit back and take things easy. It is a time to imagine what you would do if you were in your competitor's chair . . . and then do it first.

Competition is a fact of life. Wherever there are two wild animals trying to live on the same piece of land or two persons depending upon the same source of sustenance, there is competition. The customer who was a prospect to you before he bought your goods is now a prospect to your competitor. With the proper follow-through attention he will turn to you when he needs up-dating of equipment or new goods.

Writing a letter that sells goods or ideas, and following through so as to retain the customer, requires just as much specialized talent and mental ability as any other kind of advertising, if not more.

When you run into difficulties, composition of the sales or follow-up letter may give you a feeling of confusion. You may feel like throwing up your hands in despair of finding the exactly right slant or the perfect array of words. That is not unnatural. Nietzsche, the German philosopher, said in *Thus Spake Zarathustra:* "I tell you, one must still have chaos in one, to give birth to a dancing star."

The effort is worthwhile. When you set yourself to snap out of the depressing pedestrian type of letter that is so commonplace, you are raising yourself and your firm to a place where people will sit up and pay attention. As a student of sales letter writing you will generate ideas, as a philosopher you will assess the letters as to their purpose and usefulness, and as a writer you will energize them.

To summarize: the backbone of the principles of writing letters that sell is made up of these vertebrae—know why you are writing and what about; believe in what you are writing; be tactful and friendly and truthful; base your appeal on the prospect's interests . . . and check your letter and revise it.

Index